# Lecture Notes in Computer Scien

*Commenced Publication in 1973*
Founding and Former Series Editors:
Gerhard Goos, Juris Hartmanis, and Jan van Leeuwen

Andrea Asperti   Grzegorz Bancerek
Andrzej Trybulec (Eds.)

# Mathematical
# Knowledge Management

Third International Conference, MKM 2004
Białowieża, Poland, September 19-21, 2004
Proceedings

 Springer

Volume Editors

Andrea Asperti
University of Bologna
Department of Computer Science
Mura Anteo Zamboni, 7, 40127 Bologna, Italy
E-mail: asperti@cs.unibo.it

Grzegorz Bancerek
Białystok Technical University
Faculty of Computer Science
Wiejska 45A, 15-351 Białystok, Poland
E-mail: bancerek@mizar.org

Andrzej Trybulec
University of Białystok
Institute of Computer Science
Sosnowa 64, 15-887 Białystok, Poland
E-mail: trybulec@math.uwb.edu.pl

Library of Congress Control Number: 2004111460

CR Subject Classification (1998): H.3, I.2, H.2.8, F.4.1, H.4, C.2.4, G.4, I.1

ISSN 0302-9743
ISBN 3-540-23029-7 Springer Berlin Heidelberg New York

Springer is a part of Springer Science+Business Media

springeronline.com

© Springer-Verlag Berlin Heidelberg 2004
Printed in Germany

Typesetting: Camera-ready by author, data conversion by Scientific Publishing Services, Chennai, India
Printed on acid-free paper      SPIN: 11320111      06/3142      5 4 3 2 1 0

# Preface

The International Conference on Mathematical Knowledge Management has now reached its third edition, creating and establishing an original and stimulating scientific community transversal to many different fields and research topics. The broad goal of MKM is the exploration of innovative, semantically enriched, digital encodings of mathematical information, and the study of new services and tools exploiting the machine-understandable nature of the information. MKM is naturally located in the border area between digital libraries and the mechanization of mathematics, devoting a particular interest to the new developments in information technology, and fostering their application to the realm of mathematical information. The conference is meant to be a forum for presenting, discussing and comparing new tools and systems, standardization efforts, critical surveys, large experiments, and case studies. At present, we are still getting to know each other, to understand the work done by other people, and the potentialities offered by their work to our own research activity. However, the conference is rapidly acquiring scientific strength and academic interest, attracting more and more people and research groups, and offering a challenging alternative to older, more conservative conferences.

July 2004

Andrea Asperti
Grzegorz Bancerek
Andrzej Trybulec

# Organization

MKM 2004 was organized by the Institute of Computer Science, University of Białystok in co-operation with the Faculty of Computer Science, Białystok Technical University and the Association of Mizar Users.

## Program Committee

| | |
|---|---|
| Andrzej Trybulec (Chair) | University of Białystok, Poland |
| Andrew A. Adams | University of Reading, UK |
| Andrea Asperti | University of Bologna, Italy |
| Bruno Buchberger | RISC Linz, Austria |
| Roy McCasland | University of Edinburgh, UK |
| James Davenport | University of Bath, UK |
| William M. Farmer | McMaster University, Canada |
| Herman Geuvers | Catholic University of Nijmegen, NL |
| Thérèse Hardin | Pierre & Marie Curie University, France |
| Fairouz Kamareddine | Heriot-Watt University, UK |
| Michael Kohlhase | International University Bremen, Germany |
| Paul Libbrecht | Saarland University, Germany |
| Bengt Nordstrom | Chalmers University of Technology, Sweden |
| Renaud Rioboo | Pierre & Marie Curie University, France |
| Bernd Wegner | Technical University of Berlin, Germany |

## Co-referees

| | | |
|---|---|---|
| Grzegorz Bancerek | Gueorgui Jojgov | Piotr Rudnicki |
| Jacques Carette | Wolfram Kahl | Claudio Sacerdoti Coen |
| David Carlisle | Temur Kutsia | Pierre-Yves Strub |
| Luís Cruz-Filipe | Iris Loeb | Carsten Ullrich |
| Flavio de Moura | Manuel Maarek | Freek Wiedijk |
| Hazel Duncan | Lionel Elie Mamane | Wolfgang Windsteiger |
| Lilia Georgieva | Andreas Meier | Daniel Winterstein |
| George Goguadze | Immanuel Normann | Stefano Zacchiroli |
| Dimitri Hendriks | Luca Padovani | Jürgen Zimmer |
| Martin Homik | Florina Piroi | Claus Zinn |
| Klaus Jantke | Tom Ridge | |

## Organizing Committee

Roman Matuszewski (Conference Chair)  University of Białystok, Poland
Adam Naumowicz                        University of Białystok, Poland
Adam Grabowski                        University of Białystok, Poland
Mariusz Giero                         University of Białystok, Poland
Magda Polubiec
Jan Matuszewski

## Sponsoring Institution

Centrum Informatyki ZETO s.a., Białystok, Poland

# Table of Contents

# Copyright Issues for MKM

Andrew A. Adams[1] and James H. Davenport[2,*]

[1] The University of Reading, A.A.Adams@Rdg.ac.uk
[2] The University of Bath, J.H.Davenport@bath.ac.uk

**Abstract.** We present an overview of the current situation and recent and expected future developments in areas of copyright law and economics relevant to Mathematical Knowledge Management.

## 1 Introduction

The advent of digital information distribution has created both new opportunities and new challenges in all information-rich fields. The new field of MKM is itself based on this advent. As in all other fields some of the challenges for MKM are social and legal as well as technical. As Lessig [4] put forward, social norms, law, economics and technology are strongly interdependent spheres. Although the primary aims of the MKM community are technical in nature the ramifications of technology for these other areas, and the constraints of these other areas on what technology is useful, must be addressed by this community. Here, based on the reports (Deliverables 1.1 and 1.2) from Project MKMNet, we present some social and legal aspects of copyright which are central to the way in which MKM technology may develop. There is an enormous debate currently underway in society on how to move forward in a digital information age with laws and social norms based upon analogue understandings of technological possibilities. This debate is addressed below in Section 1.1, although readers interested only in the current situation and the practical implications for MKM may wish to skip over it.

### 1.1 Information Wants to be Free, People Want to be Paid

The phrase "Information Wants to be Free" has become something of a rallying cry for those who object to the restrictive practices of the so-called "copyright industries" and their representative trade bodies such as the IFIP (the international trade body representing music recording publishers). The phrase has some unfortunate aspects to it but the essence is that in the digital era it is almost impossible to control the copying and (re)distribution of information even as much as was possible in the earlier analogue era. Various variations of the phrase have been used to oppose this on philosophical, practical or economic grounds such as "if information wants to be free then who's going to pay for it?". The version

* This work was supported by EU Grant MKMNet IST-2001-37057 and UK EPSRC Grant GR/S10919.

A. Asperti et al. (Eds.): MKM 2004, LNCS 3119, pp. 1–16, 2004.
© Springer-Verlag Berlin Heidelberg 2004

we will consider in this article is that while information, by its nature, can be easily copied and redistributed, the people who produce the information and who provide value-added services making it more accessible in some way, need to pay the bills and so "want to be paid". In the midst of the industrial revolution the so-called "copyright bargain" was therefore struck which granted authors a limited monopoly on the exploitation of their creation so as to ensure that further acts of creation would be encouraged. Other voices at the time argued on both sides of this compromise, one group regarding intellectual creation as an inalienable part of the personality of the creator or creators and therefore worthy of perpetual protection, the other regarding each act of creation as building on prior creations ("If I have seen further it is by standing upon the shoulders of giants." Sir Isaac Newton; "there is no new thing under the sun" Ecclesiastes 1:9 King James version) and therefore allowing no basis for monopolistic protection.

The growth of the internet in terms of number of users, speed of access and types or amount of content has upset the copyright bargain's basic premise which is that the act of making a copy can be simply subjected to restrictions in order to make information (relatively) freely available while ensuring that creators are paid. The particular academic ramification of this problem comes with the structures that have built up around academic publishing of material. These structures may well have been reasonable as they were incrementally produced but a number of changes have placed as great a strain on them as has been seen in the music recording publishing business. Various solutions are being proposed to the problems of the current system, which we shall present in Section 6.

## 1.2    Guide to the Paper

Mathematics is an international field of study and the internet makes border-less access to information more feasible, although natural language and semantic differences between country or regional groupings provide technical challenges to MKM. Both the legal basis of copyright ownership of creative work (which includes mathematics) and the social norms/working practices in both academic and non-academic settings in various places provide challenges for international MKM efforts. In Section 2 we present a limited survey of the original ownership question for (principally) mathematical papers (other areas of mathematical knowledge, such as teaching material and computer programs are sometimes dealt with where differences are known). Once it is clear who owns the original copyright we must consider what happens to copyright when the work is published. This is usually achieved through peer-reviewed journals for mathematical papers and so in Section 3 we present information about the current practice of various publishers and owners (as is made clear in Section 2 the original author is not necessarily the initial owner) when arranging for publication. In addition to the mathematical information itself MKM is also highly concerned with metadata such as databases of citations, publication information, and extracts (such as abstracts) concerned with mathematical publishing. In Section 4 therefore we consider ownership rights and economic aspects for metadata, including an overview of ownership rights for databases. Having covered the ownership question we then turn our attention to the general situation of digital rights management (DRM) seen by some as the technological solution to a technological problem in Section 5. We then cover the issue of current and future journal publication in terms of economics, legal issues, author rights and technology in Section 6, including a brief analysis of access to older material.

## 2   Original Ownership of Copyright

The question of who has the copyright in an original piece of unpublished mathematics is interesting. For the vast majority of authors (Ph.D. students, hobbyists and retired academics apart), it could be argued that producing publishable mathematics is part of their job, and therefore, in the phrase used in English law, it is a "work made for hire", and so the employer might claim to own it. The situation in practice is more complicated, and the following examples were obtained.

**U.S. Federal Government:** Claims the rights to all material produced by employees during their normal work and does not allow for the transfer of ownership to third parties. This has specific ramifications for publication in journals (see Section 3).

**British Universities** tend to have clauses in their employment contracts that says that they do not claim this sort of copyright, though increasingly (e.g. in 1998 at Bath) they are adding clauses that say that, nonetheless, they have a licence to use it. This is required by the increasing regulation of British Universities, which may require such material to be submitted for the purposes of the Research Assessment Exercise (see www.hefce.ac.uk) or other exercises.

Technological developments in teaching software has produced a new concept, that of the Virtual Managed Learning Environment (VMLE). The modularisation of Higher Education in the UK, and the pressure on Universities to develop new sources of funding (both direct pressure from government and HEFCE and indirect pressure due to underfunding) have led to Universities viewing the contents (not the structural software which is generally off-the-shelf externally-owned or internally developed) of such VMLEs as University Intellectual Property which might be exploited for monetary gain or traded with other providers to offset production costs in other topics. However, existing academic contracts are mostly either unclear on such matters or leave copyright ownership with the academic(s) who produce such the content. Most Universities are reviewing their regulations (as mentioned above) and this is often one of the contentious issues between Universities and staff representatives (often the AUT and/or NATFHE).

However, most UK academics explicitly retain all rights in their scholarly work including the right to transfer it if required/desirable. The nebulous nature of the working day for British Academics make this an unclear area of law. Since academics generally have not signed waivers under the European

Working Time Directive[1] and many frequently work more than a forty eight hour week on a regular basis, any claim by the University to a specific piece of intellectual property the production of which was not absolutely mandated by their contract and specifically requested by their manager would be very difficult to enforce.

**German Universities** seem, from discussion at MKM '03, not to make such things explicit, but the assumption made by academics was that they had the copyright. A similar situation seems to pertain in Italy and France. The copyright law of these countries is quite divergent from that of the UK/US, in particular in the concept of "moral rights" which extend much further than required in international copyright treaties (and indeed are the source for Moral Rights existing in those treaties at all). Full transfer of copyright is not possible under these laws, only the assignment of exclusive rights to publish/exploit the work, and the concept of "work-for-hire" is missing or very weak in these jurisdictions. In the past, where publication, copying and sale of copyright material were solely physical activities located in an identifiable legal jurisdiction this was not problematic. Modern communications and electronic print media make this a highly contentious area of IP law generally.

**CWI** as a Netherlands–funded research institute, does claim the copyright.

**NAG** as a private British company does claim the copyright, and makes case–by–case decisions on whether to transfer it.

If the copyright is owned by the author or institution, then it is possible for the author or institution to publish the material on internal or external web sites[2], or submit to pre-print archives such that the Cornell (formerly Los Alamos) archive (`www.arXiv.org`). However, as the work moves towards publication, publishers may well require that the work be pulled from external web sites. There are persistent rumours, though we have been unable to substantiate it, that some Physics journals have refused papers since they are also available on the Cornell archive, which does not allow deletion.

## 3   Copyright in Published Material

The practice in the past has been for publishers, academic or commercial, to request (often demand) that the copyright in a piece of mathematics to be published[3] be transferred to them. The excuse often given is that it makes it easier for them to defend the author's rights. No-one in the network, or others we have consulted, could think of an example of this happening with articles or confer-

---

[1] Council Directive 93/104/EC, 23 November 1993.

[2] A recent classic experience was the August 2002 publication on an Indian web site of the "PRIMES is in P" paper, which went round the community within weeks, and received more rapid positive comment than a journal editor could ever hope to collect in the way of referees' comments.

[3] Book, article, conference proceedings etc.

ence proceedings, and the split of royalties on translations of books (which the publisher generally does negotiate) is often very unfavourable to the original author: typically 50:50 between author and publisher.

However, there are numerous exceptions to this principle. One important case is that U.S. (federal) Government employees are forbidden to transfer copyright, and publishers that often deal with these authors tend to have a standard clause in the copyright transfer form. At MKM '03, it was said that several European countries do not allow copyright transfer in the same sense at British and American law does. There is also the interesting question as to which law does apply if, say, a French Professor publishes in a journal produced by the American subsidiary of a Dutch company (an actual example). It was noted that many copyright transfer forms[4] are not very specific on the subject.

Publishers are not always very consistent on this subject either. As one example, the London Mathematical Society asks for copyright transfer for its paper journals (even though all these have an electronic parallel edition), but not for its all–electronic *Journal of Computation and Mathematics*. Furthermore, the spate of take–overs in the publishing industry has complicated matters. We give two examples.

- The take–over of Academic Press by Elsevier meant that, at least in 2002, there were two different sets of procedures, depending on the original history of the journal.
- The transfer of *Compositio Mathematica* from Kluwer to the London Mathematical Society, means that, in this particular case, authors are asker to transfer their copyright to the Compositio Mathematica Foundation.

Over the past few years, the International Mathematical Union has been producing guidance, suggesting that publishers (at least of articles) should not be asking for copyright transfer, and authors should not be ceding the copyright. As a result, some publishers (e.g. the American and London Mathematical Societies), now *recommend* (rather than *demand*) such a transfer. At MKM '03, several people reported that, even for publishers that did not offer such an option, it had often been possible to negotiate it.

## 3.1   Why Authors Might Want to Keep Copyright

Other than philosophical reasons[5] there are several practical reasons.

1. One may want to publish it on an internal web sites, e.g. for one's research students, and maybe classes.

---

[4] Which are generally quite brief, normally one side of A4 to avoid intimidating the authors.

[5] Which can be quite strong. It is often said that academics are the most stupid people in the world: they create something at great expense; give it away free to publishers; help, generally free of charge, with the refereeing and editing process; and then they and their libraries pay vast sums to buy the journals back.

2. One may want to publish it on an external website. There is then an issue of which version of a paper an author can self-publish:

   The author's original version (e.g. with `article.cls`);

   The publisher's version, which may well incorporate formatting that is copyright for the publisher. It is quite common for a publisher's "internal" class file to be more sophisticated than the one issued to authors.

   In either case, there is data mining that can be done with the LaTeX source, but not with, say, PDF or Postscript. But the publication of the LaTeX would imply the publication of the class file, which might prevent the previous option. Some authors feel that publishing the LaTeX might make plagiarism easier, but an advanced MKM system should make plagiarism much easier to detect.

   It was noted that LMS Journal of Computation and Mathematics publishes the PDF, but keeps the LaTeX, and has the right to re-generate a new format if PDF ceases to be the only useful publishing format. One should also note that Springer Lecture Notes in Computer Science allows articles in conference proceedings to appear on an external web site.

3. One may wish to re-use more of the paper, e.g. in a text book, than the Berne convention "fair dealing 10%" would permit. Even if the publisher ultimately allows this, it still places an administrative burden on the author, and publishers have been known to demand royalties if the author neglected to get permission.

   Indeed, in publishing a text book, most publishers will require indemnity by the author for any unacknowledged use of copyrighted material held by another. Reproducing highly similar material from one's own prior work without realising it is not impossible, particularly when trying to explain common concepts in one's research.

## 3.2   Publicly Accessible Information on Copyright Policies

Even though, as mentioned above, publishers are sometimes willing to accept or negotiate rights other than a full transfer, most authors are not aware of this. The pressure to publish placed by institutions on, particularly junior, academics may force them to accept conditions to which they object but to which they do not realise they may not be required to submit.

Even where required copyright assignment is no longer the official policy of a publishing organisation (such as the LMS), it may well be some time before their public information about publishing policies is updated. This is particularly true where commercial publishers (such as Cambridge University Press) are the physical publisher of a journal under the auspices of a learned society (as is the case for the Bulletin and Journal of the London Mathematical Society and the Journal of the Institute of Mathematics of Jussieu, all three of which are published by Cambridge University Press).

A brief investigation into the publicly published policies on copyright for journal articles produced the following results:

**AMS: The American Mathematical Society.** The AMS specifically states that they only *require* "Consent to Publish" (i.e. a non-exclusive right to print and otherwise distribute the material). However "an author is encouraged also to transfer copyright of the work to the AMS. In doing so, the author retains the right to use the work for his or her own purposes but simplifies for others the permissions process by enabling the AMS to administer it."[6] The wording of the AMS statement shows a lack of attention to the detail of copyright law. Assigning copyright to the AMS is not needed for them to administer rights negotiations and permissions to reprint, a simple assignment of those rights to the AMS would do that. What assignment of copyright does do is allow the AMS to pursue anyone violating those rights, and prevents[7] the author from negotiating payment for use of their work. There is no mention in the agreement of any sharing of payment that the AMS might negotiate/receive for such permissions.

**Oxford University Press.** As well as publishing a number of mathematic journals of its own, the Oxford University Press publishes on behalf of two external sources in Mathematics; The Institute of Mathematics and its Applications (IMA) and the Interest Group in Pure and Applied Logics (IGPL). The IMA Journals and the OUP's own journals require a transfer of copyright to the OUP (not the IMA): "It is a condition of publication in the Journal that authors assign copyright to Oxford University Press. This ensures that requests from third parties to reproduce articles are handled efficiently and consistently and will also allow the article to be as widely disseminated as possible. In assigning copyright, authors may use their own material in publications provided that the Journal is acknowledged as the original place of publication, and Oxford University Press is notified in writing and in advance."

The Journal of the IGLP situation is somewhat different. The stated purpose of this journal is to provide a fast and efficient journal publication route for a subject where timely reporting of a diverse and growing field is needed. As such, the IGPL is published online and full text articles are available for free download. There is no explicit notification on the "author submission" pages on copyright issues, but the statement regarding "Publication Policy" which includes: "We do not mind if a paper which *has already been published* in the Journal is submitted to another journal. It is the author's responsibility to inform the new publisher that the paper has already appeared in the Journal and that it will be further electronically accessible." (Emphasis in original.) seems to indicate that only the required permission to publish and maintain (presumably perpetually) the original paper are required. The information for authors on the Journal of Logic and Computation website gives no information either. The third journal of the IGPL, Journal of Language and Computation is reported to have recently switched to Kluwer

---

[6] AMS "Consent to Publish and Copyright Agreement Forms".

[7] As specified in the full text of the agreement rather than the above which was taken from the explanatory notes about the agreement.

Academic Publishers but does not yet appear on their list of journals, so no information is available online.

**Kluwer.** Kluwer Academic Press require transfer of copyright. Their reasoning for this is explained in their September 2003 copyright policy document, available on request from their legal department. This would appear to be supposedly a non-negotiable standard both for societies using Kluwer as their publishing partner and for individual authors. That is the impression given by representatives of Kluwer's legal department, although individual authors or co-publishers may have found this not to be so strict. As mentioned above publishers are sometimes reluctant to acknowledge variations in practice to avoid a flood of non-standard requests. "Important elements of the publisher's role in the scientific communication process are peer-reviewing, registration and quality assurance. In order to guarantee that the requirements of these three elements are fully met, control of the dissemination of the final article is necessary. Permitting an article to be published elsewhere on public servers without a clear connection to the peer-reviewed final article can potentially confuse readers who use the article for their own research and will not be in the interest of science. By asking for the transfer of copyright from the author to the publisher, Kluwer tries to protect the mutual interests of both the author/researcher and the publisher."

**Elsevier.** Elsevier have almost identical requirements for a transfer of copyright to Kluwer's. Their justification is quite interesting: "Elsevier wants to ensure that it has the exclusive distribution right, for all media. Such a right can be obtained through an exclusive license from authors, but there is virtually no difference between transfer and exclusive license. Given that there is virtually no difference, it seems to us that transfer does give an advantage in the elimination of any ambiguity or uncertainty about Elsevier's ability to distribute or sub-license."

In particular, the right to distribute is a separate aspect of copyright to the right to produce derivative works. Now, while it is highly unusual (though not completely unknown) for works of mathematics to be re-interpreted and adapted in another medium (which is a different process than simply transferring a printed article into a textual article online) the transfer of copyright would technically require permission from Elsevier whereas explicit rights to publish the article in all media for Elsevier would not include such rights. While it is unlikely that Elsevier in its current form would exert such rights, it is not entirely outside the bounds of possibility that such a case could arise in the future and so the current situation expects that Elsevier (and similar publishers) would always maintain their current stance on the issue. Elsevier does make a gesture in the direction of derivative works where authors retain: "The right to publish a different or extended version of the paper so long as it is sufficiently new to be considered a new work."

What the difference is between a "derivative work" and a "new work" is an interesting question, but too large for this report and so left as an exercise for the courts (see literary examples such as "The Wind Done Gone" and "Peter Pan: After the Rain" cases in the US and Canada).

Whether academic publishers honestly believe that transfer of copyright is beneficial to the academic endeavour, and whether or not they are right in this, is not the point of this report. It is clear that many if not most academic publishers have received a transfer of copyright for the material they have published in journals and sometimes in books, and that they continue to solicit such a transfer, either as a pre-requisite before publication or as a strongly supported suggestion for authors. The fact that a few major publishing houses hold such copyright could be of great benefit to making mathematics freely[8] available online in that only a small number of agreements with publishers would have to be reached to include a large portion of existing mathematics in an endeavour. It might also present a great obstacle should those companies regard these copyrights as part of their assets which they will seek to protect and from which they will seek to make further profit.

## 4    Copyright in Metadata

### 4.1    A Priori Metadata

This falls into several categories.

- Unstructured metadata added by the author, such as title, author and, generally, abstract.
- Unstructured metadata added by the publisher, such as journal, volume, page numbers, web addresses for on-line versions (which will generally be subscription-based with today's technology).
- More rarely, the above two classes could be combined, generally by the publisher, into more structured metadata, generally using the "Dublin Core" metadata standard. This would form an important part of any Mathematical Knowledge Management system, since the unstructured metadata in the first two classes varies widely between publishers, and in the absence of a uniform approach, one would need to build a case-by-case analysis into any metadata search engine, which would be tedious and error-prone.

If the author has not retained copyright in the paper, then it is fairly clear that the copyright in the metadata belongs with the publisher, though it is clearly in the publisher's commercial interest to make the metadata widely available to search engines. This is especially important if the publisher makes the on-line version of the journal (or other item) available in a binary form such as Postscript and PDF, without added external metadata where search engines, even if they had access, would not be able to harvest useful information. Where authors retain copyright it seems obvious that they grant publishers the right to use metadata along with the material.

---

[8] "Free as in speech" and/or "free as in beer" to quote Richard Stallman and the Free Software Foundation.

## 4.2    A Posteriori Metadata

The classic examples of this in the mathematical community are the *Mathematical Reviews*, *Zentralblatt für Mathematik*, or possibly *Computing Reviews*, reviews of the paper. The review is generally written by an individual, who may or may not be entitled to transfer the copyright to the reviewing organisation (see the debate in the previous section). Clearly, the review would be of no use unless the reviewing organisation had at least a licence to use the review. For the copyright in the database created by the reviewing organisation, see the next section.

## 4.3    Copyright in Databases

Few things are less certain in intellectual property rights law that the question of whether there is such a thing as "copyright in a database", as opposed to the items in a database. There is currently no international consensus, and cases are still fighting their way through the U.S. legal system and legislature. The EU does have a sui generis database right, separate from the copyright in the individual records, based on the work done in compiling and indexing such a database. "A "database" is defined by reg. 6 of the Regulations as a collection of independent works, data or other materials which are arranged in a systematic or methodical way, and are individually accessible by electronic or other means. Database right can subsist in a database regardless of whether copyright also subsists. Unlike the law of confidence, there is no requirement that the database or its contents should have any commercial or other value.[9]"

There have been few cases attempting to enforce this right so far and so the actual implementation remains something of a grey area.

## 4.4    Bibliographic Databases

Some of these are the reviewing databases, as described in the previous subsection. The on-line versions of these databases are very largely a mathematician's first source of information. Another one of great use is the "Web Of Science", produced by ISI. This can be used to find all papers that cite a given paper, thus enabling one to chase progress since a particular article. It would be a disaster for mathematics, undoing many of the advantages that information technology has brought to mathematics, if the absence of any protection for databases led these services, or the on-line version of these services, to disappear. On the other hand if the use of such services is priced out of reach of too many researchers due to over strong protection then this too would be disastrous.

The other category of bibliographic databases are those maintained, generally by individuals and their friends, of publications in a given area. One example is the "Harmonic Maps Bibliography" which can be found at www.maths.bath.ac.uk. Again, these bibliographic databases, generally accessible over the Internet, are a great asset to mathematicians trying to cope with the explosion in the mathematical literature, often said to be doubling every ten years [3].

---

[9] Quoted from the Kingsgate Chambers guide to IP Law: www.nipclaw.com/datab/.

## 4.5     Factual Databases

Many mathematical software packages are equipped with large databases of mathematical facts, which the software can search and/or use. An example of these is the database of all finite groups of order $\leq 31$ contained in the Group Theory software GAP. Again, these databases are often compiled by a team on the basis of several wider contributions. Things are complicated in this case by the fact that GAP is released under an "open source" licence.

## 5     Digital Rights Management

Digital Rights Management technology was seen, in 2001, by many, especially in the music and video industries, who claimed to be suffering greatly from Internet "piracy" to be the panacea for their woes.[10] It was felt at the time of writing the MKM proposal that mathematics could just latch on to what were clearly going to be industry-standard solutions. However, a more balanced view has now emerged, and a recent report [6] has the following in its Executive Summary.

> A principal consequence of deploying DRM technologies is to reduce the variety of tools available for accessing and modifying information goods. Thus, technological solutions threaten to worsen the imbalance between producer and user interests further.

While there were a plethora of statements about DRM on the W3C website in 2000–1, the very few later statements were significantly more pessimistic. In 2002, we read the following [5].

> Today, choosing a Digital Rights Management System (DRM) often locks you into a limited usage space for the content protected by the DRM due to limitations of the client software that plays back the content. To give customers what they want and allow broader usage, publishers and e-tailers have to offer the content in multiple formats, protected by multiple DRM systems. With the lack of a standard business rule definition language, these publishers or e-tailers have to specify the business rules separately for each DRM system they support.

As far as one can tell, this was never followed up technically, though W3C did issue the following comment[11].

> New technologies are needed to address a variety of issues around copyright and the Web. Electronic copies of a digital (intangible) item have no age: one can't distinguish between the original and the copy. The cost of copying has disappeared, which changes the whole landscape for the content industry. DRM and metadata can provide the necessary framework for a new balance and peace in the content arena.

---

[10] Often simply described as 'Napster'.

[11] http://www.w3.org/Submission/2002/05/Comment.html.

Consequently, this submission is a valuable attempt to provide input for a future DRM-Activity.

There are many Activities around DRM in different Standards bodies and Consortia around the world. MPEG is integrating DRM into MPEG-4, MPEG-7 and MPEG-21, CEN/ISSS has a Steering Group around DRM. OASIS just opened a Technical Committee on DRM to create a rights-language and Content-guard provided XrML as a contribution. None of the above mentioned initiatives federate all the stakeholders and interested parties around one table. The library community, new initiatives like the Creative Commons, like Project Gutenberg or consumer-protection associations offer welcome user perspectives too often missing from the technical design discussions of rights management systems. During the DRM-Workshop stakeholders asked W3C to help coordinate this broad variety of initiatives. This was partly done with the Workshop and the www-drm mailing-list.

DRM technologies are broadly covered by patents. This might affect the widespread use of such technology outside the very commercial sectors of the Web.

The last sentence probably implies that it is W3C's view that DRM would not be applicable for the bulk of mathematics.

Similarly, there are some proposals in MPEG-21 [1], which state that they have some connection with Digital Rights Management, but again follow-up seems to be limited, and probably not applicable to our community. The Rights Expression Language standard in MPEG-21 was approved by ISO in 2004 [2].

A further problem with the DRM technologies advocated by the music and video industries in that they tend to block all copying, whereas our community is used to "fair dealing", and indeed this is currently enshrined in most (paper-oriented[12]) copyright law. This discrepancy is brought out in the following quotation.[13]

More specifically, the content development industry, which consists of the recording industry and the movie studios, has repeatedly emphasised the need for immediate DRM solutions that stop all unauthorised copying and distribution. Meanwhile, the information technology industry is emphasising that DRM solutions should support the concept of "fair use", which allows consumers to make copies of some types of copyrighted content for their own personal use. In the US, these disagreements have led to an increase in both DRM-related lawsuits and new legislative initiatives.

---

[12] See http://www.eff.org/IP/DRM/20030916/brownback/statement.pdf for illustrations of how current interpretations in the U.S. of the DMCA are restricting this.
[13] http://www.content-wire.com/drm/drm.cfm?ccs=104&cs=2639.

## 5.1   Is P3P any Better?

A more recent initiative, the P3P project, describes itself as follows[14].

> The Platform for Privacy Preferences Project (P3P), developed by the World Wide Web Consortium, is emerging as an industry standard providing a simple, automated way for users to gain more control over the use of personal information on Web sites they visit. At its most basic level, P3P is a standardised set of multiple-choice questions, covering all the major aspects of a Web site's privacy policies.

It was originally hoped that this would also deal with issues such as copyright information as well as strictly privacy information. However, after the P3P 2.0 Workshop, the following statement appeared in the minutes[15].

> In general there was no consensus on the exact way how DRM techniques and privacy policy enforcement techniques in an enterprise should or could relate and this seems to be an interesting open question.

## 5.2   The State of Digital Rights Management

Steinmueller in [6] is pessimistic in his analysis of the future of intellectual property protection (IPP).

> The most likely scenario for future developments will be a set of continuing skirmishes between those having the greatest interests in enforcing IPP rules and those with the greatest interests in defeating IPP. Some of the vast numbers of producers and users that are in the middle of this battlefield are likely to be caught in the crossfire. They will step into various traps designed to capture those viewed as "pirates" by IPP proponents or fall victim to the opportunistic behaviour of a growing population of "claimants" who have varying degrees of legitimacy. The possibility that users will en masse be converted to a regime involving strong self-regulation of IPP transgressing behaviours is not considered seriously here. While such a regime might be conceivable in some limited domain such as the exchange of pirated copies of current hit recordings, it simply does not reflect the realities of information use that have been considered here.

## 5.3   The Current Use of DRM for Academic Papers

A number of the major publishers have begun making some or all of their publications available online. Few of these have made significant efforts to put material older than about 1990 online and many of them are only including new material. We will discuss the business models of these archives below, but will cover the issue of digital rights management for such material here.

---

[14] http://www.w3.org/P3P/#what.

[15] http://www.w3.org/2003/p3p-ws/minutes.html.

Most academic papers in mathematical sciences are typeset principally by the author using either a wordprocessor or the LaTeX (or TeX) systems. Where electronic versions are offered by the publisher these are frequently in portable document format (PDF) and sometimes in postscript, both of which are easily generated from all these input formats. Postscript does not offer much in the way of rights management, except that it can be difficult to select and copy portions of the text into an editing program, depending on the display tool used. One of the motivations for Adobe to produce the PDF specification was to allow the inclusion of some digital rights management controls in viewing and production software. It is therefore possible to place some restrictions on usage of a PDF file. In particular files may require separate passwords for opening or editing a PDF file and files may be marked as non-printable. Such restrictions are enforced by encrypting the content of the file and allowing only certain viewers to access the contents in certain ways (such as not allowing clipboard selection of the viewing screen as text and not allowing printer output. As with most DRM facilities these only discourage casual and non-technical users from violating the conditions of the files since there are always ways around such restrictions: if the material can be displayed on screen then it can always be printed via a screen shot at worst.

## 6    New Models

Academic publishing has been showing a great deal of strain in recent years. The old model of small publishing houses dedicated to publishing academic journals and monographs and making small profits on turnover has been superseded by two factors: publishing houses have been merged or taken over by large multimedia publishing organisations or, where they are attached to a University the parent organisation is more interested in the financial returns rather than in providing a non-loss-making service to academia at large. Scholarly societies who used to generate a significant proportion of their income from publishing activities are finding that the squeeze on University library budgets (caused from both ends as real-terms budgets are reduced and as prices from commercial publishers increase well beyond inflation) is causing a knock-on effect on their subscription income. When the number of institutions subscribing reduces, the cost per subscription must rise if "surplus" income for non-profit organisations is to be maintained. As these subscription rates increase many academics have looked at this model and decided that it is not the right way forward for the long term. Since many of the prestigious titles in which to publish are owned by the publishing houses new ventures are being brought forward with different models in the hope that they will eventually gain sufficient prestige (via their editorial boards, scholarly society affiliations and authors published) to supplant the expensive old-style journals. The two main models for this are the Open-Access journals and the subsidised journals. In the open access model the costs of editing and distribution (primarily maintaining web sites and printing bond copies on demand) are paid by authors. In order to avoid authors without significant funding from being barred from publishing most such journals operate an honour-based system where submitters are trusted to pay unless they really do not have funding available. In the subsidised model scholarly societies absorb most of the costs of providing fere electronic access (such as the London Mathematical Society does for its Journal of Mathematics and Computation) by subsidy from other activities including reasonably priced sale of hardbound copies to libraries. Existing publishers are also changing their practices somewhat, including offering tied-deals for access to the full archive of a journal while a current subscription exists and even bundling access to a wide-ranging set of archives in a single deal or together with a minimum-cost set of print journals subscribed to. Given the ownership of much of the existing material in papers and monographs (transferred to publishers by trusting academics over the years) it is clear that older material will always have a profit-inclusive charge attached to it. Whether profit- or surplus-generating publication of academic work can be maintained in a connected world where Google replaces the librarian for most people is still to be seen. What is certain is that knowledge management in any field cannot ignore the economics and legal aspects of ownership of creative work.

## 7    Conclusions

It is clear that appropriate use (and where necessary amendment) of both copyright law and custom and practice in publishing will be a major ideological battleground for the twenty first century. This as much if not more true for mathematical knowledge as it is for music, films, games and general textual material. Already online sources of information such as the arXive and free or "pay to publish" (rather than the prior "pay to purchase") journals are making inroads against traditional academic publishing models. Free software and open source software models are becoming economically viable beyond academic and pure research institutions, and are beginning to challenge proprietary software producers for market share.

Because of its very rich level of content (one page of mathematics can contain more hours of work, more insight and more useful results than a single page on almost other topic) and the broad applicability of mathematical information, a share and share alike attitude to mathematical knowledge has always been more prevalent than a pay-per-use approach. it is much more clear to both pure and applied mathematicians that their "seeing further" has been enabled by "standing on the shoulders of giants" (to quote Isaac Newton). As with other areas commercial publishers have gained a manner of monopoly on some of the output of mathematicians. However, unlike the music publishing world, the majority of the users are also the producers and the quality controllers of mathematical information. Thus the logic of using new technology to its utmost to aid in the creation and dissemination of knowledge as freely as possible seems unassailable and the biggest problems facing users today is how to ensure continued support for each other's work and not how to continue to support rich pickings for the middlemen.

In academia, it is well known that one must "publish or perish" and at the beginning of an academic career the question of whether to sign over copyright to a well-respected journal published by a commercial publisher in order to allow publication is not a quandary easily solved. Indeed the copyright to this very article has been signed over to Springer-Verlag to enable publication in the LNCS series. It is therefore the responsibility of more senior, usually tenured, academic staff to promote open access journals and open source or free software so that they become the standard routes to academic dissemination. They can do this by joining editorial boards of such journals (and resigning from those operated as profit-engines for commercial publishers) by publishing their own work in such places, and by dedicating as much respect in tenure and promotion decisions to such journals as to more established commercial titles. Pressure from University administrators to "exploit" mathematical "intellectual property" should not be allowed to undermine the fact that the prime purpose of academic endeavour is the production of new knowledge, and that this is better achieved both in general and in specific by exploiting new communications technologies to their fullest potential instead of closing off knowledge in a "pay-to-play" world. In the end the vast majority of academic institutions will end up paying more than they earn and most of the "earnings" will be spent on legal bills and administration, diluting still further the application of resources to the academic goal.

Mathematicians working in commercial sectors generally understand that they provide a service for the rest of their organisation, which are the profit-making parts. Even those working in the production of proprietary mathematical software often find it more beneficial to publish some of their work freely rather than keep it concealed. The emerging benefits of free and open source software development methods can provide suitable models. Those publishing material in academic publications should realise that they are already giving their work away for free and that ensuring as wide an audience as possible will bring far more benefits than giving it away to expensive-to-access routes.

# References

1. S. Devillers and A. Vetro, Delivery Context in MPEG-21, www.w3.org/2002/02/DIWS/presentations/devillers/devillers.pdf 2002.
2. ISO, Information technology – Multimedia framework (MPEG-21) – Part 5: Rights Expression Language, 2004, see www.iso.org.
3. T. Kealey, More is less, *Nature*, 405(279), May 2000.
4. L. Lessig, *Code, and other laws of cyberspace*, Basic Books, 1999.
5. RealNetworks Inc, Xcml language specification, submission to W3C, www.w3.org/Submissions/2002/05 , 2002.
6. W. Steinmueller, Information society consequences of expanding the intellectual property domain, Technical Report 38, STAR (Socio-economic Trends Assessment for the Digital Revolution), 2003, www.databank.it/star/download/E38.zip.

# Efficient Retrieval of Mathematical Statements[*]

Andrea Asperti and Matteo Selmi

Department of Computer Science
Via Mura Anteo Zamboni 7, 40127 Bologna, Italy
{asperti,selmi}@cs.unibo.it

**Abstract.** The paper describes an innovative technique for efficient retrieval of mathematical statements from large repositories, developing
and substantially improving the metadata-based approach introduced
in [10].

## 1   Introduction

The increasing amount of mathematical literature published on the web in structured, semantically rich XML-formats [16, 13, 15] and the recent combination of
these technologies with tools for automated deduction and mechanization of formal reasoning, independently pursued by several European Projects like Open-
Math, Calculemus, MKM-NET, MoWGLI and Monet has recently renewed the
interest for efficient indexing and retrieving techniques of *single mathematical
items* like theorems, definitions, examples, and so on (see e.g. [11, 2, 6, 9, 10]).

Typical techniques to query libraries of structured mathematics are based
on some kind of (first order) matching, spanning from simple pattern-matching
techniques to unification to more sophisticated queries comprising e.g. type isomorphisms [5, 4]. However, as already pointed out in [10], the straightforward
iteration of the matching operation over the whole repository of mathematical
knowledge has serious scalability problems with respect to the dimension of the
library. For instance, the MBase system [12], thanks to a clever implementation of unification, is able to iterate matching on a data base of 6000 theorems
(that is, a pretty small library) in about 1 second: if this performance is possibly acceptable for humans, is definitely too slow for the purposes of automatic
deduction, where we need to repeatedly look for applicable theorems exploring
huge trees of different possibilities.

The problem of speeding up matching and unification has already been extensively studied in the theorem proving community, but in a sensibly different
context: in particular, the knowledge base for retrieval is in that case a local
context, subject to frequent insertions and deletions, but stably loaded in RAM.
As a consequence, the typical solution is to store the data base of mathematical
items in ad-hoc data-structures, particularly optimized and integrated with the
matching algorithm, such as discrimination trees [3, 14], substitution trees [8] or
context trees [6]. As far as we know, the feasibility of scaling-up these approaches

---

[*] Partially supported by the European Project IST-2001-33562 MoWGLI.

to huge, stable repositories of available mathematical knowledge (the real context of Mathematical Knowledge Management∗) has never been addressed.

A natural way for indexing huge libraries of mathematical statements, independently introduced in HELM [10] and Mizar [2], is that to automatically extract a small set of metadata from each mathematical item, providing an *approximation* of its content, and devised to capture some simple invariants of first order matching.

In this paper, we propose a significant improvement of the technique described in [10], still relying on essentially the same Metadata Set (the HELM metadata set, originally conceived by the first author, and first published in [17]).

All examples, tests and statistics in this paper have been performed on the (HELM version) of the Coq library, composed of about 40000 mathematical objects.

## 2   Metadata as Approximations

For efficiency reasons, the metadata we are interested in are supposed to be expressible in a simple relational model. This excludes, for instance, the possibility of indexing an object with its type or with a (complex) subterm occurring in it, since these are not flat data, and we would be back to the problem of efficiently indexing and matching this information. The only flat data we may dispose of are essentially occurrences of constants. The other kind of information we may attach to these occurrences is their actual position inside the term. So, the main relation of our Metadata set is a simple ternary relation of the kind

$$Ref(source, target, position)$$

stating that *source* contains a reference to *target* at the specified *position*. By suitably describing such a position we may obviously reach the same degree of granularity of a substitution tree (where each variable marks indeed a different position), thus providing a complete description of the term. However, for limiting memory occupation, we opted for a minimal set of "interesting" positions, that, essentially just discriminates the root of the conclusion (we call this position MainConclusion) of the statement from all other occurrences.

*Example 1.* Suppose we have a statement asserting that for all $x$

$$x * 0 = 0$$

the metadata are described by the following table:

| constant | position |
|----------|----------|
| = | MainConclusion |
| * | InConclusion |
| 0 | InConclusion |

Note that variables are not indexed (it would be very difficult to take care of alpha conversion).

*Example 2.* Suppose to have a statement asserting that for all $x, y, z$

$$x * (y + z) = x * y + x * z.$$

Its metadata are described by the following table:

| constant | position |
|---|---|
| = | MainConclusion |
| * | InConclusion |
| hline + | InConclusion |

Question: in a mathematical library, how many theorems would you expect to find stating an equality between two different terms containing only $*$ and $+$?

As far as we are concerned with matching in backward reasoning, i.e. with the problem of finding generalizations of a given goal, indexing the conclusion of statements is enough. For this reason, in the rest of the paper we shall essentially work with the few metadata introduced above.

However, for other operations, like e.g. interactive support to forward reasoning, the HELM metadata set also supports indexing of hypotheses. These additional metadata are also useful in all those cases where the conclusion of the statement does not hold enough information to allow a sensible indexing. A typical, pathological case is e.g. the induction principle for natural numbers, or, more generally, the elimination scheme for an inductive type: the conclusion is a generic universal assertion containing no constant at all. On the other side, the hypothesis, listing both the type of the inductive predicate and of the eliminated data, usually provide enough information for an efficient retrieval.

The interested reader is referred to [17, 10] for an exhaustive description of the HELM Metadata Set.

## 3    Matching Conclusions

The problem of matching (for backward reasoning) consists of finding generalizations of a given goal $G$, i.e. of finding all those theorems in the repository which can be profitably applied to the given goal. If the theorem $T$ has a shape of the kind $\forall x_1, \ldots, x_n.G'$, the problem consists to look for a substitution $\sigma$ such that $G'\sigma$ can be unified with $G$ (typically, via first order unification). Since substitution can only instantiate terms (and cannot erase any subterm), every constant occurring in $G'$ must already occur in $G$: we call these constraints *atmost constraints*[1].

---

[1] We adopted the terminology of Mizar. In particular, the *only constraints* and *must constraints* of [17, 10] are respectively renamed into *atmost constraints* and *atleast constraints*.

**Definition 1.** *An* atmost constraint *is a set of constants* $atmost\{c_1,\ldots,c_n\}$. *A statement s satisfies the constraint if all constants occurring in the conclusion of s are in* $atmost\{c_1,\ldots,c_n\}$, *that is if*

$$\{x | Ref(s,x,InConclusion) \vee Ref(s,x,MainConclusion)\} \subseteq \{c_1,\ldots,c_n\}.$$

*In this case we shall write* $s \unlhd \{c_1,\ldots,c_n\}$. *We shall also write* $s \unlhd_c \{c_1,\ldots,c_n\}$ *if* $c \unlhd \{c,c_1,\ldots,c_n\}$ *and c is the (unique) constant with position MainConclusion.*

Checking that a theorem $s$ meets an *atmost constraint* with our metadata is not a very simple operation: it requires a query to the data base and then an explicit comparison of two sets (for each theorem to test). According to our measures, the cost of checking an *atmost constraint* is in fact comparable to the cost of a direct unification check *provided the theorem s is already in memory*. In fact, the real point of *atmost constraints* (not so well explained in [10]) is not to speed up filtering, but to avoid loading useless objects in the central memory. The latter can be a *very* expensive operation, especially if it requires parsing, type-checking or, even worse, downloading via web).

In any case, if we had to iterate the application of an *atmost constraint* to the whole library we would be back to the same scalability problem we started with.

Things are a bit better if we assume to work in a "first order setting", that is quite typical of automatic tactics even in higher order systems. In this case, we may assume that the head operator of the current goal $G$ is already instantiated, and thus it must appear (again in head position) in any generalization $G'$. So, with no loss of generality, we may restrict our search to the set of theorems sharing the same predicate of the goal (in position MainConclusion).

*Example 3.* Suppose we are interested in looking for theorems matching the goal $0 \leq S(0)$. We search for theorems having $\leq$ in MainConclusion and with 0 and $S$ as *atmost constraint*. In the Coq library, composed of about 40000 mathematical items (theorems, definitions, inductive types, ...), we have 263 theorems with $\leq$ in MainConclusion. Although this provides a significant reduction of the search space, iterating the evaluation of the *atmost constraint* for 263 times is a really expensive operation (especially in tactics for automatic theorem proving).

The table in Figure 1 gives the ordered list of the (top 20) constants appearing in the Coq library in position MainConclusion, together with their frequency.

The diagram in Figure 2 associates to each theorem of the library ($x$-line) the number of other theorems sharing with the former the same constant in Main-Conclusion ($y$-line); the big pick on the left is of course due to Leibniz-equality. The average value is about 596 that also provides a reasonable estimation of the average number of times we may expect to iterate the computation of an *atmost constraint* in a generic query!

| $n$ | frequency | object |
|---|---|---|
| 1 | 3978 | Coq/Init/Logic/eq.ind#xpointer(1/1) |
| 2 | 920 | Coq/Init/Logic/not.con |
| 3 | 753 | CoRN/algebra/CSetoids/cs_eq.con |
| 4 | 557 | CoRN/algebra/CSetoids/cs_crr.con |
| 5 | 438 | Coq/Init/Logic/ex.ind#xpointer(1/1) |
| 6 | 435 | Sophia-Antipolis/Functions_in_ZFC/Functions_in_ZFC/Ens.con |
| 7 | 421 | Sophia-Antipolis/Functions_in_ZFC/Functions_in_ZFC/IN.con |
| 8 | 413 | CoRN/algebra/COrdFields/leEq.con |
| 9 | 366 | Nijmegen/Coqoban/Coqoban_engine/Board.ind#xpointer(1/1) |
| 10 | 354 | CoRN/algebra/CSetoids/Ccsr_rel.con |
| 11 | 353 | Coq/Init/Datatypes/nat.ind#xpointer(1/1) |
| 12 | 350 | Coq/Init/Logic/or.ind#xpointer(1/1) |
| 13 | 333 | Coq/Init/Specif/sumbool.ind#xpointer(1/1) |
| 14 | 328 | Sophia-Antipolis/Algebra/Sets/Equal.con |
| 15 | 303 | Coq/Init/Logic/and.ind#xpointer(1/1) |
| 16 | 280 | CoRN/algebra/CSetoidFun/PartFunct.ind#xpointer(1/1) |
| 17 | 263 | Coq/Init/Peano/le.ind#xpointer(1/1) |
| 18 | 247 | Coq/ZArith/zarith_aux/Zle.con |
| 19 | 245 | CoRN/algebra/CLogic/CProp.con |
| 20 | 245 | Coq/Reals/Rdefinitions/Rle.con |

**Fig. 1.** Top 20 operators appearing in position MainConclusion

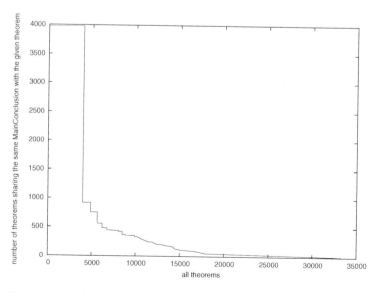

**Fig. 2.** Diagram associating to each theorem of the Coq-library ($x$-line) the number of other theorems sharing with the former the same constant in MainConclusion ($y$-line)

## 4     Atleast Constraints

A way for improving the initial filtering (preliminary to the application of an *atmost constraint*) is by requiring that more symbols of the current goal $G$ occur in the conclusion of the theorem we are looking for; we call these constraint *atleast constraints*.

**Definition 2.** *An* atleast constraint *is a set of constants* $atleast\{c_1, \ldots, c_n\}$. *A formula s satisfies the constraint if all the constants* $\{c_1, \ldots, c_n\}$ *are in the conclusion of s, that is if*

$$\{c_1, \ldots, c_n\} \subseteq \{x | Ref(s, x, InConclusion)\}.$$

*In this case we shall write* $\{c_1, \ldots, c_n\} \trianglelefteq s$ *(and* $\{c_1, \ldots, c_n\} \trianglelefteq_c s$ *if c is the constant in position MainConclusion of s.*

The interest of *atleast constraints* is that in order to find all theorems satisfying a given constraint $\{c_1, \ldots, c_n\}$ it is enough to compute

$$\bigcap_{i=1\ldots n} \{x | Ref(x, c_i, InConclusion)\}$$

that is a simple $n$-ary join operation in a relational DB.

On the other side, the big problem of *atleast constraint* is that they can potentially cut-off usefull theorems. Consider for instance, the goal is $0 \leq S(0)$. We could probably expect to find in the library, and to apply, a theorem stating that $\forall x.0 \leq x$ (provided we are talking about natural numbers). So, we may restrict ourselves to all those theorems having $\leq$ in position MainConclusion and 0 in position InConclusion, that is imposing 0 as *atleast constraint* (there are just 36 of them in the whole library). However, the same goal could also have been proved by a direct application of a theorem stating that $\forall x.x \leq S(x)$ (such a theorem can be actually found in the Coq library: `cic:/Coq/Arith/Le/le_n_Sn.con`); obviously, $\{0\} \ntrianglelefteq$`le_n_Sn.con` an the latter theorem would not be found by the above query.

The theorems containing $\leq$ in MainConclusion and satisfying $\{S\}$ as *atleast constraint* are 98. The union of this set with the previous 36 theorems give a set of 99 theorems (35 theorems contain both 0 and $S$). This is still a sensible improvement w.r.t the initial 263 candidates, but, alas, we are still neglecting all those theorems just containing $\leq$ in MainConclusion, and *nothing more*, such as, for instance, the transitivity of $\leq$.

## 5     Exactly Constraints

The considerations at the end of the previous section suggests a different approach to the computation of *atmost constraints*. First of all, we need the notion of *exactly constraint*.

**Definition 3.** *An* exactly constraint *is a set of constants* $exactly\{c_1, \ldots, c_n\}$. *A formula $s$ satisfies the constraint if the constants $\{c_1, \ldots, c_n\}$ are exactly the constants appearing in the conclusion of $s$, that is if*

$$\{c_1, \ldots, c_n\} = \{x | Ref(s, x, InConclusion)\}.$$

*In this case we shall write $\{c_1, \ldots, c_n\} \bowtie s$ (and $\{c_1, \ldots, c_n\} \bowtie_c s$ if $c$ occurs with position MainConclusion in $s$.*

The first important fact is that

$$t \trianglelefteq_c C \Leftrightarrow t \in \bigcup_{P \subseteq C} \{x | x \bowtie_c P\}$$

that is $t$ contains *at most* a set $C$ of constants if and only if for some subset $P$ of $C$, $t$ contains *exactly* the constants in $P$ (in the next section we shall see that not every subset of C has to be taken into account). The second important consideration is that *exactly* constraints may be efficiently conputed by a simple extension to the metadata set. The new relation

$$no\_concl(source, no)$$

associates to each statement *source* the number *no* of different symbols in its conclusions (the new table can be computed in few seconds from the already available metadata). Then we have

$$t \bowtie_c \{c_1, \ldots, c_n\} \Leftrightarrow \{c_1, \ldots, c_n\} \trianglelefteq_c t \wedge no\_concl(t, n)$$

that is $t$ contains exactly $\{c_1, \ldots, c_n\}$ if and only if it contains at least $\{c_1, \ldots, c_n\}$, and it just contains $n$ constants.

*Example 4.* Retrieving candidates for matching the theorem $0 \leq S(0)$ amounts to the execution of four SQL queries, corresponding to the four *exactly constraints* specified by the sets $\emptyset$, $\{0\}$, $\{S\}$ and $\{0, S\}$. The cardinality of the respective result set (for the Coq library) is given in the following table:

| exactly constraint | #result |
|:---:|:---:|
| $\emptyset$ | 60 |
| $\{0\}$ | 1 |
| $\{S\}$ | 15 |
| $\{0, S\}$ | 5 |
| total | 81 |

*Example 5.* Suppose we have the goal $x + 0 =_{nat} x$. The equality we are dealing with is Leibniz equality, and *nat* is an explicit constant appearing in the goal. So, in this case, matching the goal, amounts to solve the *exactly constraints* $\emptyset$, $\{nat\}$, $\{0\}$, $\{+\}$, $\{nat, 0\}$ $\{nat, S\}$, $\{0, S\}$ and $\{nat, 0, S\}$ with results sets as described in the following table:

| exactly constraint | #result |
|:---:|:---:|
| $\emptyset$ | 195 |
| $\{nat\}$ | 81 |
| $\{0\}$ | 0 |
| $\{+\}$ | 0 |
| $\{nat, 0\}$ | 46 |
| $\{nat, +\}$ | 9 |
| $\{0, +\}$ | 0 |
| $\{nat, 0, +\}$ | 9 |
| total | 340 |

In this case, the total number of 340 should be compared against the number of theorems satisfying an empty *atleast constraint* (with Leibniz equality in MainConclusion), that is 3978.

*Remark 1.* It never happens, in practice, that constants occur inside the conclusion of an equality statement if the type of the equality is not instantiated as well. This simple strategy allows to spare the three queries with an empty result set in the example above.

Given an *exactly constraint*, the corresponding SQL query is generated in a straightforward way; for instance the SQL query corresponding to the *exactly constraint* $\{nat, 0, +\}$ has the following shape:

```
select refObj.source
  from refObj,refObj as refObj1,
  refObj as refObj2,refObj as refObj3, no_concl
where
  refObj.occurrence
    ="cic:/Coq/Init/Logic/eq.ind#xpointer(1/1)" and
  refObj.position="MainConclusion" and
  refObj1.occurrence
    ="cic:/Coq/Init/Datatypes/nat.ind#xpointer(1/1)" and
  refObj1.position="InConclusion" and
  refObj2.occurrence
    ="cic:/Coq/Init/Datatypes/nat.ind#xpointer(1/1/1)"
  refObj2.position="InConclusion" and
  refObj3.occurrence
    ="cic:/Coq/Init/Peano/plus.con"
  refObj3.position="InConclusion" and
  refObj.source = refObj1.source and
  refObj1.source = refObj2.source and
  refObj2.source = refObj3.source and
  refObj3.source = no_concl.source and
  no_concl.no = 3;
```

The big question is of course how many different sets of *exactly constraints* we may be forced to generate for matching a given goal. If we have $n$ constants in the goal, this is obviously bounded by $2^n$, that is the cardinality of all possible subsets of a set with $n$ elements.

Thus it becomes interesting to know what could be an "expected" value for $n$, and the only sensible way to provide an estimation is again to rely on the library itself.

The table in Figure 3 gives, for several classes of terms, the repartition of the theorems according to the number $n$ of constants in their conclusion (comprising

| $n$ | $all$ | $=$ | $=_{nat}$ | $=_R$ | $cs\_eq$ | $\leq$ | $Rle$ | $leEq$ |
|------|--------|------|------|------|--------|------|------|------|
| 1 | 12635 | 195 | | | 9 | 60 | 36 | 27 |
| 2 | 6001 | 332 | 81 | 31 | 10 | 84 | 58 | 1 |
| 3 | 4049 | 616 | 132 | 57 | 8 | 54 | 78 | 94 |
| 4 | 3000 | 1017 | 203 | 122 | 13 | 24 | 23 | 31 |
| 5 | 2323 | 763 | 174 | 90 | 3 | 19 | 16 | 15 |
| 6 | 1226 | 395 | 78 | 45 | 22 | 10 | 10 | 10 |
| 7 | 875 | 216 | 48 | 38 | 22 | 6 | 8 | 5 |
| 8 | 769 | 135 | 20 | 41 | 44 | 1 | 2 | 9 |
| 9 | 496 | 65 | 15 | 35 | 69 | 1 | 4 | 13 |
| 10 | 1167 | 54 | 8 | 25 | 74 | 2 | 0 | 36 |
| 11 | 469 | 50 | 5 | 10 | 94 | 0 | 5 | 9 |
| 12 | 444 | 23 | 1 | 4 | 83 | 2 | 1 | 40 |
| 13 | 312 | 24 | 3 | 9 | 69 | 0 | 1 | 34 |
| 14 | 228 | 18 | 3 | 2 | 68 | 0 | 1 | 23 |
| 15 | 155 | 12 | 0 | 3 | 51 | 0 | 1 | 15 |
| 16 | 89 | 4 | 0 | 0 | 29 | 0 | 1 | 6 |
| 17 | 90 | 8 | 0 | 1 | 21 | 1 | 0 | 8 |
| 18 | 66 | 5 | 0 | 1 | 15 | 0 | 0 | 12 |
| 19 | 56 | 5 | 0 | 0 | 7 | 1 | 0 | 9 |
| 20 | 38 | 6 | 2 | 0 | 13 | 0 | 0 | 6 |
| 21 | 51 | 10 | 0 | 1 | 7 | 0 | 0 | 2 |
| 22 | 28 | 4 | 0 | 0 | 9 | 0 | 0 | 3 |
| 23 | 27 | 9 | 0 | 0 | 4 | 0 | 0 | 1 |
| 24 | 15 | 5 | 1 | 0 | 1 | 0 | 0 | 0 |
| 25 | 14 | 6 | 1 | 0 | 1 | 0 | 0 | 0 |
| 26 | 15 | 3 | 0 | 0 | 4 | 0 | 0 | 4 |
| 27 | 8 | 0 | 0 | 0 | 2 | 0 | 0 | 0 |
| 28 | 2 | 0 | 0 | 0 | 0 | 0 | 0 | 0 |
| $\ldots$ | | | | | | | | |
| 40 | 3 | 0 | 0 | 0 | 0 | 0 | 0 | |
| $tot.$ | 34661 | 3978 | 775 | 515 | 753 | 263 | 245 | 413 |
| $av.$ | 3.3 | 4.9 | 4.7 | 5.8 | 10.2 | 2.7 | 3.5 | 8.9 |

**Fig. 3.** Repartition of theorems with respect to the number of different constants in their conclusion

the constant with position MainConclusion). The first column refers to the whole library; the other columns are snapshots relative to the statements with the specified MainConclusion.

The average number of different constants appearing in the conclusion of statements of the Coq library is surprisingly low: 3.3. Things are a bit worse for equality statements, but we are also counting the type, and thus, according to Remark 1 the value in Figure 3 should be decremented by one.

Let us finally remark the quite anomalous behaviour of the setoid equality $cs\_eq$ and the algebraic less or equal relation $leEq$ of the C-CoRN development in Nijmegen. The problem is that in this case the formal statements are cluttered by a long series of coercions taking in charge the hierarchy of structures typical of algebraic developments. It could be possible that coercions should deserve a special treatment for indexing purposes (we are currently investigating the issue).

## 6     Prefixes

Not every subset of the constants appearing in the conclusion of a goal G should be considered for the generation of *exactly constraints*: we should only take into account subsets appearing in some prefix-tree of G. We say that $t'$ is a prefix-tree (simply, a prefix) of $t$ if $t'$ can be obtained from t by pruning subtrees (replaced by a special "empty" tree $\bot$); this is equivalent to the following definition

**Definition 4.** *The set $P(t)$ of prefixes of a tree (a first order term) $t$ is defined by the following rules:*

- $\bot \in P(t)$ *for any tree $t$;*
- *if $t = c(t_1, \ldots, t_n)$, and for $i = 1, \ldots, n$ $t'_i \in P(t_i)$, then $c(t'_1, \ldots, t'_n) \in P(t)$.*

*Example 6.* Consider the goal $S(0) * x \leq y$. The set of prefixes (neglecting variables) is $\{\bot, \bot \leq \bot, \bot * \bot \leq \bot, S(\bot) * \bot \leq \bot, S(0) * \bot \leq \bot\}$. In particular, we cannot have a prefix containing $S$ but not $*$, nor a prefix containing $0$ but not $S$. Any matching goal $G'$ must satisfy the same condition, thus imposing to have equality in MainConclusion, the set of *exactly constraint* for $S(0) * x \leq y$ is shown in the following table:

| exactly constraint | #result |
|:---:|:---:|
| $\emptyset$ | 60 |
| $\{*\}$ | 14 |
| $\{*, S\}$ | 4 |
| $\{*, S, 0\}$ | 3 |
| total | 81 |

# 7    Mixing *Exactly Constraint* and *Atleast Constraints*

When, even restricting to prefixes, the total number of *exactly constraints* is too big to allow a feasible computation, we may always employ *exactly constraints* up to a given number $k-1$ of occurrences, and then requiring *atleast constraints* for all possible subsets of $k$ constants. We call this constant $k$ the *just-factor*. The important fact is that we have to apply *atmost constraint* only to the union of the result sets of the *atleast constraints*.

*Remark 2.* The algorithm described in [10] can be considered as a degenerate case of our approach when $k = 0$.

*Remark 3.* While the result sets of different *exactly constraints* are always disjoint, this in not any longer the case for *atleast constraints* and it is worth to add an additional pass to drop repetitions.

*Example 7.* Consider again the previous example. If we decide to stop with a just-factor $k = 2$, we should consider $\{*, S\}$ as an *atleast constraint*, getting back 14 candidates with a single query (against the 4+3 theorems obtained with two queries as above). The extra 7 candidates could be filtered out by the application of the *atmost constraint*, but these would require 14 more queries (one for each statement in the result set of the *atleast constraint*).

*Example 8.* Let us consider the goal $(sinPI/3) =_R (cosPI/6)$. In Coq, the real number $n$ is treated as the sum of $n$ occurrences of 1 ($R1$); so the goal contains the 8 constants $=, R, sin, cos, div, PI, Rplus, R1$. For $k = 0$ we get the usual 3978 candidates with equality in MainConclusion. The case $k = 1$ amounts to restrict the attention to the realm of real numbers, reducing the total number of candidates to 195 (just containing equality) plus 515 statements containing $R$ (and possibly other things). On the latter 515 statements we must compute *atmost constraint*.

For $k = 2$, we have the following set of constraints:

| exactly constraint | #result |
|---|---|
| ∅ | 195 |
| $\{R\}$ | 31 |

| atleast constraint | #result |
|---|---|
| $\{R, sin\}$ | 59 |
| $\{R, cos\}$ | 65 |
| subtotal | 124 |
| subtotal (distinct) | 93 |
| total (distinct) | 319 |

Note that in this case the intersection of the result sets of the two *atleast constraints* is not empty (it contains 31 elements). At the end, we have just to compute *atmost constraints* for 93 elements: this means that in passing from a just-factor 0 to a just-factor 2 we already reduced the number of queries from $1 + 3978 = 3979$ to $4 + 93 = 97$ (2.4%).

For higher values of the just-factor things can still improve but in a much less remarkable way. In particular, for $k = 3$, the total number of queries is $7 + 51 = 58$, and for $k = 4$ is $12 + 35 = 47$.

| exactly constraint | #result |
|---|---|
| $\emptyset$ | 195 |
| $\{R\}$ | 31 |
| $\{R, sin\}$ | 0 |
| $\{R, cos\}$ | 0 |
| atleast constraint | #result |
| $\{R, sin, cos\}$ | 31 |
| $\{R, sin, div\}$ | 21 |
| $\{R, cos, div\}$ | 23 |
| subtotal | 75 |
| subtotal (distinct) | 51 |
| total (distinct) | 277 |

Note also that for $k = 4$ the subtotal of *atleast* is even greater than for $k = 3$, since we have a big number of largely overlapping sets; of course the total number of *distinct* elements is eventually either stable or decreasing.

| exactly constraint | #result |
|---|---|
| $\emptyset$ | 195 |
| $\{R\}$ | 31 |
| $\{R, sin\}$ | 0 |
| $\{R, cos\}$ | 0 |
| $\{R, sin, cos\}$ | 0 |
| $\{R, sin, div\}$ | 0 |
| $\{R, cos, div\}$ | 0 |
| atleast constraint | #result |
| $\{R, sin, cos, div\}$ | 12 |
| $\{R, sin, div, PI\}$ | 16 |
| $\{R, sin, div, Rplus\}$ | 19 |
| $\{R, cos, div, PI\}$ | 16 |
| $\{R, cos, div, Rplus\}$ | 23 |
| subtotal | 86 |
| subtotal (distinct) | 35 |
| total | 261 |

A sensible heuristic may be based on the following consideration. Suppose that the Goal $G$ has $n$ constants in position InConclusion. Then for any $k$, the number of different *exactly constraints* with more than $k$ elements is (roughly) bounded by $p(k) = \sum_{i=k+1}^{n} \binom{n}{i}$. If $p(k)$ is less than the cardinality of the result set of *atleast constraints* for $k - 1$ elements, it may look worth to generate and compute *exactly constraints* with $k$ elements; passing then to $k+1$. As a simpler, further approximation, instead of $p(k)$ we may just use the upper bound $2^n$.

For the previous example we would have the following situation (we take $n = 6$, due to the special treatment of the type $R$; for the same reason, in the case of the equality, $p(k)$ should be compared with the result set of the *atleast constraint* at level $k$, and not $k - 1$).

| k | p(k) | # − $must_k$ |
|---|------|--------------|
| 1 | 63   | 515          |
| 2 | 57   | 93           |
| 3 | 42   | 51           |
| 4 | 22   | 35           |

Our heuristic would suggest to go on (that is indeed the best decision). Using $2^n = 64$ instead of $p(k)$ we would have stopped with just-factor of 3, that is in any case a sensible choice. More generally, taking a just-factor of 3 for equality statements and of 2 for all other statements seems to be a very simple but quite effective politics.

The evaluation and tuning of the above heuristics is currently under way.

# 8    Conclusion and Future Work

In this paper we introduced a very simple but extremely effective extension of the approach described in [10] for the retrieval of statements matching a given goal $G$. Our extension is essentially based on two simple remarks:

1. an *atmost constraint* constraint $C$ may be reduced to a union of *exactly constraints* over subsets of $C$;
2. an *exactly constraint* $C$ can be simply implemented as a join of the *atleast constraint* $C$, with the fact that the statement must contain a number of constants equal to the cardinality of the $C$.

Even with very simple heuristic methods, our approach reduces the average matching time of more than ten times.

There are also additional benefits.

First of all, the approach described in [10] becomes practically useless in case the goal to match contains metavariables, since in this case the *onlyc* (responsible for the actual filtering) makes no sense. We have a similar problem, in our case, but much less dramatical since the *onlyc* would be applied (if required) to a much more smaller sets of candidates, and renouncing to this filter does not look problematic.

A second important benefit is that our approach allow to order the resulting candidates according to the dimension of the prefix of $G$ they are matching: the general idea is that a statement matching a bigger prefix is likely to be a better candidate (thus, e.g., in the case of the equality in MainConclusion, leaving symmetry and transitivity as a last resource).

From the point of view of automatic proving, our technique, although far from being resolutive, has substantially improved the automatic tactics under development in HELM, solving part of the problems, and helping to put in evidence the new and crucial weakness of the current approach: the large number of theorems having just one constant in MainConclusion and nothing else. For instance, in the case of equality we have 195 different theorems with a conclusion of the kind $n =_X m$. Typical examples are, for instance[2]:

**Singleton_inv** stating that $x$ is equal to $y$ provided $x$ is an element of $\{y\}$:

$$\forall x, y : U.x \in \{y\} \to x =_U y$$

**fun_item** stating that $u$ is equal to $v$ provided that they are the $n$-th element of a same list $e$:

$$\forall u, v : A.\forall e : List.\forall n : nat.(item\ u\ e\ n) =_A (item\ v\ e\ n) \to u =_A v$$

**Lub_is_unique** stating that $a =_U b$ provided that ($U$ is a conditionally complete partial order and) $a$ and $b$ are least upper bounds of a same subset $C$ of $U$.

$$\forall C : (Ensemble\ U).\forall a, b : U.(Lub\ C\ a) =_U (Lub\ C\ b) \to a =_U b$$

Theorems of the previous kind always match any equality goal; if moreover, as it is often the case, they generate one or more equality subgoals, we may easily expect an exponential explosion of the search-tree with a branching factor close to 100!

Several heuristic may be imagined to solve this problem, but this a completely different story that we plan to tell in a forthcoming paper.

# References

1. A. Asperti, G. Goguadze, and E. Melis, Structure and meta-structure of mathematical documents, Deliverable D1b of Project IST-2001-33562 MoWGLI, http://www.mowgli.cs.unibo.it/.
2. G. Bancerek and P. Rudnicki, Information retrieval in MML, Proceedings of the Second International Conference on Mathematical Knowledge Management, Bertinoro, Italy, February 2003, LNCS 2594, pp. 119–132.
3. J. Christian, Flatterms, discrimination nets and fast term rewriting, Journal of Automated Reasoning, 10, 1993, pp. 95–113.

---

[2] It is surprising how some of these statements may look odd and amusing when read in the "wrong" direction.

4. D. Delahaye and R. Di Cosmo, Information retrieval in a Coq proof library using type isomorphisms, in: Proceedings of TYPES 99, Lökeberg, Springer-Verlag LNCS, 1999.

5. R. Di Cosmo, *Isomorphisms of Types: from Lambda Calculus to Information Retrieval and Language Design*, Birkhauser, 1995, IBSN-0-8176-3763-X.

6. H. Ganzinger, R. Nieuwehuis, and P. Nivela, Fast term indexing with coded context trees, to appear in Journal of Automated Reasoning.

7. G. Goguadze, Metadata for mathematical libraries, Deliverable D3a of Project IST-2001-33562 MoWGLI, http://www.mowgli.cs.unibo.it/.

8. P. Graf, Substitution tree indexing, in: Proceedings of the 6th RTA Conference, Kaiserlautern, Germany, April 4–7, 1995, Springer-Verlag LNCS 914, pp. 117–131.

9. F. Guidi, Searching and retrieving in content-based repositories of formal mathematical knowledge, Ph.D. Thesis in Computer Science, Technical Report UBLCS 2003-06, University of Bologna, March 2003.

10. F. Guidi and C. Sacerdoti Coen, Querying distributed digital libraries of mathematics, in: Calculemus 2003, Aracne Editrice S.R.L., T. Hardin and R. Rioboo (eds.), ISBN 88-7999-545-6, pp. 17–30.

11. F. Guidi and I. Schena, A query language for a metadata framework about mathematical resources, Proceedings of the Second International Conference on Mathematical Knowledge Management, Bertinoro, Italy, February 2003, LNCS 2594, pp. 105–118.

12. M. Kohlhase and A. Franke, MBase: representing knowledge and context for the integration of mathematical software systems, Journal of Symbolic Computation 23:4 (2001), pp. 365–402.

13. Mathematical Markup Language (MathML) Version 2.0, W3C Recommendation 21 February 2001, http://www.w3.org/TR/MathML2.

14. W. McCune, Experiments with discrimination tree indexing and path indexing for term retrieval, Journal of Automated Reasoning, 9(2), 1992, pp. 147–167.

15. OMDOC: A Standard for Open Mathematical Documents, http://www.mathweb.org/omdoc/omdoc.ps

16. The OpenMath Standard, http://www.openmath.org/cocoon/openmath/standard/index.html

17. I. Schena, Towards a Semantic Web for Formal Mathematics, Ph.D. Dissertation, Department of Computer Science, University of Bologna, Italy, January 2002.

# Formalizing Set Theory as it Is Actually Used

Arnon Avron

School of Computer Science
Tel Aviv University, Tel Aviv 69978, Israel
aa@math.tau.ac.il

**Abstract.** We present a formalization of the axiomatic set theory ZF which reflects real mathematical practice, and is easy for mechanical manipulation and interactive theorem proving. Unlike the standard first-order formalizations, our version provides a rich class of abstraction *terms* denoting sets on the one hand, and is based on purely syntactical (rather than semantic) considerations on the other hand.

## 1    Introduction

Official formalizations of the axiomatic set theory ZF in all textbooks are based on some standard first-order language. In such languages terms are variables, constants, and sometimes function applications (like $x \cap y$). What is *not* available in them is the use of abstraction terms of the form $\{x \mid \varphi\}$. On the other hand *all* modern texts in all areas of mathematics (including set theory!) use such terms extensively. For the purpose of mechanizing real mathematical practice (including automated or interactive theorem proving), and for mathematical knowledge management in general, it is therefore important to have a formalization of $ZF$ which allows the use of such terms (and provides all other types of notation regularly employed in set theory).

Now, abstraction terms *are* used, of course, in textbooks on first-order $ZF$ (as well as in several computerized systems). However they are always introduced (at least partially) in a *dynamic* way, based on the "extension by definitions" procedure (see [7]): In order to be able to introduce some abstraction term it is necessary to first justify this introduction by proving a corresponding existence theorem in $ZF$ (or some extension by definitions of $ZF$). The complete separation we have in first-order logic between (the easy) check whether a given expression is a well-formed formula, and (the difficult) check whether it is a theorem, is thus lost. The main novelty in what we present in this paper is a language with abstraction terms which is *static*, so that the above mentioned separation is kept, and which is at the same time *complete*, in the sense that for every instance of the comprehension schema which is provable in $ZF$, there is a corresponding term which denotes the set whose existence is guaranteed by that instance.

Ideally, we would like to allow every formula $\varphi$ to be used for forming an abstraction term (according to the naive comprehension principle). Unfortunately, it is well known that this would lead to paradoxes. Historically, the guiding line

A. Asperti et al. (Eds.): MKM 2004, LNCS 3119, pp. 32–43, 2004.

behind the choice of those instances of the comprehension principle which are accepted in $ZF$ has been the "limitation of size doctrine", according to which only a collection which is not "too big" forms a set ([4, 5]). However, this criterion is not constructive: nobody has ever suggested an effective procedure, which given a formula decides whether the collection of all the objects which satisfy it is not "too big". Accordingly, $ZF$ uses instead some constructive principles to select formulas which intuitively seem to meet this criterion. These principles are usually explained and justified ([8]) on *semantic* grounds, using certain general ontological assumptions. To attain the goal of this paper we should use instead purely syntactical (rather than semantic) criteria for characterizing a sufficient big class of formulas which one can safely use (according to $ZF$) in such abstractions. For this purpose, we use a *safety relation* $\succ_{ZF}$ between formulas and finite sets of variables[1]. The intended meaning of "The formula $\varphi(x_1, \ldots, x_n, y_1, \ldots, y_k)$ is safe with respect to $\{x_1, \ldots, x_n\}$" ($\varphi(x_1, \ldots, x_n, y_1, \ldots, y_k) \succ_{ZF} \{x_1, \ldots, x_n\}$) is that for any assignment of concrete sets to the parameters $y_1, \ldots, y_k$, the class denoted by $\{\langle x_1, \ldots, x_n \rangle \mid \varphi\}$ is a set. In particular: If $\varphi(x) \succ_{ZF} x$ then the class $\{x \mid \varphi(x)\}$ denotes a set (this particular case is what interests us, but in order to define it appropriately we need to extend it to the more general relation).

## 2   The System and Its Language

### 2.1   Language

The formal definition of our language is the following (where $Fv(exp)$ denotes the set of free variables of $exp$):

**Terms:**

- Every variable is a term.
- The constants $\emptyset$ and $\omega$ are terms.
- If $x$ is a variable, and $\varphi$ is a formula such that $\varphi \succ_{ZF} \{x\}$, then $\{x \mid \varphi\}$ is a term (in which the variable $x$ is bound).

**Formulas:**

- If $t$ and $s$ are terms then $t = s$, $t \in s$ and $t \subseteq s$ are formulas.
- If $\varphi$ and $\psi$ are formulas, and $x$ and $y$ are variables, then $\neg\varphi$, $(\varphi \wedge \psi)$, $(\varphi \vee \psi)$, and $\exists x \varphi$ are formulas.

**The Safety Relation $\succ_{ZF}$:**

1. $\varphi \succ_{ZF} \emptyset$ for every formula $\varphi$.
2. $x = t \succ_{ZF} \{x\}$, $t = x \succ_{ZF} \{x\}$, $x \in t \succ_{ZF} \{x\}$, and $x \subseteq t \succ_{ZF} \{x\}$ if $x$ is a variable, $t$ is a term, and $x \notin Fv(t)$.
3. $\varphi \vee \psi \succ_{ZF} X$ if $\varphi \succ_{ZF} X$ and $\psi \succ_{ZF} X$.

---

[1] The idea of safety comes from database theory ([1,9]). See [3] for the general idea of safety relations and its connections with database theory.

4.  $\varphi \wedge \psi \succ_{ZF} X \cup Y$ if $\varphi \succ_{ZF} X$, $\psi \succ_{ZF} Y$ and either $Y \cap Fv(\varphi) = \emptyset$ or $X \cap Fv(\psi) = \emptyset$.
5.  $\exists y \varphi \succ_{ZF} X - \{y\}$ if $y \in X$ and $\varphi \succ_{ZF} X$.
6.  $\exists y \varphi \wedge \forall y (\varphi \rightarrow \psi) \succ_{ZF} X$ if $\psi \succ_{ZF} X$, $y \in Fv(\varphi)$, and $X \cap Fv(\varphi) = \emptyset$.

**Notes:**

1.  Officially, our language does not include the universal quantifier $\forall$ and the implication connective $\rightarrow$. Accordingly, in the last clause and below they should be taken as defined (in the usual way) in terms of the official connectives and $\exists$.
2.  From clauses 1 and 4 in the definition of $\succ_{ZF}$ it follows that if $\varphi \succ_{ZF} X$ or $\psi \succ_{ZF} X$, then $\varphi \wedge \psi \succ_{ZF} X$.

By inspecting the mutual recursive definitions of the sets of terms and formulas, and of the safety relation $\succ_{ZF}$, it is not difficult to prove the following two propositions:

**Proposition 1.** *$\succ_{ZF}$ has the following properties:*

 – *If $\varphi \succ_{ZF} X$ then $X \subseteq Fv(\varphi)$.*
 – *If $\varphi \succ_{ZF} X$ and $Z \subseteq X$, then $\varphi \succ_{ZF} Z$.*
 – *If $\varphi \succ_{ZF} \{x_1, \dots, x_n\}$ and $v_1, \dots v_n$ are $n$ distinct variables not occurring in $\varphi$, then $\varphi\{v_1/x_1, \dots, v_n/x_n\} \succ_{ZF} \{v_1, \dots, v_n\}$.*

**Proposition 2.** *There is a recursive algorithm which given a string of symbols determines whether it is a term of the language, a formula of the language, or neither, and in case it is a formula $\varphi$ returns the set of all $X$ such that $\varphi \succ_{ZF} X$.*

## 2.2    Logic

Basically, the logic we will use in our system is the usual first-order logic with equality. One should note however the following differences/additions:

1.  Our language provides a much richer class of terms than those allowed in orthodox first-order systems. In particular: a variable can be bound in it within a term. The notion of a term being free for substitution should be generalized accordingly (also for substitutions within terms!). As usual this amounts to avoiding the capture of free variables within the scope of an operator which binds them. Otherwise the rules/axioms concerning the quantifiers and terms remain unchanged (for example: $\forall x \varphi \rightarrow \varphi(t/x)$ is valid for *every* term $t$ which is free for $x$ in $\varphi$). We also assume $\alpha$-conversion to be a part of the logic.
2.  The substitution of equals for equals is allowed within any context (under the usual conditions concerning bound variables).
3.  In analogy to the previous rule concerning identity of terms, we may assume similar rule(s) allowing the substitution of a formula for an equivalent formula in any term or formula in which the substitution makes sense (again,

under certain conditions which will not be specified here)[2]. This would enable us, e.g., to replace the first extensionality axiom $Ex1$ below by the following analogue of the $(\eta)$ rule of the $\lambda$-calculus:

$$x = \{y \mid y \in x\}$$

(because with substitution of equivalents $\forall z(z \in x \Leftrightarrow z \in y)$ would imply $\{z \mid z \in x\} = \{z \mid z \in y\}$, and so, by $(\eta)$, that $x = y$).

## 2.3    The System $ZF^+$

Now we present the axioms of $ZF^+$, our version of $ZF$:

### Extensionality Axioms:

**Ex1**  $x \subseteq y \land y \subseteq x \rightarrow x = y$

**Ex2**  $z \in x \land x \subseteq y \rightarrow z \in y$

**Ex3**  $x \subseteq y \lor \exists z(z \in x \land z \notin y)$

### The Comprehension Schema:

- $\forall x(x \in \{x \mid \varphi\} \Leftrightarrow \varphi)$

### Peano's Axioms:

- $\emptyset \in \omega$
- $x \in \omega \rightarrow \{z \mid z = x \lor z \in x\} \in \omega$
- $\forall x(x \notin \emptyset)$
- $(\emptyset \in y \land \forall x(x \in y \rightarrow \{z \mid z = x \lor z \in x\} \in y)) \rightarrow \omega \subseteq y$

### Other axioms:

- The axiom of choice
- The regularity axiom

## 3    The Connection Between $ZF$ and $ZF^+$

The main theorem of this paper is that $ZF^+$ and $ZF$ are equivalent. For this (and in order to clarify the connections between the comprehension axioms of $ZF$ and $ZF^+$), we introduce first an intermediate system, $ZF^*$, of which $ZF^+$ is obviously an extension. Then we split the main theorem into Theorems 1 and 2 below (which together show the equivalence of all three systems).

---

[2] It makes sense to demand also that if $\varphi$ is equivalent to $\psi$, $Fv(\varphi) = Fv(\psi)$, and $\varphi \succ_{ZF} X$, then $\psi \succ_{ZF} X$. However, the crucial decidability of the safety relation will be lost if such a clause will be added to its definition. Still, it might be useful to add some particular important cases of this principle to the definition of safety.

**Definition 1.** *Let $ZF^*$ be the system obtained from $ZF$ by replacing its standard comprehension axioms (pairing, powerset, union, separation, and replacement) by the following safe comprehension schema:*

$$(SCn) \qquad \exists Z \forall x (x \in Z \Leftrightarrow \varphi)$$

*where $\varphi$ is in the language of $ZF$, $\varphi \succ_{ZF} \{x\}$, and $Z \notin Fv(\varphi)$.*

**Theorem 1.** *Every theorem of $ZF$ is also a theorem of $ZF^*$.*

*Proof.* We prove that the standard comprehension axioms of $ZF$ can be proved in $ZF^*$.

**Pairing:** $\vdash_{ZF^*} \exists Z \forall x (x \in Z \Leftrightarrow x = y \vee x = z)$, since $(x = y \vee x = z) \succ_{ZF} \{x\}$ by clauses 2 and 3 of the definition of $\succ_{ZF}$.

**Powerset:** $\vdash_{ZF^*} \exists Z \forall x (x \in Z \Leftrightarrow x \subseteq z)$ since $x \subseteq z \succ_{ZF} \{x\}$ by clause 2.

**Union:** $\vdash_{ZF^*} \exists Z \forall x (x \in Z \Leftrightarrow \exists v (x \in v \wedge v \in y))$ since $\exists v (x \in v \wedge v \in y) \succ_{ZF} \{x\}$ by clauses 2, 4, and 5.

**Separation:** $\vdash_{ZF^*} \exists Z \forall x (x \in Z \Leftrightarrow x \in y \wedge \varphi)$ since $(x \in y \wedge \varphi) \succ_{ZF} \{x\}$ by clauses 1, 3, and 4 (see second note after the definition of $\succ_{ZF}$).

**Replacement:** This is the only problematic axiom to prove. The reason is that, unlike the other comprehension axioms of $ZF$, the official formulation of replacement in the language of $ZF$ has the form of a conditional:

$$(\forall y \exists v \forall x (\varphi \Leftrightarrow x = v)) \Rightarrow \exists Z \forall x (x \in Z \Leftrightarrow \exists y (y \in w \wedge \varphi))$$

where $v, w, Z \notin Fv(\varphi)$. To prove this in $ZF^*$, let $A$ abbreviate the formula $\forall x (\varphi \Leftrightarrow x = v)$. Reasoning in $ZF^*$, assume $\forall y \exists v A$ (this is the left hand side of the implication we want to prove). This and the definition of the formula $A$ logically imply:

$$(\exists v A \wedge \forall v (A \to x = v)) \Leftrightarrow \varphi$$

But $\exists v A \wedge \forall v (A \to x = v) \succ_{ZF} \{x\}$ (by clause 6 of the definition of $\succ_{ZF}$), whence

$$\exists y (y \in w \wedge (\exists v A \wedge \forall v (A \to x = v))) \succ_{ZF} \{x\}$$

Thus $SCn$ implies:

$$\exists Z \forall x (x \in Z \Leftrightarrow \exists y (y \in w \wedge \exists v A \wedge \forall v (A \to x = v)))$$

The last two conclusions entail $\exists Z \forall x (x \in Z \Leftrightarrow \exists y (y \in w \wedge \varphi))$.

**Theorem 2.** *Every theorem of $ZF^+$ in the language of $ZF$ is a theorem of $ZF$.*

*Proof.* For simplicity, we assume that $\emptyset, \omega$, and $\subseteq$ are in the language of $ZF$ (together with the relevant axioms). We define recursively for every formula $\varphi$ of $ZF^+$ a translation $\varphi^{(I)}$ into the language of $ZF$ such that $Fv(\varphi^{(I)}) = Fv(\varphi)$:

- If $\varphi$ is an atomic formula in the language of $ZF$ then $\varphi^{(I)} = \varphi$.
- Suppose $\varphi$ is an atomic formula which contains an abstraction term. Let $t = \{x \mid \psi\}$ (where $\psi \succ_{ZF} x$) be a maximal abstraction term of $\varphi$. Define:

$$\varphi^{(I)} = \exists Z(\forall x(x \in Z \Leftrightarrow \psi^{(I)}) \wedge (\varphi(Z/t))^{(I)})$$

where $Z$ is a new variable, and $\varphi(Z/t)$ is the formula obtained from $\varphi$ by replacing every occurrence of $t$ in $\varphi$ by $Z$.
- Let $(\varphi \to \psi)^{(I)} = (\varphi)^{(I)} \to (\psi)^{(I)}$, $(\forall x \varphi)^{(I)} = \forall x(\varphi)^{(I)}$ etc.

Next, we show how to express an analogue (which is actually an extension) of $\succ_{ZF}$ within the language of $ZF$. For this we need some useful notations (in the language of $ZF$):

- $z = \{x\} \equiv_{Df} x \in z \wedge \forall y(y \in z \to y = x)$
- $z = \{x, y\} \equiv_{Df} x \in z \wedge y \in z \wedge \forall w(w \in z \to w = x \vee w = y)$
- $z = \langle x \rangle \equiv_{Df} z = x$
- $z = \langle x, y \rangle \equiv_{Df} \exists u \exists v(z = \{u, v\} \wedge u = \{x\} \wedge v = \{x, y\})$
- $z = \langle x_1, \ldots, x_n \rangle \equiv_{Df} \exists y(z = \langle x_1, y \rangle \wedge y = \langle x_2, \ldots, x_n \rangle)$ for $n \geq 3$.
- $\langle x_1, \ldots, x_n \rangle \in z \equiv_{Df} \exists y(y \in z \wedge y = \langle x_1, \ldots, x_n \rangle)$

It is easy to see that $\langle x_1, \ldots, x_n \rangle \in z \succ_{ZF} \{x_1, \ldots, x_n\}$.

Let $set_{x_1, \ldots, x_n} \varphi$ be $\exists Z \forall x_1 \ldots \forall x_n(\langle x_1, \ldots, x_n \rangle \in Z \Leftrightarrow \varphi)$ for $n > 0$, $(\varphi \to \varphi)$ for $n = 0$ [3]. Let $Set_{x_1, \ldots, x_n} \varphi$ be the universal closure of $set_{x_1, \ldots, x_n} \varphi$. Note that $Set_x \varphi$ formalizes the application to $\varphi$ of the comprehension principle. We show now by induction on the structure of a formula $\varphi$ of $ZF^+$ that if $\varphi \succ_{ZF} \{x_1, \ldots, x_n\}$ then $Set_{x_1, \ldots, x_n} \varphi^{(I)}$ is a theorem of $ZF$. [4]

1. The case $n = 0$ is trivial.
2. (a) If $t$ is a variable or a constant of $ZF$ then
   - $set_x x = t$ and $set_x t = x$ follow from the pairing axiom.
   - $set_x x \in t$ is a logically valid formula.
   - $set_x x \subseteq t$ follows from the powerset axiom.
   (b) If $t = \{y \mid \psi\}$ (where $\psi \succ_{ZF} y$) and $\varphi = p(x, t)$, where $p(x, t)$ is in $\{x = t, t = x, x \in t, x \subseteq t\}$, and $x \notin Fv(t) (= Fv(\psi) - \{y\})$, then $\varphi^{(I)} = \exists Z(\forall y(y \in Z \Leftrightarrow \psi^{(I)}) \wedge p(x, Z))$. By induction hypothesis for $\psi$ we have $\vdash_{ZF} Set_y \psi^{(I)}$. This means that $\vdash_{ZF} \exists Z(\forall y(y \in Z \Leftrightarrow \psi^{(I)}))$, and so $\vdash_{ZF} \exists! Z(\forall y(y \in Z \Leftrightarrow \psi^{(I)}))$. By part (a) we have also $\vdash_{ZF} Set_x p(x, Z)$. It is easy, however, to show that $\vdash_{ZF} (\exists! Z \varphi \wedge Set_x \psi) \to Set_x \exists Z(\varphi \wedge \psi)$ in case $x \notin Fv(\varphi)$. This implies that $\vdash_{ZF} Set_x \varphi^{(I)}$.
3. $set_{x_1, \ldots, x_n}(\varphi \vee \psi)^{(I)}$ follows from $set_{x_1, \ldots, x_n} \varphi^{(I)}$ and $set_{x_1, \ldots, x_n} \psi^{(I)}$ by the axioms of union and pairing.

---

[3] This is a generalization of the notation $Set_x \varphi$ from [7].
[4] The converse is not true. Thus $Set_x(x \neq x)$ is a theorem of $ZF$, but $x \neq x \nsucc_{ZF} \{x\}$.

4. To simplify notation, assume that $Fv(\varphi) = \{x, z\}$, $Fv(\psi) = \{x, y, z\}$, and that $\varphi \succ_{ZF} \{x\}$, $\psi \succ_{ZF} \{y\}$ (and so $\varphi \wedge \psi \succ_{ZF} \{x, y\}$). By induction hypothesis, $\vdash_{ZF} Set_x\varphi^{(I)}$, and $\vdash_{ZF} Set_y\psi^{(I)}$. We show that $Set_{x,y}(\varphi \wedge \psi)^{(I)}$ is provable in $ZF$. Reasoning in $ZF$, the assumptions imply that there are sets $Z(z)$ and $W(x,z)$ such that $x \in Z(z) \Leftrightarrow \varphi^{(I)}$ and $y \in W(x, z) \Leftrightarrow \psi^{(I)}$. Hence $\{\langle x, y\rangle \mid (\varphi \wedge \psi)^{(I)}\} = \bigcup_{x \in Z(z)}\{\langle x, y\rangle \mid y \in W(x, z)\}$. $Set_{x,y}(\varphi \wedge \psi)^{(I)}$ follows therefore by the axioms of replacement and union.

5. We leave it to the reader to show that $Set_{X-\{y\}}\exists y\varphi^{(I)}$ follows in $ZF$ from $Set_X\varphi^{(I)}$.

6. Assume that $\vdash_{ZF} set_{x_1,\dots,x_n}\psi^{(I)}$, $y \in Fv(\varphi)$, and $\{x_1,\dots,x_n\} \cap Fv(\varphi) = \emptyset$. We show that $\vdash_{ZF} set_{x_1,\dots,x_n}(\exists y\varphi \wedge \forall y(\varphi \to \psi))^{(I)}$. This is immediate from the fact that if $\{x_1,\dots,x_n\} \cap Fv(\varphi) = \emptyset$ and $y \in Fv(\varphi)$ then the formula $\exists y\forall x_1 \dots x_n((\exists y\varphi \wedge \forall y(\varphi \to \psi)) \to \psi)$ is logically valid[5], together with the following lemma (which is interesting on its own right):

**Lemma:** Assume that $\{y_1,\dots,y_k\} \cap Fv(\varphi) = \emptyset$, $\vdash_{ZF} set_{x_1,\dots,x_n}\psi$ and $\exists y_1,\dots,y_k\forall x_1,\dots,x_n(\varphi \to \psi)$ is logically valid. Then $\vdash_{ZF} set_{x_1,\dots,x_n}\varphi$.

**Proof of the Lemma:** $\exists y_1,\dots,y_k\forall x_1,\dots,x_n(\varphi \to \psi)$ logically implies the formula $\exists y_1,\dots,y_k\forall x_1,\dots,x_n(\varphi \Leftrightarrow \psi \wedge (\psi \to \varphi))$. It is easy however to see that if $\{y_1 \dots y_k\} \cap Fv(\varphi) = \emptyset$ then $Set_{x_1,\dots,x_n}\varphi$ logically follows in first order logic from $Set_{x_1,\dots,x_n}\phi$ and $\exists y_1 \dots y_k\forall x_1 \dots x_n(\varphi \Leftrightarrow \phi)$. Hence we only need to prove that $set_{x_1,\dots,x_n}(\psi \wedge (\psi \to \varphi))$ follows in $ZF$ from $set_{x_1,\dots,x_n}\psi$. But this is an instance of clauses 4 and 1.

We show now that if $\vdash_{ZF+} \varphi$ then $\vdash_{ZF} \varphi^{(I)}$. Since obviously $\varphi^{(I)} = \varphi$ in case $\varphi$ is in the language of $ZF$, this will end the proof of the theorem. Now the inference rules are essentially identical in the two systems, and our translation preserves applications of these rules. It suffices therefore to show that the translations of the axioms of $ZF^+$ are theorems of $ZF$. We leave the reader the easy task of showing this for Peano's axioms, and show here the case of the comprehension schema. Well, if $\varphi \succ_{ZF} x$ then the translation of this schema for $\varphi$ is $\forall x(\exists Z(\forall x(x \in Z \Leftrightarrow \varphi^{(I)}) \wedge x \in Z) \Leftrightarrow \varphi^{(I)})$. Now it is easy to see that this formula follows in $ZF$ from $Set_x\varphi^{(I)}$. However, the latter is provable in $ZF$ by what we have proved above (since $\varphi \succ_{ZF} x$).

**Theorem 3.** $ZF^+$, $ZF^*$ and $ZF$ are all equivalent:

- $ZF^*$ and $ZF$ prove the same theorems.
- $ZF^+$, $ZF^*$ and $ZF$ prove the same theorems in the language of $ZF$. Hence $ZF^+$ is a conservative extension of $ZF$.
- Any formulas of the language of $ZF^+$ has a translation $\varphi^{(I)}$ into the language of $ZF$ in the sense that $\vdash_{ZF+} \varphi \Leftrightarrow \varphi^{(I)}$.

---

[5] For the proof of the validity of this formula show that it follows from $\exists y_1 \dots y_k\varphi$ as well as from $\neg\exists y_1 \dots y_k\varphi$.

*Proof.* Obviously, the comprehension schema of $ZF^+$ implies $(SCn)$ (the comprehension schema of $ZF^*$). Since the usual infinity axiom is easily provable in $ZF^+$ too, it follows that every theorem of $ZF^*$ is also a theorem of $ZF^+$. This fact, together with theorems 1 and 2, entail the first two parts. It is not difficult to see that $\varphi^{(I)}$ from the proof of theorem 2 satisfies the third one.

# 4    The Expressive Power of $ZF^+$

## 4.1    Standard Notations for Sets

In the language of $ZF^+$ we can introduce as *abbreviations* (rather than as extensions by definitions) all the standard notations for sets used in mathematics. Again, all these abbreviations should be used in a purely static way: no justifying propositions and proofs are needed. Here are some examples:

- $\{t_1, \ldots, t_n\} =_{Df} \{x \mid x = t_1 \vee \ldots \vee x = t_n\}$ (where $x$ is new).
- $\langle t, s \rangle =_{Df} \{\{t\}, \{t, s\}\}$
- $\{x \in t \mid \varphi\} =_{Df} \{x \mid x \in t \wedge \varphi\}$ (where $x \notin Fv(t)$).
- $\{t \mid x \in s\} =_{Df} \{y \mid \exists x(x \in s \wedge y = t)\}$ (where $y$ is new, and $x \notin Fv(s)$).
- $\{t(x_1, \ldots, x_n) \mid \varphi\} =_{Df} \{y \mid \exists x_1, \ldots, x_n(y = t \wedge \varphi\}$ (where $y$ is new, and $\varphi \succ_{ZF} \{x_1, \ldots, x_n\}$).
- $\mathcal{P}(t) =_{Df} \{x \mid x \subseteq t\}$ (where $x$ is new).
- $s \times t =_{Df} \{x \mid \exists a \exists b(a \in s \wedge b \in t \wedge x = \langle a, b \rangle)\}$ (where $x, a$ and $b$ are new).
- $s \cup t =_{Df} \{x \mid x \in s \vee x \in t\}$ (where $x$ is new).
- $s \cap t =_{Df} \{x \mid x \in s \wedge x \in t\}$ (where $x$ is new).
- $S(x) =_{Df} x \cup \{x\}$
- $\bigcup t =_{Df} \{x \mid \exists y(y \in t \wedge x \in y)\}$ (where $x$ and $y$ are new).
- $\bigcap t =_{Df} \{x \mid \exists y(y \in t) \wedge \forall y(y \in t \rightarrow x \in y)\}$ (where $x$ and $y$ are new).

It is straightforward to check that in all these abbreviations the left hand side is a valid term of $ZF^+$ (provided that the terms/formulas occurring in it are valid terms/well-formed formulas of $ZF^+$).

**Note.**   There are two points about these definitions which are worth mentioning:

1. The validity of the term $s \times t$ is due to the fact that

$$\exists a \exists b(a \in s \wedge b \in t \wedge x = \langle a, b \rangle \succ_{ZF} x).$$

   This fact does not depend on the demand that $x \subseteq y \succ_{ZF} x$. Hence the fact that the existence of Cartesian products does not depend on the powerset axiom is reflected here by the obvious definition of a Cartesian product.

2. Our term for $\bigcap t$ is valid (and so denotes a set) whenever $t$ is valid. It is easy to see that if $t$ denotes a non-empty set $A$ then $\bigcap t$ indeed denotes the intersection of all the elements of $A$. On the other hand, if the set denoted by $t$ is empty then the same is true for the term $\bigcap t$ (such definition of intersection is known in the literature, e.g. in [6], but unlike here, it is done there by force).

## 4.2    Function Terms and the $\lambda$-Notation

In the language of $ZF^+$ we can introduce as abbreviations also the terms used in the $\lambda$-calculus (except that our terms for functions should specify the domains of these functions, which should be sets). Moreover: the reduction rules of the $\lambda$-calculus are easy theorems of $ZF^+$. To show this, we need another remarkable fact concerning $ZF^+$, namely, that the use of definite articles is available in it:

$$\iota x \varphi = \{y \mid \exists x \varphi \wedge \forall x(\varphi \to y \in x)\}$$

(where $y$ is a new variable, not occurring in $\varphi$). Here $\iota x \varphi$ (which is a valid term of $ZF^+$ by clauses 6 and 2 in the definition of $\succ_{ZF}$) intuitively denotes the intersection of all $x$ such that $\varphi(x)$. In particular: if there exists a unique $x$ such that $\varphi(x)$, then $\iota x \varphi$ denotes that $x$. Indeed, it can easily be proved[6] that

$$\vdash_{ZF^+} \exists! x \varphi \to \forall x(\varphi \Leftrightarrow x = \iota x \varphi)$$

It should again be emphasized, however, that $\iota x \varphi$ is always meaningful, and denotes $\emptyset$ if there is no set which satisfies $\varphi$, and the intersection of all the sets which satisfy $\varphi$ in case there is more than one such set[7].

Using $\iota x \varphi$ and the usual set-theoretical identification of a function with its graph we can now define $\lambda$-abstraction and function application as follows:

- $\lambda x \in s.t =_{Df} \{\langle x, t \rangle \mid x \in s\}$    (where $x \notin Fv(s)$).
- $ft =_{Df} \iota y.\langle t, y \rangle \in f$    (where $y$ is new).
- $f/s =_{Df} \{\langle x, fx \rangle \mid x \in s\}$    (where $x$ is new).

Identifying $\perp$ from domain theory with $\emptyset$, we can easily check now that rules $\beta$ and $\eta$ obtain in $ZF^+$:

- $\vdash_{ZF^+} u \in s \to (\lambda x \in s.t)u = t(u/x)$    (if $u$ is free for $x$ in $t$).
- $\vdash_{ZF^+} u \notin s \to (\lambda x \in s.t)u = \emptyset$    (if $u$ is free for $x$ in $t$).
- $\vdash_{ZF^+} \lambda x \in s.tx = t/s$    (in case $x \notin Fv(t)$).

For introducing other important notions concerning functions we need the following lemma:

**Lemma 1.** *There is a formula $OP(z, x, y)$ in the basic language of $ZF$ (i.e.: without abstraction terms) such that:*

*1.* $\vdash_{ZF^+} OP(z, x, y) \Leftrightarrow z = \langle x, y \rangle$
*2.* $OP(z, x, y) \succ_{ZF} \{x, y\}$.

**Proof:**    Such a formula was given in fact in the proof of Theorem 2. We repeat the argument: Let $Pa(z, x, y) \equiv_{Df} x \in z \wedge y \in z \wedge \forall w(w \in z \to w = x \vee$

---

[6] Note that the extensionality axioms have a crucial role in this proof.
[7] Note that $\bigcap t$ as it was defined above is just $\iota x.x \in t$, and indeed $\bigcap t$ denotes the single element of the set denoted by $t$ in case $t$ denotes a singleton.

$w = y$). Then $Pa(z, x, y) \succ_{ZF} \{x, y\}$, and $\vdash_{ZF^+} Pa(z, x, y) \Leftrightarrow z = \{x, y\}$. Let $OP(z, x, y)$ be the formula $\exists u \exists v (Pa(z, u, v) \wedge Pa(u, x, x) \wedge Pa(v, x, y))$.

We can now define:

1. $Dom(f) =_{Df} \{x \mid \exists z \exists y (z \in f \wedge OP(z, x, y))\}$
2. $Ran(f) =_{Df} \{y \mid \exists z \exists x (z \in f \wedge OP(z, x, y))\}$

## 4.3    Closure of $ZF^+$ Under Extensions by Definitions

As we noted in the introduction, in mathematical practice new symbols for relations and functions are regularly introduced in the course of developing a theory. This practice is formally based on the "extensions by definitions" procedure (see e.g. [7]). Now while new relation symbols are introduced just as abbreviations for (usually) longer formulas, new function symbols are introduced in a dynamic way: once $\forall y_1, \ldots, y_n \exists! x \varphi$ is proved (where $Fv(\varphi) = \{y_1, \ldots, y_n, x\}$) then a new $n$-ary function symbol $F_\varphi$ can conservatively be introduced, together with a new axiom: $\forall y_1, \ldots, y_n (\varphi \{F_\varphi(y_1, \ldots, y_n)/x\})$. Now a particularly remarkable property of $ZF^+$ is that this dynamic procedure is not needed for it. The required terms are available in advance, and every new function symbol we might wish to use may be introduced as an abbreviation for an already existing term.

**Theorem 4.** *For any formula $\varphi$ of $ZF^+$ such that $Fv(\varphi) = \{y_1, \ldots, y_n, x\}$), there exists a term $t_\varphi$ of $ZF^+$ such that $Fv(t_\varphi) = \{y_1, \ldots, y_n\}$, and*

$$\vdash_{ZF^+} \forall y_1, \ldots, y_n \exists! x \varphi \to \forall y_1, \ldots, y_n (\varphi(t_\varphi/x))$$

**Proof:**    Obviously, $\iota x \varphi$ is a term $t_\varphi$ as required.

An important corollary of the last theorem is that any set which has an implicit definition in $ZF^+$ has an explicit definition there, using an abstraction term. In other words: $ZF^+$ provides concrete term for every instance of the (unrestricted) comprehension schema which is provable in it:

**Corollary 1.** *Suppose $\vdash_{ZF^+} \exists Z \forall x (x \in Z \Leftrightarrow \varphi)$. Then there is a term $t_\varphi$ of $ZF^+$ such that $Fv(t_\varphi) = Fv(\varphi) - \{x\}$ and $\vdash_{ZF^+} \forall x (x \in t_\varphi \Leftrightarrow \varphi)$.*

**Proof:**    This follows from the last theorem and the extensionality axioms.

# 5    Transitive Closure and Peano's Axioms

With the exception of what we call here Peano's Axioms (our version of the official infinity axiom of $ZF$), all the other axioms of $ZF^+$ are valid in the domain of hereditarily finite sets. In [2] we have suggested that languages and logics with transitive closure operation $TC$ are the best framework for the formalization of mathematics. We show there how the special axioms for $\omega$ become redundant in such a language. Instead, all is needed is to add a clause concerning $TC$ to the definition of $\succ_{ZF}$. For completeness, we repeat the needed changes (with some improvements) here[8].

**THE SYSTEM $ZF^+_{TC}$**

**The Language:** The language of $ZF^+_{TC}$ is defined like that of $ZF^+$, with the following three changes:

1. The constant $\omega$ is removed from the language (and removing of the constant $\emptyset$ is possible too).
2. The definition of the class of formulas should be supplemented with the clause that if $\varphi$ is a formula, and $x$ and $y$ are distinct variables, then $(TC_{x,y}\varphi)(t,s)$ is a formula. The intended meaning of this formula is the infinitary disjunction of the following formulas:

$$\varphi(t,s), \exists w_1(\varphi(t,w_1)\wedge\varphi(w_1,s)), \exists w_1\exists w_2(\varphi(t,w_1)\wedge\varphi(w_1,w_2)\wedge\varphi(w_2,s)),\ldots$$

3. The definition of the safety relation $\succ_{ZF}$ should be supplemented with the following clause:
   - If $\varphi \succ_{ZF} X$, and $\{x,y\} \cap X \neq \emptyset$, then $(TC_{x,y}\varphi)(x,y) \succ_{ZF} X$.[9]

**Logic:** This should be an appropriate extension of first-order logic with rules for TC (one of which should be a general induction principle – see [2]). The exact logic necessary to get a system equivalent to $ZF$ has not been determined yet.

**Axioms:** Exactly like $ZF^+$, except for Peano's axioms (which are simply deleted). Note that now the comprehension schema has more instances.

**Theorem 5.** *The set $\omega$ of the finite ordinals is definable by a term of $ZF^+_{TC}$.*

*Proof.* $\omega = \{x \mid x = \emptyset \vee \exists y(y = \emptyset \wedge (TC_{x,y}(x = \{z \mid z = y \vee z \in y\}))(x,y))\}$

**Note.** $\emptyset$ itself may be defined already in $ZF^+$ as $\iota y.y = y$. In other words:

$$\emptyset =_{DF} \{x \mid (\exists y(y = y) \wedge \forall y(y = y \rightarrow x \in y)\}$$

Indeed, since it can be proved in $ZF^+$ that there is more than one set in the universe of sets, $\iota y.y = y$ denotes the intersection of all the sets (see the discussion above concerning the $\iota$ operator). This intersection is of course empty (a fact that can easily be proved in $ZF^+$).

## 6   Conclusion

Set abstractions of the form $\{x \mid \varphi\}$ are commonly used in mathematical practice. It is therefore very desirable that a practical formalization of Zermelo-Fraenkel

---

[8] [2] includes also a short description of $ZF^+$, without any details or proofs.
[9] It is possible to provide a general clause determining when $(TC_{x,y}\varphi)(t,s) \succ_{ZF} X$, but the details are somewhat complicated, and we omit them here.

set theory $ZF$ includes such terms. Since not all set abstractions are meaningful in $ZF$, indiscriminately allowing set abstraction terms in $ZF$ would introduce terms into $ZF$ that are actually undefined, and so before a term could be used its being defined would have to be proved. This problem is overcome in this paper by proposing $ZF^+$, a conservative extension of $ZF$ which contains a large collection of set abstraction terms of the form $\{x \mid \varphi\}$. Given $x$ and $\varphi$, $\{x \mid \varphi\}$ is a member of this collection provided $x$ and $\varphi$ satisfy a constructive syntactic condition, which we characterize by using an effective "safety" relation between formulas and (finite sets of) variables. We show that the use of these abstraction terms eliminate the need for the various comprehension axioms of $ZF$ (analogously to how function abstraction terms of Church's type theory eliminate the need for comprehension axioms in simple type theory). We also show that all the standard notations employed in books and papers for sets, functions, operations etc. can easily be implemented in our formalization as simple abbreviations.

$ZF^+$ is a compact, natural formalization of $ZF$ which directly reflects usual mathematical practice. Accordingly, it can serve as a very useful and convenient base for designing and implementing automated provers and proof-checker for set theory.

# References

1. S. Abiteboul, R. Hull, and V. Vianu, *Foundations of Databases*, Addison-Wesley, 1995.
2. A. Avron, Transitive Closure and the Mechanization of Mathematics, in *Thirty Five Years of Automating Mathematics* (F. Kamareddine, ed.), pp. 149–171, Kluwer Academic Publishers, 2003.
3. A. Avron, Safety Signatures for First-order Languages and Their Applications, to appear in *First-Order Logic revisited* (Hendricks et al, eds.), Logos Verlag Berlin, 2004.
4. A. Fraenkel, Y. Bar-Hillel, and A. Levy, *Foundations of Set Theory*, North-Holland, Amsterdam, 1973.
5. M. Hallett, *Cantorian Set Theory and Limitation of Size*, Clarendon Press, 1984.
6. B. Padlewska, Families of Sets, Formalized Mathematics, 1 (1990), pp. 147–152.
7. J.R. Shoenfield, *Mathematical Logic*, Addison-Wesley, 1967.
8. J.R. Shoenfield, Axioms of Set Theory, in: *Handbook Of Mathematical Logic* (J. Barwise, ed.), North-Holland, Amsterdam, 1977.
9. J.D. Ullman, *Principles of database and knowledge-base systems*, Computer Science Press, 1988.

# Integrated Semantic Browsing of the Mizar Mathematical Library for Authoring Mizar Articles

Grzegorz Bancerek[1] and Josef Urban[2]

[1] Faculty of Computer Science, Bialystok Technical University
ul. Wiejska 45A, 15-351 Bialystok, Poland
bancerek@mizar.org
[2] Dept. of Theoretical Computer Science, Charles University
Malostranske nam. 25, Praha, Czech Republic
urban@kti.ms.mff.cuni.cz

**Abstract.** The Mizar system is equipped with a very large library containing tens of thousands of theorems and thousands of definitions, which often use overloaded notation. For efficient authoring of new Mizar articles it is necessary to have good tools for searching and browsing this library. It would be ideal if such tools were simple, intuitive and easy to access. Particularly, they should provide interactive and integrated support during authoring Mizar articles.

We describe an approach to this task which uses the extendable MML Query tools to generate a special representation of the Mizar library (MML). This representation, so called Generated Mizar Abstracts, contains human readable form of the MML, completed by additional information which is missing or hidden in regular Mizar abstracts and texts. It also includes semantic information necessary for implementing advanced browsing in the Mizar authoring environment for Emacs (Mizar mode). Together with other functions of the Mizar mode, this allows the authors of Mizar articles to disambiguate the meaning of overloaded Mizar notations, and thus helps to start browsing at an appropriate place.

## 1    Motivation and Previous Work

### 1.1    Motivation

The goal of the Mizar project ([10], [11], [8]) is to formalize and check by computer as much mathematics as possible. This is to be achieved by writing Mizar articles; such an article usually formalizes a (small) part of some mathematical theory. These articles are then included into the Mizar Mathematical Library (MML). The stored theorems, definitions, and other Mizar constructs are later referred to when writing new Mizar articles.

The MML now consists of nearly 850 formalized articles, containing some 37000 theorems and 7000 definitions. The Mizar language has been designed (by A. Trybulec) to be easy for both reading and writing even with such high number of concepts. To achieve this end, the language supports overloading of symbols

A. Asperti et al. (Eds.): MKM 2004, LNCS 3119, pp. 44–57, 2004.
© Springer-Verlag Berlin Heidelberg 2004

which comes in two flavors. The first, the so called *ad hoc overloading*, allows the same symbol to have several completely unrelated meanings. The second is polymorphism at the level of type hierarchy (e.g. the so called *parametric polymorphism* – one functor can have different result types for different types of arguments). Such features are not specific to Mizar, they have been found useful e.g. in many modern programming languages (C++, Java, ML, etc.).

This language structure now causes that it is necessary to use Mizar-based tools (e.g. Mizar-like parser) when we want to disambiguate the exact meanings of symbols in some Mizar text. Using simpler browsing tools, like e.g. the standard tag-based browsing which is widely used for non-overloaded programming languages, can be useful, but cannot generally achieve the required precision. The goal of our work reported here was to provide such precise browsing for the MML library, and to integrate it into the Emacs authoring environment for Mizar [12], so that a functionality similar to that of advanced Integrated Development Environments (IDEs) for modern overloaded programming languages is achieved.

## 1.2   Previous and Related Work

There are several projects related to ours. The oldest of them is the Journal of Formalized Mathematics (JFM) [7], which is the electronic counterpart of the Formalized Mathematics (FM), published by the University of Białystok. JFM contains HTML-ized abstracts of the Mizar articles, which means that the symbols used in the formulas are linked to their definitions. JFM has been for long time the only tool of this kind, it is very useful even today, and at the moment it is the only "conservative" linked presentation of the Mizar abstracts, i.e. it just adds the HTML links, but does not change the text form of the Mizar abstract in any way. The main problem of the JFM is its technical implementation. It has been written with a large duplication of code, and given the fast development of Mizar, it is now outdated and very hard to maintain, to say nothing about adding new features (e.g. export of complete articles and linking of references). There are known problems in the JFM (e.g. bad browsing of selectors) that have not been repaired for some time. Our opinion is that JFM should be completely rewritten, based on a common XML-ization of the Mizar codebase and Mizar processing, and possibly merged with the functionality provided by the new MML Query tools [3].

The MML Query is another related project, and the work presented here is based on it. MML Query is a set of tools, which collects information about all Mizar *items* (e.g. symbols, constructors, theorems, definitions, etc.) from Mizar articles, and uses a database-like technology to store them, index them, and answer interactive queries about them. MML Query is not yet capable of presenting the Mizar abstracts in the same "conservative" way as the JFM can, since its first goal was mainly to capture the semantic content of Mizar articles. On the other hand it is much more flexible, and allows e.g. to recover the implicit parts of Mizar articles, like the definitional theorems or property formulas generated by Mizar automatically. The most common use of MML Query is via its HTML interface, however it has also standard command-line interface, and other output formats are easily added. We use this possibility and define a simple output format easily parsable by Emacs for the work presented here.

Finally, we can mention the earlier browsing features available in the Emacs authoring environment for Mizar. This includes tag-based browsing of MML references (i.e. theorems, definitions and schemes), which is sufficient and works well, because no overloading of their names is allowed in Mizar and every MML reference is unique. Similar tag-based functionality is also implemented for Mizar symbols (i.e. symbols for functors, predicates, etc.), however as mentioned earlier, this cannot provide the required browsing precision in the presence of overloading.

## 2     Availability and Installation

The complete system described in this article is for MML version 4.05.838 and it is about 5 MB big and unpacks to 64 MB. It is available on the web[1], but we hope that eventually this will become a standard part of the Mizar distribution.

This distribution should be directly unpacked into the directory $MIZFILES, set by the Mizar installation. The Emacs functionality is part of the Mizar mode for Emacs, which is a standard part of the Mizar distribution. Figure 1 is a screen-shot of the system in action, which can be also viewed on the web[2].

## 3     Implementation

### 3.1     Design and Overview of the Implementation

At the heart of our implementation is the notion of the *Mizar Item* (see the next section) defined by MML Query. This is a naming scheme uniquely identifying all Mizar symbols, constructors, theorems, etc. This naming scheme is the common semantic layer between MML Query and the browsing functions implemented in Emacs, and is also compatible with the naming schemes used in other Mizar related projects like MPTP [14] or MoMM [13].

Our implementation consists of the following parts:

– The customized MML Query tools (output filters) used for producing the Generated Mizar Abstracts from MML.
– The Generated Mizar Abstracts, containing a simple and easy-to-parse Emacs-based mark-up used for locating the *Mizar items* in them.
– The Emacs parsing and presentation of the Generated Mizar Abstracts, and browsing of the *Mizar items* in them.
– Additional Emacs support for disambiguating parts of the article currently developed by the author into the *Mizar items*, which allows immediate precise browsing.

---

[1] http://merak.pb.bialystok.pl/gab/gab-4.05.838.tar.gz.
[2] http://ktiml.mff.cuni.cz/~urban/snapshot3.png.

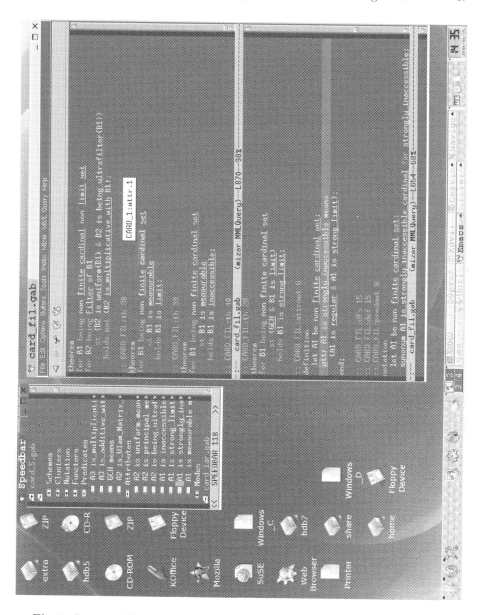

**Fig. 1.** Generated Mizar Abstract for article CARD_FIL in the Emacs browser

## 3.2    Mizar Items

For a basic overview about available *Mizar items* defined by the MML Query, it is best to have a look at their HTML-ized grammar, available at [6]. *Mizar items* are uniquely identified by their *kind*, their *Article-name* and their *Serial-number* in their article. There are many *kinds* of *Mizar items*, they can be logically divided into *Constructor-kinds*, *Notation-kinds*, *Registration-kinds* and

*Statement-kinds.* Their meaning is probably best explained on an example from the MML.

Consider the Mizar definition of the attribute `cardinal` – the first definition in the article `CARD_1` [1]:

```
definition let IT be set;
 attr IT is cardinal means
:: CARD_1:def 1
  ex B st IT = B & for A st A,B are_equipotent holds B c= A;
end;
```

This definition produces several *Mizar items*. First of all a *Constructor* item `CARD_1:attr 1` is created. This item denotes the unique Mizar attribute defined here, with its firm semantics given by this definition. This definition is also used to create a *Statement* item `CARD_1:def 1`. This is a definitional theorem created automatically by Mizar for this attribute:

```
theorem
for IT being set holds IT is cardinal
   iff
      ex B being ordinal set st
         (IT = B & for A being ordinal set
                st A,B are_equipotent
            holds B c= A);
```

The definitional theorem `CARD_1:def 1` can be explicitly quoted in Mizar proofs. Some Mizar definitions can be also used as macros, that work automatically and do not have to (and cannot) be explicitly quoted. Such macros (called definientia in Mizar) are another kind of *Statement* items, its name here is `CARD_1:dfs 1`, and its meaning is expressed as follows:

```
definiens
   let A1 be set;
To prove
     A1 is cardinal
it is sufficient to prove
   thus ex B1 being ordinal set st
       (A1 = B1 &
         for B2 being ordinal set
             st B2,B1 are_equipotent
           holds B1 c= B2);;
```

Mizar allows the authors to provide arbitrary notation for the constructors (whose role is to specify the semantics). The binding of a particular name (and arity) to a constructor is captured by *Notation* items. Here it is `CARD_1:attrnot 1` which binds the attribute symbol `cardinal` applied to one argument of the type set to the *Constructor* item `CARD_1:attr 1`. The *Notation* items provide the main method for dealing with different notations in different parts of mathematics, without influencing the semantic layer.

To sum up, the first definition in the article CARD_1 produces four *Mizar items*:

- the constructor CARD_1:attr 1
- the quotable definitional theorem CARD_1:def 1
- the unquotable definiens CARD_1:dfs 1
- the notation CARD_1:attrnot 1

One additional fact about the handling of the *Mizar items* in MML Query should be noted here. All terms and formulas appearing in them are disambiguated into the semantic (constructors) form. That means that e.g. for the above given definitional theorem CARD_1:def 1 we know for each symbol appearing there the constructor to which it actually refers. Actually, in the current version of MML Query only the constructor form is known precisely, and the human presentation is reconstructed from it, using the knowledge about the *Notation* items available at a given place. Since there is often more than one way how to do this (e.g. when multiple synonyms are available), this can cause that the reconstructed human presentation sometimes slightly differs from the original in the article.

## 3.3   The Generated Mizar Abstracts

Many of the *Mizar items* are never written explicitly in the original article. E.g. the definitional theorems can have quite complicated form, when a definition with several cases (so called *Conditional-Definiens*) is used. This sometimes causes problems to the Mizar authors, who need to know the exact form of such theorems, to be able to use them in proofs.

The purpose of the Generated Mizar Abstracts is to provide human readable presentation of various *Mizar items*, in a format similar to that of the original abstracts. We also want to allow browsing of various automatically created items (e.g. definitional theorems), which are not explicitly written in the normal Mizar abstracts.

Given these requirements, the structure of the current version of the Generated Mizar Abstracts (GABs) is following:

- Every GAB corresponds to exactly one normal Mizar abstract, and it consists of all *Mizar items* defined in the original abstract in the same order of appearance.
- Particularly, the parts of normal abstracts that are not *Mizar items* are not present in GABs. This means that e.g. comments, reservations or pragmas like *canceled* do not appear here. All variables in all items are fully qualified, while in the original abstracts, it is often necessary to search the reservations for their types.

- The items which are not explicitly written in the original abstract are by default hidden, and only their names are visible, so that the default GAB looked as close as possible to the original abstract. The presentation obviously implements functions for easy changing and customization of the visibility of items.
- Most importantly, all symbols inside terms and formulas presented in GABs are disambiguated and tagged with the appropriate constructor, which allows precise browsing.

Figure 2 is an example of the initial part of the file `card_1.gab` corresponding to the Mizar abstract `card_1.abs` [1].

### 3.4    Encoding of the Generated Mizar Abstracts

For encoding of the additional browsing information in GABs we have used a modified version of the text/enriched MIME Content-type [9, 5, 4], which we currently call text/mmlquery. This format is quite light-weight in comparison with formats like HTML or XML, and it is completely sufficient for our purpose. The generally implemented standard Emacs parser of the text/enriched format can be easily customized for the text/mmlquery format.

Following explanation of the text/mmlquery format is a paraphrase of the text/enriched syntax explanation from [9]:

> The syntax of "text/mmlquery" is very simple. All characters represent themselves, with the exception of the "<" character (ASCII 60), which is used to mark the beginning of an annotation. A literal less-than sign ("<") can be represented by a sequence of two such characters, "<<". Annotation instructions consist of annotating commands surrounded by angle brackets ("<>", ASCII 60 and 62). Each annotating command may be no more than 60 characters in length, all in US-ASCII, restricted to the alphanumeric and hyphen ("−") characters. Annotating commands may be preceded by a solidus ("/", ASCII 47), making them negations, and such negations must always exist to balance the initial opening commands.

The current version of the text/mmlquery format currently uses just the following annotation commands:

| | |
|---|---|
| $< p > ... < /p >$ | Is used to encode arbitrary parameters to other annotation commands. i.e. it corresponds to the $< param >$ command of the text/enriched format. |
| $< l > ... < /l >$ | Is used to mark the whole Mizar items in GABs, the name of the item is given as a parameter. |
| $< a > ... < /a >$ | Is used inside terms and formulas to provide the link from the symbols to the corresponding Mizar items (which are given as a parameter). |
| $< r > ... < /r >$ | Is used to mark the Mizar property formulas inside definitions (they are hidden by default). |
| $< h > ... < /h >$ | Is used to mark parts that we explicitly want to hide. This is now becoming obsolete, since all hiding of the Mizar items is now done depending on their kind. |

```
:: Article CARD_1, MML version 4.05.838
:: CARD_1:attrnot 1
definition
  let A1 be set;
  attr A1 is cardinal means
    ex B1 being ordinal set st
      (A1 = B1 & for B2 being ordinal set
          st B2,B1 are_equipotent
        holds B1 c= B2);
end;

:: CARD_1:dfs 1
definiens
  let A1 be set;
To prove
    A1 is cardinal
it is sufficient to prove
  thus ex B1 being ordinal set st
      (A1 = B1 & for B2 being ordinal set
            st B2,B1 are_equipotent
        holds B1 c= B2);;

:: CARD_1:def 1
theorem
for B1 being set holds
    B1 is cardinal
  iff
    ex B2 being ordinal set st
      (B1 = B2 & for B3 being ordinal set
            st B3,B2 are_equipotent
        holds B2 c= B3);

:: CARD_1:exreg 1
registration
  cluster cardinal set;
end;

:: CARD_1:modenot 1
definition
  mode Cardinal is cardinal set;
end;

:: CARD_1:condreg 1
registration
  cluster cardinal -> epsilon-transitive epsilon-connected ordinal (set);
end;

:: CARD_1:th 4
theorem
for B1 being set holds
  ex B2 being ordinal set st
    B1,B2 are_equipotent;

:: CARD_1:prednot 1
notation
  let A1 be cardinal set;
  let A2 be cardinal set;
  synonym A1 <=' A2 for A1 c= A2;
end;
```

**Fig. 2.** Initial part of the Generated Mizar Abstract for article CARD_1

E.g. the first existential registration in the file `card_1.gab` (see `CARD_1:exreg 1` in Fig. 1) encoded in text/mmlquery looks like this:

```
<l>:: <p>CARD_1:exreg.1</p>CARD_1:exreg 1
registration
 cluster <a><p>CARD_1:attr.1</p>cardinal</a> <a><p>HIDDEN:mode.1</p>set</a>;
end;
</l>
```

The blow-up factor caused by adding the annotations into the GABs is about 3 to 4. This is mainly caused by the long names of the Mizar items which disambiguate the Mizar symbols. We could compress the default naming scheme significantly, however as shown below in the subsection about Emacs parsing, the parsing speed is sufficient already now, and the overall size of all GABs is also reasonable – about 50 MB.

### 3.5    Using MML Query to Produce the Generated Mizar Abstracts

MML Query is a set of tools which collect information about all Mizar *items* (e.g. symbols, constructors, theorems, definitions, etc.) from the Mizar Mathematical Library, and store them in a format which is easy to index and query. The Mizar-dependent part of MML Query is based on the Mizar codebase written in object Pascal; the remaining parts are mostly written in Perl. The Perl modules implement functions like reconstruction of the human readable form of Mizar items from the internal representation, or parsing and execution of the queries written in the MML Query syntax [2]. They also implement a general plug-in mechanism for different presentations of the Mizar items and results of the queries.

For the work presented here, we have implemented a special plug-in which customizes these general presentation mechanisms to the text/mmlquery format. This is done very simply in as few as about 50 lines of Perl code. The complete creation of the Generated Mizar Abstracts from the MML Query database takes about 17 minutes on Intel Pentium 4 3GHz. MML Query is also used to generate the "raw" counterparts of the Generated Mizar Abstracts, which contain no markup and are thus suitable for processing with standard text tools like e.g. grep. The current usage of these files in our system is described in the next section.

### 3.6    Emacs Parsing, Presentation and Browsing of the Generated Mizar Abstracts

As already mentioned, the Emacs parser of the text/mmlquery format is just a customization of the unified Emacs mechanism for formatted files, which is also used for the text/enriched format. This customization is quite simple and takes only about 200 lines of the Emacs Lisp code. The parser uses the annotations from a given GAB and produces internal information necessary for presentation and browsing. This information is internally represented in two ways:

- The positions of Mizar items parsed from a given article are kept as symbol properties in the standard Emacs symbol hash-table.
- The links associated to the Mizar symbols and visibility information are kept as Emacs text properties.

Thanks to the simplicity of the text/mmlquery format, the parsing of GABs is sufficiently fast, even though Emacs Lisp is an interpreted language which is not primarily designed for speed. Complete parsing of an average GAB takes about 1–2 seconds on quite a standard computer (Intel 1.6 GHz), the largest Mizar abstract JGRAPH_4 (about 300 KB with annotations) takes about 7 seconds. These times can be further reduced to less than half by byte-compiling the Emacs Lisp code. For a comparison, note that displaying the HTML version of the GAB of JGRAPH_4 (also produced by MML Query) by the standard Emacs/W3 web browser takes about 40 seconds on the same computer, even though it is only about 100 KB bigger.

The Emacs presentation of the Generated Mizar Abstracts reuses many components which are available for normal Mizar abstracts and articles in the Emacs authoring environment for Mizar. This includes e.g. the syntax highlighting, interactive menu and speed-bar for items presented in the abstract, etc. Actually, a special submode (MML Query minor mode) of the standard Mizar mode is used for the presentation of GABs. This submode just adds or redefines the functionality, which is needed for proper presentation and browsing of GABs. This now includes the standard browsing functions like following links, and going backwards and forwards in the link history or presentation functionality like tool-tips or setting and customization of visibility of various items.

For fast grepping, we generate for each GAB its "raw" counterpart which contains no markup. The grep results are then presented in Emacs as if the grepping was done on the original GAB, the "raw" GABs are completely hidden from the user. This solves the usual problem with grepping annotated formats, without the necessity of using any specialized grepping tools or tools for stripping the markup (like perl), and is also faster then them, while the additional installation size (about 16 MB) is negligible. If perl is installed, the "raw" GABs also allow for regular expression searches spanning multiple lines in items, which is often useful in Mizar. Such features however already duplicate some of the functionality of the MML Query tools, therefore our further work in progress is a full integration of the MML Query tools into the Mizar mode as a backend for advanced queries.

### 3.7   Support for Authoring Mizar Articles

We believe that the described above features of our system make it evident, that having a GAB browser inside Emacs is a good choice, allowing reuse or customization of the vast number of available Emacs components, with very little effort and very reasonable resource requirements. This allows easy local installation and usage by an average Mizar user.

Another important feature of this system is, that it allows us to support interactive browsing even for the article which is being written by the author at the moment. This is very helpful when writing Mizar articles in advanced domains, where clashes of notation are quite often, and the author needs a good tool telling him how the formulas written by him are understood by the system.

Implementation of this feature uses parts of the Mizar system (parser and analyzer) to obtain the disambiguated (constructor) format of the formulas written by the author. Note that Mizar is not an interactive interpreter like some other proof assistants, its behavior is much more like a batch compiler. In this article we do not want to discuss the advantages and disadvantages of these different paradigms for proof assistants, nevertheless our implementation shows that even with the compiler-like approach, a fairly interactive disambiguation is not difficult to achieve (which again is also testified by the large number of Integrated Development Environments for compiled overloaded languages, with similar functionality).

We take advantage of the fact that different processing stages of the Mizar verifier use intermediate files for passing information to the next stages. The intermediate files usually contain also information about positions in the original article, so that proper error messaging was possible. Thus, for our purpose it suffices to collect the disambiguated (constructor) format from the appropriate intermediate file, and associate it with the corresponding position in the original article. This association is done using the Emacs mechanism of text properties immediately after processing, which means that even the editing actions that change positions will usually not influence the correspondence between the text in the article and its disambiguated counterpart.

In the Emacs authoring environment for Mizar this mechanism is called the *Constructor Explanations*, and when switched on by the user, a disambiguated form compatible with that used by GABs is available after Mizar processing for any formula in the article justified by simple justification. This is no serious limitation, and it will be probably completely removed after the XML-zation of the intermediate files, which is a planned feature of the Mizar system. This GAB-compatible disambiguated form of the formulas can then be used for immediate precise browsing of the symbols appearing in them, provided that the user has installed the Generated Mizar Abstracts.

## 4    Example

Finally we demonstrate our system on a simple real-life example. Consider the following simple Mizar article:

```
environ
 vocabulary ARYTM, NAT_1, XREAL_0;
 notation  SUBSET_1, NUMBERS, XCMPLX_0, XREAL_0, REAL_1, NAT_1;
 constructors REAL_1, XREAL_0, XCMPLX_0, XBOOLE_0, NAT_1;
 clusters REAL_1, NUMBERS,  XREAL_0,  ZFMISC_1, XBOOLE_0 , NAT_1;
 requirements REAL, NUMERALS, SUBSET, BOOLE, ARITHM;
begin

L1: for x being Nat holds x*x <= (x + x)*x;
```

Suppose that the user wants to know the exact meaning of the symbols in the formula L1. Simple grepping or tag-based browsing of the MML reveals that there are

- 164 definitions or redefinitions of the symbol $*$
- 99 definitions or redefinitions of the symbol $+$
- 16 definitions or redefinitions of the symbol $<=$

Instead of searching this number of possibilities, the user just switches on the menu item *Constr. Explanations ->Verbosity ->translated formula* in the Mizar mode for Emacs, and after running Mizar the following disambiguation of L1 can be obtained by clicking on the final semicolon:

```
for SUBSET_1:mode.2 ;ORDINAL1:attr.1 ; ORDINAL1:attr.2 ;ORDINAL1:attr.3
;ORDINAL2:attr.4 ;XCMPLX_0:attr.1 ; XREAL_0:attr.1 ;;NUMBERS:func.1 ;
NUMBERS:func.5 ;;XREAL_0:pred.1 NAT_1:func.2 B1 B1 ; NAT_1:func.2
NAT_1:func.1 B1 B1 ;B1 ;;
```

The underlined items are directly browsable, and e.g. clicking on the last item `NAT_1:func.1` starts browsing of the GAB of the article NAT_1, and goes to the appropriate definition:

```
:: NAT_1:funcnot 1
definition
  let A1 be Element of NAT;
  let A2 be Element of NAT;
  redefine func A1 + A2 -> Element of NAT;
  commutativity;
end;
```

The underlined items can be further explored, which loads and browses the appropriate GABs at appropriate places. Since this is a redefinition, even the symbol $+$ is linked to the constructor it redefines, i.e. `XCMPLX_0:func` 2. Clicking on the `commutativity` keyword displays the meaning of this property, which is following:

```
for A1, A2 being Element of NAT holds
A1 + A2 = A2 + A1;
```

## 5   Summary

We have presented an integrated environment for semantic browsing of the Mizar abstracts and articles being written in the Mizar mode for Emacs. This environment consists of the Generated Mizar Abstracts produced by the customization of the MML Query tools to the light-weight text/mmlquery format, Emacs presentation and browsing of these abstracts based on many reusable components of Emacs and its Mizar mode, and of functions for disambiguating the currently authored Mizar article, based on the information obtained from the Mizar verifier. This solves the problem of finding out the exact meaning of the overloaded mathematical notation used practically everywhere in Mizar, which is becoming more severe as more and more advanced mathematical articles combining different parts of mathematics are written. Our implementation reuses many components of other systems, and thus it is quite small and easy to maintain. Even though the MML is the world's largest collection of formalized mathematics, the resources required by our system are modest and it is accessible to any Mizar user as a simple and stand-alone local installation, without the necessity for installing any other specialized tools.

## 6    Future Work

As already mentioned, adding MML Query as a back-end for interactive queries is currently a work in progress. This means that answers to queries will be presented in the text/mmlquery format and immediately decoded by Emacs in the same way as the Generated Mizar Abstracts.

It would be nice to have features like presentation of whole Mizar articles (i.e. also with proofs, not just abstracts), however this is rather a general todo-item for MML Query, of which the Generated Mizar Abstracts are just a suitable presentation. Both MML Query and e.g. the *Constructor Explanations* mechanism in the Mizar mode for Emacs could be simplified and easily extended if the internal Mizar database and the intermediate processing files were using a simple XML format instead of the current fragile and illegible internal encoding. We believe that it is really high time for XML-ization of these parts of Mizar, even at the cost of temporary postponing of other works on the Mizar system.

## References

1. G. Bancerek, Cardinal numbers. Formalized Mathematics, 2(1): 377–382, 1990. http://mizar.uwb.edu.pl/JFM/Vol1/card_1.abs.html.
2. G. Bancerek, MML Query, description. http://megrez.mizar.org/mmlquery/description.html.
3. G. Bancerek and P. Rudnicki, Information retrieval in MML, In A. Asperti, B. Buchberger, J. Davenport (eds.), Proceedings of the Second International Conference on Mathematical Knowledge Management, MKM 2003, Bertinoro, LNCS 2594: 119–132.
4. N. Borenstein, "The text/enriched MIME Content-type", 09/23/1993. ftp://ftp.rfc-editor.org/in-notes/rfc1523.txt.
5. N. Borenstein, "The text/enriched MIME Content-type", 01/10/1994. ftp://ftp.rfc-editor.org/in-notes/rfc1563.txt.
6. The grammar of the Mizar library items, http://merak.pb.bialystok.pl/mmlquery/mmlquery.html#Library-item.
7. Journal of Formalized Mathematics, http://mizar.uwb.edu.pl/JFM/.

8. The Mizar Home Page, `http://mizar.org`.
9. P. Resnick, A. Walker, "The text/enriched MIME Content-type", January 1996, `ftp://ftp.rfc-editor.org/in-notes/rfc1896.txt`.
10. P. Rudnicki, An overview of the Mizar project, Proceedings of the 1992 Workshop on Types for Proofs and Programs, Chalmers University of Technology, Bastad.
11. P. Rudnicki and A. Trybulec, On Equivalents of Well-foundedness. An experiment in MIZAR, Journal of Automated Reasoning, 23, pp. 197–234, Kluwer Academic Publishers, 1999.
12. J. Urban, MizarMode: Emacs Authoring Environment for Mizar, available online at `http://kti.mff.cuni.cz/~urban/MizarModeDoc/html/`.
13. J. Urban, MoMM – Fast interreduction and retrieval in large libraries of formalized mathematics. Accepted to G. Sutcliffe, S. Schultz, and T. Tammit (eds.) – Proceedings of the IJCAR 2004 Workshop on Empirically Successful First Order Reasoning, ENTCS. Available online at `http://ktiml.mff.cuni.cz/~urban/MoMM/momm.ps`.
14. J. Urban, MPTP – Motivation, implementation, first experiments. Accepted to I. Dahn, D. Kapur, and L. Vigneron (eds.) – Journal of Automated Reasoning, First-Order Theorem Proving Special Issue. Kluwer Academic Publishers (supposed publication: end of 2004). Available online at `http://kti.ms.mff.cuni.cz/~urban/MPTP/mptp-jar.ps.gz`.

# Informalising Formal Mathematics: Searching the Mizar Library with Latent Semantics

Paul Cairns

UCL Interaction Centre, University College London
London WC1E 7DP, UK
p.cairns@ucl.ac.uk

**Abstract.** Finding required information in a library of mathematics can be problematic, just as in any other library. However, so far, there are no strong search methods based on the semantics of formal mathematics. This paper describes a new approach based on latent semantic indexing (LSI). Using this, the semantics of terms need not be explicitly defined but is indirectly inferred from a body of documents in which the terms occur. The Mizar library is used as it is a substantial resource of formal mathematics. The system described in the paper adapts Mizar articles to produce an appropriate body of documents that can be used by LSI. Preliminary tests suggest that this approach is able to provide a useful mechanism for the search and retrieval of formal mathematics.

## 1  Searching for Mathematics

Mathematical knowledge management, since its inception, has had two key themes: the organisation of mathematical knowledge; and the successful retrieval of mathematical knowledge. In this paper, we consider the retrieval task when the mathematical knowledge has already been organised and standardised, namely retrieving knowledge from the Mizar Mathematical Library (MML) [20].

Bancerek and Rudnicki [2] have already considered information retrieval in the MML. Their approach rightly criticised the poor quality of keyword and grep-based approaches. However, they do have a hypertext method of presentation that allows a person to browse the library and easily find definitions of terms by clicking on the appropriate terms in the presentation. Additionally, they developed a query language that allowed more sophisticated querying based on the structural and semantic properties of Mizar articles. This was recognised as only a first step towards full semantic search and as such may only be useful in this form to expert Mizar authors.

Other search techniques have used type isomorphisms [9], metadata [17] or a combination of metadata and reasoning [5]. With type isomorphisms or reasoning, the search engine is effectively doing some proving, albeit tailored to the particular task. As fully automated proving is still a significant research topic, this suggests that there is a limit to how far these approaches could extend. With metadata, there is of course the possibility to make a search engine very effective but then there is the overhead of who must prepare the metadata. Authors of

A. Asperti et al. (Eds.): MKM 2004, LNCS 3119, pp. 58–72, 2004.

webpages are already very poor at adding metadata and there is no suggestion that authors of mathematics are likely to be any better.

Latent semantic indexing avoids these issues entirely as the semantics of the documents to which it is applied are never explictly represented. Instead, the semantics of terms are implicitly inferred from contexts in which they occur even if, as in the case of mathematics, the contexts are sometimes the definitions of the terms.

Related to this is the notion that mathematics itself is not a formal language. Mathematics is in principle formalisable but, in practice, formalisation is hardly ever done (which is why the MML represents a valuable contribution to mathematics). I would argue that mathematics, like all human languages, functions at a level of discourse [21] rather than at a level of logic. Search that works at the level of mathematical discourse is more likely to fit better with the needs of working mathemticians.

This paper therefore treats formal mathematics as a representation of mathematical language in general. Mizar is particularly strong in providing a wide range of constructs for mathematical concepts [24] that allow its formal proofs to be more like the less formal proofs found in common mathematical texts. In this sense, the MML is actually a reliable representation of the more usual, informal mathematical language. A well-known, and indeed successful, technique in information retrieval is Latent Semantic Indexing (LSI) [6]. Rather than defining semantics through some explicit ontology, the semantics of terms are defined through their co-occurence in a large document set. This is discussed in detail in the next section but the main point is that the semantics of terms are latent in the substantial body of documents to which LSI is applied. The MML is able to provide exactly such a large set of documents from which semantics can be extracted.

After describing the details of applying LSI to the MML, I give some early results. Despite the counter-intuitive idea of ignoring the formal semantics inherent in formal mathematics, these results actually show some promising indications. The current implementation does not make full use of the MML for reasons discussed elsewhere [8] and so there are natural areas for further work and refinement of these results.

## 2   Latent Semantic Indexing

Latent semantic indexing is a method developed for doing information retrieval from natural language documents based on the general theory of latent semantic analysis (LSA) [15]. LSA has been used in a variety of text retrieval and analysis tasks including the various Text Retrieval Conferences (TREC) [23] competitions, selecting educational text and the automated assessment of essays [16].

The major task of any information retrieval system of this sort is to define the semantics of the documents and the terms in those documents. The semantics can then be used to reliably answer queries based on the documents. For example, a person seeking information using a query "wars in the Middle East" would probably be satisfied with a document about "conflicts in Iraq." This is because we recognise that "conflict" is a synonym for "war" and "Iraq" is in the "Middle East". Many text retrieval systems rely on some externally defined ontology that would make the semantic relationships between terms explicit. Thus, when given the example query the meaning of the query would be looked up and documents with a similar meaning would be returned.

With LSI, there is no such external ontology. Instead, the meaning of terms is held to be latent in the documents in which those terms appear. That is, a word gains its meaning from the many contexts in which it appears. Conversely, a document gains its meaning from the many words that occur within it. Clearly then for LSI to produce good semantics, it needs a substantial body of documents in which all the relevant terms occur in many and varied contexts. The advantage is that no work needs to be done to define an ontology for querying the documents.

For this reason, LSI seemed an appropriate tool to use and the MML the appropriate context in which to use it. Formal mathematics, in one sense, is an entire ontology of mathematical terms. However, as yet, it has not been extensively used to provide effective information retrieval. Through LSI though, the MML also represents an extensive set of documents that latently define the meanings of a huge number of mathematical terms. In addition, the ric language of Mizar reflects some of the richness of more traditional, human-oriented mathematics. LSI could tap into this to provide an alternative ontology without any extra work.

The other advantage of LSI is that its mechanism relies on some elegant mathematics that has been implemented in the GTP package [10]. GTP is written in Java. The mathematics is briefly described here to give a flavour of how it works. Followed by some details of the implementation specific to GTP.

## 2.1   The Mathematics of LSI

The occurrence of terms in documents can be simply captured in a rectangular matrix $\Delta$ where :

$$\Delta_{ij} = \begin{cases} 1 & \text{if the } i^{\text{th}} \text{ term appears in the } j^{\text{th}} \text{document} \\ 0 & \text{otherwise} \end{cases}$$

Keyword search can then be implemented by converting a query into row vector $t$ where $t_i$ is 1 if the $i^{\text{th}}$ term is in the query and 0 otherwise. Taking $d = t.\Delta$, $d$ is row vector where $d_j$ is the number of query terms occurring in the $j^{\text{th}}$ document. In particular, if $n$ is the number of non-zero entries in $t$ (that is, the number of distinct terms in the query) then $d_j = n$ means that the $j^{\text{th}}$ document contains all of the query terms.

Using singular value decomposition (SVD), it is possible to find two orthogonal matrices $U$ and $V$ and a diagonal matrix $\Sigma_D$ such that:

$$\Delta = U\Sigma_D V$$

From this equation, for a term vector $t$, keyword search would give:

$$d = t.U\Sigma_D V$$

$$d.V^{-1} = t.U\Sigma_D$$

However, we require more than keyword search. Instead, for a given query $t$, and any set of documents represented by $d$ we consider the similarity between the two vectors $t' = t.U\Sigma_D$ and $d' = d.V^{-1}$. The similarity, $s$, between vectors $t'$ and $d'$ is taken to be the cosine of the angle between them, that is:

$$s = \frac{t'.d'}{||t'||.||d'||}$$

One way to view this is that, under the transformations given, terms and documents occupy a common space based on the semantics of the terms. Now to perform a query, the term vector $t$ is generated as before. Each document is represented by the vector $d_i$ where $d_{ij} = 1$ if $i = j$ and 0 otherwise. The query is then compared to all the documents in the term/document space by finding the similarity between $t'$ and each of the vectors $d_i'$. The most similar documents are returned as the results of the query.

## 2.2    The GTP Package

Given a set of documents as either separate files or documents delimited within a single file, GTP automatically extracts terms from the documents and constructs $\Delta$. By default, a term in GTP is any alphanumeric string of characters. Also, because GTP was constructed with natural language in mind, it consults a file of common words, such as "the" and "of", and does not include a common word as a term. Mizar (like mathematics), however, has a radically different linguistic structure and punctuation from natural language. Instead, this section of GTP was replaced. Common words were simply Mizar keywords, though arguably they could be included as terms, together with ';' and ',' when used purely as separators. This means that terms could be any string of characters excluding whitespace and thus encompasses all of the constructs defined in Mizar articles.

Having defined the terms, the GTP package automatically constructs the appropriate $\Delta$ and performs the singular value decompostion. This is the main output of the first stage of GTP.

The querying process is run as a separate stage of GTP using the matrices generated from the first stage. As might be expected, the comparison process can be rather lengthy so there are some approximations that can be made to speed up matters. To facilitate discussion, in the sequel, the diagonal values of $\Sigma_D$ are referred to as the eigenvalues of $\Delta$.

The first approximation is to omit the scaling by the eigenvalues by taking $t' = t.U$. However, it produced uniformly poor results so this approximation was not used. Secondly, each eigenvalue corresponds to a factor that can be used to compare queries and documents. When the eigenvalues are very small, they can effectively be omitted from the calculation and hence speed it up. In GTP, setting the number of factors to 15 corresponds to calculating similarity based on the fifteen largest eigenvalues. The number of factors used in the test was varied as will be discussed in the results section.

In summary, to a large extent, LSI is treated here as a black box method for querying documents. The GTP implementation is untouched except to replace the code that identifies terms in the MML.

## 3     Applying LSI to Mizar

As most of the computational effort is done by GTP, the two main issues for applying LSI to Mizar are:

1. What constitutes a document?
2. How should queries be performed?

All coding was done in Java 1.4 and the Java version of the GTP package was used. Version 3.33.722 of the MML was used to generate the documents. More specifically, rather than use the full Mizar articles with proofs, only the abstracts were used in this implementation.

### 3.1     Making the MML into Documents

The decision as to what constitutes a document is crucial because this is how LSI will capture the semantics of Mizar terms. At one level, each Mizar article could be considered to be a document. However, these are substantial pieces of work with many references to a large number of terms. It was felt that with many terms in each article and a reasonable overlap between articles, using articles as documents would not distinguish sufficiently between the meanings of terms. Also, when retrieving a document, a user would probably like something more focused than a whole Mizar article. The natural choice seemed to be to divide each article into smaller parts. These parts should be both meaningful as a stand-alone entity (so not single lines of proofs) and the kind of thing that users would like to retrieve. Accordingly, a document was decided to be one of the following:

1. Theorem
2. Definition
3. Proof

As parsing Mizar articles can be problematic [8], the first stage seemed to be a proof of principle on using only theorems as documents and then only those that were in abstracts.

Simply using a theorem statement directly from a Mizar abstract was also not likely to provide an appropriate document. For example, in the following theorem [3]:

```
theorem :: ORDINAL2:1
  A c= B iff succ A c= succ B;
```

A and B would be identified as terms but without a doubt they are also used as terms in a huge number of other theorems with considerably different meanings. This would greatly confuse the semantics of the library. Also, users are not likely to find theorems about A and B interesting, but rather theorems, like this one, about successors of `Ordinals`.

In this case, A and B have already been defined as `Ordinals` in a reserve statement. A more meaningful document would be:

```
theorem :: ORDINAL2:1
  for A, B being Ordinals holds A c= B iff succ A c= succ B;
```

However, A and B still occur as terms in this document and could add noise to the LSI calculations. Instead, the document is made by replacing each occurrence of a variable by its type:

```
theorem :: ORDINAL2:1
  Ordinal c= Ordinal iff succ Ordinal c= succ Ordinal;
```

Thus Ordinals, successors and subsets all occur in the same context which LSI would use to say that the meaning of `Ordinals` is somehow defined by that of `succ` and `c=`. In addition, this document contains only terms and keywords and these latter are currently ignored.

Thus, each document is a theorem where all of the known variables have been replaced by their types. There is no further reduction of types to simpler types, for example, to say that `Ordinal` is an `epsilon-transitive epsilon-connected set`. This is because the aim is to look at the linguistic structure of the mathematics not the logical.

The process for producing the documents is given in Figure 1 and works as follows. The header of each Mizar abstract is used to generate the vocabulary used in each abstract. This means that the abstract can be reliably parsed into chunks that are either theorems, reserve statements or definitions. The reserve statements are parsed to produce of a list of variables that have a known type. The definitions are also parsed to check exactly which definition of various terms are actually in use at a given point in an article. As a by-product of parsing definitions, a catalogue is produced that states exactly where each item of vocabulary is defined together with any other useful information such as the number of pre- and post-arguments, where applicable.

The catalogue and known variables provide a context for a particular theorem. The theorem can be parsed using the context and transformed into the corresponding document as required.

The process progresses through the chunks, successively updating the context as it goes. So for instance, if a reserve statement redefines a variable as having a new type, this is carried through to the subsequent theorems and hence documents.

On the whole, the process works well. There are still some abstracts that cannot be parsed into chunks because of the use of ';' in the terms. However, this is largely due to the limitation of the current parsing technology being used,

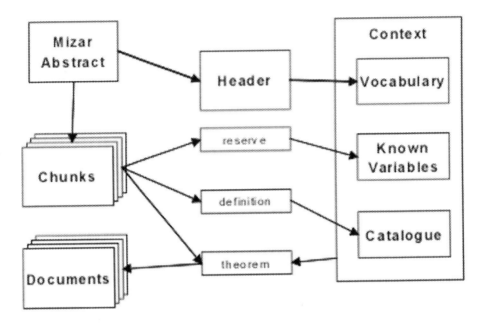

**Fig. 1.** Generating documents from theorems in an abstract

namely JavaCC [12]. It is hoped to replace this with a more versatile parser in the near future. The final document set is made up of 31251 documents that contain 3181 terms. GTP transforms this data and captures it in 106 factors, that is, 106 eigenvectors with non-zero eigenvalues, though it is not documented to what degree of accuracy GTP distinguishes a nearly zero eigenvalue from actually zero.

### 3.2     Performing Queries

If queries are to be useful to a user of the MML, the query engine most likely needs to be integrated into some larger system, such as the emacs mode for Mizar. However, at this stage, it is not clear what would constitute a useful query. This can be seen by considering the process that is done to convert a theorem in Mizar into a document for LSI. To what extent should the user do that conversion process to formulate a query? Or conversely, how much of formulating a query can be generated from a user's context of querying?

These are difficult questions in any system where complex work such as writing Mizar articles is being performed [18]. This is compounded by the fact that the full capabilities of LSI-based search are unknown.

Rather than commit at this early stage to a visual interface that may be both inappropriate and lengthy to develop, the system implemented uses a command-line approach to querying and all of the preparation of queries is done by hand.

Thus, a query is hand-written or adapted from a document based on a theorem. For example, a typical query might look like:

```
theorem set c= set implies Cl ( set /\ set ) c= Cl ( set /\ set )
```

The results from the basic GTP are the indexes of documents in the whole collection together with the strength of similarity between the document and the query. For example, GTP might produce results like:

```
4134      0.99987674
8609      0.99812323
8610      0.99809912
25838     0.99731101
```

The first number of each line corresponds to the index of a document. The second number is the strength of match with the query. The resulting documents are looked up in an index prepared at the same time as the documents were produced from the theorems. Thus, the basic results can be expanded to:

```
::theorem set c= set implies Cl ( set /\ set ) c= Cl ( set /\ set )
4134      :: CLASSES1:68   classes1        322     0.99
8609      :: FUNCT_4:6     funct_4 40      0.99
8610      :: FUNCT_4:7     funct_4 43      0.99
25838     :: TOLER_1:57    toler_1 261     0.99
```

The first line is the original query expression. Each subsequent line is a matched document in order of best match. For example, the second line tells us that document 4134 matched best and it corresponds to the theorem with the Mizar label CLASSES1:6 and it appears in the file classes1.abs [4] at line 322. The remaining three lines correspond to theorems in the articles funct_4.abs [7] and toler_1.abs [11].

These results are then turned into fragments of the corresponding abstracts to save time and effort of looking up each query result individually. So for instance, the result just described would also return the fragment:

```
4134      :: CLASSES1:68   classes1        322     0.99
theorem :: CLASSES1:68
 the_transitive-closure_of (X /\ Y) c=
   the_transitive-closure_of X /\ the_transitive-closure_of Y;
```

The results after being looked up in the index and their corresponding fragments are written to separate files.

## 4  Some Early Results

At the time of writing, a fully working system has only just been completed. This means that extensive testing has not been done. Also, as only theorems have been used, the full power of the MML has not been exploited so extensive testing would be premature. Instead, these results can be regarded as a demonstration of potential rather than a realisation of it.

The tests so far fall into three categories:

1. Can we retrieve the original theorems?
2. Can we retrieve theorems based on part of the original theorem?
3. Can we retrieve required theorems given a part of proof that needs a theorem?

The first category is there as a sanity check that when throwing documents into the the soup of LSI, they are not lost forever. The second two are moving towards more realistic queries that a user might perform. First, if you are trying to remember a theorem in full but can only remember part, can you retrieve the whole theorem? Secondly, whilst working on a proof, a user might like to find a theorem that would prove the proof step that they are currently working on. Each of these categories of tests is discussed in turn.

## 4.1    The Identity Query

It is to be hoped that any query with an actual document used in the LSI would return that document as the best matching document. However, as mentioned earlier, queries can be performed with approximations based on the number of factors used in the similarity calculation. The unapproximated SVD of the MML has 106 factors.

All of the theorems in several abstracts were used in these tests. The documents that correspond to the theorems in these abstracts were used as queries but the query was only performed using 15 factors. Nevertheless, in almost every case, the first result returned was always the original theorem. The only exceptions to this were in the situation where two theorems were virtually indistinguishable from each other.

For example, the theorems `TOPGRP_1:5` and `TOPGRP_1:6` from [14], when used as queries both returned the same two theorems *in that order*. These theorems are in fact:

```
theorem :: TOPGRP_1:5
 P c= Q implies P * h c= Q * h;
```

```
theorem :: TOPGRP_1:6
 P c= Q implies h * P c= h * Q;
```

As can be seen, they distinguish only in the order of the symbols that occur in them and as LSI does not take account of the order of terms in queries or documents, it is not surprising that these produced the same results. Also, from a user's perspective, it would not be surprising or even undesirable to have these two documents returned together.

A more surprising result from these tests came from the query based on the following theorem from [13]:

```
theorem :: TOPS_3:10
 A is boundary implies A <> the carrier of X;
```

As expected, the query returned precisely this theorem as the best match. Interestingly though the second best match was the following:

```
theorem :: TOPS_3:23
 A is nowhere_dense implies A <> the carrier of X;
```

These are clearly quite distinct theorems from general topology but the concepts of boundary and nowhere dense are very closely related. Specifically, by TOPS_1:92 [19], every nowhere dense set is boundary and hence TOPS_3:10 implies TOPS_3:23. LSI has no explicit knowledge of these theorems. The concepts of boundary and nowhere dense are simply related through frequent occurrence in related contexts. However, this vindicates the approach taken in this use of LSI in that it is the linguistic use of the concept and not the logical that in some ways defines the semantics of the concept.

## 4.2    Retrieving Full Theorems from Partial Theorems

A single theorem can often have multiple quantifiers and, usually, it is crucial to know whether a theorem is an implication, equivalence or contains negations. However, these details may not always be remembered by a human, indeed, they may be the precise reason why a person would look up a theorem.

These few tests were set up to see if, by constructing a query with a target theorem in mind, it is possible to retrieve the target. The queries were constructed using the document version of the theorem.

These preliminary results were somewhat mixed. Leaving out initial quantifiers does manage to retrieve the whole theorem. This works because in removing the variable names to convert a speculated theorem into a query, the types of the variables are replaced into the theorem. Where these types are known correctly, LSI would not distinguish between them being placed in a quantifier clause at the start of the theorem or in place of the variables as in these queries. Thus, these queries should and do work as expected.

Also, the system is reasonably successful at retrieving theorems where the logical direction of the theorem is unknown. This makes sense because in Mizar, this is usually signified with a keyword and keywords like iff and so on play no role in the search and retrieval methods as implemented here.

However, the main problem with these tests does seem to be getting the types of variables right. If the type of a variable is only partially entered, say entering only TopStruct instead of carrier of TopStruct, then the target theorem is not retrieved, at least not in the top 30 results.

Two further tests looked to retrieve a theorem when the relationship between variables in the theorem were unknown. In the first case what should have been an inequality relationship in TOPS_3:10 was guessed at by entering some likely candidates such as equality and subset as well as inequality. Everything else was as in the document version of the target theorem. In the second case, the inequality was omitted entirely. In both cases, the target theorem was retrieved as the best match.

### 4.3     Retrieving Theorems to Complete Proof Steps

In writing a Mizar article, proofs need to give full references to theorems that are required to prove proof steps. In practice, this requires an extensive knowledge of what is (and is not) in the MML and more importantly where it is. A natural task for an author would be to find a theorem that applies to their current proof goals.

The following tests looked at proof steps that required a single theorem to complete the proof. The first few were all taken from the proof of TOPS_3:3 in tops_3.miz. Topology was particularly chosen as I have some expertise in this area and hence the domaing knowledge needed to formulate queries.

The first test was trying to retrieve TOPS_1:44 [19], for the following proof step:

```
Int A c= A   by TOPS_1:44
```

Accordingly, the following query was generated:

```
theorem Int Subset of carrier of TopStruct
    c= Subset of carrier of TopStruct
```

The target theorem was indeed retrieved first by this query.
The second test was based on:

```
(Int A) /\ B c= A /\ B by XBOOLE_1:26
```

with the corresponding query:

```
theorem  set c= set implies set /\ set c= set /\ set
```

This retrieved XBOOLE_1:26 as the second result.

Subsequent queries all based on steps in the same proof, however, did not show such promise. In each case, the query formulated did retrieve theorems that were certainly in the right topic but none directly pertinent to the target proof step. These steps all involved the notions of interior and closure of subspaces in topology and its was notable that a lot of the retrieved theorems tended to include one but not both of these concepts. Perhaps these notions were poorly captured by LSI.

Two further queries (avoiding interiors and closures) were attempted, based on line 210 of tops_3.miz:

```
G c= A by TOPS_1:20
```

In this context, it was possible to formulate two queries that might have served well:

```
theorem for Subset of TopSpace holds
 ( - Subset of TopSpace ) misses Subset of TopSpace
 implies Subset of TopSapce c= Subset of TopSpace
```

```
theorem for Subset of carrier of TopStruct holds
  ( - Subset of carrier of TopStruct ) misses
    Subset of carrier of TopStruct
  implies Subset of carrier of TopStruct c=
    Subset of carrier of TopStruct
```

The target theorem was:

```
theorem :: TOPS_1:20
 K c= Q iff K misses -Q;
```

Whilst neither query retrieved this theorem, the second query did actually find the following in the top ten results:

```
theorem :: PRE_TOPC:21
  for T being 1-sorted
  for P,Q being Subset of the carrier of T holds
    P c= -Q iff P misses Q;
```

Though obviously distinct from the expected theorem, in fact, with a little work the original proof could easily be re-written to use this theorem rather than expected one. This then represents a significant success from a task-oriented perspective.

### 4.4    Summary of Results

The few tests reported here do indeed show promise though obviously the reliability of these queries is currently limited. The results are summarised in Table 1. All of the tests however did return results that could definitely be described as in the right topic for the queries. Also, as hoped for, LSI through working via the language of mathematics is also highlighting logical and conceptual links between the documents. Improving the reliability of these queries, though, is a clear priority and the current lines of development are discussed in the next section.

## 5    Conclusion and Future Work

The work done here in applying LSI to a formal mathematics library has shown the following:

– LSI can perform useful retrieval without explicit semantics
– LSI can find conceptual associations between mathematical notions
– Users can formulate query expressions for which LSI returns useful results

However, there is clearly an issue with the reliability of the queries and future work will address this.

Definitions and proofs were not included as documents in the LSI calculations. Incorporating them would increase the number of documents and could therefore

**Table 1.** Summary of Test Results

| Task | Target type | Query | Outcome |
|------|-------------|-------|---------|
| Identity | Any theorem | The target itself | Retrieves target or theorem with identical terms |
| | `TOPS_3:10` | `TOPS_3:10` | `TOPS_3:23` retrieved second because of close conceptual relationship |
| Partial | Any theorem | Target without quantifiers | Successful retrieval |
| | Any theorem | Target without correct variable types | Target not in top 30 |
| | Theorem with binary relation | Target with multiple terms to cover target relation | Successful retrieval |
| | Theorem with binary relation | Target with target relation omitted | Successful retrieval |
| Proof goals | Theorem to prove step | Guess at target theorem | Limited success |
| | `TOPS_1:20` | Guess at target theorem | Retrieved `PRE_TOPC:21` which could be applied |

better elucidate the terms in the MML. Actually, I strongly believe that proofs are the discourses of mathematics – theorems merely represent the headlines. Thus, including proofs as documents would provide a strong language-oriented foundation for the MML that I would expect LSI to exploit well.

Making proofs into documents poses two substantial obstacles. The first and easiest is that so far the Mizar language has been difficult to parse with JavaCC. Theorems and definitions use a relatively constrained subset of the full Mizar grammar and so in this implementation have been parsed using a combination of JavaCC and bespoke finite state machines. A further implementation should really use a more generic and hence robust approach to parsing though it is not clear that this would actually overcome some of the difficulties encountered so far.

The more substantial problem of including proofs as documents is the issue of how to represent a proof as a document. With theorems, this is relatively straightforward as a theorem could be viewed as a stand-alone logical statement. Proofs however represent a transformation between logical statements. Already, in trying to complete proof steps in the tests described above, I encountered issues of what exactly would constitute a sensible query in the context. Simple subsitution of variable names by the variable types, as used to turn theorems into documents, was not enough. Some patterns of how to formulate effective queries emerged and it may be possible to automate some of the query formulation task. In many ways, though, the formulation of queries can only be tackled on an empirical basis of what works well.

A wider issue that addresses the broader aim of this work is to make generating queries and understanding results easier to work with for a Mizar author.

Some form of visual interface would seem appropriate but deciding what to represent and how to represent it probably represents a significant design and evaluation effort. Related to this is whether users would want to see all the documents that were retrieved or whether in different contexts they could rely on, say, just retrieving proofs or just theorems.

In addition could further search methods or heuristics improve the reliability and therefore value of the LSI-based results? For instance, would these results be enhanced by using the filtering operations of Bancerek and Rudnicki [2]? Could the logical keywords like `iff` be used to filter suitable theorems?

In conclusion, this work shows that using search based on the implicit semantics of a formal mathematical library does in fact yield some meaningful results. With further work and empirical evaluation, it is hoped that this is a step towards a full semantic search of mathematical libraries that real mathematicians would find useful in their work.

## Acknowledgments

Thanks to Dr. Jeremy Gow for his encouragement and his comments on this paper, to Dr. Andrzej Trybulec for a useful correction to an earlier version of this paper and the anonymous referees for some very useful feedback.

# References

1. A. Asperti, B. Buchberger, and J.H. Davenport, Mathematical Knowledge Management, Proceedings of MKM 2003, LNCS **2594**, Springer Verlag, 2003.
2. G. Bancerek and P. Rudnicki, Information Retrieval in MML, in: [1], 2003, pp. 119–132.
3. G. Bancerek, Sequences of ordinal numbers, Formalized Mathematics, **1**(2), 1990, pp. 281–290.
4. G. Bancerek, Tarski's classes and ranks, Formalized Mathematics, **1**(3), 1990, pp. 563–567.
5. P. Baumgartner and U. Furbach, Automated Deduction Techniques for the Management of Personalized Documents, Annals of Mathematics and Art. Intelligence, **38**, 2003, pp. 211–288.
6. M.W. Berry and S. Dumais, Latent Semantic Indexing Web Site, accessed 29th March, 2004, http://www.cs.utk.edu/~lsi.
7. C. Byliński, The modification of a function by a function and the iterations of the composition of a function, Formalized Mathematics, **1**(3), 1990, pp. 521–527.
8. P. Cairns and J. Gow, Using and parsing the Mizar language, Electronic Notes in Theoretical Computer Science **93**, Elsevier, 2004, pp. 60–69.
9. D. Delahaye, Information retrieval in Coq Proof Library using type isomorphisms, in: T. Coquand et al. (eds.), TYPES, LNCS **1956**, 2000, pp. 131–147.
10. J.T. Giles, L. Wo, and M.W. Berry, GTP (General Text Parser) software for text mining, in: H. Bozdogan (ed.), Statistical Data Mining and Knowledge Discovery, CRC Press, Boca Raton, 2001, pp. 457–473.
11. K. Hryniewiecki, Relations of tolerance, Formalized Mathematics **2**(1), 1991, pp. 105–109.

12. Java Compiler Compiler, accessed 31st March, 2004, http://javacc.dev.java.net.
13. Z. Karno, Remarks on special subsets of topological spaces, Formalized Mathematics, **3**(2), 1992, pp. 297–303.
14. A. Korniłowicz, The definition and basic properties of topological groups, Formalized Mathematics, **7**(2), 1998, pp. 217–225.
15. T.K. Landauer, P.W. Foltz, D. Laham, Introduction to latent semantic analysis, Discourse Processes, **25**, 1998, pp. 259–284.
16. T.K. Landauer, LSA@Colorado University, accessed 31st March, 2004, http://lsa.colorado.edu.
17. B.R. Miller and A. Youssef, Technical aspects of the Digital Library of Mathematical Functions, Annals of Mathematics and Art. Intelligence **38**, 2003, pp. 121–136.
18. B. Mirel, Interaction Design for Complex Problem Solving, Morgan Kaufmann, 2004.
19. M. Wysocki and A. Darmochwał, Subsets of Topological Spaces, Formalized Mathematics, **1**(1), 1990, pp. 231–237.
20. The Mizar Mathematical Library, `http://mizar.org`.
21. L. Philips and M.W. Jørgensen, Discourse Analysis as Theory and Method, Sage Publications, 2002.
22. P. Rudnicki, An overview of the Mizar project, in: Proceedings of 1992 Workshop on Types and Proofs for Programs, 1992.
23. Text REtrieval Conference (TREC), accessed 31st March, 2004, http://trec.nist.gov.
24. F. Wiedijk, Comparing Mathematical Provers, in: [1], pp. 188–202.

# Mathematical Service Matching Using Description Logic and OWL[*]

Olga Caprotti[1], Mike Dewar[2], and Daniele Turi[3]

[1] RISC-Linz, Johannes Kepler University
A-4020 Linz, Austria
ocaprott@risc.uni-linz.ac.at
[2] NAG Ltd., Wilkinson House, Jordan Hill Rd
Oxford OX2 8DR, United Kingdom
mike.dewar@nag.co.uk
[3] Information Management Group, Dept of Computer Science
University of Manchester, Oxford Road, Manchester M13 9PL, United Kingdom
dturi@cs.man.ac.uk

**Abstract.** Web Service technology is increasingly being used to develop distributed applications, however the convention is to describe individual services in terms of the interfaces that they expose, rather in terms of the function that they perform. In this paper we describe a mechanism for encoding information about mathematical web services which is rich enough to allow a potential client to identify automatically all those services which may be capable of performing a particular task. This mechanism makes use of the Web Ontology Language (OWL) and a novel approach to Description Logic reasoning exploiting enterprise database technologies.

## 1  Introduction

Over the last few years we have seen a growth of interest in the delivery of mathematical algorithms via web or grid services. Major mathematical software packages such as Maple (via Maplets and MapleTA) and Mathematica (via web-Mathematica) now offer mechanisms for remote access and use and most recently the market leader, Matlab 7, has provided a mechanism which allows it to act as a client to any web service which is implemented according to the Worldwide Web Consortium's standards. Despite this, however, the vast majority of mathematical software packages in use today are still installed and used locally on the end-user's machine.

It is easy to envision the impact that web service technologies could have on the user community: on-demand computation could be delivered by the most competitive software directly to the laptop of a field engineer, and the results

---

[*] This work was funded by the European Union under the aegis of the MONET Project (IST-2001-34145). The authors gratefully acknowledge the work of the other partners in the project: Stilo International PLC, the Universities of Bath, Eindhoven, Nice and Western Ontario, and CNRS.

A. Asperti et al. (Eds.): MKM 2004, LNCS 3119, pp. 73–87, 2004.

could be checked by requesting that the same computation be performed by multiple service providers. Complex computations could be assembled by choreographing multiple services, for instance pipelining a computation with a visualisation of the results or verifying input data validity by online reasoners prior to the computation. Such an infrastructure is, by its very nature, decentralised and ever changing, and for it to be effective requires the use of software agents to mediate between its different elements. In the MONET project we have developed such an agent, called a *broker*, that, given a client's description of the problem which it wishes to solve, will identify those services capable of solving it. This matching process involves the storage and manipulation of a wide range of mathematical knowledge: formalisations of mathematical problems, the algorithms which can be used to solve them, the properties of particular implementations etc. In this paper we focus on the knowledge infrastructure that the broker uses to describe deployed services and clients' problems, and to match one to the other. A more general description of the MONET framework can be found in [10].

The Web Service Description Language (WSDL) is a way of describing the basic interface which a web service exposes, but it cannot be used to describe what the service actually does. When dealing with services that solve mathematical problems the subject area lends itself naturally to a precise, formalised, and unambiguous description of the abstract functionality of the service. Based on this idea, a mathematical service description language has been developed by the MONET project [18] which builds upon standards such as WSDL, RDFS, OpenMath and OWL [11, 7, 14, 21].

A key role in these descriptions is played by the MONET ontologies, which not only provide the vocabulary for describing services, but formalise the relationships between different terms in the vocabulary in a way which can be used by the service matcher. The ontologies are encoded using the Web Ontology Language (OWL) [7], the formalism chosen by the World Wide Web Consortium for the semantic web. The importance of OWL for the semantic web is motivated by its formal semantics being in Description Logics [1] (DLs), a family of knowledge representation formalisms evolved from early *frame systems* [17] and *semantic networks* [19]. DLs use an object-oriented modelling paradigm, describing the world in terms of individuals, concepts (classes) and roles (relationships); they are distinguished from their ancestors by having a precise *semantics* which enables the description and justification of automated deduction processes. In fact, they are *decidable* fragments of First Order Logic (FOL), and, as such, they inherit its classic semantics.

Computationally, the interest in DLs is that highly optimised reasoners have been developed for them. This means that we can reason over OWL ontologies in an *effective* and decidable way, and with classic FOL semantics. In particular, our mathematical service descriptions and queries can be automatically transformed into OWL descriptions using terms from the MONET ontologies. Semantically, service registration amounts to stating that a service is an instance of a given OWL description, and service matching amounts to reasoning about the asserted descriptions using the MONET ontologies to find all the instances of the user's query when expressed in OWL. This approach differs considerably from that of the related work done in the MathBroker project [2] in which registration and discovery is based upon ebXML [20].

In this particular scenario, there is no direct relation between instances. This means that reasoning over instances can be reduced to reasoning over their descriptions. From an architectural point of view, the ontology of classes can be treated as a *static* knowledge framework, while the instances are entities which need to be *dynamically* added, removed, and retrieved, and which therefore pose considerable management problems.

To tackle this problem we have developed a Java component, called *instance Store (iS)* [23], where the ontology of classes is loaded from a file into a DIG [4] compliant DL reasoner such as RACER [12], while all the assertions over the instances are added to and retrieved from a *database*. This way, in our service registration and matching we can exploit robust enterprise database technology offering *persistency*, *scalability*, and *secure* and *concurrent* transaction management[1]. All this, while ensuring both the soundness and completeness of the resulting reasoning.

This paper is structured as follows. Section 2 very briefly recalls the basic ideas of the Mathematical Service Description Language (MSDL) while the MONET ontologies are reviewed in Section 3. The matching of service descriptions with the MONET ontology performed by *iS* and the translation of MSDL to OWL are the topics of Sections 4. The final section lists a few examples of OWL queries.

## 2   Mathematical Service Descriptions

In the web service architecture, providers of services are required to advertise their availability by publishing descriptions of the functionality, availability, cost, security and accessibility of the services they maintain. In the case of mathematical web services, these descriptions are made more informative for the potential users if knowledge about certain specific aspects, which are only pertinent to mathematics, is given. The Mathematical Service Description Language (MSDL) has been designed and tailored to suit not only mathematical web services, but also mathematical queries and explanations. This section briefly recalls the basic format of a mathematical web service description, more details can be found in [18].

A mathematical service description, represented by a document in XML which conforms to the MONET schema, uses the MONET ontologies described in the following section to characterise, among others, the following aspects:

- abstract functionality by reference to a library of mathematical problems in terms of input/output and precondition/postcondition specifications,

---

[1] Indeed, in the MONET project the *iS* is deployed using the JBoss EJB container.

– algorithmic behaviour by reference to a library of algorithms, described by
  problem solved, taxonomic and bibliographical data,
– implementation details such as programming language, hardware platform,
  and algorithm features such as accuracy, memory-usage etc.
– protocol, operations and data formats by WSDL [11].

A mathematical service description for a service called nagopt is given, in
simplified form, in Figure 1 and shows the basic syntax of the XML formalism used in MONET. Classification of the services identifies it as a service

```
<service name="nagopt">
  <classification>
    <gams_class>GamsG1a1a</gams_class>
    <problem>constrained_minimisation</problem>
    <input_format>OpenMath</input_format>
    <output_format>OpenMath</output_format>
    <directive>find</directive>
  </classification>
  <implementation>
    <software>NAG_C_Library_7</software>
    <platform>PentiumSystem</platform>
    <algorithm>Safeguarded_Quadratic-Interpolation</algorithm>
  </implementation>
</service>
```

**Fig. 1.** (Simplified) MSDL description of service nagopt

that fits the GAMS taxonomy G1a1a [8] (a variant of unconstrained optimisation), uses OpenMath as its I/O format, and solves a problem to *find* a value.
In this case the description also gives additional details such as that the service is implemented using NAG's implementation of the safeguarded quadratic-
interpolation algorithm. The content of the problem and the algorithm elements is, in reality, a full URI reference that points to a library of problems and algorithm descriptions. Here for example constrained_minimisation
is a problem of the form "minimise $f(x)$ for $x$ in $[a, b]$", described at http:
//monet.nag.co.uk/problems/constrained_minimisation.

The following descriptions for the three services nagquad, nagroot, and
nagopt-variation are very similar to the one given above so we have omitted the common text replacing it by . . . .

```
<service name="nagquad">
 <classification>
  <gams_class>GamsH2a1a1</gams_class>
  <problem>definite_integration</problem>
  ...
 </classification>
 <implementation>
  ...
  <algorithm>de_Doncker</algorithm>
 </implementation>
</service>
```

```
<service name="nagroot">
 <classification>
  <gams_class>GamsF2</gams_class>
  <problem>zero_of_nonlinear_system</problem>
  ...
 </classification>
 <implementation>
  ...
  <algorithm>Powell</algorithm>
 </implementation>
</service>
```

```
<service name="nagopt-variation">
 <classification>
  <gams_class>GamsG1a</gams_class>
  <problem>constrained_minimisation</problem>
  <input_format>algstr1.cdg</input_format>
  ...
 </classification>
 <implementation>
  ...
  <platform>SR8000</platform>
  <algorithm>Quadratic_Programming</algorithm>
 </implementation>
</service>
```

We will return to these examples later in this paper when we discuss how a client formulates a query.

## 3   The MONET Ontologies

The MONET ontologies provide a vocabulary for describing queries and services, and a context for the service matcher in which the relationships between different terms in this vocabulary are made explicit. Where possible we have re-used existing vocabularies and simply re-cast them in OWL [7], the *Web Ontology Language* from the Worldwide Web Consortium. We chose OWL because it appears to be a future standard, and it is built on existing technology such as RDFS [14] and DAML+OIL [13].

The MONET ontologies are constructed in a modular way, with each "sub-ontology" referencing the external concepts it needs using the OWL `imports` statement. The current suite of ontologies is organised as follows:

**GAMS.** The Guide to Available Mathematical Software (GAMS) [8] is a service offered by the National Institute for Science and Technology which provides an online index of available mathematical software classified according to the type of problems it solves. It is heavily biased towards numerical software (commercial packages from NAG, IMSL etc. and public-domain software such as LAPACK, LINPACK and the BLAS). Unfortunately, it is extremely poor at classifying other kinds of mathematical software package (symbolic, statistical, ...) because it classifies the package as a whole rather than individual modules within the package. Nevertheless as it is the only taxonomy of this type we decided to use it as a mechanism for classifying services within the MONET framework.

   The GAMS ontology is a simple class hierarchy; each GAMS class corresponds to an OWL Class, and specialisation of a problem class is represented by a sub-class relationship. For example one-dimensional quadrature is a subclass of quadrature, and one-dimensional quadrature over a finite interval is a subclass of one-dimensional quadrature etc.

**Symbolic.** To address GAMS' shortcomings in the area of symbolic computation, the GAMS taxonomy has been extended with a small taxonomy which is a sub-class of the GAMS "O" category, *symbolic computation systems.*

**OpenMath.** OpenMath [21] is a format for the representation of mathematical expressions and objects. Constants of this language have semantics attached to them and are called symbols (for example *sin, integral, matrix, ...*). Groups of related symbols are defined in *content dictionaries.*

   The OpenMath Ontology has one root class, `OpenMathSymbol`, whose subclasses correspond to the symbols defined in a particular content dictionary. The symbols themselves are defined as further subclasses of these. We use this ontology to infer a problem type as described below.

**Hardware.** The hardware ontology is designed to describe either classes of machines or individual machines. The idea is that a user might request that a service run on a particular model of machine (e.g. a Sun Enterprise 10000), or a general class of machine (e.g. shared memory), or a machine with a certain number of processors, or .... This will be used within the *Implementation* part of an MSDL service description.

**Software.** The software ontology is designed to describe pieces of software. It is intended to be used in the implementation part of the service description and allows a user to express a preference for a service built using a particular piece of software in his or her query.

**Problems.** MONET allows for a problem to be described in terms of its inputs and outputs, pre-conditions and post-conditions, using a specially written XML Schema [9].

Within this ontology, each problem is represented as a class, which can have properties indicating bibliography entries and generalisations or specialisations of it. The most interesting property is openmath_head whose range is an object from the OpenMathSymbol class. This represents a particular symbol which can be used to construct an instance of the problem in question. So for example if a user sends the broker an integral of the form

$$\int_a^b f(x)\,dx$$

encoded in OpenMath, then the service matcher may infer that the problem which the user wants to solve corresponds to a sub-class of Problem whose openmath_head property has the value calculus1_defint.

As well as being sub-classes of Problem, particular problems may also belong to GAMS classes.

**Algorithms.** The algorithms ontology is designed to represent elements of the algorithm library in the MONET architecture. There are two subclasses in this ontology: Algorithm, which describes well-known algorithms for mathematical computations, and Complexity, which provides classes necessary for representing complexity information.

**Directives.** The directives ontology is a collection of classes which identify the task that is performed by the service as described in [9, 18], for example *decide, solve* or *prove*. In some cases the directive needs to be associated with a logical theory (e.g. *prove in theory T*) via the inTheory property.

**Theory.** The theory ontology collects classes that represents available formalised theories in digital libraries of mathematics. In the current version we use the OMDoc theories [16] in the logics and tps collections.

**Bibliography.** The bibliography ontology represents entries in well-known indexes such as Zentralblatt MATH [24] and MathSciNet [15], and allows them to be associated with particular algorithms. This allows a client to request a service which implements the algorithm described in a particular paper.

**Encodings.** The encodings ontology is a simple collection of classes which represent the formats used for encoding mathematical objects in the MONET framework – for example the formats read and written by the services or used to encode explanations.

Thus it is possible for a user to stipulate that they would like to use a service which takes OpenMath as input but returns MathML.

**MONET.** The MONET ontology imports all the ontologies described above and is used to represent complete service descriptions and queries. Not surprisingly the structure reflects that of MSDL described in Section 2 with an instance of the `Service` class having an associated `Classification` and `Implementation` class. These in turn may have properties linking them to concepts in the ontologies described above.

The design of the ontologies has been influenced by the requirements of the *instance Store* software used for reasoning and described below. The major restriction which it imposes on the ontology is that it can contain no individuals. As a consequence, many concepts which would most naturally be represented as an instance of a class (for example a particular OpenMath symbol) must be represented as a sub-class. This does not really limit the expressiveness of the ontology, but does mean that some statements are more verbose than they might otherwise be. In addition many (if not most) mathematical concepts form natural hierarchies (e.g. one concept is a special case of another), so this sub-classing approach is often required in practice.

When choosing names for concepts in our ontology we have tried to use existing URI conventions if they exist (for example the OpenMath symbol *sin* has URI `http://www.openmath.org/cd/transc1\#sin`), otherwise for existing concepts we have chosen appropriate namespaces (GAMS classes have names like `http://gams.nist.gov\#H2`) while everything we have created ourselves lives in the MONET namespace.

## 4   Service Registration and Matching

In the MONET broker services are registered by asserting them as instances of OWL descriptions automatically extracted from the services' associated MSDL descriptions. Service matching is then performed by posing a query in the form of an OWL description and then exploiting the power of DL reasoning to *infer* all services which are instances of that descriptions.

The core component in these processes is, as mentioned in the introduction, the instance Store (*iS*) – a freely available Java application [23], developed within the MONET project.

### 4.1   The Instance Store

We now describe the basic functionality of the *iS* component. (See Figure 2 for the logical functionalities performed by *iS* of service registration and matching within the MONET broker architecture and see [5] for full details on *iS*.)

*Initialisation.* The *iS* is initialised by providing a ("TBox") DL reasoner (such as RACER), a database, and an OWL ontology (e.g. the collection of MONET ontologies). The *iS* connects to the reasoner via the DIG interface [4], and, if required, loads the ontology into the reasoner after translating it to DIG. Finally, it connects to the database, creating the required tables if necessary.

*Adding and Removing Instances.* In order to add an instance to *iS*, one needs to provide a URI for it (e.g. `http://monet.nag.co.uk/service\#nagopt`) and an OWL description. The *iS* then stores this pair in the database, but also infers with the reasoner all the classes in the ontology which are more general than or equivalent to the given description, associating them with the instance's URI in the database as well. This information will be used to match queries. Removing an instance amounts then to deleting all rows in the database involving that instance.

*Retrieving Instances.* Retrieving all the instances of a given OWL description $Q$ is more complex. First, *iS* uses the reasoner to find the classes in the ontology which are subsumed by $Q$ and then retrieves the corresponding instances in the database.

Next, *iS* asks the reasoner whether $Q$ is equivalent to a class $C$ in the ontology. If that is the case then also the instances corresponding to $C$ in the database are returned and the procedure stops. If, however, the description is not equivalent to any class in the ontology, *iS* needs to retrieve all the instances of immediate parents of $Q$ and check (again through the reasoner) whether they are, in fact, instances of the given description. If they are, then the relevant instances are also returned.

Note that the computations involving the reasoner (parents, equivalents, etc) are usually performed in a fraction of a second. Coupled with the high-performance of databases this makes *iS* very efficient and scalable.

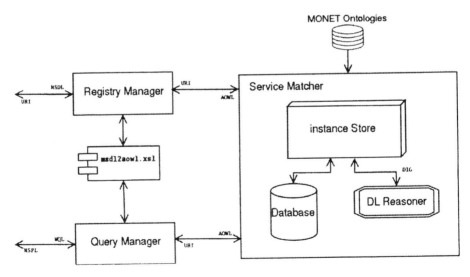

**Fig. 2.** MONET Architecture of Service Matcher and Registry and Query Managers

## 4.2    From MSDL to OWL

When a service registers itself with the broker it submits a service description in MSDL. The Registry Manager component of the broker translates this into a description in *OWL Abstract Syntax* [6] by means of an XSLT stylesheet[2] we developed (`msdl2aowl.xsl` in Figure 2). We favoured OWL abstract syntax over the XML-RDF syntax, because the former is far more concise and human readable when expressing the fragments of ontologies forming descriptions[3].

For instance, the description in OWL abstract syntax (*AOWL*) corresponding to the MSDL of Figure 1 is given in Figure 3, where for simplicity some of the restrictions "someValuesFrom(owl:Thing)" needed to ensure the existence of some value for each property are omitted. Thus

```
restriction(property someValuesFrom(owl:Thing))
```

is needed not only for `service_classification` but also for every other property in the description.

```
intersectionOf(<http://monet.nag.co.uk/owl#Service>
  restriction(<http://monet.nag.co.uk/owl#service_classification>
    someValuesFrom(owl:Thing))
  restriction(<http://monet.nag.co.uk/owl#service_classification>
    allValuesFrom(intersectionOf(<http://monet.nag.co.uk/owl#Classification>
        restriction(<http://monet.nag.co.uk/owl#gams_class>
          allValuesFrom(<http://gams.nist.gov#GamsG1a1a>))
        restriction(<http://monet.nag.co.uk/owl#service_problem>
          allValuesFrom(<http://monet.nag.co.uk/problems/constrained_minimisation>))
        restriction(<http://monet.nag.co.uk/owl#input_format>
          allValuesFrom(<http://www.openmath.org/OpenMath>))
        restriction(<http://monet.nag.co.uk/owl#output_format>
          allValuesFrom(<http://www.openmath.org/OpenMath>))
        restriction(<http://monet.nag.co.uk/owl#service_directive>
          allValuesFrom(<http://monet.nag.co.uk/owl#find>))
    ) ) )
  restriction(<http://monet.nag.co.uk/owl#service_implementation>
    someValuesFrom(owl:Thing))
  restriction(<http://monet.nag.co.uk/owl#service_implementation>
    allValuesFrom(intersectionOf(<http://monet.nag.co.uk/owl#Implementation>
        restriction(<http://monet.nag.co.uk/owl#service_software>
          allValuesFrom(<http://monet.nag.co.uk/owl#NAG_C_Library_7>))
        restriction(<http://monet.nag.co.uk/owl#service_platform>
          allValuesFrom(<http://monet.nag.co.uk/owl#PentiumSystem>))
        restriction(<http://monet.nag.co.uk/owl#service_algorithm>
          allValuesFrom(
            <http://monet.nag.co.uk/algorithm#Safeguarded_Quadratic-Interpolation>))
  ) ) ) )
```

**Fig. 3.** Description of service `nagopt` in OWL abstract syntax

Therefore, semantically, this registration corresponds to adding to the registry $\mathcal{R}$ the assertion $D(\mathtt{S})$ (in the language used by the MONET ontologies), where $\mathtt{S}$ is a constant representing the service URL:

---

[2] `http://www.cs.man.ac.uk/~dturi/ontologies/monet/msdl2owl.xsl`.

[3] For this reason we developed an OWL abstract syntax parser, now part of the OWL API [3].

$$D(\mathrm{S}) \equiv \mathtt{Service}(\mathrm{S})$$
$$\wedge \forall y. (\mathtt{service\_classification}(\mathrm{S}, y) \Rightarrow C(y))$$
$$\wedge \forall y. (\mathtt{service\_implementation}(\mathrm{S}, y) \Rightarrow I(y))$$

where

$$C(y) \equiv \mathtt{Classification}(y)$$
$$\wedge \forall z. (\mathtt{gams\_class}(y, z) \Rightarrow \mathtt{GamsG1a1a}(z))$$
$$\wedge \forall z. (\mathtt{service\_problem}(y, z) \Rightarrow \mathtt{constrained\_minimization}(z))$$
$$\wedge \forall z. (\mathtt{input\_format}(y, z) \Rightarrow \mathtt{OpenMath}(z))$$
$$\wedge \forall z. (\mathtt{output\_format}(y, z) \Rightarrow \mathtt{OpenMath}(z))$$
$$\wedge \forall z. (\mathtt{directive}(y, z) \Rightarrow \mathtt{find}(z))$$

and

$$I(y) \equiv \mathtt{Implementation}(y)$$
$$\wedge \forall z. (\mathtt{software}(y, z) \Rightarrow \mathtt{NAG\_C\_Library\_7}(z))$$
$$\wedge \forall z. (\mathtt{platform}(y, z) \Rightarrow \mathtt{PentiumSystem}(z))$$
$$\wedge \forall z. (\mathtt{algorithm}(y, z) \Rightarrow \mathtt{Safeguarded\_QuadraticInterpolation}(z))$$

## 5   OWL Queries

The simplest queries are just fragments of MSDL which provide a template for the service the user wishes to use. These queries are translated into OWL by the Query Manager component of the broker using XSLT (`msdl2aowl.xsl` in Figure 2). A simple example would consist of just a *classification* which contains a reference to a known problem (i.e. one contained in the ontology) along with values for the input data. In this case, in effect, the user is stating that he or she would like to solve this instantiation of this particular problem. Using this approach one may constrain the software or hardware the service runs on, the algorithm to be used or anything else which can be expressed in MSDL. Note that the class hierarchy in the ontology plays an important part here: given the following fragment of the algorithm ontology:

- Algorithm
  - ...
    - Quadrature
      - Automatic_Adaptive_Methods
        - ...
      - Automatic_Non-Adaptive_Methods
        - ...
      - Fixed_Abscissae_Methods

```
<monet:query xmlns:monet="http://monet.nag.co.uk/monet/ns"
             xmlns:om="http://www.openmath.org/OpenMath">
  <monet:problem >
    <monet:header/>
    <monet:body>

      <monet:output name="integral">
        <monet:value>
          <om:OMOBJ>
            <om:OMA><om:OMS name="defint" cd="calculus1"/>
              <om:OMA><om:OMS name="interval" cd="interval1"/>
                <om:OMF dec="0.0"/>
                <om:OMF dec="1.0"/>
              </om:OMA>
              <om:OMBIND><om:OMS name="lambda" cd="fns1"/>
                <om:OMBVAR><om:OMV name="x"/></om:OMBVAR>
                <om:OMA><om:OMS name="sin" cd="transc1"/>
                  <om:OMV name="x"/>
                </om:OMA>
              </om:OMBIND>
            </om:OMA>
          </om:OMOBJ>
        </monet:value>
      </monet:output>

    </monet:body>
  </monet:problem>
</monet:query>
```

**Fig. 4.** A Query Involving a natural formalisation of a Mathematical Problem

- Gauss-Hermite
- Gauss-Laguerre
- Gauss-Legendre
- Gauss-Rational
- Gill-Miller
- ...

a user could request an algorithm which used fixed abscissae and be satisfied with any one of the five alternatives.

Queries are not, however, restricted to simple templates of the service the user wants. The Query Manager can also construct OWL specifications based on other user inputs, such as that given in Figure 4. In this case the user has said that he or she would like the service to return the result of computing a particular integral, namely:

$$\int_{0.0}^{1.0} \sin(x)dx$$

This is a very natural way to express this question from a mathematical point of view but, since there is no explicit problem, taxonomy or algorithm element to help the service matcher, we need to incorporate some extra information in the ontology to enable it to identify the problem being solved. It is immediately clear to a human reader[4] that this is a definite integration problem. OpenMath

---

[4] Who is conversant with OpenMath.

has a tree structure and the root node for an OpenMath object can only be one of a small number of elements, in this case an OMA or *application* element. Since we know the structure of such elements we know that if its first child is an OMS or *OpenMath Symbol* then this is in effect the principle constructor for the object. In this case the symbol is that one used to represent definite integration (defint from the content dictionary calculus1).

Elements of the Problem Ontology may have the property openmath_head which indicates an OpenMath symbol which can be used to construct instances of that problem. In fact the definite_integration class in the Problem ontology has an openmath_head property of defint. So if the Query Manager transforms this query to a request to solve problems with an openmath_head property of defint then the reasoner will infer that any service solving the definite_integration problem is a candidate.

We now illustrate service matching by considering five queries to an elementary *iS* consisting of four services.

The first query asks for all individuals whose GAMS classification is GamsG: *iS* answers it by returning nagopt and nagopt-variation.

```
restriction(<http://monet.nag.co.uk/owl#service_classification>
  someValuesFrom(restriction(<http://monet.nag.co.uk/owl#gams_class>
          someValuesFrom(<http://gams.nist.gov#GamsG>))))
```

The second example is a query for all individuals whose implementation has Root_Finding as algorithm. In the Algorithm ontology we can find that Powell is a child of Root_Finding. And, indeed, the answer of *iS* to the query is nagroot.

```
restriction(<http://monet.nag.co.uk/owl#service_implementation>
  someValuesFrom(restriction(<http://monet.nag.co.uk/owl#service_algorithm>
    someValuesFrom(<http://monet.nag.co.uk/algorithm#Root_Finding>))))
```

We can generalise the query by replacing Root_Finding with Numeric and obtain all services as answers, since they are all numeric.

The next query is more interesting: we ask for all individuals with algorithm having a Zentralblatt bibliographic reference *0277.65028*. The answer is again nagroot, since in the Bibliography ontology we have associated that reference to Powell.

```
restriction(<http://monet.nag.co.uk/owl#service_implementation>
  someValuesFrom(restriction(<http://monet.nag.co.uk/owl#service_algorithm>
    someValuesFrom(restriction(<http://monet.nag.co.uk/algorithm#bibliographic_reference>
      someValuesFrom(intersectionOf(<http://monet.nag.co.uk/bibliography#ZentralBlatt_MATH>
       restriction(<http://monet.nag.co.uk/bibliography#bibref>
        value("Zbl_0277.65028"^^<http://www.w3.org/2001/XMLSchema#string>)))))))))
```

We now illustrate the use of negation in a query. Consider first the query where we ask for all individuals running on a platform with one processor.

```
restriction(<http://monet.nag.co.uk/owl#service_implementation>
  someValuesFrom(restriction(<http://monet.nag.co.uk/owl#service_platform>
   someValuesFrom(restriction(<http://monet.nag.co.uk/owl#number_of_processors>
    value("1"^^<http://www.w3.org/2001/XMLSchema#int>))))))
```

The answer is nagopt, nagroot, and nagquad, but not nagopt-variation since we asserted that it runs on *SR8000* which is a parallel processor. Now, if we add to the `Hardware` ontology the axiom that `Serial` and `Parallel` are disjoint, we can infer that `not(Parallel)` is equivalent to `Serial`, and hence the next query would also return `nagopt`, `nagroot`, and `nagquad`.

```
intersectionOf(<http://monet.nag.co.uk/owl#Service>
 restriction(<http://monet.nag.co.uk/owl#service_implementation>
  someValuesFrom(restriction(<http://monet.nag.co.uk/owl#service_platform>
   someValuesFrom(complementOf(<http://monet.nag.co.uk/owl#Parallel>))))))
```

In terms of the first-order deduction relation '⊢', querying for the services matching a description given in a query $Q(x)$ amounts to retrieving the set of services whose description is subsumed by the query:

$$\{\mathsf{S} \mid \mathcal{M} \vdash D(\mathsf{S}) \Rightarrow Q(\mathsf{S}) \text{ for some } D(\mathsf{S}) \in \mathcal{R}\}$$

with respect to the MONET ontologies $\mathcal{M}$ and the assertions in the registry $\mathcal{R}$.

## 6   Conclusions

The MONET ontologies are designed to model both queries and service descriptions: in that sense they are a formalism of the original MSDL language which was deliberately designed to be "ontology neutral". This was partly to make the task of authoring service descriptions more straightforward (since the language is quite compact), but mainly because OWL was then at an early stage of development. The ontologies are designed to be used by the broker and, in particular, the *iS* component which is responsible for matching queries to appropriate services. This component is, in turn, built on a Description Logic reasoner accessed through the generic DIG interface. In our case we have chosen to use RACER for this purpose, but there are several other alternatives which we could have used equally well.

We have demonstrated how one may use OWL to discover appropriate services to solve particular mathematical problems. This was intended as a proof-of-concept exercise and there are still aspects which could be improved. The ontologies themselves are somewhat sparse in some areas – our symbolic extension to GAMS for example – but we are loth to extend them purely as an academic exercise. The beauty of GAMS is that it is a categorisation of an existing set of resources and we feel that this is the right approach to take, however we are aware that it took a considerable effort to develop and it was not practical to do something on a similar scale within MONET.

One possible approach would be to allow for dynamic extension of the ontologies, so that (for example) if a service deployer registered a new problem in the Problem Library it would automatically be added to the problem ontology and the service-matcher components of the running browsers could be notified to re-initialise their versions of *iS*. This is not a perfect solution since it would allow for inaccurate or incomplete entries to be added to the ontologies, and of course it only really applies to leaf nodes.

The process of converting a query into the appropriate OWL format is important since this allows us to extend the possible mechanisms for formulating queries beyond simply asking the client to provide a fragment of MSDL. The technique we described of taking a problem description and inferring the problem type from its OpenMath structure is widely applicable and reflects the way in which human users usually interact with packages such as Maple, Matlab etc., by typing in strings such as "`int(sin(x),x=0..1)`". However there are other ways of stating mathematical problems which use the desired properties of the result such as "find all $x \in \mathcal{C} \mid x^2 = 1$". The condition here is in effect a post-condition of the problem description.

Matching on pre- and post-conditions would be a very powerful technique, partly because it would give the user much more freedom in formulating problems but also because it would help automate service orchestration. Services whose post- and pre-conditions matched could be "plugged-into" each other. However it is a well-known fact that proving that two mathematical expressions are identical is in theory undecidable [22] (although there are many mechanisms which will solve a large class of cases in practice). Given that we have access to general-purpose computer algebra systems such as Maple within the MONET framework it would not be too difficult for a broker to use them as oracles to decide whether two statements were equivalent.

Although the application we have investigated is that of advertising and discovering web services the same general framework could be used for describing and cataloguing any kind of mathematical software, or indeed for describing the individual functions available within a comprehensive software package such as the NAG Library or Maple.

# References

1. F. Baader, D. Calvanese, D. McGuinness, D. Nardi, and P. Patel-Schneider (eds.), *The Description Logic Handbook – Theory, Implementation and Applications*, Cambridge University Press, 2003.
2. R. Baraka, O. Caprotti, and W. Schreiner, Publishing and Discovering Mathematical Service Descriptions: A Web Registry Approach, Technical report, RISC-Linz Technical Report, 2004.
3. S. Bechhofer, OWL API Project, `http://sourceforge.net/projects/owlapi`.
4. S. Bechhofer, The DIG description logic interface: DIG/1.1, in: *Proceedings of the 2003 Description Logic Workshop (DL 2003)*, 2003.
5. S. Bechhofer, I. Horrocks, and D. Turi, Instance store – database support for reasoning over individuals, `http://instancestore.man.ac.uk/instancestore.pdf`, 2002.
6. S. Bechhofer, P.F. Patel-Schneider, and D. Turi, OWL Web Ontology Language Concrete Abstract Syntax, Technical report, The University of Manchester, December 2003, available from `http://owl.man.ac.uk/2003/concrete/latest/`.
7. S. Bechhofer, F. van Harmelen, J. Hendler, I. Horrocks, D.L. McGuinness, P.F. Patel-Schneider, and L.A. Stein, OWL Web Ontology Language Reference, Technical Report REC-owl-ref-20040210, The World Wide Web Consortium, February 2004, available from http://www.w3.org/TR/2004/REC-owl-ref-20040210/ .

8. R.F. Boisvert, S.E. Howe, and D.K. Kahaner, Gams: A framework for the management of scientific software, *ACM Transactions on Mathematical Software*, 11(4):313–355, December 1985.

9. O. Caprotti, D. Carlisle, A. Cohen, and M. Dewar, The Mathematical Problem Ontology: final version, Technical Report Deliverable D11, The MONET Consortium, March 2003, available from `http://monet.nag.co.uk`.

10. O. Caprotti, M. Dewar, J. Davenport, and J. Padget, Mathematics on the (Semantic) Net, in: Ch. Bussler, J. Davies, D. Fensel, and R. Studer (eds.), *Proceedings of the European Symposium on the Semantic Web*, volume 3053 of *LNCS*, pp. 213–224, Springer Verlag, 2004. May 2004.

11. R. Chinnici, M. Gudgin, J.-J. Moreau, J. Schlimmer, and S. Weerawarana, "Web Services Description Language (WSDL) version 2.0 part 1: Core language", W3c working draft, The World Wide Web Consortium, 26 March 2004, http://www.w3.org/TR/wsdl20/.

12. V. Haarslev and R. Moller, Description of the RACER system and its applications, in: R. Gore, A. Leitsch, and T. Nipkow (eds.), *Automated reasoning: First International Joint Conference, IJCAR 2001, Siena, Italy, June 18–23, 2001: proceedings*, volume 2083 of *Lecture Notes in Artificial Intelligence*, New York, NY, USA, 2001, Springer-Verlag Inc.

13. I. Horrocks et al., DAML+OIL, Technical Report REC-xslt-19991116, Joint US/EU ad hoc Agent Markup Language Committee, March 2001, available from `http://www.daml.org/2001/03/daml+oil-index.html`.

14. F. Manola and E. Miller, RDF Primer, Technical Report REC-rdf-primer-20040210, The World Wide Web Consortium, February 2004, available from `http://www.w3.org/TR/2004/REC-rdf-primer-20040210/`.

15. MathSciNet, `http://www.ams.org/mathscinet`.

16. M. Kohlhase. OMDoc: An Open Markup Format for Mathematical Documents (Version 1.2), available from `http://www.mathweb.org/omdoc/omdoc1.2.ps`.

17. M. Minsky, A framework for representing knowledge, in: P. Winston (ed.), *The Psychology of Computer Vision*, pp. 211–277, McGraw-Hill, New York, 1975.

18. The MONET Consortium, Mathematical Service Description Language: Final version, Technical Report Deliverable D14, The MONET Consortium, March 2003, available from `http://monet.nag.co.uk`.

19. M. Ross Quillian, Semantic memory, in: M. Minsky (ed.), *Semantic Information Processing*, MIT Press, Cambridge, MA, 1968.

20. OASIS/ebXML Registry Technical Committee, OASIS/ebXML Registry Services Specification v2.0, `http://www.oasis-open.org/committees/regrep/documents/2.0/specs/ebrs.pd%f`, 2002.

21. The OpenMath Society, The OpenMath Standard, October 2002, available from `http://www.openmath.org/standard/om11/omstd11.xml`.

22. D. Richardson, Some unsolvable problems involving elementary functions of a real variable, *Journal of Computational Logic*, 33:514–520, 1968.

23. D. Turi, Instance Store Project, `http://instancestore.man.ac.uk`.

24. Zentralblatt Math., `http://www.emis.de/ZMATH/`.

# C-CoRN, the Constructive Coq Repository at Nijmegen

Luís Cruz-Filipe[1,2], Herman Geuvers[1], and Freek Wiedijk[1]

[1] NIII, Radboud University Nijmegen
[2] Center for Logic and Computation, Lisboa
{lcf,herman,freek}@cs.kun.nl

**Abstract.** We present C-CoRN, the Constructive Coq Repository at Nijmegen. It consists of a mathematical library of constructive algebra and analysis formalized in the theorem prover Coq. We explain the structure and the contents of the library and we discuss the motivation and some (possible) applications of such a library.

The development of C-CoRN is part of a larger goal to design a computer system where 'a mathematician can do mathematics', which covers the activities of defining, computing and proving. An important proviso for such a system to be useful and attractive is the availability of a large structured library of mathematical results that people can consult and build on. C-CoRN wants to provide such a library, but it can also be seen as a case study in developing such a library of formalized mathematics and deriving its requirements. As the actual development of a library is very much a technical activity, the work on C-CoRN is tightly bound to the proof assistant Coq.

## 1 Introduction

A repository of formalized constructive mathematics [6] in the proof assistant Coq [13] has been constructed over the last five years at the University of Nijmegen. This is part of a larger goal to design a *mathematical assistant*: a computer system in which a mathematician can do mathematics. This covers the activities of defining (theory development), computing (programming) and proving (proof development), but ideally also editing of mathematical documents and presentation of mathematics. In such a computer system, the mathematics would obviously have to appear in a *formalized* form, i.e. as expressions in some formal language. The process of going from the informal (paper) mathematics to the mathematics that can be understood and manipulated by a computer (program) is called *formalization*.

One of the things that is very important for such a 'mathematical assistant' to be used is the availability of a large and usable library of basic results. A library will make it attractive for potential users to experiment with the system and to contribute results to its repository. Such a repository should not be just a huge collection of proved results (including the 'proof scripts' that are input for the proof assistant to carry out the proof). In our view, a library of formalized mathematics should be:

A. Asperti et al. (Eds.): MKM 2004, LNCS 3119, pp. 88–103, 2004.
© Springer-Verlag Berlin Heidelberg 2004

**Accessible:** one should be able to get a fairly fast overview of what's in it and where to find specific results;

**Readable:** once one has come down to the basic objects like definitions, lemmas and proofs, these should be presented in a reasonable way;

**Coherent:** results about a specific theory should be grouped together and theories extending others should be defined as such;

**Extensible:** contributions from other researchers should be easy to include.

How can one make such a (large) coherent library of formalized mathematics? Ideally, this should also be independent of the Proof Assistant one is working with, but right now that cannot be done. Several other projects deal with this question. The MoWGLI project [2] aims at devising system-independent tools for presenting mathematics on the web. The OpenMath [10] and OMDoc [25] standards aim at exchanging mathematics across different mathematical applications, which is also one of the aims of the Calculemus project [8]. This may eventually lead to ways of sharing mathematical libraries in a semantically meaningful way that preserves correctness, but this is not possible yet (an exception is NuPRL, which can use HOL results [29]).

So, to experiment with creating, presenting and using such a library, one has to stick to one specific theorem prover, and already there many issues come up and possible solutions can be tested. We have chosen to use the Coq Proof Assistant, because we already were familiar with it and because we were specifically interested in formalizing constructive mathematics.

This paper first describes the backgrounds of C-CoRN: its history and motivation. Then we describe the structure of the repository as it is now and the methodology that we have chosen to develop it. Finally we discuss some applications and future developments.

## 2    History

The C-CoRN repository grew out of the FTA project, where a constructive proof of the Fundamental Theorem of Algebra was formalized in Coq. This theorem states that every non-constant polynomial $f$ over the complex numbers has a root, i.e., there is a complex number $z$ such that $f(z) = 0$.

One of the main motivations for starting the FTA project was to create a library for basic constructive algebra and analysis to be used by others. Often, a formalization is only used by the person that created it (or is not used further at all!), whereas an important added value of formalizing mathematics – in our view – is to create a joint computer based repository of mathematics. For the FTA project, this meant that we did not attempt to prove the theorem as fast as possible, but that in the proving process we tried to formalize the relevant notions at an appropriate level of abstraction, so that they could be reused.

An important condition for the successful use of a library of formalized mathematics is to have good documentation of the code. There are two main purposes of documentation:

1. to show to the world what has been formalized via a 'high level' presentation of the work (in our case that would be a LaTeX document giving a mathematical description of the formalized theory);
2. to help the interested outsider to extend (or change or improve or vary on) the formalized theory.

For (1) one wants to produce a LaTeX document that 'goes along' with the formalization. This may be generated from the formalization (but it is not quite clear whether it is at all possible to generate something reasonably, and mathematically abstract, from the very low level formal proof code). Alternatively – and this is the approach followed in the FTA project – this LaTeX file may be created in advance and then used as a reference for the proof to formalize. The goal of the FTA project was to formalize an *existing* proof and not to redo the mathematics or 'tailor' the mathematics toward the proof assistant. This meant that we started from an original proof of FTA, described in [22], with lots of details filled in to ease the formalization process. The same approach has been followed throughout the rest of C-CoRN: existing mathematics is formalized, so the (high-level) mathematical content corresponds to an existing part of a book or article.

For (2), some simple scripts were created in the FTA project to be able to extract from the Coq input files a useful documentation for outsiders interested in the technical content. However, this was pretty ad hoc and not very satisfactory, and it was changed in C-CoRN, as described in Section 5.

After the FTA project was finished, i.e., after the theorem had been formally proved in Coq, it was not yet clear that it had been successful in actually creating a usable library, because all people working with the library until then were part of the project. The only way to test this would be to let outsiders extend the library. This is not too easy: due to the fact that we have tactics implemented in ML (e.g. to do equational reasoning), one cannot use the standard image of Coq and has to build a custom image first. Therefore, the first real test only came when the first author of this paper started as a new Ph.D. student to formalize constructive calculus (leading to the Fundamental Theorem of Calculus) in Coq. The FTA library turned out to be very usable. Most importantly, there was almost no need to restructure the library or redefine notions, implying that most of the basic choices that were made in the FTA project worked. (Of course, the basic library was extended a lot, with new results and new definitions.) Hereafter, the library was rebaptized to C-CoRN, the Constructive Coq Repository at Nijmegen, since the FTA and the work of the FTA project had become only a (small) part of it.

Since then, several people, working both in Nijmegen and elsewhere, have consulted, used and contributed to C-CoRN. These have found its structure (including notations, automation facilities, documentation) quite useful.

## 3   Why C-CoRN?

Formalizing mathematics can be fun. In the process of formalizing, one discovers the fine structure of the field one is working with and one gains confidence in the correctness of the definitions and the proofs. In addition to this, formalizing mathematics can also be useful. We indicate some of its possible uses:

**Correctness Guaranteed:** The formalized mathematics is checked and therefore the proofs are guaranteed to be correct for all practical purposes. This can be vital in the realm of software or system correctness, where one wants to be absolutely sure that the mathematical models and the results proved about them are correct.

**Exchange of 'Meaningful' Mathematics:** That the mathematics is formalized means that it has a structure and a semantics within the Proof Assistant. So a mathematical formula or proof is not just a string of symbols, but it has a structure that represents the mathematical meaning and its building blocks have a definition (within the Proof Assistant). These can in principle be exploited to generate meaningful documents or to exchange mathematics with other applications.

**Finding Mathematical Results:** Based on the semantics and the structure of the formalized mathematics, it should be possible to find results easier. Querying based on the (meaningful) structure is already possible (implemented in the Helm system, see [23]), but more semantical querying would be welcome. This requires adding more meta-data.

The potential uses of formalized mathematics only really become available if one can share the formalization and let others profit from it, e.g. by making it possible for them to study it, extend it or use it for their own applications or further development. A key requirement for this is that the formalized mathematics be presented. Ordinary (non-computer-formalized) mathematical results are published in articles, books or lecture notes, and are in that way shared with other mathematicians or users of mathematics. Giving a good presentation of formalized mathematics in practice, though, turns out to be quite hard. There are various reasons for this:

**Idiosyncrasies of the Proof Assistant:** When talking to a Proof Assistant, things have to be stated in a specific way, so the system understands it: definitions have to be given in a specific format, proofs have a specific form, etc. Moreover, each Assistant has its own logical foundations (e.g. set theory, type theory or higher order logic), making it easy to express some concepts (e.g. inductive definitions in type theory) and hard to express others (e.g. subsets in type theory). Because of this, mathematical theory will be defined in a specific way that best fits the idiosyncrasies of the system at hand. When presenting the formal mathematics, one would like to abstract from these 'arbitrary' choices.

**Verbosity of Formalized Mathematics:** To make the Proof Assistant understand (or be able to verify) what the user means, a lot of details have to be given. By itself, this is unavoidable (and fine, because we really want the mathematics to be verified and that doesn't come for free). But in the presentation phase, one wants to abstract from these finer details and 'view' the mathematics at a higher level. This is not so easy to achieve. Ideally it would also be possible to use the higher level (less verbose) mathematics as input for the proof assistant, but that's not easy either.

**Access to the Formalized Mathematics:** How does one find a result in the library, how does one get an overview of the material? One can query the library with syntactic means, searching a formula of a specific form, as described in [23]. This is helpful, but can a useful result still be found if it occurs in the library in disguise? Also, if a user knows that a specific lemma appears in the library, (s)he will want to apply it, which in a Proof Assistant is done by using its name. But what is the name of (the proof of) a lemma? One probably doesn't want to clutter up the names in the presentation of the math, so 'logical' naming conventions come in handy.

To really understand and work on these points, one needs a 'testbed' to experiment with. This was one of the reasons to start C-CoRN: to have a library of mathematics that people can really contribute to, read and work with.

Of course, such libraries already exist. The prominent one is the Mizar Mathematical Library (MML). However, Mizar was not good for experimenting with a library of formalized mathematics, because we would not have control over the library: one cannot just install Mizar and formalize a large library on top of the existing one. Soon the system gets slow and one has to submit the work to the Mizar library to have it integrated. Moreover, the Mizar system itself is not open in the sense that one can program one's own tools (e.g. for automation or documentation) on top of it[1]. Another important reason not to choose Mizar was that we were aiming at a library of *constructive* mathematics. For all these reasons, Coq was a good choice, with the drawback that there was only a very small initial library to begin with. (There are many 'Coq contributions', but they do not form one coherent library as discussed in Section 8.)

The main reason for working constructively is that we want to use our library, apart from studying how it conducts as a repository, to study the connections between 'conceptual' (abstract) mathematics and 'computational' (concrete) mathematics. The first (conceptual math) deals with e.g. the proof of (and theory development leading to) the Fundamental Theorem of Algebra, while the second (computational math) deals with an actual representation of the reals and complex numbers and the actual root finding algorithm that the FTA exhibits. In this paper we will not elaborate on this any further, but just point out that this was an important motivation for choosing to work with Coq. At present work is being done in program extraction from the C-CoRN library, and this relies heavily on the fact that the library is constructive.

---

[1] Right now, C-CoRN is not open either: we want to have 'central control' over the library. But the point we want to make here is that the Proof Assistant Coq, on which C-CoRN is based, *is* open.

# 4    Contents

C-CoRN includes at present formalizations of significant pieces of mathematics. In this section we give an overview of the main results in the library. So far everything has been formalized constructively. Although we do not exclude adding non-constructive theorems to the library, working constructively has some added value, as indicated in the previous section.

The C-CoRN library is organized in a tree-like fashion. This structure agrees with the dependencies among the mathematics being formalized. In Figure 1 the directory structure of C-CoRN can be seen.

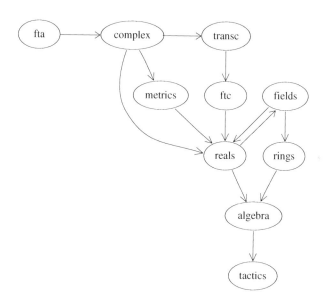

**Fig. 1.** Directory structure of C-CoRN

At the bottom of C-CoRN are the tactic files and the Algebraic Hierarchy, developed in the framework of the FTA project. Most of the tactics are to make equational reasoning easier, see [21]. In the Algebraic Hierarchy, the most common algebraic structures occurring in mathematics, such as monoids, rings and (ordered) fields, are formalized in a cumulative way and their basic properties are proved. For reasons discussed in Section 5, this formalization proceeds in an abstract way, described in detail in [19]. Furthermore, the hierarchy is built in such a way that more complex structures are instances of simpler ones, i.e. all lemmas which have been proved e.g. for groups are inherited by all ordered fields.

One might argue that tactics should not be part of a library of mathematics but are 'meta-knowledge'. However in C-CoRN the tactics are closely related to the lemmas that they depend on: these cannot be easily separated. Also lemmas and tactics can be exchanged for each other: a proof step often can be made either with reference to a lemma (declarative mathematical knowledge) or by applying a tactic (procedural mathematical knowledge). For these reasons we consider tactics to be part of the C-CoRN library.

Real number structures are defined as complete archimedean ordered fields. The C-CoRN library includes not only a concrete model of the real numbers (namely, the standard construction as Cauchy sequences of rationals) but also a formal proof that any two real number structures are equivalent and some alternative sets of axioms that can be used to define them. Thanks to these results, it makes sense to work with a generic real number structure rather than with any concrete one. This part of the library is described in detail in [18].

Among generic results about real numbers included in the library we point out the usual properties of limits of Cauchy sequences and the Intermediate Value Theorem for polynomials, which allows us in particular to define $n^{th}$ roots of any nonnegative number.

At this point the library branches in various independent directions.

One of the branches consists of the rest of the original FTA library, which contains the definition of the field of complex numbers and a proof of the Fundamental Theorem of Algebra due to M. Kneser; this work is discussed in [22]. Other important results in this part of the library include the definition of important operations on the complex numbers (conjugation, absolute value and $n^{th}$ roots) and their properties.

The second main branch deals with a development of Real Analysis following [4]. Here, properties of real valued functions are studied, such as continuity, differentiability and integrability. Several important results are included, among which Rolle's Theorem, Taylor's Theorem and the Fundamental Theorem of Calculus. Also, this segment of the library includes results allowing functions to be defined via power series; as an application, the exponential and trigonometric functions are defined and their fundamental properties are proved. Logarithms and inverse trigonometric functions provide examples of function definition via indefinite integrals.

A separate branch of the library, currently in its initial stage of development, deals with topological and metric spaces. At present this part of the library is very small; it includes simple properties of metric spaces, as well as a proof that the complex numbers form a metric space.

The sizes of the different parts of the C-CoRN library are shown in Figure 2. This data does not include the files dealing with metric spaces, as these are still in an early stage of development, nor those dealing with applications to program extraction, which will be discussed in Section 6.

| Description | Size (Kb) | % of total |
|---|---|---|
| Algebraic Hierarchy (incl. tactics) | 533 | 26.4 |
| Real Numbers (incl. Models) | 470 | 23.3 |
| FTA (incl. Complex Numbers) | 175 | 8.7 |
| Real Analysis (incl. Transc. Fns.) | 842 | 41.6 |
| Total | 2020 | 100 |

**Fig. 2.** Contents and size of C-CoRN (input files)

# 5    Methodology

In order to successfully pursue the goal of formalizing a large piece of mathematics, it is necessary to work in a systematic way. In this section we look at some of the general techniques that are used to make the development of the C-CoRN library more fluent.

We will focus on four main aspects:

**Documentation:** In order to be usable, a library needs to have a good documentation that allows the user to quickly find out exactly what results have been formalized, as well as understand the basic notations, definitions and tactics.

**Structuring:** Another important issue is the structure of the library. We feel that lemmas should be somehow grouped according to their mathematical content rather than to any other criterion; e.g. all lemmas about groups should be put together in one place, all lemmas about order relations in another, and so on. A related aspect is how to name lemmas. Experience shows that following some simple rules can make the process of looking for a particular result both easier and faster.

**Abstract Approach:** C-CoRN aims at generality. This suggests that mathematic structures (e.g. real numbers) be formalized in an abstract way rather than by constructing a particular example and working on it. We will examine some of the consequences of this style of working.

**Automation:** Finally, any successful theorem-proving environment must have at least some automation, otherwise the proving process quickly becomes too complex. We give an overview of the specific tactics that were developed for C-CoRN and show how they help in the development of the library.

## Documentation

Providing a good documentation for the formalized library in parallel with its development was a central preoccupation from the beginning of the FTA project. In fact, having a human-readable description of what has been formalized can be very useful in communicating not only content but also ideas, notations and even some technical aspects of the formalization process.

Such a documentation should at any given moment reflect the state of the library, and as such should be intrinsically linked to the script files. (This is also the idea behind Knuth's 'Literate Programming'. Aczel and Bailey use the term 'Literate Formalization' for this method applied to formalized mathematics [3].) At present, Coq provides a standard tool, called coqdoc (see [17]), that automatically generates postscript and html documentation from the Coq input files. Additional information can be introduced in the documentation via comments in the script file.

Ideally the documentation should be one with the script files; however this is not the situation in Coq. In this system the standard way to generate documentation for a library is using coqdoc, and this is the way we do it in C-CoRN.

The C-CoRN documentation includes all definitions, axioms and notation as well as the statements of all the lemmas in the library, but no proofs: being meant as *documentation*, rather than *presentation* of the library, the presence of long and incomprehensible proof scripts in the documentation would undermine its purpose. For the same reason, tactic definitions are omitted from the documentation, but not their description: although the actual code is not presented, the behavior of the existing C-CoRN specific tactics is explained as well as how and when they can be used.

In the `html` version, hyperlinks between each occurrence of a term and its definition allow the users to navigate easily through the documentation, being able to check quickly any notion they are not familiar with.

### Structuring

There are several ways that the lemmas and files in a library of formalized mathematics can be organized. The current trend in most major systems, as discussed in Section 8, seems to be adding individual files to the library as independent entities and seldom if ever changing them afterward (except for maintenance). However, C-CoRN is intended as a growing system upon which new formalizations can be made. The approach above described directly conflicts with this purpose, for it typically leads to dispersion of related lemmas throughout the library and unnecessary duplication of work.

For this reason, lemmas in C-CoRN are organized in files according to their statements and files are distributed in directories according to their subjects. Thus, different areas of mathematics appear in different directories and different subjects within one area will be different files in the same directory.

The disadvantage of this approach is that it requires some form of central control over the repository: after an extension, the library has to be reconsidered to put the definitions and lemmas in the 'right' place. This may become problematic if many files are contributed within a short time. Presently the responsibility for maintaining different parts of C-CoRN is distributed among different people: when a subject becomes extensively represented in the library, we encourage the developers of that subject to take responsibility for it. In this way we do not restrict the control of the library to a small group of people or a confined geographical location, but we manage to keep its unity. We also hope that new users will feel motivated to work in C-CoRN and extend it.

No part of the library is, strictly speaking, immutable: new lemmas can be added at any time to existing files, if they are felt to belong there. In this way, new lemmas then become immediately available to other users. In practice, though, the lower in the tree structure of Figure 1 a file is, the less often it will be changed.

Coupled with this method of working, the documentation system described above makes looking for a particular statement a simpler process than in most of the systems the authors are acquainted with. But in addition to this, naming conventions are adopted throughout C-CoRN that allow experienced users to find a specific lemma even more quickky without needing to consult the documentation. These naming conventions are too specific to be explainable in a short amount of space; the interested reader can find them throughout the C-CoRN documentation.

## Abstract Approach

One finds two approaches to formalizing algebraic operations. On the one hand one just has concrete types for various number structures, like the natural numbers, the integers, the real numbers and the complex numbers, and for each of those one defines a separate set of arithmetical operations. On the other hand – which is the approach that is followed in C-CoRN, as described in [19] – one can have a hierarchy of the commonly appearing algebraic structures in mathematics, such as groups, rings, fields and ordered fields, and then instantiate these to specific number structures. In this approach the theory of the real numbers will not refer to a specific type of real numbers, but just to a type of 'real number structure', which later can be instantiated to a concrete model[2].

This second approach has advantages and disadvantages. An advantage is that the theory that is developed for a certain structure is maximally reusable. For example, the group properties can be reused for the integers, the rational numbers, the real numbers, polynomials, vectors in a vector space, and so on. In our abstract approach each of these structures will be just an instance of the already existing algebraic type of groups, and the laws that were proved for this type will be immediately available. In the first approach the same theory has to be developed over and over again every time a new structure with the same algebraic properties is defined.

Another advantage is that the same notation will be used for the same algebraic operation. This is especially useful in a system that has no overloading, like Coq. For instance, in the first approach one has different additions on natural numbers, integers, real numbers, while in C-CoRN all of these are simply written as (x[+]y).

A third advantage is that the development of the theory will more closely follow the development of algebra in a mathematical textbook.

The main disadvantage of the abstract approach is that the terms that occur in the formalization are usually much bigger, because they have to refer to the specific structure used. Also, because of the hierarchy of the types of algebraic structures, there will be functions needed in the terms to get to the right kind of algebraic structure. This is not a problem for the user, since all these operations are implicit: the specific structure is generally an implicit argument, while the functions that map algebraic structures are coercions. But internally these terms are big, so it slows down the processing of the formalization by Coq.

---

[2] In C-CoRN this algebraic hierarchy is formalized using record types, making the abstract structures first class citizens (types) of the system. Another way to proceed (which wasn't available at the time C-CoRN was started) would be to use Coq's modules.

Another slight disadvantage of this approach is that sometimes proofs can be less direct than in the case where all functions are concretely defined. This also affects program extraction. For instance, if one knows that one is dealing with the rational numbers, a proof might be possible that gives a much better extracted program. In the case that one has to give a proof from an abstract specification, this optimization might not be available.

**Automation**

An important part of the C-CoRN library consists in tools designed to aid in its own development. Together with definitions, notations and lemmas, several automated tactics are defined throughout C-CoRN.

These tactics vary in complexity and in their underlying mechanism. Thus, there are several tactics based on Coq's `Auto` mechanism, which simply performs Prolog-style depth-first search on a given collection of lemmas. Each tactic is designed for a specific subject, such as equational reasoning in different algebraic structures (`Algebra`) or proving continuity of real-valued functions (`Contin`).

Other tactics base themselves on the principle of reflection to tackle wider classes of problems in a more uniform and more efficient way. We mention `rational`, described in detail in [19], which provides proofs of equalities in rings or fields, but can solve a much larger class of goals than `Algebra`; and `Deriv`, described in [14], a reflective tactic which can prove goals of the form $f' = g$ when $f$ and $g$ are real-valued (partial) functions. Although tactics based on reflection are usually more powerful than those based on `Auto`, they are also more time consuming when the goals are simple and usually cannot infer as much information from the context as the latter.

Finally, an interface for equational reasoning is also provided via the `step` tactic. This tactic allows the user to replace a goal of the form $R(a, b)$, where $R$ is a relation and $a$ and $b$ have appropriate types, by either $R(c, b)$ or $R(a, c)$, where $c$ is a parameter given by the user. This tactic looks through a database of lemmas that state extensionality of (various types of) relations, and chooses the one which applies to $R$. Then it applies either `Algebra` or `rational` to prove the equational side condition generated by the lemma.

The `step` tactic has been generalized to work in a much wider domain than that of C-CoRN and is now included in the standard distribution of Coq.

# 6   Applications

Besides the direct interest of formalizing mathematics *per se*, there are some interesting applications that are either being explored at present or are planned for the near future.

One of the consequences of working constructively, and therefore without any axioms, is that, according to the Curry-Howard isomorphism, every proof is an algorithm. In particular, any proof term whose type is an existential statement is also an algorithm whose output satisfies the property at hand. This allows us to obtain correct programs for free, which is an interesting possibility.

In Coq there is an extraction mechanism available that readily transforms proof terms into executable ML-programs (see [26]). Marking techniques are used to reduce the size of extracted programs significantly, as most of the information in the proofs regards *correctness* rather than *execution* of the algorithm and can be safely removed. In [15] it is described how this extraction mechanism was used to obtain, from the formalized proof of the Fundamental Theorem of Algebra, an algorithm that computes roots of non-constant polynomials. At the time of writing the extracted program is too complex and does not produce any output in a reasonable amount of time; but the same method has been used to produce a *correct* program that can compute 150 digits of $e$ in little over one minute.

Of course, the performance of these extracted programs can in no way compete with that of any existing computer algebra system. For these reasons other approaches to proving correctness of programs are known and studied in computer science. However, we feel that in situations where correctness is more important than speed, program extraction might one day be successfully used.

## 7   Future Developments

There are presently a number of different directions in which we would like to see C-CoRN extended in a near future.

One goal is to extend the library by adding new branches of mathematics to the formalization or by building upon existing ones. In particular, the following areas are considered important:

**Complex Analysis:** Presently there exist a usable algebraic theory of complex numbers and a formalization of one-variable Real Calculus. These provide a basis upon which a formalization of Complex Analysis can be built.

**Basic Topology:** There are no general topology results available in C-CoRN yet; a development of the elementary properties of topological spaces would not only extend the library, but would probably make it possible to unify different parts of the library where instances of the same general lemmas are proved for specific structures.

**Metric Spaces:** Similarly, several of the properties of the absolute value operation on real numbers and its correspondent on complex numbers are in fact instances of properties which can be proved for any distance function on a metric space. We hope that the small development currently existing in C-CoRN will enable us to prove these and other similar results in a more uniform manner.

**Number Theory:** On a different line, number theory seems to be a subject where an attempt at formalization could be very successful, since Coq is a system where it is for example very easy to use induction techniques. Furthermore, the preexistence of a library of real analysis would make it much easier to prove results which require manipulating specific integrals.

**Group Theory:** This is also a subject that would be interesting to explore in C-CoRN. Although we have built an algebraic hierarchy which includes monoids, groups and abelian groups among its inhabitants, so far most of the development has been done only when at least a ring structure is available. Formalizing important results of group theory would be an important test ground for the usability and power of the algebraic hierarchy.

On a different note, we would like to develop applications of C-CoRN. There are currently plans to do this in two different ways:

**Program Extraction:** The new extraction mechanism of Coq [26] has made it possible to extract and execute programs from the C-CoRN library, as has been explained in [16]. However, the results so far have been slightly disappointing. Recent work has shown that much improvement may be obtainable, and we hope to pursue this topic.

**Education:** A formalization of basic algebra and analysis should not only be useful for additional formalizations (by researchers) but also for students, who can use it as course material. This addresses a different audience, to which the material has to be explained and motivated (using lots of examples). We believe that a formalization can be useful as a starting point for an interactive set of course notes, because it gives the additional (potential) advantages that all the math is already present in a formal way (with all the structure and semantics that one would want to have) and that one can let students actually work with the proofs (varying upon them, making interactive proof exercises). In the *Algebra Interactive* project (see [11]), a basic course in Algebra has been turned into an interactive course, using applets to present algebraic algorithms. Another experience, on the presentation of proofs in interactive course notes, is reported in [7]. We want to investigate C-CoRN as a basis for such a set of course notes.

For usability it is very important to have good automation tactics and powerful (or at least helpful) user interfaces. Along these lines, we have some concrete plans:

**Dealing with *In*equalities:** It would be nice to have a `rational`-like tactic to reason about inequalities in ordered structures.

## 8     Related Work

The Coq system is distributed with a basic standard library. There is quite some duplication between what one finds there and what we offer in C-CoRN.

In particular the theory of real numbers by Micaela Mayero [27] is part of the standard library. This duplication extends to the tactics: what there is called the `field` tactic is the `rational` tactic in C-CoRN. However, the two theories of real numbers are quite different. Mayero's reals are classical and based on a set of axioms that constructively cannot be satisfied, while the C-CoRN reals are constructive and also have various concrete implementations. Another difference is that in the Mayero reals division is a total function which is always defined (although it is unspecified what happens when one divides by 0), which is not an option in a constructive setting. In C-CoRN, division can only be written when one knows that the denominator is apart from 0. This means that it gets three arguments, of which the third is a proof of this apartness. This difference also shows in the tactics `field` and `rational`. The first generates proof obligations about denominators, while the second does not need to do this, because this information already is available in the terms.

Besides the standard library, all significant Coq formalizations are collected in an archive of contributions. From the point of view of the Coq project, C-CoRN is just one of these contributions, although it is currently a considerable part of this archive. The contributions of Coq have hardly any relation to each other. There is no effort to integrate the Coq contributions into a whole, like we tried to do with the C-CoRN library. Everyone uses the standard library, but hardly anyone uses any of the other contributions.

Apart from Coq [13], there are several other systems for formalization of mathematics that have a serious library. The most important of these are: Mizar [28], HOL98 [33] and HOL Light [24], Isabelle/Isar [30], NuPRL/Meta-PRL [12] and PVS [31]. (Other systems for formalization of mathematics, like for instance Theorema [5] and Ωmega [32], do not have large libraries.)

The largest library of formalized mathematics in the world is the library of the Mizar system, which is called Mizar Mathematical Library or MML. To give an idea of the size of this library: the source of the C-CoRN repository is about 2 Mb, the sources of the Coq standard library together with the Coq contributions are about 25 Mb, while the source of MML is about 55 Mb. (Of course these sizes are not completely meaningful, as a Coq encoding of a proof probably has a different length from a Mizar encoding of the same proof. Still it is an indication of the relative sizes of the libraries of both systems.)

Some of the theorems that are the highlights of C-CoRN are also proved in MML, like the Fundamental Theorem of Algebra and the Fundamental Theorem of Calculus.

Unlike the Coq contributions, the MML is integrated into a whole: all Mizar articles use all the other articles that are available. So our goals with C-CoRN are similar to that of MML. However, there also are some differences. First, the MML is classical, while almost all of C-CoRN currently is constructive. More importantly, although the MML is revised all the time to make it more coherent mathematically, until recently theorems were never moved. In C-CoRN related theorems are in the same file, but in MML a theorem could potentially be found anywhere. Recently the Encyclopedia of Mathematics in Mizar project (or EMM) has been started to improve this situation, but it is still in an early stage. Another difference is that in C-CoRN arithmetic is formalized in an abstract style, as discussed above. In the MML both the abstract and concrete styles are available, but the majority of the formalizations use the latter.

Mizar users are encouraged to submit their formalizations to the MML. Mizar is not designed to allow large libraries that are separate from the MML: the performance of the system degrades if one tries to do this. When Mizar users submit their work to MML they sign a form to give up the copyright to their work, so that it can be revised if necessary by the Mizar developers. An approach on how to integrate work by others into C-CoRN still has to be developed. It will need to address the issues that (1) we want to encourage people who develop libraries on top of C-CoRN to integrate them into it and (2) we want everyone to be able to revise other people's work without getting conflicts over this. This was discussed more extensively on page 96.

The other systems mentioned above have a library similar to that of Coq. These libraries also have similarities to the C-CoRN library. For instance, in the HOL Light library both the Fundamental Theorem of Algebra and the Fundamental Theorem of Calculus are proved. The Isabelle, NuPRL and PVS libraries also contain proofs of the Fundamental Theorem of Calculus. A comparison between these proofs and the one in C-CoRN can be found in [14].

### Acknowledgments

We are grateful to everyone who has contributed to the development of C-CoRN, either by contributing files or by contributing ideas. We especially thank Henk Barendregt, Sébastien Hinderer, Iris Loeb, Milad Niqui, Randy Pollack, Bas Spitters, Dan Synek and Jan Zwanenburg. We would also like to thank the anonymous referees, whose valuable suggestions much helped improve the quality of this paper.

This work was partially supported by the European Project IST-2001-33562 MoWGLI. The first author was also supported by the Portuguese Fundação para a Ciência e Tecnologia, both under grant SFRH / BD / 4926 / 2001 and under CLC project FibLog FEDER POCTI / 2001 / MAT / 37239.

# References

1. A. Asperti, B. Buchberger, and J. Davenport (eds.), *Mathematical Knowledge Management, 2nd International Conference, MKM 2003*, LNCS 2594, Springer, 2003.
2. A. Asperti and B. Wegner, MOWGLI – A New Approach for the Content Description in Digital Documents, in: *Proc. of the 9th Intl. Conference on Electronic Resources and the Social Role of Libraries in the Future*, vol. 1, Autonomous Republic of Crimea, Ukraine, 2002.
3. A. Bailey, *The machine-checked literate formalisation of algebra in type theory*, PhD thesis, University of Manchester, 1998.
4. E. Bishop, *Foundations of Constructive Analysis*, McGraw-Hill, 1967.
5. B. Buchberger et al., An Overview on the Theorema project, in: W. Kuechlin (ed.), *Proceedings of ISSAC'97*, Maui, Hawaii, 1997, ACM Press.
6. Constructive Coq Repository at Nijmegen, `http://c-corn.cs.kun.nl/`.
7. P. Cairns and J. Gow, A theoretical analysis of hierarchical proofs, in: Asperti et al., [1], pp. 175–187.
8. The CALCULEMUS Initiative, `http://www.calculemus.net/`.

9. P. Callaghan, Z. Luo, J. McKinna, and R. Pollack (eds.), *Types for Proofs and Programs, Proc. of the International Workshop TYPES 2000*, LNCS 2277, Springer, 2001.

10. O. Caprotti, D.P. Carlisle, and A.M. Cohen, The OpenMath Standard, version 1.1, 2002, `http://www.openmath.org/cocoon/openmath/standard/`.

11. A. Cohen, H. Cuypers, and H. Sterk, *Algebra Interactive!*, Springer, 1999.

12. R.L. Constable et al., *Implementing Mathematics with the Nuprl Development System*, Prentice-Hall, NJ, 1986.

13. The Coq Development Team, *The Coq Proof Assistant Reference Manual, Version 7.2*, January 2002, `http://pauillac.inria.fr/coq/doc/main.html`.

14. L. Cruz-Filipe, Formalizing real calculus in Coq, Technical report, NASA, Hampton, VA, 2002.

15. L. Cruz-Filipe, A constructive formalization of the Fundamental Theorem of Calculus, In Geuvers and Wiedijk [20], pp. 108–126.

16. L. Cruz-Filipe and B. Spitters, Program extraction from large proof developments, in: *TPHOLs 2003*, LNCS, pp. 205–220, Springer, 2003.

17. J.-C. Filliâtre, *CoqDoc: a Documentation Tool for Coq, Version 1.05*, The Coq Development Team, September 2003, `http://www.lri.fr/~filliatr/coqdoc/`.

18. H. Geuvers and M. Niqui, Constructive reals in Coq: Axioms and categoricity, in: [9], pp. 79–95.

19. H. Geuvers, R. Pollack, F. Wiedijk, and J. Zwanenburg, The algebraic hierarchy of the FTA Project, *Journal of Symbolic Computation*, pp. 271–286, 2002.

20. H. Geuvers and F. Wiedijk (eds.), *Types for Proofs and Programs*, LNCS 2464, Springer-Verlag, 2003.

21. H. Geuvers, F. Wiedijk, and J. Zwanenburg, Equational reasoning via partial reflection, in: *TPHOLs 2000*, LNCS 1869, pp. 162–178, Springer, 2000.

22. H. Geuvers, F. Wiedijk, and J. Zwanenburg, A constructive proof of the Fundamental Theorem of Algebra without using the rationals, in: [9], pp. 96–111.

23. F. Guidi and I. Schena, A query language for a metadata framework about mathematical resources, in: Asperti et al. [1], pp. 105–118.

24. J. Harrison, *The HOL Light manual (1.1)*, 2000, http://www.cl.cam.ac.uk/users/jrh/hol-light/manual-1.1.ps.gz.

25. M. Kohlhase, OMDoc: Towards an Internet Standard for the Administration, Distribution and Teaching of Mathematical Knowledge, In *Proceedings of Artificial Intelligence and Symbolic Computation*, LNAI, Springer-Verlag, 2000.

26. P. Letouzey, A new extraction for Coq, in: Geuvers and Wiedijk [20], pp. 200–219.

27. M. Mayero, *Formalisation et automatisation de preuves en analyses réelle et numérique*, PhD thesis, Université Paris VI, December 2001.

28. M. Muzalewski, *An Outline of PC Mizar*, Fond. Philippe le Hodey, Brussels, 1993, `http://www.cs.kun.nl/~freek/mizar/mizarmanual.ps.gz`.

29. P. Naumov, M.-O. Stehr, and J. Meseguer, The HOL/NuPRL Proof Translator: A Practical Approach to Formal Interoperability, in: R.J. Boulton and P.B. Jackson (eds.), *TPHOLs 2001*, vol. 2152 of *LNCS*, pp. 329–345, Springer, 2001.

30. T. Nipkow, L.C. Paulson, and M. Wenzel, *Isabelle/HOL – A Proof Assistant for Higher-Order Logic*, vol. 2283 of *LNCS*, Springer, 2002.

31. N. Shankar, S. Owre, J. M. Rushby, and D.W.J. Stringer-Calvert, *The PVS System Guide*, SRI International, December 2001, `http://pvs.csl.sri.com/`.

32. J. Siekmann et al, Proof Development with Omega, In *Proceedings of CADE-18*, LNAI, Springer-Verlag, 2002.

33. K. Slind, *HOL98 Draft User's Manual*, Cambridge UCL, January 1999, http://hol.sourceforge.net/.

# Classifying Differential Equations on the Web

Dirk Draheim[2], Winfried Neun[1], and Dima Suliman[1]

[1] Konrad-Zuse-Zentrum für Informationstechnik Berlin
Takustr. 7, 14195 Berlin, Germany
{neun,suliman}@zib.de
[2] Freie Universität Berlin, Institute of Computer Science
Takustr. 9, 14195 Berlin, Germany
draheim@acm.org

**Abstract.** In this paper we describe the semantic analysis of differential equations given in the ubiquitous formats MathML and OpenMath. The analysis is integrated in a deployed Web indexing framework. Starting from basic classifications for differential equations the proposed system architecture is amenable to extensions for further reconstruction of mathematical content on the Web. The syntactic analysis of mathematical formulae given in the considered formats must overcome ambiguities that stem from the fact that formula particles may have different encodings, which are in principle completely arbitrary. However, it turns out that the syntactic analysis can be done straightforward given some natural heuristic assumptions.

## 1 Introduction

The motivation [15] for this work stems from several tasks we have been dealing with during recent years. We are working in the field of computer algebra, a community that has substantially contributed to the definition of mathematical encodings like MathML [13] or OpenMath [16]. We are also working in the Math-Net project [14], which collects mathematical information worldwide and tries to provide mathematicians with high quality information on mathematical subjects. Beside information on the organizational structure of the mathematical institutes, preprints and other papers on the Web are collected and analyzed to extract relevant information. Since MathML and OpenMath have gained wide acceptance by institutions like W3C and software manufacturers, it can be expected that documents will use these encodings for formulae to a larger extent.

An important detail is that MathML comes in two different styles, called Presentation Markup and Content Markup. The latter describes the mathematical content of an expression, whereas the first defines the rendering of the expression. Hence this widely used style does not contain rich information about the mathematical meaning.

We have started to reconstruct mathematical content from formulae given in MathML and OpenMath with the concrete problem of analyzing differential equations.

A. Asperti et al. (Eds.): MKM 2004, LNCS 3119, pp. 104–115, 2004.

Our current implementation supports the following orthogonal classifications:

- order
- ordinary vs. partial
- linear vs. non-linear
- homogeneous vs. non-homogeneous

Modeling with differential equations is common in science. Therefore, if a researcher looks at a collection of mathematical papers the information on the type of differential equations used therein is interesting for him or her. The information may support the researcher with respect to his or her own modeling and may lead to methods for solving considered problems. A typical example is Drach's differential equation. This is not well-known even among researchers in the field. An application for our approach could be to find all occurrences of Drach' equation in the mathematical literature.

The paper proceeds as follows. Sect. 2 discusses the problems encountered in parsing MathML and OpenMath formulae. The several classifications of differential equations are defined in a succinct declarative pseudo code style in Sect. 3. The architecture of the proposed implementation is described in Sect. 4. The paper finishes with a discussion on further work, related work, and a conclusion in Sects. 5, 6, and 7.

# 2   Parsing MathML and OpenMath

Problems arise in parsing formulae given in MathML and OpenMath formats, because different amount of semantic clarification is needed for the several formats prior to semantic processing. MathML comes along with two versions, i.e., MathML Content Markup and MathML Presentation Markup. Whereas MathML Content Markup and OpenMath are oriented towards meanings of formulae from the outset, MathML Presentation Markup is designed for the task of rendering formulae. Therefore, if targeting semantic analysis eventually, parsing MathML Presentation Markup poses significantly more problems.

## 2.1   MathML Presentation Markup

In general the several possible particles of a formula have arbitrary appropriate encodings in MathML Presentation Markup – an encoding is appropriate as long as the intended visualization is achieved. Fortunately, it is possible to assume that the vast majority of MathML Presentation Markup documents found on the Web is not directly written or edited by the authors, but produced with one of the ubiquitous mathematical software tools, i.e. Maple [12], Mathematica [18], or WebEQ [4]. Therefore, the problem of ambiguity boils down to a thorough analysis of the common tools' encodings of formula particles. Furthermore the MathML Presentation Markup standard [13] makes a couple of recommendations on how to encode certain constructs and, fortunately, the common tools more or less adhere to these recommendations. We delve into the topics of encoding

derivatives, characters, and operator and function applications. Table 1 summarizes the encodings yielded by the three leading mathematical software tools.

**Encoding of Derivatives.** There are two well-known presentations for derivatives in mathematical ad-hoc notation. Accordingly, the MathML standard pro-
poses two different Presentation Markup encodings of derivatives. For example,
the non-partial derivative of a function $f$ can be written in the following two
ways:

$$f' \tag{1}$$

$$\frac{d}{dx} f \tag{2}$$

The MathML Presentation Markup encoding for (1) is the following:

```
<mrow>
  <msup>
    <mi> f </mi>
    <mo> &#8242; </mo>
  </msup>
</mrow>
```

The MathML Presentation Markup encoding for (2) is the following:

```
<mrow>
  <mfrac>
    <mo> &DifferentialD; </mo>
    <mrow>
      <mo> &DifferentialD; </mo>
      <mi> x </mi>
    </mrow>
  </mfrac>
  <mi> f </mi>
</mrow>
```

**Character Encoding.** Unicode characters or entities can be used to encode
the same character. For example, the prime character in (1) is encoded by a
Unicode character:

```
<mo> &#8242; </mo>
```

However, an alternative encoding for this is the following:

```
<mo> ' </mo>
```

The problem to deal with many encodings for the same symbol is not difficult.
The various encodings just have to be reflected by the grammar. The problem
is rather to be aware of all possible encodings of a symbol. An allied problem
is described in Sect. 4.1: a symbol with a predefined meaning may give rise to
unsolvable ambiguity if it is not used with the intended meaning by the formula's
author.

**Operator and Function Application.** It makes a difference whether the produced MathML code contains invisible operators or not. Invisible elements can affect the appearance of the formula in browsers and may prevent ambiguity. Consider the following MathML code fragment:

```
<mi>x</mi>
<mi>y</mi>
```

Tools may visualize this code fragment as $xy$. However, it is not clear which of the following meanings the author has had in mind in writing this fragment:

- $x \times y$
- $x \wedge y$
- $x(y)$

The ambiguity of just sequencing the variables $x$ and $y$ can be overcome, if the MathML invisible operators InvisibleTimes or applyFunction are utilized. Inserting one of these elements explicitly between the identifiers $x$ and $y$ makes the meaning obvious. Even bracketing for function application cannot always adequately replace the utilization of invisible elements. Though $f(x, y)$ is unlikely to encode something different than the application of $f$ to $x$ and $y$, the formula $f(x + 1)$ still can have two different meanings, i.e. the application of $f$ to $x + 1$ or otherwise the multiplication $f \times (x + 1)$. Unfortunately, the tools Mathematica [18] and WebEQ do not enforce the production of necessary invisible operators. Therefore heuristics must be employed in parsing operator and function application, e.g. based on the assumption that certain names are rather used as function names than basic variable names and vice versa.

**Table 1.** Different encodings of formula particles by different formulae editing tools

| Encoding | Maple | Mathematica | WebEQ |
|---|---|---|---|
| derivatives | mfrac | mfrac/msup | mfrac/msup |
| character encoding | entity | Unicode | Unicode/entity |
| multiplication | explicitly | explicitly/sequencing | sequencing |
| function application | explicitly | explicitly/bracketing | explicitly/sequencing/bracketing |

## 2.2   MathML Content Markup and OpenMath

MathML Content Markup focuses on the mathematical semantics of formulae. With Content Markup it is easy to distinguish whether $fx$ means $f(x)$ or $f * x$, which makes the analysis of the formula much easier for our purposes. However, it is common sense that only a too limited subset of mathematical notation is covered by MathML Content Markup by itself. Therefore the csymbol element, which is available since the MathML version 2.0, allows Content Markup to embed elements from other notations, e.g. from OpenMath or Mathematica. In such a case heuristics must be used to find out which element is actually meant. Another problem is that MathML Presentation Markup and Content

Markup are often connected in so-called mixed or parallel markup. This way both rendering aspects and mathematical content are included in the representation of a formula. Again MathML Content Markup comes in different dialects depending on the producing tool.

OpenMath is an alternative for the encoding of mathematical formulae that is older than MathML and attempts to solve the problem in a much more rigorous way than MathML. OpenMath is strictly content oriented and enables semantically rich encodings. Each object that is used in an OpenMath encoding includes a reference to a content dictionary, which is a mathematical definition of the object. For example, the operator plus used in different rings refers to different objects in separate OpenMath content dictionaries. Thus we have to integrate content dictionaries into the parsing process. Content dictionaries are created and collected by the OpenMath Society.

## 3    Supported Classifications of Differential Equations

The supported classifications of differential equations encompass the order of an equation, the question whether an equation is ordinary or partial, whether it is linear, and whether it is homogeneous. A succinct definition of these classifications is provided in Fig. 1. Ad-hoc abstract syntax notation and declarative notation is used for this purpose. In the abstract syntax definitions all items are non-terminals. In particular, we do not specify the set of variables var and the set of operations op.

Note that the actual LISP code for the classification used in the implementation of our approach – see Sect. 4 – is, in effect not more complex than the declarative definitions given in Fig. 1. For the purpose of analyzing a differential equation an equation is simply a term composed of variables, operations, and derivatives. A derivative consists of the target function name and the derivate variables. The list of derivate variables may be empty, this way representing the genuine occurrence of the equation's target function. For the definition of linearity it can be assumed that the differential equation adheres to the common sum-of-product normal form, expressed by the abstract syntax notation normalized. Furthermore it can be assumed that the differential equation's target function is unique. In our implementation these assumptions hold because of the employed computer algebra stage and verifier stage. The homogeneity of a differential equation can be specified syntactically without detouring.

## 4    Solution System Architecture

Separation of concerns leads to a straightforward compiler stage architecture for the solution system, see Fig. 2. After finding a formula encoded in MathML or OpenMath it is parsed and an abstract syntax tree is built. We have used ANTLR [17] to build the parser. Printing the abstract syntax tree yields the formula in LISP format. If the formula represents a supported differential equation it is further processed by the REDUCE [8] computer algebra system and the

$$derivative ::= var\ var*$$
$$equation ::=\quad var$$
$$|\ derivative$$
$$|\ op\ equation_1\ \dots\ equation_n$$

$$order : \boldsymbol{equation} \to \mathbb{N}$$

$$order\ eq \overset{\text{DEF}}{=} \begin{cases} 0 & ,\ eq \in \boldsymbol{var} \\ n & ,\ eq = f\ v_1 \dots v_n \in \boldsymbol{derivative} \\ max \bigcup_{1 \le i \le n} order\ eq_i & ,\ eq = op\ eq_1 \dots eq_n \end{cases}$$

$$derivations : \boldsymbol{equation} \to 2^{\boldsymbol{var}}$$

$$derivations\ eq \overset{\text{DEF}}{=} \begin{cases} \emptyset & ,\ eq \in \boldsymbol{var} \\ \{v_1 \dots v_n\} & ,\ eq = f\ v_1, \dots v_n, \in \boldsymbol{derivative} \\ \bigcup_{1 \le i \le n} derivations\ eq_i & ,\ eq = op\ eq_1 \dots eq_n \end{cases}$$

$$ordinary : \boldsymbol{equation} \to \mathbb{B}$$
$$partial : \boldsymbol{equation} \to \mathbb{B}$$

$$ordinary\ eq \overset{\text{DEF}}{=} |derivations\ eq| = 1$$
$$partial\ eq \overset{\text{DEF}}{=} \neg\ ordinary\ eq$$

$$\texttt{normalized} ::= (\texttt{equation? derivative?})*$$

$$linear : \boldsymbol{normalized} \to \mathbb{B}$$

$$linear\ eq_1\ (f\ vars_1) \dots eq_n\ (f\ vars_n) \overset{\text{DEF}}{=} \bigvee_{1 \le i \le n} f \notin eq_i$$

$$\texttt{homogeneous} ::= (\texttt{equation? derivative})*$$

**Fig. 1.** Definition of the supported classification of differential equations. Non-terminals of the abstract syntax are used in the declarative definitions in bold face in order to denote the respective syntactic categories

formula is transformed into a normal form. Afterwards LISP programs classify the formula. The result of the classification is printed out in Summary Object Interchange Format (SOIF) because the classification is embedded into the Harvest system [1, 11], which uses SOIF data for its internal information storage and exchange.

The proposed solution is scalable with respect to functionality in several means. Future formats can be integrated easily – the abstract syntax serves as a

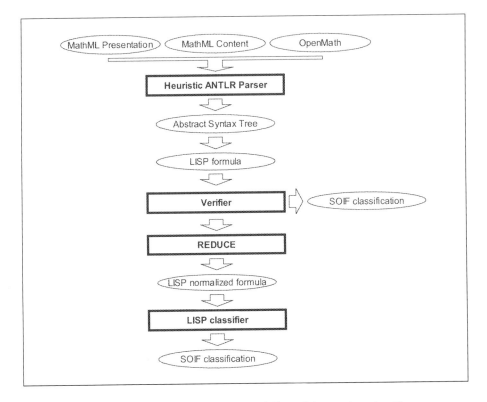

**Fig. 2.** The compiler stages of the differential equation classifier

mediator between different formats. Because of the computer algebra stage the software system is prepared for projected advanced semantic analysis.

## 4.1  Parsing Problems

First of all we assume that the MathML and OpenMath code under consideration are syntactically correct. Thus we specified non-validating grammars to reconstruct the content of the represented formulae. Parsing is aborted if it can be recognized lexically that the considered formula is actually no differential equation, for example, because it encompasses elements for encoding integrals or matrices. We cannot assume that the rules for the so-called proper grouping in Sect. 3.3 of [13] are always followed. Thus unnecessary mrow elements are escaped. Unnecessary mrow elements are those which are not nested within other elements, e.g., mfrac or msup elements. Only attributes relevant to differential equations are recognized.

The Presentation Markup grammar needs to distinguish between two kinds of identifiers, i.e., monad operators and simple variables. If an ambiguity occurs our heuristic solution decides in favor of the monad operator. For example, <mi> sin </mi> always represents the sinus function even if there is no applyFunction element next to it.

A differential equation consists of variables, numbers, differential quotients, and functions, which are bound by operators. In MathML Content Markup and OpenMath the grammar has just to follow the apply structure of the formula in order to reconstruct it. However, with respect to the actual operator structure parsing a formula encoded in MathML Presentation Markup is more complicated because the grammar has to define several internal levels to correctly obtain the priority of arithmetical operations.

## 4.2    Further Processing

After parsing a verifier checks whether a given formula actually can be considered a proper differential equation. For example, it is checked whether the target function is unique across all the equation's derivatives. If the target function is not unique the equation stems perhaps from a differential equation system, may be interesting, but not amenable to the classifications examined in this paper.

For the purpose to store the result in a unified format, the intermediate result is processed with computer algebra methods. Simplification rules are applied and a normal form is achieved. The processing identifies dependent and independent variables. As a result the derivatives and the target function are factored out so that the analysis of linearity and degree are simplified. REDUCE has been the computer algebra system of choice because it is a proven system and because REDUCE formulae can be denoted by LISP S-expressions. ANTLR generated parsers build abstract syntax trees as two dimensional presentation of the formula that can be printed out as LISP S-expressions and can be forwarded directly to REDUCE.

## 4.3    Integration into Harvest

The resulting classifier is embedded into an instance of the Harvest system – see Fig. 3 – that is hosted by the Math-Net project. Harvest is a distributed search system; the main components of Harvest are the gatherer and the broker. The gatherer collects and summarizes the resources on the Web. The broker indexes the collected information and answers queries via a Web interface. Gatherer and broker communicate using an attribute-value stream protocol, the proprietary SOIF. The gatherer triggers different summarizers for different kinds of documents. The available set of summarizers neither supports MathML nor Open-Math resources. We provided appropriate new summarizers for these resources – MathML can be found on the Web in XML files explicitly tagged as MathML or in XML files; OpenMath can be found in XML files.

## 5    Further Work

Currently we are working on the integration of a general formula search facility into our system. The problem of searching formulae, i.e., querying for formulae that match a given target formula, is different from querying formulae that match

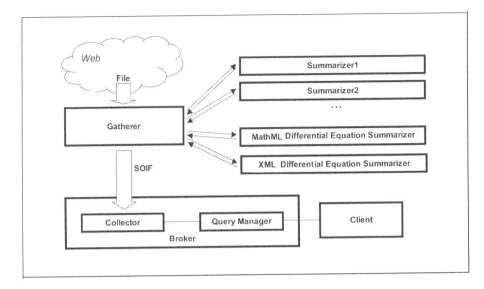

**Fig. 3.** Integration of the differential equation classifier as a summarizer into the Harvest system

given classification options. A merely textual approach for searching formulae is obviously not sufficient. Therefore each approach for searching formulae must fix a notion of similarity between formulae. Different degrees of similarity are conceivable. At a very basic level one wants to consider equivalent formulae as equal. Similarly formulae should be considered equal up to renaming of variables. However, more sophisticated similarities between formulae might be of interest. For example, two formulae are similar, if they can be constructed from each other by general term rewriting. However, subtle pragmatic questions now arise that can only be resolved by heuristic decisions: what is the appropriate granularity of term substitutions? Should it be possible to search for instances of a target formula? Or should it rather be possible to search for generalizations of a target formula?

A great deal of work with respect to questions like these has been done in the SearchFor project [3] at the INRIA Sophia-Antipolis Research Center. We are trying to utilize the results of the SearchFor system in our project. In principle, there are two basic approaches to this. In the brute force approach a converter from the S-expression format to the CAML data structure format is developed so that the SearchFor code can be reused operatively. In the reverse engineering approach the CAML code of the SearchFor system is investigated and reimplemented in LISP code.

Furthermore it would be interesting to fix formal semantics for notions of similarity between formulae. Again the knowledge about formula similarity construction that is encapsulated in the SearchFor system could serve as a cornerstone for this work.

Based on a facility for searching formulae it would be neat to offer search options for well-known differential equations or differential equation patterns, like Abel's differential equation, the Bernoulli differential equation etc.

## 6    Related Work

In [9] a PROLOG-based document object model for XML documents is proposed. Transforming XML data into the so-called ▫eld notation results in an expert system against which rule-based queries can be executed. The approach is elaborated for XML documents in general and is applied to the concrete formats MathML Content Markup and OpenMath in particular. Furthermore [9] outlines the application of the approach to the classification of ordinary differential equations with respect to Kamke's list [10]. The notion of rule-based expert system has gained remarkable consideration in the eighties for building and exploiting knowledge bases – today's working knowledge base mining relies on statistical modeling methods rather than on proof theory. However, in the case of processing mathematical knowledge it is promising to employ a logical programming language, because term rewriting problems that typically occur can be tackled by the logical programming languages' unification mechanisms. Other approaches that employ logic programming language techniques for mathematical knowledge bases are described in [2] and [6, 7].

A similar approach was used in the TILU [5] project by Einwohner and Fateman. This project provides an alternative to algorithmic integration algorithms by integral table lookup. Special conditions which arise often in integration problems, e.g., special functions in the integrand, can be used to optimize the search of the formulae.

## 7    Conclusion

We expose the following assumptions and observations:

- The Web is a huge repository; this is particularly true for mathematical knowledge.
- Sophisticated search capabilities for mathematical Web resources are required by research and education.
- MathML and OpenMath can be expected to become de-facto standards for mathematical Web resources.
- Subtle notation issues arise in handling MathML and OpenMath.

We have undertaken the following steps:

- We have chosen the classification of differential equations as a challenging starting point of our project.
- Due to its separation of concerns, the chosen system architecture is scalable with respect to further formats and further classifications.

- The implementation is used in a working instance of the Web indexing framework Harvest.

It is further work to integrate a general formula search facility into our approach.

# References

1. C.M. Bowman, P.B. Danzig, D.R. Hardy, U. Manber, M.F. Schwartz, and D.P. Wessels, Harvest: A scalable, customizable discovery and access system, Technical Report CU-CS-732-94, University of Colorado, Boulder, USA, 1994.
2. S. Dalmas, M. Gaëtano, and C. Huchet, A deductive database for mathematical formulae, in: Proceedings of Design and Implementation of Symbolic Computation Systems, LNCS 1128, pp. 287–296, Springer, 1996.
3. S. Dalmas and M. Gaëtano, Indexing mathematics with SearchFor, presented at: International MathML Conference 2000 – MathML and Math on the Web, 2000.
4. Design Science Inc., WebEQ version 3.5, 2003.
5. T.H. Einwohner and R.J. Fateman, Searching techniques for integral tables, in: Proceedings ISSAC 1995, ACM, New York, 1995.
6. A. Franke and M. Kohlhase, System Description: MBASE, an Open Mathematical Knowledge Base, in: Proceedings of CADE 2000 – International Conference on Automated Deduction, pp. 455–459, LNCS 1831, Springer, 2000.
7. A. Franke and M. Kohlhase, MBase: representing knowledge and context for the integration of mathematical software systems, Journal of Symbolic Computation, 32(4), pp. 365–402, 2001.
8. A.C. Hearn, REDUCE 2: A system and language for algebraic manipulation, in: Proceedings of the 2nd ACM Symposium on Symbolic and Algebraic Manipulation, ACM Press, 1971.
9. B. D. Heumesser, D. Seipel, and U. Güntzer, An expert system for the flexible processing of XML-based mathematical knowledge in a PROLOG-environment, in: Proceedings of the Second International Conference on Mathematical Knowledge Management, Springer, 2003.
10. E. Kamke, Differentialgleichungen: Lösungsmethoden und Lösungen, Akademische Verlagsgesellschaft, 1967.
11. K. J. Lee, Development Status of Harvest, in: Proceedings of SINN'03 Conference – Worldwide Coherent Workforce, Satisfied Users: New Services For Scientific Information, 2003, http://www.isn-oldenburg.de/projects/SINN/sinn03/proceedings.html.
12. Maplesoft Inc., Maple version 9, 2003.
13. Mathematical Markup Language (MathML) Version 2.0, W3C Recommendation, 21 February 2001.
14. Math-Net, http://www.math-net.org.
15. W. Neun, Harvesting webpages that contain mathematical information, in: Proceedings of SINN'03 Conference – Worldwide Coherent Workforce, Satisfied Users: New Services For Scientific Information, 2003, http://www.isn-oldenburg.de/projects/SINN/sinn03/proceedings.html.
16. The OpenMath Web Site, http://www.openmath.org.

17. T.J. Parr, R.W. Quong, ANTLR: a predicated-LL(k) parser generator, in: Journal of Software-Practice & Experience, vol. 25, no. 7, pp. 789–810, John Wiley & Sons, July 1995.
18. Wolfram Research Inc., Mathematica version 5, 2003.

# Managing Heterogeneous Theories Within a Mathematical Knowledge Repository

Adam Grabowski[1] and Markus Moschner[2]

[1] Institute of Mathematics, University of Białystok
ul. Akademicka 2, 15-267 Białystok, Poland
adam@math.uwb.edu.pl
[2] Department of Statistics, University of Vienna
Universitätsstr. 5, A-1010 Vienna, Austria
moschm@logic.at

**Abstract.** The problem of the integrity of a computer managed mathematical knowledge repository is in the heart of MKM since mathematical vernacular is a language permitting plenty of ways in expressing the same meaning. The users of the library are naturally forced to choose certain way among many similar ones, unless different approaches are provided by developers. Mizar is a system for formalizing mathematical content which is sufficient mature and flexible for a coexistence of different approaches of concrete subjects. Considering Mizar formalizations of ortholattice theory we discuss a useful mechanism of coping with the heterogeneity of theories in a library of mathematical facts.

## 1 Introduction

One of the questions which occur during planning and building of mathematical knowledge repositories is: should be the system centralized or rather distributed? Both approaches are tested and more or less successfully used in the field which is in the core of MKM. On the one hand, distributed, not necessarily homogeneous network of systems specialized in the different disciplines (e.g. theorem provers, model searchers, proof checkers, user interfaces etc.) together with appropriate broker architecture seems to offer a broader, more efficient structure for a mathematician to work with – from a bright idea until the successful submission of his/her work for publication.

But if we restrict our considerings to one part of mathematical activity only – e.g. to developing and enhancing of the computer checked repository of formalized mathematical knowledge, we may find the broad system ineffective and hard to use, especially if a significant part of the system lifetime is spent on a communication/translating from one standard to another. We still need efficient techniques to make larger systems work more smoothly than we may to observe nowadays.

In the paper [19] presented at the MKM 2003 in Bertinoro, important questions were formulated: what exactly means the integrity of a repository, how to deal with a library to make it (more) homogeneous. We want to shed some light

A. Asperti et al. (Eds.): MKM 2004, LNCS 3119, pp. 116–129, 2004.

onto another side: what mechanisms are sufficiently feasible to enable different approaches to the same problem or other formulations of the similar notions. Obviously, in any sense it does not mean that the repository should contain all approaches available in the literature. The computer can serve here as a kind of Kerberos which will not accept badly formulated, illogical notions (compare [3]).

Some people within MKM community (mainly not those ones who work hard introducing new standards) believe that an ordinary user of a mathematical service should not be forced to use a notion/an approach against his personal preferences. Should he change them? Or should he abandon the service? None of the solutions seem to be satisfactory here.

It may be observed that a few problems are the decisive barriers for the use of computer-managed repositories by a pen-and-paper scientist. First, too much formalism is usually strongly avoided – formal or even just rigorous mathematics seems to be a pain in the neck for an ordinary mathematician. The notion of a formal proof sketch proposed by Wiedijk in [22] may be a kind of solution. Another main problem is search and retrieval of knowledge. Here we can point out the quality of a searching tool as well as the organization of the library. We can also accent – last but not least – the heterogeneity of approaches to the chosen notion. If the author prefers e.g. certain axiomatics (even if logically equivalent to a classical base), a constraint of using another one would be a serious drawback.

In this paper we describe some of the issues concerning the formalization of ortholattices based on the lattice theory formalized in the Mizar Mathematical Library (MML for short – see [14]). We propose also a new, heterogeneous approach to the lattice theory in one of the largest libraries of (proven!) mathematical facts. The structure of the paper is as follows. In the next three sections we give an outline of the theory of lattices, posets, and ortholattices formalized in MML. In the fifth section we discuss heterogeneous approaches to considered theories. At the end we present related work and draw some final remarks.

## 2    Classical Formalization of Lattices

As the primary aim of the formalization of lattices project were Boolean algebras, let us see for the description of lattices in MML from this perspective. Since the notion of a structure is fundamental to understand abstract mathematics (as defined in [18]), we assume basic knowledge of Mizar structures and selectors, thorough exposition of the topic and an overview of the Mizar type system can be find in [1].

According to the classical definition, Boolean algebras are 6–tuples of the form $\langle B, \vee, \wedge, ', 0, 1 \rangle$, where $\vee, \wedge$ are binary operations in $B$, $'$ is a function from $B$ into $B$ and $0, 1$ are two distinct elements of $B$. The axiomatics concerned with it is well known. The structures in Mizar are implemented as partial functions on selectors, which make e.g. merging structures more natural. Considering structures as ordered tuples, one might face the problem with merging operation, because catenation of sequences will not work properly.

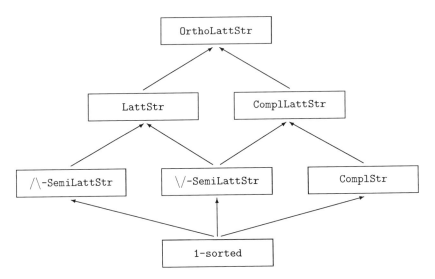

**Fig. 1.** The net of structures for lattice theory

Dependencies between underlying structures may be visualized as in Fig. 1. Arrows describe inheritance relation for selectors (fields of the structures). As it may be concluded, the backbone structure for almost all MML structures is `1-sorted` and all considered structures in the paper are descendants of it. Some of the objects have only one prefix (an ancestor) – in that case additional selectors are given. All others from the figure (besides `1-sorted`) act as items inheriting selector information. The number of multiprefixed structures in MML is relatively high (22 out of 91). Essentially structures play a role of signatures for domains. The definition of a structure provides only the typing data for operators (selectors). This information is enriched by the use of adjectives which will be explained in more detail later in the paper. Unfortunately, a user cannot define synonyms for selectors and structure names, i.e. upper and lower semilattice structures are defined separately, as well as corresponding notions. Hopefully, it will be reimplemented by the Mizar developers.

Even if synonyms for structures still cannot be defined, we may try to solve the problems concerned with it in a different way, thanks to the heterogeneous algebraic hierarchy, as we did in the case of the most famous questions answered with a help of an automated theorem prover.

In the early thirties of the previous century, Robbins posed the question if the equation which is a variant of one of the Huntington's axioms for Boolean algebras of the form

$$\big((a + b)' + (a + b')'\big)' = a,$$

where $a, b$ are arbitrary elements of the abstract algebra $\langle L, +, ' \rangle$ together with the commutativity and associativity still form a basis for the variety of Boolean algebras. For sixty years researchers could not find the answer to this question.

After McCune's solution of the Robbins problem [13] (that is, after proving that all Robbins algebras are Boolean), we decided to reuse existing formal apparatus for lattices and test the flexibility of this approach. The details of the experiment can be find in [9].

The choice of the appropriate structure was not straightforward. At a first glance, we might reuse developments from the algebraic ring theory. We wanted however to be as close as possible to Huntington's original paper where the underlying structure was $\langle B, \vee, \,' \rangle$. Moreover, intensive work with formalization of [2] (nearly 60 Mizar articles and numerous revisions of MML) made lattice theory developed in Mizar more suitable to further reuse. As a side-effect we encoded also a problem of a single axiom for Boolean algebras in terms of negation and disjunction and its 2-axiomatization due to Meredith.

We cite as an example the definition of a structure with signature (2,2,1) which may be treated as a skeleton of an ortholattice. It is prefixed by the lattice and structure with a complement operation.

```
struct (ComplLattStr, LattStr) OrthoLattStr
        (# carrier -> set,
    L_join, L_meet -> BinOp of the carrier,
            Compl -> UnOp of the carrier #);
```

The `ComplLattStr` has been introduced to keep defined notions and theorems at a satisfactory level of generality. It has two antecedents: upper semilattice – from which `L_join` is inherited, and a structure with a complement operation represented by the which field `Compl`. The `carrier` is inherited from both structures. For this structure the definition of the Robbins axiom seems to be very natural.

```
definition let L be non empty ComplLattStr;
    attr L is Robbins means          :: ROBBINS1:def 5
      for x, y being Element of L holds
        ((x + y)' + (x + y')')' = x;
end;
```

Actually, "+" is introduced as a synonymous notation for the lattice supremum operation, because it is simply shorter and easier to type. Unfortunately we could not use "'" because it is reserved for an identifier, so "'" is used instead. The attribute de_Morgan defines a natural connection (de Morgan laws) between join, meet, and complement operations.

```
definition let L be non empty OrthoLattStr;
    attr L is de_Morgan means          :: ROBBINS1:def 23
    for x, y being Element of L holds x "/\" y = (x' "\/" y')';
end;
```

Because from the Mizar structure definition only information about the arity and the type of the result on arguments of selectors can be obtained, we are forced to introduce the following attribute to ensure that the selector corresponding to the unary complement operation has actually all properties of the complement.

```
definition let L be non empty OrthoLattStr;
  attr L is well-complemented means      :: ROBBINS1:def 10
    for a being Element of L holds
    a' is_a_complement_of a;
end;
```

Table 1 summarizes used structures together with the names of the introduced new selectors (second column) together with their mother type (third column). It is easily seen which items do not introduce any new selectors. In the fourth column we give some of the adjectives defined for the appropriate structure. Inheritance mechanisms implemented in Mizar verifier allow for applying such attributes in all descendant structures. Since the adjective "Boolean" is only a shorthand for a list of some other adjectives, it is not included in the table.

**Table 1.** Basic types used in the formalization

| Structure | New selector | Type of introduced selector | Attribute |
|---|---|---|---|
| 1-sorted | carrier | set | non empty |
| ComplStr | Compl | UnOp of the carrier | |
| ∨-SemiLattStr | L_join | BinOp of the carrier | join-commutative join-associative join-idempotent upper-bounded |
| ∧-SemiLattStr | L_meet | BinOp of the carrier | meet-commutative meet-associative meet-idempotent lower-bounded |
| LattStr | none | n/a | join-absorbing meet-absorbing distributive |
| ComplLattStr | none | n/a | Robbins satisfying_DN_1 |
| OrthoLattStr | none | n/a | de_Morgan |

Now the partial correspondence between newly introduced Robbins and previously defined in MML Boolean algebras can be shown for lattices in the form of the conditional cluster registration which is cited below. Obviously, to visualize full equivalence of these algebras, the second implication should be also written with its rather straightforward proof that the Robbins equation is true in all BAs.

```
registration
  cluster Robbins join-associative join-commutative de_Morgan ->
    Boolean (non empty OrthoLattStr);
end;
```

The `OrthoLattStr` ensures that all the attributes (with "Boolean" at the top) for `LattStr` can be used. It can be read (and in fact is translated automatically) in natural language as "every lattice structure with associative and commutative join operation which satisfies Robbins axiom is also Boolean."

# 3   Orderings as an Alternative

From the mathematical point of view, an alternative approach for lattices, i.e. posets which have unique binary suprema and infima operations, is clearer and used even more often nowadays. What is especially important, it provides more homogeneous view for the theory as a whole since orderings present more general way to handle lattices, e.g. if we dropped some of the attributes of the internal relation.

Stepping from posets to lattices is done via "globalizing": a lattice $\mathcal{L}$ is a poset $\mathcal{P} = \langle P, \leq \rangle$ such that for arbitrary pair of elements of $P$ its infimum and supremum exist in $P$; i.e.:

$$\forall_{x,y \in P} \exists_{v,w \in P} \ v = inf\{x, y\} \wedge w = sup\{x, y\}.$$

Then the binary lattice operations of join and meet get identified with supremum and infimum of the set of arguments. Henceforth the basic lattice laws of commutativity, associativity, idempotence, and absorption correspond directly with partial order properties; thus one can turn from posets to an algebra of type $\langle 2, 2 \rangle$. Such a transit is justified by the common notion of semantics: a succedent $S$ follows from an antecedent $A$ only if for all possible valuations $val$ one has $eval(val, A) \leq eval(val, S)$ (with respect to the underlying poset).

Such an analogy (with logics) can be pursued furthermore. Bounds for a lattice may be introduced just mimicking the role of Boolean values as used in logics maximum $\top$ and minimum $\bot$; i.e.: $\forall_{x \in P} x \leq \top \wedge \bot \leq x$. Rewriting it into the lattice notation one gets a bounded lattice:

$$\forall_{x \in P} \ x \sqcap \top = x \wedge x \sqcup \bot = x.$$

The formal apparatus for relational structures introduced in MML looks that way:

```
struct (1-sorted) RelStr (# carrier -> set,
                           InternalRel -> Relation of the carrier #);

mode LATTICE is with_infima with_suprema Poset;
```

The adjective `with_infima` is slightly stronger than in the literature, i.e. it states for a relational structure $L$ that infima exist for arbitrary finite non-empty subset of $L$, dually is `with_suprema`. The mode `Poset` is defined naturally as `reflexive transitive antisymmetric RelStr`. The name `LATTICE` was chosen not to overload `Lattice` with its meaning as defined in the previous section.

## 4    Ortholattices

An antitone involution as already defined for "orthoposets" [15] gives way to some sort of relatively complemented lattice:

$$\forall_{x \in P}\left( x^{\mathbf{cc}} = x \,\wedge\, \forall_{y \in P}\left( x \le y \rightarrow y^{\mathbf{c}} \le x^{\mathbf{c}} \right) \right).$$

Turning $\mathbf{c}$ into a pseudocomplement results in orthocomplementation:

$$\forall_{x \in P}\ x \sqcap x^{\mathbf{c}} = \bot \,\wedge\, x \sqcup x^{\mathbf{c}} = \top.$$

Such a lattice $\langle P, \sqcap, \sqcup, \bot, \top \rangle$ is called orthocomplemented and bounded. One can observe that only one bound needs explicit assumption.

Herewith all properties of orthocomplemented lattices have been stated. However the antitonicity property of the orthocomplement is genuinely stated via order. An equivalent property in terms of lattice algebra are the de Morgan laws – with provision for the other properties; statement of one version suffices here:

$$\forall_{x,y \in P}\ (x \sqcap y)^{\mathbf{c}} = x^{\mathbf{c}} \sqcup y^{\mathbf{c}}.$$

A lattice satisfying boundedness, orthocomplementation, and admission of de Morgan laws is called an ortholattice – short for orthocomplemented lattice [11].

As above lattices are accepted as structures of type $(2, 2, \dots)$. Yet its order properties come to the fore all too often. As ubiquitous examples we have:

a) the set inclusion property is commonly used in set algebras (e.g. power set with set operations),
b) in logics the validity of implications $p \rightarrow q$ is defined via the order $eval(p) \le eval(q)$ with respect to the underlying algebraic semantics – lattice-like structures in semantics are surely not endangered by extinction.

Hence properties and (proof) argumentation are often based on order arguments. Usually join and meet operations are translated as supremum and infimum of its arguments – and vice versa. Whereby these notions get defined via order properties – especially when introduced on real numbers.

Thus an approach via order is not only some alternative but frequently desired. Above pointer to the implication tells what basic properties are looked for: partial order and negation [8]. The join and the meet can be introduced later (e.g. for technical purposes). Bounds are additional properties (for each of the approaches) which do not interfere per se with structural matters.

Henceforth basic structures should be equipped with relation and complementation. That means partial order relations for this paper. After such clarification the technical analogon is introduced in Mizar [15]: the object OrthoRelStr.

```
struct (RelStr, ComplStr)
      OrthoRelStr (# carrier -> set,
                        InternalRel -> (Relation of the carrier),
                            Compl -> UnOp of the carrier #);
```

It is a successor of the already defined simple relational structure `RelStr` and the unary operator structure `ComplStr` – very general ancestors indeed. Such constructs refer to general structures **O** of the schema:

$$\mathbf{O} = \langle \text{carrier}, \text{binary relation}, \text{unary operation} \rangle.$$

As explained in [18] this is only notion (or type in universal algebra) – properties are overdue.

There are already a lot of common relation properties in Mizar. Yet adoption of such notions is not that plain one would like; that was a reasonable aim for sake of reusability and compatibility. These notions are usually in strict formulation – the property holds only for a (proper) subset of the carrier. But fundamental poset notions are total – only total. With a little detour the partial order notion gets introduced as a shorthand:

```
definition let O non empty OrthoRelStr;
   attr O is PartialOrdered means     :: OPOSET_1:def 25
     O is reflexive antisymmetric transitive;
end;
```

A double negation property is wanted in matters of complementarity. Henceforth an involution property is introduced by an appropriate attribute `dneg` for unary functions:

```
attr O is Dneg means         :: OPOSET_1:def 7
   ex f being map of O,O st f = the Compl of O & f is dneg;
```

Because of the globalilty of the attribute it is defined via the special property of a constructor element. Thus the basic properties stated above get defined as simple combination:

```
attr O is Pure means       :: OPOSET_1:def 27
   O is Dneg PartialOrdered;
```

Of course, this is only the skeleton of the necessary properties. Mizar demands existence proofs for new notions. Thus the need for simple structures with the desired properties arises. `TrivPoset` plays such a role throughout the subject:

```
definition
   func TrivOrthoRelStr -> strict OrthoRelStr equals   :: OPOSET_1:def 5
     OrthoRelStr (# {{}}, id {{}}, op1 #);
end;
```

where `id {{}}` is an identity map on $\{\emptyset\}$, i.e. a binary relation with only one element (a pair $(\emptyset, \emptyset)$), hence nearly all properties (except a few like asymmetry) get trivial within.

Order involutivity and boundedness are still missing as the completing orthoposet ingredients. These orthocomplementarity and bound properties are defined in one step (for a unary operator on the carrier of a structure):

```
definition let PO PartialOrdered (non empty OrthoRelStr),
            f be UnOp of the carrier of PO;
  pred f OrthoComplement_on PO means      :: OPOSET_1:def 36
        f is Orderinvolutive & for y being Element of PO holds
        ex_sup_of {y,f.y},PO & ex_inf_of {y,f.y},PO &
        "\/"({y,f.y},PO) is_maximum_of the carrier of PO &
        "/\"({y,f.y},PO) is_minimum_of the carrier of PO;
end;
```

where the used predicates are defined according to its names.

Herewith the typical distinction between posets and lattices gets apparent: the existence of a supremum or infimum is not always assured – even not for bounded structures. The orthocomplementarity with `PartialOrdered` attribute suffice together for an orthoposet mode `OrthoPoset`.

Thus the `OrthoLattice` mode takes a pathway around the `OrthoPoset` (the complete development is contained in [15, 10]):

```
mode PreOrthoPoset is
     OrderInvolutive Pure (PartialOrdered (non empty OrthoRelStr));
mode PreOrthoLattice is with_infima with_suprema PreOrthoPoset;
mode OrthoLattice is Orthocomplemented PreOrthoLattice;
```

As already indicated "global" infimum and supremum (pair) properties are missing for the step towards an ortholattice mode. For conceptual (and practical) reasons a detour was taken via order involution properties and subsequent addition of orthocomplementarity instead of merging join- and meet-semilattice properties.

## 5    Handling Multiple Axiomatizations

Why the problem of handling heterogeneous approaches is so important? Many mathematical problems are often based on different approaches to the same notion and an agent managing a uniform mathematical knowledge repository is often stuck with a plenty of those choices. Furthermore, there are mathematical results only establishing connections between them. Some of the recently solved examples are – mentioned in the second section – the Robbins problem and various short Sheffer-stroke axiomatizations of Boolean lattices.

There are two main situations when dealing with multiple axiomatizations:

– different sets of operations, and consequently different structures and axioms (as Boolean posets comparing to Sheffer algebras);
– the same structure, multiple sets of axioms (e.g. 1-axiomatization for Boolean algebras based on the Sheffer-stroke vs. classical Sheffer or Meredith bases).

Regardless of the case a mutual recoding of the different theories is strongly needed.

The attempts of translation between lattices and posets within MML are not new – as well as numerous examples of elimination equivalent or redundant notions to increase uniformity of the library [19].

One of the existing – and rather not fully effective – approaches is developed in the Mizar article LATTICE3[1], via the Mizar functors establishing the communication between RelStr and LattStr with appropriate parameter and result type as cited below.

```
definition let L be Lattice;
  func LattPOSet L -> strict Poset equals      :: LATTICE3:def 2
    RelStr (# the carrier of L, LattRel L #);
end;


definition let A be RelStr such that
  A is with_suprema with_infima Poset;
  func latt A -> strict Lattice means         :: LATTICE3:def 15
    the RelStr of A = LattPOSet it;
end;
```

If the theories have e.g. different axiomatizations but the underlying structure is the same, then a conditional clusters mechanism assures the proper communication without interference from the user's side (no reference for a cluster is needed). Otherwise the common platform has to be worked out. This is how the Robbins problem has been solved.

Similarly, we have merged relational and lattice structures to obtain combined LattRelStr and introduced an adjective assured that the ordering and suprema/infima generate each other.

```
definition let L be non empty LattRelStr;
  attr L is naturally_sup-ordered means
    for x, y being Element of L holds
      x <= y iff x "|_|" y = y;
end;
```

The synonymous symbol "|_|" has been declared to cope with overloading of the symbol "\/". Authors introducing the supremum induced by a selector in LattStr and those using the same symbol for operation determined by the ordering in relational structure do not anticipate that the overloading will be dangerous since these objects have never been merged.

Now naturally_sup-ordered Lattice-like (non empty LattRelStr) can be a common type which may be used for further development of ortholattices (but equivalence of poset and lattice approach cannot be given in general as written in Section 4), Boolean algebras etc., both in binary meaning and via orthoposet. Inheritance will be crucial to use it properly. Conditional clusters also work to automatically obtain that the object with the type as above has the proper result type.

The historical motivation standing behind the approach described above is that there is a rich formal apparatus developed around binary lattices. We

---

[1] Mizar articles can be browsed at the Journal of Formalized Mathematics section in [14], the MML identifier is important here. One can find there all articles from Formalized Mathematics, however in their continuously revised form.

wanted to reuse it. But what to do if an author does not think about heterogeneity (as it often happens)? Revise the existing state? Or better rewrite everything from scratch? As it may be concluded from an experiment of Encyclopedia of Mathematics in Mizar, it is easy to be trapped by the infinite generalizations loop. EMM covers complex algebra of sets, complex numbers, and beginnings of reals, and then stopped.

The Library Committee of the Association of Mizar Users prefers a policy of continuous evolution rather than revolutionary building fragments of the library from scratch. On the one hand, the authors' rights should not be violated (while the language and library evolves, they can hardly recognize their works, however). They sign a copyright form and the Committee has the right to change their articles.

## 6    Related Work

The number of obstacles which authors of a knowledge repository may meet, is not so serious when the whole library is carefully designed by a small number of developers. That is the position of C-CoRN [5] at the moment (the number of its authors is around ten times less). Apart from that its foundations differ. Proofs in Coq are constructive compared to classical ones in Mizar. The philosophy of Coq is also different than that of the Mizar checker. The Constructive Coq Repository at Nijmegen may benefit from MML experience.

As an example of successful unification of primarily heterogeneous theories we can give also the recent redesign of the construction of complex numbers in MML. Originally defined in Mizar as pairs of real numbers, there were no way to force Mizar analyzer to understand e.g. complex zero as a real number, unless we use a casting function to provide a new type for a given variable. A new construction of reals from complex numbers with empty imaginary part together with cluster of attributes mechanism allow to clear the library and to remove some casting functions. The previous idea of the set of complex numbers $\mathbb{C}$ as a Cartesian square of set of reals seems to be satisfactory in a standalone version. However, if we require to have a natural injection of reals into the set of complex numbers without any dirty hacks, we may face serious obstacles. The same problem occurs obviously also in the case of a construction of integer numbers from naturals etc. In the case of classical mathematics, not the abstract one (where by the classical mathematics we understand this which does not use the notion of a structure, so here structure mechanisms obviously will not work), we can say about a uniformization process rather than about development of a heterogeneous theory.

Examples in group, field theory etc. arise many hard decisions: e.g. whether to introduce complement or unit element as a selector in a structure or to define it by adjectives? Even if causing many ambiguous situations, adjectives are very efficient and create with their expressive power an exclusive feature of the Mizar system.

The inheritance of theories is implemented in most systems which have their libraries. E.g. in Isabelle/HOL [16] theory Lattice is successor of the theory Bounds in similar manner as in Mizar [21].

**axclass** lattice $\subseteq$ partial-order
    ex-inf: $\exists$ inf. is-inf x y inf
    ex-sup: $\exists$ sup. is-sup x y sup

Category theory implemented in MML has pointed out that multiple fields need not be as feasible as it can be expected, and the attempt of uniformization failed because in fact there are no connections between the old (CAT) series and the new ones (ALTCAT for **alt**ernative **cat**egory theory), they are still (and will be probably) developed independently. The other reason is that the approach with the structure with large number of selectors (maximum of ten in this case) seems to be inefficient.

The freedom of choice among orderings and binary operations is important since equational reasoning is what many provers, e.g. EQP/Otter [9] are good at, and the usage of the ordering approach may decline prover's help. What remains is the question how can we deal with the results found by EQP/Otter, how to translate untyped calculations into the reasoning extensively using Mizar type system. Josef Urban's work [20] is promising, and in fact one can translate all Otter proof objects into a Mizar-like source code. Still you have to create appropriate data structure on your own.

What is important is the data structure, because proofs can be converted more or less automatically, or justification can be assured thanks to the inheritance mechanism. If we are not interested in further reusing of the notions, we can leave this issue and develop the proofs at different stages for multiple notions. That is the way freshmen can work, if they have only a narrow view at a discipline they learn. The desired knowledge repository should however offer possibly compact set of notions which enables the user via polymorphic mechanisms smooth retrieving of the appropriate workplace.

# 7    Conclusions and Further Work

The integrity of a computer managed repository of mathematical knowledge is important in the same degree as its distributivity or polymorphism. Considering integrity we have to take into account two issues: compatibility between different theories to avoid cost-consuming translations, and uniformity of the approach. Authors should have opportunity to freely choose between approaches and to communicate between all of them at all stages of their activity to enable smooth work and usage of formal apparatus which is more feasible at the chosen state.

Tools which enable in our opinion comfortable work are structures and attributes. In the Mizar system a mechanism of structures could be much improved, e.g. to enable only formalization of lower semilattices and to obtain automatically the description of upper ones etc. Such a form of transformation would ease life by saving existence proofs without posing dangerous logical problems.

The more knowledge will be retrieved, the less time an author will spend on a usual copy-and-paste job, the more creativity will be freed. Modern projects like FDL [4] and FoC [17] pay attention to such "user–friendly" issues (not to forget inheritance issues). Although more oriented towards algorithmic knowledge representation such projects point at the weaknesses and needs of "pure" proof checkers like Mizar where usability is narrowed by lack of user support and information on dependencies could be used more widely.

The experiments with heterogeneity of the approach to the lattice theory within MML are not finished since they have proven their usefulness and functionality. Using similar methods, we have developed a Boolean lattice theory in terms of the Sheffer stroke and prove its 1-axiomatization [12]. Although the structure based on the Sheffer stroke is completely different from the two described in Section 2 and 3, we successfully reused the existing formal apparatus for Boolean algebras benefitting from structures and clusters mechanism available in the Mizar system.

## Acknowledgments

The authors gratefully acknowledge the Calculemus IHP Network FP5 EU Programme for making their cooperation possible. The second author wants to thank the Theory and Logic Group of the Institute for Computer Languages (TU Vienna) for the friendly support in times when required.

# References

1. G. Bancerek, On the structure of Mizar types, in: H. Geuvers and F. Kamareddine (eds.), Proc. of MLC 2003, ENTCS 85(7), 2003.

2. G. Bancerek, Development of the theory of continuous lattices in Mizar, in: M. Kerber and M. Kohlhase (eds.), The Calculemus-2000 Symposium Proceedings, pp. 65–80, 2001.

3. B. Buchberger, Mathematical Knowledge Management in Theorema, in: B. Buchberger and O. Caprotti (eds.), Proceedings of MKM 2001, Linz, Austria, 2001.

4. R.L. Constable, Steps toward a World Wide Digital Library of Formal Mathematics, MKM Symposium, Edinburgh, UK, 2003.

5. L. Cruz-Filipe, H. Geuvers, and F. Wiedijk, C-CoRN, the Constructive Coq Repository at Nijmegen, http://www.cs.kun.nl/~freek/notes/.

6. J. Davenport, Mathematical knowledge representation, in: B. Buchberger and O. Caprotti (eds.), Proceedings of MKM 2001, Linz, Austria, 2001.

7. W. Farmer, J. Guttman, and F. Thayer, Little theories, in: D. Kapur (ed.), Automated Deduction – CADE-11, LNCS 607, pp. 567–581, 1992.

8. R. Giuntini, Quantum Logic and Hidden Variables, Bibliographisches Institut, Mannheim, 1991.

9. A. Grabowski, Robbins algebras vs. Boolean algebras, Formalized Mathematics, 9(4), pp. 681–690, 2001.

10. A. Grabowski and M. Moschner, Formalization of ortholattices via orthoposets, to appear in Formalized Mathematics, 2004.

11. G. Grätzer, General Lattice Theory, Academic Press, New York, 1978.

12. V. Kozarkiewicz and A. Grabowski, Axiomatization of lattices in terms of the Sheffer stroke, to appear in Formalized Mathematics, 2004.

13. W. McCune, Solution of the Robbins problem, Journal of Automated Reasoning, 19, pp. 263–276, 1997.

14. The Mizar Home Page, http://mizar.org.

15. M. Moschner, Basic notions and properties of orthoposets, Formalized Mathematics, 11(2), pp. 201–210, 2003.

16. T. Nipkow, L. Paulson, and M. Wenzel, Isabelle/HOL – A proof assistant for higher-order logic, LNCS 2283, 2002.

17. V. Prevosto and M. Jaume, Making proofs in a hierarchy of mathematical structures, in: T. Hardin and R. Rioboo (eds.), Proceedings of Calculemus 2003, Rome, Italy, 2003.

18. P. Rudnicki and A. Trybulec, Mathematical Knowledge Management in Mizar, in: B. Buchberger and O. Caprotti (eds.), Proceedings of MKM 2001, Linz, Austria, 2001.

19. P. Rudnicki and A. Trybulec, On the integrity of a repository of formalized mathematics, in: A. Asperti, B. Buchberger, and J. Davenport (eds.), Proc. of MKM 2003, LNCS 2594, pp. 162–174, 2003.

20. J. Urban, MPTP 0.1, in: I. Dahn and L. Vigneron (eds.), Proc. of FTP 2003, ENTCS, 86(1), 2003.

21. M. Wenzel, Lattices and orders in Isabelle/HOL, http://isabelle.in.tum.de/library/HOL/Lattice.

22. F. Wiedijk, Formal proof sketches, http://www.cs.kun.nl/~freek/notes/.

# Rough Concept Analysis – Theory Development in the Mizar System

Adam Grabowski[1] and Christoph Schwarzweller[2]*

[1] Institute of Mathematics, University of Białystok
ul. Akademicka 2, 15-267 Białystok, Poland
adam@math.uwb.edu.pl
[2] Department of Computer Science, University of Gdańsk
ul. Wita Stwosza 57, 80-952 Gdańsk, Poland
schwarzw@math.univ.gda.pl

**Abstract.** Theories play an important role in building mathematical knowledge repositories. Organizing knowledge in theories is an obvious approach to cope with the growing number of definitions, theorems, and proofs. However, they are also a matter of subject on their own: developing a new piece of mathematics often relies on extending or combining already developed theories in this way reusing definitions as well as theorems. We believe that this aspect of theory development is crucial for mathematical knowledge management.

In this paper we investigate the facilities of the Mizar system concerning extending and combining theories based on structure and attribute definitions. As an example we consider the formation of rough concept analysis out of formal concept analysis and rough sets.

## 1  Introduction

The design and the construction of mathematical knowledge repositories is in the core of mathematical knowledge management. Computer-supported processing of mathematics such as knowledge retrieval, distribution over the Internet, or development of lecture material is highly driven by the way mathematical knowledge is represented and maintained. And last, but not least, the acceptance of mathematical knowledge management systems by mathematicians themselves also depends in essence on how the knowledge in such systems is represented and developed.

Mathematicians build up mathematical theories. However, developing a new theory does not (always) mean defining and proving all from scratch: each new mathematical theory uses, refines, combines, or extends previous ones. Definitions and theorems of the constituents are then used without any major reference. So for example field theory is a refinement of group theory, field theory itself is used in the theory of vector spaces, topology and group theory are combined in the theory of topological groups, and so on. Thus almost every theory

---

* The work of the second author was partially supported by grant BW 5100-5-0147-4.

A. Asperti et al. (Eds.): MKM 2004, LNCS 3119, pp. 130–144, 2004.

relies on a number of (more) elementary theories. This phenomenon also occurs in more computer science related areas, see e.g. [9] where the verification of a probabilistic primality test algorithm required proving quite a number of group and number theoretical theorems.

This rather dynamical aspect of theories should be explicitly addressed in mathematical knowledge management systems. Developing a theory for a knowledge repository does not only contribute by introducing new notions, proving some new theorems or applying new proof methods. In principle, each theory also serves as a starting point for further development in the sense that its notions, theorems, and proofs are used to construct other theories. We believe that mathematical knowledge repositories must take this into account by providing language features that enable and support theory development. Furthermore, these should reflect the way theories are dealt within everyday mathematical life.

In this paper we focus on theory development in the Mizar system (see the website [13] of the project or [19] for details). We formalized the beginnings of the theory of rough concept analysis using different approaches – the original one as in [11] and its modifications [21]. Rough concept analysis is a synthesis of rough sets and formal concept analysis. Rough sets [17] approximate objects with respect to an indiscernibility relation. Formal concept analysis [23] is an attribute-based approach for representation and analysis of data. The combination of both thus establishes a theory for representing and analyzing uncertain data.

Both rough sets and formal concept analysis have already been formalized by the authors in Mizar [8,22], however without any intent to use them in other theories or even to combine them. Hence, rough sets and formal concept analysis provide a good example to investigate the possibilities of Mizar to glue together two independently developed theories.

The plan of the paper is as follows. In the next section we briefly introduce rough sets and formal concept analysis and review their Mizar formalization as done in [8] and [22]. Section 3 describes the combination of these two theories into rough concept analysis. Mizar language features to do so are presented. In the last two sections we discuss the Mizar approach for combination of theories and compare it to other approaches in the literature. Conclusions for the design of mathematical knowledge repositories are drawn.

## 2    Rough Sets and Formal Concept Analysis

In this section we briefly present background for the input theories. Both were developed independently, also in Mizar both were formalized in such a way. We will focus here on rough sets because of their high level of reusability in many different ways. It is well known that in classical set theory in order to define a subset $X$ of a given universe $U$ we have to specify its membership function $\mu_X : U \longrightarrow \{0, 1\}$. While for classical sets and multisets these functions are discrete-valued, in the theory of fuzzy and rough sets they are extended to a continuous case.

## 2.1    Approximation Spaces

Computers play a special role in the development of the theory of rough sets (RST for short). Even if the notion has strong mathematical flavour (although its founder, Zdzisław Pawlak is a computer scientist), it has been used from the beginning to approximate knowledge discovery and data mining process. Such an approach, called KDD-approach (for Knowledge Discovery in Databases) resulted in many practical applications, i.e. Rosetta or RSES, just to name the most important ones. We believe that KDD is also an important issue for the Mathematical Knowledge Management community.

Nobody however – as far as we know – used KDD tools for discovering the knowledge about rough sets themselves. One of the reasons probably is the lack of a proper, sufficiently big, computer-managed repository of RST knowledge. We tried to start with one of them [8], and the results are rather promising, at least in the opinion of the authors and the RS community.

RST is also an interesting subject for machine-oriented formalization for some other reasons. Since the introductory paper [17] back in 1982 numerous generalizations and improvements of the basic notions have been proposed. The community is rather young and fast-growing (the measure of acceptance ratio for presented long papers to the RSCTC 2004 Conference in Uppsala, Sweden was under 20%, there is also a subseries of LNCS, Springer, Advances in Rough Sets, devoted to the topic). On the one hand, machine-formalization of the results in such a discipline could be a challenge in itself for many reasons (the results correspond to different disciplines in mathematics and in computer science and offer many possible generalizations which could be discovered automatically etc.). On the other hand, one could reach a research frontier here relatively fast.

The theory of rough sets is a background for a methodology concerned with the analysis and modelling of classification and decision problems involving imprecise, vague, uncertain or incomplete information. As a result, it distinguishes classes of objects rather than the individuals and reflects in a formal way the very basic intuition that concept forming is finding out the similarities and the differences among objects. There are two simple models for RST in the literature. One of them is to have two sets of objects and attributes resp. forming an information system. They determine an external similarity relation clustering some objects together w.r.t. their attributes (properties). Another formal model is an approximation space, the backbone for a whole RST, which is a non-empty finite universe $U$ and the indiscernibility relation $R$ given on $U$.

Because the latter approach is more often used and methodologically simpler, we have chosen it. One of the key issues was also the possibility of further reusing. The concept of an information system can be also formalized as the descendant of the approximation space in a natural way. At the first sight, the underlying Mizar structure is RelStr, which has two fields: the carrier and the InternalRel, that is a binary relation of the carrier. The theory of relational structures has been developed and improved mainly during formalization of the Compendium of Continuous Lattices (which is described in [1] in detail). While in this context RelStr was used with attributes reflexive transitive and antisymmetric to establish posets, we decided to reuse it in our own way. First, we defined two new attributes: with_equivalence and with_tolerance which state that the InternalRel of the underlying RelStr is an equivalence resp. a tolerance relation (where a tolerance relation is a total reflexive symmetric relation, see [18]). With such defined notions, the basic definitions are as follows:

```
definition
   mode Approximation_Space is with_equivalence non empty RelStr;
   mode Tolerance_Space is with_tolerance non empty RelStr;
end;
```

Formalized theories can be treated as objects (axioms, definitions, theorems) clustered by certain relations based on information flow. The more atomic the notions are, the more is their usefulness. Driven by this idea we tried to drop selected properties of the equivalence relations. Our first choice was transitivity – therefore the use of tolerance spaces – as it seemed to be less substantial than the other two. The generalization work went rather smoothly. As we discovered soon, similar investigations, but without any machine-motivations, were done by Järvinen [10].

What is rather interesting, one of the referees among the RST community complained, that the presentation in [8] is lacking its focus between approximation and tolerance spaces. Because every approximation space is in particular a tolerance space and this is obvious also for the Mizar type checker, all theorems true in more general situations need not (from the viewpoint of the Library Committee of the Association of Mizar Users – even must not) be repeated. Some theorems holding for tolerances however are simply untrue for equivalences, so the apparent lack of focus. For many mathematicians, the uniformity and clarity of the approach is still more important than its generality.

## 2.2   Rough Sets

As it sometimes happens among other theories (compare e.g. the construction of fuzzy sets), paradoxically the notion of a rough set is not the central point of RST as a whole. Rough sets are in fact classes of abstraction w.r.t. rough equality of sets and their formal treatment varies. Some authors (as Pawlak for instance) define a rough set as an underlying class of abstraction (as noted above), but many authors claim for simplicity that a rough set is an ordered pair containing the lower and the upper limit of fluctuation of the argument $X$.

```
definition let A be Approximation_Space;
           let X be Subset of A;
   mode RoughSet of X means    :: ROUGHS_1:def 8
     it = [LAp X, UAp X];
end;
```

These two approaches are not equivalent, and we decided to define a rough set also in the latter sense. What should be mentioned here, there are so-called m odes in the Mizar language which correspond with the notion of a type. To properly define a mode, one should only prove its existence. As it can be easily observed, because the above definiens determines a unique object for every subset $X$ of a fixed approximation space $A$, this can be reformulated as a functor definition in the Mizar language.

If both approximations coincide, the notion collapses and the resulting set is exact, i.e. a set in the classical sense. Unfortunately, in the above mentioned approach, this is not the case. In [8] we did not use this notion in fact, but we have chosen some other solution which describes rough sets more effectively.

Regardless what approach we are claiming, the key notion of RST is the notion of an approximation. A lower approximation of a set $X$ consists of objects which are surely (w.r.t. indiscernibility relation of $A$) in $X$. Similarly, the upper one extends the lower for the objects which are possibly in $X$ (see [8] for detailed explanations).

```
definition let A be Tolerance_Space;
           let X be Subset of A;
   func LAp X -> Subset of A equals   :: ROUGHS_1:def 4
   { x where x is Element of A : Class (the InternalRel of A, x) c= X };
   func UAp X -> Subset of A equals   :: ROUGHS_1:def 5
   {x where x is Element of A : Class(the InternalRel of A, x) meets X};
end;
```

One of the most powerful Mizar linguistic constructions are adjectives (which are constructed by attributes). As we found Mizar modes not to be very useful within RST after we defined tolerance approximation spaces, we introduced the attribute **rough** in the following way to describe sets $X$ with non-empty approximation boundary **BndAp** $X$ (the set-theoretical difference of the upper and the lower approximations of a given set $X$).

```
definition let A be Tolerance_Space;
           let X be Subset of A;
   attr X is rough means   :: ROUGHS_1:def 7
     BndAp X <> {};
end;
```

If both the upper and lower approximation of a set $X$ coincide, **BndAp** $X$ equals $\emptyset$ and $X$ is a set in the usual sense. In Mizar script, we introduced an adjective **exact** as an antonym to the above to denote crisp sets. The apparatus of adjectives has proved its value especially when merging theories together.

## 2.3   Formal Concept Analysis

Formal context analysis (FCA for short) has been introduced by Wille [23] as a formal tool for the representation and analysis of data. The main idea is to consider not only data objects, but to take into account properties (attributes) of the objects also. This leads to the notion of a concept which is a pair of a set of objects and a set of properties. In a concept all objects possess all the properties of the concept and vice versa. Thus the building blocks in FCA are given by both objects and their properties following the idea that we distinguish sets of objects by a common set of properties.

In the framework of FCA the set of all concepts (for given sets of objects and properties) constitute a complete lattice. Thus based on the lattice structure the given data – that is its concepts and concept hierarchies – can be computed, visualized, and analyzed. In the area of software engineering FCA has been successfully used to build intelligent search tools as well as to analyze and reorganize the structure of software modules and software libraries.

In the literature a number of extensions of the original approach can be found. So, for example, multi-valued concept analysis where the value of features is not restricted to two values (true and false). Also more involved models have been proposed taking into account additional aspects of knowledge representation such as different sources of data or the inclusion of rule-based knowledge in the form of ontologies.

Being basically an application of lattice theory FCA is a well-suited topic for machine-oriented formalization. On the one hand it allows to investigate the possibilities of reusing an already formalized lattice theory. On the other hand it can be the starting point for the formalization of the extensions mentioned above. In the following we briefly present the Mizar formalization of the basic FCA notions necessary for the next section.

The starting point is a formal context giving the objects and attributes of concern. Formally such a context consists of two sets of objects $O$ and attributes $A$, respectively. Objects and attributes are connected by an incidence relation $I \subseteq O \times A$. The intension is that object $o \in O$ has property $a \in A$ if and only if $(o, a) \in I$. In Mizar [22] this has been modelled by the following structure definitions.

```
definition
  struct 2-sorted (# Objects, Attributes -> set #);
end;
```

```
definition
  struct (2-sorted) ContextStr
    (# Objects, Attributes -> set,
       Information -> Relation of the Objects,the Attributes #);
end;
```

Now a formal context is a non-empty ContextStr. To define formal concepts in a given formal context $C$ two derivation operators ObjectDerivation(C) and AttributeDerivation(C) are used. For a set $O$ of objects ($A$ of attributes) the derived set consists of all attributes $a$ (objects $o$) such that $(o, a) \in I$ for all $o \in O$ (for all $a \in A$). The Mizar definition of these operators is straightforward and omitted here.

A formal concept $FC$ is a pair $(O, A)$ where $O$ and $A$ respect the derivation operators: the derivation of $O$ contains exactly the attributes of $A$, and vice versa. $O$ is called the extent of $FC$, $A$ the intent of $FC$. In Mizar this gives rise to a structure introducing the `extent` and the `intent` and an attribute `concept-like`.

```
definition let C be 2-sorted;
  struct ConceptStr over C
    (# Extent -> Subset of the Objects of C,
        Intent -> Subset of the Attributes of C #);
end;
```

```
definition let C be FormalContext;
          let CP be ConceptStr over C;
  attr CP is concept-like means   :: CONLAT_1:def 13
    (ObjectDerivation(C)).(the Extent of CP) = the Intent of CP &
    (AttributeDerivation(C)).(the Intent of CP) = the Extent of CP;
end;
```

```
definition let C be FormalContext;
  mode FormalConcept of C is concept-like non empty ConceptStr over C;
end;
```

Formal concepts over a given formal context can be easily ordered: a formal concept $FC_1$ is more specialized (and less general) than a formal concept $FC_2$ iff the extent of $FC_1$ is included in the extent of $FC_2$ (or equivalently iff the intent of $FC_2$ is included in the intent of $FC_1$). With respect to this order the set of all concepts over a given formal context $C$ forms a complete lattice, the concept lattice of $C$.

```
theorem
    for C being FormalContext holds ConceptLattice(C) is complete Lattice;
```

This theorem, among others, has been proven in [22]. The formalization of FCA in Mizar went rather smoothly, the main reason being that lattice theory has already been well developed. Given objects, attributes and an incidence relation between them, this data can now be analyzed by inspecting the structure of the (concept) lattice; see [23,7] for more details and techniques of formal concept analysis.

## 3   Rough Concept Analysis

In this section we present issues concerning the merging of concrete theories in the Mizar system. Since we want to keep this presentation possibly self-contained and we assume basic knowledge of Mizar syntax (which is very close to the language used by mathematicians), we will illustrate them by living examples from Rough Concept Analysis and skipping most technical details. For details of the Mizar type system, see [2].

Below we enumerate ten features that proved their usability in merging the theories of RST and FCA. Though they are Mizar specific we claim that any mathematical knowledge should support the general principles of these features in one or another form in order to make theory development more feasible. We like to mention that in the course of FCA formalization the formal apparatus yet existing in the Mizar Mathematical Library also had to be improved and cleaned up.

**Data Structure.** A basic structure for the merged theory should inherit fields from its ancestors, which would be hard to implement if structures were implemented as ordered tuples (multiple copies of the same selector, inadequate ordering of fields in the result). The more feasible realization is by partial functions rather, and that is the way Mizar structures work.

```
definition
  struct (ContextStr, RelStr) RoughContextStr
    (# carrier, carrier2 -> set,
       Information -> Relation of the carrier, the carrier2,
       InternalRel -> Relation of the carrier #);
end;
```

The maximal number of fields in a single structure in the Mizar library is ten (as of a Cartesian category). The choice of having a long structure with many specialized inherited fields is what actually depends on the author. On the one hand an ordering can be defined in a natural way as an external predicate, e.g. on concepts. On the other hand, using the internal field of a structure one can benefit from the notions and theorems about relational structures. It is hard to formulate quantitative criteria in this subject, but it seems that six is a good upper approximation for a number of structure fields.

**Homogeneous Structure Hierarchy.** In Mizar the same names of fields are necessary to merge structures (the problems with multiple carriers), some automatizing could be made, though. The same names of operations or attributes will result in serious troubles if one has them together with different meanings assumed originally. As it can be observed from the previously cited example, the first two selectors have the names `carrier` and `carrier2` which is incompatible with the names of ascendant structures (`Objects` and `Attributes` occurring in `ContexStr` vs. `carrier` in `RelStr`). Since there are no synonyms for selectors in Mizar, a revision for `ContextStr` had to be made. This policy however is highly unlikely and Mizar developers should consider a language extension.

Apart from its visualization (see "Net of structures in MML" (MML stands for Mizar Mathematical Library) section at [13]), we gather basic data about structures in Table 1. As it can be concluded, the clustering of structures is good. Every fourth structure inherits its fields from at least two others, so the background for theory merging is comparatively well prepared. As a future work for the Library Committee, the number of initial (i.e. without parents) structures should be decreased.

**Table 1.** Statistical data about structures in MML

| Description | Quantity | % of total |
|---|---|---|
| descendants of 1-sorted | 72 | 79 |
| prefixed by 1-sorted | 23 | 25 |
| initial | 15 | 16 |
| standalone | 12 | 13 |
| multiprefixed | 22 | 24 |
| structures total | 91 | 100 |
| articles using structures | 533 | 64 |
| articles total | 834 | 100 |

**Forgetful Functors.** The user would have a chance to use an original part of merged object with a type of its parent, i.e. the back-translation should be provided where possible. It is provided in Mizar by the construction

the Structure-symbolof Variable

In this manner, if a `RoughContextStr` $X$ is given, the `RelStr of X` will result in the rough part of the structure $X$.

**Strict Objects.** Sometimes it is useful to deal only with the objects with the type of source theories even if we work within a target theory. The term

strict Structure-Symbol

yields an object without any additional fields than those in the input structure, e.g. `strict ContextStr` denotes the structure of a formal context without mentioning its roughness aspect.

**Inheritance of Properties.** It is natural to have notions formulated as general as possible, especially in a large repository, when unnecessary assumptions are inherited in some sense. The care is advised here, because if the definition of the lower approximation were introduced as follows:

```
definition let A be strict Tolerance_Space;
          let X be Subset of A;
  func LAp X -> Subset of A equals
  {x where x is Element of A : Class(the InternalRel of A,x) c= X};
end;
```

i.e. with tolerance space without any additional fields as a locus, this notion might not be used within RCA. There is software available in the Mizar system detecting some unnecessary assumptions, but not those searching for a more general type which may be used. Of course, the above functor has been defined in [8] without adjective `strict`.

**Free Extensions.** As it often happens, an extension of the theory to another need not be unique. There are at least three different methods of adding roughness to formal concepts [11,21]. The question which approach to choose depends on the author. The notion of a free structure in a class of descendant type conservative w.r.t. the original object is very useful.

```
definition let C be ContextStr;
  mode RoughExtension of C -> RoughContextStr means
    the ContextStr of it = the ContextStr of C;
 end;
```

Now, if $C$ is a given context, we can introduce roughness in many different ways by adjectives.

**Interferences.** Up to now, we described only mechanisms of independent inheritance of notions. Within the merged theory it is necessary to define connections between its source ingredients. Here the attributes describing mutual interferences between selectors from originally disjoint theories proved their enormous value. They may determine the set of properties of a free extension.

```
definition let C be RoughFormalContext;
  attr C is naturally_ordered means
    for x, y being Element of C holds
    [x,y] in the InternalRel of C iff
      (ObjectDerivation C).{x} = (ObjectDerivation C).{y};
end;
```

Since the relation from the definiens above is an equivalence relation on the objects of $C$ and hence determines a partition of the set of objects of $C$ into the so-called elem entary sets, it is a constructor of an approximation space induced by given formal context.

**Inherited Theorems and Clusters.** Theory merging makes no sense, if proving the same theorem would be necessary within both source and target theory. Since a new Mizar type RoughFormalContext is defined analogously to the notion of FormalContext, as non quasi-empty RoughContextStr (compare Subsection 2.3), the following Fundamental Theorem of RCA is justified only by the Fundamental Theorem of FCA. Even more, clusters providing automatic acceptance of the original theorems do it analogously within target theory. That is also a workplace for clusters rough and exact mentioned in Subsection 2.2.

```
for C being RoughFormalContext holds
  ConceptLattice(C) is complete Lattice by CONLAT_1:48;
```

**Uniform Object Naming.** We should work out a comfortable and uniform naming system for attributes. E.g. it is a rule that the structure prefixed by 1-sorted is named non empty provided its carrier is non-empty. But how it should be named to describe the 'second carrier' to be non-empty? This concerns multi-sorted structures in general. We want to find a reasonable compromise between technical naming and that close to a natural language, but the reasonable length of a name is also an important criterion. So between non empty2 and with_non_empty_carrier2 we decided to use quasi-empty.

**Synonyms for Objects.** Although uniform name spaces improve especially the searching process, sometimes having the same notationfor different notions is a serious drawback. Lattice theory can bring more appropriate examples: on the one hand we have binary suprema and infima operations in a properly defined lattice, on the other hand those in a relational structure induced by the ordering. If we merge both, the problems with identification occur, so it is reasonable to introduce a new notational synonym for one of them, e.g.

```
notation let R be RelStr,
             x, y be Element of R;
  synonym x "|_|" y for x "\/" y;
end;
```

(where "\/" stands for an original binary supremum in lattices).

# 4    Mathematical Knowledge Repositories

Mathematical knowledge management aims at providing mathematics with the help of computers. One major point in doing so is to build repositories holding the knowledge. We believe that mathematical knowledge repositories should be more than simple databases, that is the knowledge included should be verified by a prover or checker in order to avoid the inclusion of untrue knowledge. However, even then revisions may become necessary. We have seen this in the course of formalizing rough concept analysis, where renaming of the selectors of structure ContextStr was necessary in order to fully benefit from the inheritance mechanisms in Mizar. Thus the organization and maintenance of mathematical knowledge repositories is, and will stay, an ongoing process. In the following we report on the latest developments concerning MML, discuss the evolution of mathematical repositories and briefly review other approaches to theory building from the literature.

## 4.1    Mizar Mathematical Library

The Mizar Mathematical Library [13] is the (still evolving) result of a long term project that aims at developing both a comprehensive library of mathematical knowledge and a formal language – also called Mizar – for doing so. So far MML just collects articles written in the Mizar language. At the time of writing there are 834 articles with 36847 theorems/lemmas and 7093 definitions included, written by more than 150 authors.

Recently the development of the Encyclopedia of Mathematics in Mizar (EMM for short) has been started. Here definitions and theorems of MML are extracted semi-automatically into new articles with monographical character. This obviously becomes necessary having a larger number of authors who introduce definitions and theorems whenever these are convenient for the author's goals – and not when it seems reasonable to introduce them in order to get a well-developed repository. So far there are five EMM articles (XBOOLE_0, XBOOLE_1, XREAL_0, XCMPLX_0, and XCMPLX_1) including basic facts on boolean operators, real and complex numbers. Thus, in some sense, theories are built in EMM by collecting knowledge (belonging to the same topic) spread over the whole library. In parallel, work on the environment directive `requirements` continues which strengthens the Mizar checker in the following sense: requirement files contain statements that become obvious for the Mizar checker if the file is included in the environment. So far properties of real and complex numbers as well as of boolean operators and of subsets has been addressed.

In the course of developing EMM and the requirements directive we propose to also include theories based on structures and attributes such as for example groups, fields, or even RST or FCA. As a consequence these theories could be easier imported into new articles improving both the organization and reusing facilities of MML.

## 4.2 Evolution of a Repository

Though we cope mainly with the question of computer-supported mathematical theory development in this paper, machine-managed knowledge retrieval from a repository of mathematical facts is also an important issue, especially if one considers KDD-based methods usage.

The larger the database is, the easier linkages and connections can be studied. Even if MML is known as the largest library of formalized mathematics, it has a number of disadvantages. C-CoRN [4], the Constructive Coq Repository at Nijmegen, uses experience gathered when building MML. The number of people involved in this project is rather small (about 15 in total) as their library is centralized as a rule. C-CoRN grew out as a side-effect of the Fundamental Theorem of Algebra project. It is not an objection in any sense, but some obstacles might be anticipated in this way and carefully be discussed. The data structure may also profit from the uniform manner of its design. Searching for analogies, e.g. between fuzzy and rough sets, can be more successful if both are coded in similar manner or if they can be lifted to a common formal platform.

In this paper we address only issues of what Trybulec and Rudnicki [19] classify as abstract mathematics. In classical mathematics theories are hardly merged, but rather inherited. It is one of Trybulec's recent suggestions to cut MML into classical (not using the notion of a structure) and abstract mathematics to study interconnections between theories more carefully. There is also the opinion, that this will make the library more coherent, where by a 'coherence' we mean, similarly to [4], that results about a specific theory should be grouped together and theories extending others should be built on the top of them.

What we are going to do with MML is to make it better organized but we have to watch for authors' rights as well. They sign a copyright form when submitting to MML and the Library Committee of the Association of Mizar Users can revise their work. However, the copyright issues should be discussed by the MKM community since the importance of electronical repositories is growing remarkably.

It is hard to imagine a living system without any changes anyway. If the interfaces evolve, repositories can follow their development and vice versa, by exploring knowledge stored in libraries, new techniques can be worked out. In MML CVS service which is publicly available (by a usual Concurrent Version System engine with web-browsing facility) official versions of MML are archived to document revision stages. Since its initial version in May 2002, nearly 150 versions were archived (as of June 2004). It shows rather dynamic growth of the repository, especially if one takes into account that not all intermediate stages of the library were stored (some of the versions of the system consisted only of the new compilation of the executables etc.). The policy of the Library Committee of the Association of Mizar Users is that MML is archived in CVS as a whole because of the many interdependencies. Just for the record how tight this structure is, let us note here that there are nearly 500 thousand cross-citations (for definitions and theorems, internal references are not counted) between Mizar articles.

## 4.3    Other Repositories

The IMPS system [6] provides theory development in forms of the little theories approach [5]. Here theories are developed with respect to a particular set of axioms which can be compared to using a set of attributes in Mizar. To use a theorem in another context a theory interpretation is constructed. This usually includes a number of obligations ensuring basically that axioms of the old theory are mapped to theorems in the new one. Combining theories therefore can be done by establishing the axioms of the new theory and importing theorems via theory interpretations.

A similar approach can be observed in PVS [16], via the mapping mechanism it is easy to specify a general theory and have it stand for a number of instances (the latter correspond to an aggregate in Mizar). Theory declarations allow theories to be encapsulated and instantiated copies of the implicitly imported theory are generated. In Isabelle/Isar [15] there are mechanisms of merging both theories and locales. The latter modules correspond to a context rather which is a narrower notion than we dealt in this paper.

In Theorema [3] theories can be constructed by using a special language construct. This allows to explicitly state which definitions, lemmas, and theorems are part of the theory. Thus every user can construct his own theories. These theories are then used as attachments to proof attempts in this way reusing the knowledge stored in a theory. A theory may include theories again so that hierarchies of theories can be built.

Tecton [14,12] is a specification language developed mainly for the description of requirements for generic algorithms. It does include language constructs to formulate lemmas and theorems, but unfortunately no means to prove these correct. However, theories can be combined by gluing together already existing theories using the so-called refinement. This basically means that the axioms of the old theories are imported into the new one, in this way ensuring that theorems of used theories still hold. Furthermore, in doing so carriers and operators can be renamed which makes the language more flexible and user-friendly.

# 5   Conclusion

The aim of mathematical knowledge repositories is twofold: On the one hand a repository has to provide language and proof constructs to represent mathematical objects and proofs in a convenient way. On the other hand, even more important for mathematical knowledge management, the knowledge stored in a repository must be kept manageable in the sense that both retrieving and extending it is supported. Building, refining, and extending theories is an obvious approach to organize knowledge in mathematical repositories and therefore crucial for the development of mathematical knowledge repositories; in particular the flexibility of theories as known from everyday mathematical life has to be addressed. We believe that constructing – and hence refining and extending – theories using structures and attributes as presented in this paper is a step into this direction.

# References

1. G. Bancerek, Development of the theory of continuous lattices in Mizar, in: M. Kerber and M. Kohlhase (eds.), The Calculemus-2000 Symposium Proceedings, pp. 65–80, 2001.
2. G. Bancerek, On the structure of Mizar types, in: H. Geuvers and F. Kamareddine (eds.), Proc. of MLC 2003, ENTCS 85(7), 2003.
3. B. Buchberger, Mathematical Knowledge Management in Theorema, in: B. Buchberger and O. Caprotti (eds.), Proc. of MKM 2001, Linz, Austria, 2001.
4. L. Cruz-Filipe, H. Geuvers, and F. Wiedijk, C-CoRN, the Constructive Coq Repository at Nijmegen, http://www.cs.kun.nl/~freek/notes/.
5. W. Farmer, J. Guttman, and F. Thayer, Little theories, in: D. Kapur (ed.), Automated Deduction – CADE-11, LNCS 607, pp. 567–581, 1992.
6. W. Farmer, J. Guttman, and F. Thayer, IMPS – an Interactive Mathematical Proof System, Journal of Automated Reasoning, 11, pp. 213–248, 1993.
7. B. Ganter and R. Wille, Formal concept analysis – mathematical foundations, Springer Verlag, 1998.
8. A. Grabowski, Basic properties of rough sets and rough membership function, to appear in Formalized Mathematics, 2004, available from [13].
9. J. Hurd, Verification of the Miller-Rabin probabilistic primality test, Journal of Logic and Algebraic Programming, 56, pp. 3–21, 2003.
10. J. Järvinen, Approximations and rough sets based on tolerances, in: W. Ziarko and Y. Yao (eds.), Proc. of RSCTC 2000, LNAI 2005, pp. 182–189, 2001.
11. R.E. Kent, Rough Concept Analysis: a synthesis of rough sets and formal concept analysis, Fundamenta Informaticae 27(2–3), pp. 169–181, 1996.
12. R. Loos, D. Musser, S. Schupp, and C. Schwarzweller, The Tecton concept library, Technical Report WSI 99-2, Wilhelm-Schickard-Institute for Computer Science, University of Tübingen, 1999.
13. The Mizar Home Page, http://mizar.org.
14. D. Musser and Z. Shao, The Tecton concept description language (revised version), Technical Report 02-2, Rensselaer Polytechnic Institute, 2002.
15. T. Nipkow, L. Paulson, and M. Wenzel, Isabelle/HOL – a proof assistant for higher-order logic, LNCS 2283, 2002.

16. S. Owre and N. Shankar, Theory interpretations in PVS, Technical Report, NASA/CR-2001-211024, 2001.
17. Z. Pawlak, Rough sets, International Journal of Information and Computer Science, 11(5), pp. 341–356, 1982.
18. K. Raczkowski and P. Sadowski, Equivalence relations and classes of abstraction, Formalized Mathematics, 1(3), pp. 441–444, 1990, available in JFM from [13].
19. P. Rudnicki and A. Trybulec, Mathematical Knowledge Management in Mizar, in: B. Buchberger and O. Caprotti (eds.), Proc. of MKM 2001, Linz, Austria, 2001.
20. P. Rudnicki and A. Trybulec, On the integrity of a repository of formalized mathematics, in: A. Asperti, B. Buchberger, and J. Davenport (eds.), Proc. of MKM 2003, LNCS 2594, pp. 162–174, 2003.
21. J. Saquer and J.S. Deogun, Concept approximations based on rough sets and similarity measures, International Journal on Applications of Mathematics in Computer Science, 11(3), pp. 655–674, 2001.
22. C. Schwarzweller, Introduction to concept lattices, Formalized Mathematics, 7(2), pp. 233–242, 1998, available in JFM from [13].
23. R. Wille, Restructuring lattice theory: an approach based on hierarchies of concepts, in: I. Rival (ed.), Ordered Sets, Reidel, Dordrecht-Boston, 1982.

# A Path to Faithful Formalizations of Mathematics

Gueorgui Jojgov and Rob Nederpelt

Eindhoven University of Technology, The Netherlands
{G.I.Jojgov,R.P.Nederpelt}@tue.nl

**Abstract.** In this paper we are interested in the process of formalizing a mathematical text written in Common Mathematical Language (CML) into type theory using intermediate representations in Weak Type Theory [8] and in type theory with open terms. We demonstrate that this method can be reliable not only in the sense that eventually we get formally verified mathematical texts, but also in the sense that we can have a fairly high confidence that we have produced a 'faithful' formalization (i.e. that the formal text is as close as possible to the intentions expressed in the informal text).

A computer program that assists a human along the formalization path should create enough "added value" to be useful in practice. We also discuss some problems that such an implementation needs to solve and possible solutions for them.

## 1 Introduction

The de Bruijn criterion for reliability of proof-checking systems states that a proof created with arbitrarily complex techniques can be reliable as long as the final proof object can be checked by a small (i.e. manually verifiable) program. Obviously, this criterion concerns the proof construction after the problem has been translated into the language of a formal system. However, there is a stage prior to that: the transition from informal to formal and when it comes to reliability, both stages are important.

Hence there is also the question of how to create reliable formal translations of the informal mathematical problems and proofs. The process of formalizing a piece of informal mathematical text is about making explicit the intentions of the author of the text. As such, we can never be completely sure what the author of the text had intended to say and more importantly, we cannot be sure whether the piece of formal text faithfully reflects these intentions. Therefore, almost by definition the formalization is and probably always will remain a process that involves a human decision.

One way to ensure a level of reliability is to use a very weak formal system in the first translation step. The key observation is that by making an initial formal version as close as possible to the informal version, the detection of formalization errors will be much more likely. In [9, 8] a system called Weak Type Theory

A. Asperti et al. (Eds.): MKM 2004, LNCS 3119, pp. 145–159, 2004.

(WTT) is proposed that tries to conform to this idea by introducing a language to write formal mathematical texts in which the concern of the reliability of the translation is separated from (and has precedence over) the concern about the logical content of the text. The typing system of WTT is not so much focused on the formulas-as-types paradigm as on the goal of capturing the syntactic and linguistic structures of informal texts. For example, in WTT we have weak types for nouns, adjectives, sets, etc.

As regards the second stage of the formalization, there is also more to say about reliability than only the compliance with the de Bruijn criterion: in order to keep close to the intentions of the mathematical author, it is probably advisable to do proof construction more 'human-friendly', in the style of the average mathematician. The problem is evident if one looks at the user group of interactive theorem provers which in its majority consists of highly trained specialists. Their expert knowledge is not only needed to create formal texts with the tools, but also to translate informally stated problems into the language of the particular tool. In our opinion, a careful, more human-oriented tuning of both stages of proof construction, can make interactive theorem provers more widely used and more importantly, it can increase the reliability of the overall formalization.

In this paper we study to which degree WTT can convincingly perform the role of a system for initial formalization and how a WTT text can then be evolved into a fully formalized text in a full-featured type theory. To do that we will need to translate WTT texts into a type theory with incomplete proofs and terms. Such proofs and terms have missing parts that need to be proven or constructed and this is a task that is well understood and supported in modern interactive theorem provers [2]. In other words, this paper is an initial study of the feasibility of using WTT as a 'front end' for theorem provers and it does not have the purpose of proposing yet another prover.

The main line of events is hence as follows: we have an informal text of which we want to create a fully formalized version. The first step is to translate this text into WTT. As the constraints imposed are weak, the distance of the WTT text from the original can be kept minimal to reduce the chance for formalization errors. Then we will translate this WTT text into a version of our target type theory with incomplete proofs and terms and global definitions. The missing parts in these proofs and terms are explicit representations of the details that are left implicit in the informal version. Once we have the version with incomplete terms and proofs we are in the conventional domain of theorem provers.

The benefits of such an approach are manyfold. First, we have increased the reliability of the initial formulation of the informal text into a formal system. Second, the translation from the weak WTT to the strongly typed target type theory exposes many opportunities for automation and hence for creating 'added value' for the user. The third benefit, already discussed in previous work (see [7]) is that the resulting type theory text reflects the structure of the informal document we started with. This could allow us to trace back to the original informal text, any errors found during the later stages of formalization.

## 2    The Formalization Path

In this section we discuss in more detail the three translations on the path from the Common Mathematical Language (CML) through Weak Type Theory (WTT) and Type Theory with open proofs (OTT) to the final goal of a complete formalization in Type Theory (TT).

### 2.1    Step 1: From Informal Text to Weak Type Theory

In this section we illustrate the ideas explained above by showing how a piece of informal mathematics could be translated using our approach. Consider the text

---

A function from natural to naturals is *increasing* if the value of the function at a given point is strictly less than the value at the next point. We say that a function $f$ is *unbounded* if for every natural number there is an argument of the function for which the function takes a value greater than that natural number.

**Theorem 1.** *Every increasing function is unbounded.*

*Proof.* Let $f$ be an increasing function. First, using induction we will prove that $\forall x \in N(f(x) \geq x)$:

**Base** $f(0)$ is a natural number and hence $f(0) \geq 0$.
**Ind. Step** If $f(k) \geq k$ we have that $f(k + 1) > f(k)$ because $f$ is increasing. Hence $f(k+1) > k$ and this means that $f(k+1) \geq k+1$.

Now, choose an arbitrary natural number $n$. According to the above we have $f(n + 1) \geq n + 1$ and hence $f(n + 1) > n$. This means that there is an argument of the function (namely $n + 1$) for which it takes a value greater than $n$. $\qquad\square$

---

**Fig. 1.** A piece of mathematical text as written in the Common Mathematical Language (CML)

shown in Fig. 1. Looking at the structure of the text we notice that it contains two definitions (of the notions increasing and unbounded) and a theorem with its proof. This general structure is preserved in the translation of the text into WTT which is shown in Fig. 2.

Formally, the WTT text is called a book (we follow de Bruijn [4] who used this format in his pioneering Automath project). Books are lists of lines and a line is either a statement or a definition under a context. We represent the context by (nested) flags, with flag staffs denoting their scope. For example, the statement line $f(0) \geq 0$ in Fig. 2 has as context $f :$ Increasing Function and the line $f(k + 1) \geq k + 1$ has as context $f :$ Increasing Function, $k : N, f(k) \geq k$.

The syntax of the subset of WTT that we consider here is given below. It contains all essential components of WTT with exception of some extra binders

$\mathsf{Function} := (N \to N) \downarrow$

$\mathsf{Increasing} := Adj_{f:\mathsf{Function}} \forall_{n:N} (f(n+1) > f(n))$

$\mathsf{Unbounded} := Adj_{f:\mathsf{Function}} \forall_{n:N} \exists_{m:N} f(m) > n$

$\boxed{f : \mathsf{Increasing\ Function}}$

   $\boxed{f(0) \geq 0}$

   $\boxed{k : N}$

     $\boxed{f(k) \geq k}$

     $f(k+1) > f(k) \geq k$

     $f(k+1) \geq k+1$

   $\forall_{k:N} f(k) \geq k$

   $\boxed{n : N}$

     $f(n+1) \geq n+1$

     $f(n+1) > n$

     $\exists_{m:N} f(m) > n$

   $f$ is $\mathsf{Unbounded}$

$\forall_{f:\mathsf{Increasing\ Function}} f$ is $\mathsf{Unbounded}$

**Fig. 2.** Translation of the text from Fig. 1 into Weak Type Theory (WTT)

and constants that we have chosen not to include in order to keep the exposition clear.

$$
\begin{array}{rl}
\text{term} & \mathcal{T} ::= x \mid c(\vec{\mathcal{P}}) \mid \lambda_{\mathcal{Z}} \mathcal{T} \\
\text{adjective} & \mathcal{A} ::= Adj_{\mathcal{Z}}(\mathcal{S}_p) \\
\text{noun} & \mathcal{N} ::= c(\vec{\mathcal{P}}) \mid Noun_{\mathcal{Z}}(\mathcal{S}_p) \mid Abst_{\mathcal{Z}}(\mathcal{T}/\mathcal{N}/\mathcal{S}_s) \mid \mathcal{A}\mathcal{N} \mid S_s \downarrow \\
\text{set} & \mathcal{S}_s ::= x \mid c(\vec{\mathcal{P}}) \mid Set_{\mathcal{Z}}(\mathcal{S}_p) \mid \mathcal{N} \uparrow \\
\text{statement} & \mathcal{S}_p ::= x \mid c(\vec{\mathcal{P}}) \mid \mathcal{S}_p \to \mathcal{S}_p \mid \forall_Z(\mathcal{S}_p) \mid \exists_Z(\mathcal{S}_p) \mid \mathcal{T} \text{ is } \mathcal{A}
\end{array}
$$

$$
\begin{array}{rl}
\text{argument} & \mathcal{P} ::= \mathcal{S}_s \mid \mathcal{S}_p \mid \mathcal{T} \\
\text{declaration} & \mathcal{Z} ::= x:\mathsf{SET} \mid x:\mathsf{STAT} \mid x:\mathcal{N} \mid x:S_s \\
\text{context} & \Gamma ::= \emptyset \mid \Gamma, \mathcal{Z} \mid \Gamma, \mathcal{S}_p \\
\text{definition} & \mathcal{D} ::= c(\vec{x}) := (\mathcal{T}/\mathcal{S}_p/\mathcal{S}_s/\mathcal{A}/\mathcal{N}) \\
\text{line} & l ::= \Gamma \rhd \mathcal{D} \mid \Gamma \rhd \mathcal{S}_p \\
\text{book} & \mathcal{B} ::= \emptyset \mid \mathcal{B} \circ l
\end{array}
$$

For a complete description of WTT, including examples, we refer the reader to [8]. Here we will only briefly comment on some elements of the syntax used in our examples. The main weak types are term, adjective, noun, set and statement. A noun is used for indefinite descriptions, like 'a natural number greater than zero' (which is expressed by $Noun_{n:N}(0 < n)$. Adjectives are used to denote properties and may be applied to nouns ($\mathcal{AN}$ above) or to terms ($\mathcal{T}$ is $\mathcal{A}$). The operators ↑ and ↓ are used to convert a noun to a set and conversely. The binder *Set* is used for set comprehension. Statements are formed from atomic propositions (constant instances) and the usual connectives and quantifiers. The notation $\vec{\mathcal{P}}$ and $\vec{x}$ is used to denote (possibly empty) lists of objects of the corresponding category.

Fig. 2 contains the WTT text representing the informal text in Fig. 1. We have used some "syntax sugaring" (e.g. infix notation) to make the text more readable. Comparing the informal and the WTT text we can see that:

- the definitions and the statements in the text are clearly identified;
- the scope of all variables is explicitly specified either by a flag or a binder;
- no requirements are imposed on the logical validity of the statements. In particular, there is no commitment to a specific logical system (classical, intuitionistic, etc.);
- the WTT text is still readable by a mathematician;
- formalization choices to resolve ambiguities in the original text (which potentially could introduce formalization errors) have been reduced to a minimum.

## 2.2    Step 2: From Weak Type Theory to Type Theory with Incomplete Terms

Once we have translated the CML text to WTT and after making sure that the formal version faithfully captures the intended meaning of the informal one, we can look further down the formalization path.

At this point we do have to make a number of choices that may significantly influence the final result. For example, we need to choose the target system in which the fully formalized text should be represented. Here we have chosen dependent type theory as a target system but, at least in principle, we could choose also another system. We use dependent types among many other reasons also because there are versions of it that support incomplete terms which as we will see is very useful for our purposes. So, to fix the setting of the paper, in the rest of the paper we will assume that the target system is a dependent type theory in PTS style [1] which admits global parameterized definitions, constants and meta-variables [6].

The basic idea is to translate the WTT text into type theory with incomplete terms. Incomplete terms are terms with missing parts that are represented by meta-variables. We naturally obtain such terms from WTT texts because the reasoning steps are not included in WTT and because some implicit information in the WTT needs to be made explicit for the sake of the stronger typing.

To make the intended translation more intuitive, we will introduce flag notation for the type theory. Here are the main features and the differences with the flag notation for WTT: The syntax of the terms is the one of the typing system (i.e. typed λ-calculus) and the text is again structured in books consisting of lines under zero or more flags. In contrast to WTT, here all flags contain variable declarations and every line has the form

$$\boxed{\vec{x} : \vec{A}}$$
$$\bigg|\ c(\vec{x}) := M : B$$

flags in scope

definition line

where $\vec{A}$ and $B$ are types and $M$ is either a term or one of the special symbols open and prim. When $M$ is a term, the line is a definition of $c(\vec{x})$; when $M$ is open, this indicates that the line declares that $c(\vec{x})$ is a meta-variable standing for an unknown term of type $B$. When $M$ is prim, this is an indication that $c(\vec{x})$ is an uninterpreted (axiomatic) constant. The difference between a meta-variable and an axiomatic constant is that the meta-variable denotes an unknown term that we look for and hence at some point when this term becomes known, we have to convert the meta-variable declaration into a 'real' definition.

After we defined the flag notation for type theory with open terms, we need to give the rules for deciding whether a book is strongly well-typed. There are two approaches – a direct and an indirect one. The direct one is to give typing rules for flagged books. We choose the indirect one which is for each book to define a typing judgment in the standard notation and to postulate that a book is well-typed if and only if that typing judgment is derivable. This process is explained in more detail in Section 4.

In Fig. 3 we can see the OTT version of the text of Fig. 1 and Fig. 2. We notice that here all lines are in the form of definitions and have labels in the form of the constant being defined.

The process of translating a WTT book into OTT is rather involved. In this case we see that the adjectives have been translated into predicates and that the nouns have become types of sort Set. Declarations involving complex nouns like $f$ : Increasing Function are split into a declaration of an object of the type to which the noun is mapped ($f$ : Function) and an assumption that this object satisfies the predicate to which the adjective is mapped ($h$ : Increasing($f$)).

Statements of the form '$M$ is $A$' where $M$ is a term and $A$ is an adjective are translated to the propositions stating that $M$ satisfies the predicate of $A$. The logical connectives and quantifiers are straightforward to map using the usual propositions-as-types embedding.

In WTT a definition has the form $c(\vec{x}) := M$ while here we need $c(\vec{x}) := M : A$. This requires that we first translate the term $M$ and then use the type inference algorithm in the target type theory to find the type $A$.

Apart from the technical details, at this stage we are looking for a mechanism to translate as big a part as possible of the weakly well-typed WTT derivations into OTT. It is clear that there are many for which this is not possible simply because there is no possible strong typing for some weakly typed texts. However for those that this is possible, it may be difficult to do it automatically because of a number of reasons. We discuss some of the problems in Section 3. A practical implementation needs to find the right balance between performance and completeness since the more we try to expand the set of translatable WTT derivations, the more difficult problems we will confront. Where exactly this

$$\boxed{\text{Function} := (N \to N) : \text{Set}}$$

$\boxed{f : \text{Function}}$

$\text{Increasing}(f) := \forall_{n:N}(f(n+1) > f(n)) : \text{Prop}$

$\text{Unbounded}(f) := \forall_{n:N}\exists_{m:N}f(m) > n : \text{Prop}$

$\boxed{f : \text{Function}}$

$\boxed{h : \text{Increasing}(f)}$

$L_1[f,h] := \text{open} : f(0) \geq 0$

$\boxed{k : N}$

$\boxed{g : f(k) \geq k}$

$L_2[f,h,k,g] := \text{open} : f(k+1) > f(k) \geq k$

$L_3[f,h,k,g] := \text{open} : f(k+1) \geq k+1$

$L_4[f,h] := \text{open} : \forall_{k:N}f(k) \geq k$

$\boxed{n : N}$

$L_5[f,h,n] := \text{open} : f(n+1) \geq n+1$

$L_6[f,h,n] := \text{open} : f(n+1) > n$

$L_7[f,h,n] := \text{open} : \exists_{m:N}f(m) > n$

$L_8[f,h] := \text{open} : \text{Unbounded}(f)$

$L_9 := \text{open} : \forall_{f:\text{Function}}\text{Increasing}(f) \to \text{Unbounded}(f)$

**Fig. 3.** Translation of the WTT text from Fig. 2 into Type Theory with open terms in flag notation

balance lies is difficult to estimate and practical experiments are necessary to establish it.

## 2.3   Step 3: From Type Theory with Incomplete Terms to Type Theory

This is the last of the three steps in the formalization path that we discuss. So far we have a strongly well-typed flagged book in type theory with open terms and our goal is to fill in all remaining open places. These open places would typically be all proof steps in the proofs; proof obligations when using conditional definitions; terms used as witnesses which are implicit in the informal text, etc.

We should point out that the tasks required at this stage are the typical tasks performed with an (interactive) theorem prover based on type theory. We have a problem which is already formally stated and within the language of the prover and our goal is to construct terms of certain types that correspond to the open places in the OTT text.

Hence, at this point we could decide to use an interactive theorem prover to construct the missing parts and this is probably the best choice. Modern provers are complex software systems that offer a lot of help to the user in form of tactics and decision procedures for quickly making relatively large proof steps. We could mention among many others Coq [5], LEGO [10], Mizar [11], etc.

In this paper we would like to show however that the process of term construction in a theorem prover can be modeled in a natural way using flagged books. To illustrate that we take a part of the derivation in Fig. 3 and show how the basic steps of proof construction in the prover can be modeled inside the OTT.

Consider the first derivation in Fig. 4. It depicts a part of the OTT text from Fig. 3. $L_7$ there stands for the yet unknown proof of the existential statement

$$\exists_{m:N} f(m) > n$$

To do that, suppose that we have a term $ex\_intro$ representing the introduction rule for the existential quantifier. This means that we have

$$ex\_intro : \Pi U : \mathsf{Set}.\Pi P : (U \to \mathsf{Prop}).\Pi t : U.\Pi h : (Pt).\exists_{xU}(Px)$$

In other words, when applied to a set $U$, a predicate $P$ on it, an element $t$ of $U$ and a proof of $P(t)$, $ex\_intro$ would be a proof of $\exists_{x:U} P(x)$.

The second derivation in Fig. 4 shows an application of $ex\_intro$ to unknown arguments $L_7^1, L_7^2, L_7^3$ and $L_7^4$ which of course is a proof of $\exists_{x:L_7^1} L_7^2(x)$. However, our goal is to solve $L_7$ which should be of type $exists_{m:N} f(m) > n$. Hence we see that to use $ex\_intro$ to solve $L_7$ we need to solve $L_7^1$ by $N$ and $L_7^2$ by $\lambda m.f(m) > n$.

This leads to the third derivation and now we have to find the witness $m$ and a proof that $f(m) > n$. Recall however that $L_6$ is an unknown proof of $f(n+1) > n$. If we try to use $L_6$ as a last argument of $ex\_intro$, we see that in order to get a typable term, $L_7^3$ has to have the value $n+1$. This is depicted by the final derivation in Fig. 4.

Continuing in a similar way we can fill in the rest of the open goals in the derivation as this is shown on Fig. 5. For brevity we have omitted the types of the variables in $\lambda$-abstractions there.

## 3     Some Problems During the Translation of WTT Texts into Type Theory

Usually a typing system used in a theorem prover requires much stronger typing than the one required from the weakly well-typed texts. It is hence natural to expect that there will be problems when one tries to translate a WTT text to such a system. In this section we discuss several of these problems and possible solutions for them.

$\boxed{f : \mathsf{Function}}$

$\quad\boxed{h : \mathsf{Increasing}(f)}$

$\qquad\boxed{n : N}$

$\qquad\quad L_6 := \mathsf{open} : f(n+1) > n$

$\qquad\quad L_7 := \mathsf{open} : \exists_{m:N} f(m) > n$

$\boxed{f : \mathsf{Function}}$

$\quad\boxed{h : \mathsf{Increasing}(f)}$

$\qquad\boxed{n : N}$

$\qquad\quad L_7^1 := \mathsf{open} : \mathsf{Set}$

$\qquad\quad L_7^2 := \mathsf{open} : L_7^1 \to \mathsf{Prop}$

$\qquad\quad L_7^3 := \mathsf{open} : L_7^1$

$\qquad\quad L_7^4 := \mathsf{open} : L_7^2(L_7^3)$

$\qquad\quad L_7^5 := ex\_intro(L_7^1, L_7^2, L_7^3, L_7^4) : \exists_{m:L_7^1} L_7^2(m)$

$\qquad\quad L_7 := \mathsf{open} : \exists_{m:N} f(m) > n$

$\boxed{f : \mathsf{Function}}$

$\quad\boxed{h : \mathsf{Increasing}(f)}$

$\qquad\boxed{n : N}$

$\qquad\quad L_7^3 := \mathsf{open} : L_7^1$

$\qquad\quad L_7^4 := \mathsf{open} : L_7^2(L_7^3)$

$\qquad\quad L_7 := ex\_intro(N, \lambda x.f(x) > n, L_7^3, L_7^4) : \exists_{m:N} f(m) > n$

$\boxed{f : \mathsf{Function}}$

$\quad\boxed{h : \mathsf{Increasing}(f)}$

$\qquad\boxed{n : N}$

$\qquad\quad L_7 := ex\_intro(N, \lambda x.f(x) > n, n+1, L_6) : \exists_{m:N} f(m) > n$

**Fig. 4.** Sequential refinement steps. We have left out the trivial parameter list $f$, $h$, $n$ after each of the constants (e.g. $L_7^1$ should be read as $L_7^1[f, h, n]$)

## 3.1   General Problems

The path from CML to Type Theory that we explore in this paper has a number of advantages in terms of the reliability of the formalization, the fact that it is

$f$ : Function

$h$ : Increasing$(f)$

$\cdots$

$n : N$

$L_5[f, h, n] := L_4(n + 1) : f(n + 1) \geq n + 1$

$L_6[f, h, n] := le\_lt(f(n + 1), n, L_5[f, h, n]) : f(n + 1) > n$

$L_7[f, h, n] := ex\_intro(N, (\lambda m.f(m) > n), n + 1, L_6[f, h, n]) : \exists_{m:N} f(m) > n$

$L_8[f, h] := \lambda hn.ex\_intro(N, (\lambda m.f(m) > n), n + 1, L_6[f, h, n]) :$ Unbounded$(f)$

$L_9 := \lambda fhn.ex\_intro(N, (\lambda m.f(m) > n), n + 1, L_6[f, h, n]) :$

$: \forall_{f:Function}$ Increasing$(f) \rightarrow$ Unbounded$(f)$

**Fig. 5.** A possible completion of bottom part of the OTT text. The term $le\_lt$ denotes a proof of the lemma $\forall n \forall k (n \geq k + 1) \rightarrow (n > k)$

quite natural (and hence easy to use), etc. but we cannot avoid the problems that any formalization needs to solve.

Such problems are in the first place to choose the target system and how logic or other aspects of the original text will be interpreted in that system. For example, in Type Theory one distinguishes between deep and shallow embedding of a logical system. An embedding is deep when the connectives and the quantifiers are interpreted as types in the system (for example, $A \rightarrow B$ becomes $\Pi p : A.B$ or $\forall x : U.A(x)$ becomes $\Pi x : U.A(x)$). The shallow embedding is used in the so-called logical frameworks to define different logics by introducing constants representing the connectives and quantifiers. Both approaches have their pros and cons and one should make a choice based on other factors like in what context the formalization is going to be used.

### 3.2    Conditional Definitions

In Fig. 6 we see a definition of a predicate (divides$(m, n)$) under a certain condition ($m \neq 0$). Later we use this predicate with arguments $y$ and $2y$ where $y$ is declared to be a positive number. The implicit intention of the author of the text is of course that every positive number is non-zero and hence the predicate may be used. This implicit intention must be made explicit in the type theory. Fig. 7 shows how we can do this. The definition of divides which is under the condition $m \neq 0$ is translated to a definition which has one extra argument, $h : (m \neq 0)$ which is a proof of the fact that $m$ is non-zero. Adding extra proof parameters to a definition is one of the standard ways to represent partial functions in type theory and dates back to the Authomath project (see [3], p.709-710).

Next, we need to translate the instance divides$(y, 2y)$ in the last statement in Fig. 6. As the definition of divides prescribes, we need to provide a proof that $y$ is non-zero. This proof in principle should be constructed using the assumption that $y$ is a positive number. So we introduce a meta-variable $m$ representing this

$$
\begin{array}{|l}
\hline
\boxed{m, n : N} \\
\quad \boxed{m \neq 0} \\
\quad \mathsf{divides}(m, n) := \exists_{k:N}(n = km) \\
\quad \mathsf{positive} := Adj_{n:N}(0 < n) \\
\quad \mathsf{number} := N \downarrow \\
\quad \boxed{y : \mathsf{positive\ number}} \\
\quad \mathsf{divides}(y, 2y)
\end{array}
$$

**Fig. 6.** Conditional definitions

$$
\begin{array}{|l}
\hline
\boxed{m, n : N} \\
\quad \boxed{h : (m \neq 0)} \\
\quad \mathsf{divides}(m, n, \boxed{h}) := \exists_{k:N}(n = km) : \mathsf{Prop} \\
\boxed{n : N} \\
\quad \mathsf{positive}(n) := (0 < n) : \mathsf{Prop} \\
\quad \mathsf{number} := N : \mathsf{Set} \\
\quad \boxed{y : \mathsf{number}} \\
\quad \boxed{h : \mathsf{positive}(y)} \\
\quad\quad \boxed{m[y, h] := \mathsf{open} : (y \neq 0)} \\
\quad\quad L_1[y, h] := \mathsf{open} : \mathsf{divides}(y, 2y, \boxed{m[y, h]})
\end{array}
$$

**Fig. 7.** Handling of conditional definitions

proof. Note that $m$ is introduced in the same context as the occurrence of divides and hence it is in the scope of the assumption $h : \mathsf{positive}(y)$.

The actual proof of the fact that $y \neq 0$ follows from $0 < y$ is implicit in the proof and this is reflected here by the introduction of the meta-variable. We prefer to leave a proof open instead of using other methods like subtyping, decision procedures, etc. The use of such methods is not prevented or denied, we have just delayed their use and left it to the dedicated theorem prover that will work with the text with incomplete proofs.

## 3.3    The Need for Unification

As we explained above, in certain cases we may obtain objects which depend on totally or partially unknown proofs. Due to the strong typing, often we will need to check whether two objects are equal. Since every occurrence of a constant declared under a condition gets a fresh meta-variable as a representation of the unknown proof of the condition, we will find out that many constants are not equal.

For example, Consider the following declaration of the inversion function $x^{-1}$ for non-zero $x$ and the goal to prove that $x^{-1} = x^{-1}$:

$$
\boxed{x : R} \qquad\qquad \boxed{x : R}
$$

$$
\boxed{\; \begin{array}{l} \boxed{x \neq 0} \\ \quad \boxed{\begin{array}{l} inv(x) := \dots \\ inv(x) = inv(x) \end{array}} \end{array} \;}
\qquad
\boxed{\; \begin{array}{l} \boxed{h : (x \neq 0)} \\ \quad \begin{array}{l} inv(x, h) := \dots : R \\ m_1[x] := \mathsf{open} : x \neq 0 \\ m_2[x] := \mathsf{open} : x \neq 0 \\ L_1[x] := \mathsf{open} : inv[x, m_1[x]] = inv[x, m_2[x]] \end{array} \end{array} \;}
$$

The translation of the WTT text is shown to the right. Looking at the WTT text, one may think that to solve the goal a simple reference to the reflexivity of equality is enough, but in fact such an approach will fail, since the terms $inv[x, m_1[x]]$ and $inv[x, m_2[x]]$ are not $\beta$-convertible. Using unification however we could find out that to make them convertible, it is enough to have $m_2[x] := m_1[x]$.

This simple example shows how the introduction of proof parameters to objects may break the strong typing rules of the target type theory. Such problems are unavoidable however and one may need to use a form of matching or unification in order to eliminate (part of) them.

### 3.4    Set Comprehension, Adjectives and Function Spaces

In WTT we can form nouns by means of application of adjectives to existing nouns or to create sets by set comprehension which effectively introduces a kind of subtyping in the system. Consider for example the WTT text in Fig. 8. We have a second order function on the positive numbers whose type is defined using adjectives and set comprehension. One way to deal with such functions could be to extend the approach from Section 3.2 as shown in Fig. 9. The idea

$$
\begin{array}{l}
\mathsf{positive} := Adj_{n:N}(0 < n) \\
\mathsf{number} := N \downarrow \\
\boxed{f : (\mathsf{positive\ number} \to \mathsf{positive\ number}) \to Set_{k:N}(0 < k)} \\
\quad f(\lambda x : \mathsf{positive\ number}.x) > 0
\end{array}
$$

**Fig. 8.** Adjectives and function spaces

positive $:= Adj_{n:N}(0 < n)$

> $f : \Pi g : (\Pi x : N.(0 < x) \to N).\Pi H : (\Pi x : N.(0 < x) \to 0 < g(x,h)).N$
>
> > $F : \Pi g : (\Pi x : N.(0 < x) \to N).\Pi H : (\Pi x : N.(0 < x) \to 0 < g(x,h)).0 < f(g,H)$
> >
> > > $L_1 :=$ open $: f(\lambda x : N\lambda h : (0 < x).x)(\lambda x : N\lambda h : (0 < x).h) > 0$

**Fig. 9.**

is to represent functions whose range is a comprehended set into two functions. The first one produces the value and the second the proof that the value of the first satisfied the conditions. If such a function is given as an argument, the translation would expect two arguments, again one that produces the value and a second for the proof obligation (see Fig. 9).

This approach is technically complicated and it is not yet clear whether it is universally applicable (i.e. whether it is possible to do it automatically). Hence an implementation may have to limit the use of adjectives and set comprehension in function formation. We also have to keep in mind that the translation very much depends on the choice of a target type theory and hence on the possibilities to introduce subtyping there.

## 4    From Flag Notation to Typing Judgments

The flag notation that we use to represent the translation of WTT books into type theory can be converted in a straightforward manner into the usual notation with typing judgments if the target typing system supports parameterized definitions and meta-variables. Such a judgment has the form

$$\Gamma \vdash M : A$$

where $\Gamma$ is a context containing declarations and definitions, $M$ is a term and $A$ is a type. It should be read as 'in the context $\Gamma$, the term $M$ has type $A$.'

Given an OTT book in flag notation, we convert every line of the book into a parameterized definition or a declaration of a constant or a meta-variable. The parameters form a local context that is constructed by collecting all declarations in the flags under which the current line is situated. For example, in Fig. 10 we see that a primitive constant ($N$) is translated into a parameterized declaration, a definition line (divides) is translated into a parameterized definition and open definitions (m and $L_1$) are mapped into declarations of parameterized meta-variables.

This straightforward translation of flagged derivations into conventional judgment form allows us to define that a well-formed flagged derivation is well-typed if and only if its translation is derivable as a conventional judgment. Actually,

$N := \mathsf{prim} : \mathsf{Set}$

> $m, n : N$
>> $h : (m \neq 0)$
>> $\mathsf{divides}(m, n, h) := \exists_{k:N}(n = km) : \mathsf{Prop}$
>
>> $n : N$
>> $\mathsf{positive}(n) := (0 < n) : \mathsf{Prop}$
>
>> $y : \mathsf{number}$
>>> $h : \mathsf{positive}(y)$
>>> $m[y, h] := \mathsf{open} : (y \neq 0)$
>>> $L_1[y, h] := \mathsf{open} : \mathsf{divides}(y, 2y, m[y, h])$

Flag Notation

---

Conventional Notation

$N : \mathsf{Set},$
$\mathsf{divides}(m : N, n : N, h : (m \neq 0)) := \exists_{k:N}(n = km) : \mathsf{Prop},$
$\mathsf{positive}(n : N) := (0 < n) : \mathsf{Prop},$
$m[y : N, h : \mathsf{positive}(y)] : (y \neq 0),$
$L_1[y : N, h : \mathsf{positive}(y)] : \mathsf{divides}(y, 2y, m[y, h])$
$\vdash$
$\mathsf{Set} : \mathsf{Type}$

**Fig. 10.** A text in flag notation and its translation to a conventional judgment form. To distinguish between constants and meta-variables, we denote the former by $c(\ldots)$ and the latter by $m[\ldots]$

what we need is only that the context of the judgment is valid. This is the reason why we have $\mathsf{Set} : \mathsf{Type}$ after the turnstyle ($\vdash$) sign.

## 5    Conclusions and Further Research

We discussed, using examples to illustrate our approach, how a CML-text can be transformed stepwise into (1) a formal WTT-text, (2) a version in type theory with open terms and (3) stepwise, into a fully formalized text in type theory. We argued that the sketched formalization and proof construction is 'natural' in the sense that a human can easily follow the path and do the steps needed, possibly with active help of a proof assistant. Moreover, we have the conviction that the proposed approach increases the reliability of the formalization, as regards its conformity to the intentions of the mathematical author.

As topics of future work we can mention further investigation of the translation of WTT into Type Theory with open terms, including a prototype implementation. Such an implementation will gives us more understanding of the practical feasibility of the approach we advocate here.

# References

1. H. Barendregt, Lambda calculi with types, In Abramsky et al. (eds.), *Handbook of Logic in Computer Science*, pp. 117–309, Oxford University Press, 1992.
2. H. Barendregt and H. Geuvers, Proof assistants using dependent type systems, in: *Handbook of Automated Reasoning*, Elsevier Science Publishers B.V., 1999.
3. L.S. van Benthem Jutting, Checking Landau's "Grundlagen" in the Automath System, in: R.P. Nederpelt, J.H. Geuvers, and R.C. de Vrijer (eds.), *Selected Papers on Automath*, volume 133 of *Studies in Logic and Foundations of Mathematics*, pp. 701–732, North Holland, 1994.
4. N.G. de Bruijn, The mathematical language Automath, its usage and some of its extensions, in: R.P. Nederpelt, J.H. Geuvers, and R.C. de Vrijer (eds.), *Selected Papers on Automath*, volume 133 of *Studies in Logic and Foundations of Mathematics*, North Holland, 1994.
5. The Coq Development Team, *The Coq Proof Assistant Reference Manual – Version V7.4*, February 2003, http://coq.inria.fr/.
6. G.I. Jojgov, *Incomplete Proofs and Terms and Their Use in Interactive Theorem Proving*, PhD thesis, Eindhoven University of Technology, 2004.
7. G.I. Jojgov, R.P. Nederpelt, and M. Scheffer. Faithfully reflecting the structure of informal mathematical proofs into formal type theories, in: *Proceedings of the MKM Symposium 2003*, Elsevier, 2003.
8. F. Kamareddine and R. Nederpelt, A refinement of de Bruijn's formal language of mathematics, to appear in *Journal of Logic, Language and Information*.
9. R. Nederpelt, Weak Type Theory: A formal language for mathematics, Technical report, Eindhoven University of Technology, May 2002.
10. R. Pollack, The LEGO Proof Assistant, http://www.dcs.ed.ac.uk/home/lego/index.html.
11. P. Rudnicki, An overview of the Mizar project, in: *Proceedings of the 1992 Workshop on Types for Proofs and Programs*, 1992, http://www.mizar.org.

# Flexible Encoding of Mathematics on the Computer

Fairouz Kamareddine, Manuel Maarek, and J. B. Wells

Heriot-Watt University, http://www.macs.hw.ac.uk/ultra/

**Abstract.** This paper reports on refinements and extensions to the MathLang framework that add substantial support for natural language text. We show how the extended framework supports multiple views of mathematical texts, including natural language views using the exact text that the mathematician wants to use. Thus, MathLang now supports the ability to capture the essential mathematical structure of mathematics written using natural language text. We show examples of how arbitrary mathematical text can be encoded in MathLang without needing to change any of the words or symbols of the texts or their order. In particular, we show the encoding of a theorem and its proof that has been used by Wiedijk for comparing many theorem prover representations of mathematics, namely the irrationality of $\sqrt{2}$ (originally due to Pythagoras). We encode a 1960 version by Hardy and Wright, and a more recent version by Barendregt.

## 1   On the Way to a Mathematical Vernacular for Computers

Mathematicians now use computer software for a variety of tasks: typing mathematical texts, performing calculation, analyzing theories, verifying proofs. Software tools like Mathematica have been refined through many years of development. Research in mathematics, logic, and computer science has led to computer algebra systems (CAS's) and theorem provers (TPs). Languages like OMDoc [14] show good promise of having a universal way to share CAS and TP data in a mathematical software network [22].

Nevertheless, ordinary mathematicians still *write* mathematical knowledge (MK) using the traditional *common mathematical language* (CML) and typesetting tools like LaTeX. CML is mature and capable for human communication of mathematics, but unfortunately is difficult to computerize in a way that captures its essential structure.

We believe this is largely because existing computer MK representations either fail to capture the mathematical structure of natural language as used in mathematics or require writing in a rigid format [9]. Mathematical typesetting systems like LaTeX fail to capture the mathematical structure of both natural language text and symbolic formulas. Existing computer mathematics systems that capture mathematical structure either (1) do so for symbolic formulas but not natural language sentences and phrases (e.g. OpenMath or computer algebra systems), (2) handle natural language text via very complicated type systems (e.g. GF [18]), (3) require full formalization (e.g. Mizar [19] or other proof systems), or (4) otherwise restrict mathematicians' freedom to edit and display their texts in the form that best meets their needs and desires.

Theoretical approaches to this issue include De Bruijn's Mathematical Vernacular (MV) [4] and the recently developed Weak Type Theory (WTT) of Kamareddine and

A. Asperti et al. (Eds.): MKM 2004, LNCS 3119, pp. 160–174, 2004.
© Springer-Verlag Berlin Heidelberg 2004

Nederpelt [12], both of which strive toward a formalism that captures the structure of mathematical text while remaining close to the mathematician's original text.

Carrying the work of MV and WTT forward, we have been building MathLang, a framework for encoding mathematical texts on the computer. MathLang's heart is a formalism capturing the important mathematical structure of mathematical writing while keeping the flexibility of the traditional common mathematical language (CML). MathLang aims to interface computer mathematics systems with mathematicians.

MathLang analyses all mathematical texts into two interleaved parts, one for the natural language and one for the symbolic structure. The natural language part represents the text as the mathematician expects to view it. The symbolic part is automatically checked for structural correctness and contains enough semantic information to support further automatic manipulation by other available computer mathematics tools.

MathLang's design is constrained by the desire to balance the needs of ordinary mathematicians in writing MK with the needs of automated computer manipulation of MK. To support mathematicians, MathLang seeks to be (1) *expressive*, so it can handle all kinds of mathematical mental constructs, (2) *flexible*, so that ordinary mathematicians will not find it awkward to use, and (3) *universal*, so that it covers many branches of mathematics and is adaptable to new ones. To support computer manipulation, MathLang seeks to be (4) relatively *unambiguous*, so that automated processing will often be possible without human interaction, (5) sensibly *organized*, so that most desired ways of browsing the data will not be difficult, and (6) *automation-friendly*, to facilitate further more complex computations.

The language formalism of MathLang has three main features. **(1) A symbolic structure.** MathLang encodes mathematical texts via a symbolic syntax. A small set of grammatical constructions allows encoding the reasoning structure of texts. The symbolic structure is helpful for further encodings and translations. **(2) A** Cml **layer.** MathLang can coat the symbolic structure of the text with natural language information that supports a CML view of the text, like the kind of visual output that could be generated if it was written in LATEX, but also keeping the full underlying computerized structure. **(3) Automatic checking of basic grammatical conditions of the reasoning structure.** MathLang encodes the reasoning structure of a texts. A set of typing rules checks basic grammatical conditions using weak types, thus validating the good formation of the text at a grammatical level. It is very important that this checking does not require full formalization or committing to any specific foundation of mathematics.

In earlier work [13], we introduced MathLang, defined its XML-based concrete syntax, implemented a weak type checker, and tested the encoding of substantial real mathematical documents. MathLang's CML layer is new and is reported here for the first time. MathLang's symbolic structure and automated checking have had minor improvements since first reported, mainly to better support the integration of natural language text.

This article introduces MathLang's CML support in the context of explaining how the design of MathLang is evolving so that it can balance the needs both for the encoding to easily support desired computations and for the representation to be close enough to the thinking of the mathematician. Section 2 presents the MathLang philosophy while the later sections explain the capabilities of MathLang via example encodings. Although we are currently testing MathLang by encoding two large mathematical books [15, 10], this article presents encodings of shorter examples, fully developed in MathLang. Section 3 presents an example (translated earlier into WTT) and shows its encoding in MathLang via both the symbolic and CML views automatically derived by MathLang. Section 4 presents a bigger example: *Pythagoras' proof of the irrationality of* $\sqrt{2}$. We chose this proof because it has been previously used by Wiedijk as a *universal* example of proof encoding for theorem provers [20]. We encode two informal versions of this proof in MathLang: an earlier one due to Hardy and Wright as well as a more explicit (but still informal) one due to Barendregt. For all 3 example encodings presented in this paper, the CML view illustrates that (unlike WTT) MathLang indeed preserves all the original text, including the natural language part.

## 2    MathLang's Philosophy and Evolving Design

MathLang follows these goals:

1. Remain close to CML as used by mathematicians to write mathematics.
2. Act as a formal structured style which can be plugged into CAS's, TPs and other mathematical software systems.
3. Provide users of mathematics with much needed help in getting the original mathematical text into the computer by providing both a formal view of the text, and a natural language view. The formal view of the text is exactly its symbolic part and is passed to an automatic weak type checker which tests the structural validity of the text. The natural language view is automatically generated from the formal view and looks exactly like the original text.

We believe MathLang is the first framework which satisfies all the goals above. Some systems, Mizar [19] being the best example, have impressive libraries that show that much mathematics can be computerized and formalized, but they are not yet widely used by mathematicians. Abstract languages like MV and WTT are strongly based on goal 1, but fall short on goals 2 and 3, because neither provides any computer help, nor an automatic type checker to check the structural correctness of texts, nor is there a method yet of taking the translation of an original text in MV or WTT and deriving from the translation a text that looks exactly like the original one. Although MathLang has a type system which is an extension of WTT with flags and blocks, it goes well beyond MV and WTT by also working as a computer system which will communicate with other computer systems via XML and XSLT and will offer the user software help. Moreover, the merge between the abstract and the software could not have worked well to provide a view that looks so much like the original text, without both (1) the careful separation of texts into a natural language part and a formal part and (2) a careful interleaving of both parts.

Below we describe the framework MathLang following its three main features listed in Section 1. We first describe the syntax and grammar of MathLang, then we describe how the CML layer has been designed, then we explain the value that is added by MathLang's type system compared to a normal CML encoding.

## 2.1    The Symbolic Structure

The MathLang symbolic language [13] has a strict grammar that allows one to describe, with a small set of constructions, any feature that composes the reasoning content of a mathematical text.

**MathLang's Grammar.** As in MV [4] and WTT [12], an entire MathLang document is called a *book*. It is composed by a set of blocks, flags and lines. Blocks and flags are themselves composed by sub-blocks, flags and lines. A *block* highlights a piece of text as a coherent entity. It could be a section, a proof or a subproof, an example or any structure that the author wants to identify. Local constants are defined within a block (see below for more explanation). A *flag* declares variables (again, see below) and makes assumptions that will hold on a piece of text. A *line* is an atomic step of reasoning. As in common mathematical texts, a line could either make a new statement in the theory or define a new symbol (the *sentence level* groups these two possible kinds of line). Books, blocks, flags and lines compose the *discourse level*.

Four constructions are defined in MathLang to write expressions that will be the material of assumptions, declarations, definitions and statements from the discourse level. A *variable instance* refers to an already declared variable. A *constant call* uses a defined constant by referring to its definition and, in the case of a parametrized constant, by instantiating it. *Binding* an expression and a new variable is also possible with one of the many binders of the language. The last construction *attributes* an adjective to a noun to refine its meaning (again, see in the following for explanation on adjectives and nouns). These four constructions make up the *phrase level*.

Symbols used in MathLang texts are used in the *atomic level*. They could be of three kinds: *variables* that are an abstraction of a mathematical object, *constants* that are parameterizable shortcuts for mathematical objects, and *binders*.

**Grammatical Categories.** Any construction of the phase level is part of a specific grammatical category depending on the sort of the mathematical object described. In an obvious sense it depends on the symbol used to construct the expression in question. There are five of them: *terms* for elements designing a mathematical object, *sets* for sets of objects, *nouns* for kinds of mathematical objects, *adjectives* for elements that gives some attributes to a noun, and *statements* for expression that are considered as structurally valid statements. This grammatical information will be used by the MathLang type system (see Section 2.3).

**Concrete Syntax.** The *concrete syntax* of MathLang uses XML. XML-MathLang texts have level-based structure and contain grammatical information for each symbol.

## 2.2    The Layer

A MathLang author separates a CML-text into its natural language part and its symbolic part, saving the natural language part for coating purposes later, and translating the symbolic part into XML-MathLang. This XML-MathLang text is then passed into the automatic type checker of the symbolic framework to test its structural well-formedness (see Section 2.3) and thus implicitly also the original text. Figure 1 informally compares this encoding approach to others.

CmL.    The overall document is in an informal encoding.

**OMDoc's Approach.** A slightly formal structure (dashed triangle) covers the entire document. CML texts are spread all around the document. OpenMath objects are used for formal definitions (<FMP> tag). Informal definitions (<CMP> tag) are text with embedded OpenMath formulas.

**WTT.** The overall document is a formal encoding. Like N.G. de Bruijn's MV and Z. Luo and P. Callaghan's Mathematical Vernacular [16], WTT is a theoretical language and does not have any natural language representation.

**MathLang's Approach.** A computerized structure covers the entire documents. Pieces of CML transformation procedures are attached to nodes of the document's skeleton.

**TPs' Approach.** The document is a fully formal data. Usually, CML explanations are separately given (dashed blobby shapes). The natural language is produced with generic computations according to some structured text given by the programmer. (We consider here the generation of natural language texts from Coq [5], the design of an electronic library of mathematics [1], the MoWGLI project [8], work to interface Coq with $\text{T}_{\text{E}}\text{X}_{\text{MACS}}$ [2], and the documentation system of FoC [17].)

Figure 2 shows that the original CML text is first divided into a symbolic part and a natural language part and that afterward, the full original text can be retrieved, as well as a fully symbolic part which can be passed for further processing. We are currently using XSLT to express the transformations to CML. We are considering the use of the Grammatical Framework [18] for its expressiveness as a replacement of XSL. A possible intermediate stage from CML-texts to fully formalized texts (the "later computations" in Figure 2) could be to use the Mathematical Proof Language [3], a language between informal and formalized mathematics.

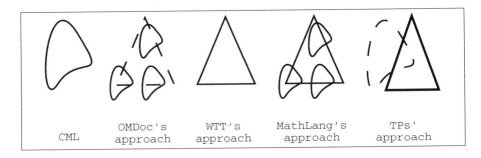

| CML | OMDoc's approach | WTT's approach | MathLang's approach | TPs' approach |

**Fig. 1.** Approaches. Informal data is represented by blobby shapes ($\wp$). Computerized and more formal data is represented by triangles ($\triangle$)

Rendering tools have been developed using XSLT to generate representations of MathLang documents. All the examples of this article have been automatically generated using these tools which work as follows given an XML-MathLang text:

- Display the information in symbolic structural view.
- Display the information in CML form (if it contains a natural language coating).

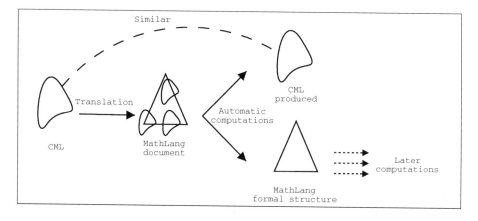

**Fig. 2.** Translation process

### 2.3    MathLang Typing

From this grammatical information given in the writing down of MathLang document, computerized analysis is possible. It gives some properties about the coherence of the text. This is done by assigning weak types to each grammatical category and construction. This weak typing remains at a grammatical level. A type theory could then be used to check the text. If a book is considered as a valid book after typing, it means that variables are well declared before being used and constants are well used according to their definitions. Because this analysis remains at a grammatical level, it therefore does not deal with the logical truth or validity of the text.

We developed an *automatic weak type checker* which analyzes the coherence of the XML-MathLang text. This automatic type checker, when given a text in XML-MathLang, checks whether the reasoning structure of the text is valid or not. In the latter case, an error message gives the reason of failure.

## 3    A Working Example

The translation of a mathematical text into a MathLang document is done by a human assisted by a computer. The MathLang writer should have a mathematical background to follow the reasoning of the mathematician author of the original text. Moreover, the MathLang writer needs to have skills in computer science to encode the document into the MathLang XML syntax. This last requirement would be avoided in the future by the development of a dedicated editor for MathLang (see Section 5).

### 3.1    The Translation Process

Four actions compose the translation process of a CML text into MathLang with presentation directives. The first two are to be done by the MathLang user. They are represented by the Translation arrow of Figure 2. The last two are initiated by the user and are automatically executed by MathLang's framework. These are the Automatic computations of Figure 2.

**Translating.** This is the main work done by the user: it reveals the reasoning structure of the original text and encodes it into MathLang. These do not require more work than a normal study of the text. The writer just needs to unfold implicit information form his understanding of the CML text (see Section 3.2).

**Adding Natural Language.** This is a crucial stage of the translation. It will not influence the *deep* MathLang encoding of the text and so will not change its validity. But it will make the MathLang document as readable as the original CML text. Because this stage is independent from type checking, this information could be added during the early translation of a piece of text or after the validating stage.

**Type Checking.** This stage is an automatic computation. The MathLang framework has a built in type checker which takes a MathLang XML document and checks its structural validity. The type checking of a MathLang XML document returns true if the program goes through the document without finding any problem. Otherwise the MathLang type checker will point an element of the document where an error has been found. The user will then need to fix it and recall the checker again.

**Producing the CML Output.** This stage is again fully automatic. It uses several XSL transformations to generate a CML text with colour annotations showing the weak types in the document. This process takes into account the presentation information given by the author to generate an output which is close to the original CML text.

To illustrate the steps to be taken by a MathLang user, we will explain the two first stages with a concrete example. We give the original text to be encoded, a representation of our MathLang encoding, and the CML output obtained from it. We use grey scale to show the belonging of text parts to a grammatical category. This helps to show in the CML MathLang output, the underlying structure of the MathLang encoding. Figure 4 contains the grey scale coding we are using in this paper.

We took our example from article [12]. By using the same example we aim to show what improvements MathLang makes over WTT. WTT was a theory describing a type system for the first level of formalization of mathematical texts. The language description was not precise enough to be used and no implementation of its ideas were available. MathLang reuses this type theory in its implementation. New constructions have been added as explained in [13].

## 3.2   The Example

Our example is a definition which defines the *difference quotient* of a function, explains what is a *differentiable* function and then states that $\sqrt{|x|}$ is not differentiable at 0. The original CML text is given by Figure 3. Figure 5 shows our MathLang encoding and Figure 6 the output we get.

---

**Definition 1.** *Let $h \neq 0$, let $f$ be a function from $A$ to $\mathbb{R}$, $a \in A$ and $a + h \in A$. Then* $\frac{f(a+h)-f(a)}{h}$ *is the* difference quotient *of $f$ in $a$ with difference $h$. We call $f$* differentiable *at $a$ if $\lim_{h \to 0} \frac{f(a+h)-f(a)}{h}$ exists. The function $\sqrt{|x|}$ is not differentiable at 0.*

---

**Fig. 3.** *Difference quotient* example: original text

**Fig. 4.** Grey scale coding

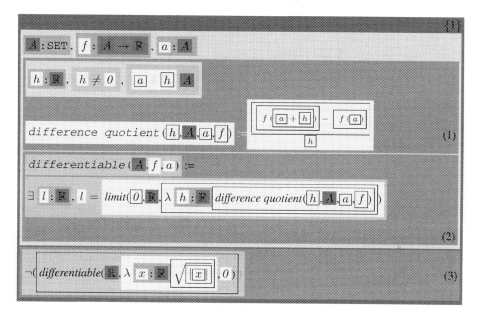

**Fig. 5.** *Difference quotient* example: symbolic structural view of MathLang

**Translating.** The original text is titled "Definition" and contains three steps. We encode it by a block (with indices {1}) to reflect the grouping of the overall definition. Then to each step corresponds one line. The first one (numbered 1) stands for the definition of the difference quotient and will be a definition line in MathLang. The second (numbered 2) will again be a definition line defining a new notion: differentiable. The last step (numbered 3) that establishes that $\sqrt{|x|}$ is not differentiable at 0 is encoded by a statement line.

*The Definitions.* In the text, we notice that both definitions have some elements in common. They use the same set $A$, the same function $f$ and the same element $a$ of $A$. These are variables. To put them in common in the MathLang document we use the flag construction that introduces context elements for several lines. In our case three variables are declared for the first two lines. The first definition also requires the declaration of the variable $h$ together with two assumptions: $h \neq 0$ and $a + h$ is in $A$.

We notice that the flag contains three elements. In the original text only four context elements are visible (the first sentence of Figure 3). The MathLang grammar forces one to strictly declare any variable. $A : SET$ that declares a set variable $A$ is an example of implicit declaration which is revealed by MathLang.

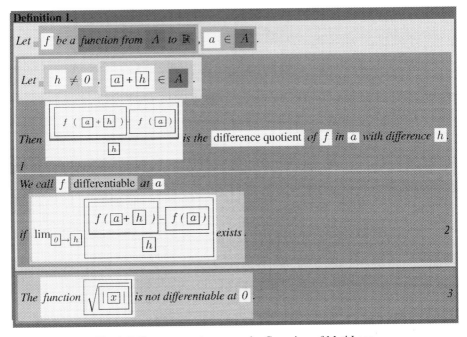

**Fig. 6.** *Difference quotient* example: CML view of MathLang

With these contexts enunciated, we give our two definitions. Here again some information will become explicit. Constant parameters should correspond to the current set of declared variables: $h$, $A$, $a$ and $f$ for the difference quotient and $A$, $f$ and $a$ for differentiable notion. The first definition uses some constants that we consider to be defined earlier on. The second definition uses the existential binder to state that a limit exists and that its value is the limit of the differential quotient when $h$ tends towards $0$. Our choice here was to reuse the constant previously defined difference quotient instead of writing again the equation.

*The Statement.* The last line with an empty context states that the function $\sqrt{|x|}$ (encoded with the $\lambda$ binder) is not differentiable at $0$. This expression uses the newly defined constant differentiable.

**Adding Natural Language.** The block including the entire text is represented with a definition LATEX environment. The sentence "Let [1], [2]." stands for the flag of our encoding where [1] and [2] are the declarations of $f$ and $a$. An empty little box in Figure 6 shows that an implicit declaration (the set $A$) took place. We do the same for the context of line 1. The order of declarations and assumptions was changed from Figure 3 to Figure 6 on purpose to show the boxes that correspond to the flag and to the context of the first line. "Then [1] is the [2] of [3] in [4] with difference [5]" is the template for our first definition. [1] being the expression of the definition, [2] the constant's name, [3] the constant's fourth parameter, [4] the third one and [5] the first one.

These associations that link one construction of the language to a natural language template could either be defined globally or locally to the document. One association could be reused at different positions. They are defined using XSL with some MathLang specific commands to easily refer to the information contained in the encoding. For example a unique command is used to colour the pieces of text according to their grammatical categories. For example, the presentation information for the line numbered 1 is as follow.

```
<template output="cml.tex" kind="xsl">
  <categ kind="par" boxed="no">
    <xsl:apply-templates select="context"/>
    <xsl:text>Then </xsl:text>
    <xsl:apply-templates select="expression"/>
    <xsl:text> is the </xsl:text>
    <xsl:apply-templates select="constant"/>
    <xsl:text> of </xsl:text>
    <xsl:apply-templates select="parameters[4]"/>
    <xsl:text> in </xsl:text>
    <xsl:apply-templates select="parameters[3]"/>
    <xsl:text> with difference </xsl:text>
    <xsl:apply-templates select="parameters[1]"/>
    <number/>
  </categ>
</template>
```

This information is a mix of XSL standard elements and MathLang specific ones. A first process will transform all these presentation data that coat the document to produce one single XSL file specific to the document in question. The second process simply consists of applying these transformation to the document itself.

## 4    Pythagoras' Proof of Irrationality of $\sqrt{2}$

In this section we give the CML-MathLang view of two versions of *Pythagoras' proof of the irrationality of* $\sqrt{2}$. We chose this proof because it has been previously used by Wiedijk as a *universal* example of proof encoding for theorem provers [20, 21]. Both original versions are included in [20]. The first one is an informal version written by G. H. Hardy and E. M. Wright (see Figure 7). Section 4.1 is the CML view of our translation into MathLang. The second one is a more explicit proof written by Henk Barendregt. We give the CML view of our MathLang translation in Section 4.2.

---

**Theorem 1 (Pythagoras' Theorem).** $\sqrt{2}$ *is irrational.*

*Proof.* If $\sqrt{2}$ is rational, then the equation

$$a^2 = 2b^2$$

is soluble in integers $a$, $b$ with $(a, b) = 1$. Hence $a^2$ is even, and therefore $a$ is even. If $a = 2c$, then $4c^2 = 2b^2$, $2c^2 = b^2$, and $b$ is also even, contrary to the hypothesis that $(a, b) = 1$.

---

**Fig. 7.** Proof of the irrationality of $\sqrt{2}$

## 4.1    The Informal Proof of Hardy and Wright

**Theorem 1 (Pythagoras' Theorem).** $\sqrt{2}$ *is irrational* .                               *1*

*Proof.* The traditional proof ascribed to Pythagoras runs as follows.

If $\sqrt{2}$ is rational with $(a\ b$                               *1*

the equation $a^2 = 2 * b^2$ is soluble                               2

Hence $a^2$ is even ,                               3

and therefore $a$ is even .                               4

If $a = 2 * c$ , then

$4 * c^2 = 2 * b^2$ .                               5

$2 * c^2 = b^2$ .                               6

and $b$ is also even ,                               7

                               8

contrary to the hypothesis that $(a, b) = 1$ .                               9

QED.                               10

## 4.2    A More Explicit Informal Proof by Barendregt

**Lemma 1.** *For* $m$, $n \in \mathbb{N}$ *one has* $m^2 = 2\,n^2 \Rightarrow m = n = 0$ . *1*

*Proof.* 1.1

Define on $\mathbb{N}$ the predicate $P(m) \Leftrightarrow \exists n . \; m^2 \quad n^2 \;\&\; m > 0$ . 2

Claim: $P(m) \Rightarrow \exists m' \quad m \quad P(m')$

Indeed suppose $m^2 = 2\,n \qquad m > 0$ It follows that $m^2$ is even . 4

but then $m$ must be even , as odds square to odds. 5

So $m \quad 2\,k$ 6 and we have $2\,n^2 \quad m^2 \quad 4\,k^2$ 7

$\Rightarrow n^2 = 2\,k^2$ 8

Since $m > 0$ , it follows that $m^2 > 0$ , 9 $\qquad n^2 > 0$ 10

and $n > 0$ . 11 Therefore $P(n)$ . 12 Moreover $m^2 = n^2 + n^2$ 13

$> n^2$ 14 $\qquad$ so $m^2 > n^2$ 15 $\qquad$ and hence $m > n$ . 16

So we can take $m' = n$ . 17

By the claim $\forall m \in \mathbb{N} . \; \neg P(m)$ since

there are no infinite descending sequences of natural numbers . 18

Now suppose $m^2 = 2\,n^2$ with $m \neq 0$ . Then $m > 0$ 19

and hence $P(m)$ . 20 *Contradiction* . 21 Therefore $m = 0$ . 22

But then also $n = 0$ . 23

24

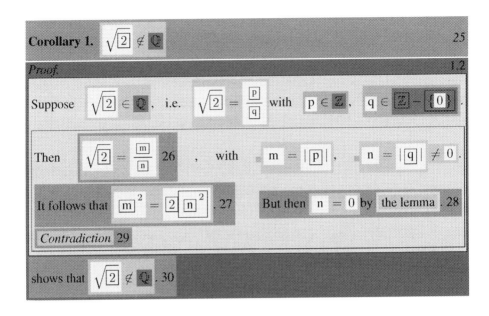

## 4.3    Discussions

*More or Less Explicit Texts.* The small set of grammatical constructions of MathLang gives all the material needed to express reasoning of different levels of precision. Both versions given here follow the same kind of structures in their demonstrations. Small steps leading to bigger ones. New statements in a certain context and definitions of new symbols. This is what MathLang is designed for: encoding these simple demonstration constructions into a structured document that eases computation. In both cases the MathLang encoding follows the reasoning structure of the text. Simple transformation procedures are then given to get the original text in return. These two versions of the same proof show the expressiveness of MathLang: we have used the same language to write a non precise proof as well as a fully explicit one. From this encoding of the proof in MathLang we get both the original text and the computerized document.

*Moving from MathLang to Other Encodings.* As we said before, the symbolic structure of MathLang texts eases both the automatic computations on the text and further translations to other languages. To illustrate this we have translated Barendregt's version of the proof into OMDoc/OpenMath.

The translation process is the same as the one carried out to obtain the CML view of MathLang documents. We spread the document with transformation information. This led to a big program that transforms automatically the MathLang document into OMDoc/OpenMath. In this transformation <CMP> (informal) and <FMP> (formal) OMDoc's tags could easily be informed. The first one using the same process as the one carried out to obtain a CML view of the MathLang text. The second one by using the symbolic structure to obtain OpenMath formulas. The third part of this translation consists in mapping the MathLang basic structures into OMDoc constructions.

For example, our MathLang translation of Barendregt's version of the proof consists of one line followed by one block, one line and one block. The first line being the definition of the lemma, the first block its proof, the second line (numbered 25) is the definition of the corollary and the second block its proof. In OMDoc the lines 1 and 25 are `<assertions>` and the blocks are `<proof>`. The predicate $P$ defined in the proof of the lemma (line 2) is a symbol definition (`<symbol>`) in the overall proof (`<theory>` in OMDoc, `book` in MathLang).

We compared this translation, that leads from a CML text to an OMDoc document via a MathLang document, to a direct translation from CML to OMDoc. The direct translation seems to be quicker but the one via MathLang has three advantages.

- The MathLang document is checked by the MathLang weak type checking. This validates the good formation of the structure of the document. Such an analysis does not exist for OMDoc and OpenMath.
- OMDoc has a formal (`<FMP>`) and an informal (`CMP`) tag for data. There are no requirements in OMDoc to have them both informed. The computerisable content of an OMDoc document depends on the author. In MathLang the main skeleton of the document fully uses symbols (similar to OMDoc's formal data), the natural language is added on top of this structured content. A MathLang-text always provides a *formal* content that could be forgotten in OMDoc.
- This structured content is encoded using a small set of MathLang constructions. These simple grammatical constructions guide the author in the translation process. It is then easier with this guiding process to obtain well structured OMDoc formal data by translating first into MathLang than directly into OMDoc.

## 5    Future Works

We described in this paper how we encode mathematics using MathLang and how we produce a CML view of this encoding. Our main future work is to ease the input of data inside the MathLang framework. Currently one requires skills in computer science to write a MathLang document. We are currently developing a user interface for MathLang based on the scientific editor $\text{T}_{\text{E}}\text{X}_{\text{MACS}}$.

As we said earlier in this paper we are starting and planing to extend the current language and framework. We aim to do it by making a use of the Grammatical Framework of A. Ranta and by moving to a second level of MathLang encoding which will include more logic and semantic.

## 6    Conclusion

By providing at the same time a computable encoding and a simple structure to produce readable output, our language MathLang tries to fill the gap between printed mathematical texts and mathematical softwares. The main problem mathematicians face when using formal systems is that it is very difficult, even for an expert, to find her way in a formal proof written by someone else. As described in this article, our system provides a direct correspondence between a symbolic structure and a CML view of a text. The original mathematical document is wisely partitioned between a natural language part and a symbolic part. The symbolic part can be used in more formal computations on the original text. This is how we imagine what could be the *new mathematical vernacular* for computers.

# References

1. A. Asperti, L. Padovani, C. Sacerdoti Coen, F. Guidi, and I. Schena, Mathematical Knowledge Management in HELM, AMAI **38(1–3)**, pp. 27–46, 2003.
2. P. Audebaud and L. Rideau, $\mathrm{T_EX_{MACS}}$ as authoring tool for publication and dissemination of formal developments, UITP, 2003.
3. H. Barendregt, Towards an interactive mathematical proof mode, in: *Thirty Five Years of Automating Mathematics*, Kamareddine (ed.), Applied Logic **28**, 2003.
4. N.G. de Bruijn, The Mathematical Vernacular, a language for mathematics with typed sets, Workshop on Programming Logic, 1987.
5. Y. Coscoy, A Natural Language Explanation for Formal Proofs, LACL, 1996.
6. J.H. Davenport, MKM from Book to Computer: A Case Study, LNCS **2594**, pp. 17–29, 2003.
7. S. Deach, Extensible Stylesheet Language (XSL) Recommendation, World Wide Web Consortium, 1999, http://www.w3.org/TR/xslt.
8. Mathematics On the Web: Get it by Logic and Interfaces (MOWGLI), http://www.mowgli.cs.unibo.it/.
9. L. Théry, Formal Proof Authoring: an Experiment, UITP, 2003.
10. Heath, The 13 Books of Euclid's Elements, Dover, 1956.
11. van Heijenoort (ed.), From Frege to Gödel: A Source Book in Mathematical Logic, pp. 1879–1931, Harvard University Press, 1967.
12. F. Kamareddine and R. Nederpelt, A refinement of de Bruijn's formal language of mathematics, Journal of Logic, Language and Information **13(3)**, pp. 287–340, 2004.
13. F. Kamareddine, M. Maarek, and J.B. Wells, MathLang: Experience-driven development of a new mathematical language, ENTCS **93**, pp. 138–160, 2004.
14. M. Kohlhase, OMDoc: An Open Markup Format for Mathematical Documents (Version 1.1), Technical report, 2003.
15. E. Landau, Foundations of Analysis, Chelsea, 1951.
16. Z. Luo and P. Callaghan, Mathematical vernacular and conceptual well-formedness in mathematical language, LNCS/LNAI **1582**, 1999.
17. M. Maarek and V. Prevosto, FoCDoc: The documentation system of FoC, Calculemus, 2003.
18. A. Ranta, Grammatical Framework: A Type-Theoretical Grammar Formalism, Journal of Functional Programming, 2003.
19. P. Rudnicki and A. Trybulec, On equivalents of well-foundedness, Journal of Automated Reasoning **23**, pp. 197–234, 1999.
20. F. Wiedijk, The Fifteen Provers of the World, University of Nijmegen.
21. F. Wiedijk, Comparing Mathematical Provers, LNCS **2594**, pp. 188–202, 2003.
22. J. Zimmer and M. Kohlhase, System Description: The MathWeb Software Bus for Distributed Mathematical Reasoning, LNCS **2392**, 2002.

# CPoint: Dissolving the Author's Dilemma

Andrea Kohlhase[1] and Michael Kohlhase[2]

[1] School of Computer Science, Carnegie Mellon University
ako@cs.cmu.edu
[2] School of Engineering and Science, International University Bremen
m.kohlhase@iu-bremen.de

**Abstract.** Automated knowledge management techniques critically depend on the availability of semantically enhanced documents which are hard to come by in practice. Starting from a detailed look at the motivations of users to produce semantic data, we argue that the authoring problem experienced by MKM is actually an *author's dilemma*. An analysis of the content authoring process suggests that the dilemma can partially be overcome by providing authoring tools like *invasive editors* aimed specifically at supporting the content creator. We present the CPoint application, a semantic, invasive editor for Microsoft PowerPoint, geared towards the OMDoc MKM format.

## 1 Introduction

Knowledge management technologies are concerned with recovering the content and semantics from documents and exploiting it for automation with an emphasis on web-based and distributed access to the knowledge. The interest in applying knowledge management tools to mathematics (Mathematical Knowledge Management, MKM) is based on the fact that mathematics is a very well-structured and well-conceptualized subject, which makes the knowledge management task simpler and more effective.

Currently, the field of MKM focuses on representation formats for mathematical knowledge (MATHML [3], OPENMATH [7], or OMDoc [19], etc.), mathematical content management systems [12, 1, 2], as well as publication and education systems for mathematics [9, 23].

While the system prototypes showcase the potential added value of explicitly representing the content and semantics of mathematical knowledge, they have failed to take off in terms of actual deployments. The main bottleneck seems to be the lack of large-scale, high-quality corpora of mathematical knowledge marked up in the respective MKM formats and the effort involved in creating these. Conventional wisdom (aka. "hope") in MKM is that the added-value applications based on semantic annotations will create a stimulus that will entice common users to invest time and effort into this exciting new technology. But the community experiences at the moment, that it is not yet sufficiently tempting. We will call this the **MKM authoring problem**.

In this paper, we will take a detailed look at the motivations of users to create MKM content and show that the MKM authoring problem is actually

A. Asperti et al. (Eds.): MKM 2004, LNCS 3119, pp. 175–189, 2004.
© Springer-Verlag Berlin Heidelberg 2004

an author's dilemma. We will then develop the concept of an invasive editor as a (partial) solution to the MKM authoring problem and present the CPOINT application, a semantic, invasive editor for Microsoft PowerPoint.

## 2    The Author's Dilemma

For a user of MKM material, the m otivation for preferring semantically rich data is simple: explicit document structure supports enhanced navigation and search, semantic markup yields context and search by content. Furthermore, the higher the degree of semantic structure, the more added-value services can feed on the material, the higher the benefit for the user.

### 2.1    What is the Author's Dilemma?

For a document author, the cost of creating a document is a priori proportional to the depth of the markup involved (assuming that the markup quality is cost-independent in an ideal world). However, once the markup quality passes a certain threshold which supports flexible reuse of fragments, document creation costs may actually go down as they are dominated by the cost of finding suitable (already existent) knowledge elements. Thus, the author is interested in a high reuse ratio, provided that retrieval costs are not prohibitive. The benefits are obvious for the author who has the opportunity to reuse her own content modules frequently, but the real payoff comes when she is part of a group of individuals that share content objects and knowledge structures freely. But why should an author share her content modules with others, who could make use of them without contributing to the common share of materials?

Cooperation is often analyzed by means of a non-zero-sum game called the **Prisoner's Dilemma** (see [4]). The two players in the game can choose between two moves, either "cooperate" or "defect". The idea is that each player gains when both cooperate, but if only one of them cooperates, the other one, who defects, will gain more. If both defect both lose, but not as much as the 'cheated' cooperator whose cooperation is not returned. The prisoner's dilemma is meant to study short term decision-making where the actors do not have any specific expectations about future interactions or collaborations.

The analogy to the document author's situation is apparent: if the author decides to invest his time and effort and others contribute as well, everyone profits tremendously from this synergy of cooperation. On the other hand, if just the author works on semantic markup, then he will gain nothing in the short run (but some in the long run). So, we can rightfully call it the **author's dilemma**.

In the prisoner's dilemma, if the decision-makers were purely rational, they would never cooperate as they should make the decision which is best for them individually. Suppose the other one would defect, then it is rational to defect yourself: you won't gain much, but if you do not defect you will have all the work. Suppose the other one would cooperate, then you will gain (especially in the long run) whatever you decide, but you will gain more if you do not cooperate (as you don't have to invest your time and effort), so here too the rational choice is to defect. The problem is that if all actors are rational, all will decide to defect, and none of them will gain anything. If we assume MKM authors to be rational, then we anticipate their non-cooperation. The MKM authoring problem is a consequence of the author's dilemma.

In order to tackle the author's dilemma we investigate the central assumption of the prisoner's dilemma that the actors do not have "specific expectations about future interactions or collaborations".

One way to get around the author's dilemma is to build or strengthen these expectations, for example by establishing targeted, cooperating research groups, open source and open content licensing, or citation indexes. Such measures[1] may well tip the scale towards cooperation and would therefore be a very worthwhile contribution to the MKM authoring problem.

In this paper, we will single out the 'real payoff' benefit, show why this argument doesn't constitute a specific expectation in the dilemma scenario, and finally dissolve the author's dilemma by changing its input parameters (costs and benefits). In particular, we will concentrate on a single author and the content authoring process.

## 2.2   The Content Authoring Process

The key intuition in MKM formats is to make semantic structures that are implicit in conventional forms of communication so explicit that they can be manipulated by machines. This explication can happen on several levels: formats like MathML [3] or OpenMath [7] allow to mark up the structure of mathematical formulae, formats like CNXML [10] mark up the document structure and allow to classify text fragments in terms of mathematical forms like "Definition", "Theorem", "Proof", etc. Formats like the logic-based Casl [11] or the development graph format [16] allow to structure mathematical knowledge into graphs of so-called "Theories", which make semantic relations (like reuse of content, semantic (in)dependence, and interpretability) explicit and available for computer-supported management. Finally, formats like OMDoc [19] attempt to combine all of these aspects of MKM into one integrated representation format for mathematical knowledge.

The explication of structure allows for a new authoring process, the **content authoring process**. In conventional document formats like LATEX, the document- and knowledge structure is inseparable from the atomic content (paragraphs of text, mathematical statements, . . . ). Therefore they have to be authored at the same time, with the exception of copy-and-paste techniques that have become available by electronic document formats. With the advent of semantic markup techniques, hypertext, and the distribution medium of the Internet, users are enabled to aggregate knowledge fragments (self-authored or from other sources) without losing the semantic context, or having to adapt notations:

---

[1] See the Connexions project for community-building efforts in this direction [14].

the more structured the knowledge fragments, the simpler their aggregation and reuse.

In fact, approaches like "Learning Objects" [15] postulate that knowledge should be represented in small units like atomic content and that all documents that can be formed using these should be represented as aggregates that mark up the structure and only reference the content. Such aggregates are lightweight, ephemeral structures that can be created on the fly and for special situations, while the learning objects form the heavyweight base of knowledge, that is expensive to create but can be reused in multiple aggregates.

Basically the same idea was realized with the semantic data format OMDoc where a document is considered to consist of a narrative document with links to a content base that is another OMDoc document (see [20]). Here, the 'learning object' is extended to a 'content object' by taking the context into consideration, enhancing it's semantic value and making it more reusable in the process.

### 2.3    Dissolving the Author's Dilemma: Creator Support

In the framework of the (new) content authoring process, we can see that the role of a document author, which used to intimately link the activities of content creation, content aggregation, and content presentation can be split up into two roles: **creator** and **aggregator**. The aggregator collects and presents atomic content, whereas the creator builds atomic content so that we might use the term **content author** as well. In fact, we expect that over time the classic academic roles of teacher, survey paper author, or science journalist will be concerned mainly with content aggregation, adding only descriptive text to existing content objects. Currently, the value of semantic markup shows itself only later in added-value services – not at the time of the actual content creation. Not surprisingly, the added-value applications have concentrated on the consumers of the semantic data and not on its producers.

If we reformulate the author's dilemma as a cost-benefit equation in these terms, it reads "The creator's loss is the aggregator's profit." In other words, the allegedly specific 'real payoff' expectation in the author's dilemma scenario really isn't one for the creator of the semantic data. The obvious conclusion consists in separating the single cost-benefit equation into one for the content author and one for the aggregating author. The author's dilemma dissolves if we can give the creator his own motivation for creating semantic data. In particular, **equipping *the creator* not only with specific content authoring support but also with added-value services will help solve the MKM authoring problem**.

Our approach to promote the creator starts with the concept of an invasive editor. Generally, authors select document creation systems (editors) with a particular purpose in mind – for instance in the face of presentational tasks. They frequently opt for editors optimized for the intended output media like data projectors (e.g. PowerPoint as presentation editor) or journals (e.g. emacs as a LaTeX-editor). As these editors optimize their output facilities to the presentational task at hand, they usually don't contain infrastructure for content markup. If an author wishes to annotate his knowledge, then he often has to leave his accustomed editor to use other tools, which is perceived as painful by experienced users. This is clearly a hurdle for an author's willingness to do semantic markup and can be alleviated by providing semantic editing facilities within the chosen editor. We call an editing facility an **invasive editor**, if it is build into an existing application and performs neglected functionalities like content markup. Such an add-on is nurtured by the existing editor in the sense that it adopts its feel, look, and location.

The apparent plus for a content author consists in the fact that she can write and markup documents in her usual work environment at the same time. But the real benefit is the following: she can improve the quality of her document by executing content checks and by visualizing the properties (e.g. stringency) of its content. In short, an invasive editor provides the potential point of entry for creator support and creator-specific added-value services in her chosen editor.

The concept of an invasive editor is latent in many modern document- or program development environments, and in fact a desired phenomenon. 'Host systems' provide scripting facilities that can be used to create interfaces to other dimensions of information in the documents. For instance, the various office suites offer some variant of VBA (Visual Basic for Applications), formatting systems like LATEX have a built-in macro processor, and computer algebra systems have embedded programming facilities. A crucial prerequisite for the suitability of a host system consists in the extensibility of the document storage format. We do not consider simple extensions like emacs modes for programming languages or semantic data formats as invasive editors, since they only provide editing facilities for dedicated file formats, and lack the added dimension.

In the Course Capsules Project (CCAPS [8, 22]) at Carnegie Mellon University we have experimented with two invasive editors with complementary characteristics: NB2OMDOC [25], an editor plug-in for MATHEMATICA as a computer-algebra-oriented and therefore mathematically interactive system, and the CPoint system for MS PowerPoint (PPT) as a purely presentation-oriented editor. We will present the latter in the next section.

# 3   CPoint – An Invasive Editor for Content in PowerPoint

Before we present the CPoint application let us consider the discrepancy between existing knowledge and its presentation in PPT. Based on this analysis, we will take a look at CPoint's forms for semantic data input, its support for content authoring, and finally demonstrate the PPT author's added-value utilities implemented by CPoint.

## 3.1   Presentation vs. Knowledge

CPoint's goal is to provide an author with an interface to explicitly store semantic information (knowledge) in the PPT slide show itself without destroying the presentational aspects of the PPT document. Critical to the task is the apparent gap between the content in a PPT document and the intended communication of knowledge in a PPT talk.

> Knowledge is the psychological result of perception and learning and reasoning
> http://www.cogsci.princeton.edu/cgi-bin/webwn

**A Priori Content.** MS PowerPoint is a visual editor and player for slides in a presentation. Thus, it exclusively addresses presentational issues — the placement of text, symbols, and images on the screen, carefully sequenced and possibly animated or even embellished by sound. Obviously, the text and the pictures carry content, and so does the structural, textual, and presentational pattern; we will call it the **a priori content**. In order to assess the quality of a priori content, we list a few typical examples: grouping information in a numbered list implies ranking information, the act of grouping text bubbles in one slide expresses a correlation, or marking text as title with presentational means classifies it accordingly. The superficial and somewhat blurred nature of the a priori PPT content is obvious, as a consequence, the knowledge that is implicit in a PPT presentation cannot be exploited for added-value services.

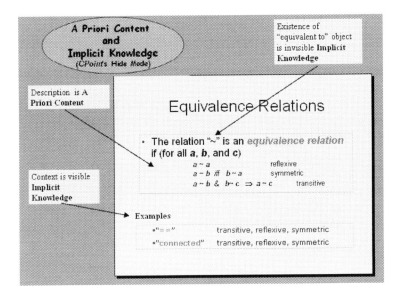

**Fig. 1.** A Priori Content and Implicit Knowledge in a PPT Presentation

**Implicit Knowledge.** The audience in a PPT talk perceives the a priori content in the PPT document together with what the lecturer says. This is followed by the user's learning and reasoning process: content becomes knowledge by categorizing the perceived information and combining it with what a user already knows. The author on the other hand already has this knowledge and while he is creating the PPT document he is using it implicitly. So the 'real' content is hidden beneath the presentation form and has to be captured and stored to make it available to MKM techniques. Figure 1 shows the interplay of a-priori content and implicit knowledge. The global context, e.g. the placement of one lecture in an entire course, is another part of the implicit knowledge. Following OMDoc, CPOINT captures this via the notion of a **collection**, encompassing a group of inter-related PPT presentations.

**Explicit Knowledge.** CPOINT provides functionality to make the implicit knowledge in a PPT presentation explicit. The PPT content author is supported in

- marking up the ontological role of a PPT object
- annotating its relation to the local and global context, i.e. to the just-learned, about-to-be-learned, and assumed knowledge elements, and
- adding background knowledge that is presupposed in the course but not presented in the slides.

We will call the resulting, explicitly annotated knowledge PPT **content** in the following. The two-stage annotation process will be described in detail in Section 3.2. For the transition from implicit to explicit knowledge see Figure 2.

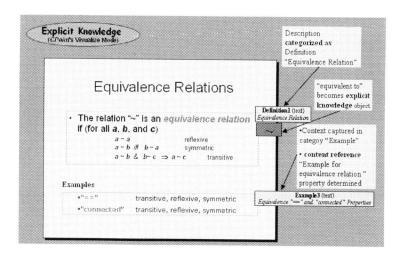

**Fig. 2.** Explicit Knowledge in a PPT Presentation

## 3.2   The CPOINT Application

CPOINT [17] is a PPT add-in that is written in VBA. To store the semantic information in the PPT files, it makes use of the fact that PPT objects can

**Fig. 3.** The CPOINT Menu Bar

be persistently 'tagged' with arbitrary strings. CPOINT is distributed under the Gnu Lesser General Public License (LGPL [13]), the newest version can be downloaded from http://cs.cmu.edu/~ccaps.

The CPOINT add-in makes its functionality available through a toolbar in the PPT menu (see Figure 3) where it is at an author's disposal whenever the PPT editor is running. The top-level structure of a PowerPoint presentation is given by slides. Each slide contains PPT objects, e.g. text boxes, shapes, images, or tables. By using CPOINT the author can attach additional information to each PPT object so that it becomes a **semantic object**.

As CPOINT wants to model the implicit knowledge in a PPT presentation and aims at facilitating the annotation process, it is geared towards the understanding process. Therefore we will continue with the application's illustration along the process' characteristics: categorizing and combining.

**Categorizing: The CPOINT Categorize Form.** The very first step in the categorizing process of an object is a naming act (title assignment) which lifts its content from e.g. mere text to a knowledge object (see Figure 4).

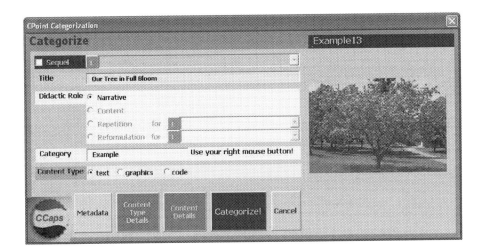

**Fig. 4.** The CPOINT Categorize Form

Classification is neither simple nor unique. First, individual styles vary a lot. Secondly, objects like texts or images may be used in different ways: An image of a tree in full bloom for instance is used narratively in a lecture about trees in computer science whereas a textual definition of a tree in the same lecture clearly contains knowledge. On the other hand the tree's picture may be definitional in a lecture about blossoms in biological science. Furthermore, objects can be pure repetitions and even though they might contain content, not all appearances are used as content objects. Analogously, a knowledge element might be described more than once in a presentation, so that the object and its reformulations are equivalent. Therefore CPOINT distinguishes an object's **didactic role** in a PPT presentation to be narrative, content, or that of a repetition or reformulation for another object.

The didactic role restricts the subsequent *category selection* – available as a drop-down menu by a right mouse click – as it is only compatible with a subset of pre-defined categories. Categories range from formal mathematical categories like "Theory", "Definition", or "Assertion" to didactic elements.

Sometimes, components of what should be categorized as a single knowledge element are spread over several slides for presentational reasons, possibly interrupted by excursions here and there. In such cases, the original assumption that (groups of) PPT objects directly correspond to knowledge objects is no longer valid. For such situations, CPOINT provides **sequel objects** that tie a component to the respective previous knowledge element part. These are not individually categorized, the first in line contains the semantic data for the sequel list.

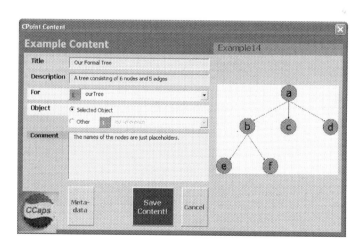

**Fig. 5.** The CPOINT Content Form for an Example

It is not always clear what an object's content is (e.g. look at 'the' object in Figure 5 and think of it as ungrouped set). In particular, the presentational information might contain more (category-independent) knowledge than is explicit. Therefore CPOINT allows to differentiate an object's **content type** to influence the conversion process. The value "text" (the default) results in a direct incorporation of the text value into the external representation. The content type "graphics" triggers the creation of a picture of the object itself and/or all underlying objects at conversion time. This is useful if only the combination of objects describe a knowledge element like a set of circles with single letters and lines between them may illustrate a tree. The content of each object is not noteworthy (e.g. a letter), but their placement in the entity is. Finally, the content type "code" is a specialization for the original application to Computer Science content in the CCAPS project. We anticipate that future applications of CPOINT will extend the repertoire of content types.

**Combining: The CPOINT Content Forms.** After a PPT object has been classified, we must make its relation to the knowledge context explicit via the respective detailed content form.

In Figure 5 we see the content form for a PPT object. Here, a specific tree (consisting of nodes and edges) is an example for the concept of a (formal) tree. In this case, the example is the PPT object itself (witnessed by the selection in the Object field of the form). If the PPT object were e.g. a text box with "Example: a directed graph unrolled" this would serve the purpose of an example (and thus would have been categorized as "example" in the previous step), but the text object itself only serves as description of another object (the directed graph) which is the real example and should be referenced in the Object field of the form.

### 3.3    CPOINT's Support for the Content Author

The following CPOINT services equip the PPT author with creator-specific tools for content authoring. Many of them directly allow the author to connect her content to a wider knowledge context of MKM materials. The CPOINTAUTHOR panel provides a tool palette for displaying and editing central CPOINT annotations of the currently selected object. While the facilities described in the last section concentrated more on the semantic annotation process for pre-existing text objects, CPOINTAUTHOR focuses on the creation of semantic objects in the content authoring process The presentational properties of these are preset by the authors personal preferences, which can be individually configured in a CSS file (Cascading Style Sheets [6]) associated with CPOINTAUTHOR.

**Visualize Mode.** As the semantic markup must not disrupt the presentational aspects of a PPT document, CPOINT provides a so-called **visualize mode** at design time. By activating it, annotation labels for semantic objects are created that contain the category information as well as the title and content type of an object. At the same time invisible objects like symbols and abstract objects are visualized. An associated **hide mode** clears the labels.

**The Navigator Button.** Generally, the purpose of a content form is to enter referential information that elucidates an object's contribution to and dependence on the knowledge context. Since such references can be local (inside the current slide show), in the current collection, or even in some external knowledge source (e.g. the MBASE mathematical knowledge base), finding and specifying reference targets is one of the major difficulties of semantic markup in general.

For each of the scopes, CPOINT determines the possible target elements (silently loading the necessary documents or connecting to external knowledge sources) and displays them in the adjoining selection box. Since this will normally be too many for a drop-down menu, the user can restrict the

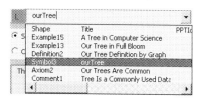

search space by various filters (e.g. category) available on right-click. In the figure on the right we can see the Navigator Button and the list of target objects in the **L**ocal presentation.

**Navigation.** As additional navigational help CPOINT offers the **GoTo** interface. The author may search for objects with certain criteria, restrict the found set by filters, determine in what presentation to look for objects, and if he selects one object, he can go to that object directly. On the right we can see that the user searched in the active PPT presentation

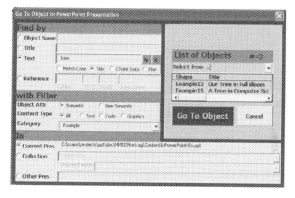

for all objects which have the word "tree" in their title and are categorized as example. The PPT show contains two yielding objects which are collected in the selection box on the upper right hand of the form.

**Export to OMDoc.** The **convert** functionality allows a user to convert a fully (CPOINT-)edited PPT presentation into a valid OMDoc document from within the PPT editor. Other OMDoc sublanguages are also supported. In particular, it can generate a document in PRESOMDOC, which is common OMDoc extended by presentational elements, and AMOMDOC which can be read by the ACTIVEMATH application.

Note, that the conversion utility recognizes TEXPOINT [24] inlays, the underlying LATEX code is conserved (as `code`) in the output OMDoc file.

**Import from OMDoc.** As a PPT document contains a lot of presentational information, CPOINT's import is based on PRESOMDOC documents. These can be **import**ed from within the PPT editor. The PRESOMDOC file is first read in, then a new PPT presentation is generated from these parsed OMDoc elements yielding the presentational information present in the document. The generalization to an import feature of OMDoc documents with the usage of an individual CSS file is at planning stage.

**Connection to the Outside World.** CPOINT exports files, which then can be **access**ed by the author directly. Furthermore, the documents are opened with an editor according to their file type and the user's personal preferences. Therefore, the author could read for instance generated OMDoc files with an emacs editor with OMDoc mode.

**Editor Notes.** An editor notes module CPOINTNOTES is available. The author can create (groups of) notes, searching in one or all groups for his notes and jumping from one to another. If an author for instance does want to supply background information, but wishes to finish creating the lecture first, he tags a missing reference by setting an editor note in the group "background" to remind him of inserting the missing references later on. At the same time he finds the phrasing of the text still wanting, so he creates another note for this object in the notes group "polish".

### 3.4   Added-Value for the Content Author

In the CPOINTGRAPHS module [18] the user is enabled to view the annotated structure in a graph format, i.e. the dependency tree of the knowledge elements is visualized. It offers several distinctive views from a general survey of theories in a collection or presentation to a single detailed theory graph. In Figure 6 we get an idea how extensive the knowledge in a course really is. Note for example, that nodes without dependencies might be considered superfluous.

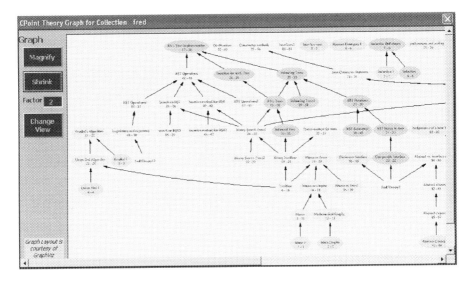

**Fig. 6.** CPOINTGRAPHS: The Theory Graph for a Course

The CPOINTAM module contains an integrated development environment for ACTIVEMATH content. It allows a user to start and stop the ACTIVEMATH application, to check for errors and to set parameters. Furthermore, it includes a utility for converting an entire PPT collection into an ACTIVEMATH course. Additionally, it implements an ACTIVEMATH guided tour button in the context menu of each object. This button causes ACTIVEMATH to create an individualized, self-contained document that leads up to the knowledge embodied in this object [23].

### 3.5    System Evaluation and Case Study

The CPOINT system has co-evolved with a large case study, the course "15-211 Fundamental Data Structures and Algorithms". 15-211 is an undergraduate course at Carnegie Mellon University (taught twice annually over a period of 10 years by a group of 10 faculty members). The current base of course materials contains about 2500 PPT slides, of which about half have been annotated in CPOINT, the rest being duplicates, variants or obsoleted versions. Our intuitions of the MKM authoring problem and many of CPOINT's auxiliary features have been shaped by this case study. Annotation time per slide (for a talented student) was about 10 minutes, which leads to a 60% MKM overhead, if we assume an average slide creation time of 15 min.

The case study revealed, that without adding background material (that is conveyed orally by the teacher during the lecture) the annotated slide show is too thin as the only resource of content for an MKM system like ACTIVEMATH. The perhaps most surprising result in the case study was that the mental model the authors had of their course materials was changed by the semantic annotation process, resulting in more structured slides, more emphasis on prerequisites, and less presentational gimmicks.

## 4    Conclusion and Future Work

In this paper, we address one of the central questions for the success of MKM techniques "Why is it so hard to motivate people to annotate their documents semantically when they agree at the same time to its usefulness and even to its exciting potential?". We characterize the underlying problem as an author's dilemma and argue, that the alleged pay-off for semantic annotation is not a specific expectation for a content author. This predictably leads to the MKM authoring problem. We propose the adoption of invasive editors with creator support and creator-specific added-value services to dissolve the content author's dilemma. We present the CPOINT system, an invasive, semantic editor in Microsoft PowerPoint and illustrate its content author support. We expect that invasive editors will lower barrier for authors, help them manage their extensive collections of presentations more effectively, even without assuming cooperation benefits by sharing materials.

However, the surprising result of research on the prisoner's dilemma is that cooperation spontaneously emerges even in such a hostile situation, if the experiment is iterated and a subset of players experiment with altruism (see [5] for details). Qualitatively, it is safe to say that cooperation emerges earlier, converges sooner, and tolerates more freeloaders, if the cooperation benefit is strengthened and the cost of unreturned cooperation is mitigated. This suggests that invasive editors will also play a role in fostering cooperation.

In the future, we envision a new PPT add-in module CPOINTPRESENTER supplementing the existing module CPOINTAUTHOR for the different roles a user can play. A presentation author (a presenter) will be supported during the composition of a presentation. He will search, find, and build new presentations based on existing knowledge elements. Here, we want to stress and facilitate the aggregator function of e.g. a lecturer. For a content author we can conceive further support by the application of information retrieval techniques to suggest categories and references for content objects. This will be particularly helpful for the migration of legacy materials to semantically enhanced formats like OMDoc. As knowledge is present in other document formats as well (probably even more so), another goal is the implementation of a CPOINT clone in MS WORD. Finally, we plan to connect CPOINT to the MBASE system [21], so that all knowledge captured in OMDoc documents and stored in an MBASE can get directly used.

### Acknowledgments

The development of the CPOINT system has been funded by the National Science Foundation under grant CCF-0113919 and a grant from Carnegie Mellon's Office for Technology in Education. The authors would like to thank Frederick Eberhardt for his markup of 15-211 and fruitful discussions on the CPOINT system.

# References

1. S. Allen, M. Bickford, R. Constable, R. Eaton, C. Kreitz, and L. Lorigo. FDL: A prototype formal digital library – description and draft reference manual. Technical report, Computer Science, Cornell, 2002. `http://www.cs.cornell.edu/Info/Projects/NuPrl/html/FDLProject/02cucs-fdl.pdf`.
2. A. Asperti, L. Padovani, C. Sacerdoti Coen, and I. Schena. HELM and the semantic math-web. In R.J. Boulton and P.B. Jackson (eds.), *Theorem Proving in Higher Order Logics: TPHOLs'01*, volume 2152 of *LNCS*, pp. 59–74. Springer, 2001.
3. R. Ausbrooks, S. Buswell, D. Carlisle, S. Dalmas, S. Devitt, A. Diaz, M. Froumentin, R. Hunter, P. Ion, M. Kohlhase, R. Miner, N. Poppelier, B. Smith, N. Soiffer, R. Sutor, and S. Watt. Mathematical Markup Language (MathML) version 2.0 (second edition). W3c recommendation, World Wide Web Consortium, 2003. Available at `http://www.w3.org/TR/MathML2`.
4. R. Axelrod. *The Evolution of Cooperation*. Basic Books, New York, 1984.
5. A. Birk and J. Wiernik. An *n*-players prisoner's dilemma in a robotic ecosystem. *International Journal of Robotics and Autonomous Systems*, 39:223–233, 2002.
6. Cascading style sheets, level 2; CSS2 specification. W3c recommendation, World Wide Web Consortium (W3C), 1998. Available as `http://www.w3.org/TR/1998/REC-CSS2-19980512`.
7. The OpenMath standard, version 2.0. Technical report, 2003. The OpenMath Society, `http://www.openmath.org/standard/om20`.

8. The course capsules project. http://aiki.ccaps.cs.cmu.edu.
9. CONNEXIONS. http://cnx.rice.edu/.
10. Basic CNXML. http://cnx.rice.edu/content/m9000/latest/.
11. Language Design Task Group CoFI. Casl – the CoFI algebraic specification language – summary, version 1.0. Technical report, http://www.brics.dk/Projects/CoFI, 1998.
12. A. Franke and M. Kohlhase. System description: MBASE, an open mathematical knowledge base. In David McAllester (ed.), *Automated Deduction – CADE-17*, number 1831 in LNAI, pp. 455–459. Springer Verlag, 2000.
13. Free Software Foundation FSF. GNU lesser general public license. Software License available at http://www.gnu.org/copyleft/lesser.html, 1999.
14. G. Henry, R.G. Baraniuk, and C. Kelty. The Connexions project: Promoting open sharing of knowledge for education. In *Syllabus, Technology for Higher Education*, 2003.
15. H.W. Hodgins. The future of learning objects, 2003.
16. D. Hutter. Management of change in verification systems. In *Proceedings Automated Software Engineering (ASE-2000)*, pages 23–34. IEEE Press, 2000.
17. A. Kohlhase. CPoint *Documentation*. Carnegie Mellon University, 2004. Technical Manual, http://www.faculty.iu-bremen.de/mkohlhase/kwarc/software/CPoint.html.
18. A. Kohlhase. CPointGraphs *Documentation*. Carnegie Mellon University, 2004. Technical Manual, http://www.faculty.iu-bremen.de/mkohlhase/kwarc/software/CPointGraphs.html.
19. M. Kohlhase. OMDOC: An open markup format for mathematical documents. Seki Report SR-00-02, Fachbereich Informatik, Universität des Saarlandes, 2000. http://www.mathweb.org/omdoc.
20. M. Kohlhase. OMDOC: An open markup format for mathematical documents (Version 1.2), 2004. Manuscript, http://www.mathweb.org/omdoc/omdoc1.2.ps.
21. M. Kohlhase and A. Franke. MBase: Representing knowledge and context for the integration of mathematical software systems. *Journal of Symbolic Computation; Special Issue on the Integration of Computer algebra and Deduction Systems*, 32(4):365–402, 2001.
22. M. Kohlhase, K. Sutner, P. Jansen, A. Kohlhase, P. Lee, D. Scott, and M. Szudzik. Acquisition of math content in an academic setting. In *Second International Conference on MathML and Technologies for Math on the Web*, Chicago, USA, 2002.
23. E. Melis, J. Büdenbender, G. Goguadze, P. Libbrecht, and C. Ullrich. Knowledge representation and management in ActiveMath. *Annals of Mathematics and Artificial Intelligence*, 38:47–64, 2003.
24. G. Necula. TeXPoint. Program Home Page at http://raw.cs.berkeley.edu/texpoint/index.htm.
25. K. Sutner. Converting MATHEMATICA notebooks to OMDoc. To appear in [20], 2004.

# On Diagrammatic Representation of Mathematical Knowledge*

Zenon Kulpa

Institute of Fundamental Technological Research, Polish Academy of Sciences
ul. Świętokrzyska 21, 00-049 Warsaw, Poland
zkulpa@ippt.gov.pl

**Abstract.** The more extensive use of diagrammatic representations as a tool for managing complexity and communication problems of mathematical knowledge is advocated in the paper. The specifics of this representation tool are introduced, including the problems with using diagrams in mathematics, issues of proper design of diagrams, specification of main usage types of mathematical diagrams and ways of their implementation. The discussion is illustrated by a number of diagrams, mostly taken from the diagrammatic notation for interval algebra recently developed by the author. These and other issues of diagrammatic representation and reasoning are investigated by the recently emerging discipline of *diagrammatics*.

## 1  Introduction

When thinking about managing some area of knowledge, one should realize first who and in which way will use it, as the form in which the knowledge should be represented and managed crucially depends on the kind of its usage. Concerning the mathematical knowledge, there are two main classes of users of it:

- M athem aticians, especially working in the same area of mathematics, and
- U sers ofm athem atics, coming from other branches of science and technology.

The second class of users of mathematical knowledge repositories seems to be much more numerous, and they will most benefit from computerization of the repositories.

Unfortunately, most of the current projects of computerizing mathematical knowledge bases are seemingly constructed by mathematicians for mathematicians only. They use the impenetrable (for non-mathematicians) theorem-proof organization of the knowledge, are based on logical representations only, and in most cases use the somewhat old-fashioned human-computer interface paradigm of a one-dimensional string of ASCII characters, ignoring the capabilities of current computer systems in setting mathematical formulae and drawing diagrams

---

* The paper was supported in part by the grant No. 5 T07F 002 25 (for years 2003–2006) from the KBN (State Committee for Scientific Research). The author is also indebted to anonymous referees of the paper for their comments and suggestions.

A. Asperti et al. (Eds.): MKM 2004, LNCS 3119, pp. 190–204, 2004.

and other visualizations. That may be acceptable for mathematicians (though one can doubt if all of them would be happy when forced to abandon their familiar mathematical notation for the illegible ASCII coding), but it is rather not acceptable for users of mathematics.

Users of mathematics have quite different needs in this respect than working mathematicians. To make the knowledge accessible to them, and managing complexity and intricacy of mathematical knowledge, one must use much more efficient knowledge representation methods, both in the sense of efficiency of encoding and storing the knowledge and efficiency of reading and absorbing the knowledge by the user. One of such efficient methods of representation of complex information is provided by diagrams. They offer readable general comprehension of some part of knowledge "at a glance," allowing also for representation of precise structural relationships. However, unfortunate expulsion of diagrams from most of mathematics arrested the development of proper design and use of good and informative mathematical diagrams. The situation changes recently – the field of diagrammatics, analogical to the field of linguistics devoted to the study of language representations, finally emerged. Using findings of research in this area (see e.g. [4, 5, 18] and article collections and proceedings like [1, 2, 7, 12]) it becomes possible to use diagrammatic representations in an efficient and reliable way to represent and manage complicated mathematical knowledge.

An example of a system trying to go in this direction is the Theorema Project (see http://www.theorema.org/) for computerized theorem proving. With it, it is possible to annotate proof steps graphically, using a system of so-called logico-graphic symbols [8]. On the other hand, tools like Maple or Mathematica, though containing a significant graphical component, do not provide a sufficient integration of these graphics tools with the mathematical base (except possibly with some rudimentary tools for graphing of functions), leaving the construction of the link between mathematics and diagrams almost entirely to the user, by means of low-level programming from basic graphical primitives in a way often much more troublesome than with common interactive graphic editors.

The paper starts with an explanation of what is understood by a diagram here and what are the main properties of this kind of representation. Then follows a summary of the use of diagrams in mathematics, especially a critical discussion of main arguments against their use here. This is followed by a discussion of main issues concerning the criteria for designing good diagrams, and the description of main types of use of diagrams in representation of mathematical knowledge, with diagrammatic examples mostly taken from the recently developed diagrammatic notation for interval algebra [18]. Finally, a short discussion of possible ways of implementing and using diagrammatic tools in mathematical knowledge bases is included. The paper is concerned mostly with diagrammatic representation of mathematical knowledge. The issue of using diagrams for reasoning (e.g., proving theorems) is only superficially touched upon. Note, however, that diagrammatic reasoning is closely related to diagrammatic representation – one must first represent the mathematical knowledge involved in order to be able to reason with it. See [4, 5, 13, 18, 27] for more on this issue.

The paper is based in significant part on discussions included in [18], with a number of modifications and additions. However, Sections 5 and 6 are entirely new, with an exception of a number of example diagrams taken mostly from [18] (though some of them are also substantially modified).

## 2     What Are Diagrams?

There is still no fully agreed consensus among researchers in diagrammatics as to the precise definition of a diagram (see e.g. [25]). Generally, a diagram is a kind of an analogical representation of knowledge, as opposed to more familiar propositional representations.

Consider an example of analogical representation, like a geographical map. In the map, size of, direction to, and distance between marks directly represent size of, direction to, and distance between real objects on the ground, say cities. In contrast, in a sentential (propositional) representation, like in the phrase "The city 250 km south of Warsaw", its parts (e.g., the word "Warsaw") or relationships between them (e.g., that "Warsaw" appears after "south" in the phrase) need not correspond to any parts and relations within the thing denoted. The same is true for a more formal propositional representation, like predicate calculus formulae. Thus, an analogical representation has a structure whose syntax parallels (models), to a significant extent, the semantics of the problem domain, while a propositional representation has a structure that has no direct bearing on the semantics of the problem domain. Diagrammatic representation can be thus defined broadly as an analogical representation presented by visual means, of some (not necessarily visual) data or knowledge. There are other, more involved definitions of the term. One definition of interest says that diagrammatic representation is a plane structure in which representing tokens are objects whose mutual spatial and graphical relations are directly interpreted as relations in the target structure.

It is important to bear in mind that the propositional versus analogical distinction is neither absolute nor sharp. There are various degrees of analogicity (see e.g. the discussion of verbal versus visual thinking in [3]), or the representation may be analogical along certain dimensions (or aspects), but propositional along others. The limiting case is reasoning directly with (or simulating) the target domain itself: if you cannot infer which lid fits the jar from the available information, try them on in turn. At the other extreme one can place, e.g., a Morse code, where the syntactic structure of dots and dashes bears little if any discernible relationship to the structure of whatever the message is about (examples taken from [6]).

The representation may thus contain elements of both kinds discussed, becoming thus a hybrid representation (called also heterogeneous [6] or multi-modal). This situation is ubiquitous in practice – it is very hard, if not impossible, to find examples of indisputably pure cases. In particular, in mathematical diagrams the propositional components are often essential, or even indispensable. They should co-exist with the diagrammatic ones, so that both complement each other, with the diagram providing a general look of the structure of the problem and formulae adding precision in important details or specifying limits of generalization of the argument, see Section 5.

Diagrammatic representations should not be confused with the term geometrical interpretation (which should be rather called "geometrical representation" anyway). The term means representing some non-geometrical knowledge in terms and notions of geometry. That may, but does not have to, involve diagrams. Note also that diagrams, even geometrical diagrams, can (and quite often do) contain visual language elements that are not geometrical (i.e., that do not represent any geometrical objects or notions), like arrowheads, various thickness or dot patterns of lines, colour, shading or cross-hatching of areas, etc.

## 3     Diagrams in Mathematics

The use of diagrams in mathematics has a long and respectable history, in the course of which various attitudes towards that use were maintained. Attitudes towards diagrams in other branches of science were usually more stable, but although they were used there extensively and without much reservations (especially in engineering and other technical disciplines), they were rarely treated as important components of scientific practice in these fields, important enough to deserve a rigorous study, not to mention a separate branch of science.

The most naturally diagrammatic field of mathematics is obviously geometry, so it is not surprising that "The Elements" by Euclid, the first mathematical text on geometry foreshadowing the modern axiomatic approach to mathematics, relied heavily on diagrams. Diagrams were later applied not only in geometry. A simple diagram of a number axis played an instrumental role in eventual acceptance of negative numbers as a respectable mathematical entity, for a long time before that called numeri ficti (fictitious numbers). A similar story repeated itself with the invention of complex plane diagram (or Argand diagram) which not only stimulated the acceptance of "imaginary numbers," but played a significant role in the development of complex analysis, see [23]. In this role, the complex plane diagram has not yet said its last word, as it is shown by recent invention of diagrammatic representations for some operations on complex numbers, until now thought to be not representable in this way [23].

However, with the invention of predicate calculus by Frege and the birth of Hilbert's program of formalization of mathematics at the end of the XIXth century, diagrams went out of fashion as a respectable research tool in mathematics and their use is considered a bad practice and actively discouraged till now. The trend went so far that some mathematicians (like Dieudonné, a member of the Bourbaki team) wrote books on geometry without a single diagram and were proud of that. The fashion persisted despite the fact that many prominent mathematicians admitted the use of visual images and diagrammatic aids in their mathematical research [10]. Diagrams were accepted at most as a secondary illustration device, suitable as an educational tool for uninitiated. As a result, the research on proper design and use of diagrams stalled, leading to easy accusations that diagrams are difficult and unreliable to use.

When proposing diagrams as a significant element of mathematical knowledge representation it is fair to consider the arguments against their use in mathematics. They can be listed under three main headings: difficulty, unreliability, and informality (of diagrams). Let us examine them in turn.

Difficulty. Even some prominent users and advocates of diagrammatic methods expressed opinions about the difficulty of using them, like Feynman [9] or Needham [23]. But while for some people it may be quite difficult to think pictorially, for others this can be actually an easier mode of thinking than the propositional one. In this respect the human population is divided roughly in half – one half being more proficient in verbal, and the other half in visual thinking. However, with the educational bias toward verbal learning and discouraging the use of diagrams, visual thinkers have rough times in school and after it, so that their visual abilities are seldom properly trained and used to their full potential. This applies especially to people seeking a career in sciences. Not surprisingly, the proportion of people for whom diagrammatic thinking is easy seems to be much smaller among scientists than in the overall population.

Besides perceiving and imagining diagrams, an effective use of them requires an actual drawing of (often many, and intricate) diagrams. With the equipment provided by human biology it is indeed difficult to produce diagrams of any complexity and accuracy – humans do not have a proper and effective visual effector, comparable in efficiency to that one we use for spoken language. Fortunately, in our times we do have technical means (namely, computers) very efficient in producing complex pictures. We can use them as a sort of prosthetic devices compensating for our deficiencies in this area.

Unreliability. It is true that, as observed by Arnheim [3]: "Perception ... is unreliable, as shown by the many optical illusions, and can refer only to actual, physically given objects, which are always imperfect." It is thus not surprising that representation of knowledge in diagrams and reasoning conducted with them are prone to various errors. This is a significant problem impeding practical use of diagrams in rigorous reasoning. This, however, applies in a significant degree to all other representations and reasoning tools. The differences here boil down to different causes and types of error situations and different ways to avoid them.

Moreover, as observed in [6], "If we threw out every form of reasoning that could be misapplied by a careless reasoner, we would have little if anything left." Thus, we must learn to live with possibly error-prone representations. Fortunately, most of these errors can be avoided by careful design and use of the appropriate visual language well adapted to the given task, augmented by the knowledge of possible error situations and methods of avoiding them. Once these situations are properly recognized, analyzed in detail, and taught to the users of diagrams, the possibility of errors in diagrams can be made no more harmful that in any other human activity. Unfortunately, the proper error-avoidance rules for diagrams are not yet fully investigated, codified and taught. This problem constitutes the important challenge for the researchers in the field of diagrammatics. Some preliminary analysis of the topic appeared in [17, 18]. From the list of possible error causes discussed there it is worth to mention the problems of diagram imprecision and particularity. Diagram imprecision (see the quote from Arnheim [3] above) may lead to various kinds of errors, like generation of impossible cases [17]. Particularity of diagrams (interpreted often as a lack of variables in diagrams) leads to problems with representing the proper range of generalization of the argument from the particular case provided in the diagram. There are various remedies for this effect, e.g., the configuration transformation diagrams discussed in Section 5.

Informality. This argument says that, by their nature, diagrams cannot be made formal enough to be acceptable as valid components of rigorous mathematical proofs. Actually, it is already disproved by many fully formalized systems of diagrammatic reasoning that have been developed, see e.g. [11, 13, 22]. However, the question has some interesting aspects worth considering in more detail.

This objection against mathematical diagrams was raised by the Hilbert's programme of formalization of mathematics. In writings of Pasch and Hilbert himself, their position on that issue is clearly stated, see the quotes discussed in [18]. The argument in these quotes says, in effect, that the formal mathematical reasoning must be restricted to mechanical manipulation of symbols, without reference to any "sense" of the underlying mathematical concepts, while diagrams, allegedly, constitute the direct embodiment of just these concepts.

Do diagrams really contain directly "the sense of geometrical concepts"? As diagrams are analogical representations, it seems reasonable to assert that. However, in practice we never attain full analogicity: a line in a diagram is not a line as understood in geometry – it is only a (often crude and approximate) representation of the appropriate geometrical concept. It then has the similar status as a symbol used in a propositional proof, containing no diagrams. From this point of view, diagrams can be considered as a different symbolic notation, useful to represent geometrical entities in the same way as certain other squiggles on paper are useful as representations of numbers, logical or arithmetic operations, and the like. Moreover, diagrams are also finite arrangements of symbols from a finite alphabet. One cannot draw an infinite line with infinite precision no more than one is able to write in a formula an infinitely precise letter "$x$" exactly identical in shape to the previous one. Thus, diagrams can also be constructed, transformed and inspected in a finitistic way, just like the formulae.

It is of course true that directness (analogicity) of diagrams, so that they seem for a human reasoner to more vividly represent the underlying mathematical concepts, their important features, and relations between them, does in a way introduce into the reasoning process the semantic reference to the concepts concerned. But that actually helps to creatively conduct rigorous reasoning, provided of course that one observes necessary precautions against misuse of the notation, as one must do also when using formulae.

Consider also that no mathematician actually works by a purely mechanical juggling of meaningless symbols. Practically, nobody even works with the pure logical notation of the predicate calculus. That would greatly impede the efficiency of mathematical work. Instead, mathematicians use, and constantly expand, quite intricate symbolic notation systems, containing also lots of essentially diagrammatic elements like two dimensional fractions, subscript and superscript systems, matrices, morphism diagrams, often very pictorial operator or relation symbols, and the like. They also to some extent use the so-called model-based reasoning, utilizing various semantic cues to navigate through the space of formal descriptions of the steps of the reasoning. The importance of such guidance in mathematical reasoning was well attested by Hadamard [10].

## 4    Designing Good Diagrams

Every representation of complex knowledge, to be sufficiently expressive, efficient, and useful, must be well designed. This obviously concerns diagrams too. Good design here must be considered on several levels.

The syntactic level concerns such requirements as sufficiently rich visual vocabulary, proper use of visual relations (to fit properties of target domain relations), and precise drawing. Mathematical diagrams historically used rather primitive visual vocabularies, which did not allow for adequate expressiveness and rich information content. A typical example of a common "textbook style" diagram is shown in Fig. 1(a) (adapted from [3]). Such diagrams must be accompanied by extensive textual explanations as shown, and thus they serve merely as additional illustration of the contents in most part communicated propositionally. Graphical medium, however, allows for much more rich visual languages, as illustrated in Fig. 1(b). For those familiar with the visual language used, the diagram can be self-explanatory; anyway, much simpler explanations suffice, and they can be made a part of the diagram itself, producing a truly hybrid representations, like in Fig. 1(c) and in diagram examples in the rest of the paper (see also [18]). In this respect, the term "proofs without words," often associated with the use of diagrams in mathematics (see [24]), is misleading. It suggests a wrong paradigm for diagrammatic reasoning – namely, that we should struggle to make purely diagrammatic proofs or representations, without the use of propositional ingredients. The proper paradigm relies instead on hybrid representations. Diagrammatic proofs are not distinguished by a lack of words (or formulae), but by the essential role a diagram plays in the reasoning.

Precise drawing is also very important – like illegible writing, sloppy drawing may lead to errors in representation and reading the data off an illegible representation. This concerns equally the overall composition and structuring of the diagram, the proper choice of visual primitives, and precise execution of details. Despite its obviousness, sloppy drawing is a very common feature of many diagrams. This is probably due mostly to the lack of training in proper design and construction of diagrams. Also, as diagrams are often considered to be of only secondary importance, especially in mathematical texts, little attention is paid to their careful design and execution.

a)

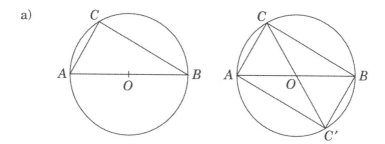

In order to prove that the triangle $\triangle ABC$ based on the diameter AB of the circle is always right-angled (i.e., $\angle ACB = 90°$), draw a line from the vertex C of the triangle through the centre O of the circle to the point $C'$ on the circle, and arrive thereby at a rectangle $ACBC'$, located symmetrically within the circle. By its position in this rectangle, the angle $\angle ACB$ at the vertex C of the triangle is an angle of $90°$.

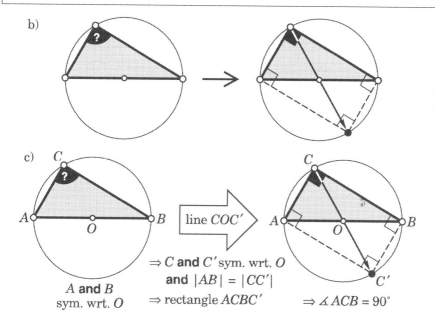

**Fig. 1.** Three main styles of mathematical diagrams: *textbook* style with textual explanation (a), *purely diagrammatic* style (b) and *hybrid* style (c)

The semantic level concerns generally the requirement of expressiveness of the representation, i.e., the possibility to express without error or confusion a sufficiently large body of data we want to represent. It may need some effort to circumvent the limitations of the Euclidean plane, and asks for the proper use of the effects of emergence and divergence (see [18] for discussion of these issues).

The pragmatic level of diagrammatic languages concerns first their effectiveness, i.e., the requirement to minimise costs of both production and using the representation, and making it less error-prone (the latter requirement is very important in such rigorous domains as mathematics). Also, the important requirement is to take into account the function, or supposed usage type, of the representation. The main usage types of mathematical diagrams are illustrated in the next section.

As the research on design of mathematical diagrams is still seriously underdeveloped, little more can be added to that listing of general issues to consider. The guidelines developed by graphic design community are seldom directly applicable to mathematical diagrams (except possibly in the area of graphing of functions, see e.g. [26], but even there the specificity of mathematical diagrams is mostly not taken into account). The next section presents thus other kinds of diagrams than graphs of functions, to illustrate other possible design problems and a sort of "guidelines-by-example."

In order to be able to produce good diagrams for a particular proof or problem, it is very advisable to develop first a comprehensive system of diagrammatic representations of objects, notions and relations in a given domain. Such a system, with its sufficiently rich visual language, provides ready-made tools and building blocks for producing unambiguous and uniformly interpretable diagrams for any particular problem within the domain. One of historical examples of such a system, of great significance to the development of its domain, is the diagrammatic notation for complex numbers plane [23]. A current example of a similar system, this time for interval algebra, constitutes the main subject of this author's research [14, 15, 16, 18, 19]. A discussion of some information design problems and solutions involved in the development of this notation can be found in [20]. The more extensive use of such diagrammatic notational systems can substantially help in managing complex mathematical knowledge.

## 5    Diagram Usage Types

Diagram usage types are defined mostly by the main goal they serve. In this short and preliminary proposal, four basic types will be discerned and illustrated by diagrammatic examples. In practice there are many intermediate cases, and diagrams that exhibit elements or features of several types, as commented upon in explanations of the examples below.

**Object Structure.** This diagram type serves the goal of showing "at a glance" how some mathematical object is constructed from its elements, what relations bind the structural elements and what properties such a structure should thus possess.

**Construction Steps.** Here the diagram shows the sequence of construction steps necessary to build some mathematical object. This may sometimes serve also as a structural description of the resulting object, see above.

**Catalogue of Cases.** The goal here is to catalogue a number of similar objects, types of objects, or reasoning cases. The main emphasis is put on comparing the objects and delineate the differences and similarities between them.

**Sequence of Transformations.** This is a sort of dynamic diagram, showing a set of transformations of the given mathematical object necessary to construct another object or to conduct some reasoning.

The exposition will be illustrated mostly by diagrams from the diagrammatic notation developed by the author [14, 15, 16, 18, 19] for interval algebra. Mathematical background had to be omitted due to the lack of space. The examples are not aimed to communicate the details of mathematics of intervals, but to show the function and look of the discussed types of diagrams.

Object Structure. Two examples of mathematical object structures are shown in Fig. 2. The set of solution types [16, 18] will be further explained below. The second example shows, in the midpoint-radius coordinates, how the set of intervals contained in the given interval $v$ (denoted by the gray triangle with the apex $v$ and the base between the interval endpoints $\underline{v}$ and $\bar{v}$) is transformed by multiplying these intervals by the interval $u$ using the ci-multiplication formula studied in [19]. The result of the mapping is the grayed heptagon above the bend axis $\mathbf{O}u \; - \ldots \mathbf{O}u \; +$. Darker gray denotes its intersection with the original triangle, and the two dark triangles to the right emphasize a part of the mapping of special interest to the mathematical argument conducted with the help of this diagram in [19]. This category of diagrams includes as a subtype various popular kinds of graphs of functions.

Construction Steps. Diagrams of this kind show how to build step by step some mathematical object, or a result of some mathematical operation. This is done usually in a sequence of steps which can be indicated with various diagrammatic means, like numbered step indicators (see Fig. 3) or sequences of "animation frames," or alternatively non-diagrammatically in the accompanying textual explanation. Showing construction steps often reveals also some aspects of the inner structure of the object constructed, thus serving in part as the object structure diagram discussed above.

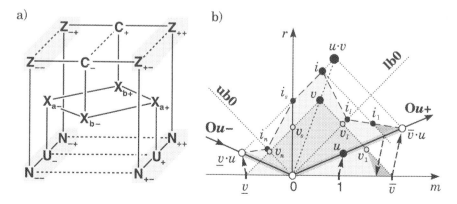

**Fig. 2.** Graph of solution types of the simple interval equation $a \cdot x = b$ (a) and structure of the mapping defined by ci-multiplication in the MR-diagram of interval space (b)

a)

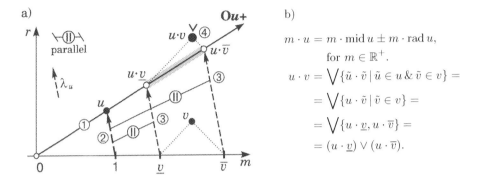

b)

$$m \cdot u = m \cdot \operatorname{mid} u \pm m \cdot \operatorname{rad} u,$$
$$\text{for } m \in \mathbb{R}^+.$$
$$u \cdot v = \bigvee \{\tilde{u} \cdot \tilde{v} \mid \tilde{u} \in u \,\&\, \tilde{v} \in v\} =$$
$$= \bigvee \{u \cdot \tilde{v} \mid \tilde{v} \in v\} =$$
$$= \bigvee \{u \cdot \underline{v}, u \cdot \overline{v}\} =$$
$$= (u \cdot \underline{v}) \vee (u \cdot \overline{v}).$$

**Fig. 3.** Construction for a product $u \cdot v$ of two positive intervals (a), compared with the formulae on which it is based (b); "$\vee$" is the *join* operation of the interval lattice

Catalogue of Cases. This is one of the most useful roles played by diagrams, especially when we want to gather and communicate systematically some organized segment of knowledge. A simple example in Fig. 4 (adapted from a diagram in [24], substantially modified) lists various types of mean formulae. It shows not only the catalogue of different formulae, but also the relationships between means, so that it plays also, to some extent, a role of a structural diagram for the space of definitions of means. This is a common (and desirable) feature of such kind of diagrams.

A more elaborate example is given by the simplified catalogue of structural types of the interval equation $a \cdot x = b$ (Fig. 5, with an explanation of the quotient sequence and quotient diagram notation in the inset). The more detailed catalogue can be found in [16, 18]. It lists additionally the exact conditions (in propositional form) for each type. It is an essentially hybrid representation; in the detailed version the propositional contents is even larger than the diagrammatic one.

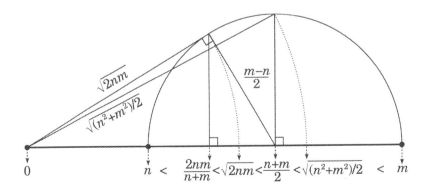

**Fig. 4.** Mean formulae and relationships between means: *harmonic, geometric, arithmetic,* and *root mean square*

Configuration Transformations. Here the diagram explains how it should be transformed, for the purpose of defining the proper range of cases for some diagrammatic argument, or a solution to a problem. In Fig. 6 it is shown how a change of position of the coefficient $a$ of the equation $a \cdot x = b$ along a trajectory through the interval space changes the structure of its solution sets (defined by quotient sequences, see Fig. 5).

There is an essential difference between this kind of diagrams and the "construction steps" diagram. The latter one shows the construction of an object by adding consecutive components, while the transformation diagram shows how the whole diagram, or some its properties, change with the change of some parameter or variable. In this way variables can be introduced into diagrammatic representations, so that such diagrams can be used to solve the particularity problem, see Section 3. They do that by showing the allowed transformations of the exemplary object $x_0$ to obtain any other object $x$ from the required class

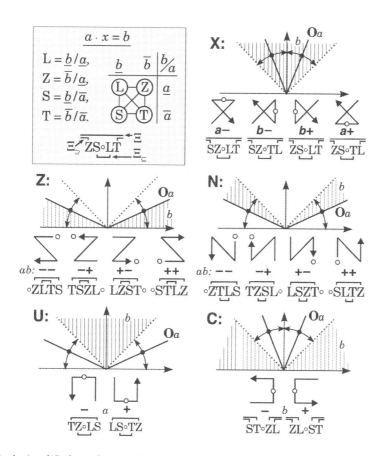

**Fig. 5.** A simplified catalogue of types and subtypes of the interval equation $a \cdot x = b$, with explanation of quotients, quotient diagrams, and quotient sequences (inset). The small circle "∘" marks the position of zero

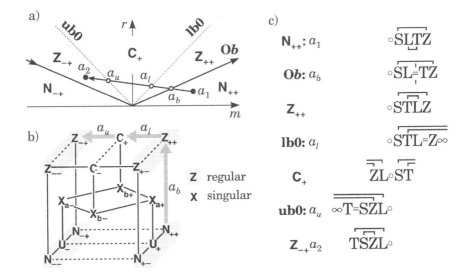

**Fig. 6.** Movement of the equation coefficient $a$ in the MR-diagram (a) with corresponding change of types (b) of solution sets structure (c)

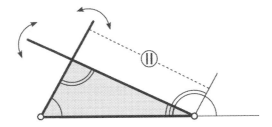

**Fig. 7.** A diagrammatic proof of the sum of angles in a triangle, using configuration transformation

$X$, see [18, 21, 27]. A simple example (adapted from [3]) is shown in Fig. 7 – rotating two sides of the triangle as indicated, one can transform the triangle to any shape without changing the reasoning leading to the thesis (assuming its invariance with respect to size and rotation of the triangle is obvious).

## 6    Implementing Mathematical Diagrams

In practical implementation of computerized repositories of mathematical knowledge, diagrams can be included in various ways. The lack of space precludes detailed discussion of the issue here, hence only general listing of a few possible approaches will be proposed.

Interactive editors for constructing mathematical diagrams by the user. They should be designed to incorporate specific needs of mathematical diagrams, in particular should contain specialized libraries of high-level building blocks and editing tools adapted to different diagrammatic notations, as mentioned at the end of Section 4.

Semi-automatic diagram generation from underlying representation, like with the existing tools (though often of low quality) for graphing functions. They should have a rarely currently available feature of interactive editing by the user of the generated diagram. The tools like the logicographic symbols of [8] also belong here.

Libraries of reference diagrams representing various pieces of mathematical knowledge (see e.g. the "object structure" and "catalogue of cases" diagrams from the preceding section). They can be, where useful, interactively animated, like some diagrams at the `http://www.cut-the-knot.com/geometry.html` site.

Interactive "diagrammatic spreadsheets" of the sort proposed in [18, 21]. The diagram, constructed by the user or provided from the reference library, is defined there as a set of graphical elements linked with appropriate constraints assuring its structural integrity during interactive transformations of the sort shown in Fig. 7. The main use of such diagrams is for interactive exploration of possible configurations of mathematical objects modelled, and in diagrammatic reasoning, especially in the cases suffering from the particularity problem.

## 7   Conclusions

To manage complex knowledge, e.g. mathematical, efficient representation tools are needed. Diagrams constitute one of such tools, as yet mostly neglected by mathematicians. Thus, the ability of diagrams to efficiently represent complex mathematical knowledge of various sorts exemplified in Section 5 should attract more attention of designers of computerized repositories of mathematical knowledge. A long-range research and implementation programme in this area is much needed. It should address such issues as codification of existing and development of new diagrammatic notations for various branches of mathematics, development of design guidelines for good mathematical diagrams, analysis of causes of, and proposing remedies for, errors in diagrammatic representations, and devising, implementing, and experimenting with new computer tools for effective mathematical diagrams generation and use.

## References

1. M. Anderson, P. Cheng, V. Haarslev, eds., *Theory and Applications of Diagrams.* Lecture Notes in AI, vol. 1889, Springer-Verlag, Berlin 2000.
2. M. Anderson, B. Meyer, P. Olivier, eds., *Diagrammatic Representation and Reasoning.* Springer-Verlag, Berlin 2002.
3. R. Arnheim, *Visual Thinking.* University of California Press, Berkeley, CA 1969.
4. D. Barker-Plummer, S.C. Bailin, The role of diagrams in mathematical proofs. *Machine GRAPHICS & VISION,* **6** (1997) 25–56.

5. J. Barwise, J. Etchemendy, Visual information and valid reasoning. In: G. Allwein, J. Barwise, eds., *Logical Reasoning with Diagrams*, Oxford Univ. Press, 1996, 3–25.

6. J. Barwise, J. Etchemendy, Heterogeneous logic. In: ibidem, 209–232.

7. A. Blackwell, K. Marriott, A. Shimojima, eds., *Diagrammatic Representation and Inference*. Lecture Notes in AI, vol. 2980. Springer-Verlag, Berlin 2004.

8. B. Buchberger, Logicographic symbols: A new feature in Theorema. In: Y. Tazawa, ed., *Symbolic Computation – New Horizons*. Tokyo Denki Univ. Press, 2001, 23–30.

9. D.L. Goodstein, J.R. Goodstein: *Feynman's Lost Lecture: The Motion of Planets Around the Sun*. W.W. Norton & Co., 1996.

10. J. Hadamard, *The Psychology of Invention in the Mathematical Field*. Princeton Univ. Press, 1945.

11. E. Hammer, *Logic and Visual Information*. Cambridge Univ. Press, 1996.

12. M. Hegarty, B. Meyer, N. Hari Narayanan, eds., *Diagrammatic Representation and Inference*. Lecture Notes in AI, vol. 2317, Springer-Verlag, Berlin 2002.

13. M. Jamnik, A. Bundy, I. Green, On automating diagrammatic proofs of arithmetic arguments. *Journal of Logic, Language and Information*, **8** (1999) 297–321.

14. Z. Kulpa, Diagrammatic representation for a space of intervals. *Machine GRAPHICS & VISION*, **6** (1997) 5–24.

15. Z. Kulpa, Diagrammatic representation for interval arithmetic. *Linear Algebra Appl.*, **324** (2001) 55–80.

16. Z. Kulpa, Diagrammatic analysis of interval linear equations. Part I: Basic notions and the one-dimensional case, *Reliable Computing*, **9** (2003) 1–20.

17. Z. Kulpa, Self-consistency, imprecision, and impossible cases in diagrammatic representations. *Machine GRAPHICS & VISION*, **12** (2003) 147–160.

18. Z. Kulpa, *From Picture Processing to Interval Diagrams*. IFTR Reports 4/2003, Warsaw, 2003. (See http://www.ippt.gov.pl/~zkulpa/diagrams/fpptid.html)

19. Z. Kulpa, S. Markov, On the inclusion properties of interval multiplication: A diagrammatic study. *BIT Numerical Mathematics* **43** (2003) 791–810.

20. Z. Kulpa, Designing diagrammatic notation for interval analysis *Information Design Journal + Document Design* **12** (2004) 52–62.

21. T.L. Le, Z. Kulpa, Diagrammatic spreadsheet. *Machine GRAPHICS & VISION*, **12** (2003) 133–146.

22. N. Miller, *A Diagrammatic Formal System for Euclidean Geometry*. Ph.D. Thesis, Cornell University, Ithaca, NY 2001.

23. T. Needham, *Visual Complex Analysis*. Clarendon Press, Oxford 1997.

24. R.B. Nelsen, *Proofs Without Words: Exercises in Visual Thinking*. The Mathematical Association of America, Washington, DC 1993.

25. A. Shimojima, The graphic-linguistic distinction: Exploring alternatives. In: A. Blackwell, ed., *Thinking with Diagrams*. Kluwer, Dordrecht 2001, 5–27.

26. E.R. Tufte, *The Visual Display of Quantitative Information*. Graphics Press, Cheshire, CT 1983.

27. D. Winterstein, A. Bundy, C. Gurr, M. Jamnik, Using animation in diagrammatic theorem proving. In: [12], 46–60.

# Predicate Logic with Sequence Variables and Sequence Function Symbols*

Temur Kutsia and Bruno Buchberger

Research Institute for Symbolic Computation, Johannes Kepler University Linz
A-4040 Linz, Austria
{kutsia,buchberger}@risc.uni-linz.ac.at

**Abstract.** We extend first-order logic with sequence variables and sequence functions. We describe syntax, semantics and inference system for the extension, define an inductive theory with sequence variables and formulate induction rules. The calculus forms a basis for the top-down systematic theory exploration paradigm.

## 1 Introduction

The goal of future mathematical knowledge management is the availability of significant parts of mathematical knowledge in computer-processable, verified, well-structured and semantically unambiguous form over the web and the possibility to easily expand, modify, and re-structure this knowledge according to specifications defined by the user. For this, mathematical knowledge has to be formulated in the frame of formal logics. Translation between presentations of mathematical knowledge with respect to different logics should be automatic. A natural standard for such logics is (any version of) predicate logic.

We believe that the goal can only be achieved by a systematic build-up of mathematics from scratch using systematic, flexible, algorithmic tools based on algorithmic formal logic (automated reasoning). By these tools, most of the work involved in building up well-structured and reusable mathematical knowledge should be automated or, at least, computer-assisted. We call the research field that enables this type of generation of large pieces of coherent mathematical knowledge "Computer-Supported Mathematical Theory Exploration".

The systems and projects like ALF [26], AUTOMATH [13], COQ [2], ELF [29], HOL [17], IMPS [1], ISABELLE [28], LEGO [25], NUPRL [12], OMEGA [4], MIZAR [3], and the others have been designed and used to formalize mathematical knowledge. THEOREMA[1] is one of such projects, which aims at constructing tools for computer-supported mathematical theory exploration. Since then, within the THEOREMA project, various approaches to bottom-up and top-down computer-supported mathematical theory exploration have been proposed and

---

* Supported by the Austrian Science Foundation (FWF) under Project SFB F1302, and Johann Radon Institute for Computational and Applied Mathematics, Austrian Academy of Sciences.
[1] http://www.theorema.org/

A. Asperti et al. (Eds.): MKM 2004, LNCS 3119, pp. 205–219, 2004.

pursued with an emphasis on top-down methods. These approaches and first results are documented in various publications and reports (see, e.g., [8, 30, 9, 10]). The approaches are summarized in the "lazy thinking paradigm" for mathematical theory exploration introduced by the second author in [9].

In general, mathematical theory exploration requires higher-order logic. The version of predicate logic used in the case studies on theory exploration [30, 9, 10] is a higher-order predicate logic with sequence variables and sequence functions. However, the proofs in the case studies are done essentially on the first-order level. In this paper we restrict ourselves to the first-order fragment of predicate logic with sequence variables and sequence functions.

Sequence variables can be instantiated with finite sequences of terms. They add expressiveness and elegance to the language and have been used in various knowledge representation systems like KIF [15] or Common Logic [18]. ISABELLE [28] implements sequent calculi using sequence variables. In programming, the language of MATHEMATICA [31] successfully uses pattern matching that supports sequence variables and flexible arity function symbols (see [7] for more details). Sequence functions can be interpreted as multi-valued functions and have been used (under different names) in reasoning or programming systems, like, e.g., in SET-VAR [5] or RELFUN [6].

The following example shows how the property of a function being "orderless" can be easily defined using sequence variables: $f(\overline{x}, x, \overline{y}, y, \overline{z}) = f(\overline{x}, y, \overline{y}, x, \overline{z})$ specifies that the order of arguments in terms with the head $f$ and any number of arguments does not matter. The letters with the overbar are sequence variables. Without them, we would need a permutation to express the same property. Definition of concatenation $\langle \overline{x} \rangle \asymp \langle \overline{y} \rangle = \langle \overline{x}, \overline{y} \rangle$ is another example of expressiveness sequence variables.

Using sequence variables in programming helps to write elegant and short code, like, for instance, implementing bubble sort in a rule-based manner:

$$\mathsf{sort}(\langle \overline{x}, x, \overline{y}, y, \overline{z} \rangle) := \mathsf{sort}(\langle \overline{x}, y, \overline{y}, x, \overline{z} \rangle) \text{ if } x > y$$
$$\mathsf{sort}(\langle \overline{x} \rangle) := \langle \overline{x} \rangle$$

Bringing sequence functions in the language naturally allows Skolemization over sequence variables: Let $x, y$ be individual variables, $\overline{x}$ be a sequence variable, and $p$ be a flexible arity predicate symbol. Then $\forall x \forall y \exists \overline{x}\, p(x, y, \overline{x})$ Skolemizes to $\forall x \forall y\, p(x, y, \overline{f}(x, y))$, where $\overline{f}$ is a binary Skolem sequence function symbol. Another example, $\forall \overline{y} \exists \overline{x}\, p(\overline{y}, \overline{x})$, where $\overline{y}$ is a sequence variable, after Skolemization introduces a flexible arity sequence function symbol $\overline{g}$: $\forall \overline{y}\, p(\overline{y}, \overline{g}(\overline{y}))$.

Although sequence variables and sequence functions appear in various applications, so far, to our knowledge, there was no formal treatment of full predicate logic with these constructs. (Few exceptions are [19], that considers logic with sequence variables without sequence functions, and [21], investigating equational theories, again with sequence variables, but without sequence functions.) In this paper we fill this gap, describing syntax, semantics and inference system for an extension of classical first-order logic with sequence variables and sequence functions. Although, in general, the extension is not very complicated, there are some subtle points that have to be treated carefully.

In the extended language we allow both individual and sequence variables/function symbols, where the function symbols can have fixed or flexible arity. We have also predicates of fixed or flexible arity, and can quantify over individual and sequence variables. It gives a simple and elegant language, which can be encoded as a special order-sorted first-order theory (see [24]).

A natural intuition behind sequence terms is that they represent finite sequences of individual terms. We formalize this intuition using induction, and introduce several versions of induction rules. Inductive theories with sequence variables have some interesting properties that one normally can not observe in their standard counterparts: For instance, Herbrand universe is not an inductive domain, induction rules can be defined without using constructors.

The calculus $\mathbf{G}^\approx$ that we introduce in this paper generalizes $\mathbf{LK}^\approx$ calculus ($\mathbf{LK}^\approx$ is an extension of Gentzen's $\mathbf{LK}$ calculus [16] with equality), and possesses many nice proof-theoretic properties, including the extended version of Gödel's completeness theorem. Also, the counterparts of Löwenheim-Skolem, Compactness, Model Existence theorems and Consistency lemma hold. $\mathbf{G}^\approx$ together with induction and cut rules forms the logical basis of the top-down theory exploration procedure [9].

The main results of this paper are the following: First, we give the first detailed description of predicate logic with sequence variables and sequence functions, clarifying the intuitive meaning and formal semantics of sequence variables that some researchers considered to be insufficiently explored (see, e.g. [11]). Second, we describe the logical foundations of the "theory exploration with lazy thinking" paradigm.

The contributions of the first author are defining syntax and semantics of languages with sequence variables and sequence functions, designing and proving the properties of the calculus $\mathbf{G}^\approx$, and showing relations between induction rules and intended models. The second author pointed out the importance of using sequence variables in symbolic computation (see [7]), introduced sequence variables and sequence functions in the THEOREMA system, defined various inference rules for them (including induction), and designed provers that use sequence variables.

We omit the details of proofs which can be found in the technical report [24].

## 2    Syntax

We consider an alphabet consisting of the following pairwise disjoint sets of symbols: individual variables $\mathcal{V}_{\text{Ind}}$, sequence variables $\mathcal{V}_{\text{Seq}}$, fixed arity individual function symbols $\mathcal{F}_{\text{Ind}}^{\text{Fix}}$, flexible arity individual function symbols $\mathcal{F}_{\text{Ind}}^{\text{Flex}}$, fixed arity sequence function symbols $\mathcal{F}_{\text{Seq}}^{\text{Fix}}$, flexible arity sequence function symbols $\mathcal{F}_{\text{Seq}}^{\text{Flex}}$, fixed arity predicate symbols $\mathcal{P}^{\text{Fix}}$, and flexible arity predicate symbols $\mathcal{P}^{\text{Flex}}$. Each set of variables is countable. Each set of function and predicate symbols is finite or countable. The binary equality predicate symbol $\approx$ is in $\mathcal{P}^{\text{Fix}}$. Besides, there are connectives $\neg$, $\vee$, $\wedge$, $\Rightarrow$, $\Leftrightarrow$, quantifiers $\exists$, $\forall$, parentheses '(', ')' and comma ',' in the alphabet.

We will use the following denotations: $\mathcal{V} := \mathcal{V}_{\text{Ind}} \cup \mathcal{V}_{\text{Seq}}$; $\mathcal{F}_{\text{Ind}} := \mathcal{F}_{\text{Ind}}^{\text{Fix}} \cup \mathcal{F}_{\text{Ind}}^{\text{Flex}}$; $\mathcal{F}_{\text{Seq}} := \mathcal{F}_{\text{Seq}}^{\text{Fix}} \cup \mathcal{F}_{\text{Seq}}^{\text{Flex}}$; $\mathcal{F}^{\text{Fix}} := \mathcal{F}_{\text{Ind}}^{\text{Fix}} \cup \mathcal{F}_{\text{Seq}}^{\text{Fix}}$; $\mathcal{F}^{\text{Flex}} := \mathcal{F}_{\text{Ind}}^{\text{Flex}} \cup \mathcal{F}_{\text{Seq}}^{\text{Flex}}$; $\mathcal{F} := \mathcal{F}^{\text{Fix}} \cup \mathcal{F}^{\text{Flex}}$; $\mathcal{P} := \mathcal{P}^{\text{Fix}} \cup \mathcal{P}^{\text{Flex}}$. The arity of $q \in \mathcal{F}^{\text{Fix}} \cup \mathcal{P}^{\text{Fix}}$ is denoted by $Ar(q)$. A function symbol $c \in \mathcal{F}^{\text{Fix}}$ is called a constant if $Ar(c) = 0$.

**Definition 1.** We define the notion of term over $\mathcal{F}$ and $\mathcal{V}$:

1. If $t \in \mathcal{V}_{\text{Ind}}$ (resp. $t \in \mathcal{V}_{\text{Seq}}$), then $t$ is an individual (resp. sequence) term.
2. If $f \in \mathcal{F}_{\text{Ind}}^{\text{Fix}}$ (resp. $f \in \mathcal{F}_{\text{Seq}}^{\text{Fix}}$), $Ar(f) = n$, $n \geq 0$, and $t_1, \ldots, t_n$ are individual terms, then $f(t_1, \ldots, t_n)$ is an individual (resp. sequence) term.
3. If $f \in \mathcal{F}_{\text{Ind}}^{\text{Flex}}$ (resp. $f \in \mathcal{F}_{\text{Seq}}^{\text{Flex}}$) and $t_1, \ldots, t_n$ ($n \geq 0$) are individual or sequence terms, then $f(t_1, \ldots, t_n)$ is an individual (resp. sequence) term.

A term is either an individual or a sequence term.

We denote by $\mathcal{T}_{\text{Ind}}(\mathcal{F}, \mathcal{V})$, $\mathcal{T}_{\text{Seq}}(\mathcal{F}, \mathcal{V})$ and $\mathcal{T}(\mathcal{F}, \mathcal{V})$ respectively the set of all individual terms, all sequence terms and all terms over $\mathcal{F}$ and $\mathcal{V}$.

If not otherwise stated, the following symbols, with or without indices, are used as metavariables: $x$, $y$ and $z$ – over individual variables; $\overline{x}$, $\overline{y}$ and $\overline{z}$ – over sequence variables; $u$ and $v$ – over (individual or sequence) variables; $f$, $g$ and $h$ – over individual function symbols; $\overline{f}$, $\overline{g}$ and $\overline{h}$ – over sequence function symbols; $a$, $b$ and $c$ – over individual constants; $\overline{a}$, $\overline{b}$ and $\overline{c}$ – over sequence constants.

**Example 1.** Let $f \in \mathcal{F}_{\text{Ind}}^{\text{Flex}}$, $\overline{f} \in \mathcal{F}_{\text{Seq}}^{\text{Flex}}$, $g \in \mathcal{F}_{\text{Ind}}^{\text{Fix}}$, $\overline{g} \in \mathcal{F}_{\text{Seq}}^{\text{Fix}}$, $Ar(g) = 2$, $Ar(\overline{g}) = 1$.

1. $f(\overline{x}, g(x, y)) \in \mathcal{T}_{\text{Ind}}(\mathcal{F}, \mathcal{V})$.
2. $\overline{f}(\overline{x}, \overline{f}(x, \overline{x}, y)) \in \mathcal{T}_{\text{Seq}}(\mathcal{F}, \mathcal{V})$.
3. $f(\overline{x}, \overline{g}(\overline{x})) \notin \mathcal{T}(\mathcal{F}, \mathcal{V})$, because $\overline{x}$ occurs as an argument of $\overline{g}$ which is of fixed arity.
4. $f(\overline{x}, \overline{g}(x, y)) \notin \mathcal{T}(\mathcal{F}, \mathcal{V})$, because $\overline{g}$ is unary.

**Definition 2.** We define the notion of atomic formula, or shortly, atom, over $\mathcal{P}$, $\mathcal{F}$ and $\mathcal{V}$:

1. If $p \in \mathcal{P}^{\text{Fix}}$, $Ar(p) = n$, $n \geq 0$, and $t_1, \ldots, t_n \in \mathcal{T}_{\text{Ind}}(\mathcal{F}, \mathcal{V})$, then $p(t_1, \ldots, t_n)$ is an atom.
2. If $p \in \mathcal{P}^{\text{Flex}}$ and $t_1, \ldots, t_n \in \mathcal{T}(\mathcal{F}, \mathcal{V})$, $n \geq 0$, then $p(t_1, \ldots, t_n)$ is an atom.

We denote the set of atomic formulae over $\mathcal{P}$, $\mathcal{F}$ and $\mathcal{V}$ by $\mathcal{A}(\mathcal{P}, \mathcal{F}, \mathcal{V})$.

The function symbol $f$ is called the head of the term $f(t_1, \ldots, t_n)$. We denote the head of $t \notin \mathcal{V}$ by $\mathcal{H}ead(t)$. The head of an atom is defined in the same way.

**Definition 3.** We define the set of formulae $\mathcal{F}ml(\mathcal{P}, \mathcal{F}, \mathcal{V})$ over $\mathcal{P}$, $\mathcal{F}$ and $\mathcal{V}$:

$$\mathcal{F}ml(\mathcal{P}, \mathcal{F}, \mathcal{V}) := \quad \mathcal{A}(\mathcal{P}, \mathcal{F}, \mathcal{V}) \cup \{\neg A \mid A \in \mathcal{F}ml(\mathcal{P}, \mathcal{F}, \mathcal{V})\}$$
$$\cup \{A \circ B \mid A, B \in \mathcal{F}ml(\mathcal{P}, \mathcal{F}, \mathcal{V}), \circ \in \{\vee, \wedge, \Rightarrow, \Leftrightarrow\}\}$$
$$\cup \{Qv.A \mid A \in \mathcal{F}ml(\mathcal{P}, \mathcal{F}, \mathcal{V}), v \in \mathcal{V}, Q \in \{\exists, \forall\}\}.$$

Free and bound variables of a formula are defined in the standard way. We denote by $\mathcal{L}_{\approx}$ the language defined by $\mathcal{F} \cup \mathcal{P}$.

# 3   Substitutions

**Definition 4.** A variable binding is either a pair $x \mapsto t$ where $t \in \mathcal{T}_{\mathrm{Ind}}(\mathcal{F}, \mathcal{V})$ and $t \neq x$, or an expression $\overline{x} \mapsto \ulcorner t_1, \ldots, t_n \urcorner^2$ where $n \geq 0$, for all $1 \leq i \leq n$ we have $t_i \in \mathcal{T}(\mathcal{F}, \mathcal{V})$, and if $n = 1$ then $t_1 \neq \overline{x}$.

**Definition 5.** A substitution is a finite set of variable bindings

$$\{x_1 \mapsto t_1, \ldots, x_n \mapsto t_n, \overline{x}_1 \mapsto \ulcorner s_1^1, \ldots, s_{k_1}^1 \urcorner, \ldots, \overline{x}_m \mapsto \ulcorner s_1^m, \ldots, s_{k_m}^m \urcorner\},$$

where $n, m \geq 0$, $x_1, \ldots, x_n, \overline{x}_1, \ldots, \overline{x}_m$ are distinct variables.[3]

Lower case Greek letters are used to denote substitutions. The empty substitution is denoted by $\varepsilon$.

**Definition 6.** The instance of a term $s$ with respect to a substitution $\sigma$, denoted $s\sigma$, is defined recursively as follows:

1. $x\sigma = \begin{cases} t, & \text{if } x \mapsto t \in \sigma, \\ x, & \text{otherwise.} \end{cases}$

2. $\overline{x}\sigma = \begin{cases} t_1, \ldots, t_n, & \text{if } \overline{x} \mapsto \ulcorner t_1, \ldots, t_n \urcorner \in \sigma, \ n \geq 0, \\ \overline{x}, & \text{otherwise.} \end{cases}$

3. $f(t_1, \ldots, t_n)\sigma = f(t_1\sigma, \ldots, t_n\sigma)$.

**Example 2.** $f(x, \overline{x}, \overline{y})\{x \mapsto a, \overline{x} \mapsto \ulcorner\urcorner, \overline{y} \mapsto \ulcorner a, f(\overline{x}), b \urcorner\} = f(a, a, f(\overline{x}), b)$.

By $\mathcal{V}ar(Q)$ we denote the set of all variables occurring in $Q$, where $Q$ is a term or a set of terms.

**Definition 7.** Let $\sigma$ be a substitution.

1. The domain of $\sigma$ is the set of variables $\mathcal{D}om(\sigma) = \{l \mid l\sigma \neq l\}$.
2. The codomain of $\sigma$ is the set of terms $\mathcal{C}od(\sigma) = \{l\sigma \mid l \in \mathcal{D}om(\sigma)\}$.
3. The range of $\sigma$ is the set of variables: $\mathcal{R}an(\sigma) = \mathcal{V}ar(\mathcal{C}od(\sigma))$.

Note that a codomain of a substitution is a set of terms, not a set consisting of terms and sequences of terms. For instance, $\mathcal{C}od(\{x \mapsto b, \overline{x} \mapsto \ulcorner a, a, b \urcorner\}) = \{a, b\}$.

Application of a substitution on a formula is defined in the standard way. We denote an application of $\sigma$ on $F$ by $F\sigma$.

**Definition 8.** A term $t$ is free for a variable $v$ in a formula $F$ if either

1. $F$ is an atom, or
2. $F = \neg A$ and $t$ is free for $v$ in $A$, or

---

[2] To improve readability, we write sequences that bind sequence variables between $\ulcorner$ and $\urcorner$.

[3] In [23] we consider a more general notion of substitution that allows bindings for sequence function symbols as well. That, in fact, treats sequence function symbols as second-order variables. However, for our purposes the notion of substitution defined above is sufficient.

3. $F = (A \circ B)$ and $t$ is free for $v$ in $B$ and $C$, where $\circ \in \{\vee, \wedge, \Rightarrow, \Leftrightarrow\}$, or
4. $F = \forall u A$ or $F = \exists u A$ and either (a) $v = u$, or (b) $v \neq u$, $u \notin Var(t)$ and $t$ is free for $v$ in $A$.

We assume that for any formula $F$ and substitution $\sigma$, before applying $\sigma$ on $F$ all bound variables in $F$ are renamed so that they do not occur in $Ran(\sigma)$. This assumption guarantees that for all $v \in Dom(\sigma)$ the terms in $v\sigma$ are free for $v$ in $F$.

# 4     Semantics

For a set $S$, we denote by $S^n$ the set of all $n$-tuples over $S$. In particular, $S^0 = \{\langle\rangle\}$. By $S^\infty$ we denote the set $\cup_{i \geq 0} S^i$.

**Definition 9.** A structure $\mathfrak{S}$ for $\mathcal{L}_\approx$ (or, in short, an $\mathcal{L}_\approx$-structure) is a pair $\langle \mathcal{D}, \mathcal{I} \rangle$, where:

- $\mathcal{D}$ is a non-empty set, called a domain of $\mathfrak{S}$, that is a disjoint union of two sets, $\mathcal{D}_{\mathrm{Ind}}$ and $\mathcal{D}_{\mathrm{Seq}}$, written $\mathcal{D} = \mathcal{D}_{\mathrm{Ind}} \uplus \mathcal{D}_{\mathrm{Seq}}$, where $\mathcal{D}_{\mathrm{Ind}} \neq \emptyset$.
- $\mathcal{I}$ is a mapping, called an interpretation that associates:
  - To every individual constant $c$ in $\mathcal{L}_\approx$ some element $c_\mathcal{I}$ of $\mathcal{D}_{\mathrm{Ind}}$.
  - To every sequence constant $\overline{c}$ in $\mathcal{L}_\approx$ some element $\overline{c}_\mathcal{I}$ of $\mathcal{D}^\infty$.
  - To every $n$-ary individual function symbol $f$ in $\mathcal{L}_\approx$, with $n > 0$, some $n$-ary function $f_\mathcal{I} : \mathcal{D}_{\mathrm{Ind}}^n \to \mathcal{D}_{\mathrm{Ind}}$.
  - To every $n$-ary sequence function symbol $\overline{f}$ in $\mathcal{L}_\approx$, with $n > 0$, some $n$-ary multi-valued function $\overline{f}_\mathcal{I} : \mathcal{D}_{\mathrm{Ind}}^n \to \mathcal{D}^\infty$.
  - To every flexible arity individual function symbol $f$ in $\mathcal{L}_\approx$, some flexible arity function $f_\mathcal{I} : \mathcal{D}^\infty \to \mathcal{D}_{\mathrm{Ind}}$.
  - To every flexible arity sequence function symbol $\overline{f}$ in $\mathcal{L}_\approx$, some flexible arity multi-valued function $\overline{f}_\mathcal{I} : \mathcal{D}^\infty \to \mathcal{D}^\infty$.
  - To every $n$-ary predicate symbol $p$ in $\mathcal{L}_\approx$ other than $\approx$, with $n \geq 0$, some $n$-ary predicate $p_\mathcal{I} \subseteq \mathcal{D}_{\mathrm{Ind}}^n$;
  - To every flexible arity predicate symbol $p$ in $\mathcal{L}_\approx$ some flexible arity predicate $p_\mathcal{I} \subseteq \mathcal{D}^\infty$;

**Definition 10.** Let $\mathfrak{S} = \langle \mathcal{D}, \mathcal{I} \rangle$ be an $\mathcal{L}_\approx$-structure. A state $\sigma$ over $\mathfrak{S}$, denoted $\sigma^\mathfrak{S}$, is a mapping defined on variables as follows:

- For an individual variable $x$, $\sigma^\mathfrak{S}(x) \in \mathcal{D}_{\mathrm{Ind}}$.
- For a sequence variable $\overline{x}$, $\sigma^\mathfrak{S}(\overline{x}) \in \mathcal{D}^\infty$.

**Definition 11.** Let $\mathfrak{S} = \langle \mathcal{D}, \mathcal{I} \rangle$ be an $\mathcal{L}_\approx$-structure and let $\sigma$ be a state over $\mathfrak{S}$. A value of a term $t$ in $\mathfrak{S}$ w.r.t. $\sigma$, denoted $Val_\sigma^\mathfrak{S}(t)$, is defined as follows:

- $Val_\sigma^\mathfrak{S}(v) = \sigma^\mathfrak{S}(v)$, for every $v \in \mathcal{V}$.
- $Val_\sigma^\mathfrak{S}(f(t_1, \ldots, t_n)) = f_\mathcal{I}(Val_\sigma^\mathfrak{S}(t_1), \ldots, Val_\sigma^\mathfrak{S}(t_n))$, for every $f(t_1, \ldots, t_n) \in \mathcal{T}(\mathcal{F}, \mathcal{V})$, $n \geq 0$.

**Definition 12.** Let $v$ be a variable and $\sigma^{\mathfrak{S}}$ be a state over an $\mathcal{L}_{\approx}$-structure $\mathfrak{S}$. A state $\vartheta^{\mathfrak{S}}$ is a $v$-variant of $\sigma^{\mathfrak{S}}$ iff $\vartheta^{\mathfrak{S}}(u) = \sigma^{\mathfrak{S}}(u)$ for each variable $u \neq v$.

The set $\mathcal{TV} = \{\mathbf{T}, \mathbf{F}\}$ is called the set of truth values. The operations $\neg_{\mathrm{TV}}$, $\vee_{\mathrm{TV}}$, $\wedge_{\mathrm{TV}}$, $\Rightarrow_{\mathrm{TV}}$, $\Leftrightarrow_{\mathrm{TV}}$ are defined on $\mathcal{TV}$ in the standard way.

**Definition 13.** Let $\mathfrak{S} = \langle \mathcal{D}, \mathcal{I} \rangle$ be an $\mathcal{L}_{\approx}$-structure and $\sigma$ be a state over $\mathfrak{S}$. A truth value of a formula $F$ in $\mathfrak{S}$ with respect to $\sigma$, denoted $\mathcal{V}al_\sigma^{\mathfrak{S}}(F)$, is defined as follows:

- $\mathcal{V}al_\sigma^{\mathfrak{S}}(p(t_1, \ldots, t_n)) = \mathbf{T}$ iff $\langle \mathcal{V}al_\sigma^{\mathfrak{S}}(t_1), \ldots, \mathcal{V}al_\sigma^{\mathfrak{S}}(t_n) \rangle \subseteq p_{\mathcal{I}}$.
- $\mathcal{V}al_\sigma^{\mathfrak{S}}(t_1 \approx t_2) = \mathbf{T}$ iff $\mathcal{V}al_\sigma^{\mathfrak{S}}(t_1) = \mathcal{V}al_\sigma^{\mathfrak{S}}(t_2)$.
- $\mathcal{V}al_\sigma^{\mathfrak{S}}(\neg F) = \neg_{\mathrm{TV}} \mathcal{V}al_\sigma^{\mathfrak{S}}(F)$.
- $\mathcal{V}al_\sigma^{\mathfrak{S}}(F_1 \circ F_2) = \mathcal{V}al_\sigma^{\mathfrak{S}}(F_1) \circ_{\mathrm{TV}} \mathcal{V}al_\sigma^{\mathfrak{S}}(F_2)$, where $\circ \in \{\vee, \wedge, \Rightarrow, \Leftrightarrow\}$
- $\mathcal{V}al_\sigma^{\mathfrak{S}}(\forall v F) = \mathbf{T}$ iff $\mathcal{V}al_\vartheta^{\mathfrak{S}}(F) = \mathbf{T}$ for every $\vartheta^{\mathfrak{S}}$ that is a $v$-variant of $\sigma^{\mathfrak{S}}$.
- $\mathcal{V}al_\sigma^{\mathfrak{S}}(\exists v F) = \mathbf{T}$ iff $\mathcal{V}al_\vartheta^{\mathfrak{S}}(F) = \mathbf{T}$ for some $\vartheta^{\mathfrak{S}}$ that is a $v$-variant of $\sigma^{\mathfrak{S}}$.

In Definition 9 we required the domain $\mathcal{D}$ to be a disjoint union of two sets $\mathcal{D}_{\mathrm{Ind}}$ and $\mathcal{D}_{\mathrm{Seq}}$. It is justified, since on the syntactic level we distinguish between individual and sequence terms, and it is natural to reflect this distinction on the semantic level. In the next section we define a calculus that is complete with respect to this semantics. Many classical results remain valid as well.

On the other side, one would naturally expect that a sequence term represents a finite sequence of individual terms. In other words, the intuition would suggest that the sequence terms should be interpreted as finite sequences of individual elements of the domain. This intuition can be easily captured by structures whose domain consists of individual elements only. We call such structures the *intended structures*. In Section 6 below we show relations between induction with sequence variables and intended structures.

# 5    The Gentzen-Style System $G^{\approx}$

In this section we present a Gentzen-style sequent calculus for $\mathcal{L}_{\approx}$.

**Definition 14.** A *sequent* is a pair of sequences of formulae. A sequent $\langle \Gamma, \Delta \rangle$ is denoted by $\Gamma \rightarrow \Delta$.

In a sequent $\Gamma \rightarrow \Delta$, $\Gamma$ is called the *antecedent* and $\Delta$ is called the *succedent*. If $\Gamma$ is the empty sequence, the corresponding sequent is denoted as $\rightarrow \Delta$. If $\Delta$ is empty, the corresponding sequent is denoted as $\Gamma \rightarrow$. If both $\Gamma$ and $\Delta$ are empty, we have the *inconsistent sequent* $\rightarrow$. Below the symbols $\Gamma, \Delta, \Lambda$ will be used to denote arbitrary sequences of formulae and $A, B$ to denote formulae. Note that $\Gamma, \Delta, \Lambda$ are sequence variables on the meta level. The set of free variables of a formula $A$ is denoted by $\mathcal{F}Var(A)$.

**Definition 15.** A *position* within a term or atom $E$ is a sequence of positive integers, describing the path from $\mathcal{H}ead(E)$ to the head of the subterm at that position. By $E[s]_p$ we denote the term or atom obtained from $E$ by replacing the term at position $p$ with the term $s$.

**Definition 16.** The sequent calculus $\mathbf{G}^{\approx}$ consists of the following 17 inference rules.

$$\frac{\Gamma, A, B, \Delta \to \Lambda}{\Gamma, A \wedge B, \Delta \to \Lambda} \ (\wedge \to) \qquad \frac{\Gamma \to \Delta, A, \Lambda \quad \Gamma \to \Delta, B, \Lambda}{\Gamma \to \Delta, A \wedge B, \Lambda} \ (\to \wedge)$$

$$\frac{\Gamma, A, \Delta \to \Lambda \quad \Gamma, B, \Delta \to \Lambda}{\Gamma, A \vee B, \Delta \to \Lambda} \ (\vee \to) \qquad \frac{\Gamma \to \Delta, A, B, \Lambda}{\Gamma \to \Delta, A \vee B, \Lambda} \ (\to \vee)$$

$$\frac{\Gamma \to \Delta, A, \Lambda \quad \Gamma, B, \Lambda \to \Delta}{\Gamma, A \Rightarrow B, \Lambda \to \Delta} \ (\Rightarrow \to) \qquad \frac{\Gamma, A \to \Delta, B, \Lambda}{\Gamma \to \Delta, A \Rightarrow B, \Lambda} \ (\to \Rightarrow)$$

$$\frac{\Gamma, \Delta \to A, \Lambda}{\Gamma, \neg A, \Delta \to \Lambda} \ (\neg \to) \qquad \frac{A, \Gamma \to \Delta, \Lambda}{\Gamma \to \Delta, \neg A, \Lambda} \ (\to \neg)$$

In the quantifier rules below

1. $x$ is any individual variable;
2. $y$ is any individual variable free for $x$ in $A$ and $y \notin \mathcal{F}Var(A) \setminus \{x\}$;
3. $t$ is any individual term free for $x$ in $A$;
4. $\overline{x}$ is any sequence variable;
5. $\overline{y}$ is any sequence variable free for $\overline{x}$ in $A$ and $\overline{y} \notin \mathcal{F}Var(A) \setminus \{\overline{x}\}$;
6. $s_1, \ldots, s_n$, $n \geq 0$, is any sequence of terms each of them free for $\overline{x}$ in $A$.

$$\frac{\Gamma, A\{x \mapsto t\}, \forall x A, \Delta \to \Lambda}{\Gamma, \forall x A, \Delta \to \Lambda} \ (\forall_{\mathrm{I}} \to) \qquad \frac{\Gamma \to \Delta, A\{x \mapsto y\}, \Lambda}{\Gamma \to \Delta, \forall x A, \Lambda} \ (\to \forall_{\mathrm{I}})$$

$$\frac{\Gamma, A\{x \mapsto y\}, \Delta \to \Lambda}{\Gamma, \exists x A, \Delta \to \Lambda} \ (\exists_{\mathrm{I}} \to) \qquad \frac{\Gamma \to \Delta, A\{x \mapsto t\}, \exists x A, \Lambda}{\Gamma \to \Delta, \exists x A, \Lambda} \ (\to \exists_{\mathrm{I}})$$

$$\frac{\Gamma, A\{\overline{x} \mapsto \ulcorner s_1, \ldots, s_n \urcorner\}, \forall \overline{x} A, \Delta \to \Lambda}{\Gamma, \forall \overline{x} A, \Delta \to \Lambda} \ (\forall_{\mathrm{S}} \to) \qquad \frac{\Gamma \to \Delta, A\{\overline{x} \mapsto \overline{y}\}, \Lambda}{\Gamma \to \Delta, \forall \overline{x} A, \Lambda} \ (\to \forall_{\mathrm{S}})$$

$$\frac{\Gamma, A\{\overline{x} \mapsto \overline{y}\}, \Delta \to \Lambda}{\Gamma, \exists \overline{x} A, \Delta \to \Lambda} \ (\exists_{\mathrm{S}} \to) \qquad \frac{\Gamma \to \Delta, A\{\overline{x} \mapsto \ulcorner s_1, \ldots, s_n \urcorner\}, \exists \overline{x} A, \Lambda}{\Gamma \to \Delta, \exists \overline{x} A, \Lambda} \ (\to \exists_{\mathrm{S}})$$

In the rule $(\approx)$ below $A$ is an atom and $p$ is a position.

$$\frac{\Gamma, (s \approx t \wedge A[s]_p) \Rightarrow A[t]_p \to \Delta}{\Gamma \to \Delta} \ (\approx)$$

Note that in both the $(\rightarrow \forall_I)$-rule and the $(\exists_I \rightarrow)$-rule, the variable $y$ does not occur free in the lower sequent. Similarly, in both the $(\rightarrow \forall_S)$-rule and the $(\exists_S \rightarrow)$-rule, the variable $\bar{y}$ does not occur free in the lower sequent.

The axioms of $\mathbf{G}^{\approx}$ are all sequents $\Gamma \rightarrow \Delta$ such that $\Gamma$ and $\Delta$ contain a common formula, and sequents of the form $\Gamma \rightarrow \Delta, s \approx s, \Lambda$. Validity and provability of sequents are defined in the standard way.

The following version of Gödel's extended completeness theorem holds for the calculus $\mathbf{G}^{\approx}$:

**Theorem 1 (Completeness of $\mathbf{G}^{\approx}$).** A sequent (even infinite) is valid iff it is provable in $\mathbf{G}^{\approx}$.

The classical results like Löwenheim-Skolem, Compactness, Model Existence theorems, and Consistency Lemma remain valid for $\mathcal{L}_{\approx}$.

The calculus $\mathbf{G}^{\approx}$ has many nice proof-theoretic properties, but is not suited for implementation because of too high non-determinism. It is a well-known problem for many sequent-based calculi (like, for instance, for the classical $\mathbf{LK}^{\approx}$ calculus). Degtyarev and Voronkov [14] survey the methods to overcome it. In our case, a variant of basic superposition with ordering and equality constraint inheritance proposed in [27] seems to be a reasonable alternative of $\mathbf{G}^{\approx}$, taking into account the fact that unification with sequence variables and sequence functions is infinitary but decidable [23]. This approach for theories with sequence variables, but without sequence functions has already been considered in [22]. To do the same for theories with sequence variables and sequence functions one needs to introduce a reduction ordering on terms involving sequence variables and functions, and an efficient algorithm for solving ordering constraints. This is a subject of further research and lies beyond the scope of this paper.

Note also that predicate logic with sequence variables and sequence function symbols can be encoded as a special order-sorted first-order theory. It requires introducing into the language an additional binary function symbol for constructing sequences, a constant for the empty sequence, and adding to the theory the corresponding axioms. Details of the translation can be found in [24].

## 6   Induction with Sequence Variables

In this section we develop a machinery to capture the natural intuitive meaning of sequence terms: representation of finite sequences of individual terms. On the semantic level it amounts to considering the intended structures, and on the inference rules level it leads to introducing induction.

We start with the definitions of *inductive domain* and *intended structure*.

**Definition 17.** Let $\mathfrak{S} = \langle \mathcal{D}, \mathcal{I} \rangle$ be a structure for the language $\mathcal{L}_{\approx}$ such that $\mathcal{D}_{\mathrm{Seq}} = \emptyset$. Then $\mathfrak{S}$ is called an intended structure for $\mathcal{L}_{\approx}$ and $\mathcal{D}$ is called an inductive domain.

Note that Herbrand structures are not intended structures for $\mathcal{L}_{\approx}$. We will write $A[v]$ to indicate that the formula $A$ contains a free occurrence of $v$.

Below we will use a special flexible arity function symbol $f$ that satisfies the following axioms:

$$\forall x \forall \overline{x} \forall \overline{y} \quad \neg (f(\overline{x}, x, \overline{y}) \approx f()),$$
$$\forall x \forall y \forall \overline{x} \forall \overline{y} \quad f(x, \overline{x}) \approx f(y, \overline{y}) \Leftrightarrow x \approx y \wedge f(\overline{x}) \approx f(\overline{y}),$$
$$\forall x \forall y \forall \overline{x} \forall \overline{y} \quad f(\overline{x}, x) \approx f(\overline{y}, y) \Leftrightarrow f(\overline{x}) \approx f(\overline{y}) \wedge x \approx y,$$
$$\forall \overline{x} \forall \overline{y} \quad (f(\overline{x}) \approx f(\overline{y}) \wedge A\{\overline{z} \mapsto \overline{x}\}) \Rightarrow A\{\overline{z} \mapsto \overline{y}\},$$

where $A$ is an arbitrary formula.

**Definition 18.** The well-founded[4] induction principle for sequence variables is formulated as follows:

$$\forall \overline{x} \ (\forall \overline{y} \ (f(\overline{x}) \succ f(\overline{y}) \Rightarrow A\{\overline{x} \mapsto \overline{y}\}) \Rightarrow A[\overline{x}]) \Rightarrow \forall \overline{x} \ A[\overline{x}] \qquad \text{(WFI)}$$

where $\succ$ is a well-founded ordering defined for terms with the head $f$.

It is not hard to show that the well-founded induction principle is valid. Since well-foundedness is an undecidable property, we will develop syntactic instances of the WFI principle that avoid direct reference to arbitrary well-founded relations. We give below some practically useful examples of such instantiation that have been used in the case studies [9, 10].

We start from auxiliary notions.

**Definition 19.** The case distinction rule from the left is the formula

$$(A\{\overline{x} \mapsto \ulcorner \urcorner\} \wedge \forall y \forall \overline{y} \ A\{\overline{x} \mapsto \ulcorner y, \overline{y} \urcorner\}) \Rightarrow \forall \overline{x} \ A[\overline{x}] \qquad \text{(LCD)}$$

The LCD rule is not valid, as the following example shows:

Example 3. Let $A[\overline{x}]$ in LCD be the atom $p(\overline{x})$. Take a structure $\mathfrak{S} = \langle \mathcal{D}, \mathcal{I} \rangle$ such that $\mathcal{D}_{\text{Ind}} = \{a\}$, $\mathcal{D}_{\text{Seq}} = \{b\}$ and $p_{\mathcal{I}}$ contains all the finite tuples over $\mathcal{D}$ whose first element is not $b$. Then LCD is false in $\mathfrak{S}$.

However, the following theorem holds:

**Theorem 2.** LCD is true in every intended model.

**Definition 20.** The suffix ordering $\succ_{\text{Suf}}$ is defined on terms with the head $f$:

$$\forall \overline{x} \forall \overline{y} \ (f(\overline{x}) \succ_{\text{Suf}} f(\overline{y}) \Leftrightarrow$$
$$\exists z \exists \overline{z} \ f(\overline{x}) \approx f(z, \overline{z}) \wedge (f(\overline{z}) \approx f(\overline{y}) \vee f(\overline{z}) \succ_{\text{Suf}} f(\overline{y}))) \qquad \text{(SO)}$$

Suffix ordering is well-founded and has the property that any term of the form $f(t_1, \ldots, t_n)$, $n > 0$, which is not minimal with respect to $\succ_{\text{Suf}}$, has individual terms as its first $k$ arguments for some $1 \leq k \leq n$.

---

[4] Also called Noetherian.

**Definition 21.** The structural induction from the left is the formula

$$(A\{\overline{x} \mapsto \ulcorner\urcorner\} \wedge \forall y \forall \overline{y}\ (A\{\overline{x} \mapsto \overline{y}\} \Rightarrow A\{\overline{x} \mapsto \ulcorner y, \overline{y}\urcorner\})) \Rightarrow \forall \overline{x}\ A[\overline{x}]. \qquad \text{(LSI)}$$

LSI can be obtained syntactically from SO and the instances of WFI and LCD: If we take

$$B[\overline{x}] := \forall \overline{y}\ (f(\overline{x}) \succ_{\text{Suf}} f(\overline{y}) \Rightarrow A\{\overline{x} \mapsto \overline{y}\}) \Rightarrow A[\overline{x}],$$
$$\text{WFI'} := \forall \overline{x}\ B[\overline{x}] \Rightarrow \forall \overline{x}\ A[\overline{x}],$$
$$\text{LCD'} := (B\{\overline{x} \mapsto \ulcorner\urcorner\} \wedge \forall z \forall \overline{z}\ B\{\overline{x} \mapsto \ulcorner z, \overline{z}\urcorner\}) \Rightarrow \forall \overline{x}\ B[\overline{x}],$$

then the following theorem holds:

**Theorem 3.** The sequent SO, LCD', WFI' $\to$ LSI is provable in $\mathbf{G}^{\approx}$.

We proved this theorem with the help of one of the provers of the THEO-REMA system. First, we proved LSI from SO, LCD', and WFI' automatically by the THEOREMA prover for predicate logic using metavariables, called PLM [20], and then translated the output into the $\mathbf{G}^{\approx}$ proof. (The calculus implemented in PLM is different from $\mathbf{G}^{\approx}$: it uses metavariables and has a restricted (incomplete) sequence unification algorithm for sequence metavariables.)

LSI has the following important property:

**Theorem 4.** LSI is true in every intended model.

The next theorem, in fact, shows that LCD can be proved from LSI:

**Theorem 5.** The sequent $\to$ LSI $\Rightarrow$ LCD is provable in $\mathbf{G}^{\approx}$.

Now we turn LSI into the inference rule:

$$\frac{\Gamma \to \Delta, A\{\overline{x} \mapsto \ulcorner\urcorner\} \wedge \forall y \forall \overline{y}\ (A\{\overline{x} \mapsto \overline{y}\} \Rightarrow A\{\overline{x} \mapsto \ulcorner y, \overline{y}\urcorner\}), \Lambda}{\Gamma \to \Delta, \forall \overline{x}\ A[\overline{x}], \Lambda} \quad (\text{SI}_{\text{left}})$$

Soundness of $\mathbf{G}^{\approx}$ and Theorem 4 imply the following result:

**Theorem 6.** If a sequent is provable using $(\text{SI}_{\text{left}})$ and the inference rules of $\mathbf{G}^{\approx}$, then it is true in every intended structure.

In the similar way we can get another instance of WFI:

**Definition 22.** The case distinction rule from the right is the formula

$$(A\{\overline{x} \mapsto \ulcorner\urcorner\} \wedge \forall \overline{y} \forall y\ A\{\overline{x} \mapsto \ulcorner \overline{y}, y\urcorner\}) \Rightarrow \forall \overline{x}\ A[\overline{x}] \qquad \text{(RCD)}$$

The prefix ordering $\succ_{\text{Pre}}$ is defined on terms with the head $f$ as follows:

$$\forall \overline{x} \forall \overline{y}\ (f(\overline{x}) \succ_{\text{Pre}} f(\overline{y}) \Leftrightarrow$$
$$\exists \overline{z} \exists z\ f(\overline{x}) \approx f(\overline{z}, z) \wedge (f(\overline{z}) \approx f(\overline{y}) \vee f(\overline{z}) \succ_{\text{Pre}} f(\overline{y}))) \qquad \text{(PO)}$$

The structural induction from the right is the formula

$$(A\{\overline{x} \mapsto \ulcorner\urcorner\} \wedge \forall \overline{y} \forall y\ (A\{\overline{x} \mapsto \overline{y}\} \Rightarrow A\{\overline{x} \mapsto \ulcorner \overline{y}, y\urcorner\})) \Rightarrow \forall \overline{x}\ A[\overline{x}]. \qquad \text{(RSI)}$$

Like LSI, we can turn RSI into an inference rule:

$$\frac{\Gamma \rightarrow \Delta, A\{\overline{x} \mapsto \ulcorner \urcorner\} \wedge \forall \overline{y} \forall y \ (A\{\overline{x} \mapsto \overline{y}\} \Rightarrow A\{\overline{x} \mapsto \ulcorner \overline{y}, y \urcorner\}), \Lambda}{\Gamma \rightarrow \Delta, \forall \overline{x} \ A[\overline{x}], \Lambda} \quad (\text{SI}_{\text{right}})$$

The counterpart of Theorem 6 holds for $(\text{SI}_{\text{right}})$.

Another useful well-founded ordering on terms with sequence variables is the length ordering defined as follows:

$$\forall \overline{x} \forall \overline{y} \ (f(\overline{x}) \succ_{\text{Len}} f(\overline{y}) \Leftrightarrow \exists z \exists \overline{z} \ f(\overline{x}) \approx f(z, \overline{z})$$
$$\wedge (f(\overline{y}) \approx f() \vee \exists u \exists \overline{u} \ (f(\overline{y}) \approx f(u, \overline{u}) \wedge f(\overline{z}) \succ_{\text{Len}} f(\overline{u}))) \quad (\text{LO})$$

If we instantiate the ordering $\succ$ in WFI with $\succ_{\text{Len}}$, we get an instance of WFI called well-founded induction principle with the length ordering:

$$\forall \overline{x} \ (\forall \overline{y} \ (f(\overline{x}) \succ_{\text{Len}} f(\overline{y}) \Rightarrow A\{\overline{x} \mapsto \overline{y}\}) \Rightarrow A[\overline{x}]) \Rightarrow \forall \overline{x} \ A[\overline{x}] \quad (\text{WFILO})$$

The next example shows that WFILO is not valid.

Example 4. Let $A[\overline{x}]$ be an atom $p(\overline{x})$ with the flexible arity predicate symbol $p$. Let $\mathfrak{S} = \langle \mathcal{D}, \mathcal{I} \rangle$ be a structure whose domain $\mathcal{D}$ is the set of all ground terms built from an individual constant $c$, sequence constant $\overline{c}$ and a flexible arity function symbol $f$. The assignment $\mathcal{I}$ is defined so that it maps each ground term to itself and the predicate $\succ_{\text{Len}}$ to the same predicate on $\mathcal{D}$. As for $p_{\mathcal{I}}$, let it be a flexible arity predicate on $\mathcal{D}$ that contains all the tuples over $\mathcal{D}$ except $\langle c, \overline{c} \rangle$. Then $\mathcal{V}al_{\sigma}^{\mathfrak{S}}(f(c, \overline{c}) \succ_{\text{Len}} f() \Rightarrow p()) \Rightarrow p(c, \overline{c})) = \mathbf{F}$ which implies that $\mathcal{V}al_{\sigma}^{\mathfrak{S}}(\forall \overline{x} \ (\forall \overline{y} \ f(\overline{x}) \succ_{\text{Len}} f(\overline{y}) \Rightarrow p(\overline{y})) \Rightarrow p(\overline{x})) = \mathbf{T}$. On the other side, $\mathcal{V}al_{\sigma}^{\mathfrak{S}}(\forall \overline{x} \ p(\overline{x})) = \mathbf{F}$. Therefore, WFILO is false in $\mathfrak{S}$ with respect to $\sigma^{\mathfrak{S}}$.

Nevertheless, WFILO is satisfied by any intended structure:

**Theorem 7.** WFILO is true in any intended structure.

Instantiating $f$ in WFILO with the tuple constructor we get the tuple induction principle formulated in [10].

WFILO can be turned into an inference rule:

$$\frac{\Gamma, \text{LO} \rightarrow \Delta, \forall \overline{x} \ (\forall \overline{y} \ (f(\overline{x}) \succ_{\text{Len}} f(\overline{y}) \Rightarrow A\{\overline{x} \mapsto \overline{y}\}) \Rightarrow A[\overline{x}]), \Lambda}{\Gamma, \text{LO} \rightarrow \Delta, \forall \overline{x} A[\overline{x}], \Lambda} \quad (\text{WFI}_{\text{len}})$$

The counterpart of Theorem 6 holds for $(\text{WFI}_{\text{len}})$.

The calculus $\mathbf{G}^{\approx}$ does not contain the cut rule, but we need it in induction proofs.

$$\frac{\Gamma \rightarrow \Delta, A, \Lambda \quad \Gamma, A \rightarrow \Delta, B, \Lambda}{\Gamma \rightarrow \Delta, B, \Lambda} \quad (\text{Cut})$$

Cut rule forms a basis for THEOREMA conjecture generation algorithm and the cascade method introduced by the second author in [8]. Informally, the cascade method works as follows: Given a goal $G$ and knowledge base $K$, if an attempt of proving $G$ using $K$ fails, cascade method tries to analyze the failing proof situation, and using the conjecture generation algorithm generates a conjecture $C$ such that $G$ might be provable using $K \cup \{C\}$. After that, it tries to prove $C$ from $K$, in the similar manner. Thus, this procedure corresponds to the application of the cut rule, and the conjecture generation algorithm can be considered as an intelligent heuristics of selecting "useful conjectures" among infinitely many possible ones.

At the end of this section we provide an example of proving by induction with sequence variables: reverse of a reverse of a list coincides with the original list. We give a "human-readable" version of the formal proof.

Example 5. We want to prove

$$\forall \overline{x} \quad rev(rev(\langle \overline{x} \rangle)) = \langle \overline{x} \rangle \tag{1}$$

under the assumptions

$$rev(\langle \rangle) = \langle \rangle, \tag{2}$$
$$\forall x \quad rev(\langle x \rangle) = \langle x \rangle, \tag{3}$$
$$\forall \overline{x} \forall \overline{y} \quad rev(\langle \overline{x}, \overline{y} \rangle) = rev(\langle \overline{y} \rangle) \asymp rev(\langle \overline{x} \rangle), \tag{4}$$
$$\forall \overline{x} \forall \overline{y} \quad \langle \overline{x} \rangle \asymp \langle \overline{y} \rangle = \langle \overline{x}, \overline{y} \rangle, \tag{5}$$
$$\forall \overline{x} \exists \overline{y} \quad rev(\langle \overline{x} \rangle) = \langle \overline{y} \rangle. \tag{6}$$

The formulae (2), (3) and (4) define the reverse function, (5) is a definition of concatenation, and (6) states that reversing a list gives again a list. Then the proof of (1) proceeds as follows:

Induction base:

$$\begin{aligned} rev(rev(\langle \rangle)) = & \quad \text{by (2)} \\ rev(\langle \rangle) = & \quad \text{by (2)} \\ \langle \rangle. & \end{aligned}$$

Induction hypothesis: We assume

$$rev(rev(\langle \overline{c} \rangle)) = \langle \overline{c} \rangle. \tag{7}$$

Induction step: We have to show that $rev(rev(\langle c, \overline{c} \rangle)) = \langle c, \overline{c} \rangle$:

$$\begin{aligned} rev(rev(\langle c, \overline{c} \rangle)) = & \quad \text{by (4)} \\ rev(rev(\langle \overline{c} \rangle) \asymp rev(\langle c \rangle)) = & \quad \text{by (3)} \\ rev(rev(\langle \overline{c} \rangle) \asymp \langle c \rangle) = & \quad \text{by (6)} \\ rev(\langle \overline{f}(\overline{c}) \rangle \asymp \langle c \rangle) = & \quad \text{by (5)} \\ rev(\langle \overline{f}(\overline{c}), c \rangle) = & \quad \text{by (4)} \\ rev(\langle c \rangle) \asymp rev(\langle \overline{f}(\overline{c}) \rangle) = & \quad \text{by (6)} \\ rev(\langle c \rangle) \asymp rev(rev(\langle \overline{c} \rangle)) = & \quad \text{by (7)} \\ rev(\langle c \rangle) \asymp \langle \overline{c} \rangle = & \quad \text{by (3)} \\ \langle c \rangle \asymp \langle \overline{c} \rangle = & \quad \text{by (5)} \\ \langle c, \overline{c} \rangle & \end{aligned}$$

which finishes the proof. Note that (6) is used once to rewrite from left to right, and in the other case from right to left.

# 7   Conclusion

We described a syntax, semantics and inference system for a logic with sequence variables and sequence functions. The calculus $\mathbf{G}^{\approx}$ for such a logic extends the $\mathbf{LK}^{\approx}$ calculus and has many nice proof-theoretic properties. Furthermore, we considered special structures, called intended structures, to reflect the intuition behind sequence variables: abbreviation of finite sequences of individual terms. We formalized this intuition using induction, and defined several versions of induction rules. The interesting feature of logic with sequence variables and sequence functions is that there is no need in introducing constructors to define inductive data types. This information is "built-in" into the logic itself.

# References

1. An Interactive Mathematical Proof System, http://imps.mcmaster.ca/.
2. The COQ Proof Assistant, http://coq.inria.fr/.
3. The MIZAR Project, http://www.mizar.org/.
4. The OMEGA System, http://www.ags.uni-sb.de/~omega/.
5. W. W. Bledsoe and G. Feng, SET-VAR, *J. Automated Reasoning*, 11(3):293–314, 1993.
6. H. Boley, *A Tight, Practical Integration of Relations and Functions*, volume 1712 of *LNAI*, Springer Verlag, 1999.
7. B. Buchberger, Mathematica as a rewrite language, in: T. Ida, A. Ohori, and M. Takeichi (eds.), *Proc. of the 2nd Fuji Int. Workshop on Functional and Logic Programming*, pp. 1–13, Shonan Village Center, Japan, 1–4 November 1996, World Scientific.
8. B. Buchberger, Theory exploration with THEOREMA, *Analele Universitatii Din Timisoara, ser. Matematica-Informatica*, XXXVIII(2):9–32, 2000.
9. B. Buchberger, Algorithm invention and verification by lazy thinking, in: D. Petcu, D. Zaharie, V. Negru, and T. Jebelean (eds.), *Proc. of the 5rd Int. Workshop on Symbolic and Numeric Algorithms for Scientific Computing (SYNASC'03)*, pp. 2–26, Timisoara, Romania, 1–4 October 2003, Mirton.
10. B. Buchberger and A. Craciun, Algorithm synthesis by lazy thinking: Examples and implementation in THEOREMA, in: *Proc. of the Mathematical Knowledge Management Symposium*, volume 93 of *ENTCS*, pp. 24–59, Edinburgh, UK, 25–29 November 2003, Elsevier Science.
11. E. Clarke, M. Kohlhase, J. Ouaknine, and K. Sutner, System description: ANALYTICA 2, in: T. Hardin and R. Rioboo, editors, *Proc. of the 11th Symposium on the Integration of Symbolic Computation and Mechanized Reasoning (Calculemus'03)*, Rome, Italy, 10–12 September, Aracne Editrice S.R.L.
12. R. Constable, *Implementing Mathematics Using the NUPRL Proof Development System*, Prentice-Hall, 1986.
13. N. G. de Bruijn, The mathematical language AUTOMATH, its usage, and some of its extensions, in: M. Laudet, D. Lacombe, L. Nolin, and M. Schützenberger, editors, *Proc. of Symposium on Automatic Demonstration, Versailles, France*, volume 125 of *LN in Mathematics*, pp. 29–61, Springer Verlag, Berlin, 1970.
14. A. Degtyarev and A. Voronkov, Equality reasoning in sequent-based calculi, in: A. Robinson and A. Voronkov (eds.), *Handbook of Automated Reasoning*, volume I, chapter 10, pp. 611–706, Elsevier Science, 2001.

15. M. R. Genesereth, Ch. Petrie, T. Hinrichs, A. Hondroulis, M. Kassoff, N. Love, and W. Mohsin, Knowledge Interchange Format, draft proposed American National Standard (dpANS), Technical Report NCITS.T2/98-004, 1998, `http://logic.stanford.edu/kif/dpans.html`.

16. G. Gentzen, Untersuchungen über das logische schließen, *Mathematical Zeitschrift*, 39:176–210, 1934.

17. M. Gordon and T. Melham, *Introduction to* HOL*: A Theorem Proving Environment for Higher-Order Logic*, Cambridge University Press, 1993.

18. Common Logic Working Group, Common logic: Abstract syntax and semantics, `http://cl.tamu.edu/docs/cl/1.0/cl-1.0.pdf`, 2003.

19. P. Hayes and C. Menzel, Semantics of knowledge interchange format, `http://reliant.teknowledge.com/IJCAI01/HayesMenzel-SKIF-IJCAI2001.pdf`, 2001.

20. B. Konev and T. Jebelean, Using meta-variables for natural deduction in THEOREMA, in: M. Kerber and M. Kohlhase (eds.), *Proc. of Calculemus'2000 Conference*, St. Andrews, UK, 6–7 August 2000.

21. T. Kutsia, Solving and proving in equational theories with sequence variables and flexible arity symbols, Technical Report 02-31, RISC, Johannes Kepler University, Linz, Austria, 2002.

22. T. Kutsia, Theorem proving with sequence variables and flexible arity symbols, in: M. Baaz and A. Voronkov (eds.), *Logic for Programming, Artificial Intelligence, and Reasoning, Proc. of the 9th Int. Conference, LPAR'02*, volume 2514 of *LNAI*, pp. 278–291, Tbilisi, Georgia, 14–18 October 2002, Springer Verlag.

23. T. Kutsia, Solving equations involving sequence variables and sequence functions, Technical Report 04-01, RISC, Johannes Kepler University, Linz, Austria, 2004.

24. T. Kutsia and B. Buchberger, Predicate logic with sequence variables and sequence function symbols, Technical report, SFB, Linz, Austria, 2004.

25. Zh. Luo and R. Pollack, LEGO proof development system: User's manual, Technical Report ECS-LFCS-92-211, University of Edinburgh, 1992.

26. L. Magnusson and B. Nordström, The ALF proof editor and its proof engine, in: H. Barendregt and T. Nipkow (eds.), *Types for Proofs and Programs*, volume 806 of *LNCS*, pp. 213–237, Springer Verlag, 1994.

27. R. Nieuwenhuis and A. Rubio, Theorem proving with ordering and equality constrained clauses, *J. Symbolic Computation*, 19:321–351, 1995.

28. L. Paulson, ISABELLE: the next 700 theorem provers, in: P. Odifreddi (ed.), *Logic and Computer Science*, pp. 361–386, Academic Press, 1990.

29. F. Pfenning, ELF: A meta-language for deductive systems, in: A. Bundy (ed.), *Proc. of the 12th International Conference on Automated Deduction, CADE'94*, volume 814 of *LNAI*, pp. 811–815, Nancy, France, Springer Verlag, 1995.

30. W. Windsteiger, Exploring an algorithm for polynomial interpolation in the THEOREMA system, in: T. Hardin and R. Rioboo (eds.), *Proc. of the 11th Symposium on the Integration of Symbolic Computation and Mechanized Reasoning (Calculemus'03)*, pp. 130–136, Rome, Italy, 10–12 September 2003. Aracne Editrice S.R.L.

31. S. Wolfram, *The* MATHEMATICA *Book*, Cambridge University Press and Wolfram Research, Inc., fourth edition, 1999.

# A Graph-Based Approach Towards Discerning Inherent Structures in a Digital Library of Formal Mathematics

Lori Lorigo, Jon Kleinberg, Richard Eaton, and Robert Constable

Department of Computer Science, Cornell University, Ithaca, NY, USA
{lolorigo,kleinber,eaton,rc}@cs.cornell.edu
http://www.cs.cornell.edu

**Abstract.** As the amount of online formal mathematical content grows, for example through active efforts such as the Mathweb [21], MOWGLI [4], Formal Digital Library, or FDL [1], and others, it becomes increasingly valuable to find automated means to manage this data and capture semantics such as relatedness and significance. We apply graph-based approaches, such as HITS, or *Hyperlink Induced Topic Search*, [11] used for World Wide Web document search and analysis, to formal mathematical data collections. The nodes of the graphs we analyze are theorems and definitions, and the links are logical dependencies. By exploiting this link structure, we show how one may extract organizational and relatedness information from a collection of digital formal math. We discuss the value of the information we can extract, yielding potential applications in math search tools, theorem proving, and education.

## 1 Introduction

Invaluable progress has been made in the development of digital libraries of math-ematics [1, 3, 4, 15, 21]. Such progress also includes content and presentation-specific representations of mathematical knowledge [13, 14, 16], including architectures for exchanging mathematical content. These efforts are bringing together otherwise disparate collections of formal mathematics, and providing rich access to mathematical knowledge.

We are interested in providing services to users and designers of formal mathematical digital libraries. One such service is the ability to search for theorems or other mathematical objects with respect to their relationship to other theorems or objects in a given collection. The kinds of inter-object relationships may include similarity of theorem statements, similarity of proof methods, even similar levels of difficulty, particularly useful in user-model based approaches and education. Another service we wish to provide is finding core or basic theorems and axioms with respect to the surrounding collection, theorems that cover or utilize heavily this core content, or theorems that seem to be authoritative and representative of a particular topic. Object dependencies of the kinds stored in the FDL can aid us in building these services.

A. Asperti et al. (Eds.): MKM 2004, LNCS 3119, pp. 220–235, 2004.

Our approach is to use the mathematical objects and their logical dependencies to build a directed graph, and apply graph-theoretic algorithms to understand and extract information from the structure. Formal mathematical lemmas and their dependencies on other lemmas or definitions in their proofs form the nodes and edges of a directed graph respectively, as do web pages and hyperlinks on the Internet. Previous research has demonstrated effective methods for gathering relatedness and other semantic information about web pages on the Internet by operating on this directed graph. Popular eigenvector-based methods that are effective in web search by finding authoritative sources include Kleinberg's HITS algorithm and Google's PageRank [9]. In addition to abilities to rank important objects, capabilities to cluster or organize data into groups based on the graph structure have been developed and exploited. Web Trawling [12] uses a graph-theoretic approach to enumerate communities on the web, based on the findings of densely bipartite sub-graphs. Recent work in [17] finds communities in networks by iteratively removing detectable edges from the network to divide the collection into related groups.

Automatically categorizing or grouping related theorems in a formal digital library is one goal we are pursuing. In this work, however, we investigate, in general, the use of link analysis methods in the formal domain. While we restrict our studies to objects that were developed using the Nuprl5 refiner and are stored in the FDL, other interactive theorem provers make the same kinds of analysis possible, by having dependency information accessible. Such systems include Coq, MetaPRL, PVS, and others. Since we operate only on logical dependencies in this analysis, any collection of mathematics from which we can extract a dependency graph would be suitable.

We apply Kleinberg's HITS algorithm to collections of formal mathematics in Section 2, where we also describe the link distributions of our chosen formal math data sets. In Section 3, we present a variation of HITS that has been tailored specifically for the formal math domain, observing varying levels of authoritativeness in this domain. We discuss future work in Section 4 and conclude in Section 5, including ways that this work opens possibilities for further automation and improvements in managing and understanding a digital library of mathematics.

## 2    HITS and Dependency Graphs

In the World Wide Web domain, hubs are web pages that point to a large number of authorities and authorities are pages pointed to by a large number of hubs. In the mathematical domain, our intuition tells us that hubs are proofs or lemmas that depend logically on a large number of authoritative lemmas or definitions, and authorities are the core definitions or theorems that are depended upon by a large number of hubs.

Kleinberg's HITS algorithm demonstrates how to find hubs and authorities on the web. After a base set of web pages and links is generated, a directed graph, $G = (V, E)$, is constructed where the vertices $V$ are the web pages, and the edges $E$ are the hyperlinks. Hubs and authorities are found by assigning hub and authority weights to the vertices, and updating these values for $k$ iterations, for some large enough $k$ so that the process approaches equilibrium, or the weight vectors become nearly stable. If $A$ is the adjacency matrix of the graph G, and vectors $x$ and $y$ are the authority and hub weight vectors, then $x$ and $y$ converge to the principle eigenvectors of $A^T A$ and $AA^T$ respectively. Then, the web pages with the c largest coordinates in x and in y when they have converged are deemed to be the c best authorities and hubs respectively.

## 2.1    Implementation and Design Choices

We implemented the algorithm in LISP, and ran the code inside of Cornell's FDL on two different collections of formal mathematics that belong to that library: the Nuprl5 Standard collection [2], and the Event Structures collection [8]. These two collections were easily accessible to us and also presented a good contrast for measuring and evaluating our results. Large collections of PVS content also currently reside in the FDL, which would have been nice to contrast with Nuprl libraries, but we did not have the dependency information yet accessible for the PVS material, though in the future we hope to experiment with other collections.

In constructing the graphs, we chose theorems and definitions to be vertices of the graph. In further analyses, we plan to add rules as well. Tactics, and code objects were also potential candidates and may of interest for different kinds of information, such as relating proof styles. We restricted the edges to be representative of logical dependences. Again, other kinds of dependencies, including pointers to documents or comment objects, could be of interest as these links become more prominent.

We considered how to define a logical dependency in the context of this link analysis. We took the logical dependencies of a theorem to be all of the objects that were needed to complete the proof of the theorem. These include definitions and other theorems. It is a matter of style whether a user chooses to create a new theorem in order to prove a current one, or not. The former would create a dependency between two theorems where the latter would not, by self-containing the proof argument. We chose to use only the direct dependencies, as maintained by the FDL. By direct, we mean theorem A depends on theorem B if and only if B is directly pointed to in the proof of A. Indirect dependencies of A would then include the direct dependencies of B. While growing the graph by adding dependencies based on dependency transitivity might account for the variable proof designs, we would lose the structures that mimic the development of the theory, and likewise, the progressive level of expertise needed to understand a theory. We thus define the out-links of a node to point to its direct logical dependencies.

For the theorems, logical dependencies were gathered from the primitive proofs of the theorems which were created during refinement in the Nuprl proof system. Primitive proofs typically have too much detail to be desirable for reading, and many users prefer to read the tactic-level proofs. Nevertheless, primitive proofs contain all of the logical information of the proof execution. And in fact, the Nuprl primitive proofs are available online as part of the HELM project [3]. We do not include any out-links for the definitions. Definition objects do not have logical dependencies, that is, any definition is valid and they may only depend on a proof if for example, we would have considered extracts as definitions. However, definitions, like theorems are built up iteratively, and the definition for greatest common denominator, for example, depends on the definition of divides. These kinds of semantic dependencies are also accessible in the FDL. To understand authoritative objects with respect to definitions, we could capture the definition-definition dependencies, as these dependencies reveal when two definitions are related. The number of definitions with respect to theorems is small and we focus here on the logical links only.

## 2.2    Nuprl5 Standard Collection

The Nuprl5 Standard collection contains theories about integers, numbers, lists, booleans, and more. Information about its dependency graph is in Table 1.

**Table 1.** Nuprl5 Standard Dependency Graph Data. Most fields should be clear. The assortativity of a network was defined by Newman in [18] and is a measure of the variance of the link distribution, or degree-degree correlations often used in social-network analysis. In practice, r is positive for social networks, where the nodes represent people, and negative for non-social networks such as the world wide web, power grids, and biological networks

| Nodes | Theorems | Definitions | Max. Outlinks | Max. Inlinks | Edges | Assortativity |
|-------|----------|-------------|---------------|--------------|-------|---------------|
| 811   | 646      | 165         | 58            | 637          | 8765  | -0.2949       |

Log-log density plots (using natural log) for the out-links and in-links are shown in Fig. 1. We observe a short incline until a peak is reached and then a decline after a peak value is met in the out-link distribution. This demonstrates a characteristic number of dependencies for the theorems. Though difficult to observe with such large variation, the tails are much longer for the in-links (we removed the end of the tail so that more data was visible since there we definition nodes with up to over 600 inlinks), which happens to be typical of the World Wide Web links.

The power law distribution, which appears as a straight line in log-log density plots, is prevalent in many growing real-world networks, such as power grids, and the Internet [5]. Our data does not closely fit a power law over the entire set of degrees, but it is nearly linear over certain intervals of degree values: after the peak in the out-link graph, and also in the earlier part of the in-link graph.

Cumulative distributions shed more visual information as to the shape and nature of our graphs. Log-log plots of the cumulative distributions are shown in Figure 2.

In the graph on the left, we observe a peak around 5-6, which is the same peak visible in the earlier graph. Also, the lower range of the in-link function

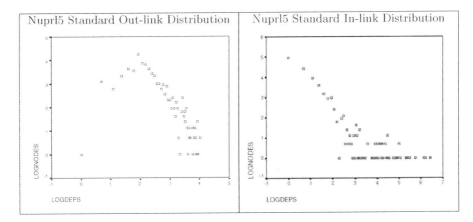

**Fig. 1.** Nuprl5 Standard Log-Log Density Plots

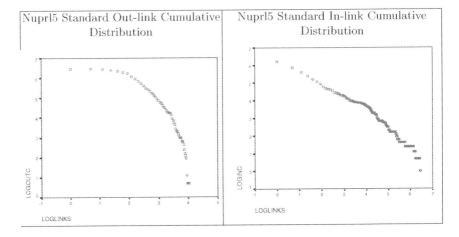

**Fig. 2.** Nuprl5 Standard Cumulative Log-Log Plots

follows a straight line, after which the data is very noisy, as shown in Figure 1 on the right.

From the above graphs, we observe a characteristic peak in the theorem out-links. Where this peak occurs may vary depending on the theory topic, or the complexity.

## 2.3    Nuprl 5 Standard HITS Results

In this section we include results from applying the HITS algorithm to our network.

The names of the top hubs and authorities of the Nuprl5 Standard collection of the FDL are listed below in decreasing order. As expected, the authorities are core, simple definitions, and the hubs are major theorems which depend on them.

**Table 2.** Nuprl 5 Standard Hubs and Authorities

| Authorities | member, all, prop, implies, and, iff, rev_implies, false, |
|---|---|
| Hubs | rem_mag_bound, select_listify_id, listify_wf, rem_eq_args_z, |
|  | rem_base_case_z, select_firstn, listify_length, mod_bounds, modulus_wf |

The authorities are the most fundamental and critical definitions in the Nuprl type theory. Hubs are objects from the list theory and the integer theory, two dominant theories in the collection. The authority values were primarily those with the greatest in-links, and likewise the hubs had large numbers of out-links. This was a trend, but not an exact representation. Rem_mag_bound, which states that the remainder of a divided by $n$ is less than $n$, for example, has 51 out-links while the maximum has 56.

In addition to finding hubs and authorities, the HITS algorithm presents an eigenvector-based approach to finding clusters or communities in a graph. While the hubs and authorities can be found from principal eigenvectors, the best hubs and the best authorities from the non-principal eigenvectors of $A^T A$ and $AA^T$ reveal communities. Furthermore, the communities that correspond to greater eigenvalues, are typically stronger. We looked for the vertices with the greatest hub weight and authority weight in the non-principal eigenvectors with the greater eigenvalues. These often are semantically related in practice. While the individual non-principal eigenvectors are thus a direct way to expose further structure in the data, we note that Ng et al. [19] observe instabilities in some cases in the use of these eigenvectors, and recommend more generally studying subspaces spanned by the non-principal eigenvectors.

Since the Nuprl Standard library has already been structured by humans around topics including lists, booleans, integers, and more, we compared the clusters found via the HITS method to the human-made categories, or topics. In some cases, the communities found could be considered as further refinements on the human-made topic structure. We set threshold values based on trial an error (an optimal threshold can perhaps be learned) as to when the corresponding eigenvalue was large enough to represent a community. The first four communities found are listed below.

The first is about lists, the second about recursive functions, and the latter two about Fibonacci numbers and atomicity in number theory. The objects in the clusters fell mainly in the human-made number theory category, and were often refinements on these human made categories.

**Nuprl 5 Standard Number Theory Example.** Hub and authority values can often best be utilized when you have already chosen a topic, as is the case in their use in Internet search. Typically, HITS seeds its search by growing its starting set of nodes. We extracted a sub-collection from Nuprl5 Standard about

226     L. Lorigo et al.

**Table 3.** Nuprl5 Standard Communities

| Community 1 | listify_length, select_listify_id, int_seg_ind, select_append_front, decidable__ex_int_seg, or, decidable, so_apply1 |
|---|---|
| Community 2 | fincr_formation, fincr_wf, fincr_wf2, equiv_rel_functionality_wrt_iff |
| Community 3 | fib_coprime, gcd_sat_gcd_p, gcd_sat_pred, fib_wf, gcd_wf, ycomb, not_wf |
| Community 4 | atomic_char, assert_of_eq_int, prime_elim, assert_of_eq_atom, le_wf |

numbers, seeded this collection by recursively adding dependencies, and ran the HITS algorithm with the new subgraph. Information about this subgraph is in Table 4.

**Table 4.** Nuprl5 Number Theory

| Nodes | Theorems | Definitions | Max. Outlinks | Max. Inlinks | Edges | Assortativity |
|---|---|---|---|---|---|---|
| 328 | 260 | 68 | 56 | 257 | 3397 | -0.2848 |

The entire graph, dense due to many connections to core definitions is difficult to visualize in a confined space. Removing all of the definitions from the graph, as well as well-formedness theorems, which correspond to each definition to say it's well formed, we obtain a more visible graph in Figure 3.

**Fig. 3.** Number Theory Theorem Dependencies

The top hubs and authorities of the Nuprl5 Number theory collection including all of its dependencies are listed below in decreasing order.

**Table 5.** Nuprl5 Number Theory Hubs and Authorities

| Authorities | member, all, implies, prop, and, iff, rev_implies, false, not |
|---|---|
| Hubs | rem_mag_bound, gcd_sat_gcd_p, gcd_sat_pred, fib_coprime, fib_wf, absval_elim, absval_pos, absval_eq, gcd_ex_n |

Since we seeded our search by adding objects that Number theory depends on, our authorities are similar to those from the entire Standard collection. If we wanted to know core definitions within number theory, we can eliminate the seeding step to get the following authorities: divides_wf, gcd_p, assoced, divides, assoced_weakening, assoced_wf.

Some of communities found from the HITS' eigenvector approach are listed below.

**Table 6.** Nuprl5 Number Theory Communities

| Community 1 | divides_of_absvals, absval_assoced, absval_wf |
|---|---|
| Community 2 | chrem_exists_aux_a, gcd_ex_n, chrem_exists_aux, atomic_char, prime_elim, gcd_exists_n, bezout_ident_n, chrem_exists |
| Community 3 | div_3_to_1, div_2_to_1, div_4_to_1, divide_wf, nequal |
| Community 4 | eqff_to_assert, eqtt_to_assert, assert_of_bnot, assert_of_band, prop |

These communities are about absolute value, Chinese remainder theorem, division, and assertion respectively. Again, the contents are not so relevant. However, we observe that the names of objects within the groupings tend to be quite similar to one another, and these similarities in naming can be taken as indicative of human judgment that the objects themselves are related.

## 2.4   Event Structures Collection

This Event Structures collection was developed by Dr. Mark Bickford, a member of both ATC-NY, a subsidiary of Architecture Technology Corporation, and Cornell's PRL Group. The objects in it define and support a logic of events, describing a semantics for distributed systems. Information about this collection's dependency graph is in Table 7.

Log-log density plots (using natural log) for the out-links and in-links are shown in Figure 4.

As in Figure 3, the functions plotted in Figure 4 are not quite linear, though probably are in a subset range. The data is noisy for objects above some link threshold. Again, we look at the log-log cumulative distributions for better clarity in Figure 5.

**Table 7.** Event Structures Dependency Graph Data. Fields are the same as in Table 1.

| Nodes | Theorems | Definitions | Max. Out-links | Max. In-links | Edges | Assortativity |
|-------|----------|-------------|----------------|---------------|-------|---------------|
| 1795  | 1306     | 489         | 210            | 708           | 16648 | -0.15896      |

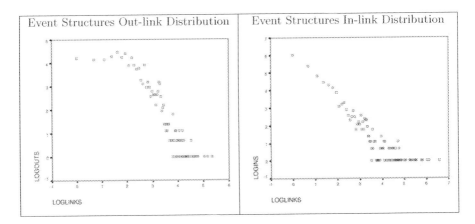

**Fig. 4.** Event Structurs Log-Log Density Plots

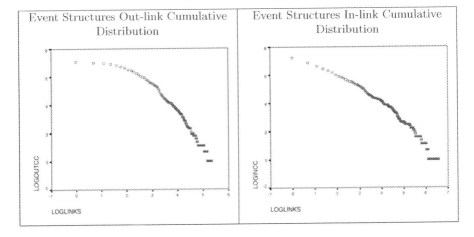

**Fig. 5.** Event Structurs Cumulative Log-Log Plots

The out-link distribution is steeper for the Event Structures collection than for the Nuprl Standard. Two factors could contribute to this. First, the Event Structures is actually built on top of the Standard collection, though the Standard collection is not included in its graph. It is an advanced collection, with large proofs about a specific topic, rather than a basic introductory collection that has more gradual variability. Second, the Nuprl Standard collection was built by several developers, and Dr. Bickford was the sole developer of the Event Structure proofs. He may have a proof signature style that may be somewhat evident in various structures of the graph. There is less of an initial incline in the out-link distribution, which is likely due to the fact that was built on top of another collection. The tails are again much longer for the in-links than for the out-links.

## 2.5     Event Structures HITS Results

Below we include results from applying Kleinberg's HITS algorithm to our network.

The names of the top hubs and authorities of the Event Structures collection are listed below in decreasing order. The names of the objects are less informative than in the Nuprl5 Standard, but the objects' contents are not entirely relevant. The authorities are fundamental lemmas, and the hubs are larger proofs which depend on them.

**Table 8.** Event Structures Hubs and Authorities

| Authorities | Id_wf, Knd_wf, IdLnk_wf, id-deq_wf, fpf_wf, fpf-cap_wf , Kind-deq_wf, fpf-dom_wf, fdf-trivial-subtype-top |
|---|---|
| Hubs | R-compat-base, R-Feasible-Dsys, sends-rule, pre-rule, d-feasible-world, R-sends-rule, R-interface-base, R-Feasible-action, R-Dsys-base-wf |

Several communities found are listed below. It is difficult to measure the strength of these communities. We include only their names, inferring that the developer used a naming scheme such that similarly named objects are similar. While it is not apparent what the communities below entail, it is evident that they are related by name.

# 3     Stratified Authority Weighting

While the hubs and authorities method assigns weights to vertices at only two levels (hub and authority), we note that there are intermediate levels of authoritativeness in the formal math domain. Math collections, unlike collections of pages on the web, consist of a small number of known kinds of objects that demonstrate varied discrete levels of authoritativeness. These kinds, or categories, are definitions, rules, theorems, proofs, and perhaps others, depending on the theorem prover and its implementation, such as extracts or hypotheses, or conjectures. Furthermore, formal theories are often built up in a step-like, or modular fashion. For these reasons, we wish to consider levels of authority.

**Table 9.** Event Structures Communities

| Community 1 | d-feasible-world, better-d-comp-step, d-comp-step2, d-comp-step, d-comp_wf, deq_wf |
|---|---|
| Community 2 | Rpreinit-P_wf, Rpreinit-init_wf, Rpreinit-ds_wf, Rpreinit-T_wf, Rpreinit-loc_wf, Rpreinit-a_wf, Rpreinit?, Rpreinit?_wf, Rpreinit-ds, Rpreinit |
| Community 3 | Reffect-f_wf, Reffect-ds_wf, Reffect-x_wf, Reffect-T_wf, Reffect-loc_wf, Reffect-knd_wf, Reffect?, Reffect?_wf |
| Community 4 | Rframe-loc_wf, Rframe-T_wf, Rframe-L_wf, Rframe-x_wf, Rframe?, Rframe?_wf |
| | prop |
| Community 5 | l_contains_disjoint, l_contains_append3, l_contains_append2, l_contains_append, l_contains_wf, l_contains-append4, l_contains |
| | prop |

## 3.1 Authority and Hub Weight Levels

We observe that the authority and hub weight values don't necessarily degrade naturally, and instead the graphs look somewhat step-like. Figure 6 shows a plot of the authority weights for the Nuprl5 Standard definitions and theorems.

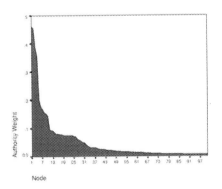

**Fig. 6.** Authority Weights

There are a couple small minor plateaus. The lower plateau, at around .7 shows the importance of the booleans, including objects such as bfalse, btrue, or, ifthenelse, and true_wf.

Next we consider only theorems, excluding wellformedness theorem, which yields step-like hub weighting. Figure 7 shows hub weights for a subset of standard theorems including integer theories, number theory, list theory, and their dependencies.

Since the Standard library is a basic collection, we expect to find more levels when combining collections built on top of Standard. Dr. Bickford built an ex-

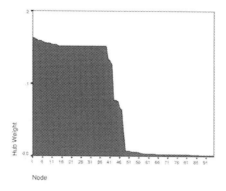

**Fig. 7.** Hub Weights

tended list theory, utlizing Nuprl5 Standard, and we plot the hub and authority weights for this collection, combined with its dependencies in Figure 8.

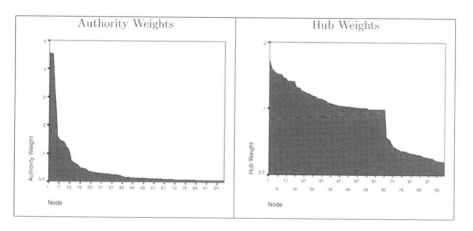

**Fig. 8.** Extended List Theory Hub and Authority Weights

We do observe slightly more structure in the hubs graph for list theory, showing its modularity. In comparing these graphs to Figures 6 and 7, we observe that there is a potentially characteristic difference between the distribution of hub weights and the distribution of authority weights.

### 3.2    Dependency-Based Levels

Instead of using HITS to find levels, we can a priori define levels based on the dependencies of the objects. We adopt the following definition of level.

Level 0 contains all objects that have no dependencies. Level $i$ contains all objects $x$, such that $x$ is not in level $j$ for any $j < i$, and $x$ depends only on objects in levels $0, \ldots, k$ for $k < j$.

Using this definition of levels, the Nuprl5 Standard collection contained a total of 19 levels. All of the definitions were in Level 0. In the Event Structures library there were a total of 31 levels. Distributions of the levels are shown in the Figure 9.

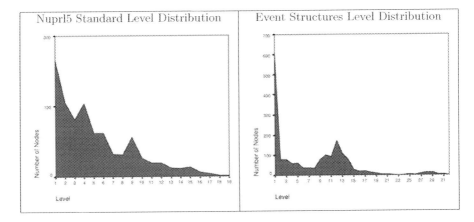

**Fig. 9.** Level Distribution

The high peaks are most interesting. These graphs reiterate in depth what we saw earlier in breadth that there is some characteristic depth (level) of proofs, just as there was in breadth (link degree). One's proof style may influence the level where there is a peak. The peak on the right is particularly noticeable; it suggests that when stratified by depth, the graph exhibits a "wide" region in the middle. In this way, it can potentially be viewed as an interesting analogue, for acyclic graphs, of the "bow-tie" model of the Web [10].

In order to extract information from these levels, one may iteratively run the HITS algorithm, iteratively finding the hubs and authorities for the graph containing the union of level $i$ and $i + 1$, for $i = 0, \ldots, m - 1$, where $m$ is the maximum number of levels. The internal HITS algorithm which runs on the adjacency matrix of a graph remains unchanged, but rather iterations of it are made according to external dependency data. The authors leave this for future work, speculating that the hubs of level $i$ and the authorities of level $i + 1$ may be similar.

## 4   Ongoing and Future Work

This work has opened for us a number of questions with applications to digital libraries of formal mathematics. We hope to be able to answer deeper questions than the hubs, authorities, and communities discussed here, and to put some of our preliminary findings to practice and testing. We wish to extend these techniques to work on other representations of mathematical objects, and contribute towards ongoing work in formal mathematical representation and presentation. Perhaps the strongest benefits may come from combining this graph-based approach with others that reveal different kinds of information when it is available, such as integrating authority measures with pattern-matching based search when searching a library of math.

Additionally, this work shows promise for an automated way of merging two collections of math from different proof assistants, by first matching up core basic definitions and then using dependency-graph analysis information to find similar proofs from two separate proof assistants. We may also use it to organize a single library, or to prepare a library for presentation by asking which objects are most influential and ought to be documented? Also, tools to visualize and interact with the digital collections surely aid us in analyzing the structures. Several theorem provers offer tree-like user interfaces and work in [7] presents methods for pruning the dependency graphs so that they are visually appealing. We are interested in how visualization in this context can aid a user searching a digital library of mathematics.

Furthermore, the scale of the amount of mathematical data is surely not even comparable to the size of the web. The HITS methods are tractable for very large data sets. We may be able to take advantage of our relatively small graph sizes to get improved results.

## 5    Conclusion

We have shown applications of WWW search techniques to a new domain, namely, formal methods, along with presenting a modified stratified method for extracting information specific for formal math. This work is exploratory and the examples above attempt to demonstrate the potential of applying the HITS algorithm and related approaches to categorizing and searching formal mathematics.

We presented two applications of HITS (1) finding Hubs and Authorities and (2) Communities, and also showed characteristics specific to the depth of proofs in the fdl library. We can conclude from these experiments that automated means can be used to discern hub, authority, and community structure in at least one particular library of formal mathematics. The automated extraction of these kinds of relationships can be useful in ranking search results, for example, in the case of the authorities, or in organizing or merging related theorems, for example, based on the community structure. These experiments also demonstrate that logical dependencies alone can be informative in extracting these relationships. Also, what was less expected were findings of strongly characteristic breadth (link-degree) and depth (level) of the library. We cannot conclude whether these characteristics are specific to Nuprl, or common to the formal math domain, but we provide here a good basis for future comparison and discovery.

## Acknowledgments

The authors wish to thank Dr. Mark Bickford for making his libraries of formal mathematics accessible to us and open for analysis. The authors also thank Dr. Stuart Allen for valuable discussions and input in the areas of formal digital libraries and mathematical knowledge management. This work was supported in part by ONR Grant #N00014-01-1-0765.

# References

1. S. Allen, M. Bickford, R. Constable, R. Eaton, C. Kreitz, L. Lorigo. FDL: A Prototype Formal Digital Library. Cornell University, Unpublished manuscript, 2002.
2. S. Allen, R. Constable, R. Eaton, C. Kreitz, L. Lorigo. The Nuprl Open Logical Environment. *Proceedings of 17th International Conference on Automated Deduction*, LNAI 1831, pp. 170-176, Springer-Verlag, 2000.
3. A. Asperti, L. Padovani, C. Sacerdoti Coen, F. Guidi, I. Schena. Mathematical Knowledge Management in HELM. *Annals of Mathematics and Artificial Intelligence, Special Issue on Mathematical Knowledge Management, Vol. 38*, Issue 1-3, pp. 27-46, ISSN 1012-2443, Kluwer Academic Publishers, 2003.
4. A. Asperti, B. Wegner. MOWGLI: A New Approach for the Content Description in Digital Documents. *Ninth International Conference "Crimea 2002" "Libraries and Associations in the Transient World: New Technologies and New Forms of Cooperation"*, 2002.
5. A. Barabasi. "Linked: How Everything Is Connected to Everything Else and What It Means", Plume Books, 2003.
6. V. Batagelj, A. Mrvar. PAJEK, Program for Large Network Analysis, `http://vlado.fmf.uni-lj.si/pub/networks/pajek/`.
7. Y. Bertot, O. Pons. Dependency graphs in Interactive Theorem Provers. *INRIA Tech Report*, 2000.
8. M. Bickford, R. Constable. A Logic of Events. *Cornell University Technical Report 2003-1893*, 2003.
9. S. Brin, L. Page. The anatomy of a large-scale hypertextual (Web) search engine. *Seventh International World Wide Web Conference*, 1998.
10. A. Broder, R. Kumar, F. Maghoul, P. Raghavan, S. Rajagopalan, R. Stata, A. Tomkins, J. Wiener. Graph structure in the web. *9th International World Wide Web Conference*, 2000.
11. J. Kleinberg. Authoritative Sources in a Hyperlinked Environment. *Proc. 9th ACM-SIAM Symposium on Discrete Algorithms*, 1998.
12. R. Kumar, P. Raghavan, S. Rajagopalan, A. Tomkins. Trawling the Web for cyber communities. *Computer Networks*, 31: 1481-1493, 1999.
13. M. Kohlhase. OMDoc: Towards an Internet Standard for the Administration, Distribution and Teaching of mathematical Knowledge. In *Proceedings of Artificial Intelligence and Symbolic Computation*, Springer LNAI, 2000.
14. M. Kohlhase. OMDoc: An Infrastructure for OpenMath Content Dictionary Information. *Bulletin of the ACM Special Interest Group for Algorithmic Mathematics*, SIGSAM, 2000.
15. D. Lozier. The DLMF Project: A New Initiative in Classical Special Functions. In *Proc. International Workshop on Special Functions - Asymptotics, Harmonic Analysis and Mathematical Physics*, Hong Kong, 1999.

16. Mathematical Markup Language (MathML) 2.0, W3C Recommendation, 21 February 2001. http://www.w3.org/TR/MathML2/.
17. M. Newman, M. Girvan. Finding and evaluating community structure in networks. *Physical Review E 69*, 026113, 2004.
18. M. Newman, J. Park. Why social networks are different from other types of networks. *Physical Review E 68*, 036122, 2003.
19. A. Ng, A.Zheng, M.Jordan. Stable Algorithms for Link Analysis. *Proc. 24th Annual Intl.*, ACM SIGIR Conference, 2001.
20. PRL Group, Department of Computer Science, Cornell University, http://www.nuprl.org/Nuprl4.2/Libraries/Welcome.html.
21. J. Zimmer, M. Kohlhase. System Description: The MathWeb Software Bus for Distributed Mathematical Reasoning. *Proceedings of the 18th International Conference on Automated Deduction (CADE 18)*, LNAI 2392, Springer Verlag, 2002.

# Theorem Proving and Proof Verification in the System SAD

Alexander Lyaletski[1], Andrey Paskevich[1,2], and Konstantin Verchinine[2]

[1] Faculty of Cybernetics, Kyiv National Taras Shevchenko University, Kyiv, Ukraine
[2] Math-Info Department, Paris 12 University, Creteil, France
lav@unicyb.kiev.ua  andrey@raptor.kiev.ua  verko@logique.jussieu.fr

**Abstract.** In this paper, the current state of the System for Automated Deduction, SAD, is described briefly. The system may be considered as the modern vision of the Evidence Algorithm programme advanced by Academician V. Glushkov in early 1970s. V. Glushkov proposed to make investigation simultaneously into formalized languages for presenting mathematical texts in the form most appropriate for a user, formalization and evolutionary development of computer-made proof step, information environment having an influence on the evidence of a proof step, and man-assisted search for a proof. In this connection, SAD supports a number of formal languages for representing and processing mathematical knowledge along with the formal language ForTheL as their top representative, uses a sequent formalism developed for constructing an efficient technique of proof search within the signature of an initial theory, and gives a new way to organize the information environment for sharing mathematical knowledge among various computer services. The system SAD can be used to solve large variety of theorem proving problems including: establishing of the deducibility of sequents in first-order classical logic, theorem proving in ForTheL-environment, verifying correctness of self-contained ForTheL-texts, solving problems taken from the online library TPTP. A number of examples is given for illustrating the mathematical knowledge processing implemented in SAD.

## 1  Introduction

The **evidential paradigm** [14] of computer-aided "doing" mathematics is considered as the core of the Evidence Algorithm programme (EA) advanced by V. Glushkov [11]. It is intended to provide a mathematician with rich and flexible languages to formalize mathematical knowledge and with methods to prove a given proposition or to verify a given proof, steps of which should be "evident" for a verificator. Thus, the notion of evidence of a proof step reflects the deductive power of proof search methods being applied.

An implementation of the evidential paradigm must satisfy the following requirements: a formal language should be expressive enough to present mathematical knowledge in a natural "human-like" form; the evidence of proof steps should evolutionary develop in accordance with the progress in the field of automated reasoning and other fields of computer mathematics; an information

A. Asperti et al. (Eds.): MKM 2004, LNCS 3119, pp. 236–250, 2004.
© Springer-Verlag Berlin Heidelberg 2004

environment should also evolve and influence the evidence of a proof step; interactive technique should permit both a man-assisted searching and cooperation with external computer mathematical services, possibly, via Internet.

The evidential paradigm is oriented to integration of numerical calculations, analytical transformations, and deduction.

**Numerical paradigm** uses the methods and techniques of operation with numbers. For a wide variety of problems of applied mathematics, these methods give an approximate (or a precise) solution by constructing finite sequences of operations over finite sets of numbers. Usually, numerical methods start with the construction of a mathematical continual model. After this, this model is transformed into its discrete representation that permits to construct different algorithms of numerical calculation for a computer [2]. As an example, we can mention famous libraries of numerical algorithms implemented as Fortran batches.

**Analytical (symbolic) paradigm** allows a computer to make complex symbolic transformations, to find analytical solution of (systems of) equations, to plot functions graphs, to build mathematical models of deterministic processes. Different computer algebra systems can serve as representatives of this paradigm.

The following reasons gave rise to this approach: (i) existence of a big number of labor-consuming tasks requiring routine analytical transformations before numeric calculations, (ii) reduction of efforts and a time spent in the case of solving a wide range of natural-scientific problems, (iii) compactness of representation and visual demonstrability of analytical solutions as compared with their numerical analogs.

**Deductive paradigm** makes use of a declarative way of representation of mathematical knowledge. This means that all existent knowledge has the form of a formal text, and additional knowledge is obtained (deduced) from it with the help of different rules of reasoning (inference rules).

The whole variety of systems that implement this paradigm can be roughly classified as follows:

- automated inference search systems (provers), such as Otter [17], Vampire [20], SPASS [25];
- interactive tactic-based proof assistants; the most well-known of them are Isabelle [18], PVS [19], and Coq [3];
- mathematical text processors: Mizar [22] and Theorema [6].

The evidential paradigm may be considered as a further development of the third type of the deductive paradigm in the direction of integration of deduction with symbolic calculations that is oriented to a declarative approach using the mentioned-above language ForTheL [24] as a communication tool between different computer mathematical services. This is one of peculiarities that distinguish Evidence Algorithm from Mizar, the system which has received a wide recognition all over the world.

A number of reasons for the appearance of integration paradigm have arisen by now (cf. CALCULEMUS Initiative, http://www.calculemus.net/). First of all, solving a really difficult problem requires simultaneously computations, analytical transformations, and automated reasoning. Also, in spite of the fact that computer algebra systems are powerful and flexible tools, results of their work often require thorough logical checking because they can be invalid in general. On the other hand, although systems of automated reasoning can guarantee the validity of results, their efficiency remains low as compared to the one of computer algebra systems because they usually lack specific decision procedures and heuristics.

Note that there exist two approaches to integrating computer mathematical services: (i) integration on the stage of design, when the construction of a software system a priori presupposes use of both of its modules and different mathematical services as its "own parts" (Mizar, Theorema, and EA) and (ii) integration on the stage exploitations, that means "assembling a new system" from systems acceptable for solving a task under consideration and available at a time when the new system is "constructed" (here a great role is played by computer mathematical services that exchange data through network with the help of special protocols). The projects OMEGA [4], OpenMath [7], and MathWeb [26] can be mentioned as investigations in the last direction; note that they contain languages for specification and exchange of data that can be used not only for solving mathematical problems, but for many other purposes.

## 2    System for Automated Deduction

By now, the first approximation to the evidential paradigm is implemented in the System for Automated Deduction, SAD [23]. The system can be used online via Internet (http://ea.unicyb.kiev.ua) for the following purposes:

- parsing and translation of ForTheL-texts (some examples can be found on the web-site);
- inference search in first-order classical logic on the basis of an original sequent calculus [8, 15, 1]; the user may supply his own problems or refer to the problems in TPTP problem library [21];
- theorem proving in the context of a self-contained ForTheL-text [9];
- verification of self-contained ForTheL-texts [16].

Any session of SAD consists of three main steps. First, SAD translates an input text (written in ForTheL or in a first order language) into its internal representation. In the translated text, the system selects a number of goals (statements to be proved) and, for each goal, determines the set of its logical predecessors (statements to be used in the proof). Finally, the system tries to deduce each goal from its predecessors. For this purpose, SAD may use its native first-order prover, as well as an external program.

There exist six main modules in SAD: [ForTheL], [FOL], [TPTP], [Reason], [Explore], and [Moses]. Below we give a brief description of them.

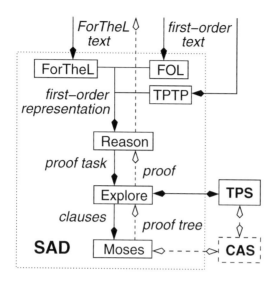

**Fig. 1.** Architecture of SAD

**Modules [ForTheL] and [FOL].** The modules [ForTheL] and [FOL] perform parsing of ForTheL-texts and first-order texts, respectively. Every of these modules converts an input text to a corresponding internal representation. This conversion preserves the structure of an initial text and translates phrases into an ordered set of first-order formulas. For input texts written in the first-order language, translation is not needed, so [FOL] just eliminates "syntactical sugar".

**Module [TPTP].** Recently, we have added a new interface module that connects SAD with the wide-known TPTP library that contains several thousands of logical problems for automated proving systems [21]. The system SAD downloads problems and axioms directly from the web-site of TPTP (one can also supply his own problem in the syntax of TPTP), and [TPTP] translates a task into its internal representation.

**Module [Reason].** This module runs a verification cycle, formulates verification tasks, and tries to solve them using its own reasoning capabilities together with the prover of SAD. In particular, [Reason] processes proofs by case analysis and by induction reasoning, simplifies a goal taking into account assumptions and affirmation written in the text, splits a complex goal to a number of simpler subgoals, and so on.

The role of the module [Reason] will be demonstrated below on an example taken from a real verification session.

**Module [Explore].** This module serves for purely technical purposes: it acts as a mediator between SAD and external theorem provers that can be used instead of (or together with) the own prover of SAD.

Module [Moses]. This module is the prover of SAD and is intended for inference search. It is implemented on the base of the sequent calculus GD (see below).

The prover looks through the search space using bounded depth first search with iterative deepening and backtracking. In order to increase the efficiency of inference search, [Moses] uses special constraints and folding-up technique [13]. Also, solutions of accumulated systems of equations are found only in reasonable cases. A special heuristics is adopted for definition application.

In order to provide SAD with equality handling capabilities, [Moses] implements a certain variation of Brand's modification method [5].

Note that since the calculus GD does not change initial premises, the prover performs operations with a tree of literal goals instead of a tree of sequents. This drastically reduces needs in computational resources.

Due to the absence of preliminary skolemization, the prover of SAD is capable to use a relevant solver for solving equation systems. The submodule of [Moses] responsible for equation handling acts as a mediator between the prover and external solvers. It checks a substitution found by such a way for admissibility and builds additional equations if necessary. The procedure computing the most general unifier is used as a default equation solver.

## 3  Linguistic Tools of SAD

The language ForTheL (Formal Theory Language) [24] is a language with formally defined syntax and semantics. It is intended for representation of mathematical texts including axioms, definitions, theorems and proofs. ForTheL is designed to be close to the natural language of real-life mathematical publications issued by human mathematicians. There are two reasons to pursue a verbose "natural" style instead of using the unified notation of some traditional logical language.

The first reason is to provide our framework with a user-friendly interface. A text composed with correct English sentences will hopefully more readable and easier to write than a collection of formulas built with quantifiers, parentheses, lambdas, junctors, and so on.

Second, a natural human text usually contains a certain useful information which lies beyond the scope of classical logic. For example, we distinguish definitions from ordinary axioms, theorems from intermediate statements inside a proof, and we tend to use them in different ways when reading a text. In a natural sentence, we meet nouns, which denote classes of entities; adjectives and verbs, which act as attributes and restrict classes; adjectives and verbs, which act as predicates and may relate different entities. However, where human language makes distinctions, the language of mathematical logic unifies: subjects, objects, attributes, predicates all become predicate symbols; axioms, theorems, definitions, ordinary statements all become formulas.

Our intention is to preserve these distinctions in formalization. We investigate how a human mathematician treats definitions as compared with axioms or lemmas, class-nouns as compared with adjectives, proofs by case analysis as compared with proofs following other schemes, and so on. Basing on these observations, we improve reasoning capabilities of a machine, we implement heuristic routines directing proof search or reducing a search space with the help of "non-logical" knowledge extracted from a formal, yet "natural-like" input text.

From the syntactical point of view, any ForTheL-text is a sequence of sections. Each section contains phrases and/or sections of lower levels. Top-level sections (such as theorems, axioms, definitions) play in ForTheL-texts the same role they do in usual mathematical texts. Typical sections of lower level are proofs, proof blocks, and proof cases. The phrases of ForTheL are either assumptions (then they begin with "let" or "assume") or affirmations.

The grammar of ForTheL-phrases imitates the grammar of English sentences. Phrases are built using nouns, which denote notions (classes) or functions, verbs and adjectives, which denote predicates, and prepositions and conjunctions, which define the logical meaning of a complex sentence. For example, "Every closed subset of every compact set is compact." is a simple ForTheL-affirmation. One can introduce a concise symbolic notation for predicates and functions and write statements in the form of usual first-order formulas.

The logical connectives along with some predicates and notions are predefined in ForTheL. All other syntactical units must be introduced explicitly. We use special introductors to declare new lexical primitives. For example, the introductor "[a divisor/divisors of x]" extends the current vocabulary with a new noun denoting an unary notion (equivalent forms of the same word may be listed with slashes). Also, one may introduce a new primitive as a synonym: "[x divides/divide y @ x is a divisor of y]" introduces a new verb.

An affirmation in a text, e.g. the statement of a theorem, can be provided with a proof section. A ForTheL-proof is a sequence of assumptions, affirmations (which may have their own proofs), and proof cases.

The simple example of a self-contained ForTheL-text is given below:

```
[a set/sets] [an element/elements of x]
[x is in/from y @ x is an element of y]
[a subset/subsets of x] [x is empty]

Definition DefSubset. Let S be a set.
  A subset of S is a set X such that every element of X is in S.

Definition DefEmpty.   Let S be a set.
                       S is empty iff S has no elements.

Axiom ExEmpty.         There exists an empty set.

Theorem.               Let S be a set.
                       S is a subset of every set iff S is empty.
```

This text will be translated into the following first-order representation.

```
Definition DefSubset. forall S (aSet(S) implies
  (forall x_1 (aSubsetOf(x_1,S) iff (aSet(x_1) and forall x_2
  (aElementOf(x_2,x_1) implies aElementOf(x_2,S)))))).

Definition DefEmpty. forall S (aSet(S) implies
  (isEmpty(S) iff not exists x_1 aElementOf(x_1,S))).

Axiom ExEmpty. exists x_1 (aSet(x_1) and isEmpty(x_1)).

Theorem. assume aSet(S).
  (forall x_2 (aSet(x_2) implies aSubsetOf(S,x_2))) iff isEmpty(S).
```

## 4   Theorem Proving in SAD

Since the internal representation of an input problem is based on a kind of the first-order language, SAD uses its prover for inference search in first-order classical logic. It was mentioned above that a special sequent formalism was developed and implemented in [Moses], the prover of SAD. In order to make this paper self-contained, we give a brief description of a certain modification GD' of the calculus GD introduced in [15] and used in [Moses].

Admissible Substitutions. Let $\Gamma$ be a set of closed formulas such that no two distinct quantifiers in $\Gamma$ bind the same variable. Let $\mathcal{V}_\Gamma$ stand for the set of indexed variables $\{\,^k v \mid v$ occurs in $\Gamma$, $k \in \mathbb{N}\,\}$. The expression $^k F$ will denote the formula $F$ with each variable $v$ replaced with an indexed variable $^k v$.

We write $F\lfloor G^+ \rfloor$ ($F\lfloor G^- \rfloor$) to denote a formula $F$ with a positive (respectively, negative) occurrence of a subformula $G$. A variable $^k v \in \mathcal{V}_\Gamma$ is said to be unknown in $\Gamma$ if for some formula $P \in \Gamma$, $P\lfloor(\forall v F)^+\rfloor$ or $P\lfloor(\exists v F)^-\rfloor$. Correspondingly, $x$ is said to be ◻xed in $\Gamma$ if for some $P \in \Gamma^*$, $P\lfloor(\forall v F)^-\rfloor$ or $P\lfloor(\exists v F)^+\rfloor$. Obviously, each variable in $\mathcal{V}_\Gamma$ is either unknown or fixed.

The set $\Gamma$ induces a partial ordering $\prec_\Gamma$ on $\mathcal{V}_\Gamma$ as follows: $^k u \prec_\Gamma {}^m w$ if and only if (a) $k = m$, and (b) a quantifier on $w$ occurs in the scope of a quantifier on $u$ (that is, some formula $F \in \Gamma$ is of the form $(\ldots \mathcal{Q}_1 u (\ldots \mathcal{Q}_2 w (\ldots) \ldots) \ldots)$.

Given a substitution $\sigma$, we define another partial ordering $\ll_\Gamma^\sigma$ on $\mathcal{V}_\Gamma$ as follows: $^m w \ll_\Gamma^\sigma {}^k u$ if and only if $^k u$ is unknown in $\Gamma$ and $^m w$ is fixed in $\Gamma$ and occurs in $^k u \sigma$.

A substitution $\sigma$ is said to be admissible in $\Gamma$ if and only if (a) $\sigma$ substitutes for unknown variables only (that is, $x\sigma \neq x$ implies that $x$ is unknown in $\Gamma$), and (b) the transitive closure of $\prec_\Gamma \cup \ll_\Gamma^\sigma$ is a partial ordering.

A substitution $\pi$ is called pasting in $\Gamma$ if and only if (a) $\pi$ just changes indexes of indexed variables (that is, $x\pi \neq x$ implies that $x$ is of the form $^k v$ and $x\pi$ is of the form $^m v$), and (b) if $^k u \prec_\Gamma {}^k v$ and $^k v \pi = {}^m v$ then $^k u \pi = {}^m u$.

Inference Rules. The main object of the calculus GD' is an a-sequent, which is an expression of the form $[\Lambda]\ \Gamma \to G$, where $\Lambda$ is a list of literals, called framed literals, $\Gamma$ is a list of formulas, called premises, and $G$ is a goal formula. In our setting, $\Lambda$ and $G$ contain indexed variables only, and $\Gamma$ does not contain indexed variables at all.

When a proof of an initial a-sequent is searched in GD', an inference tree is constructed. At the beginning of a search process the tree consists of the initial a-sequent. The tree grows from top to bottom, with the subsequent nodes generated in accordance with the inference rules of GD'.

At some moments of inference, branches in the tree may be terminated: a leaf node containing an equation of the form $\langle L_1 \approx L_2 \rangle$ (where $L_1, L_2$ are literals) is added to such a branch and no more expansions are possible on it.

Below, $F^\neg$ denotes the negation of $F$ with the negation sign moved inside $F$:

$$(\forall x\, P)^\neg = \exists x\, \neg P \qquad (P \vee Q)^\neg = \neg P \wedge \neg Q \qquad (P \supset Q)^\neg = P \wedge \neg Q$$
$$(\exists x\, P)^\neg = \forall x\, \neg P \qquad (P \wedge Q)^\neg = \neg P \vee \neg Q \qquad (\neg P)^\neg = P \qquad A^\neg = \neg A$$

The expression $^*F$ stands for $^kF$ where $k$ is a fresh index with respect to the whole inference tree. In the following inference rules, $A, B$ are unifiable atoms and $L, M$ are unifiable literals.

Goal-Splitting Rules (GS):

$(\rightarrow \forall):$ 
$$\dfrac{[\Lambda]\ \Gamma \rightarrow \forall x\, F}{[\Lambda]\ \Gamma \rightarrow F}$$

$(\rightarrow \exists):$ 
$$\dfrac{[\Lambda]\ \Gamma \rightarrow \exists x\, F}{[\Lambda]\ \Gamma \rightarrow F}$$

$(\rightarrow \supset)_1:$ 
$$\dfrac{[\Lambda]\ \Gamma \rightarrow F \supset G}{[\Lambda]\ \Gamma \rightarrow G}$$

$(\rightarrow \supset)_2:$ 
$$\dfrac{[\Lambda]\ \Gamma \rightarrow F \supset G}{[\Lambda]\ \Gamma \rightarrow F^\neg}$$

$(\rightarrow \vee)_1:$ 
$$\dfrac{[\Lambda]\ \Gamma \rightarrow F \vee G}{[\Lambda]\ \Gamma \rightarrow G}$$

$(\rightarrow \vee)_2:$ 
$$\dfrac{[\Lambda]\ \Gamma \rightarrow F \vee G}{[\Lambda]\ \Gamma \rightarrow F}$$

$(\rightarrow \wedge):$ 
$$\dfrac{[\Lambda]\ \Gamma \rightarrow F \wedge G}{[\Lambda]\ \Gamma \rightarrow F \qquad [\Lambda]\ \Gamma \rightarrow G}$$

$(\rightarrow \neg):$ 
$$\dfrac{[\Lambda]\ \Gamma \rightarrow \neg F}{[\Lambda]\ \Gamma \rightarrow F^\neg}$$

Auxiliary-Goal Rule (AG):

$$\dfrac{[\Lambda]\ \Gamma, F\lfloor B^+ \rfloor, \Delta \rightarrow A}{[\Lambda, \neg A]\ \Gamma, F, \Delta \rightarrow {}^*F^\neg}$$

$$\dfrac{[\Lambda]\ \Gamma, F\lfloor B^- \rfloor, \Delta \rightarrow \neg A}{[\Lambda, A]\ \Gamma, F, \Delta \rightarrow {}^*F^\neg}$$

Termination-by-Framed-Literal Rule (TF):

$$\dfrac{[\Lambda_1, M, \Lambda_2]\ \Gamma \rightarrow L}{\langle M \approx L \rangle}$$

Termination-by-Premise Rule (TP):

$$\dfrac{[\Lambda]\ \Gamma, M, \Delta \rightarrow L}{\langle {}^*M \approx L \rangle}$$

The following goal-drivenness constraint is applied to the inferences in GD'. Whenever an AG-rule is applied and the atom $A$ (possibly, negated) goes to the end of the list of framed literals, the corresponding occurrence of $B$ in $^*F^\neg$ must be fixed and remembered. We require that the subsequent applications of goal-splitting rules never remove that occurrence of $B$ from the proof. In other words, that occurrence of $B$ must form a literal goal after a number of splittings. Then, we require the branch containing this goal to be terminated by an application of TF-rule, with the equation $\langle A \approx B \rangle$ in the leaf.

Proof Trees. Let us consider an inference tree $T$ where every branch is terminated. Let $\Gamma$ denote the set of premises in the initial a-sequent. Let $E$ denote the overall system of substitutional equations in the leaves of the tree.

The inference tree $T$ is considered to be a proof tree whenever there exist substitutions $\sigma$ and $\pi$ such that: (a) $\sigma$ is admissible in $\Gamma$, (b) $\pi$ is pasting in $\Gamma$, and (c) $\sigma \circ \pi$ is a solution for $E$ (that is, $E\pi\sigma$ is a set of identities).

The initial a-sequent of a proof tree is called deducible in GD'.

**Theorem 1 (Soundness and Completeness of GD').** Let $\Gamma$ be a consistent set of formulas and $G$ be a formula. The sequent $\Gamma \to G$ is deducible in Gentzen's calculus **LK** [10] if and only if the a-sequent $[\ ]\ \Gamma, \neg G \to {}^0 G$ is deducible in the calculus GD'.

Note that equation solving is separated from application of inference rules. Substitutional equations may be accumulated and be sent to a solver in arbitrary moment of search. This property of GD' allows to organize a flexible proof search procedure. We underline that the calculus GD' does not rely upon preliminary skolemization, so that equations are formulated in the initial signature and a theory-specific equation solver may be used.

Let us demonstrate the deductive technique of SAD on a simple propositional problem. Assume that we want to prove the sequent $A \vee (B \vee A) \to A \vee B$. Let $\Gamma = \{A \vee (B \vee A), \neg(A \vee B)\}$. A GD'-inference used to prove the a-sequent $[\ ]\ \Gamma \to A \vee B$ is shown below:

$$
\cfrac{
\cfrac{
\cfrac{
\cfrac{[\ ]\ \Gamma \to A \vee B}{[\ ]\ \Gamma \to A} \, (\to \vee)_1
}{[\neg A]\ \Gamma \to \neg A \wedge \neg(B \vee A)} \, (AG)
}{
\cfrac{[\neg A]\ \Gamma \to \neg A}{\langle \neg A \approx \neg A \rangle} \, (TF)
\qquad
\cfrac{
\cfrac{
\cfrac{[\neg A]\ \Gamma \to \neg(B \vee A)}{[\neg A]\ \Gamma \to \neg B \wedge \neg A} \, (\to \neg)
}{
\cfrac{\cfrac{[\neg A]\ \Gamma \to \neg B}{[\neg A, B]\ \Gamma \to A \vee B} \, (AG)}{[\neg A, B]\ \Gamma \to B} \, (\to \vee)
\quad
\cfrac{[\neg A]\ \Gamma \to \neg A}{\langle \neg A \approx \neg A \rangle} \, (TF)
} \, (\to \wedge)
}{\langle B \approx B \rangle} \, (TF)
} \, (\to \wedge)
}{}
$$

Note that in any GD'-inference the premises are the same in each a-sequent. Moreover, the list of framed literals in a given node is exactly the list of the complements of literal goals above that node. So, we can present the proof tree given above in a quite abbreviated form, as the tree of literal goals. In the following inference, applications of the auxiliary-goal rule are joined with the subsequent applications of goal-splitting rules in a single inference step, and termination by a framed literal becomes termination by a contradiction in a branch:

$$
\cfrac{
\cfrac{[\ ]\ A \lor (B \lor A), \neg(A \lor B) \to A \lor B}{A}\ (GS)
}{
\cfrac{\neg A}{\langle \neg A \approx \neg A \rangle}\ (TF)
\qquad
\cfrac{\cfrac{\neg B}{B}\ (AG+GS)}{\langle B \approx B \rangle}\ (TF)
\qquad
\cfrac{\neg A}{\langle \neg A \approx \neg A \rangle}\ (TF)
}\ (AG+GS)
$$

**Fetching Problems from the TPTP Library.** As we said above, the system SAD may refer to the TPTP problem library and downloads problems and axiom sets directly from the web-site of TPTP, so that it is sufficient to give the identifier of the problem to SAD in a corresponding mode. For example, given SET001-1.p, SAD downloads first the text of the problem (comments are erased):

```
include('Axioms/SET001-0.ax').

input_clause(b_equals_bb,hypothesis,
    [++equal_sets(b,bb)]).

input_clause(element_of_b,hypothesis,
    [++member(element_of_b,b)]).

input_clause(prove_element_of_bb,conjecture,
    [--member(element_of_b,bb)]).
```

parses it, and then downloads the needed axiom set. The resulting text is transformed into an appropriate a-sequent and the inference search procedure is started. The following information will be displayed when the session finishes:

```
[Reason] inference search successful
[Main] session finished in 00:00.01
[Main] 00:00.00 in [TPTP] - 00:00.00 in [Reason] - 00:00.01 in [Moses]
```

**Theorem Proving in ForTheL-environment.** Let us consider again the ForTheL-text about empty sets given above. The following text demonstrates the output of SAD when proving the last theorem. The proposition is "evident" for SAD and the proof is found in less than a second.

The proof of the proposition has the form of a tree of literals, in a similar fashion to the proof tree given above. This inference can be transformed in the usual Gentzen-type sequent proof or in the Gentzen's natural inference.

```
Proof tree --- nodes: 17, depth: 5.
Proved in 10 msec (steps: 208, nodes: 614, depth bound: 4).

Root:
   isEmpty(S#9[1])
      -isEmpty(S#9[1])
      -aElementOf(x_1#7[2](S#9[1]),S#9[1])
         aElementOf(x_1#7[2](S#9[1]),S#9[1])
         aSubsetOf(S#9[1],x_1#8[5])
            -aSubsetOf(S#9[4],x_1#8[5])
            -isEmpty(S#9[4])
            aSet(x_1#8[5])
               -aSet(x_1#8[5])
            -aElementOf(x_1#7[2](S#9[1]),x_1#8[5])
               aElementOf(x_1#7[2](S#9[1]),x_1#8[5])
               isEmpty(x_1#8[5])
                  -isEmpty(x_1#8[7])
               aSet(x_1#8[5])
            aSet(x_1#8[5])
      aSet(S#9[1])
         -aSet(S#9[8])
  -aSet(x_2#a[1])
     aSet(x_2#a[1])
     -aSubsetOf(S#9[10],x_2#a[1])
        aSubsetOf(S#9[10],x_2#a[10])
        isEmpty(S#9[10])
     -aElementOf(x_2#4[9](x_2#a[1],S#9[10]),S#9[10])
        aElementOf(x_2#4[9](x_2#a[1],S#9[10]),S#9[10])
        isEmpty(S#9[10])
        aSet(S#9[10])
     aSet(S#9[10])
```

## 5    Text Verification in SAD

This section is devoted to the verification procedure of SAD and to the peculiarities of formalization style. We consider a real mathematical problem: Ramsey's theorem (both finite and infinite versions) as it is presented in the beginning of Graham's introductory book [12]:

**Infinite Ramsey's Theorem.** *For all $k, r \in \omega$ and any $r$-coloring $\xi : \left[\begin{smallmatrix} \omega \\ k \end{smallmatrix}\right] \to [r]$ of the $k$-element subsets of $\omega$, there is always an infinite subset $S \subseteq \omega$ with all its $k$-element subsets having the same color.*

A set hypergraph $H = H(V, E)$ denotes a set $V$ together with a family $E$ of subsets of $V$ in presupposition that every of them contains at least two elements. The chromatic number of $H$, denoted by $\chi(H)$, is defined to be the least integer $r$ such that there is an $r$-coloring of $V$ so that no edge in $E$ is monochromatic.

**Compactness Theorem.** *If $\chi(H) > t$ and all edges of $H$ are finite then there is a finite subhypergraph $G$ of $H$ with $\chi(G) > t$.*

**Finite Ramsey's Theorem.** *For all* $k, l, r \in \omega$ *there exists* $N \in \omega$ *such that if* $n \geqslant N$ *and* $\xi : \begin{bmatrix} n \\ k \end{bmatrix} \to [r]$ *is any* $r$-*coloring of the* $k$-*subsets of* $[n]$ *then some* $l$-*subset of* $[n]$ *has all its* $k$-*subsets with the same color.*

These propositions and their proofs were formalized and automatically verified in SAD. As an experiment of proving systems cooperation, the automated theorem prover SPASS [25] was used as the external prover to support verification and showed excellent results. The whole ForTheL-text consists of 490 lines of which 200 are used for preliminary facts: common elements of set and number theory, definitions and properties of functions and predicates used in the text. The rest 290 lines contain the formalization of the above text together with three proofs. Note that the above text together with two proofs (the proof of Finite Ramsey's Theorem is not given) takes approximately 130 lines in Graham's book. So, we can consider ForTheL (and the whole system SAD) as a rather economical tool for formalization of texts.

The given-above definitions and propositions are rewritten in ForTheL as follows (we replace some ASCII-notation with more readable notation of TEX).

**Theorem RamseyInf.** Let $T$ be a finite set.
  For every $(k \in \omega)$ and every countable $(S \subseteq \omega)$ and every $(c : [S/k] \to T)$
    there exists an element $u$ of $T$ and a countable $X \subseteq S$ such that
      for every $(Q \in [X/k])$ $c(Q) = u$.
**Definition DefChromC.**
  Let $H$ be a hypergraph and $L : \mathrm{Ver}\, H \to T$ for some finite set $T$.
  $L$ is chromatic for $H$ iff $H$ has no edge that is monochromatic in $H$ wrt $L$.
**Definition DefChromT.**
  Let $H$ be a hypergraph and $T$ be a finite set.
  $T$ is chromatic for $H$ iff there exists $L : \mathrm{Ver}\, H \to T$ chromatic for $H$.
**Theorem Compactness.**
  Assume $H$ is a hypergraph and $\mathrm{Ver}\, H = \omega$.
  Assume every edge of $H$ is finite.
  Let $T$ be a finite set chromatic for every finite subgraph of $H$.
  Then $T$ is chromatic for $H$.
**Theorem RamseyFin.** Let $T$ be a finite set. Let $k, l$ be numbers.
  Then there exists a number $n$ such that for every $(c : [[n]/k] \to T)$
    there exists an element $u$ of $T$ and an element $X$ of $[[n]/l]$
      such that for every $(Q \in [X/k])$ $c(Q) = u$.

We don't give here the whole ForTheL-text. Instead, we will consider a fragment from the proof of the Infinite Ramsey's Theorem that illustrates well the peculiarities of text verification in SAD.

The Infinite Ramsey's Theorem is proved by induction on $k$. In the proof of the induction step, we build a number of objects (sequences, functions, and sets) and prove their properties. The most important construction in our proof is $\{N_i\}_\omega$, a recursively defined sequence of subsets of $\omega$. This sequence is decreasing, that is $N_{i+1} \subseteq \mathrm{cdr}\, N_i = N_i \setminus \{\min N_i\}$. We want to prove a simple yet useful consequence of this fact:

For every $(i, j \in \omega)$ if $j \leqslant i$ then $N(i) \subseteq N(j)$.
proof by induction.
    Let $i, j$ be numbers so that $j \leqslant i$.
    Let $I$ be a number so that $i = \text{succ } I$.
    Case $i \leqslant j$. Obvious.
    Case $j \leqslant I$.
        Then $N(I) \subseteq N(j)$ (by IH).
        cdr $(N(I)) \subseteq N(I)$ (by DefDiff).
        $N(i) \subseteq N(j)$ (by SubTrans).
    end.
end.

The main affirmation is proved by natural induction. The systems assumes by default that the induction is held by the topmost universally quantified variable in the goal, that is, by $i$. Also, you can mention the induction term explicitly ("proof by induction on i+j.").

The verificator ([Reason]) checks that the first assumption in the proof section introduces the required variables and corresponds to the conditions in the goal. Then the appropriate induction hypothesis IH($i$) is formulated:

$$\forall x, y \in \omega \, (x < i \supset (y \leqslant x \supset N(x) \subseteq N(y)))$$

and is added to the logical context of the rest of the proof.

In our proof, the base case ($i = 0$) is obvious, since $N(0) = \omega$ by definition. Therefore, we simply omit it and consider the induction step. We assume existence of the predecessor of $i$ and prove the current goal $N(i) \subseteq N(j)$ by case analysis. Note that the goal was simplified in accordance with the first assumption.

When a sequence of proof cases is considered, the system checks that the case analysis is complete, i.e. the corresponding disjunction is valid. In our proof, the disjunction is succ $x \leqslant y \vee y \leqslant x$ and it is easily verified. Then the reasoner tries to prove the current goal for each case respectively. Note the reference to the induction hypothesis made in the second case section.

# 6 Conclusion

This paper is devoted to the description of mathematical texts processing in the framework of evidential paradigm having now the form of the implemented system SAD that is intended for different complex ways of mathematical texts processing, mainly, automated theorem proving and checking formal mathematical texts. In this connection, the system SAD exploits simultaneously a formal language for presenting mathematical texts (including theorems, their proofs, and necessary environment) in the form most appropriate for a user, as well as a formal notion of computer-made proof step based on sequent formalism of first-order logic. Mathematical text processing in SAD consists of three main steps: firstly, writing a text under consideration in a special formal language, secondly, translation of the written text into a text in the form of a set of special first-order formulas, and thirdly, proving/checking the special text with the help of sequent-type deductive tools.

Finally note that systems that constructed on the basis of the evidential paradigm (in particular, SAD) can be useful in many industrial fields such as computer-aided processing of computer knowledge, automated reasoning, checking soft and hardware, logical inference search taking into account constraints, distributed learning, e-learning, data mining from mathematical papers, construction knowledge bases for formal theories.

# References

1. Z. Aselderov, K. Verchinine, A. Degtyarev, A. Lyaletski, A. Paskevich, A. Pavlov. Linguistic tools and deductive technique of the System for Automated Deduction. In Proc. 3rd International Workshop on the Implementation of Logics, Tbilisi, Georgia, 2002, pp. 21–24.

2. N.I. Bakhvalov, N.P. Zhidkov, G.M. Kobelkon. Computational Methods (in Russian). BINOM Publisher, 2003.

3. B. Barras, S. Boutin, C. Cornes, J. Courant, J. Filliatre, E. Giménez, H. Herbelin, G. Huet, C. Muñoz, C. Murthy, C. Parent, C. Paulin, A. Saïbi, B. Werner. The Coq proof assistant reference manual – version v6.1. Technical Report 0203, INRIA, 1997.

4. C. Benzmüller, L. Cheikhrouhou, D. Fehrer, A. Fiedler, X. Huang, M. Kerber, M. Kohlhase, K. Konrad, A. Meier, E. Melis, W. Schaarschmidt, J.H. Siekmann, V. Sorge. Omega: Towards a mathematical assistant. In W. McCune (ed.), Automated Deduction – CADE-14, Proc. 14th International Conference on Automated Deduction. Volume 1249 of Lecture Notes in Computer Science, Springer, 1997, pp. 252–255.

5. D. Brand. Proving theorems with the modification method. SIAM Journal of Computing **4**, 1975, pp. 412–430.

6. B. Buchberger, T. Jebelean, F. Kriftner, M. Marin, E. Tomuta, D. Vasaru. A survey of the Theorema project. In W. Küchlin (ed.): ISSAC'97 – Proc. International Symposium on Symbolic and Algebraic Computation, Maui, Hawaii, USA, ACM Press, 1997, pp. 384–391.

7. O. Caprotti, A.M. Cohen. Integrating computational and deduction systems using OpenMath. In A. Armando, T. Jebelean (eds.), Electronic Notes in Theoretical Computer Science. Volume 23, Elsevier, 2001.

8. A. Degtyarev, A. Lyaletski, M. Morokhovets. Evidence Algorithm and sequent logical inference search. In H. Ganzinger, D.A. McAllester, A. Voronkov (eds.), Logic Programming and Automated Reasoning, Proc. 6th International Conference LPAR'99. Volume 1705 of Lecture Notes in Computer Science, Springer, 1999, pp. 44–61.

9. A. Degtyarev, A. Lyaletski, M. Morokhovets. On the EA-style integrated processing of self-contained mathematical texts. In M. Kerber, M. Kohlhase (eds.): Symbolic Computation and Automated Reasoning: The CALCULEMUS-2000 Symposium. A.K. Peters Ltd., USA, 2001, pp. 126–141.

10. G. Gentzen. Untersuchungen uber das Logische Schliessen. Math. Zeit. **39**, 1934, pp. 176–210.

11. V.M. Glushkov. Some problems of automata theory and artificial intelligence (in Russian). Kibernetika **2**, 1970, pp. 3–13.
12. R.L. Graham. Rudiments of Ramsey Theory. AMS, 1981.
13. R. Letz, G. Stenz. Model elimination and connection tableau procedures. In A. Robinson, A. Voronkov (eds.), Handbook for Automated Reasoning. Volume II. Elsevier Science, 2001, pp. 2017–2116.
14. A. Lyaletski, M. Morokhovets. Evidential paradigm: a current state. In: Program of International Conference "Mathematical Challenges of the 21st Century", University of California, Los Angeles, USA, 2000, p. 48.
15. A. Lyaletski, K. Verchinine, A. Degtyarev, A. Paskevich. System for Automated Deduction (SAD): Linguistic and deductive peculiarities. In M.A. Klopotek, S.T. Wierzchon, M. Michalewicz (eds.): Intelligent Information Systems 2002, (Proc. IIS'2002 Symposium, Sopot, Poland, June 3–6, 2002). Advances in Soft Computing, Physica-Verlag, 2002, pp. 413–422.
16. A. Lyaletski, K. Verchinine, A. Paskevich. On verification tools implemented in the System for Automated Deduction. In: Proc. 2nd CoLogNet Workshop on Implementation Technology for Computational Logic Systems (ITCLS'2003), Pisa, Italy, 2003, pp. 3–14.
17. W. McCune. Otter 3.0 reference manual and guide. Tech. Report ANL-94/6, Argonne National Laboratory, Argonne, USA, 1994.
18. T. Nipkow, L.C. Paulson, M. Wenzel. Isabelle/HOL: A Proof Assistant for Higher-Order Logic. Volume 2283 of Lecture Notes in Computer Science. Springer, 2002.
19. S. Owre, J.M. Rushby, N. Shankar. PVS: A prototype verification system. In D. Kapur (ed.), Automated Deduction – CADE-11, Proc. 11th International Conference on Automated Deduction. Volume 607 of Lecture Notes in Computer Science, Springer, 1992, pp. 748–752.
20. A. Riazanov, A. Voronkov. The design and implementation of VAMPIRE. AI Communications **15**, 2002, pp. 91–110.
21. G. Sutcliffe, C.B. Suttner, T. Yemenis. The TPTP problem library. In A. Bundy (ed.): Automated Deduction – CADE-12, Proc. 12th International Conference on Automated Deduction. Volume 814 of Lecture Notes in Computer Science, Springer, 1994, pp. 252–266. See also `http://tptp.org`.
22. A. Trybulec, H. Blair. Computer assisted reasoning with Mizar. In: Proc. 9th International Joint Conference on Artificial Intelligence, 1985, pp. 26–28.
23. K. Verchinine, A. Degtyarev, A. Lyaleyski, A. Paskevich. SAD, a System for Automated Deduction: a current state. In F. Kamareddine (ed.), Proc. Workshop on 35 Years of AUTOMATH, Heriot-Watt University, Edinburgh, Scotland, 2002.
24. K. Vershinin, A. Paskevich. ForTheL – the language of formal theories. International Journal of Information Theories and Applications **7-3**, 2000, pp. 120–126.
25. C. Weidenbach. System description: Spass version 1.0.0. In H. Ganzinger (ed.), Automated Deduction – CADE-16, Proc. 16th International Conference on Automated Deduction. Volume 1632 of Lecture Notes in Computer Science, Springer, 1999, pp. 378–382.
26. J. Zimmer, M. Kohlhase. System description: The MathWeb Software Bus for distributed mathematical reasoning. In A. Voronkov (ed.), Automated Deduction – CADE-18, Proc. 18th International Conference on Automated Deduction. Volume 2392 of Lecture Notes in Computer Science, Springer, 2002, pp. 139–143.

# Adaptive Access to a Proof Planner[*]

Erica Melis[1], Andreas Meier[1], and Martin Pollet[2]

[1] German Research Institute for Artificial Intelligence (DFKI)
Saarbrücken, Germany
{melis,ameier}@dfki.de
[2] Saarland University, Saarbrücken, Germany
pollet@ags.uni-sb.de

**Abstract.** Mathematical tools such as computer algebra systems and interactive and automated theorem provers are complex systems and can perform difficult computations. Typically, such tools are used by a (small) group of particularly trained and skilled users to assist in mathematical problem solving. They can also be used as back-engines for interactive exercises in learning environments. This, however, suggests the adaptation of the choice of functionalities of the tool to the learner. This paper addresses the adaptive usage of the proof planner MULTI for the learning environment ACTIVEMATH. The proof planner is a back-engine for interactive proof exercises. We identify different dimensions in which the usage of such a service system can be adapted and investigate the architecture realizing the adaptive access to MULTI.

## 1 Motivation

So far, the main application of mathematical systems such as computer algebra systems and theorem provers has been for assisting trained and skilled users. This user group determines many design decisions. For instance, interactive theorem proving systems try to support the proof construction by restricting choices to valid proof steps, they suggest applicable lemmas, or they produce a subproof automatically. These functionalities are useful, e.g., for interactively verifying a program and reduce the workload of the proof expert.

Another application of a mathematical system may be as a cognitive tool in a learning environment for which the user group consists of learners rather than proof experts. Empirical evidence indicates that active, exploratory learning helps to construct knowledge and skills in a learner's mind. In particular, empirical studies [13] suggest that student's deficiencies in their mathematical competence with respect to understanding and generating proofs are connected with the shortcoming of student's self-guided explorative learning opportunities

[*] This publication is partly a result of work in the context of the LeActiveMath and iClass projects, funded under the 6th Framework Programm of the European Community – (Contract IST-2003-507826). The authors are solely responsible for its content. The European Community is not responsible for any use that might be made of information appearing therein.

A. Asperti et al. (Eds.): MKM 2004, LNCS 3119, pp. 251–264, 2004.
© Springer-Verlag Berlin Heidelberg 2004

and the lack of (self-)explanations during problem solving. Such an explorative learning can be supported by tools. For this reason, the web-based adaptive learning environment for mathematics, ACTIVEMATH, integrates problem solving systems as back-engines for interactive exercising.

In an educational context the original features of typical mathematical systems are not sufficient. Rather, an educational context requires additional features for effective learning such as

- adaptivity to the learner,
- feedback on the learners activities,
- possibility to make mistakes.

In order to realize those features and to adapt to the student's context, goals, needs, capabilities, preferences, and previous activities, the setting and the user interface of tool-supported interactive exercising needs to be adaptable to the learner in a pedagogically and cognitively sound way. Thus, for interactive exercising the back-engine has to be extended so that it can process information from ACTIVEMATH's student model and pedagogical knowledge base. Similarly, information about the learner's misconceptions or performance in an exercise should be returned to the student model.

In this paper, we describe a first adaptive integration of the proof planner MULTI with the learning environment ACTIVEMATH. In particular, we discuss the different dimensions along which the usage of the proof planner MULTI can be adapted. Mostly, we describe personalization dimensions although the same setting can also be used for adaptation of accessibility and customization. We investigate the necessary extensions of MULTI and the architecture realizing the adaptive access to MULTI.

The paper is structured as follows. We start with preliminaries about ACTIVEMATH and the proof planner MULTI, since these might not be known to the gentle reader. Afterwards, we identify adaptivity dimensions of MULTI for interactive proof exercises and present the architecture for the adaptive access of MULTI. In section 5 we describe the realization of some directions of the adaptivity. Section 6 discusses potential extensions of the current approach and future work. We conclude with a discussion of results and related work.

## 2    Preliminaries

Empirical results indicate that instruction with proof planning methods, which explicitly encode mathematical steps, can be a learning approach that is superior to the traditional teaching of mathematical proof [7]. This motivates to use proof planning for maths education and the connection of the proof planner MULTI with the user-adaptive learning environment ACTIVEMATH.

The following is only a brief introduction to ACTIVEMATH and MULTI. For more details on proof planning and MULTI the interested reader is referred to [9, 8]. For more details on ACTIVEMATH see [6].

## 2.1    ACTIVEMATH, its Student Model and Pedagogical Knowledge

ACTIVEMATH is a web-based, user-adaptive learning environment for mathematics. The learner can choose learning goals to achieve a scenario. ACTIVEMATH generates learning material user-adaptively, i.e., dependent on the learner's goals, learning scenarios, preferences, and knowledge. A course generator determines the concepts that the student needs to learn for a goal chosen by the learner and selects the appropriate instructional items (explanations, definitions, examples, exercises, etc). According to pedagogical knowledge, this selection also includes the number, type, and difficulty of exercises and examples, as well as the interactivity setting of exercises (e.g., what is requested from the learner, which functionalities can be used). It assembles the instructional items in a sequence which is suggested by the scenario chosen and the pedagogical strategy following it. The adaptivity is based on a student model that includes

- the student's mastery level of concepts and skills
- the history of the learner's actions (e.g., time spent per item)
- her preferences (e.g., preferred language), the chosen learning scenario, and the learning goals as input through a questionnaire.

The student model is updated based on results of the learning activities such as reading and problem solving. That is, the student's exercise performance is evaluated and the evaluation is passed to the student model for updating it.

## 2.2    Proof Planning

Originally, the goal of the research on proof planning [2] was to prove mathematical theorems automatically. The knowledge-based approach in MULTI employs mathematical strategies, methods, and computations for this purpose. It guides the search by heuristics known from mathematical problem solving in specific mathematical areas.

Proof planning starts with a goal that represents the conjecture to be proved and with proof assumptions. It continues by applying a method (such as proof by induction) for which the application conditions are satisfied and this generates new assumptions or reduces a goal to (possibly trivial) subgoals. This process goes on until no goal is left. The resulting sequence of instantiated methods constitutes a solution proof plan.

Generally, proof construction may require to construct a mathematical object, i.e., to instantiate existentially quantified variables by witness terms. In proof planning meta-variables are used as place holders for such objects until enough information is collected to instantiate the meta-variable. A domain-specific constraint solver can help to construct mathematical objects that are elements of a specific domain. During the proof planning process the constraint solver checks the (in)consistency of constraints on meta-variables and collects consistent constraints in a constraint store. Then, it computes instantiations for the meta-variables that satisfy the collected constraints [10].

To structure the repertoire of proof planning methods and make the proof planning process more hierarchical, strategies have been introduced. One of the types of proof planning strategies is specified by a set of methods and search heuristics. Different proof planning strategies can correspond to and implement different proof ideas. In the automatic mode, the proof planner searches for applicable strategies (including object construction and backtracking) or methods in each intermediate state until it reaches a solution proof plan. Mathematics-oriented heuristics guide this search.

For new applications, MULTI has been extended with an interactive mode. In interactive proof planning, the user searches and makes the decisions, which can include the choice of strategies, of methods, and the instantiation of meta-variables.

## 3    Adaptation to the User

The proof planning service can be requested for proof examples that are (dynamically) demonstrated and for interactive exercises in which MULTI can be used as a back-engine. In these applications, the MULTI service can be adapted according to the learning scenario, the goals, the preferences, and the prerequisite knowledge of the learner. In the following, we shall discuss several adaptation dimensions together with cognitive and other variables of the learner that may affect the adaptation.

### 3.1    Proof Planning Scenarios

The first dimension of adaptation of the MULTI service is the exercise scenario. There are several types of proof exercises, e.g., those in which the student can interactively apply certain proof planning methods, freely explore, or in which the learner sketches proof steps and MULTI checks the student's steps. Accordingly, we identified several pedagogically motivated proof scenarios. They differ with respect to the overall learning goal and the employed service functionalities. The selection of a scenario is performed by ACTIVEMATH, which requests the MULTI service.

**Replay and Presentation of a Proof Plan.** Completed proof plans (or parts of proof plans) are presented to the learner. The proof plan can be presented at once or stepwise. This scenario targets an understanding of the effects of the application of individual methods, how several method applications combine to a proof plan or provide a basis for self-explaining a proof. The learner's activities in this scenario are mainly restricted to browsing the presentation of the proof plan, of methods and of the constraint store as well as replaying a proof plan step-by-step or hierarchically.

**Interactive Proof Planning.** The learner constructs a proof plan for a given problem or has to complete a given proof plan with gaps by selecting and applying methods from a pre-defined set of methods or strategies as well as by instantiating meta-variables. This scenario targets the 'technical' mastery of proof steps and proof heuristics. Moreover, the learner can realize the effects of instantiating a meta-variable and receive support for constructing mathematical objects that instantiate a meta-variable. As we shall see later (see section 5), the learner's main activities are the selection of the next step (and its details) as well as the specification of meta-variables. Other possibilities are browsing the current proof plan and requesting additional information, e.g., from the constraint store.

**Island Planning.** The learner constructs a proof sketch for a problem. This scenario targets the understanding of the proof process without details. The student is supposed to find a proof idea and to provide a structure of the proof by specifying important intermediate goals in a proof plan, so-called proof islands. The main user interactions in this scenario are adding proof islands as well as links between the islands, the theorem and the assumptions that describe which proof nodes depend from which other proof nodes. In addition, the current island plan can be browsed and additional information can be requested.

**Free Exploration.** The learner obtains full access to the proof planner. She has to state the problem and initiate the proof process. Moreover, she can freely access different kinds of proof manipulations (application of strategies, of methods, of tools, instantiation of meta-variables). This scenario is only sensible for advanced learners. It targets exploration and discovery learning.

Meta-cognitive Framework. Polya suggested a framework for teaching mathematical problem [11]. He formulates a set of heuristics cast in form of brief questions and prompts within a frame of four problem solving stages: (1) Understand the problem (2) Devise a plan (3) Carry out the plan (4) Look back at the solution. Questions and prompts for (2) are, for instance: do you know a related problem? did you use all the data? Following Polya's ideas, each of the above scenarios can be enriched with meta-cognitive scaffolding in form of context sensitive subtitles, questions and prompts. This targets a structured proof process with separated phases.

## 3.2    Other Adaptation Dimensions

Other important adaptation dimensions control the possible or preferred **problem solving strategies**, the range of method choices, domains from which mathematical objects can be drawn etc. For instance, an exercise about the limit of a sequence can be solved by the application of limit theorems proved before or by using only the definition of the limit. The choice of such a proof idea depends on the learner's capabilities and on the pedagogical strategy.

In the interactive proof planning scenario MULTI provides suggestions of method applications and meta-variable instantiations to the learner (see section 5). In this scenario an adaptation decision is whether all the suggestions have to be correct or not. This is important, since errors can be an important source of learning. As opposed to a learning context **faulty suggestions** are not appropriate for problem solving assistance. For learning, however, it might not be the best idea to make only correct suggestions because then the student might just click on any suggestion rather than learn anything.

For instance, when the student has to prove the limit of a sequence by applying theorems and she is already familiar with the theorems, then it may be too boring and not interesting to suggest only applicable theorems. Again, the decision on when to make which faulty suggestion depends on the student's situation and on her capabilities and on the pedagogical strategy.

Further dimensions for adaptation are the **user interface appearance** and the **feedback**.

Note that, so far, we focused on the realization of the adaptive application of the interactive proof planning scenario. A description of the adaptivity realized so far is given in section 5. An adaptive graphical user interface and adaptive feedback delivery are not realized so far.

### 3.3   Some Variables to Adapt to

Adaptation may depend on the learner's expertise. For instance, a student who is a novice in proving will have more difficulties to choose between many methods and therefore a large set of alternative methods to choose from should be avoided because it increases the likelihood of guessing instead of learning and reasoning.

Adaptation may also depend on the learner's activity history. For instance, it seems not to be advisable to make suggestions for a method, in case the student has not been able to apply that method for several times recently.

Many dimensions of adaptation do not only depend on the learner's aptitudes but also on the chosen pedagogical strategy. For instance, the decision when to allow for faulty suggestions will depend not only on the student's situation and on her capabilities but also on the pedagogical strategy.

## 4   Architecture

For all those adaptations of the proof planning service the actual proof planner has to be extended by a scenario management and by mediators as described below. That is, the service encapsulates mediators which provide a (Web-) communication interface and compute some of the adaptations. The communication relies on XML-RPC protocols[1] and the OMDOC language [3] and is not further considered here.

Figure 1 depicts the architecture of the proof planning service and its communication with the learning environment ACTIVEMATH including its student model and pedagogical knowledge.

The architecture separates different functionalities and different kinds of knowledge. This modularization helps to maintain and update modules and to re-use components. As a side effect, the GUI becomes more independent and

---

[1] `http://www.xmlrpc.com`

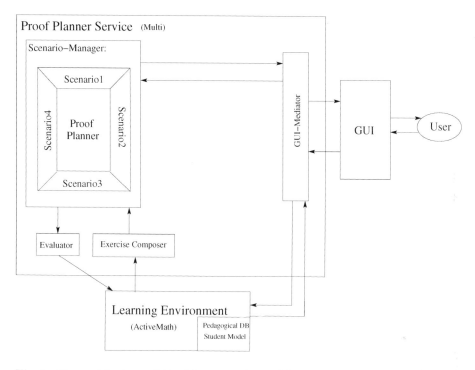

**Fig. 1.** The architecture of the MULTI service and its communication with ACTIVE-MATH and the GUI

adaptable. This part of the architecture (i.e., GUI and GUI-mediator) is, however, not yet implemented.

*Scenario-Manager.* The Scenario-Manager provides a communication shell around MULTI and realizes the different proof scenarios, which use particular proof storage and proof manipulation functionalities of the proof planner. The scenario for interactive proof planning employs – among others – the following functionalities:

– compute method application and meta-variable instantiation suggestions for the learner,
– check whether method applications and meta-variable instantiations issued by the learner are applicable,
– apply applicable steps,
– check whether proof planner can automatically complete the current proof plan,
– analyze the differences between the current proof plan fragment and a solution proof plan completed by the proof planner.

Relevant for island planning are, in particular, the functionalities:

- apply the island nodes and links specified by the user as abstract steps in the proof plan under construction,
- try to verify islands with automated proof planning or other tool support available in MULTI (e.g., with integrated computer algebra systems or automated theorem provers).

The Exercise Composer and the Evaluator provide interfaces for the communication between ACTIVEMATH and the Scenario-Manager.

Exercise Composer. When ACTIVEMATH requests a proof planning session, then the Exercise Composer computes the input for the parameters of the Scenario-Manager and the scenario. For instance, when the interactive proof planning scenario is requested, then the Exercise Composer determines the range and restriction of suggestions that the scenario component computes and provides to the learner. The Exercise Composer uses student model information for this computation.

Evaluator. At the end of an exercise the Evaluator receives an account on how complete and sound the learner solved the exercise. From this account the Evaluator computes information, which summarizes the learner's actions. The Evaluator passes this information to the persistent student model of ACTIVEMATH.

GUI. The GUI is an independent component. It will be an applet or even a standalone GUI (not integrated into ACTIVEMATH).

GUI-Mediator. The GUI-mediator is needed to adapt the presentation and feedback to the learner's needs and to configure the GUI. The GUI-Mediator realizes the communication between the GUI and the other components of the proof planning service. For each scenario, it interprets the meaning of GUI-objects and their manipulation and passes the interpretation of manipulations to the components of the proof planning service. Vice versa it translates information from the components to the GUI. This is an adaptive translation depending on information from the student model. Its main functionalities are:

- invoke and configure the GUI for a scenario and the individual learner. Adapt the GUI to user characteristics such as preferred language and to the peculiarities of the different scenarios (different scenarios require different user activities and different GUI-objects).
- interpret user interactions with the GUI and pass interpreted information to the Scenario-Manager. For instance, moving a goal-object and connecting it to assumption-objects in the GUI.
- request information/services from ACTIVEMATH, e.g., the explanation of a method or of a definition, as well as from the proof planner, e.g., the current constraint collection, and pass the results to the GUI. This is important, since the learner should be able to actively request different kinds of supporting information.

– interpret proof plan changes, feedback and messages from the proof planner components and pass them to the GUI for display. This includes the change of the proof state as well as proof planning-related messages. For instance, if a method is not applicable because its application conditions are not true, then this feedback can be displayed appropriately because it might help a learner to correct her choice of a method or its details. Since the proof planner generates feedback in a technical format the learner is not supposed to understand, the GUI-Mediator has to interpret and filter this information to provide the learner with useful, comprehensible and possibly adaptive feedback.

## 5    Adaptive Suggestions of the Glass-Box Service MULTI

The functionalities of black-box services, such as computer algebra systems, are mostly restricted to their original purpose and only few of them can be employed for means of adaptation. For instance, the computer algebra system MAPLE [12] can be called with assumptions for all following computations (e.g., $a > 0$) or certain functions can be excluded from the interaction. The restrictions may not be principled in nature and extensions similar to those described above may accommodate more adaptivity.

Compared with black-box systems the adaptive usage of glass-box systems such as MULTI can be handled more easily. The simple reason is that we have more control over the functions of the glass-box and the extended architecture allows for adaptations. In what follows, we describe some directions of the adaptivity for the interactive proof plan scenario in more detail.

### Adapting the Configuration

The list of all parameters of a scenario is called a configuration. A configuration for interactive proof planning comprises

– a proof planning strategy,
– a set of suggestion agents,
– the level of automation.

The interactive proof planner comprises an agent-based mechanism for suggesting commands, which specify a method and the arguments necessary for its application to the current proof (see [4] for a detailed description). The set of suggestion agents controls the level of freedom in the interaction with the proof planner. It can be more or less restricted, more or less guided, and it can encode tutorial strategies such as the deliberate introduction of faulty suggestions for learning from failure.

The Exercise Composer computes an initial set of agents from the specifications of methods to be considered for the exercise problem. For instance, one set of agents suggests only applicable methods with all parameters instantiated. Another set of agents suggests only a partially specified method application, which has to be completed by the student.

If the author of an ACTIVEMATH exercise wants to have a particular suggestion, e.g., a suggestion that corresponds to a typical error, then special agents can be added. The Exercise Composer evaluates these additional agents and combines them with the automatically generated ones.

Two other parameters of the interactive proof planning scenario that are determined by the Exercise Composer are 'strategy' and 'level of automation'. Proof planning strategies can implement different ideas for proving. That is, different strategies tackle a proof planning problem in a different way. If the Exercise Composer selects a strategy for the problem at hand, then it computes at least one agent for each method of the strategy. Some of the methods are pretty irrelevant for learning and therefore are applied automatically. The set of all those methods is called the level of automation.

**Selection of a Strategy**

A (proof) problem may be solvable by different (proof planning) strategies that represent different ideas of how to solve the problem. For instance, the general problem of classifying a residue class structure according to its algebraic properties (associativity, the existence of inverse elements, and isomorphy of residue classes) can be tackled by three different strategies (see [5]): the first strategy tries to solve the problem by applying known theorems, the second strategy reduces a residue class problem to a set of equations, which have to be solved, the third strategy introduces a case split over the (finitely many) elements of the residue class structure.

The Exercise Composer chooses a strategy depending on the concrete problem and on the knowledge of a learner (whether she knows the theorems that are the prerequisites of the first strategy, whether she knows the methods employed by a strategy) and her performance in previous exercises (e.g., when the other strategies have been trained already). Such configuration heuristics can be encoded by pedagogical rules. For instance

```
IF studentKnowledge(prerequisites (firstStrategy)) > medium
AND studentKnowledge(firstStrategy) < medium
THEN present exercise-for(firstStrategy)

IF  studentKnowledge(firstStrategy)  > medium
AND studentKnowledge(secondStrategy) > medium
AND studentKnowledge(thirdStrategy)  < medium
THEN present exercise-for(thirdStrategy)
```

**Selection of Agents**

If the goal is to most rapidly prove a conjecture and deep learning is unimportant, then the Exercise Composer generates agents for the configuration that check for applicability and provide only fully-specified, applicable suggestions. However, this is not a typical goal in learning to prove. Rather, learning involves to understand why a method is applicable, what a particular method is actually doing, and for which purpose it is applied. Such competencies may be better trained when input is requested from the student (rather than clicking only) or while making mistakes, discover, and correct them.

One method may correspond to several agents that differ in how specific their suggestions are, i.e., how much input is left to the student. For instance, an agent for a method, which has as arguments a goal and premises, can have suggesting agents for the premises or leave the selection of premises to the learner.

Depending on the student model and the learning goal of an exercise, the Exercise Composer chooses agents for a method that compute more or less complete suggestions. For instance, a novice learner would start with much support and fully-specified suggestions. For a more experienced learner, under-specification can force the learner to specify more input herself in order to discover and overcome misconceptions in the application of a method.

An author-specified agent may request further arguments. For instance, one method for residue class proofs uses a computer algebra system to simplify a modulo-equation. An agent added by the author requests from the student to input the resulting term in advance. During interactive proof planning this input is compared with the actual result of the computer algebra system computation. The idea behind such an agent is to stimulate the anticipatory reasoning of the learner.

### Level of Automation

The automation of the application of certain methods avoids bothering the learner with the specification of proof steps, which she already knows. Methods that decompose logical quantifiers and connectives are typical examples for automated methods. Moreover, methods that perform some normalization or re-writing of assumptions and goals can be applied automatically, in case the learner is diagnosed to understand the outcome of these methods.

## 6    Future Work

### 6.1    Extensions of the Architecture

The architecture in Fig. 1 (see section 4) enables a "one-shot" adaptive invocation of the MULTI service. That is, when the MULTI service is requested, the architecture enables the selection of a scenario and a configuration depending on the information in ACTIVEMATH. During exercising, the configuration may turn out to be inappropriate for the student. For instance, gaps or faulty suggestions may be to difficult for the student.

In order to allow for adaptation during an interactive exercise we are currently developing and integrating a local student model as well as diagnosis and feedback components into the architecture in Fig. 1.

Local Student Model. The local student model contains information about the user's actions during the proof session and mastery information relevant in that session. The local student model is maintained during the proof session only. It is initiated by the Exercise Composer with information from ACTIVEMATH's persistent student model. When a proof session terminates, the Evaluator interprets the information in the local student model and passes update information to ACTIVEMATH' persistent student model. The GUI-Mediator creates entries in the local learner history.

*Diagnose Component.* With the help of MULTI the diagnosis component analyzes the interactions of the learner as well as the proof progress during a session. It may use information in the local student model as well as information on the current proof state provided by the Scenario-Manager. The diagnosis component can change the local student model.

*Feedback Component.* The feedback component uses the diagnosed and collected information in order to compute reactions. This comprises verbal feedback for the user (via the GUI-Mediator), new suggestions, or the modification of the configuration, i.e., the scenario setting, during an exercise.

## 6.2    Deliver What the Learner Needs

Crucial for the application of MULTI for learning is a user-friendly GUI. This adaptive GUI has to hide technical details of the underlying proof engine. A first GUI will be specified based on the outcomes of Human Computer Interaction experiments with different groups of learners. Some features we identified already as crucial are a MathML-like quality of formula rendering, access of subformulas by mouse click, subformula drag&drop, and an input editor.

Beyond the mere presentation in a GUI, for many functionalities in MULTI (that can provide important information for an expert) we will have to examine by experiments whether and to which extend they are usable by particular groups of learners. As an example, consider the collection of constraints during the planning process in a constraint store and the application of a constraint solver. The constraint solver provides valuable information for proof planning such as detection of inconsistencies to guide the proof planning and construction of instantiations of meta-variables. For the usage of this information for learning we have to examine questions such as:

- for which learners is the provision of constraints suitable?
- in which form should constraints be shown to particular groups of learners?
- how should/can the consequences of actions to the constraint stores be demonstrated to learners? (e.g., the consequences of an instantiation of a meta-variable by the learner)
- which learners can deal with information such as that their current goal is inconsistent with some collected constraints?
- how should such information be provided to particular groups of learners?
- ...

## 7   Conclusion and Related Work

We described the architecture for the integration of a cognitive tool in a learning environment. For such a tool to be used for learning, additional components or features may have to be created rather than just a communication wrapper for Web-communication and brokerage.

We have shown how adaptivity can be introduced for a proof planning service in order to adapt to the context and the needs of the learner. The adaptivity is realized by extensions of MULTI as well as by the architecture that uses mediators that evaluate student model and context information to provide adaptive access to MULTI and to a GUI. The architecture emphasizes the separation of different functionalities by different components.

The concrete extensions of MULTI are tool-specific. However, such extensions can be developed for other glass-box systems as well.

For intelligent tutoring further components are necessary. In particular, we are currently designing a local student model and diagnosis and feedback components. Moreover, we started experiments to empirically test which functionalities of proof planning are suited for particular groups of learners and how to provide the functionalities to the learner in a usable way.

Aspinall describes in [1] the Proof General Kit, which provides a general architecture for the integration of proof assistants with so-called display engines. The architecture consists of a collection of communicating components centered around the Proof General Mediator, which interfaces all the components and handles the communication between the components. This approach clearly separates the GUI from the proof machinery and enables the integration of different proof assistents into a uniform framework with uniform presentations in different user interfaces. In our architecture, the mediators (the Exercise Composer and the GUI-Mediator) focus on the realization of adaptations.

### Acknowledgement

We thank numerous members of the ActiveMath-Group for their contributions in discussions.

## References

1. D. Aspinall. Proof general kit, white paper. 2002. Available from http://www.proofgeneral.org/kit.
2. A. Bundy. The use of explicit plans to guide inductive proofs. In *Proc. 9th International Conference on Automated Deduction (CADE-9)*, volume 310 of *LNCS*, pp. 111–120. Springer-Verlag, 1988.
3. M. Kohlhase. OMDOC: Towards an internet standard for the administration, distribution and teaching of mathematical knowledge. In *Proceedings Artificial Intelligence and Symbolic Computation AISC'2000*, 2000.
4. A. Meier, E. Melis, and M. Pollet. Adaptable mixed-initiative proof planning for educational interaction. *Electronic Notes in Theoretical Computer Science*, 2004. To appear.

5. A. Meier, M. Pollet, and V. Sorge. Comparing approaches to the exploration of the domain of residue classes. *Journal of Symbolic Computation, Special Issue on the Integration of Automated Reasoning and Computer Algebra Systems*, 34(4):287–306, 2002.

6. E. Melis, J. Buedenbender, E. Andres, A. Frischauf, G. Goguadse, P. Libbrecht, M. Pollet, and C. Ullrich. ACTIVEMATH: A generic and adaptive web-based learning environment. *Artificial Intelligence and Education*, 12(4):385–407, 2001.

7. E. Melis, C. Glasmacher, C. Ullrich, and P. Gerjets. Automated proof planning for instructional design. In *Annual Conference of the Cognitive Science Society*, pp. 633–638, 2001.

8. E. Melis and A. Meier. Proof planning with multiple strategies. In *First International Conference on Computational Logic*, volume 1861 of *LNAI*, pp. 644–659. Springer-Verlag, 2000.

9. E. Melis and J. Siekmann. Knowledge-based proof planning. *Artificial Intelligence*, 115(1):65–105, 1999.

10. E. Melis, J. Zimmer, and T. Müller. Extensions of constraint solving for proof planning. In *European Conference on Artificial Intelligence*, pp. 229–233, 2000.

11. G. Polya. *How to Solve it*. Princeton University Press, Princeton, 1945.

12. D. Redfern. *The Maple Handbook: Maple V Release 5*. Springer-Verlag, 1998.

13. K. Reiss, F. Hellmich, and J. Thomas. Individuelle und schulische Bedingungsfaktoren für Argumentationen und Beweise im Mathematikunterricht. In *Bildungsqualität von Schule: Schulische und außerschulische Bedingungen mathematischer, naturwissenschaftlicher und überfachlicher Kompetenzen. Beiheft der Zeitschrift für Pädagogik*, pp. 51–64. Beltz, 2002.

# Modeling Interactivity for Mathematics Learning by Demonstration

Miguel A. Mora, Roberto Moriyón, and Francisco Saiz

Escuela Politécnica Superior, Universidad Autónoma de Madrid
28049 Madrid, Spain
{Miguel.Mora, Roberto.Moriyon, Francisco.Saiz}@uam.es

**Abstract.** In this paper we present a mechanism for adding interactivity to static mathematical documents, which become interactive programs that allow students to practice the resolution of problems that involve symbolic computations. The designers that use this mechanism can work in the same environment used by students when solving the problems, and they don't need to know any programming language. The original problems can also be generalized, and sets of similar problems that can be solved using the same methods can be generated automatically. The mechanism described has been implemented in a computer system that has also collaborative capabilities.

## 1   Introduction

Explanations about mathematics methods, or examples about applications of these methods, are usually included in static documents in a style similar to textbook pages. These documents lack an important feature that is desirable in a learning environment, namely interactivity, which allows learners to get involved in the learning process in a more participative way. In this paper we present a mechanism for adding interactivity to static documents, and at the same time structuring in a hierarchical manner the presentation of the information contained in them.

In order to achieve the desired interactivity, it is essential to have an adequate level of structuring of the documents to be used. Mathematical documents usually consist of pieces of information with different levels of structure, such as formulae, graphics or text. This information is not usually structured according to rigid patterns, as opposed to computer-generated pieces of information, since for example it might correspond to pages within mathematics textbooks. In this context, semantic web efforts are well known to be addressed to the structuring of the information contained in documents, both in more general settings, [11], and in more particular ones, e.g. in mathematics [2], where they usually rely on mathematics representation languages, like MathML, [12].

Additionally, the parts that form mathematical documents, such as formulae or parts of them, are usually deeply interrelated. For instance, an explanation about a resolution method usually starts with some initial formulae and continues with a series of steps using them to generate new ones, which in turn can be

A. Asperti et al. (Eds.): MKM 2004, LNCS 3119, pp. 265–275, 2004.

utilized for new steps. A classical approach in order to deal with this issue, even though it should be mentioned that it is applied to purely numeric contexts, is the spreadsheet mechanism. On the other hand, formula evaluation is another major issue. For instance, it is usual to find the same value in a document several times with different degrees of evaluation, e.g. an arithmetical expression with parenthesis like $(3+1)^2$ that is evaluated by first evaluating the expressions between them, giving $3^2 = 9$. This also happens in the case of evaluations carried out by Computer Algebra Systems (CAS), [9], [10], where some mathematical expressions are completely evaluated. Sometimes these evaluations correspond to the resolution of a subproblem attached to a given resolution method. Besides, the degree of evaluation of the formulae is an issue that is not under a user's control.

Static documents basically serve as textbooks, with the added functionality of searching based on indexing, [2]. However, students prefer to get involved by making actions and receiving feedback from the documents. A basic example would be the case of spreadsheet documents where they not only can browse the information contained in them but they can also change values in certain cells, thereby receiving feedback showing them the result of the update of the constraints.

A richer case of interactivity corresponds to the situation where students are able to enter expressions and answers to prompts from a computer system, or to choose options presented to them. For instance, at those decision points a student can be asked to choose a resolution method and accordingly the system will enforce it. This is the case of MathEdu, [4], which provides a rich interaction capacity built on Mathematica, [10], or Calculus Machina, [7], another advanced tutoring system with other features comparable to those of MathEdu. Still, there exists today a lack of authoring tools that allow teachers to establish this kind of interactivity in a simpler way, specially starting from static documents which can serve as sources for establishing the questions. Moreover, the interactive applications developed with these authoring tools should adapt to different situations by including conditions for the applicability of the operations involved in a resolution method.

In this paper we present a mechanism of the type described above for creating a model for the interaction with the student during the resolution of problems of Mathematics. This mechanism has been implemented in ConsMath, [5], a computer system that can be used while learning parts of Mathematics that involve symbolic computations. The major features of the system are the following ones:

- ConsMath integrates both an authoring tool and an execution tool. By using the WYSIWYG authoring tool, teachers design interactive tutoring applications in an intuitive and simple way, due to the similarity of the environments used by teachers and students.
- The design process carried out by teachers is done by using programming by demonstration methods, [3], which is an important technique belonging to the field of Human-Computer-Interaction. Thus, at each instant designers work with specific examples of resolution methods, and they identify

those examples as particular cases of more general methods generating subsequently a more general and abstract model.

- By using ConsMath, an interactive application for the resolution of a certain pattern problem can be built in a simple way starting from a static document that shows the resolution for a particular problem. This initial document can be generated by the designer either from scratch or by using the ConsMath editor, which is able to import documents that include mathematical formulae written in the MathML language.
- ConsMath has been built using a collaborative framework, [6]. As a consequence of this, students can learn collaboratively and teachers can interactively monitor their actions, based on the interaction model created by teachers.

We have tested how ConsMath can be used for the design of interactive sets of problems. These tests have been performed by two math teachers. A collection of problems from the textbook [8] on ordinary differential equations has been designed. The teachers found that the resulting interactive problems are useful from the didactic point of view, the use of the tool is intuitive and simple, and they could not have developed anything similar without ConsMath. The teachers have also warned us that before using the system on a larger scale with less advanced users like students, the behaviour of the editor of math formulae should be refined. Since this editor is a third-party component, we are planning to replace it by our own equation editor in a future release.

The rest of the paper is structured as follows: in the next section we shall describe from users' perspective the use of ConsMath, i.e. teachers' point of view in the process of creating a model for the interactivity of these applications by means of specifications by demonstration, and students' point of view when using these models. We will do it by illustrating a relevant example. The following section will present a more detailed view of the system. Finally, conclusions will be presented about this work.

## 2    Using ConsMath

When working with ConsMath, students have to solve problems of Mathematics by answering the questions asked by the system. Fig. 1 shows the resolution of a problem for the computation of a limit, as it appears in the initial static document. Once the interactive problem is designed with ConsMath, the student can solve it. Then the statement is shown to him, and he has to answer the questions that are posed to him one after another. Fig. 2 shows the first question the system poses the student while solving the problem from Fig. 1.

As an example of the dialog that can take place between a student and the system, if the student decides that the first step in the resolution of the problem in Fig. 1 is substituting $\sin x$ by $x$ in the numerator, since they are equivalent infinitesimals, the system can show the student a simple case, like the computation of the limit of $(x - \sin x)/x^2$ ; this method obviously does not work. ConsMath can show the student the correct resolution of this simplified problem together with the incorrect one, both of which are generated automatically on the bases of the work done by the designer. After this, the student is asked again about the resolution of the original problem.

We shall describe now the way in which the designer can specify the dialog that takes place between the student and the system when in tutoring mode. When the designer starts his work with the initial static document, the resolution of the problem disappears and the statement of the problem stays in the screen. He can then add interactive components like the selection buttons in Fig. 2. The designer then specifies the actions to be taken when the student makes a selection by clicking on one of the possible choices; at this point the buttons disappear, the remaining part of the resolution of the problem appears again, and the designer can use it as part of the text to be shown to the student afterwards. He can also keep showing selection buttons or input fields until the problem is solved.

In order to specify the dialog that takes place in case the student makes a different choice in the first step, the designer can use the left arrow that appears in the upper part of the design window, which allows him to turn back step by step to the same situation shown in Fig. 2. Then he can click on another button and start again the corresponding specification. The same can be done at each step of the resolution.

The limit in Fig. 1 can be computed in several ways, like using L'Hôpital's rule or substituting the functions that appear by their Taylor expansion up to some degree. ConsMath, that can generate the problem randomly, is able to notice while the student is working which the possible methods of resolution are, and adapt accordingly its reaction to the answers given by the student. For example, in the case shown in Fig. 2, only the second, fourth, fifth and last possibilities are accepted. The fifth possibility gives rise to more questions that finally lead to a deadlock where the student has to recognize that the problem can not be solved, while the other possibilities can give rise to successful resolutions of the problem. Problem statements are generated randomly from statement patterns. These patterns include generalized formulae like the following one, which generalizes the formula in the problem in Fig. 1:

$$\lim_{x \to 0} \frac{A + Bx + C \sin x + Dx^2 + Ex \sin x + F \sin^2 x}{x^m \sin^n x} \tag{1}$$

where A , B , C , D , E , F , m and n can have arbitrary values within some bounds fixed by the designer. Many times the designer imposes other conditions on the initial generalized formulae. In the previous example, the designer can ask naturally for the existence of two coefficients in the numerator that are not null. In this case, when building a new specific statement, the coefficients are generated randomly one or more times until the desired condition is satisfied. ConsMath includes generators of random numbers within given intervals (integer or rational), and generators of random mathematical expressions of specific forms like polynomials or simple trigonometric functions. For example, in the previous pattern the numerator might also have been defined as a polynomial of degree 2 in x and sin x with the condition that it is not a monomial.

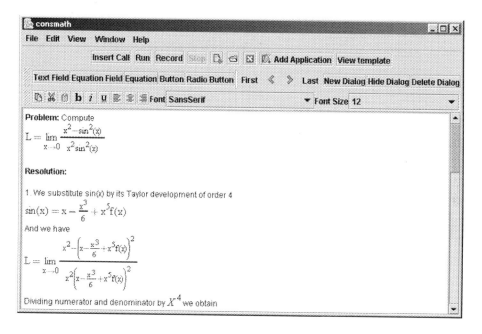

**Fig. 1.** Problem statement

During the design of a problem, designers can alternate the way each formulae is shown between the specific formulae and the corresponding generalized one. This can be done by clicking on the formula with the right button of the mouse and making the choice they want. If the formula is not generalized, the generalized view will show the same information as the specific one. By editing the generalized formulae, designers can design them, as well as they can see the effect of their design on a specific example.

When a formula depends on another one, like when substituting sin x by its Taylor expansion,

$$x - \frac{x^3}{6} + x^5 f(x) \tag{2}$$

ConsMath allows designers to propagate the generalization from the original formula to the other one by means of a spreadsheet mechanism based on the use of constraints among parts of formulae. For example, the numerator of the third formula in Fig. 1 can be generalized to

$$A + Bx + C(x - \frac{x^3}{6} + x^5 f(x)) + Dx^2 + Ex(x - \frac{x^3}{6} + x^5 f(x)) + F(x - \frac{x^3}{6} + x^5 f(x))^2 \tag{3}$$

and its value is substituted automatically in it. The same effect can also be obtained by giving the function within the limit in formula 1 a name like $Q$, and substituting sin x by formula 2 instead of the quotient in the third formula in Fig. 1. In this expression, the arrow indicates that a substitution has to be made. This can be done by just editing the generalized formula as indicated in the previous paragraph.

As said before, each time a pattern is defined in order to generalize an initial formula, the designer can specify a condition that must be satisfied. This can be done by typing a condition in the corresponding input field that depends on the variables defined in the previous generalization process. Similarly, each time the designer specifies the behaviour of the system when the student makes a choice, he can specify a condition for its application. This can be done in the same way. Hence, for example, the designer can specify that the first choice in Fig. 1 can be accepted in case $A = B = D = 0$ by just typing this condition on the corresponding input field.

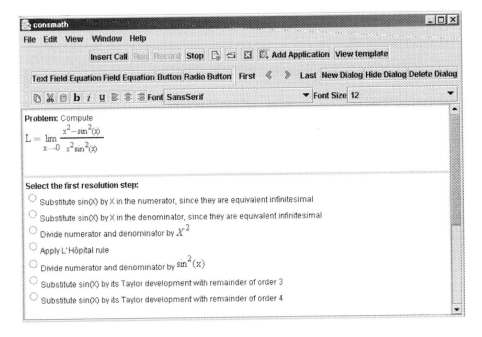

**Fig. 2.** Choice during problem resolution

Analogously, designers can specify that the questions to be asked to the students when solving problems depend on the specific problem that is being solved. For example, in case $A = B = D = 0$ in the above generalized problem, it makes sense to ask the student if he wants to factorize $\sin x$ in the numerator. This is also specified by means of conditions attached to the multiple choice buttons that show the different choices that are available in general. From this point of view, ConsMath is an adaptive system that admits different ways of resolution and reacts in different ways to the actions of the students depending on the specific problems that are being solved. Although a lot of work has been done in the last years in adaptive tutoring systems, none of them depends on deep properties of mathematical formulae and they have many limitations from the point of view of the interactive specification of the problems without the need of any programming.

## 3    ConsMath Architecture and Model

ConsMath consists of several java applications that are distributed according to a client-server architecture (Fig. 3). It allows designers to create courses as described in the previous section and, besides, both the execution and the design of these courses can be done in a collaborative manner.

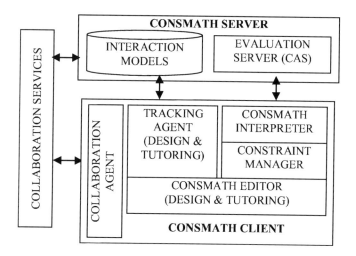

**Fig. 3.** ConsMath Architecture

In order to clarify the behaviour of ConsMath components, we will firstly describe each of them. These components are the following ones:

- An editor of mathematical texts, which supports symbolic relations among its components, and the specification of the interactivity using a programming by demonstration approach. This editor has two execution modes: the design mode (used by teachers), and the tutoring mode (used by students), which does not provide all the functionality of the design mode.
- The ConsMath server, which has a twofold functionality. Firstly, it serves as a central repository of courses or interaction templates, as courses are saved persistently creating a library, and secondly it provides mathematical expression evaluation capabilities. This second functionality is performed by using a CAS (currently Mathematica), so that that ConsMath Server acts

as a bridge between the CAS and the clients. As a consequence of these two functionalities, the ConsMath server simplifies the maintenance of the system and reduces costs, given that the clients just need the existence of one CAS running, which is at the server side, and the courses do not have to be replicated at each student's machine. The ConsMath server communicates with each client using Java Remote Method Invocation (Java RMI).

— The tracking agent is the component in charge of writing the interaction models during the design phase, and of interpreting these models in the tutoring phase.

— The constraint manager is the component that keeps all the dependencies in the document updated, sending to the ConsMath interpreter the expressions to be evaluated. Consequently, parts of these expressions need to be evaluated by the CAS, in which case the interpreter sends them to the ConsMath server for their evaluation.

— The collaboration agent is the ConsMath component which communicates with the collaboration services included in FACT, the collaboration framework used by ConsMath [6], in order to provide collaborative tutoring and designing support. The collaboration services are used by ConsMath users to participate collaboratively in the reviewing process as teachers or in the solving process as students. FACT is also written in Java and has a Client-Server architecture that communicates with the collaboration agent of each ConsMath client using Java RMI. FACT plays two main roles, firstly, it is a structured repository of collaborative sessions, which allows the users of the system, students or tutor, to collaborate in a problem resolution or review others work asynchronously, and secondly, it manages the synchronous collaborative sessions, so the users of each synchronous session share the same information and the same state of the ConsMath clients.

ConsMath users interact most of the times with the ConsMath editor. This editor can be used both by designers to create an interaction model and by students to execute this model. What designers do is to simulate user's actions and the answer of the system to these actions, by using programming by example techniques as described in the previous section. The tracking agent interprets these actions at design time to create the interaction model. When the editor is in tutoring mode, the agent listens to the actions of the student to find the answer that must be given, according to the interaction model, and reproduces this answer. In the rest of this section we will describe the document model of the ConsMath Editor, and the interaction model.

## 3.1    ConsMath Document Model

In order to simplify the interaction, ConsMath documents can be divided in subdocuments, which can be hidden or locked to prevent the interaction of students with some parts of the document when in tutoring mode.

Each subdocument is formed by HTML text combined with components that represent its non-textual part. The components that form ConsMath documents can show formulae that correspond to MathML expressions or graphical functions. These components can be editors or browsers. There are also controls for the input of MathML expressions, multiple choice controls, buttons, and list boxes.

The ConsMath's constraint manager can relate the properties of the components. For example, ConsMath allows the construction of graphics that are updated automatically depending on some formulae that appear in the document. The constraint manager allows the specification of the properties of a component as ConsMath expressions, just like in a spreadsheet. Properties of components can be values or boolean conditions, like a property that specifies if a component is visible or not. On the other hand, the expressions that can define a property can include functions to give a name to some part of the expression, creating a variable, functions that evaluate an expression, or that incorporate the value of another variable in the expression, or functions that generate a mathematical expression randomly, with an associated pattern and a condition that the expression must satisfy.

The constraint system is also responsible for the automatic conversion as needed between different types of expressions (boolean, MathML, Mathematica or OOCSMP, [1] properties). For example, the visible property of a component can be associated to a condition to indicate when that component must be shown. This condition can be written in MathML with embedded ConsMath functions. It can be specified using a WYSIWYG content MathML editor.

## 3.2     Interaction Model

The interaction model is represented by a tree where each path, from the root to each leaf of the tree, defines an abstract interaction sequence. Final interaction sequences can be more complex, because the abstract sequence can have cycles and calls to other interaction sequences, creating complex interaction models.

This model is written by the tracking agent in the design phase creating a tree with two different interlaced zones, decision zones and performance zones. Decision zones are sub-trees with information to discriminate the different situations that can be produced by the student actions. This information is acquired by the tracking agent when listening to the actions of the designer when simulating the situations that can be produced later during the execution of the model by the students. For example, the designer can simulate that the student introduces the correct answer, later the designer goes back to the initial situation by using the left arrow that appears into the upper part of the design window, as shown in figure 2, according to the explanation given in section 2, and introduces an invalid answer, creating a simple decision tree with only two alternatives.

Each leaf of a decision tree is followed by a sequence of actions, in the performance zone, that correspond to the changes in the ConsMath Document that will take place after the situation described in the previous path of the decision tree is detected. The information of the actions in the performance zones is acquired by the tracking agent by listening to the actions of the designer when in performance state. Also, performance zones can contain calls to other interaction models, or jumps to other points in the interaction tree.

In order to create the interaction model the designer navigates through the model going backward and forward creating new alternatives in a decision tree or creating new performance sequences for a particular decision path, etc. The tracking agent follows the designer actions, creating new nodes of information in the tree that represents the interaction model. A typical decision tree is formed by a sequence of events for each alternative. At run-time, when the tracking agent is listening to the events produced by the interaction of students with the current document model, and the agent recognizes one of the sequences, it emits the corresponding answer that is codified in the performance zone of the interaction tree. The answer usually consists of a new sub-document of ConsMath, with a dialog, and another decision tree, or a call to another interaction model, which usually corresponds to a subproblem call.

Also, the interaction model supports the combination, in any order, of different types of decision trees, forming more complex decision trees. These types are:

- Sequence decision tree: Is a tree where a path is matched when all events in the path take place in the order described by it.
- And decision tree: Is similar to the sequence decision, but the events can take place in any order.
- Or decision tree: In this case only one of the events described in a path of the decision tree is necessary in order to match that path.

The techniques described in this section allow the construction of a system as described in Section 2.

## Acknowledgements

The work described in this paper is part of the Ensenada and Arcadia projects, funded by the National Plan of Research and Development of Spain, projects TIC 2001-0685-C02-01 and TIC2002-01948 respectively.

## References

1. M. Alfonseca, J. Lara. Simulating evolutionary agent colonies with OOCSMP. In 17th ACM Symposium on Applied Computing (SAC'2002), track on AI and Computational Logic, Madrid, 2002, pp. 11–15.
2. A. Asperti, L. Padovani, C. Sacerdoti Coen, F. Guidi, I. Schena. Mathematical Knowledge Management in HELM. In MKM 2001 (First International Workshop on Mathematical Knowledge Management), RISC, Schloss Hagenberg, 2001.
3. A. Cypher. Watch what I do. Programming by Demonstration. MIT Press, Cambridge, MA, 1993.
4. F. Diez, R. Moriyon. Solving mathematical exercises that involve symbolic computations. Computing in Science and Engineering 6(1), 2004, pp. 81–84.

5. M.A. Mora, R. Moriyón, F. Saiz. Building mathematics learning applications by means of ConsMath. In Proceedings of IEEE Frontiers in Education Conference. Boulder, CO, 2003.

6. M.A. Mora, R. Moriyón, F. Saiz. Developing applications with a framework for the analysis of the learning process and collaborative tutoring. International Journal Cont. Engineering Education and Lifelong Learning 13(3/4), 2003, pp. 268–279.

7. D. Quinney. Computer-Based Diagnostic Testing and Student Centered Support. In C. Beevers (ed.), Computer-Aided Assessment in Mathematics Series. Learning and Teaching Support Network, 2001.

8. G.F. Simmons. Differential equations: with applications and historical notes. McGraw-Hill, 1981.

9. A. Sorgatz, R. Hillebrand. MuPAD. In Linux Magazin 12/95, 1995.

10. S. Wolfram. The Mathematica Book (fourth edition). Cambridge University Press, 1999.

11. World Wide Web Consortium (W3C). W3C Semantic Web. http://www.w3.org/2001/sw/.

12. World Wide Web Consortium (W3C). The MathML Language. http://www.w3.org/Math/.

# Extraction of Logical Structure
# from Articles in Mathematics*

Koji Nakagawa[1], Akihiro Nomura[2], and Masakazu Suzuki[1]

[1] Faculty of Mathematics, Kyushu University,
Kyushu Univ. 36, Fukuoka, 812-8581 Japan
{nakagawa,suzuki}@math.kyushu-u.ac.jp
[2] Graduate School of Mathematics, Kyushu University

**Abstract.** We propose a mathematical knowledge browser which helps people to read mathematical documents. By the browser printed mathematical documents can be scanned and recognized by OCR (Optical Character Recognition). Then the meta-information (e.g. title, author) and the logical structure (e.g. section, theorem) of the documents are automatically extracted.

The purpose of this paper is to show the extraction method of logical structure specialized for mathematical documents. We implemented this method in INFTY which is an integrated OCR system for mathematical documents. In order to show the effectiveness of the method we made a correct database from an existing mathematical OCR database, and made an experiment.

## 1   Introduction

Computers became indispensable devices for mathematics. This phenomenon can be seen by the success of mathematical systems (e.g. Mathematica, Maple) which have been being used for various other fields such as physics and economics.

In order to apply mathematics to the real world, mathematical knowledge should be stored in computers in a way that people can easily use. Even if more and more mathematics is done in formal ways, most of mathematical knowledge is still stored in papers or books. Therefore digitizing mathematical text is still important.

### 1.1   Levels of Digitization

There are several kinds of mathematics digitization. Adams gave some classifications of digitization of mathematics[1]. Based on this consideration, in this paper we introduce five levels of mathematics digitization.

---

* This work is (partially) supported by Kyushu University 21st Century COE Program, Development of Dynamic Mathematics with High Functionality, of the Ministry of Education, Culture, Sports, Science and Technology of Japan.

A. Asperti et al. (Eds.): MKM 2004, LNCS 3119, pp. 276–289, 2004.

- level 1: bitmap images of printed materials (e.g. GIF, TIFF),
- level 2: searchable digitized document (e.g. PS, PDF),
- level 3: logically structured document with links (e.g. HTML, MathML, LaTeX),
- level 4: partially executable document (e.g. Mathematica, Maple),
- level 5: formally presented document. (e.g. Mizar[6], OMDoc[4])

Currently most of mathematical knowledge is stored and used mainly in printed materials (level 1) such as books or journals. For being used actively it is preferable that mathematical text is stored in a possibly higher level of digitization. However since making documents digitized to a higher level needs quite a lot of efforts, digitization of mathematical knowledge has not been enhanced so far. Therefore we definitely need software in order to automatize the digitization process in a possibly higher level.

## 1.2   Technologies for Automatization

The automatization can be achieved step by step:

- level 1 to level 2: OCR (Optical Character Recognition),
  In order to retrieve searchable digitized document from bitmap images, OCR is used. With OCR, character sequences can be recognized from bitmap images and then they can be used for searching words. Especially recognition of mathematical formulae is the most important in recognizing mathematical documents. The mathematical formulae recognition has been well investigated, e.g. [8].
- level 2 to level 3: Extracting Logical Structure and Hyper Links,
  Obtained data after OCR are basically characters having positions in a page structured by lines and areas. They do not directly contain meta-information (e.g. author, title) of a paper and structural information (e.g. section, subsection). Also they do not have hyper links which point to internal and external documents.
- level 3 to level 4: Semantics Recognition from Presentation,
  Sometimes executable blocks (e.g. mathematical expressions, algorithms) appear in mathematical text. In level 3 mathematical expressions are described in a two-dimensional (presentational) way. We need to extract semantic expressions from these presentational expressions. Mathematica[10] has standard collections of these transformation rules which retrieve semantics of presentational expressions and one can even define their own style of notation (See `MakeExpression` function in [10]).
- level 4 to level 5: Understanding Mathematical Document,
  Usually mathematical statements such as definitions, lemmata, theorems, and proofs are written in natural languages in books or papers. Therefore for treating them in computers we need natural language processing. The first step of the natural language processing is parsing. For parsing it is common to make a corpus which is a set of grammar rules extracted from

used expressions. Making a corpus for mathematical statements was achieved by Baba and Suzuki[2]. After parsing, formalizing written mathematical description to logical formulae in a predicate logic can be achieved. Formalized statements can be used for proving in computers by theorem provers such as Theorema[3].

Since current our mathematical activities range over all digital levels, we need software which covers these all technologies from scanning to proving in a coherent manner. The ultimate goal is that scanned mathematical papers are processed and the software system gives us whether proofs are correct, though this goal is very ambitious.

Since the ultimate goal is quite ambitious, as a sub-goal we propose a mathematical knowledge browser which covers from level 1 to level 3 in Section 2. In order to make such a browser, some technologies are necessary. One of the technologies is to extract logical structure from documents after OCR. In Section 3 we discuss the method of extracting logical structure from mathematical documents. In order to show the effectiveness of the method, we made a correct database which can represent logical structure information based on an existing mathematical database for OCR, and experimented for the correct database. In Section 4 the correct database is described and the experimental result will be shown. Then we conclude the discussion in Section 5.

## 2    Mathematical Knowledge Browser

The mathematical knowledge browser helps people to do mathematics from level 1 to level 3. One of inputs for this mathematical knowledge browser is a printed mathematical document. A printed document can be scanned, and then processed by OCR. After OCR logical structure and hyper links are automatically extracted and shown to users.

We will implement this mathematical knowledge browser on an integrated OCR system for mathematical documents called INFTY[8] (INFTY can be downloaded[1]). INFTY reads scanned page images of a mathematical document and provides their character recognition results. One of the distinguished characteristics of INFTY is that it can recognize two-dimensional mathematical expressions. INFTY has a graphical user interface which can show mathematical expressions in the ordinary two-dimensional mathematical notation, and has a manual error correction interface. The recognition results can be saved in various formats, e.g. XML (called KML), HTML, LaTeX, Mathematica, and braille.

### 2.1    User Interface

The browser consists of three panes: structure pane, reference pane, browsing pane (Fig. 1). In the structure pane located in the left side, structural information is shown as a tree like a file manager. The browser pane on the right bottom and

---

[1] http://infty.math.kyushu-u.ac.jp/index-e.html

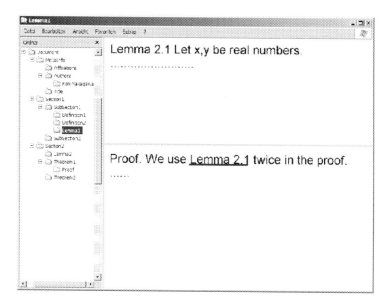

**Fig. 1.** Screen Image of Mathematical Knowledge Browser (Sketch)

the reference pane on the right top show mathematical text. By clicking a link in the browser pane, the text pointed by the link will be shown in the reference pane so that people won't lose the attention in the browser pane. For example, by clicking the link 'Lemma 2.1' the reference pane shows 'Lemma 2.1' while the browser pane does not change.

## 2.2    Showing Relationship of Mathematical Theory Structure

Usually in a mathematical paper, mathematical components (e.g definitions, lemmata, theorems) have dependencies and one can construct a graph which shows the dependencies. With the mathematical knowledge browser one can see such dependency graphs. Fig. 2 shows an example of such a graph. For example, suppose 'Lemma 3.1' is used in the proof of 'Theorem 4.2', the text 'Lemma 3.1' should appear in the proof of 'Theorem 4.2'. From this fact we can detect the dependency automatically. By this functionality, readers can recognize theory structure of a paper before reading into details.

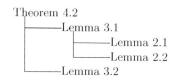

**Fig. 2.** Graph of Theory Dependency

Of course, showing theory structure is not a new idea. However the important point is that theory structure can be automatically extracted from printed mathematical documents.

## 3  Extracting Meta-information and Logical Structure

For realizing the mathematical knowledge browser, we need several technologies. One of the technologies is to extract meta-information and logical structure from mathematical documents. In this section, we discuss the method to extract automatically meta-information and logical structure.

There are several studies of logical structure extraction from documents. Extensive surveys can be found in papers[5, 7]. In these studies target documents vary from general documents to specific documents. The work presented in this paper is unique because it is specialized for mathematical documents and it extracts mathematical specific components (e.g. Theorem, Proposition). The method proposed in this paper does not need to know layout styles beforehand, while some other studies do.

### 3.1  Data Representation for Meta-information and Logical Structure

INFTY[8] produces the following nested structure as output from scanned images as input.

- 1st page (size and position in the page)
  - 1st area (size and position in the page)
    * 1st line (size and position in the page)
      · 1st character (code, size and position in the page)
      · 2nd character (code, size and position in the page)
      · ...
    * 2nd line
    * ...
  - 2nd area
    * 1st line
      · 1st character
      · ...
    * ...
- 2nd page
- ...

A document contains several pages and each page contains several areas which have positions and sizes in the page. An area can contain lines which also have their positions and sizes in the page. A line has recognized characters with positions, sizes and font styles.

INFTY produces output in a XML format called KML. We extended the KML format so that it can represent meta-information and logical structure.

For example, Fig. 3 shows a result output in the extended KML for a scanned image shown in Fig. 4. The top element is 'Doc' which contains some 'Sheet' elements representing pages. A 'Sheet' element contains some 'Area' elements whose positions and sizes are indicated by 'rect' attributes. The value of the 'rect' attribute "$left,up,right,down$" indicates the positions of left, up, right, down borders of the rectangle. An 'Area' element contains a 'Text' element having a 'Field' element. A 'Field' element has several 'Line' elements which have again several 'Char' elements.

For the need of putting additional information for meta-information and logical structure we added the 'tag' attribute for the 'Text' element in order to represent the type of the text field. The values of the 'tag' attribute are 'PageHeader', 'PageNumber', 'Caption', 'Title', 'AuthorInfo', 'AbstractHeader', 'Abstract', 'Keywords', 'Heading1', 'Heading2', 'Heading3', 'Heading4', 'Heading5', 'Text', 'ReferenceItem', 'Definition', 'Axiom', 'Theorem', 'MainTheorem', 'Proposition', 'Corollary', 'Lemma', and 'Footnote'.

## 3.2   Extraction Algorithm

The algorithm of extracting meta-information and logical structure works in two steps: segmenting areas in a page and putting appropriate tags to the areas. In Fig. 4, areas are indicated by gray rectangles and their tags are put beside the rectangles. An area can be either a special text area (page number, running header, captions of tables and figures, footnotes, and headings) or a normal text area which can be a mathematical component (e.g. theorem, definition). Later the method to extract mathematical components is described in details. After the correct process of putting tags, the conversion to a logically structured format (e.g. HTML, OMDoc) is straightforward.

**Segmentation**  Segmentations can be done in the following three ways:

- Segmentation by Spacing
  By using spacing information, scanned images are separated into several areas which can be either text areas, figure/table areas, or formulae areas.
- Segmentation by Style Difference
  For each text area, the average size of the characters contained in the area is calculated. The size of a character can be determined by the height of the character. Also boldness can be calculated by the horizontal width of a character. In an area when the styles (bold, italic, and size) of lines are obviously different from those of other lines, they are separately segmented.
- Segmentation by Keywords
  In an area, when a special keyword of mathematical components (e.g. Theorem, Lemma, Definition) comes in the beginning of a line, basically the area is segmented before the line. However sometimes there are cases that keywords do not indicate beginnings of mathematical components. This issue will be discussed in the next subsection.

```
<Doc version="1.1" language="English" ...>
 <Sheet id="1" doc_file_name="Arkiv_1997.kml"
   image_file_name="Arkiv_1997_185.tif" height="4438" width="3015" ...>
  <Area rect="148,129,1801,266" id="1" ...>
   <Text rect="148,129,1801,266" tag="PageHeader" ...>
    <Field base_char_size="16,30,13,41" sub_char_size="11,20,9,28">
     <Line id="1" rect="148,129,1086,195">
      <Char code="0141" rect="148,133,195,180" ...>A</Char>
      <Char code="0172" rect="200,151,223,180" ...>r</Char>
       ...
     </Line>
     <Line id="2" rect="149,200,1801,266">
      ...
  </Area>
  <Area rect="279,948,3022,1239" id="2" ...>
   <Text rect="279,948,3022,1239" tag="Title" ...>
   ...
  </Area>
   ...
 </Sheet>
 <Sheet id="2" doc_file_name="Arkiv_1997.kml"
   image_file_name="Arkiv_1997_186.tif" height="4432" width="3002" ...>
  <Area rect="229,169,326,215" id="1">
   <Text rect="229,169,326,215" tag="PageNumber" ...>
    <Field base_char_size="16,28,12,39" sub_char_size="11,19,8,26">
     <Line id="1" rect="229,169,326,215">
   ...
   </Text>
  </Area>
  <Area rect="1088,168,2358,228" id="2">
   <Text rect="1088,168,2358,228" tag="PageHeader" ...>
    <Field base_char_size="16,29,12,40" sub_char_size="11,20,8,27">
     <Line id="1" rect="1088,168,2358,228">
   ...
  </Area>
  <Area rect="231,405,3224,701">
   <Text tag="Theorem">
    <Field>
     <Line id="1" rect="392,405,3224,486">
      <Char code="2154" rect="392,410,452,467" bold="1"...>T</Char>
      <Char code="2168" rect="458,409,506,467" bold="1"...>h</Char>
       ...
  </Area>
 <CharInfo>... </CharInfo>
</Doc>
```

**Fig. 3.** Example of KML Output from INFTY OCR Engine

Ark. Mat., 35 (1997), 185–199
© 1997 by Institut Mittag-Leffler. All rights reserved [PageHeader]

# Extension of smooth CR mappings between non-essentially finite hypersurfaces in $\mathbf{C}^3$
[Title]

Henri-Michel Maire and Francine Meylan[1] [AuthorInfo]

## 0. Introduction
[Heading1]

Let $M$ be a real analytic hypersurface in $\mathbf{C}^3$ containing 0 and let $M'$ be the algebraic hypersurface in $\mathbf{C}^3$ defined by

$$(0.1) \qquad \operatorname{Im} w' = |z_1'|^2 + \operatorname{Re} w'|z_2'|^2, \quad (z_1', z_2', w') \in \mathbf{C}^3.$$

For any $b' < 0$, the function $(z', w') \mapsto 1/(w' - ib')$ is holomorphic in $\mathbf{C}^3 \setminus \{w' = ib'\} \supseteq M'$; therefore its restriction to $M'$ is a CR function which does not extend holomorphically around $(0, 0, ib')$. A classical argument using Baire's category theorem (see [HT, p. 125]) guarantees the existence of a CR function on $M'$ which does not extend to a full neighborhood of $0 \in \mathbf{C}^3$. In contrast, for CR mappings we have the following result.
[Text]

**Theorem 1.** *If $h: M \to M'$ is a smooth CR local diffeomorphism at 0 with $h(0) = 0$, then $h$ extends to a holomorphic mapping in a full neighborhood of 0 in $\mathbf{C}^3$.*
[Theorem]

As we shall see in Corollary 1.2, if $h$ satisfies the hypothesis of the theorem (more generally if $h$ is of finite multiplicity) then $M$ is of finite type. After Treprean's theorem we know that any CR function on $M$ extends holomorphically to *one* side of $M$; therefore Theorem 1 is equivalent to a reflection principle (cf. Baouendi and Rothschild [BR3]). Because we do not assume $M$ to be algebraic, and because $M'$ is not essentially finite, Theorem 1 does not follow from the recent results of Baouendi Huang and Rothschild [BHR] nor from those of Baouendi and Rothschild [BR2]. Notice that $M'$ is holomorphically non-degenerate in the sense of Stanton [S].

Theorem 1 may be generalized as follows.
[Text]

(1) The second author was partially supported by the Swiss NSF Grant 2000-042054.94/1. [Footnote]

**Fig. 4.** Example of Scanned Image Separated by Areas

**Putting Tags to Areas.** After the segmentation process, appropriate tags are put to these segmented areas. Here we describe criteria to decide appropriate tags for areas.

- **Title and Headings** (e.g. section, subsection)
  In order to put tags to these area, areas are ordered by the following lexico-graphic ordering through a document.

$$\langle Size, AllCapital, HCapital, Bold, Italic\rangle$$

  $Size$:     average size of characters contained in the area
  $AllCapital$:true if all characters are written in capital (e.g. SYSTEM)
  $HCapital$ : true if only head characters are written in capital (e.g. System)
  $Bold$:     true if characters are written in bold
  $Italic$:     true if characters are written in italic

  The 'Title' tag is put to areas appeared in the upper part of the first page and is written in the largest area according to the lexicographic ordering above. Headings usually start from either some numbers separated by periods or special keywords like 'Introduction', 'References', 'Bibliography' in an emphasized (large/bold/italic) font. The tags 'Heading1','Heading2', $\cdots$ are put to the second, third, $\cdots$ largest areas in the lexicographic order.
- **Author Information**
  The tag 'AuthorInfo' is put to areas which come next to the title before headings or the abstract.
- **Page Header, Footnote, and Page Number**
  The 'PageHeader'('Footnote') tag is put to areas positioned in the top (bot-tom) of pages and written in smaller fonts than the average font size of text areas in a paper. The 'PageNumber' tag is put to areas which appear on the bottom or upper right or upper left of a page and consist of numbers in Arabic style or in Roman style (e.g. i, ii, iii, and iv).
- **Mathematical Components** (e.g. definition, lemma, theorem)
  The tags for mathematical components are put to areas which start from the special keywords such as 'Theorem' and 'Definition'. Here the problem is that these special keywords do not always indicate beginnings of mathematical components. The problem will be discussed in the next subsection.

### 3.3    Two Difficulties in Extraction of Mathematical Components

Correct extraction of mathematical components are important for further pro-cessing of mathematical documents, e.g. indexing, construction of dependency graphs, and understanding of mathematical statements. Here we describe two difficulties for extracting mathematical components.

**Looking for Beginnings of Mathematical Components.** Basic idea of de-tecting beginnings of mathematical components is to look for special keywords (e.g. Theorem, Lemma, and Definition). However these special keywords do not always indicate beginnings of mathematical components.

For example in Fig. 5, the 6th line starts with the keyword 'Proposition', but it is not the beginning of a proposition declaration. It appears in text in order to refer the 'PROPOSITION 3.4' defined above. In Fig. 5 proposition com-ponents start from the keyword with all capital characters 'PROPOSITION' which

PROPOSITION 3.4. —— *Suppose that* $\alpha \geq 1$. *If* $f, g \in L^2_\alpha$ *and* $\bar{\partial}^*_\alpha f$ *and* $\bar{\partial} g$ *are in* $L^2_\alpha$ *as well, then* $(\bar{\partial}^*_\alpha f, g)_\alpha = (f, \bar{\partial} g)_\alpha$. *That is,* $f \in L^2_\alpha$ *is in* Dom $\bar{\partial}^*_\alpha$ *if and only if* $\bar{\partial}^*_\alpha f$ *is in* $L^2_\alpha$.

Since the the image of $\bar{\partial}: L^2_{\alpha, q-1} \rightarrow L^2_{\alpha, q}$ is equal to $\mathcal{K}_\alpha$ for $q \geq 1$, we have in particular that $f \in L^2_{\alpha, q}$ is in $\mathcal{K}^1_{\alpha, q}$ if and only if $\bar{\partial}^*_\alpha f = 0$. Proposition 3.4 is an immediate consequence of Proposition 3.3 and the following approximation lemma.

LEMMA 3.5. —— *Suppose that* $\mathcal{P}$ *is a first order linear differential*

**Fig. 5.** Looking for Beginnings of Mathematical Components

distinguish from other keywords like 'Proposition'. However we can not assume that keywords of beginnings are written in all capital characters, because there are many other papers which have different styles. Therefore we need a general algorithm in order to detect styles of mathematical components. In Section 3.4 the method will be described in details.

**Looking for Endings of Mathematical Components.** Looking for endings of mathematical components is not so easy task. For example, in Fig. 6, the fifth line is the ending of the lemma. In this case, the lemma is written in italic till the fifth line and from the sixth line it turns into normal font. Therefore the ending of the lemma can be detected. It is usual that lemmata or theorems are written in italic. Of course we can not assume that these components are written in italic. Additionally definitions usually are not written in italic. Another criterion can be indentation or space between lines. In this paper, we simply look for the style change from italic to normal font for mathematical components except definitions, and for definitions we look for indentation.

LEMMA 4.1.   i)  *If* $x \in H^*(G/H ; k)$ *is transgressive with respect to the bottom fibering, then the element* $p^*(x) \in H^*(G ; k)$ *is universally transgressive.*
  ii)  *If* $x \in H^*(G ; k)$ *is universally transgressive then so is* $j^*(x) \in H^*(H ; k)$.
  iii)  *If* $H^i(G/H ; k) = 0$ *for* $i < n$, deg $x < n-1$ *for* $x \in H^*(G ; k)$ *and if* $j^*(x)$ *is universally transgressive, then* $x$ *is also universally transgressive.*
  These follow from the naturality of the transgression.
  The following result is due to Borel [4] (see also Baum-Browder [2]).
  LEMMA 4.2. *We can choose generators* $a, x_7, x_{11}, \cdots, x_{8n+3} \in H^*(PSp(2n+1) ; Z_2)$ *such that* $H^*(PSp(2n+1) ; Z_2) = Z_2[a]/(a^4) \otimes \wedge (x_7, x_{11}, \cdots, x_{8n+3})$ *where* deg $a = 1$ *and* $\pi^*(x_{4i-1}) = e_{4i-1}$, $i = 2, 3, \cdots, 2n+1$, *for the projection* $\pi : Sp(2n+1) \rightarrow PSp(2n+1)$.

**Fig. 6.** Looking for Endings of Mathematical Components

When a mathematical component spreads over more than one page, failure detection of 'PageHeader', 'Footnote', 'PageNumber' causes failure of looking

**Table 1.** Lin2e Features

| Line Feature | Explanation |
|---|---|
| BK-Definition | The line begins from the keyword 'Definition'. |
| BK-Theorem | The line begins from the keyword 'Theorem'. |
| BK-Proposition | The line begins from the keyword 'Proposition'. |
| BK-Corollary | The line begins from the keyword 'Corollary'. |
| BK-Lemma | The line begins from the keyword 'Lemma'. |
| K-Italic | The keyword is written in italic. |
| K-Bold | The keyword is written in bold. |
| K-LCapital | All characters of the keyword are in large capital. (e.g PROPOSITION) |
| K-SCapital | Most of characters of the keyword are in small capital. (e.g. PROPOSITION) |
| Indented | The line is indented. |

for endings of mathematical components. Therefore detection of 'PageHeader', 'Footnote', 'PageNumber' is very important.

### 3.4    Algorithm for Detecting Styles of Mathematical Components

In a paper, for a mathematical component the formatting style is uniform in principle. The idea of the algorithm for detecting styles of mathematical components is to use the style uniformity of a mathematical component.

The algorithm for detecting styles of mathematical components is described in Fig. 7. At first features shown in Table 1 are extracted from lines, and then for each line two style values 'lineDefStyle' and 'lineCompStyle' are calculated. The variable 'lineDefStyle[i]' stores the style value of the $i$th-line and is for detecting the beginning of a definition mathematical component. The variable 'lineCompStyle[i]' is for detecting other mathematical components, since most of the cases styles of mathematical components except definitions are the same. If the line does not start from a special keyword of mathematical components, the style value becomes '-1' which means that it can not be the beginning of a mathematical component. Then the most frequent style values in a paper decide the styles of beginning lines of mathematical components and the style values are assigned to the variables 'defStyle' and 'compStyle'. Finally when the style value of a line is not '$-1$' and it coincides with the most frequent value, the line is the beginning of a mathematical component and the process of looking for the ending is executed.

## 4    Experiment

In order to see the effectiveness of the algorithm we made an experiment for a correct database.

### 4.1    Outline of Database

We added new information for logical structure to a large-scale database of mathematical documents[9, 8] and made the correct database which can be used

```
// calculating the style value for each line
for i=1 to number_of_lines(paper) {
 lf=extract_features(paper.line[i]) // extracting line features
 // The number '-1' means that the line can not be
 // the beginning of a mathematical component.
 lineDefStyle[i]= if(lf.BK-Definition, stylefunc(lf), -1);
 lineCompStyle[i]=if(lf.BK-Theorem || lf.BK-Proposition ||
       lf.BK-Corollary || lf.BK-Lemma, stylefunc(lf), -1);
}
// detecting most frequent style values
defStyle =most_frequent(lineDefStyle);
compStyle=most_frequent(lineCompStyle);
// looking for endings
for i=1 to number_of_lines(paper){
 if(!(defStyle==-1) && lineDefStyle[i]==defStyle) {
        segmentArea();
        look_for_ending_by_Indent(i);}
 if(!(compStyle==-1)&& lineCompStyle[i]==compStyle) {
        segmentArea();
        look_for_ending_by_Italic(i);}
...
};
int styleFunc(LineFeatures lf)
{ return (lf.K-Italic*2^0+lf.K-Bold*2^1+lf.K-LCapital*2^2+lf.K-SCapital*2^3
          +lf.Indented*2^4); }
...
}
```

**Fig. 7.** Algorithm for Detecting Styles of Mathematical Components

for the experiment. The documents contained in the database are 29 English articles on pure mathematics (issued in 1970 - 2000). Basically for each journal two old and new papers are selected. The numbers of pages and characters in the database are 422 and 706,279, respectively. This database is larger than other databases used in the past researches on math-OCR.

All pages were scanned in 600 dpi and binarised automatically by the same commercial scanner (RICOH imagio Neo 450). The quality of resulting page images are noisy and include a lot of abnormal characters, such as touching characters and broken characters. The maximum and minimum abnormal character rates, which represent the quality of images, are 12.6% and 0.11%, respectively.

### 4.2    Experimental Result

We implemented the algorithm within the INFTY system and compared with the correct database described above. The result is summarized in Table 2. When there are miss-recognitions of characters, the keywords used for detection are not effective for looking for beginnings of mathematical components. Therefore it is considered that 'Success'+'Miss-Recog.' approximates the real success numbers for the method described in this paper.

**Table 2.** Experimental Result

| TagName | Correct | Success | Begin-AreaErr | End-AreaErr | TagErr | Miss-Recog. | Rate1 (%) | Rate2 (%) |
|---|---|---|---|---|---|---|---|---|
| PageHeader | 425 | 418 | 1 | 3 | 3 | 0 | 98.4 | 98.4 |
| PageNumber | 398 | 381 | 11 | 0 | 6 | 0 | 95.7 | 95.7 |
| Title | 28 | 27 | 0 | 1 | 0 | 0 | 96.4 | 96.4 |
| AuthorInfo | 28 | 23 | 1 | 3 | 1 | 0 | 82.1 | 82.1 |
| Header1 | 126 | 113 | 2 | 1 | 10 | 0 | 89.7 | 89.7 |
| Header2 | 14 | 13 | 0 | 1 | 0 | 0 | 92.9 | 92.9 |
| Footnote | 16 | 10 | 5 | 0 | 1 | 0 | 62.5 | 62.5 |
| Definition | 31 | 24 | 3 | 4 | 0 | 0 | 77.4 | 77.4 |
| Theorem | 116 | 103 | 6 | 6 | 1 | 2 | 88.8 | 90.5 |
| Main theorem | 2 | 2 | 0 | 0 | 0 | 0 | 100.0 | 100.0 |
| Proposition | 91 | 83 | 5 | 3 | 0 | 0 | 91.2 | 91.2 |
| Corollary | 36 | 31 | 3 | 0 | 2 | 2 | 86.1 | 91.7 |
| Lemma | 107 | 92 | 8 | 6 | 1 | 2 | 86.0 | 87.9 |
| Total | 1418 | 1320 | 45 | 28 | 25 | 6 | 93.1 | 93.5 |

'Correct'          number of areas in the correct database.
'Success'          number of success tagging by the method proposed in this paper.
'Begin-AreaErr'  number of errors to detect beginnings of areas.
'End-AreaErr'    number of cases which detected beginnings of areas,
                        but failed to detect endings of areas.
'TagErr'           number of errors that different tags were put.
'Miss-Recog.'     number of miss-recognitions by OCR for the special keywords.
'Rate1'             success rate computed by Success/Correct $*$ 100.
'Rate2'             success rate computed by (Success + Miss-Recog.)/Correct $*$ 100.

Main reason of the failures in detecting mathematical components is that the method fails to detect endings of mathematical components because of the simple ending detection method. Improving the method will improve the recognition rate.

## 5    Conclusion

A method of extracting meta-information and logical structure from mathematical documents was presented and implemented on the base of the INFTY system. In order to show the effectiveness of the method, we made an experiment and the recognition rate was 93.1% in the practical situation including miss-recognitions of characters by OCR. We are now increasing the number of papers contained in the correct database in order to experiment for larger amount of papers.

The improvement of the recognition accuracy can be achieved by giving additional information to the system. For example, knowing journal names, which may be automatically extracted from running headers, can contribute to the accuracy, because a journal has its own format. Also when the system fails to detect logical structure, a little human interaction can contribute to the accuracy.

With the facility of automatic linking, we will be able to implement the mathematical knowledge browser based on the INFTY system. The mathematical knowledge browser can be extended to a system for editing mathematical documents. With the editor one can input mathematical statements in formalized formulae. The formalized formulae can be sent to computing, solving, proving services located in the Internet and the results can be obtained. Namely it can be used as a front-end for mathematical services. We expect this mathematical knowledge browser to become a digitalization tool for mathematics, and enhance mathematical activities.

# References

1. A.A. Adams. Digitisation, Representation and Formalisation: Digital Libraries of Mathematics. In MKM 2003 Proceedings, LNCS 2594. Springer, 2003.
2. Y. Baba and M. Suzuki. An Annotated Corpus and a Grammar Model of Theorem Description. In A. Asperti, B. Buchberger, and J.H. Davenport (eds.), *Second International Conference, MKM 2003, Bertinoro, Italy*, pp. 93–104, Feb. 2003.
3. B. Buchberger, C. Dupre, T. Jebelean, F. Kriftner, K. Nakagawa, D. Vasaru, and W. Windsteiger. The Theorema Project: A Progress Report. In *Symbolic Computation and Automated Reasoning*, pp. 98–113. A.K. Peters, 2001.
4. M. Kohlhase. OMDoc: An Infrastructure for OpenMath Content Dictionary Information. *SIGSAM Bulletin*, 34(2):43–48, 2000.
5. S. Mao, A. Rosenfeld, and T. Kanungo. Document Structure Analysis Algorithms: A Literature Survey. In *Document Recognition and Retrieval X*, number 5010 in Proceedings of SPIE, pp. 197–207, January 2003.
6. P. Rudnicki. An Overview of the Mizar Project. In *Proceedings of the 1992 Workshop on Types for Proofs and Programs*, Bastad, 1992. http://mizar.org.
7. K.M. Summers. *Automatic Discovery of Logical Document Structure*. PhD thesis, Cornell University, 1998.
8. M. Suzuki, F. Tamari, R. Fukuda, S. Uchida, and T. Kanahori. INFTY – An Integrated OCR System for Mathematical Documents. In *ACM Symposium on Document Engineering (DocEng '03), Grenoble, France, Nov. 20–22*, 2003.
9. S. Uchida, A. Nomura, and M. Suzuki. Quantitative Analysis of Mathematical Documents. Submitted.
10. S. Wolfram. *The Mathematica Book, Fifth Edition*. Wolfram Media, Inc., 2003.

# Improving MIZAR Texts with *Properties* and *Requirements*

Adam Naumowicz[1] and Czesław Byliński[2]

[1] Institute of Computer Science, University of Białystok, Poland
[2] Section of Computer Systems and Teleinformatic Networks,
University of Białystok, Poland
{adamn, bylinski}@mizar.org

**Abstract.** In this paper we report on the current state of implementation of two features of the MIZAR system – *properties* and *requirements*. These two mechanisms provide elements of basic computer algebra to strengthen the capabilities of the MIZAR checker by automation of some frequently used reasoning steps. This, in turn, allows for a notable reduction of the size of users' input in some reasonings. As a result, the size of the MIZAR library can be reduced, and, at the same time, MIZAR articles can become more like informal mathematical papers.

## 1 Introduction

The original goal of the MIZAR project was to design and implement a software environment to support writing traditional mathematics papers. Mathematical practice shows that even in formal proofs some easy background reasoning can, and in many cases should, be reduced for the sake of clarity and the comfort of both writers and readers. Although MIZAR inference checker uses model elimination with stress on processing speed (not power), its power can be extended in several ways (cf. [15]). Typically, such extensions are coded in EQUALIZER – the module responsible for the equality calculus in the MIZAR checker (cf. [20]). In this paper we describe the current state of implementation of two features which serve that goal. Namely, we discuss how certain properties can be associated with MIZAR definitions and how the requirements directive can strengthen the process of inference justification in MIZAR. Their effects can substantially reduce the amount of justification an author must provide in a proof. Used in connection with suitable management utilities these features stimulate the growth and evolution of the MML[1].

---

[1] The Mizar Mathematical Library (MML) is the official database of MIZAR articles. Its systematic collection started in 1989. At the time of this writing it contains 842 articles (about 60 MB of MIZAR texts).

A. Asperti et al. (Eds.): MKM 2004, LNCS 3119, pp. 290–301, 2004.

## 2   Properties

As described in [17], there are four main kinds of constructors in MIZAR: predicates, functors, modes, and attributes. MIZAR allows for special automated processing of certain properties of the first two types. When a symbol of a given property is included in a definition of a predicate or a functor, a suitable formula can be automatically used by the MIZAR checker in every inference step which concerns that constructor. In that case, corresponding statements and references to these statements become superfluous. Of course, the properties are paired with a justification of suitable correctness conditions which we describe in the sequel. We also discuss the restrictions which seem necessary to avoid a collapse of type system consistency.

The properties currently implemented for predicates (constructors of formulae) include: `asymmetry`, `connectedness`, `irreflexivity`, `reflexivity`, and `symmetry`, so they are applicable to binary predicates. The properties for functors (constructors of terms) are: `commutativity`, `idempotence`, `involutiveness`, and `projectivity`. The tables below present the number of occurrences of all properties in the current MML (ver. 4.09.842).

| Predicate property | Occurrences |
|---|---|
| reflexivity | 91 |
| symmetry | 85 |
| connectedness | 9 |
| irreflexivity | 8 |
| asymmetry | 4 |

| Functor property | Occurrences |
|---|---|
| commutativity | 121 |
| idempotence | 85 |
| projectivity | 9 |
| involutiveness | 8 |

Some of the occurrences are a result of specifically intended MML revisions. Others were introduced originally by authors of new contributions encouraged to use properties where applicable. It should be also possible to identify already existing MML definitions suitable for introducing properties with MMLQuery.

### 2.1   Predicate Properties

In general, a MIZAR predicate with properties is of the form:

```
definition
  let x be θ₁;
  let y be θ₂;
  pred Example_Pred x,y means
    δ(x,y);       ::  the definiens of the predicate
  predicate-property-symbol proof ... end;
  ...
end;
```

where predicate-property-symbol stands for one of the following: asymmetry, connectedness, irreflexivity, reflexivity, and symmetry (in the current implementation the properties are allowed only when the types $\theta_1$ and $\theta_2$ are equal).

The set of implemented predicate properties is not purely accidental as it may appear at first glance. One may easily check that they form the set of all meaningful universal formulae which can be obtained by combining occurrences of $P[x, y]$ and $P[y, x]$ with logical connectives (reflexivity and irreflexivity being a special case with $x = y$). Moreover, since every MIZAR predicate can have an antonym, each property must have a counterpart related to the antonym. One may observe that reflexivity automatically means irreflexivity for an antonym and vice versa. The same can be said for the pair connectedness and antisymmetry. Obviously, symmetry of an original constructor and its antonym are equivalent.

The following table contains a summary of predicate properties with suitable justification formulae. Examples of all properties taken from MML are presented below.

| Predicate property | Formula to be proved as justification |
|---|---|
| asymmetry | for x,y being $\theta_1$ holds $\delta$(x,y) implies not $\delta$(y,x) |
| connectedness | for x,y being $\theta_1$ holds not $\delta$(x,y) implies $\delta$(y,x) |
| irreflexivity | for x being $\theta_1$ holds not $\delta$(x,x) |
| reflexivity | for x being $\theta_1$ holds $\delta$(x,x) |
| symmetry | for x,y being $\theta_1$ holds $\delta$(x,y) implies $\delta$(y,x) |

We can illustrate asymmetry with the MIZAR primitive 'in' predicate. This predicate property has no accompanying justification because it is built into the MIZAR system (the article HIDDEN ([12]) which documents built-in notions).

```
definition
  let x,X be set;
  pred x in X;
  asymmetry;
end;
```

To demonstrate connectedness we can look at the redefinition of inclusion for ordinal numbers (ORDINAL1, [3]).

```
definition
  let A,B be Ordinal;
  redefine pred A c= B;
  connectedness
```

```
  proof
    let A,B be Ordinal;
    A in B or A = B or B in A by Th24;
    hence thesis by Def2;
   end;
end;
```

Here, Th24 and Def2 refer to:

```
theorem Th24:
 for A,B being Ordinal holds A in B or A = B or B in A
```

```
definition let X be set;
 attr X is epsilon-transitive means :Def2:
  for x being set st x in X holds x c= X;
end;
```

An example of a predicate with `irreflexivity` is the proper inclusion of sets (`XBOOLE_0:def` $8^2$, [7]). It sometimes happens, as in this example, that the condition is simply obvious for the checker, because in the definition block the definiens is automatically available.

```
definition let X,Y be set;
 pred X c< Y means :Def8:
  X c= Y & X <> Y;
 irreflexivity;
end;
```

As an example of the `symmetry` property we can show a predicate satisfied whenever two sets have empty intersection (`XBOOLE_0:def` 7, [7]).

```
definition
 let X,Y be set;
  pred X misses Y means :Def7:
   X /\ Y = {};
  symmetry;
end;
```

An example of `reflexivity` is the divisibility relation for natural numbers (`NAT_1:def` 3, [1]) presented below:

```
definition
 let k,l be natural number;
  pred k divides l means :Def3:
   ex t being natural number st l = k * t;
  reflexivity
```

---

[2] The phrase *Article-Identifier*:def *Definition-Number* follows the convention which identifies all MIZAR definitions in the MML.

```
proof
  let i be natural number;
  i = i * 1;
  hence thesis;
  end;
end;
```

We should note that a concept similar to predicate properties could also be implemented for modes since they are in fact special kinds of predicates. For example, reflexivity seems useful for a mode constructor like 'Subset of'.

## 2.2    Functor Properties

The binary functor properties in MIZAR are commutativity and idempotence. In general, we write a binary functor with properties in the following form:

```
definition
  let x be θ₁; let y be θ₂;
    func Example_Func(x,y) -> θ₃ means
      δ(it,x,y);
    binary-functor-property-sym bolproof ... end;
  ...
end;
```

where binary-functor-property-sym bol is commutativity or idempotence, and MIZAR reserved word 'it' in the definiens denotes the value of the functor being defined.

| Binary functor property | Formula to be proved as justification |
|---|---|
| commutativity | for x being $\theta_3$, y being $\theta_1$, z being $\theta_2$ holds $\delta$(x,y,z) implies $\delta$(x,z,y). |
| idempotence | for x being $\theta_1$ holds $\delta$(x,x,x) |

An example with both binary functor properties is the set theoretical join operator (XBOOLE_0:def 2, [7]).

```
definition
  let X,Y be set;
    func X \/ Y -> set means :Def2:
      x in it iff x in X or x in Y;
    existence proof ... end;
    uniqueness proof ... end;
    commutativity;
    idempotence;
  end;
```

With current implementation, the `commutativity` is only applicable to functors for which the result type is invariant under swapping arguments. Furthermore, `idempotence` requires that the result type be wider than the type of the argument (or equal to it).

MIZAR unary functors with properties use the form below:

```
definition
  let x be θ₁;
  func Example_Func(x) -> θ₂ means
    δ(it,x);
  unary-functor-property-symbol proof ... end;
  ...
end;
```

where unary-functor-property-symbol is `involutiveness` or `projectivity`. The system consistency is protected by the restriction that types $\theta_1$ and $\theta_2$ be equal.

| Unary functor property | Formula to be proved as justification |
|---|---|
| involutiveness | for x,y being $\theta_1$ holds δ(x,y) implies δ(y,x) |
| projectivity | for x,y being $\theta_1$ holds δ(x,y) implies δ(x,x) |

The `involutiveness` is used for example in the definition of the inverse relation (`RELAT_1:def 7`, [21]).

```
definition
  let R be Relation;
  func R˘ -> Relation means :Def7:
    [x,y] in it iff [y,x] in R;
  existence  proof ... end;
  uniqueness  proof ... end;
  involutiveness;
end;
```

As an example of the `projectivity` property we give the functor for generating the absolute value of a real number (`ABSVALUE:def 1`, [16]).

```
definition
  let x be real number;
  func abs x -> real number equals :Def1:
              x if 0 <= x
              otherwise -x;
  coherence;
  consistency;
  projectivity by REAL_1:66;
end;
```

Here, `REAL_1:66` ([14]) refers to:

```
theorem :: REAL_1:66
  for x being real number holds x < 0 iff  0 < -x;
```

Due to some problems in implementation the `idempotence`, `involutiveness`, and `projectivity` properties are still not available for redefined objects.

# 3    Requirements

The `requirements` directive, which is comparatively new in MIZAR, allows for special processing of selected constructors. Unlike the properties described in Section 2, it concerns the `environ` part of a MIZAR article (cf. [17]). With the `requirements` directive, some built-in concepts for selected constructors will be imported during the accommodation stage of processing an article (importing information from the database to create a local environment). In the MML database they are encoded in special files with extension '.dre'. As yet, the special files in use are: `HIDDEN`, `BOOLE`, `SUBSET`, `NUMERALS`, `REAL`, and `ARITHM`[3]. Below we describe how they assist the MIZAR checker with the work of reasoning so that the amount of justification an author must provide can be reduced[4].

However, the approach adopted in the MIZAR system is to use possibly minimal set of internally built-in requirements. It is preferable to use as much as possible "natural" MIZAR techniques. For instance, this is often the case with attributes where a quite powerful mechanism of cluster registrations is used to provide significant automation of reasoning (cf. 3.5).

## 3.1    Requirements HIDDEN

This directive is automatically included during accommodation of every article and therefore does not need to be used explicitly. It identifies the objects defined in the axiomatic file `HIDDEN`, i.e., the mode `set` followed by the '=' and 'in' predicates (`HIDDEN:def 1` - `HIDDEN:def 3`, [12]). Mode `set` is the most general MIZAR mode and every other mode widens to it. Thanks to the identification provided by `requirements HIDDEN` it is used internally wherever the most basic MIZAR type is needed, e.g. while generating various correctness conditions. The fundamental equality predicate '=' is extensional which means that two objects of the same kind (atomic formulae, types, functors, attributes) are equal when their arguments are equal. This particular property is used frequently by the MIZAR checker. The '=' relation is also symmetric, reflexive and transitive. Predicate

---

[3] Historically, the first `requirements` directive was `ARYTM`, introduced in 1995. It is also the one which has been changed most recently (the name was also changed into `ARITHM` in 2003).

[4] Recently, the MIZAR Library Committee decided to provide special articles covering the proofs of requirements which can be formulated as MIZAR statements (cf. [8],[6],[13],[10], and [5]).

'in' plays an important role in the 'unfolding' of sentences with the Fraenkel operator in positive and negative contexts. This allows sentences of the form ex y being $\theta$ st x=y & P[y] to be true whenever x in {y being $\theta$ : P[y]} is true and vice versa. Various features of the 'in' predicate are considered in conjunction with other requirements (cf. Sections 3.2, 3.3).

## 3.2    Requirements BOOLE

When processing an article with requirements BOOLE, MIZAR treats specially the constructors provided for the empty set ({}), attribute empty, set theoretical join (\/), meet (/\), difference (\) and symmetric difference (\+\) given in definitions XBOOLE_0:def 1–XBOOLE_0:def 6, [7]. It allows the following frequently used equations to be accepted without any external justification: X \/ {} = X, X /\ {} = {}, X \ {} = X, {} \ X = {}, and {} \+\ X = X. The empty set also gets additional properties: x is empty implies x = {}, and similarly x in X implies X is non empty. Finally, the attribute empty is added to all occurrences of the numeral 0 and, similarly, non empty to all other numerals. Additional features concerning emptiness are also described in 3.3, 3.4, and 3.5.

## 3.3    Requirements SUBSET

This requirements directive concerns the definition of inclusion (TARSKI:def 3, [18]), the power set (ZFMISC_1:def 1, [4]) and also mode 'Element of' (SUBSET_1 :def 2 with a redefinition that follows it, [19]). Inclusion and the power set are denoted as c= and bool, respectively. With this directive, X c= Y automatically yields X is Element of bool Y and vice versa (a shortcut mode notation X is Subset of Y can be used instead of X is Element of bool Y). The property of the form x in X & X c= Y implies x in Y is incorporated as well[5]. Also, when processing x in X the condition x is Element of X is generated. When BOOLE is also applied in the requirements directive, the formula x in X is equivalent to x is Element of X & X is non empty (cf. 3.2). Additionally, x in X & X is Element of bool Y yields Y is non empty.

## 3.4    Requirements NUMERALS

This directive enables special processing of the successor operator (ORDINAL1:def 1, cf. [3]). The value of succ is calculated for variables with numeric value, so for example statements like x=2 implies succ(succ(succ(x))) = succ(succ(3)) are accepted automatically. Another function of this directive is to generate the type Element of omega for any numeral, so in fact to provides the correspondence between numerals and numbers defined in the MML. With an empty requirements directive numerals are just names for (not fixed) sets. This requires also SUBSET to be present in the requirements directive in order to understand the mode 'Element of'.

---

[5] Formerly, it was an extensively used MML theorem BOOLE:11.

The attribute `natural` (`ORDINAL2:def` 21, cf. [2]) is also identified with this directive, but currently there is no special processing for it in the MIZAR checker.

## 3.5  Requirements REAL

Comparing to the previous implementation described in [15], the role of this directive has completely changed as a result of the changes in the internal representation of numeric values. The features formerly associated with `REAL` are now a part of `ARITHM` (cf. 3.6). Currently, this directive identifies the ordering relation on real numbers (`<=`) and the attributes `positive` and `negative` (`XREAL_0:def` 2-4, cf. [11]) Each occurrence of x `<=` y is processed according to the following attribute calculus:

- if x is `positive` then y is `positive`
- if y is `negative` then x is `negative`
- if x is `non` `negative` then y is `non` `negative`
- if y is `non` `positive` then x is `non` `positive`

Any negated occurrence of x `<=` y yields the following:

- if x is `non` `positive` then y is `negative`
- if y is `non` `negative` then x is `positive`

When the directive `BOOLE` is also used (the attribute `zero` is a synonym for `empty` which can be used for numbers), the checker accepts additionally the following clauses:

```
x <= y & y is non zero & x is non negative implies y is positive
x <= y & x is non zero & y is non positive implies x is negative
```

It would be possible to include also other (more specific) conditions on the attributes. But according to the adopted approach to use (when possible) "natural" MIZAR mechanisms rather than built-in knowledge, other consequences should be available to the checker as a result of processing conditional cluster registrations (`XREAL_0`, cf. [11]) as below:

```
registration
  cluster positive -> non negative non zero (real number);
  cluster non negative non zero -> positive (real number);
  cluster negative -> non positive non zero (real number);
  cluster non positive non zero -> negative (real number);
  cluster zero -> non negative non positive (real number);
  cluster non negative non positive -> zero (real number);
end;
```

This directive is also required by the MIZAR checker to automatically set the order between numerals.

### 3.6    Requirements ARITHM

Current specification of `requirements ARITHM` concerns the basic operations on complex numbers: addition (`+`), multiplication (`*`), the negative element (`-`), the inverse element (`"`), subtraction (`-`), and division (`/`) defined in `XCMPLX_0:def 4-9`, the attribute `complex` (`XCMPLX_0:def 2`), and also the imaginary unit `<i>` (`XCMPLX_0:def 1`, cf. [9]). The above functor constructors are used in EQUALIZER – the module responsible for the equality calculus in the MIZAR checker (cf. [20]) to associate every equivalence class (in a given inference step) with a unique symbolic polynomial in the canonical form:

$$a_0 + a_1 X_{i_1}^{k_{1,1}} \cdots X_{i_n}^{k_{n,1}} + \cdots + a_s X_{i_1}^{k_{i,s}} \cdots X_{i_n}^{k_{n,s}}$$

Each $X_{i_j}$ represents a term which is irreducible with respect to the above functor constructors and whose type widens to `complex number`, $a_j$ are numeric (complex) constants. Numeric values are represented as rational complex numbers (complex numbers with rational numbers as imaginary and real parts). The numerators and denominators of MIZAR numerals must not be greater than 32767 (the maximum value for a 16-bit signed integer), although all internal calculations are based on 32-bit integers. This implementation, however, is about to change in near future in order to enable calculations on integers of arbitrary length.

This apparatus allows for significant reduction of user's input in reasonings involving numbers. Quite complicated equalities are now accepted by the checker with no additional justification, like in the following example:

```
z*2*(x+y)/2-z*z = ((z*(x-(z+-1*y)))+(z*(x-(z-y))))*2"
```

where both sides are equal because they are reduced internally to the polynomial $xz + yz - z^2$. At the same time, thanks to the calculus of polynomial forms, the associativity of arithmetic operations is also solved automatically, which was often reported by users as one of the most irksome hindrances in using the MIZAR system.

## 4    Conclusions

The idea of implementing properties and requirements was based on statistical observations showing extensive usage of special constructs. Introduction of these techniques has a strong influence on the shortening of reasoning in many situations, which is immediately reflected in the maintenance of the MML.

However, the distinction between the function of properties and requirements is not always clear. In some cases, it is hard to decide which of these techniques is the best implementation. Requirements are much more flexible, but on the other hand, properties are a regular language construct and are not so system dependent. Every MIZAR user can decide whether or not to use properties for newly created definitions while a new `requirements` directive yields a partial reimplementation of the system. Moreover, some of the features currently implemented as requirements could be transformed into some kind of properties. In particular, it concerns the properties of neutral elements as described e.g. in 3.2. There is still discussion on what would be the best syntax for such a `neutrality` property.

We believe that the techniques worked out in the process of implementing `requirements ARITHM` (cf. 3.6) can also be applied more generally. It appears suitable to enable automation of reasonings concerning arbitrary ring operations, or to implement the highly desirable `associativity` property for functors. Another scope of our interest, following the authors' requests, is e.g. the implementation of `transitivity` and `antisymmetry` for predicates.

# References

1. G. Bancerek. The Fundamental Properties of Natural Numbers. *Journal of Formalized Mathematics*, 1, 1989, `http://mizar.org/JFM/Vol1/nat_1.html`.
2. G. Bancerek. Sequences of Ordinal Numbers. *Journal of Formalized Mathematics*, `http://mizar.org/JFM/Vol1/ordinal2.html`.
3. G. Bancerek. The Ordinal Numbers. *Journal of Formalized Mathematics*, `http://mizar.org/JFM/Vol1/ordinal1.html`.
4. C. Byliński. Some Basic Properties of Sets. *Journal of Formalized Mathematics*, `http://mizar.org/JFM/Vol1/zfmisc_1.html`.
5. Library Committee. Basic Properties of Real Numbers – Requirements. *Journal of Formalized Mathematics*, Requirements, 2003, `http://mizar.org/JFM/Reqmnts/real.html`.
6. Library Committee. Basic Properties of Subsets – Requirements. *Journal of Formalized Mathematics*, Requirements, 2003, `http://mizar.org/JFM/Reqmnts/subset.html`.
7. Library Committee. Boolean Properties of Sets – Definitions. *Journal of Formalized Mathematics*, Encyclopedia of Mathematics in Mizar, 2002, `http://mizar.org/JFM/EMM/xboole_0.html`.
8. Library Committee. Boolean Properties of Sets – Requirements. *Journal of Formalized Mathematics*, Requirements, 2002, `http://mizar.org/JFM/Reqmnts/boole.html`.
9. Library Committee. Complex Numbers – Basic Definitions. *Journal of Formalized Mathematics*, Encyclopedia of Mathematics in Mizar, 2003, `http://mizar.org/JFM/EMM/xcmplx_0.html`.
10. Library Committee. Field Properties of Complex Numbers – Requirements. *Journal of Formalized Mathematics*, Requirements, 2003, `http://mizar.org/JFM/Reqmnts/arithm.html`.
11. Library Committee. Introduction to Arithmetic of Real Numbers. *Journal of Formalized Mathematics*, Encyclopedia of Mathematics in Mizar, 2003, `http://mizar.org/JFM/EMM/xreal_0.html`.
12. Library Committee. Mizar Built-in Notions. *Journal of Formalized Mathematics*, Axiomatics, 1989, `http://mizar.org/JFM/Axiomatics/hidden.html`.
13. Library Committee. Numerals – Requirements. *Journal of Formalized Mathematics*, Requirements, 2003, `http://mizar.org/JFM/Reqmnts/numerals.html`.
14. K. Hryniewiecki. Basic Properties of Real Numbers. *Journal of Formalized Mathematics*, `http://mizar.org/JFM/Vol1/real_1.html`.

15. A. Naumowicz and C. Byliński. Basic Elements of Computer Algebra in MIZAR. *Mechanized Mathematics and Its Applications*, Vol. 2: 9–16, 2002, http://markun.cs.shinshu-u.ac.jp/mizar/mma.dir/2002/MMA_2002_paper_2_for_web.html.

16. J. Popiołek. Some Properties of Functions Modul and Signum. *Journal of Formalized Mathematics*, http://mizar.org/JFM/Vol1/absvalue.html.

17. P. Rudnicki and A. Trybulec. On Equivalents of Well-Foundedness. An Experiment in MIZAR. *Journal of Automated Reasoning* **23:** pp. 197–234, 1999.

18. A. Trybulec. Tarski Grothendieck Set Theory. *Journal of Formalized Mathematics*, http://mizar.org/JFM/Axiomatics/tarski.html.

19. Z. Trybulec. Properties of Subsets. *Journal of Formalized Mathematics*, http://mizar.org/JFM/Vol1/subset_1.html.

20. F. Wiedijk. Checker. Available on WWW: http://www.cs.kun.nl/ freek/notes/by.ps.gz.

21. E. Woronowicz. Relations and Their Basic Properties. *Journal of Formalized Mathematics*, http://mizar.org/JFM/Vol1/relat_1.html.

# An Investigation on the Dynamics of Direct-Manipulation Editors for Mathematics[*]

Luca Padovani and Riccardo Solmi

University of Bologna, Department of Computer Science
Mura Anteo Zamboni 7, 40127 Bologna, Italy
{lpadovan, solmi}@cs.unibo.it

**Abstract.** Mathematical expressions are pieces of structured information that could benefit from direct-manipulation approaches for document authoring. Yet, not only there is disagreement on the behaviors
of authoring tools, but also these behaviors are often ill-designed and
poorly implemented. This situation leads to dissatisfaction amid users
who prefer more classical editing approaches.

In this paper we compare the behaviors of several state-of-the-art
editors for mathematical content and we try to synthesize a set of rules
and principles to make the authoring experience pleasant and effective.

## 1 Introduction

Direct-manipulation editors for mathematical content allow an author to edit in
place a mathematical formula as this is formatted and displayed on the screen
in its traditional notation. Editing and displaying occur simultaneously and the
formula is reformatted at every modification. These editors are usually characterized by the fact that they work on a structured representation of the document,
hence they fall in the category of model-based editors.

Despite their aim of being "friendlier", direct-manipulation editors turn out
to be rather unattractive to use for both unexperienced and advanced users since
they suffer from severe usability problems. In fact, they are more challenging
to design: the use of a structured model requires the editor to implement some
kind of incremental parsing meaning that user actions are mapped on non-trivial
operations on the model. At the same time, part of the information about the
model structure is not displayed in order to reduce the user's awareness of the
model and to provide a familiar, lightweight presentation. We claim that these
are not sufficient reasons that prevent the design of a direct-manipulation editor
with good, effective usability [9, 1].

While we do not aim to describe the behavior of the perfect model-based
editor for mathematical content, we can at least try to highlight the deficiencies
in the existing tools. The goal is to synthesize a set of principles inspired by
successful text-based editors and common usability guidelines and to provide a
qualitative evaluation of the examined math editors on these bases.

---

[*] This work was supported by the European Project IST-2001-33562 MoWGLI.

A. Asperti et al. (Eds.): MKM 2004, LNCS 3119, pp. 302–316, 2004.

The structure of the paper is as follows: in Section 2 we describe the dynamics of a number of direct-manipulation editors for mathematics. We enrich the prose of the descriptions with a graphical notation whose purpose is to capture the dynamic behavior of the editors on a static medium like the paper. In Section 3 we do a little step back to the world of text editors, for which a tighter and more standardized set of rules and behaviors have emerged over the years. The analysis of these rules will be the starting point for our proposal in Section 4, where we try to classify distinct and possibly orthogonal aspects of model-based editors, in particular editors for mathematics, and list some intuitive guidelines for their development. We conclude in Section 5 with a comparison of the tested editors.

## 2   Behaviors

We began our analysis by trying out a number of currently available editors to understand how behaviors were implemented and what rationales were behind the choices. The following is the list of the products that we have tried. Some of them are just software components whose only purpose is to display and edit mathematical formulas, others are more complex applications for which editing mathematics is only an auxiliary (sometimes indispensable) functionality:

1. **Amaya** version 8.2. W eb page: http://www.w3.org/Amaya/
2. **FrameMaker** by Adobe, version 7.
   W eb page: http://www.adobe.com/products/framemaker/main.html
3. **MathType** by Design Science, version 5.2.
   W ebpage:http://www.mathtype.com/en/products/mathtype/, see also[13].
4. **Scientific WorkPlace** by MacKichan Software, version 5
   W eb page: http://www.mackichan.com/products/swp.html
5. **LyX** version 1.3.4. W eb page: http://www.lyx.org/, see also [6].
6. **Mathematica** by Wolfram, version 5.
   W ebpage:http://www.wolfram.com/products/mathematica/index.html
7. **TEXmacs** version 1.0.1.23. W eb page: http://www.texmacs.org/

The products have been chosen to represent the current state-of-the-art in both commercial and freely available software.

### 2.1   Models and Edit Points

One of the characteristics of these editors is that they are m odel-oriented rather than text-oriented. By this we mean that the internal representation of the edited document is structured and the editing commands work directly on the internal representation. This is the main source of problems because editing operations (including movements) are performed on a non-linear data structure that, once displayed, may convey only partially or approximately the overall information it represents. For example, if the model represents the sum of two entities as a binary node, because of the associativity law of addition a sum like $x + y + z$

may be displayed with no parentheses, thus concealing the actual structure which may be either one of $(x + y) + z$ or $x + (y + z)$.

Because of the structured nature of the internal application model, the information that is necessary for unambiguously specifying the point where the next editing operation will occur is made of:

- the node of the model pointed to;
- the index, also called insertion point, indicating the sub-part of the node where something has to be inserted. Terminal (or leaf) model nodes, which usually represent identifiers, numbers, and, more generally, sequences of characters, typically have as many indexes as the number of characters plus one. Non-terminal (or internal) model nodes have a number of valid indexes which may vary depending on the structure of the model.

We call the combination of these two entities edit point[1] Most editors give a visual feedback for both entities. The index is typically presented by a vertical bar called caret. The node presentation, called focus, ranges from a horizontal line spanning the node's horizontal extent on the view, a prolongated caret spanning the node's vertical extent on the view, a solid or dashed rectangle surrounding the node, and so on. Some editors like amaya have no visual feedback for the focus at all, others like lyx and texmacs emphasize all the elements from the root of the internal application model to the focus. amaya and texmacs give additional feedback at the bottom of the editing window by providing the stack of node names from the root of the document down to the edit point.

In this paper we represent the caret with ₐ or ˆ symbols and we underline the focused node. For example, sn represents a focused token node whose content are the two letters 's' and 'n', with the caret sitting in between. An insertion of the character 'i' would change the node to sin.

## 2.2    Presentation of Missing Information

Model-based editors are usually constrained by the structure of the model. For example, a node of the model representing a binary operator may be required to have two child nodes, one for each operand. However the sequential nature of the editing process prevents the document to be well-formed at all times. Missing parts of the document that are expected to be filled in are called slots. The visual feedback of slots may vary, ranging from question marks on a reverse background in framemaker, to solid or dashed rectangles in mathtype, mathematica, and lyx to nothing at all in texmacs.

## 2.3    Basic Moves

Since the purpose of editing is to change a document and since the operations that change the document are performed at edit points, one of the main concerns

---

[1] The use of the term "point" dates back to the TECO editor as documented in [12].

**Table 1.** Traversal of a horizontal group of elements

| | amaya | framemaker, mathtype, mathematica, lyx, scientific workplace, texmacs |
|---|---|---|
| (RIGHT) | $\square + \square$ | $\square + \square$ |
| | $\square + \square$ | $\square + \square$ |
| ⋮ | $\square + \square$ | $\square + \square$ |
| | $\square + \square$ | $\square + \square$ |
| | $\square + \square$ | |
| | $\square + \square$ | |
| (LEFT)* | reverse | reverse |

is how to reach edit points. We will devote this section to a comparison of the various strategies adopted by the editors. In order to do so, we present a series of tables, each of them devoted to a common mathematical construct. The tables show the movements of the caret and possibly of the focus as the user requests a sequence of actions. Actions are triggered by keystrokes: (LEFT), (RIGHT), (UP), (DOWN) represent the basic cursor movement keys. In the tables time flows from top to bottom, the keystrokes are shown in the leftmost column of the diagram whereas the cells in the other columns show the state of the various editors after the action associated with that keystroke has been executed. We denote with the word "reverse" sequences of states that mirror the corresponding states for the opposite action. We denote arbitrary subexpressions with the symbol $\square$ and assume that they are traversed with a single action.

Rows. We start with a simple list of identifiers separated by operators (Table 1). Even for this simple formula editors may have different behaviors. The amaya editor advances the caret by a little step between identifiers and operators, thus moving from the end of a node in the model to the beginning of the next one. This gives visual feedback about the focused node, which is assumed to be the one the caret is closest to, but the user has the impression of a slowed-down traversal. Conversely, the other editors provide a natural traversal behavior where one action corresponds to one step.

Scripts. Next we examine the scripting construct (Table 2), which is used for exponents, indices, integration limits, and so on. From a geometrical point of view this is the construct where bi-dimensional layout starts playing an important role since scripts are vertically shifted with respect to the main baseline.

The observed behavioral variants include: full traversal of the scripts (amaya and mathematica), deterministic traversal of a subset of the scripts (mathtype and scientific workplace), skipping of the scripts unless an explicit action is re-

**Table 2.** Traversal of scripts

| | amaya, mathematica | framemaker | | lyx | mathtype | scientific workplace | texmacs |
|---|---|---|---|---|---|---|---|
| (RIGHT) ⋮ | | | | | | | |
| (LEFT) * | reverse | reverse | reverse, but not always (see text) | reverse | reverse | reverse | reverse |

quested (framemaker and lyx, note however that lyx traverses one more edit point). A particularly original behavior is observed in the texmacs editor, in which only one of the two scripts is traversed: the script that was visited last in the previous traversal is the one to be visited during the next traversal. framemaker is also bizarre: the traversal is reversible if the state reached by (RIGHT) moves is $\Box_\Box + \Box$, but it is not reversible if the reached state is $\Box_\Box + \Box$.

The (UP) and (DOWN) keys have very different associated behaviors: from no-ops to switching between subscripts and superscripts, to jumping to the beginning or the end of the whole construct.

Radicals. Roots (Table 3) can be thought as a variant of the script construct, from both semantical and notational points of view. Still they present very different behaviors if compared to scripts. Again the traversals range from partial to full navigation of the subparts, and again framemaker presents an odd behavior that is not reversible in some cases. The mathtype editor skips the index and provides no way of accessing it except by moving the caret on a different line and finding an edit point such that a vertical movement in the opposite direction causes the caret to hit the index.

Fractions. In Table 4 we traverse fractions. This construct is characterized by a clear vertical layout which is completely orthogonal to the baseline. Here too the behaviors are very different, although slightly less bizarre, probably because there is no horizontal component in the displacement of the subparts. Again we

**Table 3.** Traversal of roots

| | amaya | framemaker | lyx, texmacs | mathematica | mathtype | scientific workplace |
|---|---|---|---|---|---|---|
| (RIGHT) ⋮ | | | | | | |
| (LEFT) ⋮ | reverse | | reverse | reverse | reverse | reverse |

**Table 4.** Traversal of fractions

| | amaya, mathematica | framemaker | | lyx | mathtype | scientific workplace | texmacs |
|---|---|---|---|---|---|---|---|
| (RIGHT) ⋮ | | | | | | | |
| (LEFT) ⋮ | reverse | reverse | reverse | | reverse | reverse | reverse |

recognize full traversals in amaya and mathematica, partial deterministic traversal in lyx, mathtype and scientific workplace (lyx has a different traversal in the opposite direction), inner traversal caused by explicit user action in framemaker, and partial, visited-last-dependent traversals in texmacs. In all cases (UP) and (DOWN) cause the caret to be moved from the numerator to the denominator or vice versa.

**Table 5.** Traversal of matrices

| | amaya, mathematica | framemaker | lyx | mathtype | scientific workplace | texmacs |
|---|---|---|---|---|---|---|
| (RIGHT) ⋮ | | | | | | |
| (LEFT)* | reverse | reverse | reverse | reverse | reverse | reverse |

**Matrices.** Finally we examine a truly bidimensional mathematical construct in Table 5, which shows the traversal of possibly fenced matrices. In framemaker the construct is skipped unless the user triggers the (DOWN) action explicitly, in which case a full traversal is performed.

## 2.4    Special Moves

Aside basic moves, most editors provide a behavior associated with the (TAB) key that causes the edit point to jump across parts of the model following varying strategies. Among the observed ones there are: cycling the empty slots of the whole formula (framemaker, mathematica and mathtype); moving to the next slot (lyx, there is no inverse action); cycling the child nodes of the focused node (scientific workplace). amaya and texmacs have no behavior associated with the ⸤TAB⸥ key.

Regarding ⸤UP⸥ and ⸤DOWN⸥ moves, they do not always behave geometrically. For example, in framemaker the ⸤DOWN⸥ key has the effect of moving the edit point down the structure to the first child of the node being edited and the ⸤UP⸥ key has the effect of moving the the edit point up the structure to the parent of the node being edited. In mathematica ⸤UP⸥ and ⸤DOWN⸥ have a context-sensitive behavior which is not always geometrical. In lyx the behavior is partially geometrical but constrained by the model structure. For example, moving from a superscript down towards the subscript (or from a subscript up towards the superscript) causes the edit point to be placed just after the base element.

## 2.5    Editing Actions

Constrained Versus Unconstrained Editing. Different editors have different concepts of a well-formed formula and consequently they constrain editing operations in very different ways. On one end is framemaker which tries to keep the formula semantically meaningful. So, for example, the user is prevented from entering a formula like $a + + b$ and parentheses must always be balanced. mathematica sometimes provides different variants of a construct, one algebraic and one typographical, that have different constraints. Other editors like amaya and lyx have a looser concept of well-formed formula and, apart from the constraints imposed by the typographical structure of the formula, they allow for much more freedom in the editing process. In mathtype editing is almost totally unconstrained, for instance it is possible to have scripts not associated with a base element.

Templates and Overlays. These concepts represent two similar ways of assisting the author in changing the structure of the document. Templates are partial formulas with empty slots. The user can insert a template in a certain point of the document, typically at the current edit point or, if the editor allows it, in place of a previously selected part of the document. Overlays are special templates in which one designated slot is filled with the document part that is referenced by the edit point or that is selected at the time the overlay is inserted. All of the tested editors implement one or the other or, more frequently, both templates and overlays.

Delete Commands. Delete commands for model-based editors are particularly delicate because the edit point may refer to internal nodes of the model. In the particular case of fractions, Table 6 shows some of the observed behaviors associated with the ⸤BKSP⸥ key (delete to the left of the caret): entering the node, similar to a ⸤LEFT⸥ move (mathematica and texmacs); entering the node and deleting recursively (amaya); deleting the whole node in one shot (framemaker and lyx); selecting the node and deleting it only if the user repeats the action (mathtype, in the table the selected fraction is shown inside a box).

**Table 6.** Different behaviors associated with the deletion of fractions

| | amaya | framemaker | lyx | mathematica | mathtype | texmacs |
|---|---|---|---|---|---|---|
| | ⬚ | ⬚ | ⬚ | ⬚ | ⬚ | ⬚ |
| (BKSP) | — | | | ⬚ | ⬚ | ⬚ |
| (BKSP) | ⬚ | | | ⬚ | ⬚ | ⬚ |

## 3    Learning from Text Editors

Although a plain text document can be seen as a monodimensional entity (a stream of characters), word processors usually introduce some structure by allowing parts of the text to be annotated with style information. So, albeit to a limited extent, even text editors are based on a somehow structured model. In their case, however, there happens to be a much stronger convergence of behaviors associated with user actions. We can characterize such behaviors, at least with respect to the kind of actions we have been examining so far, as follows:

– basic steps on the document view can be achieved by means of basic user actions (basic = one keystroke). The emphasis is on the view rather than on the model. For example the behaviors associated with the (UP) and (DOWN) keys move the edit point to another one (on a different line) that is not adjacent with respect to model structure.
– basic operations like insert or delete actions act on the smallest entity in the proximity of the edit point;
– when provided, movements and operations on the document model (movement from a word to the following or preceding ones, the deletion of a whole line, and so on) require the user to perform dedicated actions;
– there are no fake moves: each user action clearly corresponds to a definite movement of the caret in the view. The user is never required to perform extra movements to get across different elements on the model (e.g. entering a part of text which has a different style requires no extra moves if compared to continuing moving on a paragraph with the same style);
– movements are geometrically reversible: in any position except for the document border, one (LEFT) nullifies exactly one (RIGHT), one (UP) nullifies exactly one (DOWN). Modern editors have often preferred reversibility of actions over simpler geometrical movements: for example moving from the end of a line to a shorter one causes a horizontal displacement of the caret, however a reverse move restores the caret location.

Editors providing different styles have to face the problem of edit point clashing. When the caret is placed between two characters having different associated styles, which style is taken for the next inserted character? Some editors try to give the caret a different appearance (like drawing a slanted vertical bar instead of a straight one, or drawing a caret which is as tall as the current font size) but this is not always enough to disambiguate the focus in general. Most editors implement a deterministic rule like "the style of the character preceding the caret is taken" which works well in all cases but a few rare exceptions. In editors for mathematical content this solution might be impractical because the model structure is more complex and plays a much more important role.

## 4    Analysis and Proposal

Although the two kinds of editors, for structured mathematical content and for plain text, are conceptually very different, we believe that the set of behaviors they implement could and should share a large common ground. In this respect, the current state-of-the-art math editors are certainly unsatisfactory and this claim is supported by the following observations:

- the application model is exposed to the user: while working at the model level simplifies the implementation of the editor, it also forces a view of the document which often does not match the user's mental image of the mathematical formula being edited. Geometric movements, editing operations, selections should not be constrained by the model unless the user explicitly requests so;
- model-oriented and geometric navigation modes are mixed: for example, the RIGHT keystroke sometimes triggers a geometric move and sometimes it triggers a movement on the model. In other cases, see for example the framemaker editor, RIGHT/LEFT always behave geometrically, but UP/DOWN correspond to movements on the model;
- important feedback, like the placement of empty slots in amaya and texmacs, is sometimes missing;
- there is excess of useless feedback. There is no point in showing a focus if it serves no purposes in terms of feedback (moreover the focus is very model dependent by definition). Even less useful, and actually confusing, is showing the structure of the document in places that are not directly related to the edit point (see the texmacs editor);
- unexpected or ambiguous behaviors lack suitable feedback: operations that are uncommon in text editors (like deletion of a complex model node) should be carefully implemented (see deletion in framemaker and lyx);
- some actions are non-deterministic: they depend on a state of the document which is not made explicit by any form of feedback;
- simple movements are not always reversible;
- there is lack of dedicated views for model-oriented navigation and editing.

What follows is our proposal for a more uniform editing behavior.

Edit Points. It is fundamental for the application to provide effective visual feedback of the caret. The caret should give the impression of actual movement, while the focus should be displayed only if it helps disambiguating the context where actions take place. In fact the focus may be misleading when the editor implements incremental parsing rules that override the focus position depending on the requested actions. For example, upon insertion of the digit 2 from either one of the states $1_+$ and $1_+$ the editor might go into the state $12_+$. In this case the focus prior to the insertion does not necessarily indicates the model node affected by the operation.

Slots. While an empty slot occupied by the caret might need no visual feedback, parts of the document that are missing should be clearly identifiable and easily reachable.

It is often convenient to provide a quick way for moving across the slots within the document (or within a smaller scope such as a single formula). This functionality is typically accessed by the ⊞TAB⊞ key (and ⊞SHIFT⊞ + ⊞TAB⊞ for moving in the opposite direction). As there is quite general agreement on this behavior among the current editors, there are no particular principles to be listed except for reversibility. The order in which the slots are visited is also of secondary importance as the user expects the caret to jump anyway and the number of slots, which is typically very limited, makes them all reachable very quickly.

Geometric Navigation. This should be the default navigation mode as it is consistent with the "what-you-see-is-what-you-get" principle that the user edits what she sees. More precisely, the user should be allowed to traverse the document in such a way that basic move actions cause an actual, yet basic, movement of the caret in the requested direction. As formulas often occur inside text, where geometric movements are commonly accepted, these rules should apply within the formulas as well in order to guarantee adequate consistency. More specifically:

— the caret is moved to the geometrically closest and deepest edit point in the direction of the movement. The notion of "direction" we are referring to here is necessarily blurred, as in mathematical notation related parts (like a base and its associated script) are often placed with both horizontal and vertical displacements;
— in case of ambiguities (edit points at different locations that are equally distant and equally deep) the editor should behave in a deterministic way. The model structure can be used for resolving such ambiguities;
— the movement should be perceived by the user as worthwhile, the user should not be required to move across entities she has not inserted explicitly;
— movements of the caret on the view should be reversible whenever possible.

Determinism is important for avoiding the introduction of a state in the user's mental image of the document ("which node have I visited last?").

The geometric navigation mode does not guarantee in general that all the available edit points are traversed. The principle that prefers deeper edit points ensures that the caret is moved on a position where operations have the less disruptive effect on the structure of the model.

Content Navigation. As text editors normally allow the navigation at some larger granularity (like the granularity of words and paragraphs) we may expect a similar functionality for editors of mathematical formulas. An analogous concept of higher-level entity for mathematics may be that of subexpression, or subformula. Unfortunately, this concept is so broad (and often fuzzy) that it cannot be used for the implementation of a generally useful navigation mode.

It is however possible to provide simple navigation modes that are based on a smaller higher granularity, like that of tokens, with the purpose of speeding up document navigation. The principles of geometric navigation should hold at this level as well.

Model Navigation. This navigation mode is indispensable for reaching edit points that are not accessible using the geometric navigation mode alone. However, we regard this as a far less frequent navigation mode, especially because it requires the user to have a fairly clear understanding of the model structure used by the application. For these reasons we strongly advocate the use of one or more dedicated views that enable model-oriented navigation and editing functionalities. This approach is followed by so called two-view editors, such as [5, 7, 4, 10] and also by some modern Integrated Development Environments[2] where a special view is provided to show a structured outline of the edited documents.

Selection. The basic selection mode should allow for the maximum flexibility. In particular, it should be possible to select parts of the edited document that have no semantic meaning or that form incomplete subexpressions, the same way as movements and editing should be unconstrained as much as possible. Because of the complex bidimensional layout of mathematical formulas, it should be possible to refine a selection in multiple, discrete steps, rather than allowing only a one-shot action of the user.

Notwithstanding this, it is not excluded the possibility of using the application model for enabling constrained forms of selection even on the classical view. For instance, it may be important to notify the user that the selection she has made does not entirely cover a valid[3] model subpart and that subsequent paste operations might fail for this reason.

Editing. Depending on the application and on the model structure, the range of editing operations available at one specific edit point may vary significantly. In the tested editors operations mostly work at the bottommost level (the leaves of the model), while operations on the model structure are limited to selection, cut-and-paste, deletion. However, as we have already discussed in the paragraph regarding edit points in this section, editors may implement incremental parsing rules such that even simple user actions cause deep rearrangements in the structure of the document (similar approaches are presented in [15, 14, 8]). This way, the editing environment would provide for improved flexibility thus reducing training time and discomfort while keeping the actual structure of the model hidden from the user.

---

[2] See for instance Eclipse, http://www.eclipse.org
[3] The notion of validity is obviously application-dependent.

# 5    Concluding Remarks

It was during the implementation of a model-based editor for mathematical documents that we gradually realized the countless and subtle difficulties that this kind of application underlies. When we turned our attention to existing editing tool, hoping to grab some knowledge about the implemented behaviors and about the user needs and expectations, it was surprising to find out that no two editors shared exactly the same behavior on every aspect, and that several choices made by implementors seemed supported by no solid motivations. The amazing range of possibilities cannot be justified merely on the basis that different editors have different underlying document models. Although such differences do exist, the editors should still strive for providing a comfortable and familiar environment.

Precise descriptions of the dynamics of model-based editors are rare in the bibliography. Incidentally, none of the tested editors provides comprehensive documentation about their behavior, probably because the behavior cannot be easily described on a static medium like the paper. A few informal attempts in this direction can be found in [15], where a token-oriented model is proposed, and in [8]. Barfield [2] has tried to classify tree-editing operations and some of his ideas influenced the navigation modes in Section 4.

Comparisons of document editors have usually the aim of measuring their effectiveness in terms of rate of accomplished tasks, average number of errors, and so on. In the case of text editors, most of the work was carried out during the eighties. Of particular relevance are Roberts et al. [11] and Borenstein [3]. Some interesting statistics about document editors can also be found in Whiteside et al. [16], where the importance of movement actions is highlighted. This is one of the reasons why we have devoted so much effort in understanding and analyzing geometric moves in the examined editors. It is reasonable to assume

**Table 7.** Scores of the tested editors

|  | amaya | framemaker | lyx | mathematica | mathtype | scientific workplace | texmacs |
|---|---|---|---|---|---|---|---|
| Edit point feedback | ● | ● | ○ | ● | ● | ● |  |
| Edit point accessibility | ○ |  | ● | ○ | ● | ○ | ● |
| Geometric moves |  |  | ○ | ○ | ○ | ● | ○ |
| Reversibility of moves | ○ |  | ● | ● | ● | ● | ● |
| Deterministic moves | ● | ○ | ● | ● | ● | ● | ○ |
| Model view | ● |  |  |  |  | ○ | ○ |
| Slot navigation |  | ● | ○ | ● | ● | ○ |  |
| Selection flexibility | ● | ○ | ○ | ○ | ○ | ○ | ○ |
| Model structure | ○ | ● | ○ |  |  | ○ | ○ |

that a similar suite of tests can be prepared for editors for mathematical content, but to the best of our knowledge no formal comparison has been developed so far.

At last, we could not refrain from summarizing the usability of the tested editors. For each of the features investigated in this paper we have given a measure of usability of its implementation. In Table 7 an empty cell means "not implemented" or "poor support", a ∘ symbol means "partial support" and a • symbol means "good support". We have also given a rough measure of the complexity of the model used by the editors. Intuitively, the more complex the model the more difficult it is to implement behaviors that respect our proposals. The results are clearly subjective and approximate. In fact, in many cases we could only guess about the model structure adopted by the editor. However, the table provides us with a rather strong feeling that direct-manipulation editors can be significantly improved, and that this might justify their unpopularity among both unexperienced and expert users.

# References

1. Apple Computer, Inc. "Apple Human Interface Guidelines", March 2004, http://developer.apple.com/documentation/UserExperience/Conceptual/OSXHIGuidelines/

2. L.G. Barfield, Editing Tree Structures, Technical Report CS-R9264, Amsterdam, 1992.

3. N.S. Borenstein, The evaluation of text editors: a critical review of the Roberts and Morgan methodology based on new experiments, Proceedings of the SIGCHI conference on Human factors in computing systems, pp. 99–105, San Francisco, California, 1985.

4. K.P. Brooks, A Two-view Document Editor with User-definable Document Structure, Digital Systems Research Center, Palo Alto, CA, November 1988.

5. J. Fine, Instant Preview and the TEX daemon, TUGboat, 22(4), pp. 292-298, December 2001.

6. L.E. Jackson, H. Voß, LyX – An Open Source document processor, TUGboat, Vol. 22, Number 1/2, pp. 32-41, March 2001.

7. D. Kastrup, Revisiting WYSIWYG Paradigms for Authoring LATEX, Proceedings of the 2002 Annual Meeting, TUGboat, Volume 23, No. 1, 2002.

8. J.-F. Nicaud, D. Bouhineau, T. Huguet, The Aplusix-Editor: A New Kind of Software for the Learning of Algebra, LNCS 2363, pp. 178–187, Springer-Verlag, Berlin, 2002.

9. D.A. Normal, The Psychology of Everyday Things, Basic Books, Inc., Publishers, New York, 1988.

10. L. Padovani, Interactive Editing of MathML Markup Using TEX Syntax, to appear in the Proceedings of the International Conference on TEX, XML and Digital Typography, 2004.

11. T.L. Roberts, T.P. Moran, The evaluation of text editors: methodology and empirical results, Communications of the ACM archive, Volume 26 , Issue 4, New York, NY, USA, April 1983.

12. R. Stallman, GNU Emacs Manual, for Version 20.1, Thirteenth Edition, Free Software Foundation, Cambridge, MA, USA, 1997.

13. P. Topping, Using MathType to Create TEX and MathML Equations, Proceedings of the 1999 TEX Annual Meeting, TUGBoat, Volume 20, No. 3, 1999.

14. M.L. Van De Vanter, Practical Language-Based Editing for Software Engineers, in Proceedings of Software Engineering and Human-Computer Interaction: ICSE '94 Workshop on SE-HCI: Joint Research Issues, LNCS 896, pp. 251–267, Springer-Verlag, Berlin, 1995.

15. M.L. Van De Vanter, M. Boshernistan, Displaying and Editing Source Code in Software Engineering Environments, Proceedings of the Second International Symposium on Constructing Software Engineering Tools, CoSET'2000.

16. J. Whiteside, N. Archer, D. Wixon, M. Good, How do people really use text editors?, Proceedings of the SIGOA conference on Office information systems, pp. 29–40, New York, NY, USA, 1982.

# Intuitive and Formal Representations: The Case of Matrices

Martin Pollet[1,2,*], Volker Sorge[2,**], and Manfred Kerber[2]

[1] Fachbereich Informatik, Universität des Saarlandes, Germany
pollet@ags.uni-sb.de
[2] School of Computer Science, The University of Birmingham, England
{V.Sorge|M.Kerber}@cs.bham.ac.uk

**Abstract.** A major obstacle for bridging the gap between textbook mathematics and formalising it on a computer is the problem how to adequately capture the intuition inherent in the mathematical notation when formalising mathematical concepts. While logic is an excellent tool to represent certain mathematical concepts it often fails to retain all the information implicitly given in the representation of some mathematical objects. In this paper we concern ourselves with matrices, whose representation can be particularly rich in implicit information. We analyse different types of matrices and present a mechanism that can represent them very close to their textbook style appearance and captures the information contained in this representation but that nevertheless allows for their compilation into a formal logical framework. This firstly allows for a more human-oriented interface and secondly enables efficient reasoning with matrices.

## 1 Introduction

A big challenge for formalising mathematics on computers is still to choose a representation that is on the one hand close to that in mathematical textbooks and on the other hand sufficiently formal in order to perform formal reasoning. While there has been much work on intermediate representations via a 'mathematical vernacular' [3, 12, 5], most of this work concentrates on representing mathematical proofs in a way that closely resembles the human reasoning style. Only little attention has been paid to an adequate representation of concrete mathematical objects, which captures all the information and intuition that comes along with their particular notation. Logicians are typically happy with the fact that such concepts can be represented in some way, whereas users of a formal system are more concerned with the question, how to represent a concept and how much effort is necessary to represent it. Depending on the purpose of the representation it is also important how easy it is to work with it.

In this paper we examine one particular type of mathematical objects, namely matrices. Let us first take a closer look how the matrix concept is introduced in a mathematical textbook. Lang [8, p.441] writes:

---

* The author's work is supported by EU IHP grant Calculemus HPRN-CT-2000-00102.
** The author's work is supported by a Marie-Curie Grant from the European Union.

A. Asperti et al. (Eds.): MKM 2004, LNCS 3119, pp. 317–331, 2004.

"By an $m \times n$ **matrix** in $R$ one means a doubly indexed family of elements of $R$, $(a_{ij})$, $(i = 1, \ldots, m$ and $j = 1, \ldots, n)$, usually written in the form

$$\begin{pmatrix} a_{11} & \cdots & a_{1n} \\ & \cdots & \\ a_{m1} & \cdots & a_{mn} \end{pmatrix}$$

We call the elements $a_{ij}$ the **coefficients** or **components** of the **matrix**."

Mathematicians do not work with the definition alone. The definition already introduces the representation as a rectangular form in which the elements of a matrix are ordered with respect to their indices. Matrices can be viewed as collections of row or column vectors, as block matrices, and various types of ellipses are used to describe the form of a matrix. The different representations are used to make the relevant information directly accessible and ease reasoning.

Depending on the exact logical language, one would consider a matrix as a tuple consisting of a double indexed function, number of rows, number of columns, and the underlying ring. And opposed to mathematics, one has to stick to this definition during all proofs. The (logical) view that a matrix is a tuple, which mainly bears aspects of a function, is not adequate from a mathematical point of view. If we look at a concrete matrix such as a $2 \times 2$ matrix containing only the zero element this matrix $Z$ is a constant. This means in particular that for any matrix $M$, the product $M \cdot Z$ is equal to $Z$ without the necessity to do reasoning about tuples and lambda expression. This is analogous to the relationship between the formal logical and mathematical view of the natural number four, which logically is the ground term $s(s(s(s(0))))$, while mathematically it is the constant symbol 4.

In this paper we show how to abstract from the functional representation of concrete matrices and how to attach structural information for matrices to the formal representation by so-called annotated constants. The structural information can be used for reasoning, which simplifies proof construction since some of the reasoning steps can be expressed as computations. The connection to the formal content allows the verification of the abstract proof steps in the underlying logical calculus.

In the next section we will have a closer look at different types of matrices that we want to be able to represent. In section 3 we will introduce annotated constants as an intermediate representation for mathematical objects. In section 4 we will discuss how concrete matrices, block matrices and ellipses can be represented and manipulated as annotated constants. We conclude with a discussion of related and future work in section 5.

## 2    Matrices – Examples

In this section we give an overview of some important cases of matrices and their representations as they appear in algebra books (e.g. [8, 6]). We do not intend to give an exhaustive overview. However, we believe that the cases covered here will allow for generalisations and adaptations to others. We discuss some of the representational issues, for which we propose solutions in the subsequent sections of the paper.

## 2.1   Concrete Matrices

A matrix is a finite set of entries arranged in a rectangular grid of rows and columns. The number of rows and columns of a matrix is often called the size of that matrix. The entries of a matrix are usually elements belonging to some algebraic field or ring. Matrices often occur in a very concrete form. That is, the exact number of rows and columns as well as the single entries are given. An example is the following $2 \times 3$-matrix:

$$M = \begin{pmatrix} 3 & 2 & 7 \\ 1 & 0 & 4 \end{pmatrix}$$

Matrices of this form are fairly easy to represent and handle electronically. They can simply be linearised into a list of rows, which is indeed the standard input representation of matrices for most mathematical software, such as computer algebra systems. Since both the size of the matrix is determined and all the elements are given and of a specific type, manipulations of the matrix and computations with the matrix can be efficiently performed, even if the concrete numbers are replaced by indeterminates such as $a, b, c$.

While concrete matrices often occur in many engineering disciplines, pure mathematics goes normally beyond concrete sizes, but will speak of matrices in a more generalised fashion.

## 2.2   Block Matrices

Block matrices are matrices of fixed sizes, typically $2 \times 2$ or $3 \times 3$, whose elements consist of rectangular blocks of elements of not necessarily determined size. Thus, block matrices are in effect shorthand for much larger structures, whose internal format can be captured in a particular pattern of blocks. Consider, for instance, the general matrix of size $(n + 1) \times (n + 1)$ given as

$$M = \left( \begin{array}{c|c} a & v^T \\ \hline 0 & A \end{array} \right)$$

in which $a \neq 0$ is a ring element (scalar), $0$ is the zero vector of size $n$, $v^T$ is the transpose of an arbitrary vector $v$ of size $n$, and $A$ is a matrix of size $n \times n$.

A block matrix can be emulated with a concrete matrix by regarding its elements as matrices themselves. This can be achieved by identifying, scalars with $1 \times 1$ matrices, vectors with $n \times 1$ matrices, and transposed vectors with $1 \times n$ matrices. While this enables the use of the techniques available for concrete matrices to input and represent block matrices, manipulating block matrices is not as straightforward. Since the elements do no longer belong to the same algebraic ring (or indeed to any ring), computations can only be carried out with respect to a restricted set of axioms. In particular, one has to generally forgo commutativity when computing with the single blocks. Again this can be simulated to a certain extend. For instance, the inverse of the above matrix can be computed by using a computer algebra system that can deal with non-commutativity, as demonstrated in section 4.2. Computations concerning two block matrices, such as matrix addition or multiplication can be simulated as well. However care has to be taken that the sizes of the blocks are compatible.

## 2.3   Ellipses

While block matrices can capture simple patterns in a matrix in an abstract way, more complex patterns in generalised matrices are usually described using ellipses. Consider for instance the definition of the following matrix $A$:

$$
A = \begin{pmatrix} a_{11} & b & \cdots & b \\ 0 & \ddots & \ddots & \vdots \\ \vdots & \ddots & \ddots & b \\ 0 & \cdots & 0 & a_{nn} \end{pmatrix}
$$

The representation stands for an infinite class of $n \times n$ matrices such that we have a diagonal with elements $a_{ii}$, $1 \le i \le n$, all elements below the diagonal are zero, while the elements above the diagonal are all $b$. A matrix of this form is usually called an upper triangle matrix.

In the context of matrices we can distinguish essentially two types of ellipses:

1. Ellipses denoting an arbitrary but fixed number of occurrences of the same element, such as in $(0 \cdots 0)$.
2. Ellipses representing a finite number of similar elements that are enumerated with respect to a given index set $(a_1 \cdots a_n)$[1].

Both types of ellipses are primarily placeholders for a finite set of elements that are either directly given (1) or can be inferred given the index set (2).

Another important feature of ellipses in the context of matrices are their orientation. While for most mathematical objects, such as sets or vectors, ellipses can occur in exactly one possible orientation, in two-dimensional objects such as matrices we can distinguish three different orientations: horizontal, vertical, and diagonal. Thereby ellipses are not only placeholders for single rows, columns or diagonals but a combination of ellipses together can determine the composition of a whole area within the matrix. For example the interaction of the diagonal, horizontal and vertical ellipses between the three 0s in $A$ determines that the whole area underneath the main diagonal defaults to 0.

Matrices with ellipses are well suited for manipulation and reasoning at an intuitive abstract level. However, already their mere representation poses some problems. While they can be linearised with some effort, a two-dimensional representation of the object is preferable, as this eases to determine the actual meaning of the occurring ellipses. It is even more challenging to mechanise abstract reasoning or abstract computations on matrices with ellipses.

---

[1] Here the notion of an index set is not necessarily restricted to being only a set of indices for a family of terms, but we also use it with a more general meaning of enumerating a sequence of elements as for instance in the vector containing the first $n$ powers of $a$, $(a^1 \cdots a^n)$.

## 2.4    Generalised Matrices

While ellipses already provide a powerful tool to express matrices in a very general form by specifying a large number of possible patterns, one sometimes wants to be even more general than that. Consider for instance the following definition of matrix $B$:

$$B = \begin{pmatrix} a_{11} & \star & \cdots & \star \\ 0 & \ddots & \ddots & \vdots \\ \vdots & \ddots & \ddots & \star \\ 0 & \cdots & 0 & a_{nn} \end{pmatrix}. \text{ Also written as: } \begin{pmatrix} a_{11} & & \star \\ & \ddots & \\ 0 & & a_{nn} \end{pmatrix}$$

Matrix $B$ is very similar to $A$ above, with the one exception that the elements above the main diagonal are now arbitrary, indicated by $\star$, rather than $b$. This is a further generalisation as $B$ now describes an upper triangle matrix of variable sizes $n \times n$, where we are only interested in the elements of the main diagonal $a_{ii}$, $1 \leq i \leq n$, but we don't care about the elements above the diagonal. While such a matrix can be represented with the same representational tools as the matrix $A$ above, it will be more difficult to deal with when we actually want to compute or reason with it.

In the following we shall describe how we can handle concrete matrices, block matrices, and ellipses. In order to extend our approach to cover generalised matrices as well, we would need to handle "don't care" symbols, in addition. We do not go into this question in this paper.

# 3    Intermediate Representation – Annotated Constants

In this section we present the concept of annotated constants, a mechanism that provides a representational layer that can both capture the properties of the intuitive mathematical representation of objects, as well as connect these objects to their corresponding representation in a formal logic framework. Annotated constants are implemented in the Omega system [10] and therefore the logical framework is Omega's simply typed lambda calculus (cf. [1]). We have first introduced annotated constants in [11] in the context of mathematical objects, such as numbers, lists, and permutations. For the sake of clarity we explain the idea in the following using the much simpler example of finite sets.

Let us assume a logical language and a ground term $t$ in this language. Let $c$ be a constant symbol with $c = t$. An annotated constant is then a triple $(c, t, \mathbf{a})$, in which $\mathbf{a}$ is the annotation. The annotation $\mathbf{a}$ is any object (making use of an arbitrary data structure) from which $c$ and $t$ can be reconstructed. Think of $c$ as the name of the object, $t$ as the representation within logic, and $\mathbf{a}$ as a representation of the object outside logic.

Finite Sets: Finite sets have a special notation in the mathematical vernacular, for example, the set consisting of the three elements $a$, $b$, and $c$ is denoted by $\{a, b, c\}$. We can define this by giving the set a name, e.g., $A$, and a definition in logic as a ground term. Important knowledge about sets with which it is appropriate to reason efficiently is: sets are equal if they contain the same elements regardless of their order, or the union of two sets consists of the elements which are a member of one of the sets and so on. This type of set manipulation has not so much to do with logical reasoning as it has with computation. The union of two sets, for instance, can be very efficiently computed and should not be part of the process of search for a proof.

Annotated constants for finite sets are defined with the attributes

**Annotation for Finite Sets:** The data structure of sets of the underlying programming language is used as annotation and the elements of the set are restricted to closed terms, e.g., the set containing the three constants $a$, $b$, and $c$ in the concrete example.

**Constant Symbol:** We give the set a name such as $A$. Even more appropriate for our purpose is to generate an identifier from a duplicate free ordering of the elements of the set, for the example $A_{\{a,b,c\}}$.

**Definition:** The definition of the set corresponds to a lambda term in higher-order logic, e.g., $\lambda x. (x{=}a \vee x{=}b \vee x{=}c)$. In order to normalise such terms it is useful to order the elements of the set, that is, we wouldn't write the term as $\lambda x. (x{=}b \vee x{=}a \vee x{=}c)$. Since the annotation has to represent the object completely the formal definition can be constructed from the annotation.

The basic functionality for handling annotated constants is implemented on the term level of the Omega system. In first approximation, an annotated constant is a constant with a definition and has the type of its defining term $t$. As such it could be replaced by its defining term during the proof or when expanding the proof to check formal correctness. Typically, this is not done, but annotated constants are manipulated via their annotations. The defining term of an annotated term is used only when necessary.

The manipulation of operations and verification of properties is realised as procedural annotations to functions and predicates. A procedural annotation is a triple $(f, \mathbf{p}, T)$, where $f$ is a function or predicate of the logical language, $\mathbf{p}$ is a procedure of the underlying programming language with the same number of arguments as $f$ and $T$ is a specification (or tactic) for the construction of a formal proof for the manipulation performed by $\mathbf{p}$. The procedure $\mathbf{p}$ checks its arguments, performs the simplification, and returns a simplified constant or term together with possible conditions for this operation.

For example, the procedure for the union of concrete sets $\{a, b\} \cup \{c, d\}$ checks whether the arguments are annotated constants for concrete sets, and returns the annotated constant which has the concatenation of $\{a, b\}$ and $\{c, d\}$ as annotation. Analogously the property $\{1, 2, 3\} \subset \mathbb{Z}$ holds, when all elements of the annotation of the set are constants which have as annotation an integer as data structure.

The proof specification $T$ is used to formally justify the performed step. Thereby an annotated constant is expanded to its formal definition and the computation is reconstructed by tactic and theorem applications. This expansion will be done only when a low level formal proof is required, certainly not during proof search.

**What Are the Advantages of Using Annotated Constants?**

Firstly, annotated constants provide an intermediate representation layer between the intuitive mathematical vernacular and a formal system. With annotated constants it is possible to abstract from the formal introduction of objects, allow the identification of certain classes of objects and enable the access of relevant knowledge about an object directly. Annotations can be translated into full formal logic expressions when necessary, but make it possible to work and reason with mathematical objects in a style that abstracts from the formal construction.

Secondly, annotations allow for user friendly input and output facilities. We extended Omega's input language to provide a markup for an annotated constant to indicate the type of the object it represents. For each kind of annotated constant the term parser is extended by an additional function, which parses annotations and transforms these annotations into an internal representation. During parsing additional properties can be checked and errors in the specification can be detected. In this way it is possible to extend syntactic type checking. An additional output function for each kind of annotated constant allows to have different display forms for presenting formulas to the user.

Thirdly, procedural annotations enable an efficient manipulation of annotated constants. Theses procedures can access information without further analysis on (lambda) terms (which define annotated constants formally) and allows to compute standard functions and relations very efficiently. These operations and properties become a computation on the data structures of annotated constants.

## 4    Matrices as Annotated Constants

In this section we show how annotated constants can be used to implement the different representations for matrices presented in section 2.

### 4.1    Concrete Matrices

Concrete matrices of fixed sizes, for example,

$$M = \begin{pmatrix} 3 & 2 & 7 \\ 1 & 0 & 4 \end{pmatrix}$$

can be represented in higher-order logic as a 4-tuple: $(f, 2, 4, \mathbb{Z})$ where $f$ is the lambda expression[2]

$$
\lambda i \lambda j. \quad
\begin{aligned}
&\text{if} && i = 1 \wedge j = 1 && \text{then } 3 \\
&\text{elseif} && i = 1 \wedge j = 2 && \text{then } 2 \\
&\text{elseif} && i = 1 \wedge j = 3 && \text{then } 7 \\
&\text{elseif} && i = 2 \wedge j = 1 && \text{then } 1 \\
&\text{elseif} && i = 2 \wedge j = 2 && \text{then } 0 \\
&\text{else} &&&& \quad\; 4.
\end{aligned}
$$

---

[2] The conditional   if $P$ then $m$ else $n$ can be defined in higher-order logic by the description operator $\iota$. The expression $\iota y. S(y)$ denotes the unique element $c$ such that $S(c)$ holds, if such a unique element exists. A conditional can thus be defined by $\iota k. (P \wedge (k = m)) \vee (\neg P \wedge (k = n))$, which returns $m$ if $P$ holds, else $n$ (for more details see [1]).

When we look at the concrete matrix the information connected to this representation is, that the position of all the elements is specified and that the number of rows and columns of the matrix are immediately perceivable. When we look at the formal representation, then even to access an element at a certain position requires reasoning, even non-trivial reasoning when, for example, the first condition is given as $f$ $\lambda i \lambda j$. if $P(i,j)$ then 3 elseif ... where $P(i,j)$ is some equivalent formulation of $i = 1 \wedge j = 1$.

Also in order to multiply two concrete matrices, reasoning about the corresponding lambda expressions is necessary. For instance, the transpose of $M$ is

$$M^T = \begin{pmatrix} 3 & 1 \\ 2 & 0 \\ 7 & 4 \end{pmatrix}$$

which can be represented as a 4-tuple $(f^T, 4, 2, \mathbb{Z})$ where $f^T$ is the function you get by swapping the arguments of $f$, i.e. $\lambda j \lambda i$ rather than $\lambda i \lambda j$. The product $M \otimes M^T$ is a matrix $(f *_4 f^T, 2, 2, \mathbb{Z})$, in which the function is computed component wise as the sum of products of ring elements, that is, $\lambda i \lambda j$. if $i = 1 \wedge j = 1$ then $3 \cdot 3 + 2 \cdot 2 + 7 \cdot 7$ elseif ..., which requires considerable reasoning to arrive at the result. We argue that although this can be done in logic, it is not appropriate, analogously as it is not appropriate to compute a product such as $20 \cdot 15$ by reasoning with the definition of $\cdot$ in the constructors 0 and $s$ over the natural numbers.

We therefore define annotated constants for concrete matrices as follows:

**Annotation for Concrete Matrices:** The data structure of arrays, where the elements are in the logical language and all of them have the same type $\alpha$. All places of the array must be filled with constants of the logical language, as for instance in our example matrix $M$.

**Constant:** A constant $A$ of the logical language of type $\mathbb{Z} \times \mathbb{Z} \to \alpha$.

**Definition:** The lambda expression representing a double indexed function of the form $\lambda i \lambda j$. $f(i,j)$, where $i$ and $j$ range over the integer intervals $[1, m]$ and $[1, n]$, respectively and every $f(i,j)$ is an element of a ring $F$. In other words $f(i,j)$ corresponds to a matrix entry in the $i^{\text{th}}$ column and the $j^{\text{th}}$ row. To guarantee that a double indexed function actually constitutes a matrix it has to fulfil the property M atrix$(f, m, n, F) \equiv \forall i \in [1, m], j \in [1, n] : f(i,j) \in F$. A concrete example for such a lambda expression is the double indexed function representing $M$ above.

For annotated constants representing concrete matrices the operations for summation and multiplication of matrices, scalar multiplication, and transposing a matrix are annotated by corresponding procedures. With the tactic *simplify* which applies all possible simplifications specified in annotated procedures, a proof step performing the matrix multiplication $M \otimes M^T$ is:

$L_1$.  $\{0,1,2,3,4,7\} \in R$          (open)
$L_2$.  $Ring(R,+,\cdot)$          (open)

$L_3$.  $P = \begin{pmatrix} 62 & 31 \\ 31 & 17 \end{pmatrix}$          (open)

$L_4$.  $P = \begin{pmatrix} 3 & 2 & 7 \\ 1 & 0 & 4 \end{pmatrix} \otimes \begin{pmatrix} 3 & 2 & 7 \\ 1 & 0 & 4 \end{pmatrix}^T$    (simplify $L_1, L_2, L_3$)

The line $L_3$ contains the matrix which is the result of the simplification. Since the matrices consist of integers, which are annotated constants again, the simplification can compute the result of arithmetic operations on integers. The lines $L_1$ and $L_2$ contain the side conditions of the computation. Note that the necessary conditions on the size of the matrices M $\mathrm{atrix}(\left(\begin{smallmatrix} 3 & 2 & 7 \\ 1 & 0 & 4 \end{smallmatrix}\right), 2, 3, R)$ and M $\mathrm{atrix}(\left(\begin{smallmatrix} 3 & 2 & 7 \\ 1 & 0 & 4 \end{smallmatrix}\right)^T, 3, 2, R)$ are available from the annotation and thus can be checked during the expansion of the tactic *simplify*.

## 4.2   Block Matrices

A block matrix of the form $M = \left(\begin{array}{c|c} a & v^T \\ \hline 0 & A \end{array}\right)$ can be formally expressed in logic as a tuple $(f, n+1, n+1, F)$, in which $f$ is a function from the indices into the ring, $\{1, \ldots, n+1\} \times \{1, \ldots, n+1\} \to F$ defined as

$$\lambda i \lambda j. \quad \begin{array}{llll} \text{if} & i = 1 \wedge j = 1 & \text{then } a \\ \text{elseif} & i = 1 \wedge 2 \le j \le n+1 & \text{then } v_{j-1} \\ \text{elseif} & 2 \le i \le n+1 \wedge j = 1 & \text{then } 0 \\ \text{else} & & a_{i-1,j-1} \end{array}$$

If we assume $a \ne 0$ and $\det(A) \ne 0$, we can then show that the set of matrices of the above form constitute a subgroup of the group of invertible matrices with respect to matrix multiplication. This is, however, not straightforward using the lambda expression, since a lot of the structural information is needed for the argument, which is lost in the lambda term. What we really want to do is to lift the argument about $2 \times 2$ block matrices to a sound argument about general matrices.

In effect the argument can be collapsed into a single computation. By emulating the block matrix with a $2 \times 2$ matrix over a non-commutative ring we can compute its inverse using the computer algebra system Mathematica [13] together with the NCAlgebra package [9] for non-commutative algebra. If we replace the block matrix with a matrix of the form

$$\begin{pmatrix} a & b \\ 0 & c \end{pmatrix}, \text{the corresponding inverse matrix is } \begin{pmatrix} a^{-1} & -a^{-1} \cdot b \cdot c^{-1} \\ 0 & c^{-1} \end{pmatrix}.$$

Note that $-a^{-1} \cdot b \cdot c^{-1}$ can not be further simplified to $-\frac{b}{a \cdot c}$, since matrix multiplication is non-commutative. This computation on concrete matrices can be used to determine the inverse of the original block matrix by simply substituting $v^T$ for $b$ and $A$ for $c$:

$$\begin{pmatrix} a^{-1} & -a^{-1} \cdot v^T \cdot A^{-1} \\ 0 & A^{-1} \end{pmatrix}$$

With the additional fact that $a^{-1}$ and $A^{-1}$ exist if and only if $a \neq 0$ and $\det(A) \neq 0$, the property can be proved.

Block matrices are implemented as annotated constants in the following way:

**Annotation for Block Matrices:** The data structure of $2 \times 2$ arrays $\begin{pmatrix} A & B \\ C & D \end{pmatrix}$ where the elements $A, B, C, D$ are either annotated constants for matrices or double indexed lambda functions. All elements must have the same type. In addition, for annotated constants representing matrices the following conditions must hold for the number of rows $row(A) = row(B) = r_1$, $row(C) = row(D) = r_2$, and $col(A) = col(C) = c_1$, $col(B) = col(D) = c_2$ for the number of columns.

**Constant:** A constant of type $\mathbb{Z} \times \mathbb{Z} \to \alpha$ representing the matrix.

**Definition:** Block matrices are expanded into a lambda term of the form

$$
\lambda i \lambda j. \; \begin{array}{llll}
\text{if} & 1 \le i \le r_1 & \wedge\ 1 \le j \le c_1 & \text{then } A(i,j) \\
\text{elseif} & 1 \le i \le r_1 & \wedge\ c_1 + 1 \le j & \text{then } B(i, j - c_1) \\
\text{elseif} & r_1 + 1 \le i & \wedge\ 1 \le j \le c_1 & \text{then } C(i - r_1, j) \\
\text{else} & [\text{i.e.,} r_1 + 1 \le i \wedge c_1 + 1 \le j] & & D(i - r_1, j - c_1),
\end{array}
$$

where the $A(.), B(.), C(.), D(.)$ denote double indexed functions, possibly generated by expansion of concrete matrices.

The annotated constants for block matrices allow us to combine matrices given by lambda expressions with concrete matrices. The operations for matrices then work directly on the individual blocks of the block matrices. Given double indexed functions $u_{ij}, v_{ij}, A_{ij}, B_{ij}$ the tactic $simplify$ applied to the formula in $L_8$ results in the following proof situation:

$$
\begin{array}{llll}
L_1. & Matrix(u_{ij}, 1, 2, R) & & (open) \\
L_2. & Matrix(v_{ij}, 1, 2, R) & & (open) \\
L_3. & Matrix(B_{ij}, 2, 2, R) & & (open) \\
L_4. & Matrix(A_{ij}, 2, 2, R) & & (open) \\
L_5. & \{0, 1\} \in R & & (open) \\
L_6. & Ring(R, +, \cdot) & & (open)
\end{array}
$$

$$
L_7. \quad M = \begin{pmatrix} (1) & u_{ij} \oplus (v_{ij} \otimes B_{ij}) \\ \begin{pmatrix} 0 \\ 0 \end{pmatrix} & A_{ij} \otimes B_{ij} \end{pmatrix} \quad (open)
$$

$$
L_8. \quad M = \begin{pmatrix} (1) & v_{ij} \\ \begin{pmatrix} 0 \\ 0 \end{pmatrix} & A_{ij} \end{pmatrix} \otimes \begin{pmatrix} (1) & u_{ij} \\ \begin{pmatrix} 0 \\ 0 \end{pmatrix} & B_{ij} \end{pmatrix} \quad (simplify \; L_1, \ldots, L_7)
$$

Line $L_7$ contains the result of the matrix multiplication and lines $L_1$ to $L_6$ the side conditions on the objects involved, which cannot be inferred from the annotations.

We describe the simplification stepwise. First the sub-blocks of the matrices are multiplied, resulting in

$$\left(\begin{array}{c|c} ((1)\otimes(1))\oplus\left(v_{ij}\otimes\begin{pmatrix}0\\0\end{pmatrix}\right) & ((1)\otimes u_{ij})\oplus(v_{ij}\otimes B_{ij}) \\ \hline \left(\begin{pmatrix}0\\0\end{pmatrix}\otimes(1)\right)\oplus\left(A_{ij}\otimes\begin{pmatrix}0\\0\end{pmatrix}\right) & \left(\begin{pmatrix}0\\0\end{pmatrix}\otimes u_{ij}\right)\oplus(A_{ij}\otimes B_{ij}) \end{array}\right).$$

Already at this point the side conditions regarding the double indexed functions $u_{ij}, v_{ij}, A_{ij}, B_{ij}$ are generated. The requirements for the size can be reconstructed from the sizes of the concrete matrices together with the condition from the matrix multiplication. Then simplification is applied to the content of each sub-block, starting with simplification of the arguments of an operation.

For concrete matrices operations are performed as described in section 4.1. For the simplification of operations containing both concrete matrices and double indexed functions we only consider the following cases:

- multiplications involving the zero matrix (i.e., a concrete matrix containing only the zero element of the underlying ring) are replaced by the zero matrix;
- summations with the zero matrix are replaced by the double indexed function;
- multiplication with a concrete diagonal matrix, containing the same element on the diagonal is replaced by scalar multiplication with said diagonal element.

Simplifying the above block matrix with respect to the rules for multiplication then yields

$$\left(\begin{array}{c|c} (1)\oplus(0) & 1\cdot u_{ij}\oplus(v_{ij}\otimes B_{ij}) \\ \hline \begin{pmatrix}0\\0\end{pmatrix}\oplus\begin{pmatrix}0\\0\end{pmatrix} & \begin{pmatrix}0&0\\0&0\end{pmatrix}\oplus(A_{ij}\otimes B_{ij}) \end{array}\right)$$

Further simplification employs the rules for addition and also scalar multiplication on $1\cdot u_{ij}$ resulting in the formula given in $L_7$ of the above proof.

The simplification for operations on matrices with mixed representations could also be carried out differently, namely by introducing concrete matrices, that is

$$\begin{pmatrix}a\\b\end{pmatrix}\otimes u_{ij}\rightarrow\begin{pmatrix}a\cdot u_{11} & a\cdot u_{12}\\b\cdot u_{11} & b\cdot u_{12}\end{pmatrix}$$

and then apply simplification on the elements of the matrix. For $a=b=0$ the result will be the same as for our simplification, but in the general case, the result is a concrete matrix having elements of the double indexed mixed with the elements of the concrete matrix. This means the structure of the initial blocks would be lost or hard to recognise.

While our example works with $3\times 3$ matrices represented as $2\times 2$ block matrices, the argument can be extended to arbitrary $n\times n$ matrices still represented as $2\times 2$ block matrices of the form:

$$\left(\begin{array}{c|c} \dfrac{(1)}{\begin{matrix} 0 \\ \vdots \\ 0 \end{matrix}} & \begin{matrix} u_{ij} \\ \\ A_{ij} \end{matrix} \end{array}\right)$$

But in order to do this we need an adequate treatment of ellipses.

## 4.3     Ellipses

While block matrices already allow us to combine concrete matrices using arbitrary double indexed functions, they only enable us to combine rectangular shapes. Using ellipses we can further generalise the representation of matrices. We then need to generalise also the simplifications introduced in the last section to matrices with fixed but arbitrary sizes. If we consider our example matrix

$$A = \begin{pmatrix} a_{11} & b & \cdots & b \\ 0 & \ddots & \ddots & \vdots \\ \vdots & \ddots & \ddots & b \\ 0 & \cdots & 0 & a_{nn} \end{pmatrix}$$

then $A$ can be represented in higher-order logic as a 4-tuple: $(f, n, n, \mathbb{Z})$ where $f$ corresponds to the lambda expression:

$$\lambda i \lambda j.\ \begin{array}{lll} \text{if} & i = j & \text{then } a_{ij} \\ \text{if} & i < j & \text{then } b \\ \text{else} & & 0 \end{array}$$

Compared to the concrete instances above, the higher-order representation is concise. Nevertheless, in mathematics one develops particular methods for reasoning with matrices of non-concrete sizes, which follow a particular pattern, such as triangle matrices, diagonal matrices, and step matrices. Since these patterns are not necessarily obvious given the lambda term alone it is desirable to have the explicit representation of matrices with ellipses available for reasoning.

Ellipses are realised using annotated constants as well. They are categorised into horizontal, vertical, and diagonal ellipses and have the following four attributes that connect them within the matrix and determine their meaning:

**Begin:** A concrete element that marks the start of the ellipsis.

**End:** A concrete element that marks the end of the ellipsis.

**Element:** The element the ellipses represents; this can either be a concrete element such as 0 or $b$, or a schematic element such as $a_{\chi,\xi}$. Here $\chi$ and $\xi$ are schematic variables that indicate that they are iterated over.

**Range:** In case the element is concrete (e.g. 0 or $b$), no range is given. If the ellipsis has a schematic term as element, the integer ranges for the necessary schematic variables are given. In our example we have $1 \le \xi \le n$ and $1 \le \chi \le n$ meaning that both $\xi$ and $\chi$ take values from 1 to $n$ with increment 1.

The values for the attributes are determined during parsing of the expression. Thereby not all combinations of ellipses are permitted. Essentially, we distinguish three basic modules a matrix can consists of:

1. points, i.e. single concrete elements.
2. lines, i.e. an ellipsis or a sequence of ellipses of the same form together with concrete elements as start and end points. An example of a line comprised of more than one ellipsis is for instance the main diagonal of $A$ where two diagonal ellipses constitute a line from $a_{11}$ to $a_{nn}$.
3. triangles, i.e. a combination of a horizontal, a vertical and a diagonal line. Since we only allow for one type of diagonal ellipsis, the we can get exactly

two different types of isosceles right triangles:

Both start and end elements of an ellipsis are determined by searching for a concrete element in the respective direction (i.e., left/right, up/down, etc.) while ignoring other ellipses. Both element and range are computed given the start and end: If the start and end terms are the same then this term is taken to be the element the ellipsis represents and no range needs to be computed. In case they are not the same we try to compute a schematic term using unification. Although the unification fails it will provide us with a disagreement set on the two terms, which can be used to determine the position of possible schematic variables. If the disagreement set is sensible, that is, it consists only of terms representing integers, the schematic term is constructed and the ranges for the schematic variables are computed.

We illustrate how exactly ranges are computed with the help of some examples. Consider the vector $(a_1^n \cdots a_n^1)$, the schematic term is then $a_\xi^\chi$ and the ranges are $\xi \in \{1, \ldots, n\}$ and $\chi \in \{n, \ldots, 1\}$. Since these ranges are both over the integer and compatible, in the sense that they are of the same length, the ellipsis is fully determined. As an example of incompatible ranges consider the vector $(a_1^k \cdots a_n^1)$; without further information on $n$ and $k$ the computation of the ellipsis will fail. Currently the increment of the range sets is always assumed to be 1. The computation of possible index sets is currently more a pragmatic one and rather simple. It is definitely not complete since there are many more possible uses of indices conceivable in our context.

An ellipsis is said to be computable if we can determine both begin and end element, if the element is either a concrete element or a schematic term, and if sensible and compatible integer ranges can be computed. Otherwise parsing of an ellipsis will fail. An ellipsis within a matrix gets the same type as the elements of that matrix. This means ellipses are generally treated as ordinary terms of the matrix, in particular with respect to input, display, and internal representation. For instance, our example matrix $A$ is input as the $4 \times 4$ matrix

```
((a(1,1)  b       hdots  b      )
 (0       ddots   ddots  vdots  )
 (vdots   ddots   ddots  b      )
 (0       hdots   0      a(n,n)))
```

and is also represented internally as a $4 \times 4$ array. However, the simplifications can use the information provided by the ellipsis during the reasoning process.

When a matrix containing ellipses is expanded into a lambda term the expansion algorithm translates the ellipses into appropriate conditions for the if-then-else statements. Thereby the matrix is first scanned and broken down into its components, i.e. points, lines, and triangles. These can then be associated with corresponding index sets and translated into a lambda expression. For instance the diagonal ellipsis in our example matrix $A$ above can be simply translated into the conditional if $i = j$ then $a_{ij}$, while the areas above and below the main diagonal where a horizontal, a vertical, and a diagonal ellipsis bound the area in which all the elements are either 0 or $b$. In an additional optimisation step neighbouring triangles are compared and can be combined to form rectangular areas.

The simplification for operations on matrices are extended to the cases where matrices contain ellipses. For example, the sum of matrices where both matrices contain ellipses at the same positions results in a matrix containing the sum of concrete elements and the ellipses between those elements. The multiplication of a diagonal matrix containing the same element on the diagonal is reduced to scalar multiplication with this element.

## 5     Conclusions

Formal representations of mathematical objects often do not model all important aspects of that object. Especially some of the structural properties may be lost or hard to recognise and reconstruct. In our work we investigated these structural properties for the case of matrices where there exist different representations for different purposes. Each representation has certain reasoning techniques attributed to it.

We modelled the structural knowledge about concepts with the help of annotations, which are used to identify objects and to store information about them. We implemented the different representations for matrices as annotated constants and showed how basic simplifications are performed. The representations for block matrices and ellipses allow us to represent matrices of a general form. Annotations are also used for manipulations of objects. Instead of deduction on formulas, many manipulations can be reduced to computations on annotations. Since we are able to express general matrices, we can express general properties and theorems based on our formalism. With simplifications performed on generalised matrices we are now able to express complex reasoning in the form of computational steps. In future work we want to investigate how this can further aid in the construction of actual proofs. Remember that we currently deal annotated constants, that is, only with ground terms. Thus, it would be useful to extend the work in a way that allows also to deal with variables.

Annotations preserve the correctness by their implementation as constants of the formal language. The proof construction is split into a phase where steps are performed based on the richer knowledge contained in annotations and a verification phase where these steps are expanded to calculus level proofs. The expansion is currently only implemented for a subset of the operations. The expansion mechanism for proof steps using annotations needs to be simplified and generalised. The use of canonical forms should help keeping this expansion simple.

Our work compares to de Bruijn's idea of a mathematical vernacular [3], which should allow to write everything mathematicians do in informal reasoning, in a computer assisted system as well. In this tradition, Elbers looked in [4] at aspects of connecting informal and formal reasoning, in particular the integration of computations into formal proofs. Kamareddine and Nederpelt [5] have formalised de Bruijn's idea further. While the approach to a mathematical vernacular is general, to our knowledge no attempt has been made to incorporate concrete objects like matrices directly. In the Theorema system Kutsia [7] has worked with sequence variables which stand for symbols of flexible arity. Sequence variables have some similarities to our ellipses. However, as opposed to sequence variables our ellipses allow only fixed interpretations. Moreover sequence variables can be viewed as an extension of the logical system which allows to deal with these expressions within the logic. The main emphasis of our work is to allow for representation within logic and extra-logical manipulation of expressions at the same time. Bundy and Richardson [2] introduced a general treatment for reasoning about lists with ellipses in a way that they consider an ellipsis as a schema which stands for infinitely many expressions and a proof about ellipses stands for infinitely many proofs, which can be generated from a meta-argument.

# References

1. P.B. Andrews. *An Introduction to Mathematical Logic and Type Theory: To Truth Through Proof.* Kluwer, 2nd edition, 2002.
2. A. Bundy and J. Richardson. Proofs about lists using ellipsis. In *Proc. of the 6th LPAR*, volume 1705 of *LNAI*, pp. 1–12. Springer, 1999.
3. N.G. de Bruijn. The mathematical vernacular, a language for mathematics with typed sets. In *Selected Papers on Automath*, pp. 865–935. Elsevier, 1994.
4. H. Elbers. *Connecting Informal and Formal Mathematics.* PhD thesis, Eindhoven University of Technology, 1998.
5. F. Kamareddine and R. Nederpelt. A refinement of de Bruijn's formal language of mathematics. *Journal of Logic, Language and Information*, 13(3):287–340, 2004.
6. M. Köcher. *Lineare Algebra und analytische Geometrie.* Springer, 1992.
7. T. Kutsia. Unification with sequence variables and flexible arity symbols and its extension with pattern-terms. In *Proc. of AICS'2002 & Calculemus'2002*, volume 2385 of *LNAI*. Springer, 2002.
8. S. Lang. *Algebra.* Addison-Wesley, Second Edition, 1984.
9. NCAlgebra 3.7 – A Noncommutative Algebra Package for Mathematica. Available at http://math.ucsd.edu/~ncalg/.
10. Omega Group. Proof development with Omega. In *Proc. of CADE-18*, volume 2392 of *LNAI*, pp. 143–148. Springer, 2002.
11. M. Pollet and V. Sorge. Integrating computational properties at the term level. In *Proc. of Calculemus'2002*, pp. 78–83, 2003.
12. M. Wenzel and F. Wiedijk. A Comparison of Mizar and Isar. *J. of Automated Reasoning*, 29(3–4):389–411, 2002.
13. S. Wolfram. *The Mathematica book.* Wolfram Media, Inc., 5th edition, 2003.

# Mathematical Libraries as Proof Assistant Environments

Claudio Sacerdoti Coen[*]

Department of Computer Science, University of Bologna
Mura Anteo Zamboni 7, 40127 Bologna, Italy
sacerdot@cs.unibo.it

**Abstract.** In this paper we analyse the modifications on logical operations – as proof checking, type inference, reduction and convertibility – that are required for the identification of a proof assistant environment with a distributed mathematical library, focusing on proof assistants based on the Curry–Howard isomorphism.

This identification is aimed at the integration of Mathematical Knowledge Management tools with interactive theorem provers: once the distinction between the proof assistant environment and a mathematical library is blurred, it is possible to exploit Mathematical Knowledge Management rendering, indexing and searching services inside an interactive theorem prover, a first step towards effective loosely-coupled collaborative mathematical environments.

## 1 Introduction

The main goal of Mathematical Knowledge Management (MKM) is the creation of large distributed libraries of mathematical knowledge and the development of tools to manage, render, data mine, index and retrieve the notions in these libraries. Mathematical Knowledge Management does not study the process of new mathematical knowledge creation by a mathematician, but is expected to have a substantial impact on it: the better the existent knowledge is grasped and retrieved, the quicker the process of creation. For instance, recent studies [2, 3] implement an authomatic knowledge discovery framework by tightly integrating Mathematical Knowledge Management with authomatic theorem proving: the existent mathematical knowledge is used to derive new definitions, to guess interesting properties and to drive the theorem prover by suggesting well known proof techniques; the theorem prover is used to detect the properties that hold and prune out wrong guesses.

It is not known whether all the expectations will be met or whether the mathematicians will not adopt the Mathematical Knowledge Management tools finding them useless. Nevertheless, we already have evidence of the necessity for them in the restricted domain of interactive theorem proving. The mathematician that deals with formal mathematics has to develop her own theories on top

---

[*] Partially supported by 'MoWGLI: Math on the Web, Get it by Logic and Interfaces', EU IST-2001-33562.

of large bases of apparently trivial facts that nevertheless need to be proved and retrieved. Mathematical Knowledge Management techniques are necessary since large knowledge bases can be developed only collaboratively and since often the facts in them are so obvious event not to have a name easy to remember, so to be effectively retrieved only using the advanced indexing techniques developed in MKM.

Proof assistants – also called interactive theorem provers – are based on the notion of environment, that is the knowledge base that is local to one development and that is interactively augmented. Logical operation (as proof-checking) and extra-logical utilities (as rendering and searching) operate on the proof assistant environment only.

To achieve full integration with Mathematical Knowledge Management tools, the natural path is blurring the distinction between a distributed mathematical library and the environment of a proof assistant, consequently replacing every extra-logical utility that is limited to the environment only with the corresponding Mathematical Knowledge Management tool that operates over the whole distributed library.

In this paper we analyse the necessary modifications on the logical operations for the identification of the proof assistant environment with a distributed mathematical library, focusing on the proof assistants based on the Curry-Howard isomorphism.

In Sect. 2 we present the Calculus of Constructions as a paradigmatic example of the logic of a proof assistant based on the Curry-Howard isomorphism. In particular, we detail the classical presentation of the reduction and typing rules of the calculus, and we analyse the role of the environment in this presentation.

Since the rules are not syntax oriented, implementations are based on an alternative version that also handles the environment in a completely different way. This operational presentation of the rules is described in Sect. 3. Both set of rules are not well suited for the replacement of environments with distributed mathematical libraries.

In Sect. 4 we present a third original version of the rules that differs from the operational presentation in the way environments are constructed: instead of the operational "bottom up" construction of the environment, based on well-typed extensions of the current environment, we present a "top down" approach where the environment is considered to be a subset of the mathematical library and where the environment necessary to type-check a definition can be dynamically inferred during type-checking.

Intuitively, in the classical approach the environment is a consistent space of mathematical notions, that can only be augmented if its consistency is preserved. No notion outside this consistent space is accessible and no operation can be performed on it. In our approach, instead, there is a much larger space of connected and maybe conflicting mathematical notions, that is the mathematical library. We can associate to every point in the space an environment that is the minimal consistent subspace that contains the point and that is closed for references (i.e. occurrences of lemmas and definitions). It is possible to operate on the whole space as long as inconsistent subspaces are not considered at once.

Section 4 analyses the practical relevance of the contribution presented in this paper, whereas Sect. 5 describes future work.

## 2     The Calculus of Constructions

In this section we present a variant of the Calculus of Constructions (CoC) [5] as a paradigmatic example of a calculus used to implement proof assistants based on the Curry-Howard isomorphism. The given presentation is obtained by removing from the Calculus of (Co)Inductive Constructions – the calculus of the Coq proof assistants[1] – all the rules that deal with local definitions and (co)inductive types. The part of the calculus that deals with universes is preserved, but is simplified (hence making it less expressive). The motivation is the complexity of the omitted rules, that are largely orthogonal to the topic addressed in this paper. Nevertheless, in the author's PhD. dissertation [9] the whole Calculus of (Co)Inductive Constructions is considered.

Since CoC is (an extension of) a Pure Type System, we could adopt Pure Type Systems extended with constants as our paradigmatic example. Nevertheless, the generalization of what we propose to Pure Type Systems is a trivial exercise and casts no additional light on the topic. Moreover, our formalization has the additional benefit of being closer to the calculus actually implemented in the proof assistant Coq.

### 2.1     Syntax

Let $\mathcal{V}$ be a denumerable family of variable names, $x, y, z, \ldots \in \mathcal{V}$.

Let $\mathcal{C}$ be a denumerable family of constant names, $c, c_1, \ldots, c_n \in \mathcal{C}$.

Well formed terms (represented by $t, f, u, T, U, N, M$) are inductively defined as follows.

$$
\begin{array}{lll}
t ::= & x & \text{identifiers} \\
| & c & \text{constants} \\
| & \textbf{Set} \mid \textbf{Prop} \mid \textbf{Type}(j) & \text{sorts} \\
| & (t\ t) & \text{application} \\
| & \lambda x : t.t & \lambda\text{-abstraction} \\
| & \Pi x : t.t & \text{dependent product}
\end{array}
$$

Identifiers are references to locally bound variables, whereas constants are references to global definitions that are collected in an ordered list called an environm ent The terms **Set**, **Prop** and **Type**$(i)$ are called sorts and are indexed by $s$. Sorts are the types of a type. In particular, the sorts $Prop$ and $Set$ are used to type respectively propositions and data types. Every sort is typed by another sort $Type(i)$ characterized by a greater index $i$ (the index of $Prop$ and

---

*Set* is 0). A $\lambda$-abstraction $\lambda x : t_1.t_2$ is a function whose input $x$ is of type $t_1$ and whose output is the expression $t_2$. A dependent product $\Pi x : t_1.t_2$ is the type of all the functions whose input $x$ is of type $t_1$ and whose output is of type $t_2$. The variable $x$ is bound in $t_2$ both in $\lambda$-abstractions and dependent products. Free variables, substitution and $\alpha$-conversion are defined as usual. Terms are syntactically identified up to $\alpha$-conversion.

## 2.2 Environments and Contexts

As environments are ordered lists used to collect global definitions, contexts are ordered lists used to collect local declarations. Contexts and environments are formally defined by the following grammar:

$$
\begin{array}{lll}
\Gamma ::= [] & \text{empty context} \\
\quad | \ \Gamma.(x : T) & \text{declaration of } x \text{ of type } T \\
E ::= [] & \text{empty environment} \\
\quad | \ E.(c : T := t) & \text{definition of } c \text{ as } t \text{ of type } T
\end{array}
$$

We assume that no variable $x$ is declared twice in a context and that no constant $c$ is declared twice in an environment. The typing rules of the calculus enforce this invariant.

We write $(x : T) \in \Gamma$ if $x$ is declared in $\Gamma$ to have type $T$. Similarly, we write $(c : T := t) \in E$ if $c$ is defined in $E$ to be $t$ of type $T$.

## 2.3 Reductions and Convertibility

The syntax of the CoC allows to define and apply functions. The reduction rules of the calculus describe how the result of a function application is computed. We define two reduction rules: $\delta$-reduction and $\beta$-reduction.

$\delta$-reduction states that a constant occurrence can be replaced with its definiendum:

$$c \triangleright_\delta t \quad \text{if } (c : T := t) \in E$$

$\beta$-reduction substitutes the application of a function to its argument with the body of the function, replacing the formal parameter with the actual argument:

$$(\lambda x : T.M \ N) \triangleright_\beta M\{N/x\}$$

Additionally, the substitution operator $M\{N/x\}$ takes care of avoiding capturing of free variables of $N$.

The reflexive, symmetric, transitive and context-aware closure $=_{\beta\delta}$ of $\delta$-reduction and $\beta$-reduction is called convertibility. The reduction rules form a strongly normalizable rewriting system [11]. As a consequence, convertibility is a decidable property: to decide whether two terms are convertible we can test $\alpha$-convertibility of their normal forms. More efficient algorithms based on weak head reduction are used in real world implementations [8, 9].

Since convertibility is a decidable equivalence relation, it is practical to identify terms up to convertibility. Concretely, this means reducing the number of human provided deduction steps of a proof by replacing them with machine performed computational steps.

## 2.4    Typing Rules

We give the typing rules of CIC by mutually defining two judgements. The first one, $E[\Gamma] \vdash t : T$, asserts that $t$, in an environment $E$ and a context $\Gamma$ that depends on $E$, has type $T$. The second one, $\mathcal{WF}(E)[\Gamma]$, asserts that $E$ is a valid environment – i.e. it is acyclic and it comprises only well-typed definitions – and that $\Gamma$ is a valid context in $E$ – i.e. it is acyclic and it comprises only well-typed variable declarations. An environment $E$ is acyclic when each constant definition $d$ may refer only constants defined before $d$ in $E$. Similarly, a context $\Gamma$ in $E$ is acyclic when each variable declaration $d$ may refer only constants in the environment $E$ or variables declared before $d$ in $\Gamma$. Cyclic environments and contexts must be avoided since in general they correspond to non well-founded (and logically inconsistent) recursive definitions. Finally, we will see that $E[\Gamma] \vdash t : T$ implies $\mathcal{WF}(E)[\Gamma]$ for each couple of terms $t$ and $T$.

The rules of the two judgements are given in Table 1. The Conv rule is the one responsible for the identification of convertible terms. The version proposed here is a major simplification of the corresponding rule adopted in the Coq system and adapted from ECC [7]. In the original rule the equivalence relation $=_{\beta\delta}$ is replaced by an order relation $\leq_{\beta\delta}$ that admits cumulativity between universes. Cumulativity grants that each term of type $\mathbf{Type}(i)$ is also of type $\mathbf{Type}(j)$ for each $j > i$ (and is expressed by the rule $\mathbf{Type}(i) \leq_{\beta\delta} \mathbf{Type}(j)$. The order relation can also be extended to relate non-convertible function spaces (and sigma types, if available) when their input types (in contra-variant position) are convertible and their output types (in co-variant position) are in $\leq_{\beta\delta}$. The choice of the less expressive version of the rule avoids further complications that are orthogonal to our proposal.

This version of the typing rules is the one usually presented in theoretical dissertations about the Calculus of Constructions, since it is the presentation that more easily allows to prove metatheoretical results. Notice, however, that this formulation is not syntax directed: to type-check a term $t$ it is always possible to apply both the Conv rule and the rule – or the rules when $t$ is a dependent product – that match the syntactic structure of the term. Thus implementations are usually based on an alternative syntax directed presentation of the typing rules of the calculus.

In Sect. 3 we will present the syntax directed version of the typing rules of the calculus. Before that, let's analyze the way the environment is handled in the typing rules already given.

## 2.5    Environment Handling

First of all, by inspection of the typing rules of the $E[\Gamma] \vdash t : T$ judgement we notice that the environment $E$ is never modified (i.e. the same environment is used both in the conclusion and in every hypothesis). Moreover, every internal node of the derivation tree but conversion nodes (rules Prod-SP–Conv) does not directly exploit the environment. The conversion rule access the environment to compute $\delta$-reduction steps, but without checking its validity. On the contrary,

**Table 1.** Typing rules, original formulation

WF-Empty

$$\mathcal{WF}([])[[]]$$

WF-Var

$$\frac{E[\Gamma] \vdash T : s \quad s \in \{\mathbf{Prop}, \mathbf{Set}, \mathbf{Type}(i)\} \quad x \notin \Gamma}{\mathcal{WF}(E)[\Gamma, (x : T)]}$$

WF-Const

$$\frac{E[[]] \vdash T : s \quad s \in \{\mathbf{Prop}, \mathbf{Set}, \mathbf{Type}(i)\} \quad E[[]] \vdash t : T \quad c \notin E}{\mathcal{WF}(E; c : T := t)[[]]}$$

Ax-Prop

$$\frac{\mathcal{WF}(E)[\Gamma]}{E[\Gamma] \vdash \mathbf{Prop} : \mathbf{Type}(n)}$$

Ax-Set

$$\frac{\mathcal{WF}(E)[\Gamma]}{E[\Gamma] \vdash \mathbf{Set} : \mathbf{Type}(n)}$$

Ax-Acc

$$\frac{\mathcal{WF}(E)[\Gamma] \quad n < m}{E[\Gamma] \vdash \mathbf{Type}(n) : \mathbf{Type}(m)}$$

Var

$$\frac{\mathcal{WF}(E)[\Gamma] \quad (x : T) \in \Gamma}{E[\Gamma] \vdash x : T}$$

Const

$$\frac{\mathcal{WF}(E)[\Gamma] \quad (c : T := t) \in E}{E[\Gamma] \vdash c : T}$$

Prod-SP

$$\frac{E[\Gamma] \vdash T : s_1 \quad E[\Gamma, (x : T)] \vdash U : s_2 \quad s_1 \in \{\mathbf{Prop}, \mathbf{Set}\} \quad \text{or} \quad s_2 \in \{\mathbf{Prop}, \mathbf{Set}\}}{E[\Gamma] \vdash \Pi x : T.U : s_2}$$

Prod-T

$$\frac{E[\Gamma] \vdash T : \mathbf{Type}(n_1) \quad E[\Gamma, (x : T)] \vdash U : \mathbf{Type}(n_2) \quad n_1 \leq n \quad n_2 \leq n}{E[\Gamma] \vdash \Pi x : T.U : \mathbf{Type}(n)}$$

Lam

$$\frac{E[\Gamma, (x : T)] \vdash t : U \quad E[\Gamma] \vdash \Pi x : T.U : s}{E[\Gamma] \vdash \lambda x : T.t : \Pi x : T.U}$$

App

$$\frac{E[\Gamma] \vdash t : \Pi x : U.T \quad E[\Gamma] \vdash u : U}{E[\Gamma] \vdash (t\ u) : T\{u/x\}}$$

Conv

$$\frac{E[\Gamma] \vdash T_1 : s \quad E[\Gamma] \vdash t : T_2 \quad E[\Gamma] \vdash T_1 =_{\beta\delta} T_2}{E[\Gamma] \vdash t : T_1}$$

all the leaves of a derivation tree (rules Ax-Prop–Const) check the validity of the environment by testing $\mathcal{WF}(E)[\Gamma]$. Due to our previous observation, this means that a proof of $\mathcal{WF}(E)[\Gamma]$ for the same version of $E$ and $\Gamma$ is required at each leaf of the derivation tree. Of course, this is totally unreasonable from an implementation point of view. Thus the operational presentation of the rules will take care of this, granting that a couple $(E, \Gamma)$ will be checked only once.

Let's focus now on the derivation rules of the $\mathcal{WF}(E)[\Gamma]$ judgement. The applications of this rules are stratified: first of all the WF-Var rule is applied several times to remove one after the other all the declarations in the context $\Gamma$; then the WF-Const rule is applied several times to remove one after the other all the definitions in the environment $E$. Finally a single application of the WF-Empty rule ends the proof. In the first phase – the applications of the WF-Var rule – the environment $E$ is also never modified.

From the previous observations we conclude that the only rule that destructures the environment $E$ is the WF-Const rule. The WF-Const rule checks for well-formedness of the environment $E'$ obtained removing from $E$ its last element; then it checks for the well-typedness of the definition in the environment $E'$. By induction on the height of the derivations we can easily prove that eventually every element of $E$ is checked for well-formedness in a derivation of $\mathcal{WF}(E)[]$. Interestingly, however, this check is apparently done "on demand": the well-formedness of the environment $E$ is not checked before starting the proof of $E[\Gamma] \vdash t : T$, but only during its proof, whenever an occurrence of a constant is met. However, every constant in $E$ is checked, even if it does not occur in $\Gamma$, $t$ and $T$. In the latter case, the thinning lemma [11] states the uselessness of the check, since unused constants can be removed from the environment without affecting well typedness. This suggests that checking "on demand" can be improved to avoid unused definitions.

The previous observations imply that the standard presentation of the type-checking rules is not appropriate for a direct implementation, especially if the environment is substituted by a large and distributed mathematical library, since

– the parts of the library that are not useful to type-check the term under consideration are checked anyway;
– each object in the library is checked more than once.

In the next section we analyse the standard operational presentation of the type-checking rules, discussing how the environment is handled.

## 3    Syntax Directed Type Checking Rules

The syntax directed (or operational) version of the reduction and type-checking rules of CoC solves at once two problems of the previous presentation: each definition in the environment is checked at most once; and at most one type-checking or reduction rule can be applied to a given term (respectively to a couple of terms).

Thanks to the latter remarkable property the operational presentation of the rules yields an efficient algorithm that does not require backtracking. However, in this paper we are more interested in the first property.

The key idea that underlies the management of the environment is the following already noticed invariant: the environment is consulted, but it is never modified during the type-checking of a term $t$ in the context $\Gamma$. Thus it is possible to define the (current) environment as an abstract data type with two methods: the first one returns the definition of a constant $c$ in the environment; the second one appends a definition to the environment. The latter method checks for the well-typedness of the definition before appending it. The initial environment is the empty environment (that is always well-formed). The invariant that is granted by the two method implementations is the well-formedness of the environment. Thus, in the following typing rules, we can always assume the environment $E$ to be well-typed.

The expression $\mathrm{whd}(E, t)$ that occurs in the typing rules compute the weak head normal form of $t$ in the environment $E$. The judgement $E[\Gamma] \vdash t \downarrow t'$ is a syntax directed formulation of the convertibility judgement. It satisfies the property $E[\Gamma] \vdash t \downarrow t'$ iff $E[\Gamma] \vdash t =_{\beta\delta} t'$. A set of rules for the $E[\Gamma] \vdash t \downarrow t'$ judgement that yield and efficient implementation can be found in [8, 9].

The rules of the typing judgement are given in Table 2. The premise $(c : T := t) \in E$ of the BU-Const rule is implemented by calling the first method of the abstract data type that implements $E$ on the constant name $c$. The definition $(c : T := t)$ is the result of the method invocation.

**Table 2.** Typing rules, operational formulation

BU-Ax-Prop

$$\frac{}{E[\Gamma] \vdash \mathbf{Prop} : \mathbf{Type}(i)}$$

BU-Ax-Set

$$\frac{}{E[\Gamma] \vdash \mathbf{Set} : \mathbf{Type}(i)}$$

BU-Ax-Acc

$$\frac{n \leq m}{E[\Gamma] \vdash \mathbf{Type}(n) : \mathbf{Type}(m)}$$

BU-Var

$$\frac{(x : T) \in \Gamma}{E[\Gamma] \vdash x : T}$$

BU-Const

$$\frac{(c : T := t) \in E}{E[\Gamma] \vdash c : T}$$

BU-Prod

$$\frac{E[\Gamma] \vdash T : S_1 \qquad whd(E[\Gamma], S_1) = s_1}{E[\Gamma, (x : T)] \vdash U : S_2 \qquad whd(E[\Gamma, (x : T)], S_2) = s_2}{E[\Gamma] \vdash \Pi x : T.U : s_2}$$

BU-Lam

$$\frac{E[\Gamma] \vdash T : S \quad whd(E[\Gamma], S) = s \quad E[\Gamma, (x : T)] \vdash t : U}{E[\Gamma] \vdash \lambda x : T.t : \Pi x : T.U}$$

BU-App

$$\frac{E[\Gamma] \vdash t : S \quad whd(E[\Gamma], S) = \Pi x : U.T \quad E[\Gamma] \vdash u : U' \quad E[\Gamma] \vdash U \downarrow U'}{E[\Gamma] \vdash (t\ u) : T\{u/x\}}$$

To grant the well-formedness of the environment, a definition $(c : T := t)$ is appended by the second method only if the following conditions are satisfied:

$$c \notin E \quad E[[]] \vdash T : S \quad \mathrm{whd}(E[[]], T) = s \quad E[[]] \vdash t : T' \quad E[[]] \vdash T' \downarrow T \quad (*)$$

As already stated in the introduction of the paper, the major drawback of this management of the environment is that the environment must be constructed in a "bottom up" fashion, checking in advance all the results that will be needed for the mathematical result the user wants to develop. Since it is common to discover the need for a lemma during the development of a proof, the bottom up environment construction can be an annoying limitation.

For instance, let us consider the following scenario: the user knows (or finds using a search engine) that there is a lemma in the mathematical library that she would like to use. The lemma is not part of the current environment and it depends on other lemmas and definitions that are not part of the current environment. Thus she is obliged to add to the environment all these lemmas and definition in the right order, i.e. without appending a definition that relies on another definition not appended yet. If she is able to append all the lemmas and definitions, comprising the wanted lemma, then the obtained environment is well-formed and she can apply the lemma.

Since we cannot expect the user to perform by hand the previous mechanical operations, we can delegate them to an external software agent. However, this solution is not efficient, since all the terms of all the definitions that must be added to the environment are browsed twice: the first time to collect all their dependencies to compute their topological sorting; the second time to type-check them. Moreover, bugs in the topological sorting algorithm are difficult to detect since they manifest themselves by producing non well-formed environments whereas well-formed environments can be produced.

Finally, notice that the syntax directed type-checking judgement is not a complete formal description of the type-checker, since the data type and its implementation must also be described, as well as the additional constraints $(*)$.

In the following section we propose yet an alternative formulation of the type-checking judgement. The formulation proposed is syntax oriented, yielding an algorithm that can be mechanically implemented. The environment is managed in a "top down" fashion, being constructed (identified) only on demand, in a "call-by-need" fashion. Concretely, an environment is a consistent subset of a larger (and possibly inconsistent) mathematical library. Thus the user is always free to use at any time a lemma in the library that is not yet in the environment. Finally the judgement proposed is self-contained, no longer requiring an external data type.

## 4    Mathematical Libraries as Environments

Let $\mathcal{L}$ be a (possibly inconsistent) mathematical library (i.e. a set of constant definitions $(c : T := t)$). An environment $E$ is a consistent subset of $\mathcal{L}$. We define two mutual judgements, $\langle \Phi \rangle E[\Gamma] \vdash t : T \bowtie E'$ and $\mathrm{fetch}(\Phi, E, c, E', (c : T := t))$, with the following semantics:

- $\mathrm{fetch}(\Phi, E, c, E', (c : T := t))$ holds when the environment $E \subseteq \mathcal{L}$, assumed to be consistent, can be extended to a new consistent environment $E' \subseteq \mathcal{L}$ such that $E$ is a prefix of $E'$, no constant in the set of constant names $\Phi$ is defined in $E'$ and $(c : T := t) \in E'$ where $(c : T := t) \in \mathcal{L}$.

  Concretely, the judgement defines a function whose input is the triple $(\Phi, E, c)$ and whose output is the couple $(E', c : T := t)$. We say that $E'$ is the (minimal) context extension of $E$ that includes $c$. The set of constant names $\Phi$ is a technical trick used to detect cycles in the constructed environment extension.

- $\langle \Phi \rangle E[\Gamma] \vdash t : T \bowtie E'$ holds when $t$ has type $T$ in the environment $E'$ and in the context $\Gamma$ and $E'$ is an extension of $E$ (assumed to be consistent) such that all the constants in the set of constant names $\Phi$ are not defined in $E'$.

  Concretely, the judgement defines a function whose input is the tuple $(\Phi, E, \Gamma, t, T)$ and whose output is the minimal environment extension $E'$ in which the input is well-typed.

The rules of the two judgements are given in Table 3. The following two theorems, whose proof can be found in the author's PhD. dissertation [9], state the equivalence of the proposed judgement with the standard presentation.

**Theorem 1 (Soundness).** For each environment $E$, context $\Gamma$, list of references $\Phi$ and term $t$ such that the intersection between the domain of $E$ and $\Phi$ is empty, if $\mathcal{WF}(E)[\Gamma]$ and $\langle \Phi \rangle E[\Gamma] \vdash t : T \bowtie E'$ then

- $\mathcal{WF}(E')[\Gamma]$
- the intersection between the domain of $E'$ and $\Phi$ is empty
- for each couple of terms $t', T'$ such that $E[\Gamma] \vdash t' : T'$ we also have $E'[\Gamma] \vdash t' : T'$
- $E'[\Gamma] \vdash t : T$.

**Theorem 2 (Completeness).** For each environment $E$, context $\Gamma$ and term $t$, if $\mathcal{WF}(E)[\Gamma]$ and $E[\Gamma] \vdash t : T$, then there exists an unique term $T'$ such that $\langle \emptyset \rangle E[\Gamma] \vdash t : T' \bowtie E$ and $E[\Gamma] \vdash T =_{\beta\delta} T'$.

## Practical Relevance

The main aim of this paper is the development of a type-checker that blurs as much as possible the distinction between the logical environment and the mathematical library, giving to the user the feeling of building her own development on top of the whole library. All the mathematical results in the library must seem to be always available, even if they have not been type-checked and put in the environment so far.

The typing judgement proposed satisfies at once several properties that altogether yield almost mechanically the implementation of a type-checker that satisfies our needs. Indeed

**Table 3.** Typing rules, proposed new operational formulation

TD-Ax-Prop
$$\langle\Phi\rangle E[\Gamma] \vdash \mathbf{Prop} : \mathbf{Type} \bowtie E$$

TD-Ax-Set
$$\langle\Phi\rangle E[\Gamma] \vdash \mathbf{Set} : \mathbf{Type} \bowtie E$$

TD-Ax-Acc
$$\langle\Phi\rangle E[\Gamma] \vdash \mathbf{Type} : \mathbf{Type} \bowtie E$$

TD-Var
$$\frac{(x : T) \in \Gamma \quad or \quad (x : T := t) \in \Gamma}{\langle\Phi\rangle E[\Gamma] \vdash x : T \bowtie E}$$

TD-Const
$$\frac{fetch(\Phi, E, c, E', (c : T := t)) \qquad \langle\Phi\rangle E'[\Gamma]}{\langle\Phi\rangle E[\Gamma] \vdash c : T \bowtie E'}$$

TD-Prod
$$\frac{\langle\Phi\rangle E[\Gamma] \vdash T : S_1 \bowtie E' \qquad\qquad whd(E'[\Gamma], S_1) = s_1}{\langle\Phi\rangle E'[\Gamma, (x : T)] \vdash U : S_2 \bowtie E'' \qquad whd(E''[\Gamma, (x : T)], S_2) = s_2}{\langle\Phi\rangle E[\Gamma] \vdash \Pi x : T.U : s_2 \bowtie E''}$$

TD-Lam
$$\frac{\langle\Phi\rangle E[\Gamma] \vdash T : S \bowtie E' \quad whd(E'[\Gamma], S) = s \quad \langle\Phi\rangle E'[\Gamma, (x : T)] \vdash t : U \bowtie E''}{\langle\Phi\rangle E[\Gamma] \vdash \lambda x : T.t : \Pi x : T.U \bowtie E''}$$

TD-App
$$\frac{\langle\Phi\rangle E[\Gamma] \vdash t : S \bowtie E' \quad whd(E'[\Gamma], S) = \Pi x : U.T \quad \langle\Phi\rangle E'[\Gamma] \vdash u : U' \bowtie E'' \quad E''[\Gamma] \vdash U \downarrow U'}{\langle\Phi\rangle E[\Gamma] \vdash (t\ u) : T\{u/x\} \bowtie E''}$$

TD-fetch-Const-hit
$$\frac{(c : T := t) \in E}{fetch(\Phi, E, c, E, (c : T := t))}$$

TD-fetch-Const-miss
$$\frac{c \notin \Phi \qquad (c : T := t) \in \mathcal{L}}{\langle\Phi; c\rangle E[[]] \vdash T : S \bowtie E' \qquad whd(E'[[]], T) = s}{\langle\Phi; c\rangle E'[[]] \vdash t : T' \bowtie E'' \qquad E''[[]] \vdash T' \downarrow T}{fetch(\Phi, E, c, E''; (c : T := t), (c : T := t))}$$

- the type-checking rules are syntax oriented;
- every object in the environment is checked only once;
- every object in the library is checked at most once, and only if necessary;
- the environment necessary to type-check a term is reconstructed on-the-fly during type-checking;
- the typing judgement is self-contained and fully describes the type-checker kernel.

Soundness (theorem 1) grants two useful implementation properties. The first one is what we name *minimal environment reconstruction*: given a term $t$, if $\langle\emptyset\rangle\emptyset[[]] \vdash t : T \bowtie E$, then $E$ is the smallest well-formed environment required to type-check $t$.

We call the second property *environment extension*: in order to check a new term, definition or declaration for well-formedness, we do not have to throw away the already computed and well-formed environment. We can simply invoke the type-checking procedure passing the current environment as the initial environment. In case of success, the returned environment is the minimal extension of the initial environment that grants the well-formedness property.

Environment reconstruction paves the way to the notion of trusted information source. A trusted information source is a subset of the distributed library of knowledge that is closed (in the sense that it is well-formed) and that we can trust to be also consistent. Concretely, trusting an information source $\mathcal{L}'$ amounts to adding a new inference rule that deals with the fetch relation, and to slightly change the reduction rule that deals with $\delta$ reduction:
O-fetch-Const-trust

$$\frac{(c : T := t) \in \mathcal{L}'}{\text{fetch}(\Phi, E, v, E; (c : T := t), (c : T := t))}$$

The rule for $\delta$–reduction is changed by replacing the premise $(c : T := t) \in E$ with the premise $(c : T := t) \in E$ or $(c : T := t) \in \mathcal{L}'$.

Basically, the new rule above means that a declaration or definition in a trusted information source $\mathcal{L}'$ can always be considered as well-formed. Equivalently, it says that $\mathcal{L}'$ can always be considered as a subset of any well-formed environment.

The proposed typing judgement, extended with trusted information sources, has been implemented in a proof-assistant kernel prototype developed in project HELM[2] (Hypertexual Electronic Library of Mathematics) [1] and it has already been in use for a couple of years. The prototype consults the HELM mathematical library of about 40000 lemmas and definitions extracted from the Coq proof assistant [10]. The library is physically distributed among several repositories. One of the repositories provides the standard library of the Coq proof assistant, that is granted to be closed and consistent. Thus the repository is considered a trusted information source, whereas all the other repositories are untrusted.

Recently, the kernel of the proof-assistant prototype has been embedded in a fully fledged tactic-based interactive theorem prover, that implements also refinement and unification. Unification is an extension of convertibility that handles missing or incomplete information: two open terms can be unified if there exists a substitution that makes them convertible. In a similar way refinement is an extension of convertibility that handles missing or incomplete information: an open term is refinable when there exists a substitution that makes it well-typed.

In the author's PhD. dissertation [9] the technique presented in this paper is extended to cover also unification and refinement. Thus the user of the HELM proof-assistant is never exposed to the notion of environment: all she knows about is the mathematical library that she can search, render and data mine and that she can freely extend, as long as no inconsistency is added. The searching, rendering and data-mining components of the prototype are off-the-shelf MKM

---

[2] http://helm.cs.unibo.it

services developed in project HELM and in project MoWGLI[3] (Math on the Web: Get it by Logics and Interfaces).

## 5   Future Work

The Calculus of Constructions and its extensions – as the Calculus of (Co)Inductive Constructions adopted by Coq – is formalized by imposing a linear ordering over the sorts **Type**: $\mathbf{Type}(i) \leq \mathbf{Type}(j)$ whenever $i < j$. The ordering is just used to avoid circularities, that may correspond to logical inconsistencies. No assumption is made in the meta-theory of the calculus about its linearity.

However, implementations of the Calculus of Constructions are usually based on a different sorts representation, where the order relation is a partial order that is automatically inferred by the system and that can be represented as an acyclic graph. The benefits of this solution are twofold: on the one hand the user is given the illusion to work in a simpler (but inconsistent, [4]) impredicative system that has only one sort **Type : Type**; on the other hand the system is more flexible in the definition of new sorts and new constraints about the sorts.

For instance, in the classical presentation it is not possible to add a new sort $\mathbf{Type}(i)$ between $\mathbf{Type}(1)$ and $\mathbf{Type}(2)$ unless every sort $\mathbf{Type}(j)$ such that $j \geq 2$ is shifted. Even worse, given two logically unrelated sorts $\mathbf{Type}(n)$ and $\mathbf{Type}(m)$ we are obliged to artificially fix an order – say $n < m$ – unless we are using a partial order. Once the order $n < m$ is fixed, the usage of a lemma that generates the logical constraint $m < n$ is rejected even if the detected cycle does not correspond to a real logical inconsistency.

As a future work, we are planning to detail and implement a version of the typing judgement that is based on a partial order implemented as an acyclic graph. Since constraints (arcs) among the sorts are introduced during type-checking, we must extend our judgement to build the sorts graph on-demand during environment reconstruction and extension.

One interesting property of this approach with respect to the usual implementation is that the sorts graph inferred by the environment reconstruction procedure is minimal, in the sense that no constraint can be relaxed without losing the well-typedness of the declaration.

Unfortunately, in case of failure during an environment extension we are not allowed to conclude that the given term, declaration or definition is not well-typed. For instance, it may be the case that no well-formed extension of the current environment grants well-formedness, simply because of a conflicting set of constraints. Nevertheless, it may be the case that some of the conflicting constraints are derived from parts of the initial environment that are not necessary to type-check the given input [6]. Thus, to conclude that the input is not well-formed, we are obliged to repeat the check starting from the empty environment.

Notice that the problem we have just noticed is not a side-effect of our special handling of the environment. Indeed, our approach is the only one that allows

---

[3] http://mowgli.cs.unibo.it

to overcome the problem, by reconstructing the minimal necessary environment. In the Coq system, for instance, when such a case is met the only solution is to factorize out of the required modules[4] all the definitions necessary to type the incriminated definition. Basically this amounts to perform by hand the operation of environment reconstruction.

It should be noted, however, that the cases where the problem arises are very uncommon. All the cases known by the author are to be found in the encoding of set theories and the theory of categories where big and small sets (or categories) are mixed together in the same development. Nevertheless, once again we feel that, in the context of mathematical knowledge management, the problem must be faced in a serious way, since it can deeply hinder the possibility of extending or reusing a development in the long term.

To integrate the inference of the sorts graph $\gamma$ in the environment reconstruction procedure, all the rules need to be given the sorts graphs an additional input and output. Moreover, the fetch relation becomes also responsible for extending the system of constraints by adding the constraints that are required to type-check the reference object. Thus, in order to obtain a sound implementation, we need to keep, for any object in a trusted information source, the minimal set of constraints imposed during its type-checking. Let $\mathcal{K}$ be the map that associates the constraints to a reference $r$. The fetching rule is changed in the following way:

TD-fetch-Const-trust

$$\frac{(c : T := t) \in \mathcal{L}' \qquad \mathcal{WF}(\gamma \sqcup \mathcal{K}(c))}{\mathrm{fetch}(\varPhi, \langle E, \gamma \rangle, c, \langle E; (c : T := t), \gamma \sqcup \mathcal{K}(c) \rangle, (c(v_1, \ldots, v_n) : T := t))}$$

where $\gamma$ is the set of constraints in input, $\sqcup$ is the operation that merges two set of constraints and $\mathcal{WF}(\gamma \sqcup \gamma')$ is the new judgement that checks if the merge of two set of satisfiable constraints is satisfiable (i.e. it does not contain any cycles).

# References

1. A. Asperti, F. Guidi, L. Padovani, C. Sacerdoti Coen, and I. Schena. Mathematical Knowledge Management in HELM. In Annals of Mathematics and Artificial Intelligence, 38(1): 27–46, May 2003.
2. B. Buchberger. Computer-Supported Mathematical Theory Exploration: Schemes, Failing Proof Analysis, and Metaprogramming. Technical report, September 2004, RISC, Austria.
3. S. Colton. Automated Theory Formation in Pure Mathematics Series: Distinguished Dissertations. 2002, XVI, 380 p., ISBN: 1-85233-609-9.
4. T. Coquand. An Analysis of Girard's Paradox. In Proc. Symposium on Logic in Computer Science, pages 227-236, Cambridge, Massachusetts, 16-18 June 1986. IEEE Computer Society.

---

[4] A Coq module roughly corresponds to a mathematical development. They are the minimal compilation units of the Coq system.

5. T. Coquand and G. Huet. The Calculus of Constructions. Technical report 530, INRIA, May 1986.

6. J. Courant. Explicit universes for the calculus of constructions. In V.A. Carreño, C. Muñoz, and S. Tahar (eds.), Theorem Proving in Higher Order Logics: 15th International Conference, TPHOLs 2002, volume 2410 of Lecture Notes in Computer Science, pages 115-130, Hampton, VA, USA, August 2002. Springer-Verlag.

7. Z. Luo. *An Extended Calculus of Constructions.* PhD thesis, University of Edinburgh, 1990.

8. R. Harper and R. Pollack. Type checking with universes. Theoretical Computer Science, 89:107–136, 1991.

9. C. Sacerdoti Coen. *Mathematical Knowledge Management and Interactive Theorem Proving.* PhD thesis, University of Bologna, 2004.

10. C. Sacerdoti Coen. From Proof-Assistants to Distributed Libraries of Mathematics: Tips and Pitfalls. In Proc. Mathematical Knowledge Management 2003, Lecture Notes in Computer Science, Vol. 2594, pp. 30–44, Springer-Verlag.

11. B. Werner. *Une Theorie des Constructions Inductives.* PhD thesis, Université Paris VII, 1994.

# Efficient Ambiguous Parsing
# of Mathematical Formulae[*]

Claudio Sacerdoti Coen and Stefano Zacchiroli

Department of Computer Science, University of Bologna
Mura Anteo Zamboni 7, 40127 Bologna, Italy
{sacerdot,zacchiro}@cs.unibo.it

**Abstract.** Mathematical notation has the characteristic of being ambiguous: operators can be overloaded and information that can be deduced is often omitted. Mathematicians are used to this ambiguity and
can easily *disambiguate* a formula making use of the context and of their
ability to find the right interpretation.

Software applications that have to deal with formulae usually avoid
these issues by fixing an unambiguous input notation. This solution is
annoying for mathematicians because of the resulting tricky syntaxes
and becomes a show stopper to the simultaneous adoption of tools characterized by different input languages.

In this paper we present an efficient algorithm suitable for ambiguous
parsing of mathematical formulae. The only requirement of the algorithm
is the existence of a "validity" predicate over abstract syntax trees of
incomplete formulae with placeholders. This requirement can be easily
fulfilled in the applicative area of interactive proof assistants, and in
several other areas of Mathematical Knowledge Management.

## 1 Introduction

Mathematicians are used to well established and ambiguous notational conventions. To design a software application which have to deal with mathematical
formulae, we have to consider this habit.

Sometimes a mathematician who is reading a formula, solves the ambiguity
using the notion of context: for instance, if $f$ is known to be a scalar value, then
$f^{-1}$ is the inverse value $1/f$; if $f$ is a function, then $f^{-1}$ is probably the inverse
function of $f$.

More often the context is not sufficient and the ambiguity is solved by picking
the only interpretation that makes sense or the interpretation that is more likely
to have one. For instance, without additional information, a mathematician is
like to interpret $\phi^2(x)$ as $(\phi \circ \phi)(x)$ although $\sin^2(x)$ is probably interpreted as
$(\sin x)^2$.

Associating precedences to operators does not always solve ambiguity problems as shown by the combined usage of conjuction and equality operators:

---

[*] The authors have been partially supported by 'MoWGLI: Math on the Web, Get it
by Logic and Interfaces', EU IST-2001-33562.

A. Asperti et al. (Eds.): MKM 2004, LNCS 3119, pp. 347–362, 2004.

$A \wedge B = B \wedge A$ is usually interpreted as equality of conjuctions whereas $x = y \wedge y = x$ as conjuction of equalities.

Using unambiguous grammars computer scientists avoid ambiguity problems in programming languages and programmers are used to learn them from scratch along with their ad hoc syntactical rules. Mathematicians can of course do the same with new proof assistants or other Mathematical Knowledge Management (MKM) applications. Notwithstanding this fact, there are motivations for trying to recognize ambiguous mathematical inputs in the MKM context. In the following paragraphs we try to identify some of them.

Different mathematicians adopt for the same concept different notations. We do not want to give up this possibility for technical reasons. In MKM indeed there are several situations where the user has to write or read a mathematical formula without knowing the context, in which notations are defined. Let us consider a search engine for mathematical results, as the one described in [5]. The user enters a statement to retrieve all its proofs. In order to do so, she has to pick a notation and use symbols and constants that are not fixed by any context. Thus the search engine has to be able to parse the ambiguous sentence, disambiguate it and perform the search modulo the context.

A feature that is usually provided to the user of a Computer Algebra System (CAS) or a proof assistant is that of defining new notations, which are stored in the context. Sooner or later it will happen that a user needs to merge together two contexts where the same notation is used for different concepts. If these systems do not handle overloading, the easiest form of ambiguity, at least one of the two notations is actually masked and the user has to redefine it, creating a break point in the notational uniformity of the whole development. The Mizar[10] library committee has already faced several times these kind of problems, that were solved by changing one of the two notations and updating the whole Mizar library.

Among the topics of MKM there are digitalization and enhancement of already existing mathematical knowledge. Since the notation used in already existing mathematical documents is ambiguous, ambiguity must be addressed in both phases. Morever, since the amount of such documents is huge, we should minimize as much as possible the amount of disambiguation work left to the human.

In this paper we outline an efficient algorithm which can be used to perform ambiguous parsing in applications pertaining to the MKM area. The algorithm can be seen as an improvement of the algorithm for ambiguous parsing used in type based parsers as the one of the Grammatical Framework [11]. Type based parsing imposes a type system over the grammar of the language that must be recognized, and uses the typing judgement to prune wrong interpretations. In the context of mathematical formulae no additional type system needs to be imposed since arity, domain and codomain information associated to mathematical operators can play the role of a type system that supports the required operations.

In Sect. 2 we present the classes of efficient and modular parsing algorithms we are interested in; in Sect. 3 we describe refinement, the predicate needed to validate formulae fragments; the algorithm itself is presented in Sect. 4 and analyzed in Sect. 5, where several future research directions are also outlined; final remarks and conclusions are given in Sect. 6.

## 2    Requirements

Traditionally, compilers have been implemented as pipelines of phases. The first phase, lexing, takes in input a stream of characters and produces as output a stream of tokens. These tokens are the input for the parsing phase which in turn produces as output one or more abstract syntax trees (or ASTs for short). The semantic analysis phase finally takes in input ASTs and enriches their nodes with semantics information. Each phase can fail, aborting the whole process.

The parsing phase is in charge of recognizing if the input phrase pertains to a predefined grammar or not. This grammar is said to be unambiguous if, for any given input phrase, there exists at most one AST; otherwise the grammar is an ambiguous grammar.

The output of the parsing phase for an unambiguous grammar is either a parse error or the unique AST for the input formula. This property does not hold for ambiguous grammars. In that case the output of the parsing phase is no longer a single tree, but rather a set of trees.

Ambiguous grammars are just one aspects of ambiguity, the other one we will consider is introduced by the semantic analysis phase. We say that an AST is an ambiguous AST when the semantic analysis phase can associate to it more than one semantics – whatever the semantics is.

When this kind of ambiguity has to be considered, the output of the semantic analysis phase is a set of semantics for each AST in the input set. Let us consider the formula $(1+2)*3^{-1} = 1$, and suppose we are in the applicative area of proof assistants. This formula exhibits the latter aspect of ambiguity described, since each symbol in it can have many different semantic interpretations:

1. each number can be a natural, integer, rational, real or complex number;
2. "$-1$" can either be the application of the unary operator "$-$" to 1, or the integer, rational, real or complex number $-1$;
3. "$=$" can represent many different equalities (Leibniz's polymorphic equality an equivalence relation over natural or real numbers, ... );
4. "$+$" and "$*$" can be defined over naturals, integers, ...;
5. if subtyping does not hold, implicit coercions can be inserted to inject a number of one type in a "super type";
6. since different representations of a concept have different computational properties, several representations of, say, natural numbers may be available.

Similar observations can be made in applicative areas other than that of proof assistants. For instance, some of them applies directly to CASs. In the rest of the paper we want to address the two forms of ambiguities at the same time.

We say that an algorithm performs am biguous parsing when it associates to an input formula $E$ the set of all the semantics for $E$. This means that we are considering the second and third phases of a traditional compiler as just one macro phase. The motivation is efficiency: we want to be able to detect semantically wrong formulae already during the parsing phase, without generating a multitude of ASTs that later on cannot be assigned any meaning.

At the same time, we do care about the modularity induced by the distinction of the two phases. Thus these are the two requirements that we want our algorithm to satisfy:

1. The algorithm should be com positional: the semantic analysis phase should be as separate as possible from the parsing phase.
2. The algorithm should be effcient: semantic errors must be detected as early as possible, preventing further parsing and semantic analysis of already incorrect interpretations.

The apparent conflict between the two requirements manifest itself in implementations that fulfil one requirement sacrificing the other. For instance, let us consider again the formula $(1 + 2) * 3^{-1} = 1$. The naive compositional algorithm (NCA for short) performs parsing first, returning a huge set of ASTs, one for each combination of the possible interpretations of each symbol. For instance, one possible output is the tree whose root is equality over real numbers and whose second argument is the Peano number 1. Then semantic analysis proceeds at pruning out the most part of the combinations: for instance, every tree whose root is the equality over real numbers and whose second argument is not a real number is pruned. Unfortunately, this algorithm is not efficient, since several trees are parsed and analyzed even if looking at the root and its second argument already provides enough information to prune them out. However, due to its triviality, NCA is the most commonly used algorithm [11].

Let us now consider the most efficient top-down algorithm, which generates every possible interpretation for the root, and for each interpretation calls itself on the two arguments remembering what the expected type of the argument was. The expected type is used to pick for the second argument of the root the only interpretation that respects the type. Corresponding efficient bottom-up algorithms can be easily built as well. Clearly this algorithm is not compositional, since it performs type checking already during the parsing phase, and just on a fragment of the tree.

In Sect. 4 we propose a compositional and yet efficient algorithm for ambiguous parsing of mathematical formulae, showing that the conflict is only ephemeral. The main assumption underlying the algorithm is the availability of the refinement operation described in the next section. Intuitively, the function allows to detect semantic errors on partial ASTs and thus it can be used already during the construction of the AST set that is the output of the parsing phase.

To the authors knowledge the algorithm is new, despite its apparent simplicity. Its novelty was also confirmed by private communication with Aarne Ranta, who is the main author of Grammatical Framework (GF) [11] and without any doubt one of the major experts in this field.

## 3   Refinement

The crucial ingredient of our parsing algorithm is the function that performs semantic analysis of the abstract syntax tree of the formula. Its goal is to detect invalid formulae. Since the most common mistake in a formula is the application of an operator to arguments outside its domain, this function is likely to be a sort of type deriver. Indeed, every foundational system used to encode the formulae has its own version of a (weak) "type" system.

Let us consider several kind of formulae encoding used in the mathematical practice and in MKM. Set theory is the most widely used foundation among mathematicians. In principle, every operator in set theory is untyped (or uni-typed), since every term is a set and set theoretical operations can be applied to any set. For instance, the natural number zero can be defined as the empty set and the natural number one as the set $\{\emptyset\}$. Thus the formula $0 \in 1$ is perfectly valid. Notwithstanding this, mathematicians that work in set theory use to consider natural numbers as a sort of abstract data type, forgetting their concrete definition and considering "well typed" only the applications of operators whose domain is the same or a subset of the set the argument belongs to.

The logical foundation that Computer Algebra Systems are commonly based on is some variant of multi-sorted first order logic. The arity and sorts of the symbols define the type system that prevents wrong applications inside formulae.

The type system becomes a truly first class citizen in mathematical reasoning tools based on type theory. The majority of Proof Assistants (PA), with the significant exception of Mizar[10], are based on type theory, where a type is assigned to every term, and a product (or arrow type) is assigned to operators. The application is well-typed if the type of the argument matches the domain of the product.

Type systems can be classified according to the presence or absence of dependent products. A non-dependent product $T_1 \rightarrow T_2$ types functions whose output type $T_2$ does not depend on the actual argument. On the contrary, a dependent product $\varPi x : T_1. T_2(x)$ types functions whose output type $T_2(x)$ is a function of the actual argument $x$. Dependent type systems allow to express tighter constraints on the arguments of an operator, rejecting a larger number of wrong formulae and making the disambiguation algorithm more effective, but also more complex.

Type derivers are programs that check whether a type can be assigned to a formula, and that can optionally return the computed type. Thus they can be exploited as pruning functions for NCA: after generating every AST, the type deriver is used to prune invalid ASTs. To implement our efficient version of the algorithm we need an extension, called refiner, of a stronger version of the type deriver able to deal with incomplete formulae. However, our algorithm is fully generic, since it is not based on a particular calculus or a particular type system. The only necessary requirement is the possibility to represent incomplete formulae and the existence of a refiner.

An incomplete formula is a formula where non linear placeholders for subformulae occur. Every non linear placeholder $?_i$ where $i$ is a natural number replaces the occurrence of a subformula. Occurrences of equal placeholders replace equal subformulae. In type theory literature, placeholders are called metavariables [8, 13, 7].

In type theory for instance, to obtain a typed calculus with metavariables from a typed calculus of closed terms (where no metavariable occurs), metavariable occurrences are added to the term grammar, and a typing context for metavariables is added to the typing rules. The typing context associates a type to each metavariable, that is the type of the term replaced by the metavariable. In the case of dependent products, the type of the metavariable in the typing context is replaced by a sequent, that describes the type of the replaced term and the free variables that (may) occur free in the replaced term, together with their type. For instance, the formula $\forall x : \mathbb{Z}.x = ?_1$ is well typed if the sequent $x : \mathbb{Z} \vdash ?_1 : \mathbb{Z}$ is associated with $?_1$, stating that $?_1$ is a term of type $\mathbb{Z}$ parametric in $x$ also of type $\mathbb{Z}$.

**Definition 1 (Refiner).** A refiner is a function whose input is an incomplete formula $t_1$ and whose output is either:

- an incomplete formula $t_2$ where $t_2$ is a well-typed formula obtained by assigning a type (or a sequent) to each metavariable in $t_1$ and, in case of dependent types, by instantiating some of the metavariables that occur in $t_1$;
- the special constant $\epsilon$ if there exists no well-typed formula $t_2$ that can be obtained by assigning a type (or a sequent) to each metavariable in $t_1$ and by instantiating some of the metavariables;
- the special constant $\bot$ when neither one of the two previous cases can be verified by the algorithm.

Whereas type checking is usually decidable, refinement is usually a semidecidable problem. Thus, in the literature, refinement algorithms are usually described to return either a refined term $t_2$ or the $\bot$ answer [7]. In the Ph.D. thesis of the first author of this paper [12] an algorithm that returns the three previous answers is described as a simple modification of the classical algorithm. Notice that if $refine(t) = \bot$ then no information is actually provided: the formula could either be refinable or not. As a consequence, our disambiguation algorithm can only exploit the other two answers, and the refiner will be more and more useful as long as it minimizes the number of $\bot$ outputs.

A simple example should clarify the usage of the refinement algorithm. Let us consider the incomplete mathematical formula $?_1 = \sqrt{?_2}$ represented in set theory and in a type theory of total functions with dependent products, and let's try to refine it. We use juxtaposition for operator application, following the usual $\lambda$-calculus convention.

- Set theory: $?_1 = \sqrt{?_2}$ is encoded as $(= ?_1 \ (sqrt \ ?_2))$ where $=$ is the polymorphic equality over arguments that belongs to one set and $sqrt$ is a function whose domain is the set $\mathbb{R}_0^+$ of non negative real numbers and whose codomain is the set $\mathbb{R}$ of real numbers.

  $refine(= ?_1 \ (sqrt \ ?_2))$ returns $(= ?_1 \ (sqrt \ ?_2))$ since the term is well-typed once the type $\mathbb{R}$ is assigned to $?_1$ and the type $\mathbb{R}_0^+$ is assigned to $?_2$.

– Dependently typed type theory of total functions: $?_1 = \sqrt{?_2}$ is encoded as $(= ?_3 \; ?_1 \; (sqrt \; ?_2 \; ?_4))$ where $=$ is the monomorphic ternary operator whose first argument is a type and whose other arguments are terms of that type; $sqrt$ is the binary operator whose first argument $x$ is of type $\mathbb{R}$ and whose second argument has dependent type $(\geq \; x \; 0)$ (i.e. it is a proof of $x \geq 0$). $refine(= ?_3 \; ?_1 \; (sqrt \; ?_2 \; ?_4))$ returns $(= \mathbb{R} \; ?_1 \; (sqrt \; ?_2 \; ?_4))$ since the term is well-typed once that $?_3$ is instantiated with $\mathbb{R}$, the sequent $\vdash ?_1 : \mathbb{R}$ is assigned to $?_1$, the sequent $\vdash ?_2 : \mathbb{R}_0^+$ is assigned to $?_2$ and the sequent $\vdash ?_4 : (\geq \; ?_2 \; 0)$ is assigned to $?_4$.

Notice that, in the case of dependent type theories, the refiner sometimes needs to instantiate metavariables that occur in the argument of an operator whose type is a dependent product. For instance, in the previous example the type of the monomorphic equality is $\Pi T : Type. \; T \to T \to Prop$ and $?_3$ is the argument of the formal parameter $T$. Thus the type $\mathbb{R}$ of the third operator argument $(sqrt \; ?_2 \; ?_4)$ must match the type $T = ?_3$ and this holds only instantiating $?_3$ with $\mathbb{R}$.

In the next section we will describe our disambiguation algorithm that is based on refinement instead of the simpler type derivation.

# 4   The Algorithm

Our algorithm for efficient ambiguous parsing is based on two components: a parser and a disambiguator. The parser component is similar to the homonymous phase of a traditional compiler pipeline in the sense that it actually checks if the input token stream belongs to a given grammar. The main difference with a traditional parser is that this one, instead of returning a set of ASTs, acts lazily immediately returning a pair. The first projection of this pair is a description of the choices which have to be made in order to obtain a term (i.e. an unambiguous interpretation of the input). We call such a description an interpretation domain. The second projection of the pair returned by the parser is a function that returns a term once applied to an oracle (called interpretation) that guides its choices.

The second component of our algorithm, the disambiguator, "drives" the parser by feeding with interpretations its output. Interpretations can be totally or partially defined over the interpretation domain. When the parser is faced with a choice that is not considered in a partial interpretation, it generates a placeholder. A partial interpretation approximates a total one since the generated open term matches the closed term of the total interpretation. The disambiguator builds total interpretations by repeated approximations, using the refiner described in Sect. 3 to prune those approximations that lead to not well-typed terms.

The clear distinction between parser and disambiguator ensures that our algorithm is compositional; the efficiency is in turn granted by the refiner which permits to prune interpretations as soon as they lead for sure to not well-typed terms. Let us analyze more formally the ideas sketched so far.

Let $\mathcal{T}$ be the set of well formed terms and let $\mathcal{S}$ be a set of symbols that can have more than one interpretation (that we call choice) in the input.

**Definition 2 (Interpretation).** Interpretation domain, interpretation codomain and interpretation are mutually defined in the following way:

- an interpretation domain is a finite set whose elements are couples $(s, l)$ where $s$ (the symbol to be interpreted) is an element of $\mathcal{S}$ and $l$ (the list of possible choices) is a list of functions from interpretations to $\mathcal{T}$;
- an interpretation codomain is a set whose elements are either the element "?" (implicit term) or functions from interpretations to $\mathcal{T}$;
- an interpretation is a total function from interpretation codomain to interpretation codomain, subject to the following condition: for each element $i = (s, [t_1 ; \ldots ; t_n])$ of the interpretation domain, if the interpretation applied to $i$ returns a function $t$, then $t \in \{t_1, \ldots t_n\}$.

An interpretation $\phi$ is partial when there exists an interpretation domain item $i$ such that $\phi(i) = ?$.

In ML notation Def. 2 is:

```
type symbol                          (* abstract data type *)
type term                            (* abstract data type *)
type interpretation_domain_item =
  Item of symbol * (interpretation -> term) list
and interpretation_codomain_item =
    Implicit
  | Term of (interpretation -> term)
and interpretation =
    interpretation_domain_item -> interpretation_codomain_item
```

Intuitively, an interpretation domain item describes all the possible ways to interpret a given symbol. An interpretation codomain item is either an implicit term (refusal of choosing an interpretation for the symbol) or just one interpretation among the possible ones. Thus, an interpretation is just a kind of oracle that, given a set of choices and a set of answers for each choice, associates to each choice either an answer among the one proposed or the "no choice" term.

We let $D$ range over interpretation domains, $\phi$ range over interpretations and $t_\uparrow$ over functions from interpretations to terms. Let us now define the parser.

**Definition 3 (Parser).** A parser is a function that maps its input (a token stream) to a couple $(D, t_\uparrow)$ where $D$ is an interpretation domain and $t_\uparrow$ is a function from interpretations defined over $D$ to terms.

Operationally, the parser can be obtained mechanically from a traditional parser for non-ambiguous grammars, either top down, bottom up, or general, by lifting its output from terms to functions, from interpretations to terms. An example in OCamlYacc[1] syntax should clarify the previous statement. Let us

---

[1] OCamlYacc is a tool, similar to Yacc, that produces bottom up OCaml parsers from LALR(1) grammars.

consider the OCamlYacc production that parses the formula $t!$ (the factorial of $t$) and returns an OCaml value representing the resulting term:

```
expr: expr BANG { Bang ($1) }
```

Applying the mechanical lifting transformation, the production becomes:

```
expr:
  expr BANG {
    let dom, mk_expr = $1 in
    dom, fun interp -> Bang (mk_expr interp) }
```

The first component of the output is the domain of the subexpression. The second component is a $\lambda$-abstraction over an interpretation, that becomes the argument of the subexpression (that is now lifted and needs an interpretation in input).

The interesting case is the case of ambiguous parsing, i.e. the case when the parser must make a choice. The solution is simply to add all the possible choices to the output domain, and makes the interpretation function perform the choice. Example:

```
expr:
  expr EQ expr {
    let ((dom1, mk_expr1), (dom2, mk_expr2)) = ($1, $3) in
    (union (union dom1 dom2)
      (EQ,
       [ fun interp ->  (* decidable equality over naturals *)
           APPL [eq_nat; mk_expr1 interp; mk_expr2 interp];
         fun interp ->  (* leibniz's equality *)
           APPL [eq; ?; mk_expr1 interp; mk_expr2 interp] ])),
    fun interp ->
      match interp EQ with
      | Implicit -> ?  (* fresh metavariable *)
      | Term mk_term -> mk_term interp }
```

If the oracle `interp` given in input satisfies Def. 2, then `interp EQ` will be either `Implicit` (refusal to choose) or one of:

```
1.  Term (fun interp ->  (* decidable equality over naturals *)
      APPL [eq_nat; mk_expr1 interp; mk_expr2 interp] )
2.  Term (fun interp ->  (* leibniz's equality *)
      APPL [eq; IMPLICIT; mk_expr1 interp; mk_expr2 interp] )
```

From the latter example it should be clear in which sense the parsing phase proceeds "lazily" and also in which sense interpretations behave as oracles for the parsers. The last and more interesting component is the disambiguator.

**Definition 4 (Disambiguator).** A disambiguator is a function whose input is a couple $(D, t_\uparrow)$ where $D$ is an interpretation domain and $t_\uparrow$ a function from interpretations defined over $D$ to terms. The output of the disambiguator is the set $\{t \mid \exists \phi \text{ of domain } D \text{ s.t. } t = t_\uparrow(\phi) \text{ and } t \text{ is well-typed}\}$

All the couples parser, disambiguator are clearly compositional. We will now present an efficient algorithm satisfying the specification for a disambiguator. The idea of the algorithm is to build the set of interpretations that produces well-typed terms by progressive refinements, starting from the interpretation that always refuses to choose and progressing towards an interpretation that always returns some lifted term. At each refinement step, the function $t_\uparrow$ is applied to obtain an open term, that is immediately fed to the refiner. The refiner function acts as a sort of validator, rejecting partial instantiations that already produce ill-typed open terms. In the case of dependent types it may also provide positive information, in the sense that it may automatically instantiate several metavariables, constraining the set of future choices.

The simplest version of our algorithm – that does not exploit refiner positive information – can be sketched in pseudo-code as follows:

$$\textbf{let } refine(t) = \text{a refiner according to Def. 1}$$

$$\textbf{let } update(\phi, s, t'_\uparrow)(s') = \begin{cases} \text{Term } (t'_\uparrow) \textbf{ if } s' = s \\ \phi(s) \quad \textbf{otherwise} \end{cases}$$

$$\textbf{let } disambiguate(D, t_\uparrow) =$$
$$\quad \textbf{let } \phi_0 = \lambda x. Implicit$$
$$\quad \textbf{let } \Phi = \begin{cases} \{\phi_0\} \textbf{ if } refine(t_\uparrow(\phi_0)) \neq \epsilon \wedge refine(t_\uparrow(\phi_0)) \neq \bot \\ \emptyset \quad \textbf{otherwise} \end{cases}$$
$$\quad \textbf{foreach } (s, l) \in D$$
$$\qquad \Phi := \{\phi' \mid \phi \in \Phi \wedge t'_\uparrow \in l \wedge \phi' = update(\phi, s, t'_\uparrow) \wedge refine(t_\uparrow(\phi')) \neq \epsilon\}$$
$$\quad \textbf{return } \{\phi \mid \phi \in \Phi \wedge refine(t_\uparrow(\phi)) \neq \bot\}$$

The following is an example of the application of the algorithm to the formula $(5/2)!$ where $/$ can be either the integer division $/_\mathbb{N}$ or the real division $/_\mathbb{R}$, 2 and 5 can be natural or real numbers and the factorial operator can be applied only to natural numbers. Only the first iterations of the main loop are reported.

$$D = \begin{cases} / \mapsto [/_\mathbb{N} : \mathtt{nat} \to \mathtt{nat} \to \mathtt{nat} \; ; \; /_\mathbb{R} : \mathtt{R} \to \mathtt{R} \to \mathtt{R}] \\ 2 \mapsto [2 : \mathtt{nat} \; ; \; 2 : \mathtt{R}] \\ 5 \mapsto [5 : \mathtt{nat} \; ; \; 5 : \mathtt{R}] \end{cases}$$

$$\phi_0 = \begin{cases} / \mapsto Implicit \\ 2 \mapsto Implicit \\ 5 \mapsto Implicit \end{cases} \qquad \begin{aligned} & refine(t_\uparrow(\phi_0)) = \\ & \quad refine(?_1!) = \{?_1 : \mathtt{nat}\} \end{aligned}$$

$$\Phi_0 = \{\phi_0\}$$

$$\phi_1 = \begin{cases} / \mapsto /_\mathbb{N} \\ 2 \mapsto Implicit \\ 5 \mapsto Implicit \end{cases} \qquad \begin{aligned} & refine(t_\uparrow(\phi_1)) = \\ & \quad refine((?_1/_\mathbb{N}?_2)!) = \{?_1 : \mathtt{nat} \; ; \; ?_2 : \mathtt{nat}\} \end{aligned}$$

$$\phi'_1 = \begin{cases} / \mapsto /_\mathbb{R} \\ 2 \mapsto Implicit \\ 5 \mapsto Implicit \end{cases} \qquad \begin{aligned} & refine(t_\uparrow(\phi_1)) = \\ & \quad refine((?_1/_\mathbb{R}?_2)!) = \epsilon \end{aligned}$$

$$\Phi_1 = \{\phi_1\}$$

# 5    Analysis and Future Improvements

The algorithm presented in the previous section is surely efficient according to our notion of efficiency since at each iteration of the for loop the set of interpretations $\{\phi' \mid \phi \in \Phi \wedge t'_\uparrow \in l \wedge \phi' = update(\phi, s, t'_\uparrow)\}$ is immediately pruned by means of the check $refine(t_\uparrow(\phi')) \neq \epsilon$. Pruning prevents further parsing of the user provided formula (since parsing is a lazy operation) and reduces the number of applications of the semantic analyser (the refiner in our implementation). More formally, we can try to estimate the computational complexity of the algorithm in order to compare it with that of NCA.

Estimating precisely the cost of the parsing phase is very complex since it is interrupted by pruning. Moreover, the overall time spent by the algorithm is dominated by the semantic analysis. Thus we ignore the parsing time and we define the computational cost of the algorithm as a function of the number of calls to the refiner.

Let $\Phi_i$ be the value of the $\Phi$ variable at the $i$-th loop of the algorithm. The number of refine operations invoked is $\Sigma_{i=1}^{|D|} |\Phi_i|$.

The worst case of the algorithm is obtained when pruning always fails. Thus $\Sigma_{i=1}^{|D|} |\Phi_i| > |\Phi_D| = \Pi_{(s,l) \in D} |l|$. The latter formula is the number of abstract syntax trees computed by NCA. Thus, in the worst case, our algorithm is more expensive than the NCA. However, the worst case is extremely unlikely when $|D|$ is big, since it corresponds to a term where a lot of ambiguous symbols occur with the following property: each symbol is completely independent of the others and it can be resolved independently from the other choices.

The optimal case of the algorithm is obtained when pruning reduces the set $\{\phi' \mid \phi \in \Phi \wedge t'_\uparrow \in l \wedge \phi' = update(\phi, s, t'_\uparrow)\}$ to a set of cardinality $c$ where $c$ is the number of valid interpretations. Thus $\Sigma_{i=1}^{|D|} |\Phi_i| = \Sigma_{i=1}^{|D|} c = c|D|$. Since $c$ is usually a small value – how many different valid interpretations of a formula usually hold? – the latter expression is smaller than $\Pi_{(s,l) \in D} |l|$ already for small values of $|D|$, and it becomes smaller and smaller when $|D|$ (the number of ambiguous symbols in a formula) increases.

It is now evident that the computational complexity of the algorithm is greatly influenced by the pruning rate: the more invalid partial terms will be detected, the smaller the $|\Phi_i|$, the lower the overall time spent by the algorithm. In particular, to obtain an average performance close to the optimal case we should minimize $|\Phi_i|$ for each $i$ by pruning invalid interpretations as early as possible.

The choice of the strategy used to pick the next element of the domain $D$ in the `foreach` loop of the algorithm greatly influences the pruning rate. Let us consider the following trivial example: $(f\ (g\ x)\ (h\ y))$ where all the atoms are ambiguous (i.e. $f, g, x, y$ are all elements of the disambiguation domain $D$).

The strategy that sorts $D$ according to the visit in preorder of the syntax tree refines in succession the terms $(f\ ?_1\ ?_2)$, $(f\ (g\ ?_3)\ ?_4)$, $(f\ (g\ x)\ ?_4)$ and so on. Since the type of a function constraints the type of its arguments, refining the first term already rejects interpretations of $f$ that are not binary, and refining the

**Table 1.** Comparison between our algorithm and NCA

| NA | PA | I | NA | PA | I | NA | PA | I | NA | PA | I | NA | PA | I | NA | PA | I |
|---|---|---|---|---|---|---|---|---|---|---|---|---|---|---|---|---|---|
| 1 | 2 | -1 | 32 | 33 | -1 | 32 | 33 | -1 | 128 | 38 | 90 | 512 | 45 | 467 | 1680 | 35 | 1645 |
| 1 | 4 | -3 | 32 | 33 | -1 | 42 | 13 | 29 | 128 | 38 | 90 | 512 | 41 | 471 | 1792 | 51 | 1741 |
| 1 | 6 | -5 | 32 | 33 | -1 | 63 | 83 | -20 | 128 | 38 | 90 | 896 | 51 | 845 | 2688 | 54 | 2634 |
| 3 | 5 | -2 | 32 | 40 | -8 | 63 | 83 | -20 | 128 | 38 | 90 | 896 | 51 | 845 | 3584 | 55 | 3529 |
| 4 | 6 | -2 | 32 | 39 | -7 | 63 | 19 | 44 | 160 | 38 | 122 | 896 | 51 | 845 | 3584 | 54 | 3530 |
| 4 | 7 | -3 | 32 | 33 | -1 | 96 | 37 | 59 | 192 | 108 | 84 | 896 | 49 | 847 | 7168 | 63 | 7105 |
| 8 | 7 | 1 | 32 | 33 | -1 | 128 | 40 | 88 | 192 | 111 | 81 | 896 | 47 | 849 | 8192 | 60 | 8132 |
| 14 | 24 | -10 | 32 | 33 | -1 | 128 | 43 | 85 | 224 | 46 | 178 | 1024 | 42 | 982 | 14336 | 62 | 14274 |
| 21 | 13 | 8 | 32 | 33 | -1 | 128 | 42 | 86 | 224 | 45 | 179 | 1280 | 44 | 1236 | 21504 | 65 | 21439 |
| 32 | 32 | 0 | 32 | 33 | -1 | 128 | 42 | 86 | 224 | 47 | 177 | 1280 | 43 | 1237 | 21504 | 60 | 21444 |
| 32 | 33 | -1 | 32 | 33 | -1 | 128 | 39 | 89 | 256 | 40 | 216 | 1280 | 43 | 1237 | 36864 | 79 | 36785 |
| 32 | 38 | -6 | 32 | 33 | -1 | 128 | 38 | 90 | 320 | 20 | 300 | 1536 | 54 | 1482 | 53760 | 65 | 53695 |
| 32 | 33 | -1 | 32 | 39 | -7 | 128 | 38 | 90 | 480 | 41 | 439 | 1536 | 48 | 1488 | 53760 | 67 | 53693 |

$NA$ = Trivial compositional algorithm (number of refinements)
$PA$ = Proposed algorithm (number of refinements)
$I$ = Improvement = $NA - PA$

second term rejects interpretations of $g$ whose output type does not match the type of the first argument of $f$. Thus at each step several partial interpretations are pruned. If the type of the function constraints the possible interpretations of the operands to just the choices that are prefixes of the final valid interpretations, then we are facing the optimal case of the algorithm.

Any other strategy that consider a subterm without first considering its parents in the abstract syntax tree yields to less pruning. For instance, the term $(f\ (?_5\ x)\ (?_6\ y))$ can be successfully refined for each interpretation of $f$, $x$ and $y$ such that $f$ is a binary operator. The reason is that the refiner can always attribute to $?_5$ the type $T_1 \to T_2$ where $T_1$ is the type expected by $f$ and $T_2$ is the type of $x$.

The strategy that sorts $D$ by preorder visiting the syntax tree is not always optimal, but it behaved particularly well in all the benchmarks we did on our implementation, exhibiting an average case really close to the optimal one. Table 1 compares the number of invocations of the refiner using our algorithm and using NCA. The table has been obtained parsing all the statements and definitions of all the theorems that deals with real numbers in the standard library of the Coq proof assistant.

As expected our algorithm performs more refinements than NCA when the number of ambiguous symbols – and thus also the number NA of syntax trees – is small. In this case only a few more refinements are performed. When the size of the domain – logarithmic in the number of NA of syntax trees – grows, the number of refinements performed by our algorithm grows only linearly in the size of the domain. Note that this is the expected behaviour for the optimal case of the algorithm when the number of valid interpretations $c$ is fixed. Indeed, only

5 of the 79 statements admit more than one valid interpretation. We conclude that in practice the average case of our algorithm is close to the optimal case.

Notice also that there is a trivial heuristic to predict whether our algorithm is convenient over NCA: it is sufficient to look at the number $NA$ of syntax trees and apply our algorithm whenever $NA$ is higher than a given threshold (32 in our benchmark).

We should further observe that the computational cost of a refinement is not constant, being a function of the term to refine, and it is extremely difficult to approximate. Still, it is surely small for small terms. Thus the calls to the refiner performed by our algorithm are in the average case cheaper than those performed by NCA, since at least half of our calls are on prefixes of the syntax tree.

Moreover, using preorder visit, the computational cost of the computation of $t_\uparrow(\phi)$ and $refine(t_\uparrow(\phi))$ can be lowered. Indeed, at each iteration of the for loop, $t_\uparrow$ is applied to an interpretation $\phi'$ that differs from $\phi$ only by instantiating more implicit arguments that are leaves of the generated term tree. Thus, the term returned by $t_\uparrow(\phi)$ is a prefix of the term returned by $t_\uparrow(\phi')$. This suggests that the cost of the computation of $t_\uparrow(\phi')$ could be greatly reduced by changing $t_\uparrow$ so that its exploit the knowledge about the partial result $t_\uparrow(\phi)$. Similarly, when $refine(t_\uparrow(\phi))$ is defined and different from $\bot$, its value can easily be exploited in the refinement of $t_\uparrow(\phi')$.

Combining these two optimizations, we can easily make the cost of the two operations at each iteration negligible, still being compositional. These optimizations have not been implemented yet, they are planned as future work.

Another optimization derives from the positive information computed by the refinement function, that is the map that associates a sequent or an instantiation to each metavariable. For instance, if the refine operation assigns to $?_1$ the type $\mathbb{R} \to \mathbb{R}$, an interpretation that instantiates $?_1$ with logical negation can be rejected without even trying to refine the associated term. This corresponds to remembering in $\Phi$ also the refinement map associated with each term and to adding a new pruning test over $\phi'$ based on the unification of the type of the term generated by $t'_\uparrow$ with the type assigned to $s$ in the map. This optimization is also planned as future work.

An interesting topic that was completely skipped so far is the construction of the interpretation domain by the parser. MKM tools provide at least two sources of information that can be exploited to construct the list of possible choices for each symbol. The first one is related to the ambiguities that arise from the resolution of an identifier. Indeed, it is not unusual to have several objects in a distributed library that are given the same name (e.g. "reflexive_property", "domain" or simply "P"). Thus to every identifier we can associate several objects. The parser needs to retrieve for each identifier the list of all the objects whose name is equal to the identifier. The task can easily be performed making the parser consult a search engine for mathematical formulae as the one developed in the MoWGLI project [5] or the similar, but less generic one, developed by the Mizar group [2].

The second source of information is represented by XML notational files that describe the mathematical notation associated with definitions in MKM libraries. Indeed, several projects provide XSLT stylesheets to render mathematical formulae encoded in content level markup as MathML Content, OpenMath or OMDoc. Since there exist large classes of operators that share a similar notation, these stylesheets are usually generated from more concise descriptions of symbols arity and precedence levels [9, 4, 6]. These descriptions could be exploited also in the implementations of our disambiguation algorithm.

Finally we should address the case where the disambiguator returns more than one well-typed term. Depending on the kind of processing required on the terms, the system may either proceed in parallel on all the generated terms, or ask the user to choose the term she was interested in. In the latter case the system can identify all the choices that are still ambiguous, and present to the user a human readable description of each choice.

## 6    Concluding Remarks

Our disambiguation algorithm has been implemented and integrated both in the MoWGLI search engine and in the HELM proof assistant prototype [12]. The former is a Web-Service for retrieving lemmas and definitions from the distributed HELM library by matching their type against a user provided pattern. The lemmas and definitions are XML encodings of those in the library of the Coq proof assistant [3]. We developed a Web interface for the search engine that allows users to enter patterns as mathematical formulae with placeholders.

The usual mathematical notation is available and it is disambiguated using our algorithm. In case of multiple interpretations of the formula the search engine can ask the user to identify the only interpretation she is interested in, or it can perform the search according to each interpretation. For instance, it is possible to look for theorems stating $?_1 + ?_2 = ?_2 + ?_1$ retrieving at once the commutative property for the addition over Peano natural numbers, binary positive numbers, integers, rationals and real numbers.

The performance analysis presented in Sect. 5 is confirmed by our implementation: the time spent in the disambiguation of the formula is negligible with respect to the time spent in the search and in the network transmission.

The HELM proof assistant prototype implements an interactive reasoning tool based on the logic of Coq, adopting the HELM distributed library as its own library. One main difference with respect to the Coq system is the size of the context. Whereas in Coq the context corresponds to only a subset of the whole library, in our prototype all the definitions and theorems in the library are in scope. Thus we must face a much higher degree of ambiguity, since several mathematical notions have been redefined several times in the library of Coq and since there exists several formalizations of the same mathematical concept. Another important difference is that Coq behaves as a compiler, whereas our tool is more interactive. Thus every Coq input must have exactly one interpretation, since in case of multiple valid interpretations it is not possible to ask to the user what interpretation she meant. We observed that disambiguation time is negligible with respect to the validation time of a single proof step.

Comparing our solution with that adopted in the forthcoming release of the Coq system (version V8.0) is surely interesting. Whereas in the previous versions of the system the grammar did not allow overloading, in version 8.0 overloading is admitted thanks to the introduction of notational scopes. A scope is a region of text where only some parsing rules are active. For instance, there exists a scope where "*" is interpreted as the multiplication between Peano numbers and another one where it is interpreted as the product of two types. A syntactical device is given to the user to change the current scope, even in the middle of a formula. Scopes are associated with the arguments of the constants, so that when an argument of type **Set** is met the scope that handles "*" as a type product is opened.

The reader should notice that associating a scope to a constant argument is weaker than associating a scope to the type expected for an argument. For instance, the identity function $id$ has type $\Pi T : Set.T \rightarrow T$ and $(id\ nat\ 0)$ is a correct application where the type $T$ is instantiated with the type $nat$ of natural numbers, and 0 has the expected type $T = nat$. However, associating the scope of natural numbers notation to the second argument of $id$ independently from the value of the first argument is a mistake. More generally, we observe that scopes behaves as a new kind of types, much in the spirit of those of Grammatical Framework [11]. This new type system is imposed in parallel with the already existent type system of Coq, that is not exploited. On the contrary, our algorithm is based on the refinement operation provided by the underlying logic of Coq.

For sure, one benefit of this duplicate and weaker type system is its generality: since it is independent from the underlying logic, it can be made part of the notation description and it can be reused with several backends. Nevertheless, there are major drawbacks. First of all, as shown in the previous examples, disambiguation is less effective than that based on our technique, since scopes are chosen by exploiting the context only in a minimal way. More explicitly, imposing a weak type system when a stronger one is available is not appealing at all and requires strong motivations that we do not see.

Secondly, there is a problem of consistency between the two type systems: since the notational types are assigned by the user without any consistency check, it may happen that a wrongly assigned notational type prevents the user from inserting valid Coq terms. Adding another layer of consistency checking is both theoretically and practically complex, especially when compared with the simplicity of the algorithm proposed in this paper.

# References

1. A. Asperti, F. Guidi, L. Padovani, C. Sacerdoti Coen, and I. Schena. Mathematical Knowledge Management in HELM. In Annals of Mathematics and Artificial Intelligence, 38(1): 27–46, May 2003.

2. G. Bancerek, P. Rudnicki. Information Retrieval in MML. In Proceedings of the Second International Conference on Mathematical Knowledge Management, MKM 2003. LNCS, 2594.

3. The Coq proof-assistant, `http://coq.inria.fr`.

4. P. Di Lena. Generazione automatica di stylesheet per notazione matematica. Master thesis, University of Bologna, 2003.

5. F. Guidi, C. Sacerdoti Coen. Querying Distributed Digital Libraries of Mathematics. In Proceedings of Calculemus 2003, 11th Symposium on the Integration of Symbolic Computation and Mechanized Reasoning. Aracne Editrice.

6. M. Kohlhase. OMDoc: An Open Markup Format for Mathematical Documents (Version 1.1). OMDoc technical recommendation.

7. C. McBride. Dependently Typed Functional Programs and their Proofs. Ph.D. thesis, University of Edinburgh, 1999.

8. C. Munoz. A Calculus of Substitutions for Incomplete-Proof Representation in Type Theory. Ph.D. thesis, INRIA, 1997.

9. W. A. Naylor, Stephen Watt. Meta Style Sheets for the Conversion of Mathematical Documents into other Forms. On-Line Proceedings of the First International Conference on Mathematical Knowledge Management, MKM 2001.`http://www.emis.de/proceedings/MKM2001/`.

10. The Mizar proof-assistant, `http://mizar.uwb.edu.pl/`.

11. A. Ranta. Grammatical Framework: A Type-Theoretical Grammar Formalism, manuscript made available in September 2002, to appear in Journal of Functional Programming.

12. C. Sacerdoti Coen. Knowledge Management of Formal Mathematics and Interactive Theorem Proving. Ph.D. thesis, University of Bologna, 2004.

13. M. Strecker. Construction and Deduction in Type Theories. Ph.D. thesis, Universität Ulm, 1998.

# An Architecture for Distributed Mathematical Web Services

Elena S. Smirnova, Clare M. So, and Stephen M. Watt

Ontario Research Centre for Computer Algebra (ORCCA)
Department of Computer Science, University of Western Ontario
London, Ontario, Canada. N6A 5B7
{elena,clare,watt}@orcca.on.ca

**Abstract.** This paper describes technologies to create and maintain a
problem solving environment based on a framework for distributed mathematical web services. Our approach allows clients to access mathematical computational facilities through a uniform set of network protocols,
independent of the software packages that provide the end functionality.
The author of a mathematical web service need know only the specifics of
the system in which the mathematical computations are performed, e.g.
Maple, Mathematica or Fortran with NAG library. Whatever additional
network service code that is necessary (e.g. Java, WSDL, etc), is generated
and configured automatically. This paper presents a brief architectural
overview of the entire framework, and then gives a detailed description of
the design and implementation of the tools for mathematical servers for
this environment. A set of mathematical web services currently deployed
are described as examples.

## 1   Introduction

Over the past decades mathematical software systems have become increasingly
powerful and complex. Each major system has its own strengths and areas in
which it surpasses the others, often provided by complex packages or libraries.
This picture changes constantly as new versions of systems are released. Considerable expertise required to know which package is the best for which problem at
any given time. Users are therefore often unaware of existing software solutions
to their mathematical problems. Even if they are aware they may not be willing
to maintain up-to-date licenses for multiple software systems only occasionally
used. We see this situation becoming more challenging over time, and its solution
is the object of the MONET project.

MONET is a European ESPRIT project for *Mathematics On the NET*, with the
goal of designing a framework for the provision and brokerage of mathematical
web services. The partners in this consortium are the Numerical Algorithms
Group Ltd (NAG), the University of Bath, Stilo Technology Ltd, the University
of Manchester, the Technical University of Eindhoven, the University of Nice,
and the Ontario Research Centre for Computer Algebra at the University of
Western Ontario. The architecture devised by the MONET consortium involves

A. Asperti et al. (Eds.): MKM 2004, LNCS 3119, pp. 363–377, 2004.

(1) a number of software components, including brokers, planners and servers, (2) various ontologies representing mathematical problem domains and services, and (3) specific languages to communicate mathematical problems, results and explanations. An overview of this architecture is given in Section 2, and a detailed description is given in the report [1]. While the best approach for service brokers and planners remains the subject of on-going research, the strategy for providing the specific mathematical services can be declared complete. This is the main subject of the present paper.

We have developed an approach whereby (1) the author of a mathematical web service need know only the software system he or she uses to provide the service, and (2) the user of the mathematical service need not be aware of the implementation language. For example, an expert in symbolic computation, proficient in Maple, can develop a set of Maple packages solving a specific problem. This expert can then use our framework to create a mathematical web service to solve this problem. Without additional effort on the part of the service author, the service will accept requests in a system-neutral protocol, based on OpenMath [9][10]. We describe this architecture for mathematical web services in Section 3. A number of issues arising in the implementation are described in Sections 4, 5 and 6.

We believe that both services and clients benefit from this architecture. Clients do not have to have the necessary mathematical software installed locally, and are not required to know the syntax and calling sequences of multiple mathematical software packages. Service providers can expose their most recent mathematical software to a larger target audience, reduce maintenance costs for old versions, and potentially derive transaction-based revenue. Once a sufficient number of services are deployed, the MONET framework could be applied to a wide spectrum of applications, including professional technical services, mathematical education and distance learning, and research support in a number of domains. As mathematical systems become ever more complex, this approach to service discovery and planning could conceivably be used within individual systems.

In order to place our work in context in the world of mathematics-related web services, we refer to some other projects in this area, including M Base [25] and H-Bugs [11]. MBase is a extensive database for mathematical theory, symbol, definition, axiom and theorem. It contains a variety of mathematical knowledge description, but does not particularly aim to offer any implementation of algorithms or methods for the solution of mathematical problems. H-Bugs is an investigation to distributed system based on MONET architecture, as demonstrated, for theorem proving. The main topic of this paper is the description of the architecture for providing m athem atical com putation web services within the MONET framework.

As a first example, we have developed and deployed the following symbolic mathematical web services at University of Western Ontario [1] (see Fig. 1): Arith-

---

[1] URL: http://ptibonum.scl.csd.uwo.ca:16661/MonetServiceClient/

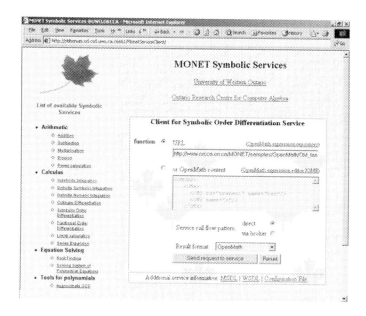

**Fig. 1.** MONET web services page at University of Western Ontario

metic expression simplification, Indefinite integration, Definite symbolic integration, Definite numeric Integration, Ordinary differentiation, Fractional-order differentiation, Symbolic-order differentiation of rational functions, Limit calculation, Series expansion, Approximate GCD, Root-finding service (including parametric solutions) and Solving systems of polynomials.

# 2   General MONET Architecture

## 2.1   Main Components

There are three components in MONET architecture: client, broker and server (see Fig. 2). Servers expose their services by registering with brokers. Clients send queries to a broker asking if web services for solving specific kinds of mathematical problems are available. Brokers resolve clients' queries by looking for suitable mathematical services available and passing the clients' requests to them. After this, services try to solve the given mathematical problems using the capacities of their mathematical solving engines. Finally, clients obtain the result of the computation and possibly a meaningful explanation.

## 2.2   Mathematical Broker

The Mathematical Broker presented in [5] is a special component in this architecture. It is assumed to be a sophisticated search engine and planner for complex mathematical problems. Its goals are to match the characteristics of

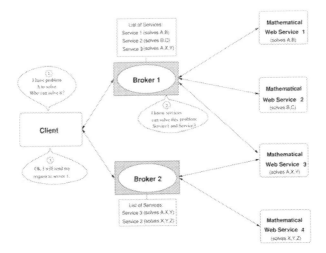

**Fig. 2.** The general scheme of the MONET Architecture

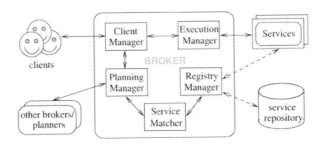

**Fig. 3.** The general scheme of the MONET Broker

given mathematical problem to web services available and, if no single service can solve the given problem by itself, to divide the problem into smaller portions that can be solved by available services. In general, matching requests for arbitrary mathematical problem is intractable. However, we seek to provide a solution for a wide range of problems that appear in practice.

## 2.3   Languages and Standards Used

Languages and standards have been developed by the OpenMath society and the MONET consortium to describe mathematical problems and communicate the results in an unambiguous way. OpenMath[9][10] is an extensible standard to encode the semantics of mathematics in a system-neutral format. It was chosen for communicating mathematics in this architecture because, unlike Content MathML, it can be extended natively to cover new areas of mathematics by writing new Content Dictionaries. The Mathematical Service Description Language

(MSDL)[4] is a specialized format that describes mathematical web services in the MONET architecture. It is needed when servers register the services with brokers. There are others languages developed by MONET consortium, but these two are used by servers to expose and provide services.

# 3     Architecture of Mathematical Web Services

In the MONET architecture mathematical web services are provided without revealing their implementation structure. A mathematical web service can be provided by a stand-alone C program, or by an interface to a package from a system such as Axiom[22], Derive[23], Maple[20], Mathematica[21] or Matlab[24]. This approach aims to be flexible and extensible, to allow easy switching between mathematical systems, and to allow the easy creatoin of new services.

In this section we describe the architecture we have designed for the construction of such a Mathematical Web Server. In our description we show the service being provided by a Maple program, but in principle any other package could be used.

## 3.1     Mathematical Web Server Environment

The first design decision for the Mathematical Server is that all services deployed on it to run independently, each reachable at its own unique URL and offering its own functionality. All of these services are enclosed within a specially designed software package, sometimes called the wrapper tool, and may be maintained by several managers. Together, these form the Mathematical Web Server Environment.

One of the essential components to the Mathematical Web Server is its mathematical engine, usually provided by a a package within some computer algebra system.

The general scheme of organization for the Mathematical Server is shown in Figure 4. It shows that each mathematical service is assigned to several components, which all together are responsible to fulfill service's functions.

The principal information about each service is provided by the service configuration file that contains tree parts: (1) a formal service description, using MSDL [4], (2) a service interface to a mathematical software system, and (3) an actual service implementation provided as code for that system. It is possible for alternative implementations to be given, in which case parts (2) and (3) have multiple components.

The wrapper tool is a container for a generic mathematical service, and its specific behaviour is determined by the service configuration file.

Outside the mathematical engine, there are two core managers to maintain the network interface to this mathematical server environment: one is responsible for new service creation and installation, and the other for invocation of a service installed.

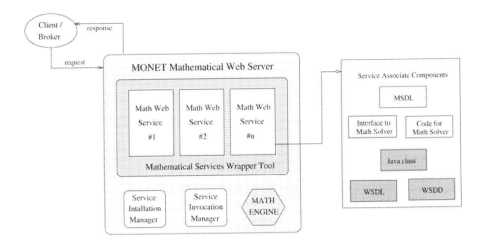

**Fig. 4.** The general scheme of MONET Mathematical Server Architecture

## 3.2    Mathematical Service Organization

Mathematical Services are organized in such a way that the author of a new service need not know about web servers and services, Java or the various XML technologies in order to create a new service. Instead, the service's authors provide code written for a mathematical system that implements their service. The author must separately indicate the name of the main function that enters this implementation.

As shown in the Figure 4, each service is associated with three original pieces of information and three generated components. The original information about the service includes the formal service description given in MSDL, service interface to the mathematical engine of the server and code for the service implementation to be executed by mathematical engine. Generated associates of the service are service core Java class, web service deployment descriptor (WSDD) [8] and web service description language file (WSDL) [7].

**Service Configuration File.** The original information about a mathematical service is provided by the service author and stored in an XML-based configuration file. This file is the item in the mathematical service infrastructure that uniquely and completely represents the service implementation.

The service description file consists of three parts: the service MSDL skeleton (to be completed automatically during service installation), service interface to mathematical engine (for example Maple or Axiom), and service implementation (code written in the language of the mathematical system used).

The structure of the configuration file has the pattern indicated below.: Note that a file may contain descriptions for more than one service, especially if it makes sense when several services share parts of an implementation.

```
<mathServer>
    <msdl>
        <service name="sevice_A">
            {MSDL skeleton for service A}
        </service>
        {MSDLs for other services}
    </msdl>

    <services>
        <service name="service_A" call="function_call_for_service_A"/>
        {interface for other services}
    </services>

    <implementation language = "math_solver_name">
        {implementation for each service using
          the languageof the corresponding solver}
    </implementation>
</mathSever>
```

The configuration file for each service should be available for the wrapper tool at any time after the service is installed on the Mathematical Server.

**Generated Service Associates.** The configuration file statically describes service functionalities. In order to fulfill them dynamically we still need additional descriptors and implementation tools. Those components are service implementation Java class, WSSD and WSDL files.

All of them are automatically created by the Mathematical Solver Environment installation engine: a Java class is created according to the information provided in the service configuration file, then both WSDD and WSDL descriptors are derived from this Java class API.

These generated components are then used to deploy, expose and run the service. During service installation, the created Java class is placed in a proper location in the web server file system, so it is ready to maintain service calls. WSDD is used to deploy service on the web server, and WSDL is exposed to the outside world to provide MONET brokers and clients with the information about service interface (see Fig. 5).

**Realization of Service Functions.** The main functions of each mathematical web service are carried out by a combination of a service core Java class, the server Invocation Manager and information from the service configuration file.

The main idea of the service organization is that its Java class receives all requests from the outside (client or brokers), extracts information about mathematical arguments (if any) passed with the request and then calls service invocation engine. The Invocation Manager in turn creates a program for the solving engine in real time, using information from service configuration file and the mathematical arguments from the service call. This program is passed to the server's mathematical engine for execution. The result is retrieved by the same Invocation Manager, wrapped into a service response message and sent back to the client or broker (see Fig. 6).

# 4    Details of the Architecture Implementation

## 4.1    Technologies Used

The list of technologies involved in the process of developing Mathematical Web Server includes several network protocols: SOAP [6], TCP, HTTP, etc., various products from Apache software foundation: Jakarta Tomcat [16], Axis [17] and Ant [18], different computer algebra systems such as Maple [20] and Axiom[22], as well as Java SE [14] from Sun Microsystems.

## 4.2    Core Components of the Mathematical Web Server Architecture

As mentioned in section 3, the implementation of the Mathematical Web Server includes installation and invocation managers. The installation manager takes care of new service creation and maintaining (installation/deinstallation). The invocation manager is an engine that handles calls to services from the outside. There is also a third component of Mathematical Web Server; it is responsible for installation of mathematical server itself.

## 4.3    Mathematical Web Server Installation

The Mathematical Web Server installation process sets up a web server in order to prepare it for running mathematical web services.

Assuming Apache Tomcat and Apache Axis are already installed on a web server, the procedure of setting it up for MONET Web services is performed by running a script from the installation kit.

## 4.4    Mathematical Web Service Installation

The Mathematical Service Installation Manager is implemented as a combination of Java programs and shell scripts. Each of the Java programs is responsible for carrying out one or more steps of service installation process. The whole instillation is driven by a manager script. As described in the section 3.2, all necessary information about a service is provided in its configuration file. In order to install a service, the Installation Manager needs to have access to this file. To register a new service with the MONET Broker, the Installation Manager also requires the URL of the Broker.

While installing a new service(see Fig. 5), the Installation Manager

- parses configuration file to extract the information about service interface,
- creates Java class that will implement the service on the web server,
- generates server deployment descriptor (WSDD),
- deploys the service on the web server,
- retrieves WSDL (descriptor of web service interface to clients) created by the server,
- according to the current service installation, updates its MSDL skeleton to a FULLY functional mathematical service descriptor.

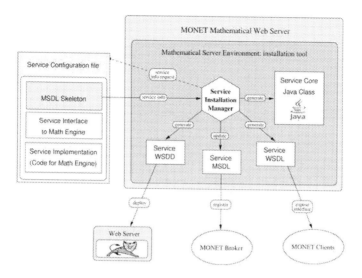

**Fig. 5.** MONET Mathematical Service Installation

After installation is complete the service can be seen from outside by MONET clients and brokers, and it is ready to handle requests from them.

## 4.5 Mathematical Service Invocation

When a mathematical service receives a request with a mathematical query, the service core Java class retrieves the input arguments from this query and calls the service Invocation Manager.

The Mathematical Service Invocation Manager is implemented as a combination of several Java libraries and auxiliary packages for mathematical engine systems, designed to fulfill service functions according to the information provided in the service configuration files.

The following steps (also shown as scheme in the Fig. 6) are executed every time a mathematical service is invoked:

1. The service Java class calls the Invocation Manager with the following parameters
   - the reference to the service configuration file
   - an array of mathematical arguments from the query to the service
   - optional mathematical formats, if client set preference for encoding of service input and output (see section 5).
2. The Invocation Manager parses the configuration file and extracts the service implementation and service interface.
3. The service arguments, by default encoded in OpenMath, get parsed and prepared for the conversion to the internal syntax of the mathematical engine.
4. The Invocation Manager generates the program to be executed by the mathematical solving engine. This is based on the implementation part from the

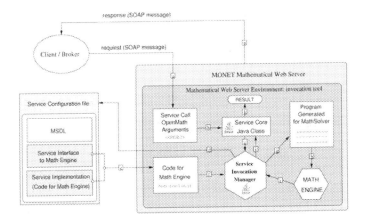

**Fig. 6.** MONET Mathematical Service Invocation

service configuration file, the service interface to this system and the mathematical arguments from service request.

5. The generated code is passed to the mathematical engine for execution.
6. The result from mathematical engine returns to the Invocation Manager. There it gets converted to an appropriate mathematical format and encoding (see section 5.2), afterward it is passed back to service core Java class.
7. The service Java class wraps the answer into a message using the SOAP object exchange protocol and sends it back to the MONET client.

## 5     Mathematical Web Service Input and Output

### 5.1     Input Format

All MONET mathematical services accept input arguments as OpenMath expressions. Each expression can be encoded as plain string, an XML DOM object[13] or a RIACA OpenMath object[12]. The reason to support all of these encodings was to experiment with a choice of possible interfaces to clients and brokers while using the same service.

A string is the simplest way to format a request. This does not require any extra libraries, nor serialization tools on a client side. However, in case of string-based inputs there is a hight probability of submitting invalid OpenMath within service requests.

An XML Document Object Model (DOM) is used to represent parsed XML documents in as a tree structure. It is a moderately more complex encoding of OpenMath objects that at least can ensure that the passed arguments represent are valid XML.

The RIACA format is specially designed to represent OpenMath objects. It guaranties that inputs sent are valid OpenMath, but in this the case client has to know about the RIACA library, have it installed locally and perform the serialization of RIACA objects when sending SOAP messages with service queries.

## 5.2  Output Format

The mathematical services currently implemented return string object encoding OpenMath expression, containing the list of results or error message.

**MEL Format.** If requested by a client, the answer from a service can be wrapped in a service response object, using the MONET Mathematical Explanation Language (MEL) [2] ontology. We do not offer this option by default, since when the result from a service is sent back to the MONET Broker, the later will provide the wrapping, possibly including supplementary information, such as explanation from a Planning Manager or Execution, etc.

**Additional Mathematical Formats for Service Output.** In addition, our current implementation of MONET mathematical services supports several other mathematical formats to encode service results. Users may set their preferences while calling a service, and the result can be given in any of the following formats: OpenMath, Content MathML, Presentation MathML and LaTeX. This is an experimental facility that can be used in environments that integrate several formats into represent mathematical objects.

## 5.3  Conversion Between OpenMath and Math Engine Language

Conversion between OpenMath and language of the chosen solvers is important in offering mathematical web services. All mathematical expressions must be encoded in OpenMath, a system-neutral format, but not all solvers can accept input and return output in OpenMath.

Conversion between OpenMath and strongly-typed languages, such as Axiom, is not difficult because type information is apparent in both formats. Conversion between OpenMath and dynamically typed languages, such as Maple, does not have a trivial solution because the semantic information for expressoins in these languages is often implicit. It is not practical to force all service authors to use only solvers that use strongly-typed languages, because solvers that use dynamically-typed expressions can be very useful in practice. We use Maple to demonstrate the challenges and our solution in converting between OpenMath and a dynamically typed language. Similar issues would be encountered when service authors try to offer mathematical web services using another mathematical engine having a dynamically-typed language.

The conversion between OpenMath and Maple is described using a collection of Mapping files, typically one for each OpenMath CD in use. Mapping files describe the correspondence between OpenMath and Maple, and a single mapping file is used to drive both directions of the conversion. An entry in a mapping file contains a fragment of OpenMath markup and the corresponding structure of Maple command. When designing the mapping files, some differences between OpenMath and Maple are generalized. Order of arguments and corresponding Maple command are taken into account. If the mapping file's design cannot be used to describe the conversion, a Maple procedure can be attached instead.

Converting from OpenMath to Maple is mostly straight-forward. The correspondence can usually be determined by the OpenMath symbol (`<OMS>`) alone.

Difficulties in this direction of conversion still exists because of the differences in the design of the languages or in the form of certain expressions.. For example, the partial differentiation operation in Maple takes a list of bound variables to indicate with respect to which the differentiation is to be done. The corresponding OpenMath function takes the indexes of bound variables in a list to achieve the same purpose. In the worst case, an OpenMath expression may not have a Maple correspondence at all. In this case, the converter throws an error notifying the users that certain OpenMath symbols are not handled by this converter.

Maple to OpenMath conversion is less straight-forward because a Maple expression is subject to ambiguities. Ambiguities exist in a Maple expression because Maple is a dynamically-typed language and the meaning of an expression cannot be determined by the symbolic function compositions alone. As a simple example, Maple uses the same function call ("diff") for both univariate and partial differentiation. OpenMath has two distinct symbols (<OMS>) for these mathematical concepts. Some ambiguities can be resolved by inspecting the number of types of arguments. For ambiguities that cannot be resolved in this manner, we develop and employ policies to specify what to do with such cases. The first policy is to resolve the ambiguity by an extra Maple procedure supplied when the converter is invoked. An example strategy in this policy is to choose first possible OpenMath correspondence found. Second policy is to generate a pseudo OpenMath representation that can be dealt with later. In the worst case, the third policy is used to throw an error notifying the user that such ambiguity cannot be resolved.

# 6    Using Other Mathematical Engines with the Server

As mentioned in section 3.2, different math engines can be used with this service architecture. For the author of the service, switching between mathematical engines means only editing the service configuration file. For the developer of a Mathematical Server, changing its mathematical engine requires replacing components of the Invocation Manager that are specific to the mathematical software used, however the second part of the Mathematical Server – Installation Manager remains the same.

## 6.1    Changes to Service Configuration File

The configuration file allows an author to specify the name of the mathematical engine, and give an implementation for the engine with that name. It also permits to have more than one implementation for the same service, using alternative mathematical engines. For example the service for definite integration may use system Derive, Axiom or Mathematica instead of Maple, or it may use all four of them. In this case all that is required from the author of the service is to change the implementation part of service configuration file. If one decides to use all of the above computer algebra systems to implement definite integration service, its configuration file might be re-written as the following:

```
<mathServer>
 <msdl>
  { MSDL for Definite Integration Service }
 </msdl>

 <services>
  <service name="DefiniteIntegrationService" call="monetDefInt"/>
 </services>

 <implementation language = "maple">
   monetDefInt:=proc(function,var,lower_limit,upper_limit);
          int(function,var=lower_limit..upper_limit);
   end:
 </implementation>
 <implementation language = "derive">
   monetDefInt(f,x,a,b,e) := PROG( e:=INT(f,x,a,b), return(e))
 </implementation>
 <implementation language = "mathematica">
   monetDefInt[f_,x_,a_,b_] := Integrate[f,{x,a,b}]
 </implementation>
 <implementation language="axiom">
)clear completely
monetDefInt(f,x,a,b)==
  integrate(f,x=a..b)
 </implementation>
</mathServer>
```

## 6.2    Changes to the Mathematical Server Components

In order to enable capabilities of Mathematical Server to handle services using various mathematical engines, the developer of a particular instance of the mathematical server has to replace the elements of the Invocation Manager that depend on the mathematical engine. These are the code generation, the tools for conversion between OpenMath and the language of this system and an adapter that allows to plug the system software into Mathematical Server environment.

Essentially, this means providing new code for Java classes implementing these functions. The good news is that the stubs of these classes, once created, can be reused by simply pointing to the location of their files during Mathematical Server installation. Currently we have created such code stubs for two computer algebra systems: Maple and Axiom. None of this is completely straightforward, but fortunately these tasks need be done only once for each system.

The whole structure of Mathematical Server, as well as its tools assigned to install and maintain new services remain the same, since they do not depend on the mathematical engine.

## 6.3    Current Status and Future Work

We have successfully applied this technique to switch between two computer algebra systems, Maple and Axiom. We have not yet experimented with substituting the mathematical engine with a Fortran program using NAG libraries, but we believe that the organization of the web server and mathematical web services will easily allow this.

## 7   Conclusion

We have described an approach to providing mathematical web services in which authors wishing to provide services need know only the mathematical software packages with which they are already familiar. No knowledge is required of Java, WSDL or other web technologies. We see this as a significant benefit over previous approaches, given the rarity of individuals with expertise in both web technologies and mathematical software.

For each mathmatical software system used to implement services, a translator program to and from OpenMath must be provided. This is required only once for each system, however.

The client-side interface to the mathematical services is suitable for use both by software systems and end users. It is currently used to serve a test web site providing a selection of symbolic mathematical services at `http://ptibonum.scl.csd.uwo.ca:16661/MonetServiceClient`. It is also used for on-going experimentation with complex service brokers that plan solution strategies combining services from different mathematical software systems.

## References

1. S. Buswell, O. Caprotti, and M. Dewar, MONET Architecture Overview, Deliverable 4, The MONET Consortium, 2002.
2. Y. Chicha, J. Davenport, and D. Roberts, *Mathematical Explanation Ontology*, Deliverable 7, The MONET Consortium, 2004.
3. O. Caprotti, D. Carlisle, A.M. Cohen, and M. Dewar, Mathematical Problem Description Ontology, Deliverable 11, The MONET Consortium, 2003.
4. S. Buswell, O. Caprotti, and M. Dewar, *Mathematical Service Description Language* , Deliverable 14, The MONET Consortium, 2003.
5. W. Barbera-Medina, S. Buswell, Y. Chicha, M. Gaetano, J. Padget, M. Riem, and D. Turi, Broker API, Deliverable 18, The MONET Consortium, 2003.
6. W3C, Simple Object Access Protocol (SOAP) 1.1, `http://www.w3.org/TR/SOAP`, 2003-2004.
7. W3C, Web Services Description Language (WSDL) 1.1, `http://www.w3.org/TR/wsdl.html`.
8. W3C, Web Service Deployment Descriptor (WSDD) 1.1, `developer.apple.com/documentation/WebObjects/Web_Services/Web_Services/chapter_4_section_7.html`.
9. OpenMath, `http://www.openmath.org/cocoon/openmath`, 1999-2004.
10. An OpenMath v1.0 Implementation, S. Dalmas, M. Gaetano and S. M. Watt, Proc International Symposium on Symbolic and Algebraic Computation (ISSAC 1997), pp. 217-224, ACM Press 1997.
11. Brokers and Web-Services for Automatic Deduction: a Case Study, C. Sacerdoti Coen and S. Zacchiroli, Proc. Calculemus 2003.

12. RIACA OpenMath Library, http://www.riaca.win.tue.nl/products/openmath/lib/1.3/api , 2001–2004.
13. *Document Object Model* , http://www.w3.org/DOM/.
14. Java Standard Edition, Sun Microsystems Inc, http://java.sun.com, 1995–2004.
15. The Apache Software Foundation, http://httpd.apache.org, 1996–2004.
16. Apache Jakarta Project, Apache Software Foundation, http://jakarta.apache.org/tomcat, 1999–2004.
17. Apache Axis, Apache Web Services Project, http://ws.apache.org/axis, 1999–2004.
18. Apache Ant, Apache Software Foundation, http://ant.apache.org, 2000–2004.
19. JavaServer Pages Technology, Sun Microsystems, Inc. http://java.sun.com/products/jsp, 1999–2004.
20. Maple, Maplesoft, a division of Waterloo Maple Inc. 2004, http://www.maplesoft.com, 2004.
21. Mathematica, Wolfram Research, Inc., http://www.wolfram.com, 2004.
22. Axiom, Software Foundation, Inc., http://savannah.nongnu.org/projects/axiom, 2000–2004.
23. Derive, LTSN Maths, Stats & OR Network, http://www.chartwellyorke.com/derive.html 2000–2004.
24. MatLab, The MathWorks, Inc., http://www.mathworks.com/products/matlab, 1994–2004.
25. The MBase Mathematical Knowledge Base. http://www.mathweb.org/mbase/.

# The Categorial Type of OpenMath Objects

Andreas Strotmann

Universität zu Köln, ZAIK/RRZK
strotmann@rrz.uni-koeln.de

**Abstract.** We introduce a fundamental concept found in the formal semantics of language, categorial type logics, into the field of knowledge communication language design in general, and into mathematical content markup language design in particular.

Categorial type logics permit the specification of type systems for knowledge communication languages that are both *complete* wrt. language structure and *extensible* wrt. the lexical component.

We apply this concept to OpenMath, and propose a categorial type logic for that language which matches well with its intended semantics. The proposed type logic is a simpler version of the well-established **L2** categorial type logic, from which it inherits decidability and other useful mathematical properties.

As a practical result, we report a serious problem in the OpenMath 1.0 specification.

## 1 Introduction

We have long argued [12] that content markup languages need to obey the Compositionality Principle which requires that "the meaning of a compound expression is a function of the meaning of its parts and of the syntactic rule by which they are combined."[11] Many languages for communicating or processing mathematics have non-compositional features [12] that frequently turn out to be bugs [16, 14], but the core of OpenMath [1, 4] does comply with this principle [16].

Mathematically, the compositionality principle has been modeled in the literature as a requirement for the existence of an interpretation that acts as a homomorphism from a syntactic algebra to a semantic algebra. From a more practical computer scientist's perspective we have noted that it implies that

> "a language for expressing semantics for exchange among computer programs [...] define[s] a basic interpretation procedure – how to interpret the parts, and how to interpret the combinations of parts. [...] [C]ompositionality means that one is able to provide a firmly grounded scaffolding from which one can work to extend the scope of [the] language by adding only lexical entries, while keeping the scaffolding intact." [12]

The challenge for the practical designer of languages like OpenMath is to provide such a basic interpretation that can act as a semantic scaffolding for their

A. Asperti et al. (Eds.): MKM 2004, LNCS 3119, pp. 378–392, 2004.
© Springer-Verlag Berlin Heidelberg 2004

language. This exercise can be a valuable design tool for content communication languages, as we will show here by applying it to OpenMath.

A *skeleton semantics* for a compositional language, as we termed it [12], i.e. a compositional semantics that respects the syntactic structure of a language, has been studied in formal linguistics under the general heading of "categorial grammar," and it is in this sense that we use the term "categorial" here.

The interested reader is invited to consult M. Moortgat's survey of *Categorial Type Logics* [13] for a justification and history of this terminology, and for an in-depth treatment of both the notions and the notations we use in the following.

## 2    Problems of a Formal Semantics for Content Markup

The specification of a semantics for content markup languages like MathML-Content [6] or OpenMath is a thorny issue. Both languages have side-stepped the issue by declaring their semantics "informal" and thus, open to interpretation.

In the case of OpenMath, however, two proposals for OpenMath type systems were published simultaneously with Version 1.0 of the Standard [4], in order to provide a more ("Strong" OpenMath [5]) or less (Small Type System [7]) detailed semantics for OpenMath objects. The idea is that many type theories exist, all of them equally valid, and since any formal semantics induces a type theory, any number of such semantics for OpenMath must be allowed to co-exist.

No such publication seems to exist for MathML Content markup, perhaps because the MathML philosophy specifically declares its semantics informal.

On the other hand, developers of another knowledge communication language, the Knowledge Interchange Format (KIF) [9], provide a fully formal semantics (although not a type theory) for their language. Ontologies based on KIF have included "engineering mathematics" [10], making KIF directly comparable with MathML and OpenMath despite its quite different designated application area of intelligent agent communication.

The main reason for avoiding the specification of a formal semantics for a content markup language, for example in the form of a formal type system, appears to be grounded in two conflicting demands on such a language and its semantics. On the one hand, a content markup language needs to be extensible in order to allow the marking-up of novel concepts in the language, but on the other hand a formal semantics for a knowledge communication language needs to be complete in the sense of providing an interpretation for all possible legal sentences in that language.

Another problem is that different type theories make different choices when it comes to weighing type inference power (and thus the set of constructs that are interpreted correctly) against automatic validation speeds (or indeed decidability). Defining too weak a formal type theory, it can be argued, would risk prohibition of even quite common scientific formalisms, but would allow one to require "conforming" applications to implement it. A powerful formal type theory, on the other hand, may be able to specify the semantics for a wide range of such formalisms, but its proof theory might be prohibitively expensive to implement or run, or even undecidable.

The concept of a categorial semantics in general, and of a categorial type system in particular, tries to provide a good compromise between the extremes of both these dimensions.

On the one hand, a categorial semantics is complete with respect to the syntactic structures provided by a content markup language, but it is at the same time extensible with respect to the lexical ingredients of the language. By providing a clean conceptual interface to "external" type theories on atoms of the language, it acknowledges that different formal semantics are possible and, indeed, useful, but by providing a single common structural semantics for the language it makes sure that any two such semantics agree at least on the basic meanings of an expression.

On the other hand, a categorial semantics of a content markup language can in principle be kept simple enough to be implemented easily, so that its ease of implementation or its inference power would depend on the application's choice of a more or less complex "external" lexical semantics, on which choice the categorial semantics itself is agnostic.

## 3   Origins of Categorial Semantics

As mentioned earlier, we have "stolen" the concept of a categorial semantics from Formal Semantics, a.k.a. Montague Semantics, a branch of Formal Linguistics, where categorial types are a fundamental tool for studying the structure of the semantics of language, and *Categorial Type Logics* [13] have been studied extensively.

We therefore adapt a formalism from this field, known as the Lambek calculus [13], for the purpose of illustrating its usefulness in the much more recent field of content markup language design. We thus follow a historical precedent in that a seminal paper for such a calculus [2] applied it both to natural language sentences and to mathematical formulas.

A categorial semantics for a language can only exist if the language obeys the twin principles of *Strong Compositionality* and *Lexicalism*. The strong compositionality principle requires that the semantics of a language be a homomorphism between its syntactic and semantic algebras. Lexicalism, in addition, requires all atoms of the language to be assigned a semantics (or a type) exclusively via a *lexicon*, leaving the semantics of compound expressions of the compositional language to be induced via semantic constructors.

The Lambek calculus [13] is originally one of syntactic categories only (hence the term *categorial*). However, via the homomorphism between syntactic and semantic algebras postulated by the strong compositionality principle, the syntactic Lambek calculus immediately translates to a semantic one.

The semantic version of the Lambek Calculus is thus commonly understood as a type logic, where syntactic categories are homomorphically mapped to semantic types., and it is this interpretation that we will apply to the content markup language OpenMath in the following.

## 4 Lambek Types and the Lambda Calculus

As a gentle introduction to the Lambek calculus, we will briefly show how it can be used in a type theory for the Lambda calculus.

Lambda calculus expressions of the form $fxy$ (i.e., applications) are assigned the type $F \bullet X \bullet Y$, where upper-case letters denote the type of the corresponding variables denoted in lower-case letters, and $\bullet$ denotes type-level application. Lambda abstraction expressions of the form $(\lambda x.f)$, on the other hand, are assigned the type $X \backslash F$ in this calculus.

Given this definition, the Lambda calculus expression $((\lambda x.(\lambda y.fxy))x)y$ has the Lambek type $((X \backslash (Y \backslash (F \bullet X \bullet Y))) \bullet X) \bullet Y$, for example.

The Lambek calculus then has type-level equivalents of Lambda Calculus reduction rules. $\beta$-Reduction, for example, which says that

$$\frac{(\lambda x.f)x}{f} \beta \text{ , corresponds to } \frac{(X \backslash F) \bullet X}{F} \beta_{lr} \text{ .} \tag{1}$$

In other words, (right) application cancels (left) abstraction just like multiplication cancels division.

Notice how the *left* abstraction notation $X \backslash F$ causes it to become visually separated from its canceling *right* application $F \bullet X$. We therefore propose to use in the following the more intuitive though clearly equivalent *right* abstraction notation $F/X$ instead of $X \backslash F$, which produces the following categorial version of the Lambda Calculus $\beta$-reduction rule:

$$\frac{(F/X) \bullet X}{F} \beta_r \tag{2}$$

In this notation, the Lambda calculus currying rules for binary functions,

$$\lambda x.\lambda y.f \equiv \lambda x.(\lambda y.f) \quad \text{and} \quad fxy \equiv (fx)y \text{ ,} \tag{3}$$

the associativity rules for lambda abstraction for application, correspond to the following categorial type-level equivalences:

$$F/Y/X \equiv (F/Y)/X \quad \text{and} \quad F \bullet X \bullet Y \equiv (F \bullet X) \bullet Y \tag{4}$$

Notice how the switch to the more intuitive right abstraction division notation induces a reversal of the ordering of the variables (or rather, their types) in the type-level equivalent formula. This is a small price to pay for an otherwise nicely intuitive formalism, where cancelling factors are always directly adjacent.

This is therefore the variation on Lambek's notation for categorial type logics that we propose to use in the following for content markup languages, since these languages, like the Lambda Calculus that they tend to be based on, are

A. Strotmann

essentially prefix notations that do not need to distinguish between right- and left-hand side arguments. Again, we follow established precedent here, since this is actually closer to the notation $\frac{A}{B}$ used in Ajdukiewicz's seminal paper [2, 3] for a non-directional categorial calculus.

## 5  Categorial Type of OpenMath Objects

We will now develop a categorial type logic for OpenMath objects as defined in the OpenMath Standard Version 1 [4]. Following the compositional approach, we will examine each *structural syntactic* constructor of OpenMath and give it a *categorial* interpretation. In other words, we will propose a categorial type constructor as homomorphic image for each syntactic category of OpenMath.

In this context, we will use the notations used in the OpenMath Standard [4] to write OpenMath objects, and the notation in [13] for type assignment: if $\Omega$ denotes an OpenMath object, we let $\tau(\Omega)$ denote its type. More generally, we will let $\tau_\eta(\Omega)$ denote its type given an environment $\eta$ of type variable bindings.

In OpenMath 1.0, OpenMath objects are defined as abstract data structures that are either basic OpenMath objects or compound OpenMath objects. Compound OpenMath objects are either OpenMath application objects, OpenMath binding objects, OpenMath attribution objects, or OpenMath error objects; basic OpenMath objects are OpenMath symbols, OpenMath variables, OpenMath integers, OpenMath floating point numbers, OpenMath bytearrays, or OpenMath character strings.

OpenMath objects may also be viewed as the result of parsing their *encodings*, i.e. as an abstract syntactic structure. It is in this interpretation that we use their definition as a basis for our categorial analysis in the following.

### 5.1  OpenMath Application Objects

An *OpenMath application object* has the syntax $\mathbf{application}(a_0, \ldots, a_n)$ , where the $a_i$ are arbitrary OpenMath objects and $n \geq 0$.

Given its intended meaning as *application*, we can define the categorial type of an OpenMath application object as:

$$\tau_\eta(\mathbf{application}(a_0, \ldots, a_n)) := (\tau_\eta(a_0) \bullet \ldots \bullet \tau_\eta(a_n)) \tag{5}$$

This can also be expressed as the axiom schema[1]

$$\frac{\tau_\eta(\mathbf{application}(a_0, \ldots, a_n))}{(\tau_\eta(a_0) \bullet \ldots \bullet \tau_\eta(a_n))} \; oma_n \tag{6}$$

This is essentially the same as definitions used in both the Small Type System [7] and Strong OpenMath [5] type system proposals for OpenMath, and it is rather straightforward.

---

[1] Note that this extends the usual Lambek notation for type-level application to the nullary case, by writing $(\tau_\eta(a_0)\bullet)$ for $n = 0$.

## 5.2    OpenMath Attribution Objects

*OpenMath attribution objects* have the form $\textbf{attribution}(a_1\ b_1, \ldots, a_n\ b_n, e)$. The *attribute names* $a_i$ are restricted to be OpenMath symbols, whereas the *attribute values* $b_i$ and the *body* $e$ are arbitrary OpenMath objects.

Neither of the two existing proposals for OpenMath type systems deals with general OpenMath attribution objects. This is understandable since semantically, the attributions are meant to provide additional information about the body OpenMath object without actually "changing" its meaning. This is true only for OpenMath 1, however: OpenMath 2 will introduce the concept of semantic attributes that *are* allowed to change meanings.

As a categorial type definition for an OpenMath attribution object with a single attribute we propose

$$\tau(\textbf{attribution}(a\ b, e)) := (\tau(a) \bullet \tau(b)) \bullet \tau(e) \tag{7}$$

or, as a proof schema with the unchanged environment $\eta$ made explicit,

$$\frac{\tau_\eta(\textbf{attribution}(a\ b, e))}{(\tau_\eta(a) \bullet \tau_\eta(b)) \bullet \tau_\eta(e)}\ omattr_1 \tag{8}$$

The OpenMath Standard declares that the following syntactic equivalence holds for OpenMath attribution objects:

$$\textbf{attribution}(a_1\ b_1, a_2\ b_2, e) \equiv \textbf{attribution}(a_1\ b_1, \textbf{attribution}(a_2\ b_2, e)) \tag{9}$$

from which we get the following fully general type assignment for OpenMath attribution objects:

$$\frac{\tau_\eta(\textbf{attribution}(a_1\ b_1, \ldots, a_n\ b_n, e))}{(\tau_\eta(a_1) \bullet \tau_\eta(b_1)) \bullet (\ldots ((\tau_\eta(a_n) \bullet \tau_\eta(b_n)) \bullet \tau_\eta(e)) \ldots)}\ omattr_n \tag{10}$$

The OpenMath 1 intention that attributions not modify the meaning of the attributed object is modeled in our framework by restrictions on the signatures of attribute name symbols – an approach that is compatible with changes in this policy in OpenMath 2. We discuss OpenMath lexical semantics below.

## 5.3    OpenMath Binding Objects and OpenMath Variables

An *OpenMath binding object* has the form $\textbf{binding}(b, v_1, \ldots, v_n, e)$. The components of an OpenMath binding object are its *head* $b$, called a *binder* if it is an OpenMath symbol, its *bound variables* $v_1 \ldots v_n$, and its *body* $e$. The binder and the body are both arbitrary OpenMath objects, and the bound variables are either OpenMath variables or OpenMath variables embedded as the body of an OpenMath attribution object.

Caprotti and Cohen [5] deal with OpenMath binding objects only in the case of a single, explicitly typed bound variable. Their proposal can be expressed in our formalism roughly as

$$\tau(\textbf{binding}(b, \textbf{attribution}(\texttt{type}\ t, v), e)) := \tau(b) \bullet \tau(t) \bullet (\tau(e)/\tau(t)) \tag{11}$$

Since we are aiming to be fully general, however, we need to define a categorial type for all OpenMath binding objects, typed or untyped and with an arbitrary number of bound variables. We therefore offer the following simplified type assignment for OpenMath binding objects:[2]

$$\tau(\mathbf{binding}(b, v_1, \ldots, v_n, e)) := \tau(b) \bullet (\tau(e)/\tau(v_n)/\cdots/\tau(v_1)) \qquad (12)$$

This corresponds to an interpretation of an OpenMath binding object as forming an abstraction over the variables $v_1 \ldots v_n$ with body $e$ and applying the binder $b$ to the resulting abstraction: $\mathbf{binding}(b, v_1, \ldots, v_n, e) \equiv b(\lambda v_1. \cdots \lambda v_n.e)$.

These type assignments have a nicely simple form, but they do not yet formalize sufficiently the fact that variable binding modifies the environment $\eta$ of type assignments to variables. The following axiom schema does this properly in the case of OpenMath variables $v_1 \ldots v_n$:

$$\frac{\tau_\eta(\mathbf{binding}(b, v_1, \ldots, v_n, e))}{\tau_\eta(b) \bullet (\tau_{[v_1:V_1,\ldots,v_n:V_n|\eta]}(e)/V_n/\cdots/V_1)} \; omb_{v_1:V_1,\ldots,v_n:V_n} \qquad (13)$$

This still ignores OpenMath binding objects in which the bound variable OpenMath objects are not simple OpenMath variables but attributed OpenMath variables. In the case of a single bound variable with a single attribution, we get, by combining (7) and (12):

$$\frac{\tau_\eta(\mathbf{binding}(b, \mathbf{attribution}(a_1 \; b_1, v), e))}{\tau_\eta(b) \bullet (\tau_{[v:V|\eta]}(e)/((\tau_\eta(a_1) \bullet \tau_\eta(b_1)) \bullet V))} \; omb_{v:V} \qquad (14)$$

Since generalizing this formula to arbitrary numbers of variables and attributions per variable yields a rather unwieldy formula, we will leave it as an exercise to the reader.

For *OpenMath variables*, the categorial type is generally $X$ – a type variable:

$$\frac{\tau_{\eta_{x:X}}(x)}{X} \; omv_x \qquad (15)$$

where $\eta_{x:X}$ stands for the type assignment $X$ for the variable $x$ in the environment $\eta$, i.e. the environment $\eta$ contains, for each type variable name, a type assignment that is itself a variable, namely, a type variable. Any concrete type assignment for a variable in an OpenMath object needs to be deduced via type inference mechanisms and unification of type variables.

Care needs to be taken therefore that several occurrences of a variable in the same scope are properly assigned the same type variable as their lexical meaning assignment, and that the same variable name in different scopes is

---

[2] Note that we have lost the type information that was present in Caprotti and Cohen's proposal; by providing a general type semantic for OpenMath attribution objects and by giving appropriate signatures to type symbols we can easily recover this information in our framework.

assigned different type-level variables in the type assignment. That is the task of the environment parameter $\eta$ of the type assignment $\tau_\eta(\Omega)$.

Letting $\eta_{x:X}$ stand for the type assignment $(x : X) \in \eta$ such that if the list $\eta$ contains the type assignments $(x : X_1), (x : X_2), \ldots$ in this order, then $X = X_1$ (i.e. letting the environment $\eta$ act as a stack of type assignments for variables in the standard fashion), we can now see that the above definition for type assignments for variables, bindings, and attributions combine to give the expected results:

$$\cfrac{\cfrac{\cfrac{\cfrac{\tau_{[]}(\mathbf{binding}(a, v, \mathbf{application}(f, v, v)))}{\tau_{[]}(a) \bullet (\tau_{[v:V]}(\mathbf{application}(f, v, v))/\tau_{[v:V]}(v))} \; omb_{v:V}}{\tau_{[]}(a) \bullet (\tau_{[v:V]}(\mathbf{application}(f, v, v))/V)} \; omv_v}{\tau_{[]}(a) \bullet ((\tau_{[v:V]}(f) \bullet \tau_{[v:V]}(v) \bullet \tau_{[v:V]}(v))/V)} \; oma_2}{\tau(a)_{[]} \bullet ((\tau_{[v:V]}(f) \bullet V \bullet V)/V)} \; omv_v$$

but

$$\cfrac{\cfrac{\cfrac{\cfrac{\cfrac{\tau_{[]}(\mathbf{binding}(a, v, \mathbf{application}(f, v, \mathbf{binding}(b, v, v))))}{\tau_{[]}(a) \bullet (\tau_{[v:V]}(\mathbf{application}(f, v, \mathbf{binding}(b, v, v)))/\tau_{[v:V]}(v))} \; omb_{v:V}}{\tau_{[]}(a) \bullet (\tau_{[v:V]}(\mathbf{application}(f, v, \mathbf{binding}(b, v, v)))/V)} \; omv_v}{\tau_{[]}(a) \bullet ((\tau_{[v:V]}(f) \bullet \tau_{[v:V]}(v) \bullet \tau_{[v:V]}(\mathbf{binding}(b, v, v)))/V)} \; oma_2}{\tau_{[]}(a) \bullet ((\tau_{[v:V]}(f) \bullet V \bullet \tau_{[v:V]}(\mathbf{binding}(b, v, v)))/V)} \; omv_v}{\cfrac{\tau_{[]}(a) \bullet ((\tau_{[v:V]}(f) \bullet V \bullet (\tau_{[v:V]}(b) \bullet (\tau_{[v:V_1, v:V]}(v)/\tau_{[v:V_1, v:V]}(v))))/V)}{\tau_{[]}(a) \bullet ((\tau_{[v:V]}(f) \bullet V \bullet (\tau_{[v:V]}(b) \bullet (V_1/V_1)))/V)} \; omv_v} \; omb_{v:V_1}}$$

## 5.4   OpenMath Error Objects

*OpenMath error objects*, semantically speaking, only carry the meaning that an error occurred. For the sake of completeness, we therefore simply note that, in a type inference chain, their occurrence would therefore simply trigger a "fail" condition, or $\bot$:

$$\frac{\tau_\eta(\mathbf{error}(\ldots))}{\bot} \; omerr \tag{16}$$

## 5.5   OpenMath Symbols

As in [13], "in accordance with the categorial tenet of *radical lexicalism*, we assume that the grammar for [our language] $\mathcal{L}$ [= OpenMath] is given by the conjunction of [its] general type logic with [its] language-specific lexicon $\text{LEX}(\mathcal{L})$ [which is] characterized in terms of a type assignment function" that assigns a set of applicable categorial types to a lexical item. The type assigned to a lexical item therefore does not need to be unique, as one of the earlier type systems for

OpenMath stipulated, but it is assumed that there are only a finite number of distinct alternatives. [13]

In the case of *OpenMath symbols*, OpenMath realizes LEX in the form of OpenMath content dictionaries and zero or more associated "signature" declarations. Signature declarations depend on the type system they are embedded in. At least two such systems have already been defined for OpenMath, but none cover all existing OpenMath content dictionaries.

We discuss common patterns of categorial signatures of OpenMath symbols below.

## 5.6    Other Basic OpenMath Objects

In addition to OpenMath variables, OpenMath distinguishes several different kinds of constant leaf objects, or *basic OpenMath objects*. Since they are syntactically distinguished, we need to discuss categorial type assignments for each.

In the interest of a "pure" categorial semantics, we could assign all constant basic OpenMath objects the type $X$ – i.e., unknown, variable. However, OpenMath integers are one example where the intent is quite clearly that they be representations of integers, and their type thus $\mathbb{Z}$.

Both strategies are sanctioned for a categorial OpenMath grammar that we quoted above, so that we will not propose a specific choice here.

## 6    Categorial Type Inference Rules and OpenMath

Now that we have defined the basic translations for OpenMath object structures into categorial types, we need to choose which categorial type inference rules should apply to them in order to complete the categorial type logic.

### 6.1    $\beta$-Reduction

A type-level version of $\beta$-reduction applies to OpenMath types to capture the intended meanings of OpenMath application objects and OpenMath binding objects. The categorial $\beta$-reduction inference rule schema for OpenMath is:

$$\frac{(A/B_1 \cdots /B_n) \bullet B_n \cdots \bullet B_1}{A} \; om\beta_n \tag{17}$$

This simply means that applying an $n$-ary function object with argument types $B_1 \ldots B_n$ to $n$ arguments of the correct type in the correct order results in an element of the result type of the function object.

Note that in linguistic applications, we only find a single inference rule of this type for $n = 1$. This is because in the Lambda calculus (which is used in linguistic applications) both application and abstraction obey an associativity law. OpenMath as such does *not* obey these laws (see below), so that we have to use a rule schema for the type-level version of $\beta$-reduction for all $n \geq 0$.

## 6.2   Currying

OpenMath 1.0 provided very limited support for another type inference rule that is usually found in such contexts, namely the currying rules:

$$\frac{(A/B/C)}{((A/B)/C)} \, /assoc^* \quad \text{and} \quad \frac{A \bullet B \bullet C}{(A \bullet B) \bullet C} \bullet assoc^* \, . \tag{18}$$

Neither of these rules, however, is defined for OpenMath objects in full generality. The only currying rule that the OpenMath 1.0 Standard clearly specified holds for OpenMath binding objects and corresponds to the type inference rule

$$\frac{D \bullet (A/B/C)}{D \bullet ((D \bullet (A/B))/C)} \, om/assoc \, . \tag{19}$$

This rule is modeled on the abstraction currying rule $/assoc*$ above which we could attempt to recover from the OpenMath binding object currying rule $om/assoc$ by letting $D = (X/X)$ and applying the $\beta$-reduction rule $om\beta$.[3]

Unlike for OpenMath binding objects, no currying rule is defined for Open-Math application objects in the OpenMath 1.0 Standard – the usual symmetry between application and abstraction currying is broken. Since the currying rules are actually derived from the observation that

$$(x, y \mapsto f)(a, b) = ((x \mapsto (y \mapsto f))(a))(b) \, , \tag{20}$$

a rule that applies only if both application *and* abstraction are curried, we have reason to be worried.

We thus perceive a mismatch between the categorial type system that we propose on the one hand, and the definitions of the OpenMath Standard 1.0 on the other. This may be due to problems in the categorial semantics approach we advocate, or it may be due to problems in the OpenMath definition – we show here that the OpenMath 1.0 definition was in error. Indeed, we will show that it is impossible to define a correct syntactic rule for currying OpenMath objects.

The reason is that the particular way that OpenMath binding objects are structured is asymmetric with respect to the way that OpenMath application objects are structured, and this asymmetry dooms any attempt to introduce a

---

[3]

$$\frac{(X/X) \bullet (A/B/C)}{A/B/C} \, om\beta_1, X = A/B/C$$

and

$$\frac{\dfrac{(X/X) \bullet (((Y/Y) \bullet (A/B))/C)}{(X/X) \bullet ((A/B)/C)} \, om\beta_1, Y = A/B}{(A/B)/C} \, om\beta_1, X = (A/B)/C$$

Note that we have to cheat a bit by giving each copy of $D$ a different copy of its signature ($X/X$ vs. $Y/Y$) in the second derivation in order to achieve this result.

general-purpose currying rule for OpenMath application objects and OpenMath binding objects.

To see this we consider again the type-level version of the OpenMath binding object currying rule (19):

$$\frac{D \bullet (A/B/C)}{D \bullet ((D \bullet (A/B))/C)} \; om/assoc \qquad (21)$$

Notice that the $(D \bullet (A/B))$ in the second line of this rule, that is the type of the values returned by elements of $D$ when applied to elements of $(A/B)$, must match the $A$ of the first line, that is the type of the body of the OpenMath binding object: an OpenMath binding object needs to return the same result type as its body returns in order for this currying rule to even make sense.

Quantifiers have predicates as bodies, which return truth-values, and they themselves also return truth-values. Similarly, operators that are induced by $n$-ary associative functions (e.g. $\sum$ induced by $+$, or the "big" version $\bigcap$ of $\cap$) all return the same type of value as their bodies do. With the currying rule an axiom of Lambda calculus, all the binder symbols defined in early OpenMath versions in fact obeyed this currying rule!

Not all binders fit this model, however, just as not all $n$-ary functions are associative. Here are a few well-known counter-examples:

**the** : $\iota$ as in $\iota x.P(x)$: "*The unique $x$ such that $P(x)$ is true*". The body $P$ returns a truth value, while the generalized quantifier $\iota$ returns an object from some arbitrary domain.

**some** : $\epsilon$ as in $\epsilon x.P(x)$: Chooses "*some $x$ that satisfies $P(x)$*".

**sequence** : $(A_i)_{i \in \mathbb{N}}$ – the *sequence* of all $A_i$ where $i$ ranges over the natural numbers, for example. The body returns *elements* of the sequence, but the binder returns a *sequence* of such elements.

**set of** : $\{x \mid P(x)\}$ – the *set of* all $x$ that satisfy $P(x)$.

The first two in this list were not defined in early versions of the OpenMath content dictionaries, and the final one was defined as a multi-argument operator rather than a binder, so that this problem was not immediately apparent.

However, the class of counter-examples is clearly open-ended, as it includes at least one element per non-associative $n$-ary operator in mathematics. It clearly contains important concepts that OpenMath will need to represent. Hence, the class of counter-examples is anything but negligible.

The currying rule for OpenMath binding objects is therefore irreparably broken. Based on the results reported here, OpenMath version 1.1 has therefore removed the currying rule completely to fix this major bug in OpenMath 1.0.

## 7    On a Lexical Semantics of OpenMath

Recall that "the grammar for [OpenMath] is given by the conjunction of [its] general type logic with [its] language-specific lexicon" LEX(OpenMath) which assigns categorial types to lexical items.

The detailed lexical semantics of the *full* set of OpenMath symbols, i.e. the full definition of LEX(OpenMath), is explicitly not within the scope of this paper – the whole point of a categorial semantics is the ability to factor out that aspect of meaning. It *is*, however, of interest here to study what *kinds* of signatures an OpenMath categorial type logic might have to support, i.e. what entries in LEX(OpenMath) might look like, and if the mechanisms we have introduced so far are up to the task of handling them. Space constraints only allow us to cover the most important aspects of this question here, however. Additional details are discussed in [15], and a full treatment will be the subject of a later publication.

Regular constants, functions, or relations typically can be assigned signatures such as $\tau(\mathtt{pi}_{\mathrm{nums1}}) := \mathbb{R}$ or $\tau(\mathtt{sin}_{\mathrm{transc1}}) \in \{(\mathbb{R}/\mathbb{R}), (\mathbb{C}/\mathbb{C})\}$; as type inference rules:

$$\frac{\tau(\mathtt{pi}_{\mathrm{nums1}})}{\mathbb{R}} \text{ LEX } ; \qquad \frac{\tau(\mathtt{sin}_{\mathrm{transc1}})}{\mathbb{C}/\mathbb{C}} \text{ LEX }, \qquad \frac{\tau(\mathtt{sin}_{\mathrm{transc1}})}{\mathbb{R}/\mathbb{R}} \text{ LEX} \qquad (22)$$

Note that we use concrete mathematical type constants such as $\mathbb{R}$ for the reals and $\mathbb{C}$ for the complex numbers in these examples instead of the type variables that we have used in our examples so far. This is in keeping with the OpenMath philosophy that signatures of OpenMath Symbols are given modulo a concrete type system.

Here is a simple example of how the categorial and a concrete lexical type system might interact profitably to infer the type $\mathbb{R}$ of $\sin \pi$:

$$\frac{\dfrac{\dfrac{\tau(\mathbf{application}(\mathtt{sin}_{\mathrm{transc1}}, \mathtt{pi}_{\mathrm{nums1}}))}{(\tau(\mathtt{sin}_{\mathrm{transc1}}) \bullet \tau(\mathtt{pi}_{\mathrm{nums1}}))} \, oma}{((\mathbb{R}/\mathbb{R}) \bullet \mathbb{R})} \text{ LEX}}{\mathbb{R}} \, \beta$$

Binder symbols have slightly more complex signatures, as they include type variables: $\tau(\mathbf{the}_{\mathrm{quant42}}) := \mathbb{T}/(\mathbb{T}/X)$. An attribute name has a signature which ignores the attribute and returns the type of the attributed object unchanged: $\tau(\mathbf{mathml}_{\mathrm{presentation}}) := (X/X)/\mathrm{MmlPresType}$.

Our examples use concrete types "plugged" into the categorial type system we propose from a concrete type system chosen purely for illustration purposes. This illustrates the usefulness, but also the limitations of the concept of a categorial type system: it mirrors very well the partitioning of the OpenMath language into the fixed definition of the structure of OpenMath objects on the one hand and the open and extensible set of OpenMath symbol definitions in OpenMath content dictionaries on the other, defining the former, "plugging in" the latter.

The important difference between this approach and previous type system proposals for OpenMath is that in our example above the signatures of symbols do not consist solely of constructors and constants of a separate type theory, but utilize standardized categorial type constructors for application and abstraction in conjunction with constants from a sample concrete type theory.

Simple and elegant though this idea may sound in theory, it immediately brings up the practical question of how a categorial type theory like the one we propose, on the one hand, and a concrete "plug-in" lexical type theory, on the other, would interact mathematically and proof-theoretically.

To see that this question is not quite trivial, consider the deceptively simple example formula $(\sin \pi = 0)$ expressed in OpenMath. A few predicates such as equality are polymorphic, applicable to elements of any type at all. We can express this easily in the categorial framework by using type variables instead of constant type names in the signature: $\tau(\mathtt{eq}_{\mathrm{relations1}}) :=_{\mathrm{LEX}} 2/X/X$. With this definition in place, we can now deduce that $(\sin \pi = 0)$ stands for a truth value:

$$
\cfrac{\tau(\mathbf{application}(\mathtt{eq}_{\mathrm{relations1}}, \mathbf{application}(\mathtt{sin}_{\mathrm{transc1}}, \mathtt{pi}_{\mathrm{nums1}}), 0))}{\cfrac{\tau(\mathtt{eq}_{\mathrm{relations1}}) \bullet (\tau(\mathtt{sin}_{\mathrm{transc1}}) \bullet \tau(\mathtt{pi}_{\mathrm{nums1}})) \bullet \tau(0)}{\cfrac{(2/X/X) \bullet ((\mathbb{R}/\mathbb{R}) \bullet \mathbb{R}) \bullet \mathbb{Z}}{\cfrac{(2/X/X) \bullet \mathbb{R} \bullet \mathbb{Z}}{\cfrac{(2/X/X) \bullet \mathbb{R} \bullet \mathbb{R}}{2} \; \beta_2(X = \mathbb{R})} \; \mathbb{Z} \subset \mathbb{R}} \; \beta_1} \; \mathrm{LEX}} \; oma
$$

This derivation uses two important new details. First, as a new aspect of the categorial type logic, it uses unification to deduce a possible value for the type variable $X$ from the structure of the $\beta$-reduction rule in the $\beta_2(X = \mathbb{R})$ inference step. Second, it includes a derivation step that is true only in the plugged-in concrete lexical type theory ($\mathbb{Z} \subset \mathbb{R}$), in this case, a deduction based on a simple type hierarchy.

Together, these make the question of an interaction between a categorial type logic and a "plug-in" lexical type theory quite non-trivial. Luckily, this question has been studied in a general form in the categorial semantics research area of formal linguistics, from where we "stole" the idea in the first place – another good reason to explore a linguistics parallel for a general theory of content markup languages. In [13] we find that the categorial type logic that we propose for OpenMath is a simpler version of the **L2** type logic, the positive features of which it thus inherits. In addition, [8] "explores the consequences of layering a Lambek calculus over an arbitrary constraint logic," and "[provides] for [such a] hybrid language a simple model-theoretic semantics, [where] the proof system for the underlying base logic" (in our context, the type logic for a concrete "plug-in" type system) "can be assumed to be a black box that performs *entailment checking*" (such as subtype checking for the plugin type system).

## 8 Summary and Outlook

In this paper we have introduced the formal linguistics concept of a *categorial type logic* as surveyed in [13] into the field of content markup language design.

The concept of a categorial type logic, especially in the form of a Lambek calculus that we adapted here to our use, applies to a language that obeys the compositionality principle. In [16] we argued that OpenMath [4, 1] is the first knowledge communication language to meet this requirement; it is thus OpenMath that we apply this new concept to in this paper, with some success.

- We have proposed a basic categorial type logic for OpenMath 1.1 that matches well with the intended semantics of core OpenMath.
- The basic categorial type logic is a simpler version of the well-known and extensively studied restricted second-order polymorphic **L2** categorial type logic [13] (without associativity, i.e. currying), and it inherits decidability and other useful mathematical properties from it.
- The interaction between a categorial type logic of this kind, and a very general class of "plug-in" lexical type theories, has been studied in the linguistics literature, and we get decidability of the combined (or rather, layered) type logic given decidability of the plug-in lexical type theory [8].
- Categorial type logics thus allow us to specify a complete categorial semantics for OpenMath, which fully supports extensibility both with respect to its "lexicon" (i.e. OpenMath content dictionarys) and with respect to the support for multiple competing lexical type theories. Previous type system proposals for OpenMath have been incomplete in that the type semantics of some core OpenMath constructions were not fully specified.
- Problems with the OpenMath 1.0 Standard [4] that we discovered using this tool, are, on our suggestion, fixed as of OpenMath 1.1.

A price that we have had to pay for this success in the case of OpenMath is that the resulting categorial type logic is non-associative, which would correspond to a loss of currying in an underlying Lambda calculus. However, as we have seen, this price is a direct consequence of a specific design decision for OpenMath that we have thus been able to show would need to be seriously reconsidered in future versions of OpenMath, namely, the decision to represent OpenMath binding objects with a header element instead of using the Lambda calculus as a basis for OpenMath.

As a design guideline for future versions of OpenMath in particular, and for all content markup and knowledge communication languages in general, we therefore suggest aiming for a design that supports a categorial type logic **L2** with full support for currying and with those restrictions on second-order quantification that make it decidable [13]. This suggestion has profound consequences for the range of admissible syntactic structures of such languages.

It remains to study in more depths the consequences of these ideas for lexical type systems for OpenMath, since we were only able to scratch the surface of this topic here. MathML would also benefit from a definition of a categorial semantics for its content markup language, as would other knowledge communication languages.

In summary, the concept of a categorial grammar, and the compositionality principle it derives from, have been shown to be a powerful design tool (or design principle, resp.) for content markup languages.

## Acknowledgments

I am indebted to O. Caprotti, M. Kohlhase, and L.J. Kohout as well as several anonymous reviewers for insightful discussions of the material presented here.

# References

1. J. Abbott, A. van Leeuwen, A. Strotmann. OpenMath: Communicating mathematical information between co-operating agents in a knowledge network. J. of Intelligent Systems, 1998, special issue: Improving the Design of Intelligent Systems: Outstanding problems and some methods for their solution **8**, 1998.

2. K. Ajdukiewicz. Die syntaktische Konnexität. Studia Philosophica **1**, 1935, pp. 1–27.

3. K. Ajdukiewicz. Syntactic connexion. In S. McCall (ed.), Polish Logic 1920–1939. Oxford University Press, 1967, pp. 207–231, translated from [2].

4. O. Caprotti, D. Carlisle, A. Cohen (eds.). The OpenMath standard – version 1.0. Technical report, Esprit Project OpenMath (2000) URL: `www.nag.co.uk/projects/OpenMath/omstd/`.

5. O. Caprotti, A. Cohen. A type system for OpenMath. Technical report, Esprit Project OpenMath, 1998.

6. D. Carlisle, P. Ion, R. Miner, N. Poppelier (eds.), Mathematical Markup Language (MathML) 2.0: W3C Recommendation. URL: `www.w3.org/TR/2001/REC-MathML2-20010221/`, 21 February 2001.

7. J. Davenport. A small OpenMath type system. SIGSAM Bulletin (ACM Special Interest Group on Symbolic and Algebraic Manipulation) **34**, 2000, pp. 16–21.

8. J. Dörre, S. Manandhar. On constraint-based Lambek calculi. In P. Blackburn, M. de Rijke (eds.), Specifying Syntactic Structures. CSLI Publications, 1997.

9. M. Genesereth, R. Fikes. Knowledge Interchange Format, Version 3.0 Reference Manual. Technical Report Logic-92-1, Computer Science Department, Stanford University, Stanford, CA, USA, 1992.

10. T. Gruber, G. Olsen. An ontology for engineering mathematics. In J. Pietro Torasso (ed.), Proceedings of the 4th International Conference on Principles of Knowledge Representation and Reasoning, Bonn, FRG, Morgan Kaufmann, 1994, pp. 258–269.

11. T. Janssen. Compositionality. In J. van Benthem, A. ter Meulen (eds.), Handbook of Logic and Language. Elsevier, Amsterdam, 1996, pp. 417–473.

12. L. Kohout, A. Strotmann. Understanding and improving content markup for the Web: from the perspectives of formal linguistics, algebraic logic, and cognitive science. In J. Albus, A. Meystel (eds.), Proc. of IEEE Internat. Symp. on Intelligent Control, IEEE Internat. Symp. on Computational Intelligence in Robotics and Automation & Intelligent Systems and Semiotics (A joint conf. on the Science and Technology of Intelligent Systems), Piscataway, NJ, IEEE & NIST, IEEE, 1998, pp. 834–839.

13. M. Moortgat. Categorial type logics. In J. van Benthem, A. ter Meulen (eds.), Handbook of Logic and Language. Elsevier, Amsterdam, 1996, pp. 93–177.

14. A. Strotmann. Limitations of the Knowledge Interchange Format as a general purpose content communication language. J. of Intelligent Systems **12**, 2002.

15. A. Strotmann. Content markup language design principles, 2003, Dissertation, The Florida State University.

16. A. Strotmann, L. Kohout. OpenMath: compositionality achieved at last. SIGSAM Bulletin (ACM Special Interest Group on Symbolic and Algebraic Manipulation) **34**, 2000, pp. 66–72.

# Author Index

# Lecture Notes in Computer Science

For information about Vols. 1–3107

please contact your bookseller or Springer